A Companion to
Old and Middle English
Literature

A Companion to Old and Middle English Literature

EDITED BY
Laura Cooner Lambdin
AND
Robert Thomas Lambdin

GREENWOOD PRESS
Westport, Connecticut • London

Library of Congress Cataloging-in-Publication Data

A companion to Old and Middle English literature / edited by Laura Cooner Lambdin
and Robert Thomas Lambdin.
    p. cm.
   Includes bibliographical references (p.) and index.
   ISBN 0-313-31054-8 (alk. paper)
   1. English literature—Old English, ca. 450–1100—History and criticism—Handbooks,
manuals, etc. 2. English literature—Middle English, 1100–1500—History and
criticism—Handbooks, manuals, etc. I. Lambdin, Laura C. II. Lambdin, Robert T.
PR166 .C66 2002
829'.09—dc21   2001057726

British Library Cataloguing in Publication Data is available.

Library of Congress Catalog Card Number: 2001057726
ISBN: 0–313–31054–8

First published in 2002

Greenwood Press, 88 Post Road West, Westport, CT 06881
An imprint of Greenwood Publishing Group, Inc.
www.greenwood.com

Printed in the United States of America

The paper used in this book complies with the
Permanent Paper Standard issued by the National
Information Standards Organization (Z39.48–1984).

10 9 8 7 6 5 4 3 2 1

We dedicate this book to
Carol Cooner Bridges and
Luther Leonard Bridges,
our aunt and uncle
and the godparents
of our second daughter, with
love and thanks for
years of loving kindness.

Contents

Introduction

A Companion to Old and Middle English Literature is an essential reference guide for period scholarship because it examines English medieval literature comprehensively by genres. Written by academics who recognized this critical need, the text classifies early British literature by time and type using genres in an effort to significantly increase our understanding of textual meaning and historical context. Using structure as an evaluative critical tool of judgment, genres allow us to more fully know a piece of literature by what it is and what it is not. Previously, no book existed that defined, classified, and critically studied the bulk of Old and Middle English writings, so the scope and depth of this text fills a gap in literary studies. Thus this volume is not only for scholars, but also for any reader of the era's literature.

This volume is intended to guide readers by encouraging and relishing categorical interpretations of extant, primarily canonized, medieval works through comparison with other literary pieces of the period that share a similar organization, style, or theme and have, therefore, previously been classified by literary critics as also belonging to that particular genre. With a grateful nod to Marxist criticism in particular, we note that culture, history, and prevailing ideologies shaped medieval writers' purposes in ways now largely unfathomable but still completely undeniable. Undoubtedly, literature is ultimately a social act, allowing new interpretations and evaluations with each historical era and each reader. Reproducing the spirit and vitality of the medieval period is, despite the anachronistic current attempts made by various groups at festivals, impossible; however, we can best recapture a glimpse of early England through the comprehensive approach of classifying and categorizing its literature into genres and then contemplating audience and purpose.

We must assume that a medieval author knew the artistic conventions and structures of typical literary types, and that his or her text was shaped by that knowledge. Tradition is coercive, and while we cannot be certain how much Greek and Roman knowledge seeped into early England, we can see that medieval texts are clearly authored along similar lines. Classical literary divisions, for example, Aristotle's categories of epic, lyric, and drama, were certainly not coerced imperatives, if they were even known. We admit to the openness and instability of literary texts, but find value in comparing the attitude, structure, subject, audience, and purpose in certain remarkably similar works.

The majority of medieval works are clear-enough examples of a certain genre to benefit from a study through comparison of the distinctions, characteristics, and components within that grouping. Recognition of form and shared literary devices intelligible to writer and reader adds significant pleasure and is invaluable at clarifying objectives in many cases. Mikhail Bakhtin's "jolly relativity," the shaping effects of carnivals and festivals that allowed literary genres to be subverted and mocked, clearly occurred; however, as Bakhtin asserts, this phenomenon was not evident until the questioning humanism of the Renaissance. The medieval era seems a transition period between classical restraint and Renaissance exuberance.

Genre lines are clearly drawn, and few medieval works resist classification. They share defensive, aesthetic criteria involving several common denominations and devices. While medieval works also do not seem to be especially experimental, they rarely reflect the stylized aesthetic purity or rigid unity of later neoclassical principles. There is little of the purposeful genre shifting that occurred often in works from 1840 to 1940 when an author knew but sidestepped the formal expectations and structural patterns of genre.

Medieval authors seemed in firm control of form. Of course, we must acknowledge the heterogeneous qualities encouraged by the long tradition of oral transmission necessitated by an almost completely illiterate audience. This same heterogeneous quality reminds us now that the reasons many texts seem to reflect the concerns of all social classes is that the earlier pieces were recited by traveling minstrels to royal courtly audiences, urban bourgeois, and country folk alike. The storyteller was unlikely to imagine an entirely new tale in each group, but he surely would add elements of particular interest to each audience, and some of these newly interwoven parts remained in the next telling or even in the mind of the next teller. After a text had been recited by many scops for all audiences, an extra layer of piety was probably purposefully added by the clerics who transcribed it because the scribes were, after all, employed by the church.

Didactic works and hagiography are obviously intended for moral instruction. Chivalric romances are inherently courtly. Ballads reflect the canniness of common folk. The principles of inner form—audience, purpose, attitude, emotional tone—are no less obvious among genres than the outer forms of meter, structure, and organization. Certain genres, like drama with its mystery and morality plays, can be divided into subdivisions based primarily upon inner form. There are even a few works that share traits and overlap genres somewhat, but we have no medieval texts that defy classification or seem experimental to the point of requiring a separately named form.

Happily, it seems that during the "Dark Ages," perhaps reflecting strict classical restraints, writers made efforts to adhere to perceived rules of categories. The *Companion* discusses each fascinating genre, giving its primary characteristics and then many prominent examples. Further, each chapter includes a critical survey of the literary history of that genre, with particular attention given to the more recent critical studies. A bibliography follows at the conclusion of each chapter as well as a comprehensive bibliography at the end of this urgently needed and infinitely useful reference tool. All translations of poetry have been made by the authors and/or contributors.

A Companion to
Old and Middle English
Literature

1

Old English and Anglo-Norman Literature

Robert Thomas Lambdin and Laura Cooner Lambdin

When one considers Old English literature, those texts composed prior to the Norman Conquest of 1066 or so, five distinct types come immediately to mind: epic, lyric, charms and riddles, didactic prose, and chronicles. While it is often easy to glamorize this era as one of castles, heroes, and farmers involved in feudal loyalty and honest agrarian lifestyles, the truth is that this was a time of hardship, and the literature reflects these difficult lifestyles. In what is today England, the land was covered by thick forests; lurking in these dark abysses were savages and beasts waiting for any unsuspecting prey. Here were found tribes of peoples today commonly known as the Anglo-Saxons; it must be noted that this term was created solely as a means to distinguish the British Saxons from those of the Continent (Greenfield 6). It is also used to define the language of England from the seventh to the twelfth centuries, although the bulk of extant material dates from around 900 through 1050. The language was spoken in four dialects: Northumbrian, Mercian, Kentish, and West Saxon. The latter is the dialect of most of the best-known literature from this time (Moore, Knott, and Hulbert 1).

Old Saxon was the language of the continental Saxons who spoke it throughout North Germany. The earliest extant document from this group is the *Heliand*, a metrical paraphrase of the Gospels (Moore, Knott, and Hulbert 2). This early biblical document sets the stage for what we would find in England at this time. The works are steeped in the fantastic while including elements of the newly accepted and fairly popular religion of Christianity. In a land as bleak and isolated as England, it is easy to see how a religion that provided a sense of hope would be adopted into both the previously pagan culture and the literature.

In England the land itself dictated the way inhabitants should eke out their existences. Hunting and fishing were crucial for food, goods, and shelter. The United Kingdom is a land surrounded by water, so the sea often looms large in the area's literature. Sailing was not only a means of survival; in lyric and epic poetry it allowed for visions of mythological creatures and hyperbolic retellings of everyday events. When the hard days of harvesting, hunting, and seafaring came to an end, nights of feasting and mead drinking began and produced their own legends.

The tales told and songs sung were often in honor of those who exhibited great courage and could teach others survival lessons. Ironically, intermingled into these tales of remarkable feats was the inevitable tinge of melancholy. This was not the idyllic land of legends; it was one with harsh winters and short springs and summers. Human life was often brief and filled with constant loss, so the heroes usually sought glory and immortality in the songs passed from bard to bard or scop to scop. The musical retellings were not only a way of teaching, but also the only real form of public entertainment on the cold nights of the long, harsh winters. Oddly, the works also show a society that embraced peace and reveled in virtue.

The same weather patterns that made socializing indoors important also begot tales of the mysterious and the horrible: dragons that burned down villages and ogres that ripped men asunder. Yet these works functioned to amuse large groups during long periods of confinement. This illustrates the importance of the banquet and the mead halls as places of social and political interaction. Traveling gleemen and scops would vie for honor in their singing and tale-telling techniques. Whoever painted the best word pictures and kept the audience enthralled would win the prize. As Greenfield finds, there is little doubt that the earliest Old English verses were meant to be recited while accompanied by a harp (72).

In these isolated halls evolved the hierarchical and, ultimately, feudal political structure of a government ruled by a king whose underlings, the territorial lords and earls, oversaw the serfs who worked solely for their ruler. This transition was one of the key elements of the epic poems of this time. Epic poems are long narratives that follow the deeds of a great hero, focusing mainly upon one or two important periods and events that reflect his valor. As with much of the literature of this period, the epic poems are rooted in popular myths and traditions of the people. This was a period where the poetry was essentially parallel and alliterative. Most Old English poetry is made up of two half-lines consisting of two accented syllables. The other unaccented syllables varied, but each half-line had at least four syllables. The two halves were then related by consonantal alliteration (Smith, "Riddles" 439).

Initially, epics were sung by minstrels who may have remained in one place but who more likely traveled from settlement to settlement for fresh audiences. Minstrels learned their stories by imitating the great storytellers; over time, the most memorable works were eventually written down. However, because they were originally transmitted orally, emendations and deletions to stories naturally occurred based upon the preferences of particular audiences. For example, a minstrel would likely be more handsomely paid if he incorporated the name of and kind words about the king in whose mead hall he was performing. This helps explain much of the convoluted and hyperbolic rhetoric we see in the extant material.

It is because these works were initially sung that we should not be surprised that almost all surviving Old English poetry exists in only four manuscripts: The *Beowulf* Manuscript, or Cotton Vitellius A.xv, the Exeter Book, the Junius Manuscript, and the Vercelli Manuscript. All date from around 1000 and are composed in the West Saxon dialect of AElfric. The manuscripts' dates are uncertain because of the nature of their oral transcriptions; however, most critics agree that the bulk of these poems date from the late seventh to the early ninth centuries. This is not to say that there is no disagreement, as some critics find the texts to be from as early as the seventh to as late as the tenth century. The most common poems from this time are epic, allegory, and riddles and charms (Greenfield 78–79). There is no extant prose work.

The heroes of the epics were always vigorous young men who performed glorious deeds for the sake of their valor; any reward was unimportant for their motivation. The freewheeling integration of myths and legends into historically accurate tales allows for twisting and elimination of some of the truths that shaped these events. The most famous Old English epic is *Beowulf*, a text dated to sometime around the ninth century. The unknown author of this long poem had a great grasp of construction of a tale. The rhythm of the text varies based upon the accent of words and alliteration. The lines are composed of two halves separated by a caesura, or pause, allowing a presenter to create a rather musical effect (and to breathe) even though there is little or no true rhyme scheme to *Beowulf*. This effect is produced by the inclusion of two strongly accented syllables in each half-line, for a total of four strongly accented words per line. The poet's use in each line of three to four words that begin with the same sound or letter also added poetic flavor through alliteration.

Beowulf seems to have been composed principally in West Saxon. It survives today in one manuscript that has been partially damaged by fire. Somewhat difficult to study as a written work, *Beowulf* was probably composed to be chanted or sung. As an oral work, the poem probably evolved over a long period of time with many additions and deletions based upon audience, purpose, and artistic merit. This freedom allowed the scops to add totally new episodes or expand or contract old ones as interested a particular group. Also, examination of the text exposes that somewhere late in its construction the poem became "Christianized": elements of Christianity were layered over an originally pagan text. This is fairly typical because the clerics who transcribed these originally pagan poems worked for the church and would naturally encourage didactic messages where possible.

Set on the coast of the North Sea around 512, *Beowulf* is presented in two distinct parts, each demonstrating the virtue and integrity of Beowulf the hero.

Two major events chronicle the deeds of Beowulf as a youth and as an old man; the first is the killing of Grendel and his mother, and later is the slaying of the ferocious dragon. The action takes place over an interval of many years, from Beowulf's heroic heights to his kingly end. Perhaps this is meant to suggest that once a young man gains stature as a hero, he remains one. True to typical epic construction, the poem includes and was probably based upon many Danish myths, legends, and beliefs. An audience likes to be reminded of what it already knows.

The poem is extremely valuable in its explicit views of the harsh and pagan lives it explores. The protagonists and supporting characters display undying faith in *wyrd* (fate), which is clumsily integrated with the Christian belief that man should have faith only in God and his grace. Thus many seemingly incongruous aspects can be explained as later layering of the Christian morality audiences expected by the Middle English period. Some of the clumsier religious aspects can be attributed to the earliness of Christian belief. The people of the audience as a whole were still in transition. Scribes apparently altered certain aspects of the poem to make it better adhere to Christian dogma. Despite this tampering, one of the poem's greatest assets to scholars lies in its presentation of a fairly clear view of ancient England. We see a culture that emphasized the glory of individual courage and integrity, as well as a society dependent upon the loyalty of all members of the tribe. It is not the hero who creates the mythological elements; it is the bards who sing through years of oral transmissions to motivate and inspire others. The hero is elevated as one of the few who stand out against the masses who quiver in mere adequacy. Beowulf is honored as a leader who is consistently selfless and who serves his people by physically saving them from monsters.

In this way the epic serves to show the great pride this culture had in its ancestors, much like a Memorial Day or Veterans' Day parade today. Simultaneously, the poem served to show how technique could elevate the bard to greatness in much the same way as he honors the epic hero. The work is steeped in alliteration, never an easy task in the composition process. Its propensity for hyphenated words demonstrates a creative nuance for the ages. But it is *Beowulf*'s use of kennings (figures of speech using description) that truly demonstrates the inception of the wonderful growth of English as a descriptive language. While this intricate construction is free flowing, the work contains very little humor because it concerns very serious business: the survival of the Danes. It may be that the formal rhetoric was aimed at the hierarchy, but it is probably true that even when people were listening to the tale told by a bard, they had little to laugh about; their world was still one of brutality and coldness. Regardless, the poem demonstrates that these peoples had a grand curiosity and awareness concerning their ancestors, for special passages are dedicated to the genealogy of the great men, ancestors of characters of the epic.

The story in *Beowulf* is well known. The huge mead hall Heorot, built by Hrothgar, the king of the Scyldings, is constantly being attacked by the huge monster Grendel. A descendant of Cain, Grendel despises the noise produced at the raucous hall and decides to try to put an end to it. He enters the hall and takes thirty men. This trend continues until the Scyldings, with good reason, fear entering the hall. For an additional twelve years Grendel keeps the hall quiet.

Word of this comes to the Geats, so Beowulf sets out to assist Hrothgar. On their arrival, the Geats feast with the Scyldings. They enjoy a wonderful evening filled with revelry and boasting about their great deeds. Beowulf and his men then retire to Heorot and wait for the monster to appear. Their wait is short, as Grendel enters and kills one of Beowulf's men. Beowulf, who has been sleeping in another house, follows the monster into a deep bog, where an epic battle occurs. The Geat slays the monster with the sword of a giant and cuts off his head, taking the prize with him back to Heorot. Grendel's mother then comes to take the head back. After another great battle, Beowulf slays the mother and displays Grendel's head in Heorot. He then returns with great honor to his homeland and the court of Hygelac.

When the king and his sons are killed in battle, Beowulf is made king. He rules in peace for fifty years until a cup is stolen and guarded by a dragon. Accompanied by his friend Wiglaf, Beowulf kills the monster but in the process is mortally wounded himself. After his death he is sent to eternity in a large funeral pyre, leaving the land in the same heroic way that he lived.

This wonderful poem is interspersed with both Christian and pagan elements, showing the religious transition that occurred in England during the period of its transmission. Of import in the poem concerning Christian elements are the poem's many mentions of God and the concept of faith; there are also many biblical references, including a song of creation, Grendel's family line being linked to Cain, and a discussion of the Flood.

Perhaps the greatest conflict between the Christian and the pagan elements is the role of *wyrd* or fate in the poem. In Anglo-Saxon times the concept of fate was seen in a hero's willingness to test it. Often he would match his courage against heavy odds. Unlike modern media, where the "good guy" usually wins, in this time the heroes were often killed. This end result was not as important in the concept of *wyrd*; the hero's unwavering courage in the face of these insurmountable odds (R. Lambdin, "Wyrd" 524). The way a man met death bravely spoke volumes about his character, much like the Greek concept of a man returning from battle either with his shield or on it. It is obvious that over the course of time the Christian element was introduced, but the idea that Beowulf is sent to his final resting place in a huge funeral pyre shows that this movement could not totally eliminate the pagan influences. Further, Beowulf is able to slay the monster using a sword forged by giants, supernatural creatures. The hero's ability to stay under water for enormous amounts of time suggests that he too is somewhat more than human. Throughout literature heroes generally have at least one superhuman quality that sets them apart.

However, *Beowulf* is also an ambiguous work that does not seem to allow a consensus among the critics, who often disagree about a particular context in which to place the poem. Also called into question is the way that Beowulf the hero should be perceived. Is he primarily Christian, or do his pagan elements overshadow him? Others postulate that the author integrates the two conflicting ideologies as a means of tolerance for the pre-Christians; in essence, their heroic achievements were admirable (Hagen, *"Beowulf"* 55–56).

The greatness of *Beowulf* serves as a wonderful introduction to the other genres of literature, both prose and lyric poetry, that are such vital parts of Old English. While it may seem that the poetry of this age is greater than the prose, each is not without its strong points. There may be more lyric poetry because it was more entertaining to a scop's audience. Also, poetry is composed with meter and rhyme scheme and is thus easier to remember. Most of the Old English poems were orally handed down from generation to generation long before they appeared in written form. The music of the lyric poetry as it may have been sung by the gleemen is lost except as it exists in the intricate composition of many of the poems. Each line usually has three alliterative syllables—two in the first section and one in the second.

The myths and legends included in some of the works would have been easily picked up by the wandering minstrels who added local stories for greater flavor. Indeed, adding area names and places was probably a business necessity because the greater the story's local flavor, the more sellable it was to the market. The more renown the minstrel accomplished, the more worthy he would seem. Kings and nobles of this time would be more likely to choose only the most accomplished entertainers for their courts and feasts. This would enhance the likelihood that these works would eventually be composed in manuscripts on vellum. The ruling elite was the only group outside the church with the means and education to encourage the process.

Most of the lyric poems from this time have the same characteristics. Freedom is one of the dominant themes. This is easy to comprehend because of the ruthless nature of the attacking peoples and the constant threat of oppression. The domination of nature and disease also is a major theme. Plagues wiped out entire villages; droughts damaged crops and food supplies. Storms eliminated fleets of ships. The harsh climate and conditions conspired to make these cultures glorify any heroic overcoming of obstacles. Monetary rewards were viewed as fleeting; however, the promise of one's name being immortalized in a minstrel's song or a bard's poem was the greatest reward.

Among the earliest examples of poetry that showed the stark realities one must overcome is *Widsith*, a poem that is musical in the sense that a gleeman sadly sings of the upper echelon that he has known. This work is one of the many Old English elegies. The elegy is a poem that is usually a meditation about a particular theme. The genre dates back to classical times, as there are both Greek and Roman elegies. Originally these were poems reflective of elements of death, love, and war; however, over the years the elegy evolved to the point that it was only a poem of mourning (Chalmers 175–176). In *Widsith* the title character's name actually translates to "faraway." This may mean that the poem is meant to demonstrate many of the conventions of storytelling. The list of mead halls, gifts given, geography, and chronology presented would have been impossible for a single scop to undertake (Elton Smith, *"Widsith"* 514–515). The character reports on the grief and the hardships of one whose mead hall has been overthrown. The social import of this destruction is great, as is seen in *Beowulf*, for the socializing in this type of setting was of the utmost import to these people. A mead hall was the place where information was exchanged, political alliances were solidified, and life was celebrated.

Another of the Old English elegies is "The Wanderer," found in one manuscript, the Exeter Book. The poem is presented in the form of the *eardstapa* or "earth stepper" and shows the agony of isolation of one who has been exiled (Hagen, "Wanderer" 506). From a bard's point of view, it would have been difficult for an established singer who had been at the top of the ladder in his hall to be bumped back to the bottom where he must go and start anew. This would result in the somber melancholy prevalent in "The Wanderer" and other poems of the *ubi sunt* motif. With the protective haven of his hall destroyed, the poem illustrates how the protagonist must travel through water and bad weather in solitude to perform the only kind of work he knows.

Here we see the themes of solitude and isolation prominent in many of these poems. Yet despite it all, the wanderer remembers how generous his lord was to him. Now the lord is dead, and the singer wanders alone. Although the scop is forced to wander in solitude until his nights in the mead halls, he is also true to the concept of *comitatus*. Finally, the poem serves to remind us that life is fleeting: the material things one has can disappear; it is the spiritual things that truly matter. Indeed, life and fame are fleeting. The human condition of mutability, a change rarely for the better, is consistently displayed. The poem's conclusion offers hope for Christian salvation; however, the isolation of exile presented may be interpreted to be a mirror of the futility of human existence (Hagen, "Wanderer" 507).

Perhaps the first English lyric, *Deor's Lament* displays the bard's lamentation at being dismissed from the court of Heodenings. Deor, the bard of the court, had been usurped and eclipsed by a rival poet. Here the poet presents his plight in dire terms; indeed, the tone dictates the feeling that this dismissal may be comparable to other tragic situations, a kind of mock-heroic technique. Elton Smith (*"Deor's"* 148) notes that the poem's construction, six strophes with a recurrent refrain, is uncharacteristic of Anglo-Saxon verse and also makes dating the poem difficult. Thus this work may actually be a translation of an older Old Norse poem.

In strophes one and two we are presented the story of Weland, who is tortured by Nithad; he then extracts his revenge upon Beodihild. These actions are then examined as to their effect on the characters, and each strophe ends with the refrain "That sorrow passed, so may this." The poem is unique because it refers to historical figures who had been commemorated in lays. Also, it is one of the first compositions to be written in strophic form with a refrain; only one other poem, *Wulf and Eadwacer* (composed sometime before 940) uses this device. Finally, *Deor's Lament* works well because it takes the centrist position in the contrast between courage and misfortune. In this world there is no way of escaping the final truth: life ends.

Unknown are both the date and the author of "The Seafarer," another poem found in the Exeter Book. This work reflects upon the natural world more positively than works previously discussed and shows the great fondness these people felt toward the sea. The poem's structure suggests a dialogue between an old salt and a younger man who is keen to go on his first voyage. The older character recounts the hardships of sea life. The perceived glamour simply does not exist; however, there is a distinct magnetism that comes from the ocean; this systematically produces an irresistible desire to return to sea adventures.

"The Seafarer" is important because of the obvious metaphorical implications it posits concerning the relationship of man to both the sea and the land. It characterizes life on land as one of ease and comfort. The poem examines this image as it progresses to its allegorical conclusion: the troubles dictated by the seaman mirror the troubles of life. To this the characters respond that the call of the ocean is the call of God. Clearly the implication here is the ideation that the path to heaven is filled with vigorous trials and problems that must be overcome, lest the adventure of life end in tragedy.

Hagen ("Seafarer" 455) finds that this poem's construction has caused great critical controversy because it is constructed in two distinct halves, one descriptive, the other didactic. Early editions of the text purged the poem's conclusion, believing it to be a later addition. However, more recent critiques of the poem have found the seafaring motif to be somewhat of a constant throughout; this serves to eliminate the contextual problems. Also, many see the poem to work in tandem with "The Wanderer" because of the similar themes of exile and estrangement.

Another example of similar testing is *The Fight at Finnsburgh*, composed sometime before *Beowulf*. This is evident because lines 1068–1159 of *Beowulf* allude to the "epic song of Finn" (Elton Smith, "*Fight*" 196). It is clear that this poem was composed as an epic lay; unfortunately we have only fifty lines of the piece. This portion begins with Hnaef, ruler of the Scyldings, reveling with his men in their mead hall one evening. The Frisian Finn is detected as he and his men approach the hall bent on attacking. Hnaef rouses his troops and encourages them to be brave in battle. Key among the warriors are Siegferth, Eaha, and Ordlaf, who hie to the doors of the hall to protect it. The Frisian Guthere conversely urges Garulf, a young lad of great determination, to retreat from the battle, but the neophyte has no intention of backing down and yells to his leader, "Who is holding the door?" From behind the barrier comes the reply of Siegferth, the hero, who identifies his status and says smartly, "I am ready for you." Garulf is slaughtered by the Scylding Siegferth, and the ensuing battle rages for five days. Unfortunately, this is where the fragment ends.

Around 937 *The Battle of Brunanburgh* was composed. Found in the *Anglo-Saxon Chronicle* under the year 937, this work concerns the great victory of Alfred's heirs, Æthelstan and Edmund, over an army composed of Scots, Danes, and Britons. In the battle that takes place at Bruna's Burg, the enemy army is decimated by the valiant chiefs. The Scots and the Danes are massacred in droves; at one point five young and valiant kings lie dead on the battlefield, the victims of incredible swordplay. Anlaf, who heads the fleet of the invaders, is able to escape alive, while Constantine and his men are forced to a hasty retreat by the two heirs. In the end it is noted that there has never been such a slaughter on this island. More than half the lines of this poem are exact quotations taken from other Anglo-Saxon poems; thus Hagen (*"Brunanburgh"* 49) notes that this poem may be one of the earliest forms of an anthology. While the depiction of the battle is tense and seemingly historical, the poem is presented in sparse detail. The poem is strong in its general outline of the events surrounding the battle and exhibits a somber tone. However, what may be most striking about this work is that there are no Christian elements found in it. Church clerics who later transcribed it left the text as an action adventure story about fighting and heroes.

Another poem that glorifies war, *The Battle of Maldon* was composed around 991 and is important for scholarly examination because it demonstrates many of the elements of the heroic works, especially the notion that personal glory comes by the deliverance of selfless acts. This work glorifies the deeds of Earl Byrhtnoth against the Viking invaders under the command of Anlaf. The Vikings have sacked Stone, Sandwich, and Ipswich and are bent on doing the same to Maldon, which lies on the banks of the river Panta. Here the water branches, and the Danes congregate on the island formed by this river.

In typical form, the poem begins with Byrhtnoth exhorting his men to fight bravely for their honor. When the Vikings offer peace if the earl pays tribute, Byrhtnoth answers that his men will give the Vikings darts, spears, and swords for ransom. He then urges his men to advance, but since the tide is high, neither army is able to push the battle. When the tide ebbs, Byrhtnoth is too bold and pushes his luck a bit too far; he allows the Vikings to cross the bridge because he overestimates his own strength. This error gives the Vikings the advantage, and the Athelings are systematically killed. Among the dead and wounded is a relative of Byrhtnoth. Indeed, the earl himself is slain by a poisoned spear. With his dying breath he urges his men to resist to their fullest and then heroically dies, commending his spirit to God.

The Battle of Maldon is a classic composition in the scheme of Old English poetry. The work remains true to the code of *comitatus*. Heeding the word of their fallen leader, the Athelings continue the fight. Byrhtnoth's close friends Ælnoth and Wulmær are also killed and fall next to the earl. However, the English seem to be motivated by the valor of these leaders, and a counterattack is mounted. The poem ends with the brave Godric leading the attack. Critics generally agree that the theme of heroism in the face of defeat is expanded here to include the traditional Germanic expectations of loyalty to one's lord. Much of the criticism of the work centers upon the apparent pride of Byrhtnoth's decision to allow the Vikings to cross the causeway (Hagen, "*Maldon*" 51).

As the dogma of Christianity permeated the everyday world of the English, it faced the difficult task of usurping earlier beliefs. Many pagan thoughts had to be supplemented gently to appease the general populace in this transition to a Christian society. Chiefly exemplifying this fine line are the charms that offer a cross-composition that includes pagan superstition and folklore and the invocation of the Christian God. This mix was often explained as a means to make the incantation more effective. We could say that for insurance all possible help was invoked, but the works seem more sincere in tone, suggesting a culture in honest transition from one belief system to another. Perhaps the greatest example of this shifting process is the charm "Land Remedy," which was meant to ensure fertile fields. In "Land Remedy" the old earth goddess Erce is invoked as the mother of men. However, her image is described as becoming fruitful when it is in "God's embrace." It is only the synergism of the two that assures the bountiful harvest. Other charms were composed to give remedy against sudden stitches, dwarves, swarms of bees, and cattle thieves.

Typical charms were composed in three parts. First was the naming of the means to be used in the implementation of the charm. Next came the short narrative that described how the evil arose. If this was unknown, the work could list a time when the charm was effectively used. Finally, the charm presented the incantation wherein was mentioned the technique needed for the alleviation of the problem. Charms continued to be popular forms for establishing a link between religious elements and demonstrating a descriptive technique that would be evident later in the riddles that appeared around the eighth century. Elton Smith ("Charms" 91) notes that Anglo-Saxon religion must have assumed that piety begets material return—a stark contrast to the usual biblical allusion that the only true treasure is Heaven.

Composed anonymously, the riddles are very interesting forms of writing covering a wide range of topics. Many of the riddles seem to have been translated from Latin (Elton Smith, "Riddles" 439). These works tend to be more descriptive than literary and served to demonstrate facets of the ordinary life of England. Straight to the point, the riddles display little if any humor, thus demonstrating that these were meant to be intellectual activities. Of particular note is the idea that riddles usually are one of four distinct types. The first described some item in the natural world. A second type could be vehicles to present some elements of folklore or tales. The riddles were also used to describe typical life in England. Finally, there are the charms that are simply brilliant descriptive poetry presented in the form of a game wherein the poet employs description to make readers see and feel unnamed objects. Here the riddles are descriptions of various objects or phenomena.

Included in the subject matter are various storms, the sun, an iceberg, fire, a swan, and a shield and sword. This interesting cross between natural and man-made items adds to the difficulty in identifying the subjects of the works. For example, the varying storms (one on land and one at sea) present a constant subject with a degree of difference. The storm on land moves with malice while burning people's halls or spoiling the houses and causing death. This contrasts greatly with the surge of the storm at sea that rages loudly and beats the shores, causing the depths of the sea to envelop all that crosses it.

Destruction is also seen in the "Sun" riddle, where some living creatures are burned up by the heat while others are simply distressed. However, the bleak notion surrounding the storms is replaced at the end of the sun riddle because the sun can also gladden many with its bright rays and warmth. This preoccu-pation with the power of heat is also presented in the "Fire" riddle, in which all are warned of the cruelty of fire to those who allow it to grow too proud. The riddle "Iceberg" conversely demonstrates the cold irony of these monsters of the sea. While they look wondrous, they are ravaging beasts that decimate ships and crews. Of particular note here is the oxymoronic notion that the ice-berg's laughter was terrible, a striking precursor to the revelation of its sharp edges waiting to pierce the hull of any ship that ventured too close.

Other riddles deal with the accoutrements of war. Obviously the value of items such as spears and shields would be steep, and while today we may not hold them in such high esteem, instruments of war were invaluable possessions at this time. In the "Shield" riddle, the item is personified to demonstrate the strife that has been inflicted upon it. The lone figure has been wounded by a knife and stricken by a sword. This relentless onslaught has made this protective piece demonstrate human capabilities concerning the ever-present threat of bat-tle, for it has grown weary of battle; it is tired of being struck by blades. Cer-tainly this touching insight emphasizes the brutal aspects of this period. Perhaps the author of this piece had seen too many battles lost or too many of his relatives or friends killed in war. This counters the adulation given to the sword in its riddle, in which it is seen as a wondrous creature. This staff is beloved by its lord and elaborately decorated. It is clear that the composer of this riddle feels little if any of the strife posited by the author of the "Shield."

A final type of riddle concerns not the abstract, such as the sun, or the vicious, such as the sword, but more real or living creatures. Here we find works that beguile in their presentations while cleverly demonstrating a keen awareness of the natural elements of the animal world. The beauty of the swan's motion is highlighted in the riddle "Swan." Here the poet notes that these birds silently gad about, whether they are on land, sea, or in the air. This seemingly effortless existence does not go without notice. Even more amazing to the poet in this area is the ability of the swan to fly high into the clouds where it can look down on men. The power of this capability is awesome.

The riddles obviously showed a keen desire to manipulate and demonstrate a grasp of the vernacular. This may explain why so many riddles were copied and passed about. This knowledge would also be demonstrated in a vastly different way. As noted, the writings of this period were gradually Christianized for many reasons. Foremost is the fact that Christianity had become the most popular religion in Britain at this time. Further, since the monasteries were the centers of culture, it is only natural that literature that was Christian in tone grew and developed; few new ideas were created, for these were mostly the works of monks and were composed in Latin, the tongue of the church.

However, the influences were great and twofold. One school of Christian influence came from the Augustinian influence from Rome. Evidently this was very popular around Essex, although no literature of this type survives. The second came from Ireland and was influenced by Bishop Aidan. Starting in the monasteries of Northumbria, especially Jarrow and Whitby, this school's authors include the heavyweights of this period, Bede, Cynewulf, and Cædmon.

Bede (673?–735), also known as the Venerable Bede, is regarded as the first English professional scholar. He spent his entire life preparing for work in the monastery. Eventually he lived in the Monastery of St. Paul in Jarrow, known then as the most learned spot in Western Europe. Here Bede held a position that would be best described today as that of a university professor. His works, mostly composed in Latin, pertained to many subjects, including Bible commentary, hagiography, science, and history. Perhaps his most significant work is the *Ecclesiastical History of the English People*, completed in 731. This work is still considered to be a major source for English history from 597 to 713. The *History* is important because Bede gathered his findings from all the written works he could find, from oral traditions, from visitors, and from eyewitnesses. For their efforts, Bede actually cited many of his sources (Esther Smith, "Bede" 54–55). Unabashed plagiarism ran rampant in the medieval and Renaissance periods, so Bede's habit of giving credit to his predecessors for materials not his own is rare indeed.

Bede's *Ecclesiastical History* covers the time from the Roman Caesar's invasion to 731. The book is notorious for its somber, straightforward account of the events of history. The work's critical faculty shows Bede's ability to remove himself from the events. After his death in 735, the work was continued by other monks. Perhaps the most important aspect of this text is that it is the sole work that provides insight into the ancient times of Britain, and we are fortunate that it seems reasonably credible. It is also here that we see the shift from the previous normal reference of *annus mundi* (year of the world) to *annus domini* (year of the Lord) (Esther Smith, "Bede" 54).

Book I: Preface is dedicated to King Ceowulph. Obviously Bede relied heavily upon the archives of the Roman church as tools for the composition of this book. Perhaps his principal aid was Abbot Albinus. *Preface* begins with an extensive description of England's topography, climate, and soil. Then the history begins, starting with Caesar's Roman conquest of England. Also included are the Britains' struggles with the Scots and Picts. Ironically, these skirmishes led to the Britains asking the Romans for help in constructing a great wall. Once this task was completed and the Romans withdrew, the book relates the hardships endured by the people, especially when the Angles arrived from the Continent and conquered them. This portion is then concerned with the travels of Bishop Aidan and notes several of his miracles. He is credited with giving sight to a blind child and preventing St. Alban's Monastery from burning. Perhaps the most touching portion of the work is Bede's depiction of Hilda, the abbess of Bede's home monastery at Whitby. Her life and death are detailed in a way that shows Bede's obvious closeness to her.

The Story of Cædmon, composed around 690, shows that Cædmon was an illiterate laborer attached to the monastery at Whitby. After he had been driven in shame from a feast table, he went to a stable and dozed off. In a dream he was given the gift of writing verses that presented his interpretation of the biblical Scriptures. Unsure of what he should do, Cædmon showed his works to Hilda, the abbess at Whitby; she urged him to give up his secular ways and join the monastery. From then on he lived the quiet, simple life of a monk.

One of Bede's writings centered on the missionary work of Paulinus, who had been sent to further Augustine's work. Bishop Paulinus's most famous convert was probably King Edwin of Northumbria. He had married a Christian, Ethelberga, on condition that she remain a Christian. Paulinus tried for years to convert the pagan king; his efforts were aided by letters from Pope Boniface. Yet Edwin continued to be unmoved until he had a vision. Edwin's counselors advised that because of this vision the king should accept this new religion. One of Edwin's counselors eloquently noted that the present life is unknown, much like the flight of the sparrow. After Edwin embraced Catholicism, most of his subjects followed. This time is known as a remarkably peaceful era where even women could walk the country unescorted. This marked a substantial victory for this fledgling faith, as Northumbria was at the apex of its power. Also, because the main function of written texts during this period was to educate, Bede, along with his counterparts Benedict Biscop and Ceolfrith, helped establish the library at Jarrow as one of the most impressive of this time (Esther Smith, "Bede" 55).

Cædmon, the seventh-century laborer turned monk, discussed Bede and wrote a great amount of works. Included in his canon are the *Paraphrase* and *Judith*. The *Paraphrase* is a retelling of Genesis, Exodus, and a portion of Daniel. Noted for being composed in the vernacular, this work opens with Cædmon's famous hymn. *Judith* is another poetic interpretation of a biblical book, although there is some doubt about its author, as some believe that a follower of Cædmon was responsible for writing it. Elton Smith ("Cædmon" 72) notes that translation of much of Cædmon's works is somewhat difficult because of his overuse of kennings, or figures of speech using description to illustrate. For example, "sea" would be noted as "whale-road" (Curtis, "Kennings" 331). Obviously these imprecise terms could lead to some confusion.

Cædmon's Hymn is a short poem noted for its fervor in praising God. One of the earliest extant Old English poems, it is a simple work that exalts the Creator of all things who will survive forever. Nine lines of alliteration, the poem praises the awesome power of God especially appreciates the excellence of his works, which include the earth and heaven. Oddly, the hymn itself was an addition to a Latin text; it appears as a marginal gloss. Thus some critics believe that the Old English version may simply be a paraphrase of the Latin. However, since variations of the hymn are found in different manuscripts, others give credence to the notion that the work reflects a background of oral transmission (Hagen, "Cædmon's Hymn" 73).

It is conceivable that Cædmon composed *Exodus*, but it is by no means certain. This paraphrase of Exodus 13–15 concerns Moses' leading the Israelites out of Egypt. Guided by two pillars of fire, they are led out of the wilderness. As they note the Egyptians behind them, the Israelites prepare for battle until the waves of the Red Sea part, allowing them passage. When the Egyptians attempt to follow, they are obliterated by the sea. The poem ends with Moses urging the Israelites to follow the will of God and to keep his laws, followed by a song of thanksgiving and the division of the Egyptian goods as spoils of war. While the work is a good account of these actions, it is puzzling in its digressions that are brought into the poem as the Israelites cross the Red Sea. It is here that we are given the story of Noah and then Abraham's aborted sacrifice of Isaac. Cædmon's *Exodus* is important on many levels; perhaps the most intriguing is its seemingly opposite thematic conventions compared to those of *Beowulf*. As noted, *Beowulf* is largely a pagan work with the Christian elements added into it. *Exodus* seems to be the exact opposite: thematically it is a Christian work with large sections that emulate pagan ideas. Because the Anglo-Saxons loved battle scenes, the poem heightens with great detail the conflicts between the Israelites and the Egyptians, providing vivid images, especially honoring the shields and accoutrements of battle, as well as providing grisly images of birds circling the mass corpses of the vanquished Egyptians.

Perhaps the most grotesque scene developed in Old English literature is seen in the drowning of the Egyptians. Here the poet adds much greater detail than is found in the Bible. The horror of this scene is magnified to demonstrate the great power of God as he obliterates the Egyptian horde. It is with great horror that the reader hears of the intensity of the wrath, so that even the blue sky was turned red with the blood of the Egyptians. Clearly *Exodus* may be seen as functional as well as literary. How better for a fledgling religion to grab its converts than to threaten them into submission with the potential for damage from the omnipotent God? In this way Cædmon the poet may be seen as both one of the early great leaders of the church and an important contributor to the literature of this time.

Of major import is the fact that Cædmon saw fit to present the story of *Exodus* and most of his other works by adapting the pagan vernacular of the common people for Christian purposes (Hagen, "Cædmon's Hymn" 73). Perhaps it is safe to say that Cædmon must have realized the difficulty that the people had in understanding the dogma of Catholicism. Few were fluent enough in Latin to comprehend the levels of intensity or depth of wisdom found in the biblical texts. Thus the majority of people must have had to depend upon storytellers and clerics' versions of the Bible. This would add more difficulty to an already-complicated subject.

Cædmon was followed by Cynewulf (c. 750), who is his peer in his contributions to the literature of religious poetry in Northumbrian dialect. Other than Cædmon, Cynewulf is the only Old English poet whom we can call by name. Curiously, there is absolutely nothing known about his life; all that survives this wonderful author are his poems, which include *The Elene* and *The Christ. The Elene* concerns itself with the finding of the true cross. The rood appears to Emperor Constantine. After a long period of searching, the true cross and the exact site of the Crucifixion are discovered by Constantine's mother, the empress Helen.

One of the more curious facets of Cynewulf's works is his propensity for working his name into his poems, using both runes and Roman cryptograms. It is supposed that Cynewulf was either a priest who is known to have executed a decree in 803 or a bishop of Lindisfarne who died in 781. Like those of Cædmon, his works are somewhat difficult to translate because of his use of kennings. Also, his poems are seen to be more descriptive and revealing than those of Cædmon (Elton Smith, "Cynewulf" 113).

In *The Ascension* Cynewulf touches only briefly upon the birth of Christ before relating the tale of the disciples' meeting with Jesus at Bethany. This is where he revealed his last command for the disciples to be joyful in heart, for he would never leave them but would continue to love them forever. Then Jesus ascended to heaven, much to the delight of a beautiful throng of angels and to the sadness of the disciples. Here the poet comments upon the blessings that Jesus' ordeal brought to all men, which include a free choice between the glory of heaven and the perpetual angst of hell. Also, he considers the varying talents presented to all: some receive wisdom, others musical talents or athletic prowess. Finally, the poem touches upon the church's inspiration gleaned from the Ascension, wherein it is afforded the opportunity not only to overcome its heathen force but also to spread the truth of Christianity throughout the world. Following a passage on the Judgment Day, Cynewulf's customary runic signature is found, here in the texture of the paragraph. Here the runes stand both for letters and for words suggested by the letters.

Perhaps the most powerful section of *The Christ*—not normally ascribed to Cynewulf—is *Doomsday*. This portion is the author's very detailed vision of universal destruction, the Last Judgment, eternal happiness for those worthy, and eternal suffering for the damned. In specific terms the poem examines these horrors and blessings. It is relentless in its details of the fate of the wicked who will be swallowed up by the hot flames of hell. In stark contrast to this horrific vision are the blessings bestowed by God upon the good folk who are able to watch the torment rain upon the damned. The piece is interesting in the notion that despite all their ills, the most miserable experience of those in hell is their contemplation of the bliss of those in heaven.

While *The Phoenix* may not have been composed by Cynewulf himself, it is a work that clearly shows his influence. The poem is a derivation of a Persian legend that has been amended to include Christian allegory. In the work the Phoenix serves as a metaphor for Christ, who has died and been reborn. The initial portion of the poem glamorizes a kind of idyllic land comparable to a new Eden; the land is described as temperate, with only fertile plains and crystal-clear water. The Phoenix is initially a dull gray-colored bird; the only remarkable thing about him is his song. After a millennium the bird has aged and retires to Syria, where his sweetly smelling nest is ignited by the sun, consuming the bird. However, the Phoenix is then reborn as a beautifully plumed creature. In his claws he carries the ashes and bones that he is returning to his native dwelling—a testament to the eternal life granted by God's grace (Elton Smith, "Cynewulf" 114).

After Cynewulf, one of the wisest and greatest kings of England, Alfred (849–899), made his mark in the literary field. He united the West Saxons and then conquered the Danes at Ethandun in 878. During his tenure as ruler, schools were founded, cities were rebuilt, a fair code of laws was compiled, and justice was reformed. It is because of his eclectic tastes and accomplishments that he is the only English monarch known as "the Great" (Esther Smith, "Alfred the Great" 7). Perhaps the most educated ruler of this period, Alfred was renowned as a patron of both literature and learning. This was possible because the period of his reign was one of great peace and order. Of paramount concern to him was the transcription of great Latin texts into the dialect of the West Saxons. In this endeavor he chose four books for transcription in the fields of history, geography, ethics, and religion: Bede's *Ecclesiastical History*, Orosius's *History of the World*, Boethius's *Consolation of Philosophy*, and the practical treatise of instruction for the clergy, Gregory's *Pastoral Care*. While these works are extremely important in the schema of Old English literature, perhaps Alfred's greatest achievement was his directive for the preparation of the *Anglo-Saxon Chronicle*.

The *Anglo-Saxon Chronicle* provides a piecemeal rendition of the history of Britain from pagan times to 1154. Obviously, since Alfred died around 899, additions had to be made to the original text. Three updates have been noted, one for the period of 894–924, another for the years 925–975, and an addition for the years 983–1018. The work then continued until the Norman invasion of 1066. When the vernacular of the ruling class shifted from Latin to French, the updates of the *Chronicle* ceased (McDonald, "*Anglo-Saxon*" 16).

The *Chronicle* starts with pre-Roman Britain and extends to the twelfth century in some manuscripts. It is arranged chronologically and records events that must have impressed the clerics charged with its compilation. While most of the accounts are nonsecular, some of the entries are concerned with historical events and are vividly portrayed. It is perhaps most notable as a record of the time; also of significance is that it is written in the native tongue rather than Latin.

From the *Chronicle*, the portion for 1066 stands out for obvious reasons, relating the Norman Conquest. Harold II was Earl Godwin's son; Godwin held most of the real power in England for a while. Harold's brother Tostig plotted with King Harold of Norway to take the throne of England. Simultaneously, William of Normandy was sailing to England as Harold II was marching to York to put down Tostig's rebellion. He eventually obliterated the rebel forces, slaying the Norwegian king and many of his allies.

In the interim, William had claimed a hold on another portion of England, constructing a castle at the port city of Hastings. Harold II's large army marched two hundred miles in five days to confront this foreign force, and the two armies met at Appledore. There many men were slaughtered on each side, including Harold II. William's army eventually claimed the battle and the throne of England. Given the size and strength of William's army, the English claimant to the throne, Edgar Atheling, submitted, and William the Conqueror took control of England.

William proved to be a thorough administrator, as is seen in the Domesday Book, otherwise known as the Book of the Day of Assessment, from 1088. The king was concerned about all that was happening in England and by whom its land was occupied. He sent his men all over the land into every area to discover how large each shire was, what lands belonged to the king, what stock was on this land, and how much the king should be paid by each shire each year. It is noted that every ox, cow, and pig was hand counted for this report. This is extremely important because this is the only real survey of this type made in medieval Europe, and it provides an invaluable record of social conditions. All inhabitants from the time of Edward the Confessor (1042–1066) are listed. This volume is still available in London's Public Record Office (R. Lambdin, "*Domesday*" 151).

After the conquest of 1066 by the Normans, French became a major influence on the English language. The first Anglo-Normans looked down upon the Saxon vernacular and spoke only French; this was seen best in the court, public documents, and transactions. This language barrier served to be divisive as the conquering Normans distanced themselves from the Saxons, integrating only when necessary. In this genre chronicles and other works from Latin sources were popular additions to Anglo-Norman works (R. Lambdin, "Anglo-Norman" 14).

Thus Old English became the language of the artisans and the oppressed, although, as is usual in the natural progression of language, derivations of the native French evolved and French words were imbedded in the vernacular of the common folk; after all, conquerors and the conquered had to communicate. The invasion spawned four distinct languages: Northumbrian was the language in the north, while Mercian was spoken in the Midlands. In the south the West Saxon language ruled, while in the court only French was used. However, because French became the language of the government, English soon lost its distinct forms and inflections. Eventually Mercian became the standard tongue.

This occurred for a variety of reasons. Foremost was that the Midlands district contained both London, the capital and home of the royal court, and Oxford, the center of learning. Also, because the Midlands lay between the north and the south, it was only natural that the language served as a cusp. Thus Mercian gradually spread throughout the island.

It is here that we see the shift from the somber brutality of the Anglo-Saxon literature to the glorified tales of love and adventure found a bit later. Very prominent in this period are the metrical romances, which were literally tales in verse form. Many of these works centered upon the reign of Charlemagne and his counterparts, as exemplified by the *Chanson de Roland*. Also popular during this period were tales from the Mediterranean Sea area, especially of Alexander the Great and the classical stories of the fall of Troy. Obviously, heroes are a major part of these works. Perhaps the most famous to evolve from the area of Britain are those regarding King Arthur and his Knights of the Round Table.

For three hundred years French was a major influence on the culture of England and affected the society in several ways both politically and socially. Politically, the Norman Conquest actually led to the union of England, for it provided a sense of nationalism while the king's power increased under the feudal system. This established a global economy as England stepped up its ties with the Continent in terms of commercial, political, and religious interaction. Slowly these influences overhauled England's legal and political systems. This continued until the fourteenth century when few works were composed in the French vernacular of England, although Continental French continued to be used in some works, such as John Gower's *Mirour de l'omme* (R. Lambdin, "Anglo-Norman" 14).

Socially, this period created some timeless themes that remain symbols of the age. A new spirit of vigor and beauty fused with a love of the mother goddess of the earth to establish the code of chivalry and exaltation of women. This worship of all things female mixed with the current Christian religious zeal and created the cult of the Virgin Mary. Still, because of the invasion, English was not the language of literature for several centuries; French and Latin usurped it in this regard. Norman architecture was introduced and also spread throughout the island.

William was a harsh ruler who levied heavy taxes on his subjects. He militarily reduced his opposition and then confiscated all of the land of the vanquished. Thus every inch of England belonged to the king. William retained one-sixth of all the land for himself and granted about one-half of the remaining land to loyal Normans. This systematic taking of parcels did not sit well with the natives. However, he countered this ill will by establishing a strong and orderly government. While he ruled, there were rarely internal quarrels because all was aimed at the greater good of the country. The Norman influence led to the establishment of a feudal society in England. Manorial lords reaped the profits from the peons and also supplied the men for the king's army. Thrice annually the manorial lords convened and advised in the creation of laws. All nobles spoke French, while the legal documents were composed in Latin.

Also, the church was allowed to retain its lands. Pope Alexander II had blessed William's endeavors, and in return William instituted the Cluniac reforms. Under these reforms, older bishops were replaced by Normans, such as Lanfranc, who enforced the strict doctrines of the church, such as celibacy. He also reorganized monasteries and established new schools. The jurisdiction of the church was given its own court system, although the king retained the right to veto any decree (Curtis, "William" 518).

After William died, he was succeeded by two of his sons. During Henry I's reign the conventions of chivalry were firmly entrenched. Chivalry, a term derived from the term *chevalier* or "horseman," is usually seen to refer to customs associated with knighthood and evolved to include the training of young knights and squires to hunt, fight, and serve their lords (R. Lambdin "Chivalry" 97). In its most outrageous form chivalric knights adopted the code of courtly love that required the knight to dedicate his quests to a lady, whether or not they were romantically involved. This code flourished for a short time and then dissipated.

The time of Henry I is seen to have been one of peace, prosperity, and gaiety. All seemed to be content, from the peasants to the nobles. Sport and hospitality dominated their lives. However, it was not a time that was conflict free. The general populace loved the cockfights, feasting, and revelry that transpired during this era, but the church looked down on and tried to suppress such activity that did nothing to further Christianity that celebrated God's grace. The church pushed for pilgrimages and celebrations of the lives of saints as substitutes. However, the church's efforts seemed futile and were stepped up when the people simply used these days as times of revelry. Eventually even the monasteries were tainted by the gallivanting merrymaking of this period.

As an offshoot of this hedonistic time, new monastic orders arose. The Cistercians advocated simplicity and dignity, devoting their time to studying and manual labor. They raised livestock and exported wool. Also, the crusading movement established the precursors to the guilds, the Templars. After Henry I's death Stephen took the throne, and England was rocked by civil war and anarchy that did not end until the Angevin Henry II ascended to the throne in 1154. During his reign there was conflict between the king and the church; he was also responsible for great constitutional and legal reform. The towns of England grew at tremendous rates, which was good for the Crown when Richard I (1189–1199) needed to fund the Third Crusade. After Richard died, John (1199–1216) ruled viciously; his reign was marked by horrible conflicts between nobles and the king. Eventually the nobles forced John's hand and were victorious. The result was the creation of the Magna Carta and the development of Parliament, which would continue to grow in power and add to later conflicts. Wars between the nobles and the Crown continued when Henry III (1216–1272) ruled. Also during this period England attempted to take over Ireland, and the English kings continued the attempts of their Saxon predecessors to take over

Wales and Scotland. Edward I (1272–1307) was the first king to systematically attempt to conquer England's neighbors. Although he was unsuccessful, Edward I did make a name for himself in his expansion and reform of England's courts and legal system.

The literature of this period (c. 1066–1350) lacked the harsh tone of the previous Anglo-Saxon time. Instead, the works are bright and clever verses that show an obvious love of words and language. The themes were mostly romantic, and the characters were usually historical figures, religious figures, or imaginary figures. No matter which of these types the author chose, his end result was romantic in idea or deed. The primary reason these works existed was to entertain. Geoffrey of Monmouth (1084–1154) related the Arthurian legend, demonstrating that imagination and fancy were prevalent in the works that pushed love and adventure as themes. For the first time, Arthur the legend became Arthur the character. This was normal for Geoffrey, who seemed to seek out stories of the fantastic and odd legends from a multitude of sources, including William of Malmesbury and Henry of Huntingdon. Geoffrey claimed to use a very old Anglo-Saxon verse that had been lent to him, but the existence of such a text has been called into doubt by most historians, as medieval authors of this period typically made up authority figures and sources. Thus it is inferred that Geoffrey's works may be more creative than literal. Indeed, in Geoffrey's works we find the first known story of King Lear as well as treatments of Brutus, Aeneas, and the Holy Grail (McDonald, "Geoffrey" 225).

Since Arthur seemed to mirror the splendor of this period, many other authors also chose to write about this king, and so Arthurian legends became very popular. The embellishment of the Arthur tales spilled over into the histories of the time, which were no longer composed in the monotonous factual tone of the *Anglo-Saxon Chronicle*. While the character had appeared in earlier Welsh and French sources, the English Arthur is generally seen to be more rugged and violent than his predecessors, although he is ever identified as the first Christian king. What remained consistent from one Arthur to the next was that for the most part he was worthy of emulation. Also, many characters, such as Lancelot, the Lady of Astolat, Merlin, Guinevere, Morgan Le Fay, Tristan, Isolt, and Gawain are some of the most compelling in all of literature, perhaps because their tragic endings were spurred by erotic love in all its various forms.

Modern authors still find new ways to present the Arthurian legends, but are not as captivated as the Victorian Alfred Tennyson or the Pre-Raphaelite Brotherhood. For example, Dante Gabriel Rossetti's influence on William Morris during this time can be seen in the "vividness, the symbolism, and the bright clear pictures" of Morris's works (L. Lambdin and R. Lambdin, *Camelot* 72–73). First mentioned in the ninth-century chronicle *Historia Brittonum* (c. 800), a work attributed to the Welsh Nennius, Arthur does not appear again until the middle of the tenth century, when he is given a brief mention in the *Annales Cambriae* (c. 950). Here the Arthur character has Christian elements imposed upon him; for example, he fought for three days at the Battle of Baden while bearing the cross of Christ on his shoulders. Until Geoffrey's work, most references to Arthur are scant, with little substance (L. Lambdin, "Arthurian Legend" 20–21).

The earliest Arthurian romances are those of the Frenchman Chrétien de Troyes, who was associated with the Countess Marie, daughter of Eleanor of Aquitaine. He is responsible for the interlacing of court life, courtly love, and chivalry into the tales. His *Erec et Enide* (c. 1170), *Lancelot* (c. 1179), *Yvain* (c. 1179), and *Perceval* (c. 1180–1190) all contain the models of courtly love integrated with polite conversation. These works were sophisticated folks' guides to proper etiquette presented beautifully in poetry (L. Lambdin, "Chrétien" 97).

In fact, most of the works, regardless of type, were composed in verse. Layamon's historical *Brut* appears in end-rhyme. Layamon was an Anglo-Saxon priest of Worcestershire who around 1205 composed the *Brut*, a copy of Wace's *Roman de Brut* (c. 1155). The *Brut* begins with Aeneas's departure from Troy and ends with Cadwalader's departure to Rome. However, the bulk of the work is devoted to King Arthur, the great hero who was a warrior leader with special abilities that had been given to him by elves (L. Lambdin, "Layamon" 353). Numerous metrical romances demonstrate the popularity of this genre. Both historical and legendary figures had their stories told as verse tales. The Anglo-Normans immortalized such stock characters as Robin Hood, Charlemagne, and Aeneas in verse tales.

Perhaps the best poetic example of this is *Sir Gawain and the Green Knight* (c. 1370), often seen as the cornerstone of Anglo-Norman literature. While the nobles were glorified in their share of works, this period is noted for its inclusion of the common folk who loved to hear the ballads that sang of King Horn and Robin Hood. This period also gives us a vast array of religious writings. The *Ancrene Riwle* (c. 1220), or the rules for an anchorite, was one of the first prose works to set definite rules demonstrating the proper ways for those determined to devote their lives to religion. The *Cursor Mundi* even dared to put biblical history into metrical romance, while Orm's *Ormulum* paraphrased the lessons of the Gospels.

Among the most prominent twelfth-century authors were Giraldus, Wace, and Walter Map. Giraldus presented his autobiography as a means to demonstrate his dedication to his religion while attacking monastic orders. Wace is responsible for the *Roman de Brut* (c. 1154), one of the best histories of this time; it is also noted for its Arthurian references. Layamon based his *Brut* upon this work. Walter Map represents a third type of author, the courtier class. He is a curious author because he was born an aristocrat, yet he hated the court. Thus his satirical *Courtier's Trifles*, composed in Latin, preaches moral lessons to those most unlikely to heed them, the nobility.

Attesting to the popularity of histories during this time is the sheer bulk of volumes that are extant. Histories of England were produced by William of Malmesbury, Henry of Huntingdon, and Geoffrey of Monmouth. Geoffrey's

History of the Kings of England (c. 1136) is perhaps the best known, although it is a prose romance rather than a true history. It, too, contains Arthurian matter, showing the popularity of this subject. The story of Abbot Samson, who is widely acknowledged as one who revolutionized monastic life, is found in Jocelin of Brakeland's *Chronicle of St. Edmundsbury.*

Further, in the twelfth and thirteenth centuries there is an abundance of chronicles, perhaps because of a growing nationalistic sense. The Crusades had brought knowledge of a bigger world to England. Thus the general populace was stimulated by a keen interest in the workings of the church, the mystery of the Orient, and a fascination with chivalry, patriotic reflections of a superior country. While many chronicles were composed in Latin, a huge amount of these were composed in English; indeed, they are some of the first works written in the native tongue since the Norman Conquest. *Poema Morale* (c. 1200), an account of heaven and hell and the nature of good deeds leading to eternal life in heaven, and *The Ormulum* (c. 1150) are two of the best known of this type. *Cursor Mundi* (c. 1300) also was composed in English, as was Robert Mannyng's *Handlynge Synne* (c. 1303). A deeply religious work concerning the philosophy of love is Richard Rolle's *Prick of Conscience* (c. 1325).

Finally, the works of two great philosophers serve as the connection between the literatures of Old and Middle English. Roger Bacon and Duns Scotus were well respected during this period. Sometime around 1250 Bacon composed three major volumes, *Opus Majus, Opus Minus,* and *Opus Tertium. Tertium* is a scientific work, while *Majus* attempts to draw a connection between philosophy and theology. *Minus* takes up the argument of *Majus,* but expands it to include a discussion of the faulty interpretation of Scripture. Duns Scotus (c. 1300) advocated faith over reason and was quite popular for a while. Curiously, Scotus fell into such disfavor that to be associated with his works and ideas became an embarrassment; the term "dunce" is a derivative of his name.

While it is clear that the works of the Anglo-Saxons will never be considered one of the great literatures of the world, as Michael Alexander (9) notes, they do provide for us a glance into a harsh, lonely past. The poetry belongs to an oral tradition that is probably as old as these Germanic tribes themselves. The very notion that the poets of the courts and the clerics of the church together served as the keepers of the traditions is exciting. In terms of mutability, the wealth is gone but the names remain—Beowulf, Ælfric, Alfred, Bede, each a mystery, yet all immortalized because of their deeds or accomplishments. It is through the works of this time that we can capture the pure thrill of the battle.

The extreme violence that occurred between the tribes and the invaders is both gruesome and lyrical due to the words of the scops that have frozen some of these incidents in time. The thrill of accomplishment is contrasted sharply with the dialectic of defeat and isolation, as when the scop has lost his position and is exiled in "The Wanderer." The didacticism of the works may attempt to beat the audience into Christian submission, but their theoretical importance cannot be overlooked. This was the way that the masses were instructed. The majority of people probably understood little if any of what they heard in church because they did not speak Latin. The religious aspects spun into the tales of the mystics and the heroes worked well on two levels. First, they reinforced the message of the grace of Christianity. Second, they showed the power of greatness. It is true that this might not be the best literature in the world, but its timelessness and function cannot be overlooked, and its basic sincerity cannot be forgotten.

SELECTED BIBLIOGRAPHY

Abraham, Lenore. " 'Caedmon's Hymn' and the 'Gethwaernysse' ('Fitness') of Things." *American Benedictine Review* 43.3 (September 1992): 331–44.

Alexander, Michael. Introduction. *The Earliest English Poems.* New York: Penguin, 1966.

Blacker, Jean. *The Faces of Time: Portrayal of the Past in Old French and Latin Historical Narrative of the Anglo Norman "Regnum."* Austin: University of Texas Press, 1994.

Bozoky, Edina. "From Matter of Devotion to Amulets." *Medieval Folklore* 3 (Fall 1994): 91–107.

Bragg, Lois. "The Modes of the Old English Metrical Charms." *Comparatist* 16 (May 1992): 3–23.

Chalmers, Rebecca. "Elegy." *Encyclopedia of Medieval Literature.* Ed. Robert Thomas Lambdin and Laura Cooner Lambdin. Westport, CT: Greenwood Press, 2000. 175–176.

Cherniss, Michael D. "The Oral-Traditional Opening Theme in the Poems of Cynewulf." *De Gustibus: Essays for Alain Renoir.* Ed. John Miles Foley, J. Chris Womack, and Whitney A. Womack. New York: Garland, 1992. 40–65.

Clemoes, Peter. *Interactions of Thought and Language in Old English Poetry.* Cambridge: Cambridge University Press, 1995.

Curtis, R. Churchill. "Kennings." *Encyclopedia of Medieval Literature.* Ed. Robert Thomas Lambdin and Laura Cooner Lambdin. Westport, CT: Greenwood Press, 2000. 331.

———. "William I (the Conqueror)." *Encyclopedia of Medieval Literature.* Ed. Robert Thomas Lambdin and Laura Cooner Lambdin. Westport, CT: Greenwood Press, 2000. 517–518.

Frantzen, Allen J. *King Alfred.* Boston: Twayne, 1986.

Garmonsway, G.N., ed. and trans. *The Anglo-Saxon Chronicle.* London: Dent, 1990.

Greenfield, Stanley B. *A Critical History of Old English Literature.* New York: New York University Press, 1965.

Guerin, M. Victoria. *The Fall of Kings and Princes: Structure and Destruction in Arthurian Tragedy.* Stanford, CA: Stanford University Press, 1995.

Hagen, Karl. "*Battle of Brunanburgh, The.*" *Encyclopedia of Medieval Literature.* Ed. Robert Thomas Lambdin and Laura Cooner Lambdin. Westport, CT: Greenwood Press, 2000. 49–50.

———. " 'Battle of Finnsburgh.' " *Encyclopedia of Medieval Literature.* Ed. Robert Thomas Lambdin and Laura Cooner Lambdin. Westport, CT: Greenwood Press, 2000. 50–51.

———. *"Battle of Maldon, The." Encyclopedia of Medieval Literature*. Ed. Robert Thomas Lambdin and Laura Cooner Lambdin. Westport, CT: Greenwood Press, 2000. 51–52.

———. *"Beowulf." Encyclopedia of Medieval Literature*. Ed. Robert Thomas Lambdin and Laura Cooner Lambdin. Westport, CT: Greenwood Press, 2000. 55–56.

———. " 'Caedmon's Hymn.' " *Encyclopedia of Medieval Literature*. Ed. Robert Thomas Lambdin and Laura Cooner Lambdin. Westport, CT: Greenwood Press, 2000. 73.

———. " 'Seafarer, The.' " *Encyclopedia of Medieval Literature*. Ed. Robert Thomas Lambdin and Laura Cooner Lambdin. Westport, CT: Greenwood Press, 2000. 455.

———. " 'Wanderer, The.' " *Encyclopedia of Medieval Literature*. Ed. Robert Thomas Lambdin and Laura Cooner Lambdin. Westport, CT: Greenwood Press, 2000. 506–507.

Jones, W. Lewis. *King Arthur in History and Legend*. Cambridge: Cambridge University Press, 1911.

Lacy, Norris J., ed. *The Arthurian Encyclopedia*. New York: Garland, 1986.

Lambdin, Laura Cooner. "Arthurian Legend." *Encyclopedia of Medieval Literature*. Ed. Robert Thomas Lambdin and Laura Cooner Lambdin. Westport, CT: Greenwood Press, 2000. 20–28.

———. "Chrétien de Troyes." *Encyclopedia of Medieval Literature*. Ed. Robert Thomas Lambdin and Laura Cooner Lambdin. Westport, CT: Greenwood Press, 2000. 97–98.

———. "Layamon." *Encyclopedia of Medieval Literature*. Ed. Robert Thomas Lambdin and Laura Cooner Lambdin. Westport, CT: Greenwood Press, 2000. 353–354.

Lambdin, Laura Cooner, and Robert Thomas Lambdin. *Camelot in the Nineteenth Century: Arthurian Characters in the Poems of Tennyson, Arnold, Morris, and Swinburne*. Westport, CT: Greenwood Press, 2000.

Lambdin, Robert Thomas. "Anglo-Norman." *Encyclopedia of Medieval Literature*. Ed. Robert Thomas Lambdin and Laura Cooner Lambdin. Westport, CT: Greenwood Press, 2000. 14–15.

———. "Chivalry." *Encyclopedia of Medieval Literature*. Ed. Robert Thomas Lambdin and Laura Cooner Lambdin. Westport, CT: Greenwood Press, 2000. 97.

———. *"Domesday Book." Encyclopedia of Medieval Literature*. Ed. Robert Thomas Lambdin and Laura Cooner Lambdin. Westport, CT: Greenwood Press, 2000. 151.

———. "Wyrd." *Encyclopedia of Medieval Literature*. Ed. Robert Thomas Lambdin and Laura Cooner Lambdin. Westport, CT: Greenwood Press, 2000. 524.

Lehnert, Martin. *Poetry and Prose of the Anglo-Saxons*. Vol. 1. *Texts*. 2nd rev. ed. Halle: VEB Max Niemeyer Verlag, 1960.

Mackey, Louis. "Eros into Logic: The Rhetoric of Courtly Love." *The Philosophy of (Erotic) Love*. Ed. Robert C. Solomon and Kathleen Higgins. Lawrence, University Press of Kansas, 1991. 336–351.

McDonald, Richard. *"Anglo-Saxon Chronicles." Encyclopedia of Medieval Literature*. Ed. Robert Thomas Lambdin and Laura Cooner Lambdin. Westport, CT: Greenwood Press, 2000. 15–17.

———. "Geoffrey of Monmouth." *Encyclopedia of Medieval Literature*. Ed. Robert Thomas Lambdin and Laura Cooner Lambdin. Westport, CT: Greenwood Press, 2000. 224–226.

Moore, Samuel, and Thomas A. Knott, revised by James R. Hulbert, *The Elements of Old English.* 10th ed. Ann Arbor, MI: George Wahr Publishing, 1977.

Niles, John D. " 'Editing' *Beowulf*: What Can Study of Ballads Tell Us?" *Oral Tradition* 9.2 (October 1994): 440–467.

O'Keeffe, Katherine O'Brien, ed. *Old English Shorter Poems: Basic Readings.* New York: Garland, 1994.

———. "Orality and the Developing Text of *Caedmon's Hymn.*" *Anglo-Saxon Manuscripts: Basic Readings.* Ed. Mary P. Richards. New York: Garland, 1994. 221–250.

Olsan, Lea. "Latin Charms of Medieval England: Verbal Healing in a Christian Oral Tradition." *Oral Tradition* 7.1 (March 1992): 116–142.

Ostman, Jan Ola. " 'The Fight at Finnsburh': Pragmatic Aspects of a Narrative Fragment." *Neuphilologische Mitteilungen* 95.2 (1994): 207–227.

Scragg, Donald, ed. *The Battle of Maldon, AD 991.* Oxford: Blackwell, 1991.

Smith, Elton E. "Caedmon." *Encyclopedia of Medieval Literature.* Ed. Robert Thomas Lambdin and Laura Cooner Lambdin. Westport, CT: Greenwood Press, 2000. 72–72.

———. "Charms." *Encyclopedia of Medieval Literature.* Ed. Robert Thomas Lambdin and Laura Cooner Lambdin. Westport, CT: Greenwood Press, 2000. 90–91.

———. "Cynewulf." *Encyclopedia of Medieval Literature.* Ed. Robert Thomas Lambdin and Laura Cooner Lambdin. Westport, CT: Greenwood Press, 2000. 113–115.

———. *"Deor's Lament." Encyclopedia of Medieval Literature.* Ed. Robert Thomas Lambdin and Laura Cooner Lambdin. Westport, CT: Greenwood Press, 2000. 148–149.

———. *"Fight at Finnsburgh, The." Encyclopedia of Medieval Literature.* Ed. Robert Thomas Lambdin and Laura Cooner Lambdin. Westport, CT: Greenwood Press, 2000. 196–197.

———. "Riddles." *Encyclopedia of Medieval Literature.* Ed. Robert Thomas Lambdin and Laura Cooner Lambdin. Westport, CT: Greenwood Press, 2000. 439–440.

———. *"Widsith." Encyclopedia of Medieval Literature.* Ed. Robert Thomas Lambdin and Laura Cooner Lambdin. Westport, CT: Greenwood Press, 2000. 514–516.

Smith, Esther. "Alfred the Great." *Encyclopedia of Medieval Literature.* Ed. Robert Thomas Lambdin and Laura Cooner Lambdin. Westport, CT: Greenwood Press, 2000. 6–7.

———. "Bede, St., The Venerable." *Encyclopedia of Medieval Literature.* Ed. Robert Thomas Lambdin and Laura Cooner Lambdin. Westport, CT: Greenwood Press, 2000. 54–55.

Spaeth, J. Duncan. *Old English Poetry: Translations into Alliterative Verse with Introductions and Notes.* New York: Gordian Press, 1967.

Stork, Nancy Porter. "Maldon, the Devil, and the Dictionary." *Exemplaria* 5.1 (Spring 1993); 111–134.

Wright, Charles D. "The Pledge of the Soul: A Judgement Theme in Old English Homiletic Literature and Cynewulf's 'Elene.' " *Neuphilologische Mitteilungen* 91.1 (1990): 23–30.

2

Religious and Allegorical Verse

Gwendolyn Morgan

To speak of religious or allegorical verse in England during the ninth through the fifteenth centuries is to embrace the vast majority of extant Anglo-Saxon poetry and a goodly portion of that composed in Middle English. Allegory, especially in the high Middle Ages, was frequently more of a characteristic than a mode, and religion informed everyday life to a far greater degree than we expect today. Consequently, a study that attempted to address such breadth would necessarily run to multiple volumes. Moreover—and herein lies the essential problem—religion was not clear cut, despite the fact that Catholic Christianity existed as the only official religion in Western Europe. A plethora of recent studies on the issue have shown that the Christianization of Europe, especially in the rural areas, was frequently nominal until the twelfth or thirteenth century. After that time, two Christianities existed side by side through the sixteenth and even seventeenth centuries: first, the mainstream classical form upheld by the church; and second, a folk religion, a blending of pre-Christian beliefs, practices, and deities with the more essential elements of the mainstream religion that often seemed heretical to church officials. Where, then, does one draw the necessary boundaries in defining medieval religious and allegorical verse?

In order to facilitate a discussion that is neither redundant of the more standard treatments of religious poetry nor so broad as to cease to be helpful, let us first consider only that verse that is both religious and allegorical, thereby eliminating most sermons, the religious epics, clerical ballads, and so forth, which receive sufficient treatment elsewhere in this volume. This leaves us with a body of verse that can legitimately be called "wisdom literature," which, in the words of Morton Bloomfield (17), provides "rules of conduct or control of the environment" while attempting to "suggest a scheme of life [and] to control life by some kind of order." In other words, wisdom literature embodies an essential-spiritual view of the world and, through its understanding, a means to affect or manipulate it. To perform these functions, it is almost by necessity allegorical, since one needs to extrapolate to the general or universal from the specific in order to define cosmic order. All in all, it is wisdom literature that provides a unified spiritual and philosophical—religious and allegorical—vision of existence for any particular culture.

While the wisdom literature of a society tends to manifest itself in specific forms of poetry, not all examples of these forms are necessarily wisdom literature, nor does the latter limit itself exclusively to them. Rather, it runs through and across the standard literary categories of elegy and epic, lyric and ballad, defined more by purpose and universality than by formal expression. In whatever form, it offers insight into the essential perspectives of society. The slippery nature of wisdom literature is particularly evident in the early English canon, since the medieval period in Britain embraces two completely different cultures and languages and hence two spiritual as well as poetic traditions. These, of course, are the Anglo-Saxon—until the last, primarily an oral culture and tenacious of its pre-Christian traditions—and the postconquest literate and continentally influenced high medieval society.

The Anglo-Saxon poetic corpus includes considerably less Christian allegorical verse than does that in Middle English. True, a goodly amount of standard religious poetry, ranging from the early *Cædmon's Hymn* to *The Dream of the Rood*, the epics *Elene* and *Judith*, and a variety of clerical translations of biblical or Latin texts, does survive, but none of these are what we could call allegorical. In the main, allegory does not seem to have been a primary mode of the Anglo-Saxons. Notable exceptions do, however, exist. Two texts usually classified as elegies, "The Wanderer" and "The Seafarer," are clearly allegories of the journey of human life toward a Christian afterlife. Similarly, the bestiary pieces, especially "The Panther" and "The Whale," are allegorical descriptions of different aspects of the Christian deity. However, it is in the riddles and the metrical charms that the most comprehensive view of the Anglo-Saxon universe, its spiritual possibilities, and the secret to living within it find their fullest expression. Thus, I would assert, these two characteristically Old English genres comprise the true wisdom literature of preconquest England. Two collections of riddles, for a total of ninety-five, are found in the Exeter Book miscellany, while the twelve metrical charms are scattered throughout a variety of manuscripts, ranging from medical compendia (the *laeceboc* and the *lacnunga*) to a paraphrase of the New Testament (the *Heliand*) and the collected writings of St. Jerome and Bede. The eclectic nature of these repositories is in concert with the universal nature of wisdom literature; moreover, that all are church-sanctioned sources suggests clerical acceptance of the verse recorded therein. Both facts confirm the importance of the charms and riddles, too frequently dismissed as trivia, in Anglo-Saxon culture.

What, then, characterizes Anglo-Saxon wisdom literature? First and foremost, it expresses a tendency to synthesize differing views of life, attempting to reconcile the seemingly irreconcilable into a coherent expression of the nature of existence. Rather than polarize opposites in the manner of Neoplatonic medieval Christianity, the vision expressed in the charms and riddles embraces these opposites as different aspects of the same thing—two sides of the same coin—both essential to the natural order. This same inclusive impulse pervades even their spiritual intimations, for the charms and riddles embrace pagan perceptions seemingly as readily as Christian, not, as earlier scholars would have it, as incidentally surviving remnants of a forgotten pagan past but as part and parcel of a living spiritual perception. Riddles, by their very nature, are well suited to such a task, for their primary feature is to mislead the hearer to a mundane answer and then suddenly surprise with a completely different solution to which its clues, interpreted on a different level, apply equally well. The majority of Anglo-Saxon specimens take this one step further, pointing out the contradictions inherent in an object itself. Consider, for example, Riddle 74:

> Ic waes faemne geong,   feaxhar cwene,
> ond aenlic rinc   on ane tid;
> fleah mid fulgum   ond on flode swom,
> deaf under yþe,   dead mid fiscum,
> ond on foldan stop,   haefde ferð cwicu.
>
> [I was a young girl,   a gray-haired queen,
> and an honored warrior   in an hour;
> flew with birds   and swam on the flood,
> dove under waves,   dead among fishes,
> and walked on land,   had a living soul.]

Despite a plethora of nineteenth- and early-twentieth-century attempts to solve this riddle, the meager and unsatisfactory selection of proposed solutions ("swan," "cuttlefish," and "siren") indicates the difficulty of applying all its clues to a single entity. Recently, however, Morgan proposed "reflection." This answer should have been arrived at earlier if scholars had not been so conditioned by Christian Neoplatonic binaries that forbid a thing to be both male and female, human and animal, dead and alive at the same time. Yet a reflection is exactly this, for it is the living thing that casts it yet has no life of its own; it adopts the form and gender of its source and so can appear on land or sea even in a cloudy sky, appearing to walk, swim, or fly appropriately. Such traits amply express the reconciliation of opposites into merely different aspects of the same thing that characterizes the Anglo-Saxon riddles. The same impulse appears in the metrical charms, which can at once credit both Odin and the Christian God with creation, appeal to pagan sympathetic magic and spirits with the same efficacy as to Christ and his saints, recognize spells as good or evil, and bless and curse at the same time.

The inclusive, conciliatory tendency in the ancient English world view is directly connected to a sense of potential as both negative and positive, and to a recognition that sometimes both are necessary to existence. For example, Charm 1, "Against Unfertile Land," suggests that if magical spells can be used for evil (to curse the land), so might the same be used for good, although we might prefer to call positive spells "prayers"; additionally, the speaker herein recognizes that his magic is of the same ilk as that used by his enemies and that if the latter is stronger or better formed, it will overcome his own. Thus if there is to be good magic, there can be bad; if there is bad, there can be good. This same dualism of potential appears throughout the riddles. A horn may bring music or be used for drinking and thus contribute to the enjoyment of life; used in hunting or battle, it is the harbinger of death. Yet even the death it portends is dualistic, for hunting is both sport and a source of food, and hence life; moreover, battle may bring triumph or defeat.

The Anglo-Saxon view, therefore, asserts an ambiguity in human existence far more profound than that depicted by the high medieval Wheel of Fortune, one that reveals that all aspects of creation have a dark side. Embodied also in the seemingly unqualified acceptance of this perception is a sense that the world makes no special provisions for humanity, that is, it is not the world created by God for man, as it is in the orthodox Christian view, but rather holds unseen risks and unexpected disaster, which explains why, in general, Old English poetry depicts nature as untrustworthy. Human nature, too, is not necessarily essentially good, another area in which the established Anglo-Saxon cultural view militates against the Christian. The essence of such perceptions finds its ultimate expression in the Anglo-Saxon concept of *wyrd*. Unlike fate or fortune, *wyrd* lies not under the control of God, ultimately carrying out his divine plan in ways that human intellect is merely incapable of perceiving, but rises above all deities. An unknowable, unstoppable, uncaring force, it simply is; it neither favors nor despises man any more than it does any other aspect of creation; it simply operates according to its own logic, completely divorced from concerns of human existence.

The duality inherent in the Anglo-Saxon vision thus accounts not only for its repeated expression in the everyday subjects of the riddles but for the acceptance of magic and pagan deities alongside Christian prayer and the Trinity in the charms. Moreover, it explains why the speakers in "The Wanderer" and "The Seafarer" seem so sad, why, in fact, these poems are elegies rather than celebrations of Christian reward in the afterlife. Consider, for example, that the speaker in the latter poem expresses a genuine regret for the warmth of society, family, and creature comforts that he has forgone to make his voyage. Consider also that the speaker in "The Wanderer" mourns the loss of his gold-lord and the security of his position in a band of warriors, ruing the loss of friends and home with an equal intensity and expressing nothing but regret that he must make his (allegorical) voyage alone. Even his memories of lost splendor are dominated by their sweetness and his yearning for it, not by an understanding of their necessary transience in comparison to the Christian heaven, which ap-

pears only as a poor consolation in the final six lines of the poem. Such a
perception makes it difficult indeed to accept the simple polarities of good and
evil, God and Satan, inherent in the essentially optimistic religion of Christianity.
For some centuries, indeed, they are not fully accepted, which results in a qualified, somber view even in the overtly Christian pieces. Here, then, is the expression of Anglo-Saxon "folk Christianity," at times hardly capable of being
called Christianity at all: the incorporation of the church's teachings into an
already-comprehensive vision of the cosmos as yet other expressions of its dualistic potential and nature.

As was noted earlier, examples of Anglo-Saxon wisdom literature are found
scattered throughout the traditional genre categories, notably in the elegies "The
Wanderer" and "The Seafarer," but it is most concentrated within the riddles
and metrical charms. Riddle 1, solved as a storm, is one of the many more
obvious expressions of the dualism and reconciliation of opposites that characterizes Old English wisdom literature:

> Hwylc is haeleþa þaes horsc   ond þaes hygecraeftig
> þaet þaet maege asecgan,   hwa mec on sið wraece?
> Þonne ic astige strong,   stundum reþe,
> þrymful þunie,   þragum wraece,
> fere geond foldan,   folcsao baerne,
> raeced reafige.   Recas stigað
> haswe ofer hrofum.   Hlin bið on eorpan,
> waelcwealm wera.   Þonne ic wudu hrere,
> bearwas bledhwate,   beamas fylle
> holme gehrefeð,   heahum meahtum
> wrecen on waþe   wide sended.
> Haebbe me on hrycge   þaet aer hadas wreah
> foldbuendra,   flaesc ond gaestas,
> somod on sunde.   Saga hwa mec þecce,
> oþþe hu ic hatte,   þe þa hlaest bere.

> [What is as wicked as man   or so mind-crafty
> that it might be said   in my coming is sorrow?
> When I fall in force,   fiercely cruel,
> powerfully crashing,   I sometimes punish,
> fire the fields,   burn folk-dwellings,
> waste buildings.   Smoke rises
> black over roofs.   A din is on earth,
> bitter death to men.   Then I drop on woods,
> forests flower,   trees fill
> from my rainy roof,   by high right
> borne on my journeys   and widely sent.
> I have on my shoulders   that which once wreathed
> earth-dwellers,   flesh and spirit,
> completely together.   Say what covers me,
> or how I am called,   that which I bear.]

In this relatively short poem, a multitude of dualisms manifest themselves. A storm may destroy villages and bring death to men as well as life to the woods and fields. It is both punishment and reward and recalls in its description of the water it carries in its clouds, which "once wreathed earth-dwellers . . . completely," both the primordial state prior to the Creation and the destruction of the world by the Flood. Even the duality of man—flesh and spirit—is evoked. In this way, Riddle 1 is typical of the vast majority of the surviving examples, but the real complexity of the religious perceptions of the Anglo-Saxons is perhaps best illustrated by comparing Riddles 30a and 30b. Identical except for five small but significant changes in wording, both refer to a constellation that is also a wooden object that brings joy to men and women. In 30b, purification is suggested by its destruction, and it appears as an object of worship rather than as a simple instrument of joy. Solved, respectively, as a harp and a cross, the two riddles amply express the very different aspects of Anglo-Saxon culture, the one a communal, bardic society, the other a Christian nation.

Of the metrical charms, "Against Unfertile Land" perhaps offers the most comprehensive vision because it combines pagan magic with Christian ritual and the rhetoric of both traditions in its efforts to restore fertility to the soil. On the pagan side, the charm employs sympathetic magic (cutting turfs from all geographic points and blessing them, anointing a plow with a mixture of every desired tree and plant as well as the milk of cows to be raised on the land, and so on), invokes Erce as the earth mother, and calls upon a sky God to fertilize her. Drawing on Christian symbols, it includes taking the sod to church and having a priest say mass over it, placing crucifixes in the soil, and invoking the four gospelers, the Virgin Mary, Christ, the Pater Noster, and the Ave Maria in the same prayers that include Erce and her consort. Even the timing of the ritual and physical actions call upon the seasons and the sun, as well as the Christian sense of left as the truly sinister side. As a whole, then, "Against Unfertile Land" is a magnificent example of Anglo-Saxon folk religion and an excellent illustration of its tendencies to reconcile spiritual perceptions rather than oppose them.

Finally, the bestiary pieces, although they are clearly Anglo-Saxon recreations of Latin originals, cannot be omitted from any examination of Old English religious and allegorical verse. They are, admittedly, wholly Christian in their doctrine, "The Partridge" or "The Dove," "The Panther," and "The Whale" representing the different aspects of the Trinity (Holy Ghost, Son, and Father, respectively). As more specific discussions of all these genres lie elsewhere in this volume, there is no need for fuller discussion of their more general attributes here.

Sadly, except for mainstream clerical compositions of clearly Christian sensibility, the wisdom literature of the Anglo-Saxons was almost entirely neglected through the 1800s. Late in that century and into the first quarter of the twentieth, a flurry of interest in solving the riddles occurred, amply summarized in Krapp and Dobbie's edition of the Exeter Book. This interest soon petered out, however, and very little indeed was attempted with the charms or the bestiary beyond literal understanding. The same tends to hold true up to the present, although growing recognition of the importance of popular culture in recent decades, especially in the religious-studies arena, has stimulated interest in the charms and riddles at least as religious artifacts, if not as wisdom literature. In other fields, Gregory Jember has defended the riddles as essential expressions of Anglo-Saxon culture and its world view, although his interest tends to lie in the overall genre of riddles themselves rather than in the Old English tradition as wisdom literature. Until very recently, most assessments of the charms have found their pagan characteristics to be merely incidental fossils of a dead past, or at best an adaptation of earlier pagan tradition to Christian purposes, much in the manner that the ancient symbols of holly and mistletoe have found their way into traditional Christmas decor. For a good summary of this view, refer to Karen Louise Jolly's article. Most recent work with charms and riddles has been done by Morgan, who defends them as significant wisdom literature and elucidates the dualism of the world view they embody. By and large, however, the area of Old English wisdom literature remains a rich mine for the interested scholar, one that must be explored before our understanding of the Anglo-Saxon sensibility can begin to claim any kind of comprehensiveness.

The neglect shown in the treatment of Anglo-Saxon wisdom literature is, fortunately, not evident in that of the high Middle Ages, probably because the latter is much more obviously Christian and hence more compatible with our preconceived view of the period. The Norman culture underlying mainstream high medieval English culture was firmly Christian and literate when it arrived with the Norman Conquest, and so initially a replacement rather than a symbiosis or assimilation of cultural expressions, including poetry, occurred. Thus we suddenly find allegory everywhere in literature, as opposed to its paucity during the Anglo-Saxon period, and the Christian religion imbues most genres to a very high degree indeed. The two frequently go hand in hand, although we do find political allegory as well, and except where the popular culture of the day—surviving almost solely in the folk ballad—appears, the world view from the twelfth through the fifteenth centuries is very much of a piece.

Religious allegorical verse of the high Middle Ages tended to develop in specific genres, the best realized being the morality play and a reworking of the version of the dream vision. However, we should not ignore the fact that wisdom literature here, too, crosses genre boundaries. It appears in the typology of the cycle plays and such symbolic scenes as the gift giving that closes the Wakefield *Second Shepherd's Play*, where the tennis ball, the bird, and the cherries respectively represent Christ's dominion of the world, the soul or the Holy Ghost, and the appearance of life in death represented by the Savior's coming. We find it again in the various exempla, those moral tales providing instructions for proper conduct (including the beast fables), and again in the Marian lyrics, in which the Blessed Virgin figures as the adored courtly mistress of the poet, who is, like the courtly lover, inspired to great deeds (moral behavior) through love of her inherent goodness. Religious overtones even color many of the stories of Chaucer's apparently secular *Canterbury Tales* and various allegories such as *The Parliament of Fowls* and *The House of Fame*. Some Christian sermons, too, such as those by Richard Rolle, are frequently allegorical. Finally, in the most famous romance of the period, Thomas Malory's *Morte d'Arthur*, we find a comprehensive combination of spiritual vision and several levels of allegory.

The vision expressed in English high medieval wisdom literature is solidly mainstream Christian, although perhaps somewhat darker in tone than that of its continental equivalent. It evinces a complete acceptance of Christian Neo-platonic binaries: one either follows God or the Devil, and all things in the world proceed from either one or the other and are therefore inherently either good or bad. The omnipotence of the Christian God prevents any attempt to understand the cosmos except through the Scriptures (which are themselves, of course, mediated by representatives of the church) or to manipulate it except through prayer. It follows from this that since man cannot understand God's plan, he should live his life in imitation of Christ; thus the greatest virtues are piety, humility, selflessness, acceptance of one's lot (as obedience to God's plan), and eschewing pleasures of the flesh and of this world in general in favor of spiritual purity. Life under these guidelines is much less complex than in the Anglo-Saxon view, especially since detailed plans for such behavior are laid out explicitly in such sermons as Mannyng's *Handling Sin* and the dream visions. Consider, for example, *Winner and Waster*, a short alliterative poem usually ascribed to Richard Rolle. In the form of a debate on economic troubles of the fourteenth century, it is, in fact, a sermon on how the good, humble laborer (the "salt of the earth") fulfills God's plan while the shirker, or "waster," not only harms the commonweal but rebels against natural order and harmony. The poem was possibly one of the sources for Langland's *Piers Plowman*, perhaps the best known of high medieval dream visions, which incorporates the sentiment into a heavy-handed allegory in which a town (the earth) stands between the tower of Truth and the dungeon of Wrong. The people, tempted by the pleasures of the flesh (the Seven Deadly Sins) are exhorted in a sermon by Conscience to seek Truth, and hence salvation. Those willing to labor honestly with Piers are then guided by him to the tower. In the process the characters meet with such personifications as Reason, Lady Meed (earthly reward and pleasure, another form of temptation), Repentance, and Clergy. Ultimately, the dream vision is a solid confirmation of the social hierarchy, although it does address the problem of corruption in the clergy. The anonymous *Pearl*, another dream vision, ad-dresses the problem of earthly versus heavenly rewards through a more specific situation. Here a jeweller has lost his "pearl without price," which saddens him beyond all reason. He falls asleep, and the pearl appears to him as a maiden dressed in white, dwelling in the New Jerusalem, who chastises him for thinking more of his earthly pleasure than of her (and, by extension, his) eternal reward in heaven. Not yet ready to enter heaven, the jeweller is sent back to complete his journey of life and to strive for his own place in the hereafter, much consoled by his vision. For obvious reasons, *Pearl* is generally believed to be an allegorical elegy for a lost child, but whether or not this is true, the lesson remains the same: man must accept his earthly lot, not put too much value on earthly joys, and strive for entry into heaven. Thus the poem echoes what in England is a particularly strong penchant for the *contemptus mundi* tradition.

The same inclination dominates the most famous of English medieval morality plays, *Everyman*. Here, too, Everyman must learn that rewards of this world ("Goods," "Kindred," "Fellowship," "Cousin") are fleeting and untrustworthy, and that only reliance on the gifts of God, both natural ("Five Wits," "Beauty," and "Strength") and spiritual ("Knowledge" and "Discretion"), can lead to salvation through the willing performance of Good Deeds and Confession of his sins. Ultimately, following the counsel of his Good Deeds, Everyman is saved and lies only briefly in his grave before ascending to heaven. So it is with all the moralities, other particularly fine examples of which include *Mankind* and *The Castle of Perseverance*.

Turning from such clearly religious wisdom literature to that usually conceived as secular, we need not scratch the surface very deeply to find a level of religious allegory operating in concert with the more worldly strains of a tale. In the romance *Sir Gawain and the Green Knight*, for example, if we set aside the problems of the chivalric code and courtly love, we find that Gawain's great failing is his lack of faith in God, initially represented by the image of the Virgin on the inside of his shield, which, significantly, is removed with the rest of his armor when he enters Bercilak's castle of pleasures. He keeps faith with his host and remains strong against the temptations of the lady until the latter reminds him of his mortality and offers to preserve him in his upcoming battle by giving him a magic girdle. This, of course, leads to the small punishment the giant metes out and, more important, becomes the source of his shame, for which he atones by forever wearing the girdle as a sign of his newfound humility. Even more than *Sir Gawain and the Green Knight*, Malory's *Morte d'Arthur* carries a level of Christian allegory in its obvious equation of the "once and future king," the savior of Britain who dies for his people but will return in his nation's time of need, to Jesus, his sacrifice, and the Second Coming. After all, what is Camelot but perfection on earth with an ideal Christian behavioral code recognized in the Knights of the Round Table, whose ultimate quest is that for the Holy Grail? Thus underlying the Normanized Celtic heroic myth with its primary allegorical level nostalgically looking back to the great King Henry V is another assertion of the need to strive for God and the transience of worldly achievements.

These two romances have an additional importance to a discussion of medieval wisdom literature, for they both betray their pre-Christian folk roots in native Celtic lore. These roots are not limited to the characters and tales themselves, but emerge in the magical elements, which are not, the reader will note, exclusively evil. In *Sir Gawain and the Green Knight* the magic of Bercilak and Morgan le Fay is a tool by which the hero is taught a Christian lesson;

moreover, Bercilak's oasis of pleasure appears in the thorny wilderness of Gawain's trials specifically in answer to a prayer he utters for help and succor. In *Morte d'Arthur* Arthur could not have been even conceived, let alone have come to kingship, without the agency of Merlin, a sorcerer surfacing frequently in the various Celtic mythic cycles, and after Arthur attains the throne, the wizard continues to guide him in establishing the most perfect of earthly kingdoms. True, Arthur's great adversaries are witches, but they are not adherents of Devil worship; rather, they are simply evil manifestations of the same magic that Merlin manipulates for good. Thus in these aristocratic expressions of folk myth, the peculiar version of Christianity characterized by the blending of pagan perceptions with church teachings witnessed in Anglo-Saxon wisdom literature continues into the high Middle Ages.

Unfortunately, it is only by looking through such aristocratic texts as these romances that we can catch glimpses of high medieval folk religion, for the populace remained largely non- or only marginally literate throughout the period, and those commoners who did achieve literacy were by and large employed within church institutions. As is clear from the discussion of the subject in this volume, medieval balladry comes to us as the only substantial body of folk poetry from the period, and very little of it addresses religion per se. It is worth noting, however, that there are a number of ballads (e.g., "Thomas Rhymer") that draw upon pre-Christian perceptions of the supernatural, although these are certainly not allegorical or overtly religious and thus lie beyond the scope of this chapter. As a result, we can only examine the wisdom literature of mainstream society in the English high medieval period and suggest that scholars interested in folk religion look to theological, art, and anthropological studies.

SELECTED BIBLIOGRAPHY

Adams, Robert. "*Mede* and *Mercede*: The Evolution of the Economics of Grace in the *Piers Plowman* B and C Versions." *Medieval English Studies Presented to George Kane*. Ed. E.D. Kennedy, Ronald Waldron, and Joseph Wittig. Wolfeboro, NH: D.S. Brewer, 1988. 217–232.

Alford, John A. "The Idea of Reason in *Piers Plowman*." *Medieval English Studies Presented to George Kane*. Ed. E.D. Kennedy, Ronald Waldon, and Joseph Wittig. Wolfeboro, NH: Boydell and Brewer, 1988. 199–216.

Andrew, Malcolm, and Ronald Waldron. Introduction. *The Poems of the Pearl Manuscript*. Berkeley: University of California Press, 1979.

Bloomfield, Morton. "Understanding Old English Poetry." *Annuale Mediaevale* 9 (1968): 5–25.

Boitani, Piero, and Anna Torti, eds. *Religion in the Poetry and Drama of the Late Middle Ages in England*. Cambridge: Brewer, 1990.

Flint, Valerie I.J. *The Rise of Magic in Early Medieval Europe*. Princeton, NJ: Princeton University Press, 1991.

Frye, Northrop. "Charms and Riddles." *Spiritus Mundi: Essays on Literature, Myth, and Society*. Bloomington: Indiana University Press, 1976. 123–147.

Grendon, Felix. "The Anglo-Saxon Charms." *Journal of American Folklore* 22 (1909): 105–137.

Hamilton, Marie Padgett. "The Meaning of the Middle English *Pearl*." *PMLA* 70 (1955): 805–824.

Jackson, W.T.H. "Allegory and Allegorization." *The Challenge of the Medieval Text*. Ed. Joan M. Ferrante and Robert W. Hanning. New York: Columbia University Press, 1985. 157–171.

Jember, Gregory. Introduction. *The Old English Riddles: A New Translation*. Denver: Society for New Language Study, 1976.

———. "Prolegomena to a Study of the Old English Riddles." *Journal of the Faculty of Liberal Arts, Saga University* 19 (1987): 155–178.

Jolly, Karen Louise. "Anglo-Saxon Charms in the Context of a Christian World View." *Journal of Medieval History* 11 (1985): 279–293.

Krapp, George Philip, and Elliott Van Kiirk Dobbie, eds. *The Exeter Book*. New York: Columbia University Press, 1936.

Mackenzie, W.R. *The English Moralities from the Point of View of Allegory*. Boston: 1914.

Morgan, Gwendolyn. "Essential Loss: Christianity and Alienation in the Anglo-Saxon Elegies." *In Geardagum* 11 (1990): 15–33.

———. "Dualism and Mirror Imagery in Anglo-Saxon Riddles." *Journal of the Fantastic in the Arts* 5.1 (1992): 74–85.

———. "Duality in *Piers Plowman* and the Anglo-Saxon Riddles." *Connotations* 1.2 (1991): 168–172.

Morgan, Gwendolyn, and Brian McAllister. "Reading Riddles 30A and 30B as Two Poems." *In Geardagum* 14 (1993): 67–78.

Owst, G.R. *Literature and Pulpit in Medieval England*. 2nd rev. ed. Oxford: Blackwell, 1961.

Pickering, O.S., ed. *Individuality and Achievement in Middle English Poetry*. Suffolk: D.S. Brewer, 1997.

Russell, J. Stephen, ed. *Allegoresis: The Craft of Allegory in Medieval Literature*. New York: Garland, 1988.

Ryan, Lawrence V. "Doctrine and Dramatic Structure in *Everyman*." *Speculum* 32 (1957): 722–735.

Scott, Charles T. "Some Approaches to the Study of the Riddle." *Studies in Language, Literature, and Culture of the Middle Ages and Later*. Ed. E.B. Atwood and A.A. Hill. Austin: University of Texas, 1969.

Spearing, A.C. *Medieval Dream-Poetry*. Cambridge: Cambridge University Press, 1976.

Tucker, P.E. "The Place of the Quest of the Holy Grail in the *Morte Darthur*." *Modern Language Review* 48 (1953): 391–397.

Vinaver, Eugène. Introduction. *The Works of Sir Thomas Malory*. 2nd ed. Oxford: Oxford University Press, 1967.

Williamson, Craig, trans. *A Feast of Creatures: Anglo-Saxon Riddle Songs*. Philadelphia: University of Pennsylvania Press, 1982.

Zeeman, Elizabeth. "Piers Plowman and the Pilgrimage to Truth." *Essays and Studies* 11 (1958): 1–16.

3

Alliterative Poetry in Old and Middle English

Scott Lightsey

Simply defined by the stressed repetition of sounds, alliteration is the " 'rum, ram, ruf,' by lettre" of Chaucer's Parson's complaint. This simplicity belies alliteration's metrical complexities and its central position in the history of English versification. Long before the enormously varied and complex alliterative output of Chaucer's time, alliteration was the dominant poetic form in Old English poetry. Before that it was the first poetic form of the Germanic tribes of central Europe. Consequently, alliteration is deeply tied to the Germanic origins of English language and poetics and spans centuries, even contributing to the popularity and persistence of modern English terms like "cyberspace" and "World Wide Web." But as a poetic form, its impact is deeply significant for the history and cultural continuity of medieval English literature.

Alliteration antedates Germanic literacy, originating in the continental proto-Germanic languages of prehistoric Europe. Early Germanic tribes used oral recitals of alliterative poetry to transmit their cultural heritage, the legends and lives that gave them an identity as a people. In this manner alliterative poetry could be said to be deeply intertwined with the social life of the Germanic people, including those who spread alliterative poetry westward as they migrated to Britain after the Roman withdrawal.

The earliest surviving example comes from the Galleus Horn, an early-fifth-century artifact carved with an alliterative runic inscription:

Ek hlewagastiR HoltijaR   horna tawido
[I, Hlewagast, Holtís son, made the horn] (Russom, *Beowulf* 1)

This early continental alliterative line shares characteristics with the Old English alliterative poetry employed over four hundred years later in the epic poem *Beowulf*:

God mid Geatum   Grendles dæda
[Good amid the Geats, Grendel's deeds] (l. 195)

The attributes shared by these lines indicate some of the basic rules of English alliteration. They both alliterate, and we would say that the Old English line is metrically bound by the alliterating [g], just as the earlier line is bound by [h]. Both lines alliterate on accented syllables. Also, there is no restriction on the number of unaccented syllables between stresses. Although these lines are separated by the sea and several centuries, the continuities of style between them suggest that the conventions of alliterative poetry have deep linguistic and cultural roots.

English verse is expressed in a long line composed of two half-lines, the first half-line called the on-verse and the second half-line the off-verse. These are separated by a metrical pause or caesura but remain bound together by the alliterating initial sounds. Consonant sounds alliterate with like consonants, but vowels and diphthongs all may alliterate with one another. Alliteration exploits speech rhythms native to accentual languages, emphasizing the tendency toward word-initial stress in the Germanic languages from which English is descended. This allows the poet to compose using regular stress, but to do so in lines of varying numbers of syllables.

Stress in alliterative verse is linguistically significant, generally falling on syllables whose importance coincides with prose phrasal stress so that the most semantically important words are highlighted by the meter. Old English alliterative half-lines are generally categorized by one of five types of stress outlined by Sievers in 1893. Despite a few refinements in the hundred or so years since they were established, these basic types are still used in critical discussions of scansion in Old English poetry. Each half-line may be characterized as follows, with "/" representing stressed syllables, "\" representing minor stress, and "x" representing one or more unstressed syllables:

Type A: /x/x
Type B: x/x/
Type C: x//x
Type D: //\x or //x\
Type E: /\x/

Each line must have at least one alliterating sound in the on-verse and might have two in the off-verse. The first stressed alliterating syllable in the off-verse is called the headstave, and its alliteration dictates the alliteration of the entire line. Structurally, the verse depends on stressed syllables, and the number of unstressed syllables may vary. In this example from Pope's normalized edition of *Cædmon's Hymn*, the half-lines alliterate on the sound [m]:

Metodes meahta / and his mod-geþanc
[The maker's might and his thought]

We could scan this example from Cædmon and see that the on-verse is type A since it scans "/xx/x" and the off-verse is type B since it scans "xx/x/." The intervening unstressed syllables in the on-verse and the anacrusis of the off-verse do not significantly affect the meter.

It also should be noted that although these critical examples of the verse are typeset to distinguish between half-lines, in the original manuscripts Old English verse was not neatly arranged in paired half-lines, but rather was written continuously. Alliteration could be distinguished only by hearing the poetic rhythm as the poem was spoken or sung aloud.

Internal evidence, such as the image of men singing to a harp passed in the hall in the Venerable Bede's Cædmon story, the poetic voice's reference to singing performance in *Widsith* (ll. 104–5), and the references to singer and harp in *Beowulf* (ll. 89–90) suggest that Old English alliterative poetry was performed to the accompaniment of a harp. The instrument found among the relics in the sixth-century Sutton Hoo ship burial confirms the poetic image of the singing scop, the "shaper" or storyteller who performed stories in verse. John Pope and Andreas Heusler have emended Sievers's method of scansion to accommodate the idea of a singing performance.

The preliterate origins of this poetry suggest that alliterative poetry, in addition to its linguistic affinity for languages with initial stress, may have arisen in part as a mnemonic aid to the scop during oral presentation. Early alliterative poetry allowed the illiterate composer to recite his verse using a style called oral formulaic composition by Albert Lord. This method offset the limits of memory by employing a set of stock formulae or phrases on a range of traditional motifs. The story singers had to memorize thousands of lines of verse, and the repetitive patterns and phrasing of Old English poetry allowed the singer to perform lengthy narrative works from memory.

The style was flexible, and slight variations could be introduced according to the necessities of performance and audience. This variation, called apposition, allowed the poet to reiterate previous themes, expanding the poem without requiring additional material. Such changes nevertheless maintained the structural and thematic continuity of the alliterative poem, preserving its overall character as it was handed down through pagan history to the Christian clerics who first recorded alliterative verse in written form.

As England was re-Christianized in the seventh century, literate English clerics began to record this native verse, and the flexible and likely variant formulaic aspects of any given oral composition were frozen in manuscripts. These could then be read aloud, maintaining the repetitive similarity of phrasing and verse forms in scribally transmitted preliterate compositions such as *Beowulf*. In the transmission from oral to literate forms these works acquired Christian flavoring. The Exeter Book riddles and other alliterative Old English works show evidence of Latinate influence in their content, and many Latin works were rendered in alliterating half-lines when they were translated into the vernacular. This selection of "The Whale" from the Old English version of the Latin *Physiologus* is one such example:

> Is þæs hiw gelic   hreofum stane(1. 8)
> [His mien is like rough stone]

That the Latin form was transformed into alliterative meter suggests the depth of English investment in the native verse form underlying the use of the vernacular.

Toward the end of the first millennium, as northern invaders were pressing English culture further southward, the depredations of the Danes caused the loss of much of the thriving English manuscript culture. Most surviving manuscripts are from the south, and the near uniformity of transmission in the West Saxon and Anglian dialects now makes it almost impossible to construct a plausible timeline for most Old English compositions. With only a few exceptions, linguistic information on provenance also is discouraged by the lack of manuscript evidence, so that scholars must often judge matters of age and chronology according to metrical evidence. The surviving Old English alliterative verse is a small body of diverse works ranging from translations of Latin to folk epics and chronicle poetry of military encounters. Among these surviving works is the earliest known Germanic epic, *Beowulf.*

Beowulf is a secular heroic poem, the earliest English epic, and exists in a single copy, the manuscript Cotton Vitellius A.xv. The 3,182 alliterating lines of this elegiac poem offer an unprecedented access to the literary life of the turn of the millennium, when it was recorded, and that culture's view of an otherwise almost undocumented earlier pagan culture. Images of pagan practices and the general tone of grim Germanic heroism are conveyed in regular alliterating long lines, comprised mainly of type-A half-lines, with a relatively even distribution of the other four types. Note how even in the simplest line the often-guttural effect of Old English is softened by the rhythmic combination of consonant and vowel alliteration:

> Aledon þa   leofne peoden(1. 34)
> [Laid they down the king they loved]

The poem betrays an extreme artistic sensitivity in the use of alliteration. The poet also exploits the versatility of alliterative style through the use of attendant features of Old English poetic style such as litotes or understatement, compounds, and metaphorical kennings such as the word *hron-rade* ("whale-road," 1. 10) for sea, and by relating long and apparently digressive matter to the central narrative through structural parallels and thematic contrasts rendered in a highly competent alliterative style.

In contrast to the highly artistic qualities of *Beowulf*, the surviving 325 alliterating lines of the fragment known as *The Battle of Maldon* consciously exploit the heroic themes found in *Beowulf*. The unknown poet clearly was not as versatile as the *Beowulf* poet. There is little to distinguish the poem metrically, since it was recorded in a highly repetitive and largely unremarkable style that only occasionally rises to something like this example of interlocked alliteration:

"Gehyrst þu sælida   hwæt þis folc segeð?" (1. 45)
[Hear you seafarer what these folk say?]

Note how the line alliterates on [h], [s], and [þ]. The use of alliteration here is also significant because the poet, conscious of the value of archaic themes from the Old English alliterative tradition, aligns his poem thematically and stylistically to elevate a military encounter that occurred in the year 991 to the tone of a heroic folk epic in only a few hundred lines. The cultural identification with alliterative style, as well as the nationalist themes from Old English poetry, produces in *The Battle of Maldon* a lesser but significant cousin to the metrical power achieved in *Beowulf*.

Very little alliterative verse survives in Old English. The problems associated with the destruction of manuscripts by the Vikings were exacerbated by the disappearance of written records in the vernacular after English rule in Britain was suddenly ended by the Norman victory in 1066. According to extant manuscript evidence, in the years after the Norman Conquest the Anglo-Saxon literary culture suddenly died away, replaced by Norman writings rendered in favored continental forms. Romance languages lend themselves readily to end-rhyme, and rhymed French poetry displaced the native alliterative verse that had been used in popular folk- and court-centered compositions before 1066. From the eleventh century onward, little record of Old English alliterative meter exists. Between the end of the Anglo-Saxon period and the explosion of alliterative verse in the fourteenth century, the scarcity of documentation in extant manuscripts offers only a fragmented record, giving many critics the impression of a distinct break in the metrical practice of alliteration between the Old and Middle English periods.

However, the waning of the Old English manuscript culture does not necessarily imply the end of the Old English alliterative style; according to some scholars, the classical alliterative style died during this period, but others hold that alliterative poetry continued to develop alongside the English language in the sparsely documented centuries of French influence. The idea of a rupture in the tradition is unanimous, but the idea of complete discontinuity is disputed on grounds that the alliterative verse of the Old English period may have in effect "gone underground," preserved in the vernacular speech of the English under Norman rule. According to this theory, the vernacular poetic turned alliterative poetry once again into an oral form practiced among the illiterate, largely English lower classes before reemerging with the development of Middle English in the wake of the elite Norman culture's linguistic and social dominance. Oral transmission leaves little ground for evidence, and this argument has fallen into disfavor in recent years. Despite the fact that theories of continuity necessarily stand on sparse available evidence, they are nevertheless worthy of attention given their importance in the evolutionary character of this lively debate, and in recent years a growing consensus has held that some form of continuity is probable.

The manuscript record offers little evidence of the use of alliteration between the eleventh and fourteenth centuries, and only a handful of works remain to suggest continuities between Old and Middle English styles of alliteration. Alliterative verse in this period underwent changes, becoming widely varied in style and in general difficult to classify closely using the Sievers types applicable to older English literature.

There are in fact a small but significant number of alliterative poems in manuscripts dating from the twelfth and thirteenth centuries. Dates of composition are difficult to determine, but many works, such as the *First Worcester Fragment*, carry internal evidence suggesting earlier composition, and their alliteration is metrically continuous with the earlier alliterative style. A twelfth-century manuscript, Cambridge Ff.I.27, includes the twenty-one-line *Description of Durham*, which is probably the latest extant poem written in the rigorous alliterative style of earlier Old English verse:

> ðær monia wundrum gewurðað / ðes ðe writ seggeð (1. 20)
> [there many marvels occur, as the book says]

In this line the interlocked alliteration preserves the Old English model, but subsequent alliterative verse of this sparsely documented period shows more variation or flexibility in style and includes the charm *Against a Wen* in MS Royal 4.A.xiv, dating from the mid-twelfth century; *The Grave*, a mid-twelfth-century poem of twenty-five alliterating verses preserved in MS Bodleian 343; and the *Death Fragment*, MS Trinity College, Cambridge, B.14.39. Scarce longer works from this period include the *Proverbs of Alfred*, MS Jesus College, Oxford, 29, also existing in a badly corrupt copy bound with the *Death Fragment*; and *The Departing Soul's Address to the Body*, a 349-line poem in MS Worcester Cathedral Library 174, bound with the 23-line *First Worcester Fragment*.

Alliterative works such as the poems of the Katherine Group tread the line between poetry and a prose analogue of the rhythmic prose alliterative style of earlier writers like Wulfstan. As part of the debate over alliterative continuity, these works are growing in importance, and critical study will continue to define more closely the irregularities of these transitional alliterative works. But no issue of the transitional period overshadows the metrical interest and controversies generated by slightly later works that appeared during the long apparent hiatus in the alliterative style between 1250 and 1350.

Caught in the controversy over possible transition is Layamon's *Brut* (MS Cotton Caligula A.ix, c. 1225, and MS Cotton Otho C.xiii, c.1275). The poem is a lengthy chronicle account of the history of the Britons, divided into three episodic sections of vernacular legendary material. The poem's approximately 30,000 alliterating lines record the period from the fall of Troy to the life of King Arthur, and from Arthur's death to Æthelstan's expulsion of the Britons to Wales.

The poem exhibits some of the four-stress meter of the earlier alliterative style, but it also includes a great deal of five-, six-, and even seven-stress meter, and in addition to the alliteration, two in five lines contain end-rhyme. Whereas Old English alliteration typically carried a double alliteration in the first half-line, the *Brut* in many on-verses carries only single alliteration. The use of rhyme, assonance, and syllabic rhythms suggests that this poem bears little formal similarity to Old English alliteration, and the debate over whether and what sort of poetry it is has been thoroughly treated by Brehe, who argues that *Brut* is rhythmic prose. Among recent scholarship suggesting that there are indeed continuities between Old and Middle English alliterative styles, transitional-period works such as the thirteenth-century *Bestiary* figure prominently. The *Bestiary*, from British Museum MS Arundel 292, dates from the middle of the thirteenth century and is a Middle English translation of the Latin *Physiologus* of Theobald. Edwin Duncan argues that the poem shares formal characteristics with both earlier and later forms of alliterative verse, making it a possible link between Old and Middle English alliterative forms (31).

Although not poetry in the strict sense, the alliterative prose of early writers like Wulfstan and the later works by Richard Rolle and the author of the *Ancrene Wisse* has suggested to Kubouchi and others the possibility of prose origins for the later alliterative verse. Whatever may be made of the intervening period, the extant manuscript evidence indicates the appearance of a highly developed alliterative style in the later fourteenth century, and scholars have debated the manner of its origins for decades.

In the mid-fourteenth century alliterative poetry reappears as a dominant force in the verse production of England, demonstrating affiliations with a variety of classes, contents, and causes. It has long been thought that this body of work was a colloquial expression of the northwest Midlands, since this is the dialect of most of the corpus. It is in fact a vital part of the national literature, interacting with a variety of forms and social circumstances. Middle English alliterative poetry such as the content of the Harley manuscript lyric *The Blacksmiths* treats urban themes, and Langland's *Piers Plowman* is rendered in a style and using a vocabulary specifically geared toward a broader national audience, his success attested by the more than fifty manuscripts of his work and by his influence on other poets. The alliterative *Morte d'Arthur* exemplifies the suitability of the alliterative form for conveying matters of nationalist importance, and the popularity of alliterative poetry continued to extend into the translation of Latin works into late Middle English alliterative classics like the *Wars of Alexander*.

In general, the genre of alliterative poetry continued to exhibit a high level of literacy and scholarly awareness. According to David Lawton, "There [was] no corpus of Middle English poetry more clerkly, literate and essentially bookish than the alliterative" (6). Contrary to earlier assumptions that the Middle English alliterative line is not as rigorously metrical as that in most Old English poetry, Hoyt Duggan and others have suggested that Middle English alliterative meter is every bit as rule bound as its Anglo-Saxon antecedent (Duggan 223ff.).

In the mid-fourteenth century alliterative poetry assumes a very different character from the Old English forms discussed earlier. General description must here suffice, since the variety of alliterative verse forms is almost as great as the number of extant poems, so free were poets' hands with the alliterative style. The later alliterative line is looser, employing a four- or five-stress line, usually with three alliterating words and at least two stresses after the caesura. Unlike the rigid Old English verse, the Middle English alliterative line could take a larger range of accented syllables and is defined most clearly by the simple presence of alliteration flanking a strong medial pause or caesura. The variety of the meter and the flexibility it demonstrates in a wide range of uses should not be taken as an indication of structural decay of the form, but rather as a display of the power of English alliterative poetry to thrive among the many upheavals, linguistic and political, that characterize the fourteenth century.

The unique manuscript British Museum Cotton Nero A.x preserves the only copies of four disparate poems on disparate themes: *Pearl*, *Cleanness*, *Patience*, and *Sir Gawain and the Green Knight*. These works display a range of alliterative styles under the hand of a single author, indicating the self-consciousness with which variants on the style were produced, much as one would expect of French troubadour lyric.

Pearl employs end-rhyme to separate the verse into stanzas according to matched pairs of rhyming sounds. Although three of four lines contain alliterating words, the structure relies on an iambic accentual pattern rather than on the alliteration guiding the other poems in the manuscript. The admixture of rhyme and stanzaic form used by the poet actually renders alliteration structurally unimportant in the case of *Pearl*, which employs alliteration only stylistically (Duggan 232). *Patience* is marked in the margins of the manuscript with a double stroke on every fourth line, leading editors to denote these groups as stanzas. While a basic four-line syntax prevails, there is no clear metrical requirement to render the poem stanzaically. *Sir Gawain and the Green Knight* is a formal variant in which the long lines are organized into verse paragraphs of variable length, each completed with a single-stress line termed the bob, followed by a final quatrain or wheel of three-stressed alliterating lines, end-rhyming with the bob on the second and fourth line. While the poem is structurally dependent upon alliteration for its form, the tendency toward rhyming accentual verse is indisputable.

The flexibility with which the author manipulates alliteration for various effects in these four poems suggests some of the expansive qualities of alliterative poetry in the fourteenth century. Middle English poets could freely mix the natural tendencies of English to alliterate initial sounds with the flexibility of the continental end-rhyme, producing a richer variety of form than what was available under the system of Germanic alliteration and grammar.

William Langland, one of the greatest Middle English poets to use alliterative verse, avoided the highly ornate diction and compiled detail employed by his contemporaries. Instead, he used a plain or simplified alliterative style and vocabulary intended to convey his matter to a non-Midlands audience, possibly in the environs of London. The success of this style is evident in the number of surviving manuscripts and in the spawning of the poems of the *Piers* tradition, a series of works influenced by the politics as well as the plain alliterative style of Langland's work. The social critique in Langland's verse, conveyed in such a powerful poetic form, resonated with followers who produced an extensive literature of alliterative verse in the *Piers* tradition.

Piers Plowman uses alliterative verse to remarkable effect, exploiting the style's ability to switch rapidly from rhetorically elevated diction to simple, homely tones. The poet uses a range of effects in a widely varied line, sometimes reducing alliteration by repeating sounds on semantically unimportant words and often leaving the verse devoid of formal devices. The effect is one of marked simplicity masking a powerful poetic, often reflected in lines whose alliterating stress diminishes in the off-verse, dissipating the buildup of stress in the line. Typical of his more ornate style is this line from 15.74 of the B-text, alliterating on [t], [m] and [s]:

> And tellen men of þe ten comandementʒ   and touchen þe seuene synnes

This single line displays complex interlocked and serial alliteration, and often the poet exploits the cohesive effect of alliteration by interlocking over several lines in order to sustain an idea. Critical debate has yet to resolve the exact nature of his unique and flexible alliterative line, although the consensus holds that formal aspects of Langland's alliteration are more highly regulated than previously thought.

Just as the English investment in the vernacular and its forms was displayed in the Old English alliterative translation of the Latin *Physiologus*, so too Middle English writers translated Latin into their native alliterative idiom. A translation of the Latin *Historia de Preliis*, the *Wars of Alexander* is extant in two fifteenth-century manuscripts, Oxford Bodleian MS Ashmole 44, and Trinity College, Dublin, MS D.4.12. The late date of the manuscripts does not rule out an earlier composition, though such matters are difficult to pin down. What is of particular interest to students of alliterative poetry is the matter and manner of translation of this late-antique Latin epic into a fourteenth-century English context (Turville-Petre, *Alliterative Revival* 98–99), for example, the emphasis in the translation on religious asceticism among the Brahmins and the tendency toward rendering monstrous and marvelous elements in extreme detail for the amusement of an audience similarly interested in piling up of detail in poems such as *Sir Gawain*.

If the lack of a large manuscript record gives the extant corpus of Middle English alliterative poetry an impression of idiosyncrasy, the variety of alliterative verse in such a small corpus should also attest the originality and power of the alliterative form. Further, as the preceding discussion spanning hundreds of years of alliterative poetry suggests, there is no "standard" alliterative form in English, but rather a rich and varied body of poetry developing over several centuries and undergoing numerous formal and cultural changes.

Studies of alliterative poetry usually address themselves to either Old or Middle English before organizing around either metrical studies or literary analyses and textual criticism. In addition to these period-specific studies of alliterative verse, a range of critical analyses address the possible continuities between Old and Middle English alliterative poetry, attempting to bridge the actual gaps in evidence as well as those caused by critical methodologies that could not admit the possibility of continuity. Editions, translations, and recordings are also important parts of the study of alliterative poetry.

For students not yet equipped to read Old and Middle English, there are many modernized translations. Those seeking such editions should read carefully the translator's comments on methodology, lest they be misled by the format of an edition intended to address theme and narrative at the expense of poetic form. Examples such as Marie Borroff's excellent translation of *Sir Gawain and the Green Knight* tend to preserve the basic aspects of the meter while making the matter of the poem accessible to modern audiences. Student editions such as J.R.R. Tolkien's *Sir Gawain and the Green Knight*, E. Talbot Donaldson's version of *Piers Plowman*, and A.V.C. Schmidt's translation of the *Piers Plowman* B-text provide excellent access to the poems through modernized language, leaving metrical matters to more advanced texts. Additionally, parallel texts such as Howell D. Chickering's edition of *Beowulf* provide excellent comparative resources for the beginning translator.

Additionally, spoken-word recordings are available to help students and professionals improve their ear for alliterative verse in performance. Caedmon Records produces compact-disc versions of spoken-word performances, and the Chaucer Studio makes available a vast range of cassette tape recordings of readings in a variety of Old and Middle English dialects by prominent scholars. Recent among these is Alan Gaylord's compact disc of readings of alliterative poetry sung to demonstrate the poetic properties of the form in performance.

The scholarship on Old English alliterative poetry is vast. R.D. Fulk's *History of Old English Meter* is widely regarded as the place to begin. His introduction is an excellent historical review of the study of early alliterative meter, and subsequent chapters detail linguistic and metrical evidence in support of his conclusions on the chronology of Old English poetry. Geoffrey Russom's works on the linguistic aspects of Old English poetics address the deeper issues underlying alliterative form, and he appears among the major scholars anthologized in McCully and Anderson's *English Historical Metrics*, a collection that covers the range of Old and Middle English metrics, with a heavy emphasis on alliterative verse.

Many studies addressing alliterative poetry in Middle English take up the issue of continuity, beginning with Oakden in his second volume and including R.M. Wilson in *Early Middle English Literature*. David Lawton's *Middle English Alliterative Poetry* addresses the range of critical issues raised in the field. Turville-Petre's *The Alliterative Revival* is, as the title suggests, of the school favoring discontinuity, and Salter's work on *Piers Plowman* complements this perspective.

Studies such as Ralph Hanna's chapter in *The Cambridge History of Medieval English Literature* take the field to task for imposing terms like "revival" and "colloquial" with the consequence of creating unnaturally deterministic temporal and geographical rifts in the scholarship on the alliterative form. Similarly expansive models of approach are sure to evolve as scholars expand current methodologies and editors produce increasingly versatile, flexible electronic editions.

These critical studies of Old and Middle English are based on a wealth of helpful facsimiles and editions. The foundational series for the study of alliterative verse in Old English is *The Anglo-Saxon Poetic Records* (*ASPR*) edited in six volumes by Krapp and Dobbie. For many Old English poems, *ASPR* still provides the definitive edition, but particular editions are preferred for major poems. Examples include the Klaeber edition of *Beowulf*. Middle English alliterative poetry is widely varied, and critics often forgo broad studies to address the poetics of individual texts. For example, Derek Brewer and Jonathan Gibson's *A Companion to the Gawain-Poet* offers a range of perspectives in poetics, culture, and textual study. Individual editions too carry invaluable information, such as the critical apparatus of Duggan and Turville-Petre's *Wars of Alexander*. The most widely available editions of Middle English alliterative verse are the Early English Text Society (EETS) volumes, and such individually published single editions are supplemented by collections of less well known alliterative verse, which abound in editions such as Turville-Petre's *Alliterative Poetry of the Later Middle Ages: An Anthology*.

Finally, it is worth noting that non-medieval-specific studies of English metrics may offer insight into the history of the alliterative verse form beyond the confines of medieval studies. Jakob Schipper collects examples of alliterative verse demonstrating the changing use of the form down to the nineteenth century. Among these we find an example of the affective power of medieval alliterative form:

> If thus the king's glory / our gain and salvation
> Must go down the wind / amid gloom and despairing (120)

Here nineteenth-century medievalist poet William Morris enlivens the themes of his poetry by using alliterative meter evocatively, signaling what he felt were his primitive Germanic cultural affiliations.

Due to the variety of alliterative verse and the number of centuries over which English poets developed and exploited the form, it is considerably simpler to define it than it is to describe its complex position in the history of medieval English literary form and social movement. Alliterative verse is so varied in its forms, contents, and applications that in this space may be offered only the briefest introduction. But perhaps the major factor in the lively and ongoing critical interest in alliterative meter has to do with its variety and durability. Scholarly debates centering on issues of meter and the continuity between Old and Middle English alliteration are currently being supplemented by new investigations into the social and political importance of alliteration and the relationship of alliterative verse to the dominant French rhyming conventions of Middle English. Controversies will continue to abound in the field, making it one of the most vital areas of inquiry for medievalists interested in the verse production of England during the first thousand years of insular literacy.

SELECTED BIBLIOGRAPHY

Borroff, Marie, trans. *Sir Gawain and the Green Knight*. New York: Norton, 1967.

Brehe, S.K. " 'Rhythmical Alliteration': Ælfric's Prose and the Origin of Laȝamon's Metre." Ed. Françoise Le Saux. *The Text and Tradition of Laȝamon's Brut*. Cambridge: D.S. Brewer, 1994. 65–87.

Brewer, Derek, and Jonathan Gibson, eds. *A Companion to the Gawain-Poet*. Cambridge: D.S. Brewer, 1997.

Cable, Thomas M. *The English Alliterative Tradition*. Philadelphia: University of Pennsylvania Press, 1991.

Chickering, Howell D., Jr., trans. *Beowulf: A Dual-Language Edition*. Garden City, NY: Anchor, 1977.

Donaldson, E. Talbot, trans. *Will's Vision of Piers Plowman*. Ed. Elizabeth D. Kirk and Judith H. Anderson. New York: Norton, 1990.

Duggan, Hoyt N. "Meter, Stanza, Vocabulary, Dialect." *A Companion to the Gawain-Poet*. Ed. Derek Brewer and Jonathan Gibson. Cambridge: D.S. Brewer, 1997.

Duggan, Hoyt N., and Thorlac Turville-Petre. *The Wars of Alexander*. Oxford: Published for the Early English Text Society by the Oxford University Press, 1989.

Duncan, Edwin. "The Middle English *Bestiary*: Missing Link in the Evolution of the Alliterative Long Line?" *Studia Neophilologica* 64 (1992):25–33.

Frantzen, Allen. "The Diverse Nature of Old English Poetry." *Companion to Old English Poetry*. Ed. Henk Aertsen and Rolf H. Bremmer, Jr. Amsterdam: VU University Press, 1994. 1–17.

Fulk, R.D. *A History of Old English Meter*. Philadelphia: University of Pennsylvania Press, 1992.

Gaylord, Alan T. *The Poetics of Alliteration: Readings of Medieval English Alliterative Verse*. Supplement to *Medieval Perspectives*, vol. 14. Chaucer Studio Occasional Readings, no. 26. [Provo, UT]: Chaucer Studio; [Richmond, KY]: Southeastern Medieval Association, 1999.

Gollancz, Israel. Introduction. *Pearl, Cleanness, Patience, and Sir Gawain, Reproduced in Facsimile from the Unique Manuscript Cotton Nero A.x. in the British Museum*. Early English Text Society, Original Ser. 162. London: EETS, 1923.

Hanna, Ralph. "Alliterative Poetry." *The Cambridge History of Medieval English Literature*. Ed. David Wallace. Cambridge: Cambridge University Press 1999. 488–512.

Heusler, Andreas. *Lied und Epos in Germanischer Sagendichtung*. Darmstadt: Wissenschaftliche Buchgesellschaft, 1960.

Hutcheson, B.R. *Old English Poetic Metre*. Suffolk: D.S. Brewer, 1995.

Kiernan, Kevin S. *Beowulf and the Beowulf Manuscript*. New Brunswick, NJ.: Rutgers University Press, 1981.

Klaeber, Friedrich, ed. *Beowulf and the Fight at Finnsburg*. Boston: Heath, 1922.

Krapp, George Philip, and E.V.K. Dobbie, eds. *The Anglo-Saxon Poetic Records*. New York: Columbia University Press, 1931–1954.

Kubouchi, Tadao. *From Wulfstan to Richard Rolle: Papers Exploring the Continuity of English Prose*. Cambridge: D.S. Brewer, 1999.

Lawton, David, ed. *Middle English Alliterative Poetry and Its Literary Background: Seven Essays*. Cambridge: D.S. Brewer, 1982.

Lord, Albert Bates. *The Singer of Tales*. Cambridge: Harvard University Press, 1960.

McCully, C.B., and J.J. Anderson. *English Historical Metrics*. Cambridge: Cambridge University Press, 1996.

Oakden, James Parker. *Alliterative Poetry in Middle English*. 2 vols. Manchester: Manchester University Press, 1930–1935.

Pope, John C. *The Rhythm of Beowulf*. 2nd ed. New Haven, CT: Yale University Press, 1966.

———, ed. *Seven Old English Poems*. Indianapolis: Bobbs-Merrill, 1966.

Russom, Geoffrey. *Beowulf and Old Germanic Metre*. Cambridge: Cambridge University Press, 1998.

———. *Old English Meter and Linguistic Theory*. Cambridge: Cambridge University Press, 1987.

Salter, Elizabeth. *Piers Plowman: An Introduction*. Cambridge, MA: Harvard University Press, 1962.

Schipper, Jakob. *A History of English Versification*. Oxford: Clarendon Press, 1910.

Schmidt, A.V.C., trans. *Piers Plowman: A New Translation of the B-Text*. New York: Oxford University Press, 1992.

Sievers, Eduard. *Altgermanische Metrik*. Halle: Max Niemeyer, 1893.

Stevick, Robert D. "The Oral-Formulaic Analysis of Old English Verse." *Speculum* 37 (1952):382–389.

Tolkien, J.R.R., and E.V. Gordon, eds. *Sir Gawain and the Green Knight*. 2nd ed. rev. by Norman Davis. Oxford: Clarendon Press, 1967.

Turville-Petre, Thorlac. *Alliterative Poetry of the Later Middle Ages: An Anthology*. Washington, DC: Catholic University of America Press, 1989.

———. *The Alliterative Revival*. Cambridge: D.S. Brewer, 1977.

Wilson, R.M. *Early Middle English Literature*. London: Methuen, 1939.

4
Balladry

Gwendolyn Morgan

The folk-song tradition of balladry, expressing popular perceptions on a particular issue or a world view in general, comes to us as the only substantial poetry corpus of the medieval English commoner. Oral in nature, balladry tends to a high degree of superficial change (i.e., variation in surface expression), but the consistency in underlying narrative is surprisingly strong. Nonetheless, balladry remains a slippery term, and the genre eludes all but the most general of classifications. Formally, for example, although certain theorists insist upon very specific rhyme and metrics, both the medieval genre and its modern descendant defy such limitations: most examples employ stanzas of two or four lines, but others pattern stanzas on up to eight or ten lines; four stresses per line may be the most common, but meters range from three to seven stresses; the most usual rhyme schemes are alternating (*abab*) and couplet, but others surface with sufficient frequency to belie any rule. In other words, loose formal guidelines exist, but they are no more than guidelines. Even what would seem a universal formal characteristic—that ballads are set to music (which, incidentally, accounts for the regularity of formal characteristics within any specific example)—cannot be taken for granted, for the earliest surviving example in the English canon is almost certainly a clerical composition, literary in origin, and by the late twentieth century, this arguably had become the norm.

The most notable mechanical attribute of medieval balladry is the vocabulary of stock lines and phrases shared by the genre as a whole. These are formulaic descriptions that attach themselves frequently to completely unrelated ballads. Consider, for example, that any number of heroes and heroines call for their servants to "saddle me the black, the black / or saddle me the brown"; that many a lover sets his mistress on a "milk-white steed / and himself on a dappled grey"; that Robin Hood, Johnny Cock, Adam Bell, and other such outlaws all meet "under the greenwood tree"; that towers and the hair of maidens both shine "like the gold so red"; and so forth. These stock expressions serve a number of purposes. At the most basic level, they help maintain rhyme schemes, as their usual appearance as the second and/or fourth line of a stanza reflects. Additionally, they act as a shorthand to express commonplaces necessary for coherence but that are in themselves irrelevant to the heart of the story. But most important, stock phrases offer a performing balladeer time to think on his feet, whether he is calling upon memory for an old song or composing a new one. This latter point requires some expansion.

In a literate culture such as our own, a variety of written modes may be employed to permanently record news, opinions, history, philosophy, behavioral norms, spiritual perceptions, and so forth. In an oral culture, such pieces of information can only reside within human memory, and certain individuals (scops, bards, balladeers) possess the mental acumen and language skills to perform the function of recording and preserving the society's store of them. The context of medieval balladry was one in which the strict hierarchy of the feudal system separated the literate aristocracy from the non- or marginally literate commoner, and hence the latter fell back upon the oral mode for expression. Song, because of its supporting musical structure, provides a formal regularity that particularly facilitates such extensive demands on memory, relieving the poet of the need to consider metrics and rhyme schemes, or their variation; he needs only add words to "slots" already provided. To increase efficiency in storing vast amounts of raw information, the singer simply retains skeletal versions of individual tales, using the stock vocabulary to flesh them out. Any particular singer during any particular performance may select different formulaic phrases to expand the memorized outline, and this, along with inevitable variation in unimportant detail (whether from personal preference, error, or faulty memory) in part explains the multiple variations distinguishing ballad versions and analogues.

The formal simplicity resulting from these techniques of retention and performance necessarily leads to a loosening in the relationship of form to content in balladry. True, a lively lilt would be unlikely to serve as an appropriate vehicle for a tragic love story, but the fact remains that subject matter has little to do with patterns in meter or rhyme, poetic density, or even basic sound play. Moreover, the manipulation of variations in these patterns to reflect moments of pathos, crisis, or emphasis simply does not appear. Indeed, this lack of correlation between subject and expression is a primary distinction setting the genre apart from other poetic modes. That the musical mode of balladry is one reason for this has already been noted. Another, however, is that the ballad generally eschews extensive description and emotive expression, presenting instead rather bald narrative. Entering the drama of its story "in the fifth act" (to use a critical cliché), it presents crisis and denouement, but tends to ignore the events that led up to them; it concentrates on action and result rather than motive. Any attempt to set the scene or to delineate character is virtually nonexistent, dismissed with stock phrases so commonplace as to be meaningless. In concert with this minimalist approach to the story is the famous "impersonality" of the ballads, that is, a general lack of overt moral commentary or philosophizing on action or character. Indeed, the narrator is infrequently a real presence, usually appearing only to call his audience to attention or assert the veracity of his tale, and this reflects the relationship of balladry to the earlier epic oral tradition and the prestigious position of the bard within the culture that produced it. Nonetheless, despite all this apparent objectivity, to assume that balladry offers no judgment on the behavior of its characters is a mistake. It is merely that such judgment is implicit, shown in a concern for cause-and-effect relationships in the action.

As an oral mode, balladry at its simplest functions as a kind of "verbal newspaper," recording significant events in one geographic area and passing them on to others, and it should not, therefore, surprise us to find that the majority of ballads have their bases in actual events. These events range from sordid, local occurrences (consider the infanticide described in *The Cruel Mother*) to the commemoration of landmark occurrences (such as the border skirmishes presented in *Durham Field* and *Chevy Chase*) and political events (for example, the disastrous loss of the king's ship, intended to carry home his royal bride, immortalized in *Sir Patrick Spens*). This newspaper function accounts for the composition of a ballad within a short time after the event described. Yet newspapers are incomplete without editorial comment, and even those reports that are seemingly most objective express opinion; so, too, with balladry.

As was noted earlier, while overt moral or other commentary on the action and characters is by and large absent from the ballads, it is implicit in their usual ironic mode, which often stretches into parody. Thus the absurdity or disaster of a ballad situation itself directs the audience to the obvious conclusion: rejection of behavior or thinking that leads to undesirable results. Consider the following stanzas from *Sir Patrick Spens*, describing the aftermath of a shipwreck in which all are lost:

> O our Scots nobles were right loath
> To wet their cork-heeled shoes,
> But long before the play was done,
> Their hats, they swam above.
>
> . . .
>
> Half over, half over to Aberdour
> It's fifty fathoms deep,
> And there lies good Sir Patrick Spens
> With the Scots lords at his feet.

The ballad opens with a political rival directing the king to send Sir Patrick on a long sea voyage, an ill-considered suggestion given the time of year, as both Sir Patrick and his sailors know. Moreover, Patrick is sensitive to the plot afoot.

Nonetheless, his honor and feudal obligation to the king require him to obey the order, which ends in total loss, leaving the ship destroyed, all hands drowned, and the mission of the king undone. Yet the ballad forestalls any movement toward sympathy or pathos. Its closing vision is comedy: the nobles' hats float on the surface of the water after their owners have submerged to spend eternity lying at the feet of a heroic, but nonetheless very dead, Sir Patrick in a parodic reversal of feudal hierarchy and chivalric obligation. Moreover, terming the endeavor a mere "play" suggests the artificiality and absurdity of a social code demanding such self-defeating behavior over the dictates of common sense.

Indeed, this very rejection of aristocratic idealism constitutes the value system propounded by the ballads and hence, we may assume, embraced by the subculture that produced them. Heroism, rejected as self-indulgent at best and more frequently downright foolish and destructive, gives way to canniness; romanticism and courtly love must succumb to the needs of everyday survival; the optimism of spiritual salvation is eclipsed by the bitterness of worldly existence. Only pragmatism leads to success in medieval folk song. The mothers of *Lord Randal* and *Edward, Edward*, for example, concern themselves not with sorrow at the imminent deaths of their sons—the deaths are unavoidable—but with the inheritance portions left behind to the family. Similarly, various discarded mistresses, such as those from *Fair Annie* and *The Lass of Rock Royal*, worry over lost means of support for themselves and the legitimacy of their children rather than broken hearts. Rape, in *The Knight and the Shepherd's Daughter*, drives the heroine not to shame or suicide but to a healthy demand for redress at court in the form of marriage and the security it offers. Earl Brand, like Sir Patrick Spens, pays for his chivalry with death: the old man he refuses to kill despite the advice of his beloved immediately returns with their enemies. Thus this emphasis on common sense and the basic needs of survival, and with it tacit rejection of idealistic behavior lying beneath the guise of honor or love, continues throughout the genre.

We need not search long to find the reason for such a coldly practical approach to life, for the ballads' world view reflects the bleak existence of the medieval commoner. Quite simply, the universe is a dangerous, unforgiving, and untrustworthy place that makes no special allowances for humanity. Consider the following vision of existence from the thirteenth-century *Riddles Wisely Expounded*:

> Hunger is sharper than the thorn,
> Thunder is louder than the horn.
>
> Longing is longer than the way,
> Sin is more ready than the day.
>
> God's flesh is better than the bread,
> Pain is more fearful than is death.

. . .
Thought is swifter than is the wind,
Jesus is richer than the king.

Sulphur is yellower than is the wax,
Silk is softer than is the flax.

Gone is the world created by God for man, and in its place we find thorns,
thunder, wind, and a human lot defined by hunger, pain, death, and unfulfilled
longing. The prosaic comparisons made to the sacraments ("God's flesh") and
Jesus' sacrifice, and the basic need implicit in them, undercut any spiritual consolation that they should recall, for clearly the speaker knows only flax, not silk,
and conceives the king as so rich that only Jesus himself might be more so.
Moreover, human behavior, in which sin occurs more frequently than the sun
rises, seems unlikely to earn redemption. Indeed, throughout the ballad universe,
humanity is generally cruel and self-serving, certainly untrustworthy: around
every corner lurks one who would lie, cheat, rape, steal, maim, kill, or simply
refuse to pay for good services rendered. Even the framework of *Riddles Wisely
Expounded* confirms these perceptions, for a demon posing as a chivalric knight
and proposing courtly love has posed the riddles in the first place, and the
maiden has defeated him only by calling upon her life experience to answer
them correctly. The best one can do, in the ballads, is to look to one's own
survival, to rely on one's wits, to expect nothing, to trust nobody. It is a bitter
vision indeed.

Just as the ballads record and transmit specific events and general perceptions,
they also function to reflect social change and sway opinion. Certainly the prop-
agandistic possibilities of folk song were exploited early. *London Lickpenny*, for
example, provides criticism of aristocratic exploitation of the working class,
Queen Eleanor's Confession popular opinion on the queen's morals, and several
ballads dating to 1264 and 1275 satiric rejection of the policies of Henry III and
Richard of Alemaigne, respectively. Such ballads, to continue the newspaper
analogy, constitute the editorials. Yet, as we have seen, the perceptions of a
society are more than reactions to current events: behavioral standards and systems of belief transcend the immediate and are more profound and resistant to
fluctuation. It is this essential world view that *Riddles Wisely Expounded* exemplifies and that remains unchanged over the next several centuries, appearing
in other ballads as diverse as *The Gardener, Hind Etin,* and *The Unquiet Grave.*
This sensibility—bitter, commonsensical, and pragmatic in the extreme—
clashes violently with the ideology expressed in the chivalric code with its paradigms of true knighthood, courtly love, and Christian piety. In this way, in the
field of popular folk song, the underclass conducted its philosophical warfare.

Just as balladry undercuts and rejects the romanticism and idealism of the
courtly code, which dominated mainstream literature of the period, so does it
negate the old misconception of supreme piety and reverence for the church as

the primary factors directing the commoner's thinking. Not for the underprivileged medieval Englishman the vision of unimpeachable divine order in the universe that human society reflected, nor a mild acceptance of his lot in this life in exchange for heavenly rewards. Rather, the almost complete absence of a religious sensibility from the ballad corpus suggests a general lack of spiritual consolation. References to religion are scant indeed, and when they do appear, they almost invariably reflect an angry resentment of ecclesiastical abuses, turning monks, abbots, and bishops into villains or the butts of jokes. Only one religious ballad of popular origin, *The Bitter Withy*, survives, and this reflects class antagonism and a desire for retribution in the here and now rather than a humble bowing of the head to supposed divine will. Consider its tale: the child Jesus asks to play ball with "lords' and ladies' sons," but they reject and ridicule him because of his low birth. His immediate reaction is to lure the noble children to their deaths, and although Mary spanks him for this "misbehavior," he remains unrepentant: instead, he curses the withy, whose branch Mary employs in the beating, to be "the very first tree / that withers at the heart." In this way the ballad not only credits Jesus with very human class jealousy and vengeful desires (so much for turning the other cheek), but reflects a good deal of satisfaction in the lower class's triumph over its oppressors. On the whole, however, Christianity simply does not figure in medieval popular folk song, seemingly irrelevant to or impotent in the face of the commoner's bitter existence.

Yet one subset of the ballads does attempt a reconciliation of the commoner's world view with that of the aristocrat. Songs of the yeomanry, so called because of their social origin and affiliation, provide an uneasy marriage between chivalric idealism and common sense, reflecting an important social phenomenon accompanying the breakdown of the feudal system. As the middle classes grew in wealth and numbers, and consequently in influence, they encroached upon the traditional province of the aristocracy, entering its ranks through marriage or the purchase of titles; challenging its authority, both in Parliament and popular uprising; infiltrating the households of the nobility in positions of influence; and establishing trade guilds that wielded considerable economic as well as political and social power. In urban areas known as the "citizen class," in the rural areas as the yeomanry, these successful commoners embraced as part of their rise in stature the idealism of the class to which they aspired. Yet because their success was also due to their established value system, they did not abandon their reliance on wit, pragmatism, and hard work. From a union of the two are their heroes—Robin Hood, Johnny Cock, Adam Bell, and their ilk—born. The 450-line *Gest of Robin Hood* epitomizes yeoman balladry. Its hero, overtly identified not as an out-of-favor aristocrat but as a yeoman, rules his forest band on the model of feudal obligation, where rank is attended by privilege and honor. Similarly, his character traits are courtly, for he worships women (he will not attack any party that includes females), takes the Virgin Mary as his courtly mistress, observes the codes of hospitality and fair play, holds honor as the most sacred of human qualities, is skilled at arms (not incidentally, specifically the bow, the weapon of the yeoman class), and defends the weak against evil oppressors. On the other hand, Robin is also noted for his audacity and trickery; he is a master of disguise; he experiences no moral qualms in robbing the rich (even of the ecclesiastical persuasion); he flaunts transgressions of the (admittedly unjust) law and its representatives. In the single most important motif of the yeoman ballads, he poaches the king's deer despite his fiercely avowed loyalty to the Crown. That the yeoman heroes are always outlaws indicates the continued marginalization of the class. That they are better at being chivalric and pious than their social superiors indicates not only the corruption rampant in the aristocratic and clerical institutions but also the yeomanry's fitness for membership in the ruling class. That they live from successfully poaching the king's deer and ultimately obtain forgiveness, respect, and honor at his hand can only be considered a metaphor for the social changes taking place during the fourteenth and fifteenth centuries. Hence the yeoman ballads are not so much a literature of ideological revolt as one of the assimilation for which the middle classes strived.

Balladry, then, is best understood and classified according to the cultural functions it performs and the world view and opinions it expresses, rather than its formal attributes. It represents, during the English Middle Ages, the division not only of class but of culture in British society, and consequently of the concerns of that culture, ranging from everyday behavior to general world view. Within what has been defined as a single genre, we find the divisions that merit, in mainstream literature, critical consideration as separate genres, but that in balladry merely become subclasses—domestic ballads, romantic ballads, comic ballads, political ballads, ballads of chivalry and of the yeomanry, and so forth. Ultimately, and quite simply, balladry is the collected "literature" of a culture, separate and distinct from that of the ruling classes that comes to us as the received canon. All this means, also, that balladry is the first recognizable popular-culture product in the English tradition.

From its misty inception sometime during the tenth or eleventh century through its heyday in the fourteenth and fifteenth and down to the present era, the ballad alone of poetic forms has enjoyed uninterrupted popularity. As literacy increased during the sixteenth and seventeenth centuries, the ballad lost its preeminent position as the only, or even the primary, means for transmitting the perceptions of the people who produced it, and became more regularly used in its function as a vehicle for sociopolitical criticism and satire. Although, thanks to the enduring universality of their vision of the universe and their entertainment value, earlier traditional ballads continued to be sung, new compositions were limited to topics of immediate popular concern or interest. In these the broadside tradition was born. Later attempts to appropriate the ancient form led to a great outpouring of "literary" ballads in the nineteenth century, and today ballads of all three forms exist (and are composed) in abundance. All three classifications (traditional, broadside, and literary), however, ultimately derive from the medieval period.

The traditional or folk ballad is the most prolific in the early periods, arising from the popular consciousness and expressing its vision of the universe and behavioral norms, regardless of the subject through which they were exemplified. Originally arising primarily in rural areas (as did British society), it performed the functions of all the various types of literature in a lettered society. Some critics see it as the uninterrupted evolution of the earlier epic tradition, but although it is certainly in part rooted there, its connections to other song forms, primarily the carol, harvest songs, and thyme songs, cannot be ignored. All, however, see it as a genuine folk product. Broadside balladry, too, began in the Middle Ages, originally part and parcel of the traditional ballad and only gradually, as urbanization, literacy, and, later, the availability of cheap printing increased among the population as a whole, emerging as a separate entity. It continued its development as a distinct variety in the cities, reflecting the specific and immediate concerns of laborers and the new middle classes represented by trade guilds, entrepreneurs, and civic leaders. During the late seventeenth and eighteenth centuries the parodic or satiric ballad reached its peak, compositions appearing almost daily to ridicule, criticize, or condemn various current events; cheaply and carelessly reproduced on "broadsheets," available for a pittance from street vendors or simply anonymously posted in public locations, the type earned for itself the name "broadside." The distinction between traditional and broadside ballad, both still alive and healthy in the world of popular folk song today, is perhaps best illustrated by an example from the Canadian scene of the mid-1970s. The popular American western ballad *You Picked a Fine Time to Leave Me, Lucille* is a true folk product, telling a tale of love and betrayal in modern rural America. Decades later, during the tenure of Canadian prime minister Pierre Trudeau, whose policies and long term of office were coming under fire, the ballad was adapted within days of Trudeau's wife leaving him. The chorus satirically reflected not only the prime minister's personal discomfiture, but his political troubles and the populace's eroded confidence in him:

> You picked a fine time to leave me, Margaret,
> I've got three hungry children
> And I'm losing Quebec.
> You say I've got Horner, but I can't hug Horner;
> What do you mean, "wanna bet?"

Even a mere twenty years later, the names "Trudeau" and "Horner" and the actions of their owners have begun to fade, although many will still recognize the strains of the original ballad peering through the adaptation, and the unsympathetic parody of the latter. If the original American version is a traditional folk ballad, timeless in its depiction of betrayed trust, broken home, and hard rural life ("I've got four hungry children and a crop in the field"), the Canadian

parody is a broadside, having meaning only in a very specific, time-bound political situation; no one sings or records it now, its import having disappeared
with the next general election.

Unlike the broadside, the literary ballad has always been distinct from the
genuine popular product, but it nonetheless appeared very early. Indeed, the
oldest (late-twelfth- or early-thirteenth-century) extant English ballad, *Judas*, is
probably literary in origin, an example of a medieval practice of "rehabilitating"
folk song. Early on, ballads earned disapproval from mainstream society for
their rebellious and irreverent nature, and a number of low-level clerics attempted to bring balladry more in line with the received view by writing new,
religious verses to established popular tunes. *Judas* and *Herod and Saint Stephen*
are probably the best known of such endeavors, and although they cannot be
considered products of true popular culture, they are nonetheless an integral part
of the history of the genre. The aristocracy also occasionally composed ballads,
but the efforts of both the nobility and the clergy always bear the earmarks of
their ideologies and are ill matched with the body of true medieval folk song.

As class boundaries continued to disintegrate, social mobility brought the
ballad tradition into increasingly literary circles, and by the high Renaissance
such poets as Christopher Marlowe, Sir Walter Ralegh, and John Donne were
composing verse in ballad or mock-ballad form. The practice fell off in the
Restoration and the eighteenth century, although popular composition (primarily
of the broadside variety) continued, but arose again with the romantic poets
(consider Wordsworth and Coleridge's *Lyrical Ballads*), who sought inspiration
in the simplicity of rural life and folk tradition. Continuing through the Victorian
era with the like of Thomas Hardy, the ballad survives today as traditional folk
song, literary endeavor, and political satire throughout the English-speaking
world.

Because of the elusive nature of the ballads' definition, in considering representatives it is perhaps best to offer a well-known example of each subject
classification and then proceed to a comparison between folk, literary, and clerical approaches to the genre. Approximately half of the surviving ballads fall,
in light of their mundane subjects, into the category of "domestic songs." These
are the most universal in nature, concerned with themes and motifs that, through
everyday experiences, express the commoner's vision of existence. We have
already examined *Riddles Wisely Expounded* as a representative of this type.
Better known is *Edward, Edward*, a song in question-and-answer form (also like
Riddles and the almost equally well known *Lord Randal*), in which a young
man returns home with a bloody sword and answers a series of questions posed
by his mother. He first asserts that he has killed his hawk, then his horse (both
with explicit associations of nobility of character, generosity, and loyalty), but
his mother knows that neither is the true case. He finally confesses to having
murdered his father, with a later implication that he did so on the advice of his
mother. After ensuring that Edward's fate will be death, the mother quickly
proceeds to an examination of his will—what will his wife, his children, and

herself receive of his possessions? In what appears to be exceptional bad grace, Edward curses his "towers and halls / 'till they fall down," his wife and children to beggary (for no apparent reason), and his mother to hell for her part in the murder. The significance of the exchange is twofold. First, the emphasis throughout the ballad remains upon pragmatics: what has he done, what is the penalty, who will inherit what? Never is motive or repentance an issue, nor is the mother concerned for anyone's fate but her own. Second, the sordid nature of the deed itself and the fact that his mother apparently advised Edward to commit the murder, along with Edward's total disregard for his innocent wife and children, bespeak a dim view of human character, but one nonetheless in concert with the bleakness of the common vision. So, too, with *Lamkin*, another domestic song. Here Lord Wearie contracts with the mason, Lamkin, to build a castle but then refuses to pay for his labor and instead goes off across the seas on unexplained business. True to his threat (which Wearie ignores), Lamkin murders his wife and son, aided by the child's nurse, in retribution. Although the two culprits are hanged upon Wearie's return, the ballad concentrates in the main on the murders themselves, justified by the nurse's cry "What better is the heart's blood of the rich than of the poor?" To the unrelieved general pessimism of the ballads *Lamkin* thus adds a testimony to aristocratic abuse of the laborers and a goodly dose of class jealousy and rebellion, once again accurately reflecting social conditions of the Middle Ages.

Next in number are the romantic ballads, those dealing with the love relationship between the genders. Still sung today, *Barbara Allen* is the best known of these. A young man pines away for love of the title character, who, when summoned to his deathbed, pragmatically responds that there is nothing she can do for him, and why should she care since either she does not know him (version A) or he deserves his fate for slights he paid her earlier (version B)? Overtaken by remorse after his death, however, Barbara Allen declares that she, too, will die in consequence. Sadly, *Barbara Allen* is atypical of medieval romantic ballads in that it supports the fiction (to the medieval commoner) of true, transcendent love and punishes the heroine for not succumbing to it. Usually the opposite is true: those who indulge such idealism ultimately meet a bad end, while those who guide such interests with healthy concerns for family, wealth, and everyday life tend to make out better. Consider, for example, *The Gardener*, in which a young man woos a maiden with promises of garbing her in flowers from his garden, suggesting that they live together there in idyllic pastoral existence. The young woman, however, is much too sensible to accept his offer and turns his metaphor on its head in her response:

> The hailstones shall be on thy head
> And the snow upon thy breast,
> And the east wind shall be for a shirt
> To cover thy body next.

Thy boots shall be of the tangle [seaweed]
Which nothing can betide;
Thy steed shall be of the wan water:
Leap on, young man, and ride!

Obviously this young woman knows what is important in everyday life. So, too, does the heroine of *Hind Etin* learn, years after she elopes to the woods with a low-born lover. Seven children later, Etin explains to his young son why his mother is so miserable: she was a king's daughter and could have had an easy life had she not indulged their foolish passion. Fortunately for all involved, the child goes to his grandfather, explains the situation, and returns all to the king's good graces. The title characters of *Lord Thomas* and *Fair Annet* are not so lucky, however. After wrestling with the issue of pragmatics versus true love, Lord Thomas opts for the former. Sadly, Annet decides to attend the wedding, Thomas goes back on his decision, and he, Annet, and the bride die in a triple murder-suicide. Such is the penalty of true love.

A less known ballad, but one that encompasses all the motifs of the romantic songs, is *The Douglas Tragedy*. In this song another pair of star-crossed lovers elope, but during their escape the hero is mortally wounded. He dies later that night, and his bride dies shortly thereafter of grief. The penultimate stanzas are from balladry's common stock vocabulary:

Lord William was buried in St. Mary's church,
Lady Margaret in Mary's choir;
Out of the lady's grave grew a bonny red rose,
And out of the knight's a briar.

And they two met, and they two plait,
As fain they would be near;
And all the world might know right well
They were two lovers dear.

The motif of the sympathetic grave plants originates in medieval courtly romances, the earliest known occurrence being in versions of *Tristan and Iseult*. In the romance they stand as the final image of transcendent courtly love. Adapted by ballads, however, the grave plants meet bitter fates. The two stanzas just quoted are followed by this closing commentary on the efficacy of romantic idealism:

But by and rode the Black Douglas
And, oh, but he was rough!
For he pulled up the bonny briar,
And threw it in St. Mary's loch.

Once again borrowing images from aristocratic literature only to subvert them, the ballads transform this symbol of all that is best about romance into one depicting all that is wrong with it. Only the means of destruction varies. Sometimes, as in this ballad, it is a human rival; in others it is accident, as when an old woman cuts off the lover's knot in *Lord Lovel* or when a careless clerk does the same in *Fair Margaret and Sweet William*; in still others the culprit is nature itself, as in *Lady Alice*, when a "cold, northeasterly wind" simply breaks the stalk. Whatever the cause, the sympathetic grave plants are rarely allowed to stand unmolested, surely as significant a commentary on the efficacy of romantic love as the fact that the lovers themselves almost invariably die.

Of the yeoman ballads, *A Gest of Robin Hood* epitomizes the genre, of which the standard motifs and hero have been discussed earlier. Other good examples of this subset include *Adam Bell* (who might just as well be Robin Hood) and *Johnny Cock*. Of all ballad types, this class is the most consistent, for while plot details vary, the hero is always a good yeoman outlawed for poaching the king's deer who fights against unjust officials of the law and the church; a master of arms and disguise, he defends the poor and helpless and is usually pardoned by the king and raised to his household. Even plot details—archery contests, the robbing of rich clerics, the narrow escape of the hero's party from entrapment in a castle after defeating twenty times their number—tend to remain the same.

Surviving religious ballads, except for *The Bitter Withy*, are all literary clerical compositions. Nonetheless, any study of medieval balladry would be incomplete without reference to *Judas* and *Herod and Saint Stephen*. Both are very short, simplistic, and heavy-handed in their symbolism. The former, representing the oldest complete manuscript version of an English ballad, characterizes Judas as an idiot so foolish as to be robbed of the thirty pieces of silver Jesus has given him to purchase food. Worried that he will be upbraided, he betrays the very man whose anger he seeks to avoid in order to recoup his losses, and to make matters worse, he refuses the gold offered him for the betrayal, stating instead that he must have the thirty pieces of silver to replace those that were stolen. Obviously the song partakes of the medieval tradition of ridiculing evil (thereby reducing its power) and traditional biblical characters who are against Christ. *Herod and Saint Stephen* is even less interesting, recounting only the miracle of a roasted fowl (borne on a platter to Herod by Stephen) rising and crowing in confirmation of Jesus' birth and foreshadowing his resurrection. Both these songs are typical of clerical rewrites and lack the strength of vision (however negative) or manipulation of motif evident in the folk products.

Sir Patrick Spens (discussed at length earlier) stands as the best-known example of the ballads of chivalry, in which knightly deeds either meet with disaster or ridicule or are simply reduced to insignificance in the face of common sense. In *The Boy and the Mantle*, for example, an elflike child visits Arthur's court with magical articles that expose the knights as cowards and cuckolds and Guinevere as a "bitch and a witch and a whore bold," the latter an accurate if somewhat bald assessment. The ballad sensibility simply does not allow for cloaking deeds in fancy phrases, and the boy merely tells it as he sees it. *The Marriage of Sir Gawain* (an analogue to Chaucer's "Wife of Bath's Tale") also exposes both Arthur and Gawain as cowards, leaving the loathly lady with her wisdom and common sense firmly in control. It is *The Twa Corbies*, however, that serves as a particularly fine example of the commoner's view of the courtly tradition, especially when it is juxtaposed to its literary analogues, *The Three Ravens* and *The Corpus Christi Carol*.

Of these ballads, it was once thought that *The Twa Corbies* was a much later cynical variation of the idealistic *Three Ravens*, and despite the obvious affinities in story, image, and form, *The Corpus Christi Carol*, as its name implies, was not even considered a ballad and therefore left out of any comparisons. However, fragments of *The Twa Corbies* have since been located in earlier manuscripts, and given its consistency of vision with the main ballad corpus, it now has been accepted as a medieval folk composition, while its analogues are viewed as literary ballad imitations. Which of the two secular pieces came first is still debated, although in the context of the present discussion this hardly matters. Nonetheless, starting this comparison with *The Three Ravens* is perhaps best, for its aristocratic value system will be most familiar to readers of medieval literature. In it three ravens discuss breakfast possibilities, one observing that a slain knight lies close by, but that he is too well guarded by his hawks and hounds for them to ravage his body. At this point the knight's beloved buries him and then herself dies of love. The imagery clearly supports the chivalric code, for the knight's shield lies over his body like a badge of honor, and the loyalty of the heraldic companions—the hawks and hounds—attests to his worthiness. Moreover, the body itself lies in a "green field" until it is laid to rest in "an earthen lake," both Edenic images of rebirth. The devotion of the lady, kissing his wounds, dying in her bereavement, is worthy of courtly love, and the canonical hours (prime, evensong) that punctuate the action, as well as the final closing apostrophe to God to "send every gentleman / such hawks, such hounds, and such a leman," suggest an underlying and compatible Christian sensibility.

While *The Three Ravens* supports the aristocratic ideology on all levels, its companion piece seems equally to undercut it:

> "In behind yon old foul dike,
> I know there lies a new-slain knight,
> And nobody knows that he lies there
> But his hawk, his hound, and lady fair.
>
> "His hound is to the hunting gone,
> His hawk to fetch the wild fowl home,
> His lady's taken another mate,
> So we may make our dinner sweet.

You'll sit on his white neck-bone,
And I'll peck out his bonny blue eyes;
With a lock of his golden hair,
We'll thatch our nest when it grows bare.

Many a one for him makes moan,
But none shall know where he is gone.
O'er his white bones, when they are bare,
The wind shall blow for ever more.

Here again is the familiar bleak vision of the ballads. Without prospect of resurrection, the body lies hidden in a stagnant ditch, abandoned by the companions
that should symbolize loyalty and fidelity. No sense of honor, only one of futility
and hopelessness, dominates the scene. Yet the matter-of-fact tone of the corbies,
seeking only to survive and thatch a bare nest, is echoed by the new pursuits
of the hound, hawk, and lady: in true, pragmatic fashion all have gone on with
the business of living rather than indulge futile obsession with that which cannot
be changed. Together the poems offer two sides of the same coin, the same
situation evaluated according to opposing value systems, and the result of a
comparison is a succinct means of summing up the ideological conflict from
which they spring.

The Corpus Christi Carol represents the third side of the medieval tripartite
society, the church. It transforms the dead knight into the eternally bleeding
body of Christ, the lady love into the Virgin Mary, who weeps at his feet, and
the hawk into a metaphor for the Holy Ghost. The colors gold, purple, and red
complete the iconography. Yet rather than leave anything to misinterpretation,
this clerical adaptation becomes as heavy handed as those discussed earlier in
describing a stone at the head of the bed with "*Corpus Christi* written thereon."
No room for error exists. Its form identical to that of *The Three Ravens* (and
therefore slightly different from that of *The Twa Corbies*), the poem was likely
written as a companion piece to the aristocratic version, both of which may or
may not have been "rehabilitations" of the popular piece. Whatever the case, its
reverent and somber optimism again serves to emphasize the complete absence
of any similar religious sensibility from the main ballad corpus. The world view
of medieval balladry, regardless of subject, and even in more humorous modes,
remains cynical, pragmatic, and ultimately dark.

While medieval balladry itself stretches back to the tenth century, its literary
and critical history begins only in the eighteenth. Prior to this time, the ballads
were not considered poetry at all by those in charge of the canon, but rather the
trivial amusements of the family gathering or, in its worse light, a means of
propagandizing and rabble-rousing. However, in their search for a British "national character," the eighteenth-century antiquarians conducted the first timid
ventures at constructing an English literary history. Unfortunately, as it came to
them, the ballad was held in well-established contempt, for by the seventeenth
and eighteenth centuries the broadside version, which caused the political elite

no end of trouble, dominated. Political figures of the time even came to view it as an essential means of controlling public opinion. As early as 1703, for example, Fletcher of Saltoun noted that "if a man were to make all the ballads, he needed not care who should make the laws of the nation" (quoted in Friedman 71), and shortly afterwards Richard Steele observed in issues 135 and 502 of the *Spectator* (c. 1712) that Queen Elizabeth had her minister of state review current ballads to determine and manipulate the tide of popular opinion. In 1722 Daniel Defoe asserted in "The Ballad Maker's Plea" that balladry's primary function was "a useful incentive to mischief" (59). Later, Horace Walpole is known to have suggested that his party secretly compose and disseminate ballads against the French Revolution and even in support of themselves. He nonetheless was aware that he was wielding a double-edged sword and cautioned against a colleague's suggestion of their casual appropriation for other purposes. Thus the earliest analyses of and attempts to understand or imitate ballads were almost purely political.

Nonetheless, operating under the influence of John Dryden's theory of the linear development of poetry (*Of Dramatic Poesie*, 1668), Joseph Addison argues in his noted "Chevy Chase Papers" (*Spectator* nos. 70–74) that "the sentiments of that ballad are extremely natural and poetical, and full of the majestic simplicity which we admire in the greatest of ancient poets," and that the ballad's lack of refinement was no excuse for "prejudice . . . against the greatness of the thought." In other words, the ballads reflected an esteemed English national character, rooted deeply in the past, that produced singularly noble and profound sentiments and thoughts despite the rudeness of expression. An anonymous 1715 tract, *A Pill to Purge State-Melancholy*, echoes the opinion. Even so, it was not until the great antiquarian movement blossomed in the second half of the eighteenth century, with the works of Thomas Percy, Thomas Warton, and Joseph Ritson, that the ballad received a broader interest and defense. All remained concerned with the ballad's reputation as a rabble-rousing tool, but they also continued the defense begun by Addison, asserting its value as a key to the "history, the poetry, the language, the manners, or the amusements of our ancestors" (Ritson, "Advertisement" to *Ancient Songs and Ballads*). Not perceiving the deliberate irony of the ballads or understanding the oral nature of their form, however, the eighteenth-century literati never analyzed the ballads for formal merit, Percy even going so far as to indulge in what Samuel Johnson called "enthusiastic improvement" of the pieces in his Folio Manuscript before he published them in his *Reliques of Ancient English Poetry* (1765). The latter is the first significant work of ballad scholarship, recording and justifying a large number of ancient examples. Following close on its heels, Warton's *History of English Poetry* (1774), while lamenting the satirical, invective broadside, nonetheless asserted that certain ancient songs "have transmitted to posterity the praises of knightly heroism, the marvels of romantic fiction, and the complaints of love" (59). The opinion expressed in Ritson's 1802 *Dissertation on Romance and Minstrelsy* also subscribes to this antiquarian impulse.

While the antiquarians of the eighteenth century at least recognized balladry as meriting a place in the English literary tradition, they also planted the seeds for a continued misunderstanding of the ballads that endured until the 1950s. In their eagerness to see the early songs as reflecting the ideals of the chivalric code, the re-creations of which dominated perceptions of nationalism in their own age—and in their belief that early poetic expression was clumsy and crude, awaiting their own refinements for improvement—they germinated the idea of the ballads as imperfect, crude reflections of the courtly romance. That illiterate commoners were necessarily less intelligent or poetically talented, that their emotions and understanding were less developed, seems an impossible belief today, yet that is exactly what underlies the perception of the ballads as poor imitations of courtly themes, motifs, and tales. Such is antiquarians' mixed blessing upon the literary history of the ballad.

Throughout the eighteenth century the only significant activity in ballad composition remained in the broadside variation, which enjoyed unprecedented and uninterrupted success until it petered out in the mid-nineteenth century. In the tradition of folk balladry, while transmission of ancient songs flourished, only limited new composition took place. It remained for the romantic poets, especially William Wordsworth and Samuel Taylor Coleridge, to resurrect the genre, albeit in literary form, with *Lyrical Ballads* (1798). They chose to imitate balladry because, as Wordsworth expresses it in his preface, "poems . . . written upon more humble subjects, and in a still more naked and simple style," better lend themselves to expression of pure and essential emotion, being more elemental and closer to the natural world. Proceeding from the same basis as the ballad's eighteenth-century defenders, Wordsworth manages to elevate the stature of the ancient form another notch in literary history, asserting that the very simplicity that the antiquarians found defective was a quality to be desired in poetry. Even so, he continued the assumption that traditional songs were sometimes subject to faulty or unpolished expression, which should be corrected. Thus Wordsworth unwittingly perpetrated two important errors in understanding medieval balladry: first, that simplicity of form indicated simplicity of thought; and second, that crudeness (including the genre's hard-headed practicality, merciless irony, and sardonic treatment of idealized subjects) was unintentional and merely the result of inexpert poetics. Despite these two important but brief attempts to secure a place for balladry in the mainstream literary canon, the tradition by and large remained ignored or scorned in literary criticism. Needless to say, however, true folk ballads continued to be sung and composed, and a few mainstream poets, notably Thomas Hardy, continued to follow Wordsworth's lead in appropriating the form for "serious" literary compositions.

By the turn of the twentieth century, medieval studies as a discipline had finally been established in curricula of higher learning. Literary studies followed suit and began to consider all medieval forms, not merely those of the ruling classes, and the ballad once again commanded interest, even more than it had done before. In 1882–1898 Francis Child produced *The English and Scottish*

Popular Ballads, which remains the most comprehensive compilation of folk song from all periods. Organized roughly according to date but without any attempt at critical analysis and using the most arbitrary of selection criteria, Child's work is nonetheless a monumental achievement for students of folk song and popular culture. However, early critical studies continued very much in the same vein as those of the antiquarians, considering balladry as a popular, de-based form, a poor imitation of courtly literature. Attempts to connect it to the epic tradition as a natural development also conclude that it was a kind of evolutionary dead end, rendered unnecessary by near-universal literacy. Popular culture not having yet been recognized as important to students of the arts and humanities, early critics dismissed the survival of the tradition as unimportant and continued in the view of the genre as crude, inexpert poetry of an unimportant class, imitative and derivative, without value as true literature. Finally, in the 1950s M.J.C. Hodgart produced the first serious study of medieval balladry. Recognizing that the ballad folk inhabited, and portrayed in their poetry, a very different, darker, more cynical universe than their social betters, and that such a universe precipitated a different value system, Hodgart also admitted that certain examples of the genre had moments of artistry. Nonetheless, he continued to assume that the ballads of chivalry and romance, in particular, were bad courtly imitations, and to judge their artistic merit by the standards of mainstream medieval literature, concluding that in general the balladeers were bad poets. Arthur K. Moore, in his article "The Literary Status of the English Popular Ballad," attempted to invalidate this latter conclusion, examining intricate imagery and symbolism in the medieval corpus. Unfortunately, no significant work, other than source studies, appeared after Moore's defense until the 1990s, when Gwendolyn Morgan produced two books and a number of articles defending the ballads as true popular culture, with a consistent and coherent world view expressed effectively through competent poetic craft. The ballad today remains a neglected area of study, although its significance is slowly growing as the importance of popular-culture and social-history studies increases. As an art form, the ballad is enjoying yet another revival, particularly in the area of popular country and western music, cowboy poetry, and literary parody. In other words, balladry has come full circle, returning to the social classes and purposes whence it sprung.

SELECTED BIBLIOGRAPHY

Addison, Joseph, and Richard Steele. *The Spectator*. Ed. George A. Aitken. New York: Longmans, Green, & Co., 1898.

Buchan, David. *The Ballad and the Folk*. London: Routledge and Kegan Paul, 1972.

Child, Francis, ed. *The English and Scottish Popular Ballads*. 5 vols. Boston: 1882–1898.

Defoe, Daniel. "The Ballad Maker's Plea" (1722). *Daniel Defoe: His Life and Recently Discovered Writings*. Ed. William Lee. New York: Franklin, 1969. 3: 59.

Entwistle, William J. *European Balladry*. Oxford: Clarendon Press, Oxford University Press, 1939.

———. " 'Sir Aldinger' and the Date of the English Ballads." 1953. Rpt. in *Saga Book of the Viking Society for Northern Research* 13 (1980): 97–112.

Fowler, Davd C. *A Literary History of the Popular Ballad*. Durham, NC: Duke University Press, 1968.

Friedman, Albert B. *The Ballad Revival*. Chicago: University of Chicago Press, 1961.

Furrow, Melissa M., ed. *Ten Fifteenth-Century Comic Poems*. New York: Garland, 1985.

Garbáty, Thomas J. "Rhyme, Romance, Ballad, Burlesque, and the Confluence of Form." *Fifteenth-Century Studies: Recent Essays*. Ed. Robert F. Yeager. Hamden, CT: Archon, 1984. 283–301.

Gerould, Gordon Hall. *The Ballad of Tradition*. Oxford: Clarendon Press, 1932.

Hart, Walter Morris. *Ballad and Epic*. 1907. Rpt. New York: Russell & Russell, 1967.

Henderson, T.F. *The Ballad in Literature*. New York: Haskell House, 1966.

Hodgart, M.J.C. *The Ballads*. 2nd ed. London: Hutchinson, 1962.

Ker, W.P. *Epic and Romance: Essays on Medieval Literature*. 1897. Rpt. New York: Dover, 1957.

Leach, MacEdward, and Tristram Coffin, eds. *The Critics and the Ballad*. Carbondale: Southern Illinois University Press, 1961.

Lloyd, A.L. *Folk Song in England*. London: Panther, 1969.

Long, Eleanor. " 'Young Man, I Think You're Dyin': The Twining Branches Theme in the Tristan Legend and in English Tradition." *Fabula* 21 (1980): 183–99.

Lord, Albert. *The Singer of Tales*. Cambridge, MA: Harvard University Press, 1960.

Moore, Arthur K. "The Literary Status of the English Popular Ballad." *Comparative Literature* 10 (1958): 1–20.

Morgan, Gwendolyn. *Medieval Balladry and the Courtly Tradition*. New York: Peter Lang, 1993.

———, ed. and trans. *Medieval Ballads: Chivalry, Romance, and Everyday Life*. New York: Peter Lang, 1996.

Motherwell, William. *Minstrelsy Ancient and Modern*. 1827. Rpt. Detroit: Singing Tree, 1968.

Nygard, H.O. "Ballad Source Study." *Journal of American Folklore* 65 (1952): 1–12.

Oates, Joyce Carol. "The English and Scottish Traditional Ballads." *Southern Review* 15 (1979): 560–566.

Pearsall, Derek. *Old English and Middle English Poetry*. London: Routledge and Kegan Paul, 1977.

Percy, Thomas. *Reliques of Ancient English Poetry*. 1765. Rpt. London: Russell & Russell, 1921.

Pinto, Vivian de Sola, and Allan Edwin Roday, eds. *The Common Muse*. London: Chatto and Windus, 1957.

Porter, James, ed. *The Ballad Image*. Los Angeles: University of California Press, 1983.

Pound, Louise. *Poetic Origins and the Ballad*. New York: Macmillan, 1921.

Richmond, W. Edson. *Ballad Scholarship: An Annotated Bibliography*. New York: Garland, 1989.

Ritson, Joseph. *Ancient Songs and Ballads*. 1790. 3rd ed. Ed. W. Carew Hazlitt. London: Reeves and Turner, 1877.

———. *A Dissertation on Romance and Minstrelsy*. London: Payne and Foss, 1802.

Vargyas, Lajos. *Researches into the Medieval History of Folk Ballad*. Trans. Arthur H. Whitney. Budapest: Akademiai Kiado, 1967.

Warhaft, S., and J. Woodbury. *English Poems, 1250–1660*. Toronto: Macmillan, 1961.

Warton, Thomas. *History of English Poetry*. 1774. Ed. René Wellek. New York: Johnson Reprint Corp., 1968.

Wilgus, D.K., and Barre Toelken. *The Ballad and the Scholars*. Los Angeles: University of California Press, 1986.

Wilson, R.M. *The Lost Literature of Medieval England*. London: Methuen, 1952.

Wimberly, L.C. *Folklore in the English and Scottish Ballads*. New York: Frederick Ungar, 1959.

5

The Beast Fable

Brian Gastle

A fable, simply put, is a short didactic narrative that serves to exemplify the morality of specific human behaviors and characteristics. Its most common form has traditionally been and still is that of the beast fable, a relatively short verse or prose narrative or description focusing on animals rather than on human characters, for "although fables do not have to contain animals, animals have always bulked large in fable collections and in fable theory" (Ziolkowski 18). The beast fable uses animals to represent human characteristics, and indeed, many of the characteristics we associate with animals today—the sly fox and the deceptive snake, for example—stem from the beast-fable tradition. This is not to say that humans do not appear in beast fables, but rather that they take a back seat to the animals, who are there to represent the morality of the tale. The animal characters become the vehicle for overtly moralistic and sometimes-satiric commentary on human behavior and society, pointing a moral that is often explicitly spelled out at the end of the fable.

There are actually three distinct genres of beast fable. A beast or animal fable proper—sometimes referred to as an apologue—is a short narrative in verse or prose using animals as the main characters and concluding with an explicitly defined moral relating to the human characteristics displayed by the animals. A second type of story, the beast or animal epic, is a variant of the beast fable. The main difference between the beast fable and the beast epic is that the focus of the beast epic is upon its narrative, whereas the focus of the beast fable is upon didacticism: the fable is used to teach something, sometimes about the animal, but usually about humans. The beast epic's narrative is usually much more developed than the beast fable's narrative, as are the characters. In fact, the fable's characters tend to be types rather than fully developed characters in and of themselves. Modern works like Richard Adams's *Watership Down* or

George Orwell's *Animal Farm* qualify as part of the animal-epic tradition, given their extremely well developed characters and complicated narrative structure. A third medieval genre closely linked with the beast fable is the bestiary. Bestiaries were very common in the Middle Ages, and while they have changed a great deal, we can still see vestiges of the tradition in reference materials on nature like the Audubon or Peterson field guides. Medieval bestiaries describe animals, both real and fabulous, as part of a natural history, providing contemporary scientific information, legendary characteristics, and often an interpretive reading of the animal in the context of Christian doctrine. Their focus is primarily descriptive and interpretive rather than narrative. In these bestiaries the beasts are not characters, as they are in animal epics; rather, they are described in varying amounts of detail in order to place them within a particularly Christian cosmology. Bestiary entries usually conclude with an allegorical interpretation of the animal, much like the moral interpretation attached to beast fables; it is usually a warning or praise of a specific human characteristic or behavior, or, in the rare instances of fables where the allegory is clearly political, in praise of a specific political, historical, or religious figure. Its clearly generic reliance upon a didactic conclusion undoubtedly contributed to the beast fable's popularity during the Middle Ages, especially among members of the church who found the genre particularly appropriate for sermon exempla.

The Old English and Middle English beast-fable tradition owes a great deal to its Latin precursor, the proliferation of which "may well have been stimulated by the renewed educational activity at the imperial courts from the time of Charlemagne onwards" (Mann 556). Like the beast-fable genre itself, the sermon genre necessitated a juxtaposition of entertainment and edification, and lively stories were often sought to reinforce the lesson of the day's sermon; the beast fables were easily recognizable and appreciated for their folklore characteristics. But the beast fable benefited from a long literary tradition as well.

The most familiar of all collections of classical beast fables is Aesop's, which medieval writers would not have known in the original. Aesop apparently lived in the sixth century B.C.E., and his fables are still popular today. But the Aesopean fables we have today, like the versions that were available to medieval writers, are compilations of fables from both before and after Aesop's life. Medieval authors knew of Aesop primarily through a fourth-century Latin work in prose called the *Romulus*, which claimed to be a translation of Aesop's Greek works. A second popular collection of fables by Avianus, a second-century C.E. poet, which was thought to be Aesop's also provided a literary antecedent for medieval fable writers. A second-century C.E. manual on writing, the *Art of Speaking* by Hermogenes, suggests that beast fables can assist in the education of the young if the fables are "plausible," by which Hermogenes implies that certain animals maintain innate characteristics applicable to humanity. Later medieval English versions appended increasingly complex allegorical interpretations (specifically Christian ones) to the fables, a tradition of appendage that began, albeit sporadically, in Anglo-Saxon England. Like their classical antecedents, early English animal tales tended to focus primarily upon descriptions of the natural history of animals, and these descriptions found their way into the earliest of English animal-tale collections, the bestiaries.

THE OLD ENGLISH *PHYSIOLOGUS* AND *THE PHOENIX* FROM THE EXETER BOOK

While animal stories were clearly popular throughout the Middle Ages, only three examples of Old English bestiary descriptions are extant: an Old English *Physiologus* usually attributed to Cynewulf describes the panther, the partridge, and the whale. These three entries are believed to be derived from the Latin *Physiologus*, a metrical bestiary of twelve chapters by Bishop Theobald, possibly abbot of Monte Cassino from 1022 to 1035. Theobald's version itself is based on a fourth-century Greek text or a lost text possibly written in Alexandria. The Old English *Physiologus* is believed to have been composed sometime in the eighth or ninth century and, like much of Anglo-Saxon literature, was composed by an author now unknown.

The three *Physiologus* entries in The Exeter Book appear on folios 95b–98a. The third entry, the partridge, is fragmentary, containing only a dozen or so lines of verse; "eight lines of religious application, and four of exhortation by the poet, and especially the part descriptive of the partridge, must be conjecturally restored by reference to the treatment in the fuller versions, which are based upon Jer. 17.11" (Cook 7). This break in the text occurs after only the first line of the poem, "Hyrde ic secgan gēn   bi sumum fugle wundorlīcne." [So, too, I have heard tell a wondrous tale about a certain bird]. The lines following the break in the manuscript are devoted to a reading of the missing description in which we are admonished to abandon sin and "forsake the black iniquities of hell." This exhortation to return to God accords with the *Physiologus* tradition's standard symbolic meaning for a partridge, and although that bird is never identified explicitly, it seems clear that the "fugle" referred to in the first line is a partridge.

In fact, of the other *Physiologus* entries in the Exeter Book, only the description of the panther is complete. The description of the whale, or the asp-turtle, is some eighty-nine lines long, but is missing one to two lines in the epilogue. The introductory section of "The Whale" concludes with its infamous scientific name, "fastitocalon," which links the behemoth to the more common sea-turtle. The poem goes on to describe this boulderlike monster as one that deceives sailors into thinking that it is an island on which it is safe to land. When the sailors become complacent, the whale submerges, killing its unwary occupants. The significance of this animal is then related by the poet, "Swā bið scinn[en]a þēaw, dēofla wīse" [Such is the way of demons, the wont of devils] (32). The whale is a representative demonic figure, luring men to their destruction in the same way the devil seduces humanity into slothful and inattentive behavior. The poem describes how this beast can lure other animals to their doom by exuding a special perfume, drawing all creatures into its hell-like mouth. Indeed, many of the more common representations of hell mouths in later medieval iconography owe a great deal to the description of the whale in the bestiary tradition.

Like the whale, the panther in the Old English *Physiologus* also exudes a pleasant smell, which attracts animals and humans alike, but the significance of the panther is diametrically opposed to that of the whale, for the panther is a friend (*frēond*) to all except the dragon, the beast most often associated with Satan. "The Panther" describes the beauty of this beast's coat, likening it to Joseph's, and extols the panther's gentle nature, beauty, and goodness. The religious significance of the panther is underscored when the poem states that the beast rests for three days after eating. The epilogue to the poem suggests that, like God granting good grace to men for their salvation, the panther graces us, and other animals, with its sweet nature, sounds, beauty, and scent.

The only other substantial Old English work in the beast-fable tradition is *The Phoenix*, which is also extant in the single manuscript of the Exeter Book (ff. 55b–65b) and is also by an unknown author, although it has often been attributed to Cynewulf. At 677 lines, it is a substantial description of the mythological bird that is consumed by fire and is reborn from its own ashes. It should be no surprise that the allegorical interpretation of the phoenix is strongly linked to Christian doctrines of resurrection and the Judgment Day. Beyond the remarkable description of the mythical beast, its attributes (such as its penchant for being dipped into water or clapping its wings together three times) are used to refer both to Christ's miraculous resurrection and to the ultimate resurrection of the virtuous on Judgment Day: "The phoenix's rebirth foreshadows man's future resurrection, but is also a symbol of Christ's past resurrection" (Blake 33). According to Blake, *The Phoenix* derives its description of the phoenix from a fourth-century Latin poem usually attributed to Lactantius, *Carmen de Ave Phoenice*, and its subsequent allegorical interpretation from Ambrose's *Hexaemeron* (17–24). Much medieval poetry was, of course, derived from earlier sources, and what makes *The Phoenix* such a luminous example of the bestiary tradition and Old English poetry in general is the synthesis and juxtaposition, rather than the mere translation, of its classical and Christian sources—a poetic style that was to serve as a precursor to most later Middle English beast poetry.

THE MIDDLE ENGLISH *BESTIARY*

The Middle English *Bestiary*, also referred to as the Middle English *Physiologus*, dates from the middle of the thirteenth century and survives in a single manuscript, British Library MS Arundel 292. It is a poem of around eight hundred lines in Early East Midland dialect, treating thirteen beasts: the ant, the dove, the eagle, the elephant, the fox, the stag (hart), the lion, the siren (mermaid), the panther, the serpent, the spider, the turtledove, and the whale. Twelve of these entries derive, like the Old English *Physiologus*, from the Latin *Physiologus* of Theobald, and the thirteenth, the dove, is drawn from Alexander

Neckam's *De Naturis Rerum* (Ward and Waller 227). Each description is followed by a treatise describing the Christian allegorical significance of the animal. These morals are a familiar part of the bestiary tradition. What the Middle English *Bestiary* brings to this tradition is a lively synthesis of verse forms. The poem is written primarily in six-syllable couplets, akin to the hexameter lines of the earlier Latin version, but the alliteration, rhyme, and assonance common to early Middle English works are also regularly used by the poet.

While the previous English bestiary works divided their descriptions into two main parts, a natural history and an accompanying allegorical, moral, or religious interpretation, the poet of the Middle English *Bestiary* actually labels these sections with accompanying rubrics: *natura* and *significatio*. The basic characteristics regarding both their *natura* and their *significatio* are as follows (note the similarities with earlier entries, such as the Old English panther):

Beast	Natura	Significatio
Lion	Hunts on a hill.	God is the Lion ruling in heaven.
	Awakes at birth only after three days.	Resurrection after the third day.
	Never closes eyes in sleep.	God constantly watches over us.
Eagle	Renews its youth by flying toward the sun.	Man renews himself by attending church and praying.
Snake	Sheds its skin.	Man should abandon wickedness.
	Flees a naked man but attacks a clothed man.	The devil only attacks those clothed in sin.
Ant	Works constantly, saving for the winter.	Work hard and prepare for doomsday.
Hart	Eats snakes and quenches venom with water.	Drink from God's well to quench sin.
	They stay together to help each other.	Help one another to avoid sin.
Fox	Cunning and steals fowl.	The devil plays the fox, tricking us.
	Feigns death to lure carrion birds.	He feigns honesty to destroy us.
Spider	Hides, after making her web, to lure prey, then drinks its blood.	A man who betrays others drinks the blood of his fellow man.
Whale	Its sweet breath lures fish.	The devil lures with sweet words.
	Sailors drown, thinking it an island.	His followers will drown in their sins.
Mermaid	Half beautiful woman, half fish, the siren lures ships to destruction with her beautiful voice.	Like a wolf in sheep's clothing, liars and perjurers can steal both possessions and souls.
Elephant	The huge elephant can be laid low by a trap—leaning on a cut tree, he falls—but a young one will help him up.	Adam fell by a tree, and it took young Christ to raise up him and all others.

Turtledove	The turtledove takes one mate, and should he die, she embraces him in her heart as if he were alive.	Our soul should be married only to Christ nor ever hold another as its spouse.
Panther	Beautiful and sweet-smelling, other animals follow it. Sleeps for three days after feeding.	Christ is more beautiful than any man and led humanity to salvation after three days of death.
Dove	The dove has seven attributes: (1) she has no bile in her; (2) she does not steal; (3) she lives on seeds, not on worms; (4) she is a mother to other birds; (5) her cry is sorrowful; (6) she watches for the hawk; and (7) she nests in solid rock.	So too should we (1) be humble, (2) not live by thieving, (3) live by the teachings of Christ, (4) treat our fellow people well, (5) bewail our sins, (6) beware of the devil, and (7) place our trust in God.

The final entry, "The Dove," is perhaps the most peculiar because of its simplicity. It contains virtually no physical description of the bird, but is rather a brief (the shortest entry in the Middle English *Bestiary* at eighteen lines) litany of characteristics, and rather than incorporating a section for each, every characteristic (*natura*) is followed immediately by a one-line *significatio*. This variant might be explained by the fact that the dove is the one beast not found in the *Bestiary*'s Latin source.

THE FOX AND THE WOLF

Written around the latter half of the thirteenth century, the 295-line *Fox and the Wolf* survives in a single manuscript, Bodleian Library, Oxford, Digby 86 (written at the Priory of Worcestershire). The poem is part of the French tradition of Reynard the Fox stories; the *Roman de Renart* contains more than twenty similar stories, or branches. "The Fox and the Wolf" belongs to branch 4 of the *Roman de Renart*. French Reynard stories, in which the fox "symbolizes the clever man who deludes society, is brought to judgement, but escapes by cunnung" (Barnhart 104), proliferated in the thirteenth century, and the Middle English *Fox and the Wolf* most certainly benefits from that tradition.

In this version of the story, the hungry fox enters the courtyard of a household through a break in the wall without, as the poet states, leave of either the "haiward" (the guardian of the fields) or the "reve" (the manorial sheriff). Upon entering the courtyard, the fox spies a cock, Chauntecler, and his attendant hens just inside the doorway of the house (chicken coop). The fox then tries to trick the fowl into believing that he is a physician, since he has "leten ine hennen blod." But the cock is not fooled and sends him on his way. Soon thereafter the fox becomes as thirsty as he was hungry and chances upon a well. Not understanding the mechanism of the well, which incorporates two counterbalanced buckets, the fox climbs into one bucket and promptly falls to the bottom of the well, whereupon, after bemoaning his fate, he hears his friend, the wolf, walk by. Knowing that few would voluntarily change places with him, the fox tricks the wolf into believing that he is dead and in paradise, with plenty of sheep and goats to eat. The gullible wolf, after confessing his sins to the wily fox (including the time the wolf thought he saw the fox sleeping with the wolf's wife), jumps into the other bucket. As they pass each other in the well, the fox rising to the top as the perplexed wolf sinks to the bottom, the fox confesses that he plans to escape the well and leave the wolf to his fate. The poem ends with a brief description of a local friar, Ailmer, finding the wolf in the well and, thinking that the wolf is the devil, calling his brothers to stone and club the beast.

Even this cursory summary makes clear the seemingly disparate sections of the poem. The fox's entry into the inner courtyard has little to do with the subsequent parts of the poem, especially the well scene, and yet it is significant for placing the fox within an allegorical tradition of the hungry tempter/foe looking for a chance to steal into the inner sanctum of the soul. This introductory scene differentiates this fox, this Renart, from earlier, especially Aesopic, versions of this animal tale. The fox's subsequent conversation with the cock is somewhat confusing, since he refers to a number of chickens that he has eaten, an event about which the cock seems to be aware, yet one that the reader does not see firsthand. This confrontation between Chauntecler and Renart is a familiar one, and one that is echoed later in Chaucer's "Nun's Priest's Tale," but the focus on and of the dialogue appears to be peculiar to the Middle English *Fox and the Wolf*. The fox uses recognizable medical practices and terms, such as his offer to bleed the cock to alleviate a problem with his spleen—both to attempt to seduce the cock nearer and to exhibit his clearly superior intellect.

The third section of the poem, Renart's adventure with the well and the wolf, redirects the social criticism of the poem away from the secular realm (physicians) and toward the sacred. It is a familiar medieval critique of a gullible layman taken in by a false ecclesiastic. But the poem is more complicated than this plot implies, for the fox himself is overcome by his own thirst, and it is this excessive passion that leads to his downfall, much like his own false diagnosis of the cock's excessive spleen. In fact, as Honegger points out, there are striking similarities between Renart's attempted deception of the cock and his subsequent successful deception of the wolf: the fox's hunger in the former and his thirst in the latter; the desire for both the cock and the wolf to fly/jump down to the fox; the fox's pretense of being a physician in the henhouse and his pretense of being in paradise in the well; and the offer by the fox to help (treat or shrive) both (187). But the wolf is tricked while the cock is not. Chauntecler's beast-fable history might account for this difference, as he is traditionally a more sympathetic figure than the wolf. Or the tale may be focusing, as Honegger suggests, upon the ability of Chauntecler to reject the lying fox who attempts a repositioning of power in the henhouse (187–88).

The fourth and final section of the poem is common to stories such as these. The poem moves into the human world for both narrative and moral purposes.

The comic conclusion of the tale depends, in part, upon the slapstick reaction of the priests upon seeing the wolf in their well-water bucket and the ensuing thrashing of the wolf. It also foregrounds the difference between the bestiary or *Physiologus* interpretations of the wolf and the later significance of that animal in the *Roman de Renart*. Often, in the bestiary tradition, "the devil bears the similitude of the wolf" (White 59), and yet it is the fox here who is the seducer, tempter, and liar. While these allegorical elements hearken back to the Aesopic beast fable and later bestiary traditions, the focus of *The Fox and the Wolf* is clearly upon its comic narrative, endowing these animals with a depth of character unheard of in those other forms. This narrative focus makes *The Fox and the Wolf* an excellent example of the later Middle English beast epic, a genre that Chaucer shortly reinvests with the explicit moral exemplum of the fable proper.

CHAUCER'S "NUN'S PRIEST'S TALE"

Chaucer's "Nun's Priest's Tale" is certainly the most famous medieval English beast narrative, and it is also one of the most popular of Chaucer's tales among medieval scholars. The composition date of "The Nun's Priest's Tale" is much more specific than those of many other earlier works, yet still frustratingly vague. The poem refers to the Peasants' Revolt of 1381, and Chaucer died in 1400. While many Chaucerians have tried to date the tale more specifically, none have done so with any great certainty (Pearsall 29–30). External evidence for dating of the poem is even less helpful since there are no manuscripts extant of Chaucer's work that date from his lifetime. The two earliest manuscripts, the Hengwrt and the Ellesmere, were produced within a decade of Chaucer's death. The Ellesmere is generally considered to be the later of the two and was apparently compiled under conspicuous editorial guidance.

The plot of Chaucer's tale, in some respects, is simpler than that of *The Fox and the Wolf*. This 625-line tale begins with a brief description of the household of a poor widow who owns, among other animals, a rooster and a house of seven hens. This rooster, Chauntecleer, is renowned throughout the land for his crowing, and his favorite paramour among the hens is the fair Pertelote. One day, while Chauntecleer and Pertelote are sleeping beside one another on his perch, Chauntecleer experiences a nightmare about being accosted in his yard by a beast like a hound with yellow-red fur and black-tipped ears and tail. When he relates his dream, and his fear of it, to Pertelote, she berates Chauntecleer for his cowardice. What ensues is a 250-line debate over the validity of dreams, incorporating references to biblical sources, exempla, and a variety of classical authorities on dreams, including Cato, Macrobius, and Scipio. Pertelote seems to convince Chauntecleer that he should not worry about his dreams, but this resolution is one of the most problematic moments of the tale, for Chauntecleer concludes his acquiescence to her by reciting the well-known Latin proverb "Mulier est hominis confusio"—which literally translates as "woman is the ruin of man"—but Chauntecleer translates that proverb erroneously, saying, "woman is mannes joye" (3166). After this argument Chauntecleer and Pertelote kiss and make up, and the lascivious nature of the cock is reinforced by the poem as he "fethered" Pertelote twenty times and "trad" her just as often.

The tale then goes on to describe how a fox crept into the henhouse yard at night and hid until daytime. When Chauntecleer emerges in the morning to crow, he sees the fox hiding in the bushes. Before Chauntecleer can flee, the fox assures him that he means Chauntecleer no harm and only wants to hear the beautiful crowing about which he has so often heard. The fox's flattery convinces Chauntecleer to stretch out his neck to crow, whereupon the fox catches him and bears him off into the woods. The narrator (Chaucer's Nun's Priest) at this point, in one of his frequent intrusions into the narrative, states "allas" that Chauntecleer flew from the beams of the henhouse, "allas" that his wife convinced him not to believe in dreams, and that all this took place on a Friday.

As the fox carries Chauntecleer off into the woods, outdistancing the pursuing animals, the widow and her two daughters come at Chauntecleer's cry of distress, and Chauntecleer convinces the fox to mock his pursuers. When the fox opens his mouth to do so, Chauntecleer flies to safety in the top of a tree, and no amount of cajolery by the fox can bring him down. At the end of the tale, Chaucer's Nun's Priest recites an explicit moral for the fable: such it is to be reckless and negligent and trust in flattery. He concludes by stating that we should all take the "moralite" of this tale and take the fruit but "lat the chaf be stille" (3443). The beauty and skill exhibited by "The Nun's Priest's Tale" derives from two aspects: the tale itself and the placement of that tale within *The Canterbury Tales* as a whole.

The opening of the tale places the narrative within a tradition as familiar as that of *The Fox and the Wolf*, moving from a casual description of the human world to a specific characterization of two of the three main figures. Chauntecleer is typical for a cock in both the bestiary and beast-fable tradition. His singing is more than merely pleasant; it is renowned throughout the land. Bestiaries praised the cock for its crowing not only because it was pleasant but also because it evoked the cleansing of the human soul after it "crows" its confession. Like Peter's reformation upon the crowing of the cock after denying Jesus for the third time, the cock's crow signified repentance. But the beast-fable tradition tended toward a different focus for the cock. Sometimes wise, sometimes stupid, the cock in the Aesopean tradition tended to represent masculinity and patriarchal order among the female hens of the henhouse, and we can certainly see this tradition emerge in "The Nun's Priest's Tale." Chaucer primarily focuses not only on Chauntecleer's lascivious nature, but upon his prodigious ability to satisfy his carnal desires, being able to copulate with Pertelote over twenty times in one morning after they reconcile their argument on dreams.

The argument on dreams in "The Nun's Priest's Tale" may be found among some, but not all, of Chaucer's source material, which includes Marie de France's "Del Cok e del Gupil," similar episodes from branch 2 of the Old

French *Roman de Renart*, and sporadic borrowings from medieval authorities on dreams and their interpretations. This argument on dreams occupies a major position in the tale, although it has little to do with the development of the plot (but much to do with the development of Chauntecleer's character). While the tale is marked at the onset as a beast fable or beast epic, it quickly repositions itself within the debate genre, with Chauntecleer believing in the validity of dreams and Pertelote refuting that belief. The debate begins with Pertelote concerned about Chauntecleer, and, as Donald Howard and James Dean point out, much of the humor of this section (and of the tale in general) derives from Chaucer occasionally pointing out to the reader that this academic debate is being conducted by chickens (n. 240), as with Pertelote's reference to Chauntecleer as her "herte dere," which with a strongly pronounced Middle English final "e" would sound much like a clucking hen (n. 244). Both Chauntecleer and Pertelote, but especially Chauntecleer, use the debate to foreground their learned nature, but it is Chauntecleer especially who seems to want to appear well versed and educated. However, his attempt to appear superior is undercut by the fact that he describes the fox in perfect detail yet does not know what the beast is—besides, of course, the fact that Chauntecleer is a chicken.

While the dream debate has little to do with the subsequent plot development, other than to foreshadow the coming of the fox, it does foreground Chauntecleer's pride and enables the reader to better take the "moralite" of the tale, as the Nun's Priest desires the pilgrims to do. Perhaps the most common position on the morality of the tale is that it is an allegory of the Fall of Man. Chauntecleer, seduced by the fox by means of Chauntecleer's own hubris, "falls" from the beams of the chicken coop into the waiting mouth of the demonic tempter. In part, this fall is facilitated by the erroneous counsel of his wife. When he does manage to escape, he flies upward into the treetops, toward heaven, wherein he remains safe so long as he does not repeat his sin and lapse once again into the mouth of the devil. This reading of the fox fits the allegorized bestiary tradition, wherein the fox lures birds as the devil lures souls, but it is a marked divergence from *The Fox and the Wolf*, the *Roman de Renart*, and other medieval beast fables, wherein the fox is often a sympathetic character and is lauded for his clever nature. This particular allegorical reading is also not without its flaws, for Chauntecleer relies upon his own devices, or more appropriately upon the devices he has learned from the demonic fox, to lead himself to salvation. Faith, repentance, confession, absolution, and prayer have little to do with Chauntecleer's salvation, yet they were mainstays of medieval theology devoted to salvation. While the Nun's Priest urges the pilgrims to take the "moralite" of the story, implying that there is more to the story than a fox, a cock, and a hen or merely that the pilgrims should not trust flattery, the true nature of that moral is ambiguous.

Perhaps this should not be a surprise given Chaucer's propensity for ambiguity, or the ambiguous nature of the Nun's Priest himself. Apart from the narrative structure of the tale, Chaucer further complicates this tale by assigning it to the Nun's Priest, one of the most meagerly described characters on the pilgrimage. The tale is appropriate for a clerical tale teller. The content is sententious, patriarchal, and not a little sexist. It is also a fine example of the requital motif woven throughout *The Canterbury Tales*, for "The Nun's Priest's Tale" follows directly after the Monk's *De Casibus Virorum Illustrium*, a collection of stories relating the tragic downfall of famous men. The Monk's tale is interrupted by the Knight, who comments that the Monk's constant focus on tragic downfall is too much for most men. Of course, the Knight, one of the highest-ranking members of the pilgrimage, would be especially susceptible to the fate implied by the turning of Fortune's Wheel. Even though the Host wants the Nun's Priest to tell a tale of hunting, "The Nun's Priest's Tale" is a far more appropriate response to the tragedies of the Monk. As a divine comedy, Christianity relied upon the hope of resurrection and salvation from the Fall. In his tale the Nun's Priest is critical of the Monk, who neglects this most basic focus of his vocation. Chauntecleer achieves salvation, whereas all of the characters in the Monk's stories are left in death and despair. As a further link between the tale and the narrator, the few traits revealed about that narrator seem to dwell on his masculinity, much as the Nun's Priest himself dwells upon the masculinity of Chauntecleer. Apart from the Host's desire for a hunting tale from this priest, the Host describes, in the epilogue to the tale, the muscles of the priest, how the Nun's Priest would be a "trede-foul aright" (3451), although the validity and position of that epilogue is debatable. While "The Nun's Priest's Tale" may seem to raise more questions than it answers, it is that problematizing of the genre that seems to be Chaucer's main contribution to the beast-fable tradition. Part bestiary, part fable, the tale's complicated interaction of plot, characters, and narrator also places it within the beast-epic tradition.

JOHN LYDGATE (EARLY FIFTEENTH CENTURY)

In the early fifteenth century John Lydgate compiled the first real collection of late medieval beast fables in Middle English, the *Isopes Fabules*, as well as separate longer fables such as "The Churl and the Bird" and "The Debate of the Horse, Goose, and Sheep." The fables in *Isopes Fabules* focus upon the moralization of the animals rather than on any real narrative, much like the earlier bestiary tradition, but the 387-line "Churl and the Bird" is an excellent example of the later tradition that juxtaposed moral "sentence" with narrative "solaas." A churl captures a bird who then refuses to sing because she is in prison. She tells him that she will give him three "wisdoms" if he lets her free, to which he agrees. She tells him not to believe everything he hears, not to desire the impossible, and not to regret the past. She then tells him that he should not have let her go, since she contains a magical treasure, an "iagounce," inside of her. Upon hearing this, the churl laments his bad fortune. The bird then goes on to berate the churl, since he should not have given credence to her lie, nor desired the stone that he could not have, nor regretted what was done.

Lydgate translates seven fables in his *Isopes Fabules*: the tale of the Cock and the precious stone, the fable of the Lamb devoured by the Wolf, the tale of the Frog and the Mouse, the tale of the Hound and the Sheep, how the Wolf deceived the Crane, the fable of the Sun's marriage, and the fable of the Hound that bore the cheese. Each fable begins with a brief moral statement that is later expanded and discussed directly after the fable. Perhaps of more interest to Lydgate scholars than these fables and their attendant morals is the autobiographical material found in the introduction to the fables, in which Lydgate describes himself in typically self-effacing rhetorical terms.

The morals of "The Churl and the Bird" might seem clear, and indeed the narrator restates them in the "Verba Auctoris," or words of the author, at the end of the poem, but in the final "Lenvoi," Lydgate redirects that moral to the issues of freedom foregrounded at the bird's capture, stating that whosoever has freedom has "all suffisaunce" (376). The poem's conclusion is more social commentary than it is didactic moral statement. Both the bird and the poet berate the churl for being churlish, for the bird suggests that a rude churl cannot be taught "termys of gentilnesse" (343).

ROBERT HENRYSON (LATE FIFTEENTH CENTURY)

The second significant collection of late medieval Middle English animal fables after Lydgate's *Isopes Fabules* was written by Robert Henryson, a late-fifteenth-century Scottish poet, usually referred to as one of the Scottish Chaucerians. In his collection, the *Morall Fabillis of Esope the Phrygian* (written in Middle Scots, a northern dialect of Middle English), Henryson uses familiar Aesop tales for their didactic purpose as exempla. Like Lydgate's prologue to the *Isopes Fabules*, Henryson's prologue to his *Morall Fabillis* praises poetry for its beauty, but unlike Lydgate, Henryson goes on to laud the moral and didactic virtues of poetry, which he suggests can be corrective. This is a common trope of medieval (and later) poets and is reinforced as a trope through the continuing modesty Henryson exhibits through his apology for his lack of skill. Henryson's collection is much more substantial and developed than earlier Aesopean collections. It is almost 3,000 lines long, averages "230 lines per fable and 43 lines per *Moralitas*" (Gopen 1), and contains thirteen fables apart from the 63-line prologue. Many of these tales are versions of earlier Aesopean fables, but Henryson incorporates some new religious allegorical elements and fables like *The Preiching of the Swallow* and *The Tale of the Paddok and the Mous*.

OTHER BEAST FABLES

These several beast fables, beast epics, and bestiaries by no means comprise an exhaustive list. It would be virtually impossible to offer such a list given the rather vague nature of the genre. Medieval church fathers such as Ambrose, Augustine, and Gregory used animals for sermon exempla, although these animal stories are almost exclusively in Latin. The genre reached a height in thirteenth and fourteenth-century collections of English preachers, like Jacques de Vintry's *Sermones Vulgares et Communes* (Rowland 5), and in biblical animal exempla, such as can be found in the fourteenth-century *Piers Plowman*. The variety and number of Latin fables speak to the international nature of the beast fable and of medieval literature in general. After receiving an education in Paris, Odo of Cheriton returned to England and completed a collection of eighty-one fables in Latin around 1221. These Latin fables include three Middle English proverbs, and his work is perhaps one of the first collections of beast epics in England (Honegger 176–777). Just prior to Odo of Cheriton, at the end of the twelfth century, Marie de France completed her *Ysopet*, perhaps the most famous collection of medieval fables written in England (in French) in the Middle Ages before Caxton's 1484 translation and edition of Aesop's fables.

The literary argument, or debate, of the thirteenth-century *The Owl and the Nightingale* owes a great deal to the beast-fable, animal-epic, and bestiary traditions, although no bestiary actually treated these particular animals. As can be seen from the argument between Chauntecleer and Pertelote in "The Nun's Priest's Tale," the debate itself influenced the beast fable as well. *The Parliament of Three Ages'* list of animals as the poacher stalks a deer relies upon the beast-fable tradition, as does the allegorical and narrative use of animals in *Winner and Waster*. Perhaps the most famous medieval poem in this vein is *Sir Gawain and the Green Knight*, wherein it is crucial to understand the allegorical and symbolic use of the three animals (the deer, the boar, and the fox) hunted by the host as his wife visits Sir Gawain. Perhaps the most fantastic of all bestiary-like works, *Mandeville's Travels*, develops the natural-history tradition of the bestiary without assigning a moral value to the animals in question.

CRITICAL SURVEY

While there have been many studies of individual beast fables, beast epics, and bestiaries, few have attempted a methodical study of the genre in medieval English literature. One of the best places to start is also one of the most recent works. Thomas Honegger's 1996 book *From Phoenix to Chauntecleer: Medieval English Animal Poetry* is just such a study. In three main sections—one devoted to the *Physiologus* tradition (including the Old English *Physiologus*, the Old English *Phoenix*, and the Middle English *Physiologus*), the second to bird poems (including *The Owl and the Nightingale, The Thrush and the Nightingale, The Cuckoo and the Nightingale*, and *The Parliament of Fowls*), and the third to the beast-fable and beast-epic traditions (focusing on *The Fox and the Wolf* and "The Nun's Priest's Tale")—Honegger meticulously discusses issues of authorship, dating, manuscript history, sources, analogues, and critical history before supplying a formal analysis of each work, usually within the allegorical and moral framework of the beast-fable tradition. In addition, his thirty-two-page bibliography is extremely thorough. Unfortunately, apart from a brief statement concerning the tradition after 1400, his study ends with Chaucer.

One of the publications that has promoted the study of the medieval (and other) beast fables has been *Bestia*, the yearbook of the Beast Fable Society. This journal publishes articles relating to all aspects of all beast fables from virtually every historical period and cultural context, as does the International Reynard Society. As its World Wide Web home page states, the International Reynard Society was founded "to group together medievalists and other scholars in . . . the associated fields of the so-called 'Beast Epic' of Reynard the Fox, the Fable tradition, and the short comic narrative genre exemplified by the Old French Fabliaux." Since its inception, it has expanded its focus to include "wider moral, satirical and allegorical textual studies, as well as areas of iconography and art history, and to attract fellow-scholars working in similar fields in both the Classical and modern periods" (<http://www.hull.ac.uk/french/fox.html>).

While its scope is not limited to medieval fables, Mary Ellen Snodgrass's *Encyclopedia of Fable* is an excellent source both for approaching individual fables from the Middle Ages and for placing those fables within a broader historical and cultural context. The encyclopedia is useful for keeping track of the big picture, although most critical studies of the beast fable tend rather toward specialization of material. In *Bestiaries and Their Users in the Middle Ages*, for example, Ron Baxter focuses upon the history behind the bestiary, especially its Latin history, its development in the later Middle Ages, and actual book production of bestiaries, and provides information about readership, authorship, and medieval material culture. For bestiaries in particular, one of the most profitable research foci has been on the texts as visual documents rather than as literature. Baxter shares this focus with many of the chapters in *Beasts and Birds of the Middle Ages*, a collection edited by Willene Clark and Meradith McMunn. These chapters represent the recent movement in medieval studies toward more interdisciplinary approaches to texts, especially the influence of manuscript studies and material culture on literary and social history.

For bestiaries, like much of medieval literature in general, it is better to cast a wider net than the merely language-specific studies of Old and Middle English bestiaries and the *Physiologus* tradition. One of the best earlier works on the bestiary tradition is Florence McCulloch's *Mediaeval Latin and French Bestiaries*. In her first two chapters she provides an excellent history of the bestiary and *Physiologus* traditions as well as a review of research up to the date of her work. Her work for Chapel Hill's Studies in the Romance Languages and Literatures series heralded the beginning of the genre's increased critical attention; the past three decades have seen the emergence of numerous scholarly editions, translations, and facsimiles.

In fact, the best place to start research on many individual beast fables, epics, and bestiaries is by examining the critical introductions of these relatively recent editions. The 1893–1934 Early English Text Society (EETS) edition of the

Exeter Book was reprinted in 1987–1988 and the Middle English *Physiologus*, edited by Hanneke Wirtjes, was issued in 1991; both include the editorial apparatus for which EETS is widely known. *The Phoenix* is available in a separate edition, edited by N.F. Blake. Blake's revised (1990) edition includes an excellent overview of the language, manuscript history, the phoenix story, dating, and sources. Its bibliography is selective, and it includes for context other versions of *The Phoenix*, including the *Carmen de Ave Phoenice*, selections from Ambrose's *Hexaemeron, The Prose Phoenix*, and an Old Norse version of the poem. Unfortunately, *The Fox and the Wolf* has not been revisited by editors quite so recently. Garbáty includes the poem in his anthology *Medieval English Literature*, but provides little information on scholarship. A complete edition appears in Bennett's and Smithers's anthology *Early Middle English Verse and Prose*.

Both the bestiary and Aesopean fables have been popular among modern readers, and while most modern editions of fables derive from a variety of sources, "modern" bestiaries are quite medieval with respect to both their textual sources and their lavish illustrations. T.H. White's translation of the Latin *Physiologus* offers instruction and pleasure to scholars and popular audiences alike. Interspersed with black-and-white drawings based on the manuscript images of the beasts, the text is copiously annotated in the witty style that has made White so popular. Another popular translation of the Latin *Physiologus* is Richard Barber's translation of MS Bodley 764 for the Folio Society. While it contains virtually no critical apparatus, it does contain beautiful color facsimile versions of all the miniatures.

Certainly the medieval beast fable that has received the most critical attention has been Chaucer's "Nun's Priest's Tale." The most detailed survey of this tale may be found in Derek Pearsall's variorum edition of the tale, published in 1983. Pearsall's discussion of the criticism of the tale is particularly insightful, placing research within argumentative contexts rather than merely listing and describing it chronologically. The variorum edition is a good companion survey to *The Riverside Chaucer*, the standard critical edition of Chaucer's works, which includes substantial critical and bibliographic commentary on the tales. While Beryl Rowland's *Blind Beasts* is not devoted to the beast fable directly, it offers a survey of Chaucer's use of animals, which, of course, is heavily indebted to both the bestiary and beast-fable traditions. As Chaucer and other medieval poets well knew, the difficulty (or perhaps the beauty) of the beast fable lies in the uncertainty of meaning inherent to the fable even as the fable or bestiary attempts to define the moral or anagogic relevance of the animal. Arnold Clayton Henderson's article "Medieval Beasts and Modern Cages: The Making of Meaning in Fables and Bestiaries" is a study of the ways in which the animals of medieval fables resist static interpretation and meaning. It suggests, for example, that "The Nun's Priest's Tale" contains as many "meanings" as have been put forth by various readers.

That variety and ambiguity seem to be the reasons for the beast fable's general and enduring popularity. Humans are fascinated by the animal world and attempt, wherever possible, to impose their humanity (both virtues and vices) upon it. Twentieth-century versions of the bestiary and beast-fable traditions range from television cartoons to animal documentaries, from Sunday comic strips to naturalists' field guides. These versions, like their forebears, provide the elements required by *The Canterbury Tales'* storytelling game: they are both edifying and entertaining. More than mere anthropomorphism, the beast fable makes a point (and an art) of saying more about its tellers than about its subjects.

SELECTED BIBLIOGRAPHY

Barber, Richard, ed. and trans. *Bestiary*. Woodbridge, Eng.: Boydell Press, 1993.

Barnhart, Clarence L., ed. *The New Century Handbook of English Literature*. Rev. ed. New York: Appleton-Century-Crofts, 1967.

Baxter, Ron. *Bestiaries and Their Users in the Middle Ages*. Stroud: Sutton; London: Courtauld Institute, 1998.

Bennett, J.A.W., and G.V. Smithers, eds. *Early Middle English Verse and Prose*. Oxford: Clarendon Press, 1966.

Benson, Larry D., ed. *The Riverside Chaucer*. 3rd ed. Boston: Houghton Mifflin, 1987.

Blake, N.F., ed. *The Phoenix*. 2 Rev. ed. Exeter: University of Exeter Press, 1990.

Clark, Willene B., and Meradith T. McMunn, eds. *Beasts and Birds of the Middle Ages*. Philadelphia: University of Pennsylvania Press, 1989.

Cook, Albert Stanburrough, ed. and prose trans. *The Old English Physiologus*. Verse trans. James Hall Pitman. Yale Studies in English 63. New Haven, CT: Yale University Press, 1921. Rpt. in *Translations from the Old English*. Hamden, CT: Archon Books, 1970.

Elliott, Charles, ed. *Robert Henryson: Poems*. Oxford: Clarendon Press, 1963.

The Exeter Book. Ed. George Philip Krapp and Elliott Van Kirk Dobbie. The Anglo-Saxon Poetic Records. New York: Columbia University Press, 1936.

The Exeter Book. Ed. W.S. Mackie and Israel Gollancz. Early English Text Society O.S. nos. 104, 194. London: K. Paul, Trench, Trübner and Co., 1895–1934, Millwood, NY: Kraus Reprint, 1987–1988.

Garbáty, Thomas J., ed. *Medieval English Literature*. Lexington, MA.: Heath, 1984.

Gopen, George D., ed. and trans. *The Moral Fables of Aesop by Robert Henryson*. Notre Dame, IN: University of Notre Dame Press, 1987.

Henderson, Arnold Clayton. "Medieval Beasts and Modern Cages: The Making of Meaning in Fables and Bestiaries." *PMLA* 97 (1982): 40–49.

Honegger, Thomas. *From Phoenix to Chauntecleer: Medieval English Animal Poetry*. Swiss Studies in English 120. Tübingen and Basel: Francke Verlag, 1996.

Howard, Donald R., and James Dean, eds. *The Canterbury Tales: A Selection*. New York: New American Library, 1969.

International Reynard Society (Beast Epic, Fable & Fabliau). Online. 2 May 2000. http://www.hull.ac.uk/french/fox.html.

Jacobs, John C., ed. and trans. *The Fables of Odo of Cheriton*. Syracuse, NY: Syracuse University Press, 1985.

Mann, Jill. "Beast Epic and Fable."*Medieval Latin: An Introduction and Bibliographical*

Guide. Ed. F.A.C. Mantello and A.G. Rigg. Washington, DC: Catholic University of America Press, 1996. 556–561.

McCulloch, Florence. *Mediaeval Latin and French Bestiaries*. University of North Carolina Studies in the Romance Languages and Literatures, 33. Chapel Hill: University of North Carolina Press, 1960.

McKnight, George Harley, ed. *Middle English Humorous Tales in Verse*. Boston and London: Heath, 1913.

Morris, Richard, ed. *An Old English Miscellany Containing a Bestiary, Kentish Sermons, Proverbs of Alfred, Religious Poems of the Thirteenth Century, from Manuscripts in the British Museum, Bodleian Library, Jesus College Library, Etc.* Early English Text Society OS 49. London: 1872.

Pearsall, Derek, ed. *The Nun's Priest's Tale*. Vol. 2, pt. 9, of *A Variorum Edition of the Works of Geoffrey Chaucer*. Norman: University of Oklahoma Press, 1983.

Rowland, Beryl. *Blind Beasts: Chaucer's Animal World*. Kent, OH: Kent State University Press, 1971.

Snodgrass, Mary Ellen. *Encyclopedia of Fable*. Santa Barbara, CA: ABC-CLIO, 1998.

Spiegel, Harriet, ed. and trans. *Fables of Marie de France*. Toronto: University of Toronto Press, 1987.

Ward, A.W. and A.R. Waller, eds. *The Cambridge History of English Literature*. Vol. 1. Cambridge: Cambridge University Press, 1949.

White, T.H., ed. and trans. *The Bestiary: A Book of Beasts*. New York: Capricorn Books, 1960.

Wirtjes, Hanneke, ed. *The Middle English "Physiologus."* Early English Text Society Original Series 299. Oxford: Oxford University Press, 1991.

Ziolkowski, Jan M. *Talking Animals: Medieval Latin Beast Poetry, 750–1150*. Philadelphia: University of Pennsylvania Press, 1993.

6
Breton Lay

Shearle Furnish

The Breton lay in the form known to modern readers originated in twelfth-century French courtly writing. The most famous examples are the twelve lays of Marie de France as collected in the British Museum manuscript Harley 978. However, a body of anonymous French lays is also extant from the period and influenced perhaps equally with Marie the later tradition in Middle English. The term *lay* may have meant for Marie not so much her own brief romantic narratives in octosyllabic couplets, but rather the tradition of oral performance from Celtic Brittany to which her work pays memorial homage. Thus Marie's poems might represent no more than the narrative verse residue of a body of work that also once incorporated song and instrumental accompaniment. Nonetheless, the literary genre that she and other French writers created has survived its antecedents and enjoyed a wide influence, including that exerted on a small body of Middle English poetry of the fourteenth and fifteenth centuries. Some of this English poetry is loosely translated from the French, and literary historians have typically viewed the entire tradition as derivative and, with just a couple of exceptions, generally inferior to its French models.

The Breton lay in Middle English is a brief, romantic narrative in octosyllabic couplets or tail-rhyme stanzas, its plot taking the shape of a turn of Fortune's wheel rather than the quest. It invariably possesses or claims affinities of some sort with Celtic tradition: fairy lore, setting in Brittany, or simply the author's confession of influence. Unlike courtly romance, the Breton lay concerns family drama more than martial prowess, but like Marie's lays and chivalric romances such as Chrétien's *Conte del graal*, the Breton lay in Middle English frequently concerns the nurture, maturation, and social integration of its hero or heroine.

The extant Middle English Breton lays appear earliest in an influential manuscript of the middle fourteenth century, the Auchinleck Manuscript (Advocates'

19.2.1, no. 155, at the National Library of Scotland). It is thought that Geoffrey Chaucer read or even may have possessed this manuscript for a time, and its influence can be seen in his contributions to the genre, "The Franklin's Tale" and "The Wife of Bath's Tale," as well as in other stories in *The Canterbury Tales*. James Boswell's father gave the manuscript to the faculty of the University of Edinburgh, and it was well known to Walter Scott. Three early Middle English lays appear in the Auchinleck Manuscript: *Sir Orfeo, Lay le Freine*, and *Sir Degaré*. Another early poem in couplets is *Sir Landevale*, a translation of Marie's *Lanval* and the principal source of Thomas Chestre's *Sir Launfal*. In addition to these, Chaucer's tales and four lays written in tail-rhyme stanzas make up the whole body of tales usually thought of as the Breton lays in Middle English. The tail-rhyme lays, except for Chestre's later and northern in provenance, are *Sir Launfal, Emaré, Sir Gowther*, and *The Erle of Tolous*.

That the Breton lay is a distinct genre in Middle English is controversial. No single, simple definition of the type is widely embraced, and discussions typically characterize it by a loose collection of general features. Among these are relative brevity (they range from 400 to 1,200 lines), direct dependence upon Celtic fairy tale, authorial allusions to the literary tradition in French, and family drama as the principal theme rather than martial prowess or courtly love. Aside from this loose assortment of characteristic features, the Breton lay in Middle English is not obviously distinct from the verse romance of the age, and many commentators consider the form no more than a subset of that immense tradition.

The unique version of *Lay le Freine*, in the Auchinleck Manuscript, opens with a prologue that—like Marie's prologue to *Equitan*, by which it may be influenced—sketches the lineaments of the Breton lay:

> We redeþ oft & findeþ ywrite
> & þis clerkes wele it wite,
> layes þat ben in harping
> ben yfounde of ferli þing.
> Sum beþe of wer & sum of wo
> & sum of ioie and mirþe also
> & sum of trecherie & of gile,
> of old auentours þat fel while,
> & sum of bourdes and ribaudy,
> & mani þer beþ of fairy.
> Of al þinge þat men seþ
> mest o loue for soþe þai beþ.
>   In Breteyne bi hold time
> þis layes were wrouȝt, so seiþ þis rime,
> when kinges miȝt our yhere
> of ani meruailes þat þer were
> þai token an harp in gle & game
> & maked a lay & ȝaf it name.

The most famous and beautiful poem in the genre, and one that illustrates many of these attributes, is *Sir Orfeo*, which in other manuscripts bears a version of the *Lay le Freine* prologue. *Sir Orfeo* is the tragic story of Orpheus and Eurydice transformed by the influences of Celtic fairy lore, medieval exegesis, and chivalric romance. Orfeo, a minstrel of great skill and renown and king of a city the poem identifies as at once Thrace and Winchester, rules happily with his queen Heurodis. One day, while she sleeps under a tree in their orchard, the King of the Fairies visits her dreams and commands her to be ready the following day, for then he will return and take her away forever. Orfeo attempts to defend her with military force, but even surrounded by the shield wall of his troops, she vanishes at the appointed hour. Grief stricken and perhaps also overcome by guilt or shame, Orfeo sets his steward in charge of his kingdom, sheds all trappings of his royal condition, and exiles himself to the wilderness with no comfort but his harp, upon which he plays in the intervals of his suffering. Just as in the classical tale, his playing charms the brute creatures.

Ten years pass in this way, during which Orfeo sometimes experiences eerie visions of the Fairy King's company and, finally, the vision of his queen among them. Suddenly charged with purpose, he follows them into the fairy kingdom, a beautiful place beyond a mountainous barrier, like that ruled by the hawk-knight in Marie's *Yonec*. There, posing as a minstrel, he plays for and delights the king, who grants him a boon. Claiming his wife, he returns to his own land, where, after joyful reunion with his loyal steward, he and Heurodis reign happily for the rest of their lives.

Justifiably famous for its poetry and dramatic tension, *Sir Orfeo* is also critically important to literary history. In it we see an important example of how medieval authors encountered classical texts. *Sir Orfeo*'s romantic transformation of what was tragic in classical tradition is not so much a misinterpretation as it is a medieval incorporation or appropriation of ancient ideas. Because Orfeo and his queen return from the fairyland of the taken and the dead, some readers have seen a melding in the poem of Celtic legend, classical myth, chivalric quest, and Christian allegory. Because Orfeo is both a king and a minstrel, other readers have seen in the hero exegetical connections between Orpheus and David, as well as between Orpheus and Christ. In addition to these literary associations, the emphasis upon Orfeo's harp and minstrelsy surely indicates the poet's artistic self-consciousness and the poem's sophisticated self-reflexivity.

To examine *Sir Orfeo* as a type of the Breton lay, however, one gives particular attention to the elements specially emphasized in the prologue to *Lay le Freine*: the fairy, marvels (or *aventure*), and love. The Fairy King in *Sir Orfeo* is, on the one hand, a romantically transformed Pluto, lord of the underworld and the dead. As such, he represents both the inexorable natural law that takes Eurydice and the potentate to whom the heroic husband must make his appeal. On the other hand, the Fairy King is also the hero's rival or Jungian shadow, like the Green Knight or Lancelot's Meleagant. Like the Green Knight, he challenges the hero in his own court, departs in marvelous circumstances, and provides the ultimate test of the hero's prowess. Significantly, in both poems the particular form this prowess takes is not martial but courtly. Gawain treats Bercilak's lady with honor and upholds his obligations in the Christmas game of exchanged blows. Orfeo charms the fairy court with his music and defeats his rival in a contest of courtesy, not arms. In both cases a certain grace under pressure does honor to the hero while he is a guest in the enemy's castle.

Also like the Green Knight, but much more like Meleagant, the Fairy King menaces the mortal realm and possesses a prominent trait of violence. Upon waking from her troubled sleep, Heurodis cries horribly, rubs her limbs in a distracted way (the Middle English says that she "fretted" them), and tears at her face until it bleeds. When at length she is able to explain her anguish, she recounts how the Fairy King accosted her and reports the threats with which he enforced his demand:

> & ȝif þou makest ous ylet,
> whar þou be þou worst yfet
> & totore þine limes al
> þat noþing help þe no schal,
> & þei þou best so totorn,
> ȝete þou worst wiþ ous yborn.

Filtered through Dame Heurodis's agitated report comes a sense of the Fairy King's inexorable and adamant power. He tells her that resistance is useless and, worse, would be met with violence and maiming. In *Sir Orfeo*, then, as in *Sir Gawain and the Green Knight* or Chrétien's *Le Chevalier de la charrette*, the alien's land lies parallel to the mortal realm and is governed by a court that resembles and matches in many ways the hero's mortal court. In these poems the fairy or alien invades and menaces the mortal court.

It is not always thus, however, either in the chivalric romances or in the lays. Just as in Chrétien's *Le Chevalier au lion* it is Arthur's knight Yvain who invades the alien land, in Marie's *Lanval* and in Middle English adaptations including Thomas Chestre's *Sir Launfal*, the realm of the fairy is a refuge for the exiled mortal and harbors no designs on what is Arthur's. The hero, who feels alienated and disappointed at court, finds fairyland attractive and inviting and ultimately flees there permanently. The realm of the fairy is not always apparent in the lays as a distinct geographical entity lying apart from the mortal court, and on occasion when there is another land, such as the country of le Freine's suitor Guroun, it is not apparently an enchanted world. In *Sir Degaré* the sudden appearance of the fairy knight who becomes the hero's father seems the realization of an ideal suitor who can overcome the possessiveness of the lady's father—in other words, the realization of a wish-fulfillment fantasy. That the fairy knight rapes her shows that he is made, as it were, in the irrational, possessive image of her father, the only other man she knows, and indicates symbolically the suitor's sufficient power to counteract the father's power. Again in this English poem, where a mysterious intruder displaces a possessive lord, the resemblance to Marie's *Yonec* is compelling, but in *Sir Degaré* there is no literal realm of the fairy. So the concept of the fairy need not be concretized in a fairyland but simply in an extraordinary event. Le Freine's suitor functions in much the same way, taking her away from her native land, where she is a foundling, and seeming to promise her an identity and a role. In this other world of wish fulfillment she immediately finds the role of patroness or liege lady and eventually discovers, more than just identity as her lord's wife, her birth identity with its attendant features of social legitimization and status.

Closely related to the element of the fairy otherworld, of course, is magic or marvels. One of the more consistent features of the Breton lays is their commemoration of "ferli thing." *Sir Orfeo* dramatizes several marvels, including the Fairy King's covert visitation of Heurodis as she sleeps in her husband's ostensibly secure orchard, her anticlimactic but eerie vanishing the next day just as her abductor warned ("Ac ȝette amiddes hem ful riȝt / þe quen was oway ytuiȝt"), Orfeo's charming of brute nature by his playing, his several hallucinatory visions of the fairy retinue during his time of exile, and the fantastic landscape and architecture of his rival's kingdom. As the Fairy King himself reminds Orfeo, even the hero and heroine themselves illustrate a marvel, for in the ten years of Orfeo's wilderness exile, he has aged noticeably and shows the rigors of privation, yet Dame Heurodis is apparently unchanged in her beauty.

In this feature of enchantment or marvels, *Sir Orfeo* plainly demonstrates its relationship to Marie and the French tradition. The speaking white hind and empty bark of *Guigemar* and the hawk-knight of *Yonec* represent the type to which the marvels in *Sir Orfeo* correspond. It is sometimes remarked that the Middle English tradition is more likely to rationalize or naturalize fairy marvel than is the French tradition; however, in both Marie's collection and in the Middle English tradition one finds a variety and breadth of treatment. In Marie's *Equitan* and *Laüstic*, for instance, there is no magic at all, though there are symbolic objects that correspond, in the power they exert on characters, to the marvelous events of other lays. *Le Fresne*, a tale of the same sort, appears among the Middle English poems as *Lay le Freine*. Versions of *Sir Degaré* other than that in the Auchinleck Manuscript rationalize the prominent fairy elements of that poem.

Among the stanzaic lays there are marvels aplenty, but with the very significant exception of *Sir Launfal*, in none of them is enchantment ascribed to the fairy. *Emaré*, an analogue of the Constance story, employs in a way reminiscent of *Guigemar* a boat cast adrift but guided purposefully to various destinations. Abandoned on the sea first by her outraged father and later by the jealous husband who rescued her, Emaré endures a sequence of trials culminating in miraculous arrival in Rome. Also reminiscent of the fairy magic in other lays, Emaré's costly heirloom cloak and afterwards her son exercise a mysterious power to compel the affections of other characters. *Sir Gowther*, an analogue of the anonymous French *Tydorel* and the Robert the Devil tradition, makes even more explicit a process of Christianization apparent in Emaré's destiny in Rome. Sir Gowther, a demon's son, is saved and turned toward Christian heroism by the miraculous intervention of heaven in both his and his beloved's lives. Climaxing a series of other miraculous gifts that enable his acts of prowess against enemies of Christendom, his beloved's apparent return to life and sudden gift of speech after lifelong muteness signal Gowther's redemption. Like other lays mentioned here, *The Erle of Tolous* contains no marvels at all, strictly speaking, but does present an account of erotic attraction that seems a rationalized vestige of fairy power somewhat less explicit than Emaré's cloak. Clearly, all the English lays dramatize the marvelous, whether that notion is represented by fairy magic, the exercise of erotic fascination, hagiographic miracle, or just the working of coincidence as destiny, as in *Lay le Freine* and *Sir Degaré*.

For Marie, love is clearly the greatest of marvelous powers, as well as the unifying theme of her collection. It is wrong, however, for literary historians to generalize, as they sometimes have done, that her lays concern courtly love and the English concern married love. It is more accurate to observe that both traditions anatomize love and that both dramatize exalted and debased forms of love inside and outside of marriage. For example, Marie's *Equitan* fosters the reader's sympathy for the seneschal, whose marriage is abused by his wife and his king. *Bisclavret*, too, tells of a good marriage abused by malicious adultery. *Guigemar* and *Milun*, though they begin in conventional situations of courtly adultery, resolve in the marriage of protagonists, and in this respect they are more like *Sir Degaré*, *Lay le Freine*, and *The Erle of Tolous* than otherwise. Marie's *Eliduc* also dignifies marriage.

For their part, the English lays occasionally do dramatize a courtly affair in a sympathetic manner. Such is le Freine's relationship with her lord at the time she leaves the convent. It may not be fair to introduce *Lay le Freine* here, since that poem is a translation of Marie; however, *The Erle of Tolous* develops the affection and mutual assistance of the titular hero and his empress in such a way that it obliquely criticizes, if not dismisses, the lady's marriage. Chaucer, whose sensitivity to the nuances of the genre is especially keen, composes "The Franklin's Tale" to dramatize both a courtly suit and a married love. Even though Aurelius does not receive his lady's favors, nonetheless the discipline of love produces finally a leap forward in his character when he learns to release her in love rather than abduct her in lust and deceit, as do Meleagant, Orfeo's rival, Degaré's father, or the knight protagonist of "The Wife of Bath's Tale." Rather than attempt to perceive a general attitude in either tradition toward marriage or love, it is more useful to observe how, in any lay of either national tradition, differences are drawn between the way love is ennobled and the way love is abused.

Sir Orfeo, for instance, is often mentioned as characteristic of the way the English tales in the genre concern married love. Indeed, the bond between Orfeo and his lady is exquisitely described and central to the story, exactly as in the antique versions, but the poet's great achievement does not depend upon the fact that they are married. (A later, rather pious redaction in the Ashmole Manuscript does emphasize married love.) Rather, the poem's greatness lies partly in the pathos of their conversation on the day her dreams are invaded and, later, in their wordless communication of grief when he spies her among the retinue of fairy ladies:

> ȝern he biheld hir & sche hi[m] eke,
> ac noiþer to oþer a word no speke.
> For messais þat sche on him seiȝe
> þat had ben so riche & so heiȝe,
> þe teres fel out of her eiȝe.

True to the spirit of Marie, here the poet indicates the great power of love as a shaper of character and destiny when, in the next moment, Orfeo abandons exile and follows the fairy retinue and his wife to the court of his rival. The incident is in many ways reminiscent of the passage in *Yonec* where the lady suddenly leaves her tower and follows her mortally wounded beloved to his own kingdom, a place she had never before known. That lady and her hawk-knight represent both a sympathetic courtly adultery and the great power of love. In appreciating *Sir Orfeo*, then, one should emphasize not the marriage but rather the love.

Although the Breton lays attracted considerable attention from nineteenth-century philologists, two volumes essentially define the circumstances for continued interest in the Middle English poems during the twentieth century. One is an edition from 1930, Walter H. French and Charles B. Hale's *Middle English Metrical Romances*, which presents five of the lays as a group under the rubric "The Matter of Britain." Though most of the lays in it have enjoyed individual editions, individual lays or groups have since been anthologized frequently, and there have been two comprehensive collections, nonetheless scholarly studies consult French and Hale frequently to this day. The other influential book at the beginning of modern literary study of the lays, in 1927, is Roger Sherman Loomis's *Celtic Myth and Arthurian Romance*.

From the beginning, literary historians were interested in the Celtic antecedents of the genre and viewed the lays as heir to folk tradition. In 1953 G.V. Smithers examined lays in both language traditions for "the basic story-pattern" or folktale type "to which some of these works can be reduced" (61). Concentrating at length on versions of the Lanval story, *Sir Degaré, Sir Orfeo, Sir Gowther*, various French lays, and even couplet and metrical romances, Smithers began to draw out the intertextual associations that show in the English poems the transmission, anyway, if not the conscious awareness, of their literary antecedents. Smithers and other early close readers established the utility of comparative analysis that remains valuable to contemporary readers, as, for example, to Piero Boitani's insightful and concise description of the genre (54–56). Boitani and other contemporary readers now see the Breton lays in Middle English as much more sophisticated and self-aware than did earlier generations of scholars. Smithers, on the other hand, saw the continued development of the genre as a process of corruption of Marie's elegant conceptions. Likewise, George Kane, who thought "The Franklin's Tale" the best of the tradition, called *Emaré* a failure and *Lay le Freine* "a technically unremarkable little story" (47) and asserted that *The Erle of Tolous* "has great faults of structure" (35), *Sir Gowther* "is not very skilfully told" (32), and *Sir Launfal* has "a mealy-mouthed and sanctimonious opening" (34). At no period of their study have the anonymous lays, especially the stanzaic lays, compared very favorably to the urbanity of Marie, Chrétien, or Chaucer, but more recent readers have held them in substantially higher regard than did Kane.

For Kane and other writers in midcentury, including Mortimer Donovan, John Beston, and the editor A.J. Bliss, the later tradition of the Breton lay represented the decline of a courtly literary genre into a less elegant minstrel tradition with a popular audience. Beston concluded that "some of the English lays are skillfully told, some are merely competent; but it is broadly true that the English lay did not achieve a great deal beyond translation . . . and retelling" (336). Donovan went so far as to assert that "only the twelve Breton lays of Marie de France can be called, strictly, 'true' lays" (179). Something very close to this view is still apparent by 1990 in A.C. Spearing's "Marie de France and Her Middle English Adapters." Spearing argues that "Thomas Chestre either failed to grasp or failed to value the true nature of the Lanval story." In remarks reminiscent of Kane, Spearing calls Chestre's poem "a fascinating disaster" (148) and "the vision of aristocratic life seen from below stairs" (153). The poem, Spearing asserts, has "the extreme and powerful badness found in other works of self-pitying self-revelation that also at times plead to be rescued by being read as deliberate self-parody" (156). Those holding this view that Marie's art is incompletely understood or poorly imitated by later poets especially implicate the stanzaic lays in this decline. They note with varying levels of dissatisfaction the confusion of the genre with romance elements and hagiography, as well as the frequent use of minstrel formulae and tag lines in the metrical stanzas. However, more recent commentators than Kane and Donovan have perceived greater literary sophistication in the lays. B.K. Martin's defense of *Sir Launfal* and Derek Brewer's willingness to take *Sir Degaré* seriously are instances of the eventual recuperation of the tradition, facilitated in part by a renewed general acceptance of the lays as folk material appropriated to literary uses, just as Smithers suggested. More sophisticated and historically responsible assessments of the audience of medieval romance have also prevailed in the meantime, led perhaps most importantly by R.W. Hanning in 1981.

One early movement in the recuperation of literary reputation for the anonymous lays was Laura Hibbard Loomis's discovery of the Auchinleck Manuscript's influence on Chaucer. Thus the very standard to which the lays were held and found lacking was discovered to be in their debt. Subsequent readers learned that even though the cutting burlesque of "Sir Thopas" might be aimed at Chestre's *Sir Launfal*, on the other hand the clerk of Orleans's marvelous entertainment of Aurelius and his brother was almost certainly dependent on *Sir Orfeo*, and in part even the dynamics of the love triangle at the heart of "The Franklin's Tale."

As with the taxonomy of species in nature, so with forms of medieval romance, scholars have tended to fall into two categories we could call, after the example of popular science, splitters and lumpers. In biology, splitters are relatively quick to declare new species where others may see only racial variations. In literary history, splitters tend to see the differences among the lays and among the romances; they find neither term very stable for the identification of generic boundaries; they tend to divide and subdivide either category into smaller family units such as "liaison with the fairy mistress," "wish-fulfillment fantasy," or "tales of loss and recovery." Splitters are by far the more numerous critical readers of the Breton lays: John Finlayson and Mortimer Donovan are important examples. Lumpers, or those who despite difference see strong threads of generic resemblance running through the tradition—who, in other words, see one species with numerous specimens—are fewer. Those who see one generic tradition have tended to concentrate on narrative technique and formal structure. Constance Bullock-Davies and Rosemary Woolf might be called lumpers.

One of the more insightful recent studies also might be characterized in this way. David Harrington offers a definition of the Middle English lays according to thematic criteria different from those observed in other studies. Although he would exclude *Sir Degaré*, he sees the genre otherwise united by "social and ethical values that distinguish them in important ways" from other medieval narrative (74). Noting the general subordination of martial prowess in the English lays, Harrington calls their most important crises and plot devices "tests of gentleness" (83). "The overall impression," he continues, "is of characters striving for mutual respect or love through ethical behavior" (87). The lays "offer speculative models of how men and women might live and love together" (93). Harrington's definition suggests that the tradition of the Breton lays is more consistent than others have seen it, and that in many important ways the whole tradition of English lays is true to the tradition of Marie. Published reactions to his article have so far been mixed; Donna Crawford, for example, finds Harrington "attending to only half the story" (51). Nonetheless, his is a very intelligent set of brief readings of the poems. Coupled with the recent appearance of Laskaya and Salisbury's fine collection, Harrington's views should assure a continued critical interest in the Breton lays in Middle English.

SELECTED BIBLIOGRAPHY

Editions

Bliss, A.J., ed. *Sir Launfal*. London: Thomas Nelson, 1960.
————, ed. *Sir Orfeo*. London: Oxford University Press, 1954.

French, W.H., and C.B. Hale, eds. *Middle English Metrical Romances*. New York: Prentice-Hall, 1930.

Laskaya, Anne, and Eve Salisbury, eds. *The Middle English Breton Lays*. TEAMS Middle English Texts Series. Kalamazoo, MI: Medieval Institute, 1995.

Rickert, Edith, ed. *The Romance of Emaré*. EETS E.S. 99. London: Kegan Paul, Trench, Trübner, 1908.

Rumble, Thomas C., ed. *The Breton Lays in Middle English*. Detroit: Wayne State University Press, 1965.

Sands, Donald B., ed. *Middle English Verse Romances*. New York: Holt, Rinehart and Winston, 1966.

Shepherd, Stephen H.A., ed. *Middle English Romances*. Norton Critical Edition. New York: W.W. Norton, 1995.

Studies

Arthur, Ross. "Emaré's Cloak and Audience Response." *Sign, Sentence, Discourse: Language in Medieval Thought and Literature*. Ed. Julian Wasserman and Lois Roney. Syracuse, NY: Syracuse University Press, 1989. 80–92.

Beston, John B. "How Much Was Known of the Breton Lai in Fourteenth-Century England?" *The Learned and the Lewed*. Ed. Larry D. Benson. Cambridge, MA: Harvard University Press, 1974. 319–336.

Bettelheim, Bruno. *The Uses of Enchantment: The Meaning and Importance of Fairy Tales*. New York: Knopf, 1975.

Boitani, Piero. *English Medieval Narrative in the Thirteenth and Fourteenth Centuries*. Trans. Joan K. Hall. New York: Cambridge University Press, 1982.

Brewer, Derek. "Medieval Literature, Folk Tale, and Traditional Literature." *Dutch Quarterly Review of Anglo-American Letters* 11 (1981): 243–256.

————. *Symbolic Stories: Traditional Narratives of the Family Drama in English Literature*. Cambridge: D.S. Brewer, 1980.

Briggs, Katherine M. "The Fairies and the Realm of the Dead." *Folklore* 81 (1970): 81–96.

Brown, Carole Koepke. " 'It Is True Art to Conceal Art': The Episodic Structure of Chaucer's *Franklin's Tale*." *Chaucer Review* 27 (1992): 162–85.

Bullock-Davies, Constance. "The Form of the Breton Lay." *Medium Ævum* 42 (1973): 18–31.

Calin, William. *The French Tradition and the Literature of Medieval England*. Toronto: University of Toronto Press, 1994.

Colopy, Cheryl. "*Sir Degaré*: A Fairy Tale Oedipus." *Pacific Coast Philology* 17 (1982): 31–39.

Cook, Robert. "Chaucer's Franklin's Tale and *Sir Orfeo*." *Neuphilologische Mitteilungen* 95 (1994): 333–336.

Crawford, Donna, " 'Gronyng wyth Grysly Wounde': Injury in Five Middle English Breton Lays." *Readings in Medieval English Romance*. Ed. Carol M. Meale. Cambridge: D.S. Brewer, 1994. 35–52.

Cross, Tom Peete. "The Celtic Elements in the Lays of *Lanval* and *Graelent*." *MP* 12 (1915): 585–644.

Davies, Constance. "Classical Threads in 'Orfeo.' " *MLR* 56 (1961): 161–166.

Donovan, Mortimer J. *The Breton Lay: A Guide to Varieties*. Notre Dame, IN: University of Notre Dame Press, 1969.

Doob, Penelope Reed. *Nebuchadnezzar's Children: Conventions of Madness in Middle English Literature*. New Haven, CT: Yale University Press, 1974.

Evans, Murray J. *Rereading Middle English Romance: Manuscript Layout, Decoration, and the Rhetoric of Composite Structure*. Montreal: McGill–Queen's University Press, 1995.

Finlayson, John. "The Form of the Middle English Lay." *Chaucer Review* 19 (1985): 352–367.

Friedman, John Block. *Orpheus in the Middle Ages*. Cambridge, MA: Harvard University Press, 1970.

Frye, Northrop. *The Secular Scripture: A Study of the Structure of Romance*. Cambridge, MA: Harvard University Press, 1976.

Furnish, Shearle. "Civilization and Savagery in Thomas Chestre's *Sir Launfal*." *Medieval Perspectives* 3 (1988): 137–49.

————. "The Modernity of *The Erle of Tolous* and the Decay of the *Breton Lai*." *Medieval Perspectives* 8 (1993): 69–77.

Gros Louis, Kenneth R.R. "The Significance of Sir Orfeo's Self-Exile." *RES* 18 (1967): 245–252.

Hanning, Robert W., "The Audience as Co-Creator of the First Chivalric Romances." *Yearbook of English Studies* 11 (1981): 1–28.

————. "Poetic Emblems in Medieval Narrative Texts." *Vernacular Poetics in the Middle Ages*. Ed. Lois Ebin. Kalamazoo, MI: Medieval Institute, 1984. 1–32.

Hanning, Robert W. and Joan Ferrante, eds. and trans. *The Lais of Marie de France*. Durham, NC: Labyrinth Press, 1982.

Harrington, David V. "Redefining the Middle English Breton Lay." *Medievalia et Humanistica* n.s. 16 (1988): 73–95.

Hill, D.M. "The Structure of 'Sir Orfeo.' " *Mediaeval Studies* 23 (1961): 136–153.

Hume, Kathryn. "The Pagan Setting of the *Franklin's Tale* and the Sources of Dorigen's Cosmology." *Studia Neophilologica* 44 (1972): 289–294.

————. "Why Chaucer Calls the *Franklin's Tale* a Breton Lai." *PQ* 51 (1972): 365–379.

Johnston, Grahame. "The Breton Lays in Middle English." *Iceland and the Mediaeval World: Studies in Honour of Ian Maxwell*. Ed. Gabriel Turville-Petre and John Stanley Martin. Victoria, Australia: Wilke, 1974. 151–61.

Kane, George. *Middle English Literature: A Critical Study of the Romances, the Religious Lyrics*, Piers Plowman. London: Methuen, 1951.

Lane, Daryl. "Conflict in *Sir Launfal*." *Neuphilologische Mitteilungen* 74 (1973): 283–287.

Lerer, Seth. "Artifice and Artistry in *Sir Orfeo*." *Speculum* 60 (1985): 92–109.

Loomis, Laura Hibbard. "Chaucer and the Breton Lays of the Auchinleck MS." *SP* 38 (1941): 14–33.

————. *Mediaeval Romance in England*. London: Oxford University Press, 1924.

Loomis, Roger Sherman. *Celtic Myth and Arthurian Romance*. New York: Columbia University Press, 1927.

Lucas, Peter J. "An Interpretation of *Sir Orfeo*." *Leeds Studies in English* 6 (1972): 1–9.

Marchalonis, Shirley. "*Sir Gowther*: The Process of a Romance." *Chaucer Review* 6 (1971): 14–29.

Martin, B.K. "*Sir Launfal* and the Folktale." *Medium Ævum* 35 (1966): 199–210.

Mitchell, Bruce. "The Faery World of *Sir Orfeo*." *Neophilologus* 48 (1964): 155–59.

O'Brien, Timothy D. "The 'Readerly' Sir Launfal." *Parergon* 8 (1990): 33–45.

Ogle, M.B. "The Orchard Scene in *Tydorel* and *Sir Gowther*." *Romanic Review* 13 (1922): 37–43.

Reilly, Robert. "*The Earl of Toulouse*: A Structure of Honor." *Mediaeval Studies* 37 (1975): 515–523.

Rosenberg, Bruce A. "The Three Tales of 'Sir Degare.' " *Neuphilologische Mitteilungen* 76 (1975): 39–51.

Shippey, Thomas A. "Breton *Lais* and Modern Fantasies." *Studies in Medieval English Romances: Some New Approaches*. Ed. Derek Brewer. Cambridge: D.S. Brewer, 1988. 69–91.

Smithers, G.V. "Story-Patterns in Some Breton Lays." *Medium Ævum* 22 (1953): 61–92.

Spearing, A.C. "Marie de France and Her Middle English Adapters." *Studies in the Age of Chaucer* 12 (1990): 117–156.

Speirs, John. *Medieval English Poetry: The Non-Chaucerian Tradition*. London: Faber and Faber, 1957.

Strohm, Paul. "The Origin and Meaning of Middle English Romance." *Genre* 10 (1977): 1–28.

Warden, John, ed. *Orpheus: The Metamorphoses of a Myth*. Toronto: University of Toronto Press, 1982.

Woolf, Rosemary. "Later Poetry: The Popular Tradition." *History of Literature in the English Language*. Vol. 1, *The Middle Ages*. Ed. W.F. Bolton. London: Barrie and Jenkins, 1970. 267–311.

7
Chronicle

Emma B. Hawkins

According to *The Oxford English Dictionary*, the word *chronicle* derives directly from Latin *chronica* (ultimately from Greek χρονικά) by way of Old French and originally referred to " 'things' or 'matters of time.' " Thus chronicles are records of facts or events, in order of date. But so, too, are annals. The distinction between the two depends upon how developed the historical entries are. Chronicles are more "rhetorically polished" than annals, which are "a mere succinct listing of events in the order in which they occurred" (Kennedy, *Chronicles* 2598). The typical Old or Middle English chronicle was primarily historical and utilitarian rather than literary in intent, was restricted in space for the sake of maintenance and preservation, and required some degree of regular and timely upkeep. Nevertheless, as a genre it still permitted moderate variation. Events from the past and the present, of both great and small importance, and with either a significant connection or none at all were included. The scope of coverage ranged from universal to local. Items of interest were rendered in prose and poetry. Although accurate and objective reporting was vital, emotionally charged personal judgments as well as mythical and legendary elements were included.

In England the concept of the chronicle probably originated with the keeping of Easter tables wherein clerics would make a list of successive years, calculate the day upon which Easter would fall in each year, and then record the year and the Easter calculation, one per line. This single line, along with the margins, provided space sufficient for brief notations of a historical nature. Even so, Charles Plummer is convinced that the purpose of the early chronicles was not to serve merely as "a device for arranging a store of events," or as a means for "reducing the accumulations of history to literary order," or as "a method, a system of registration" for placing events in their corresponding chronological slots (2: xix). Instead, the goal was more basic and simple: "to keep apart the ever-receding years which tend to melt into one another in the haze of unassisted memory" (2: cxiv).

The *Anglo-Saxon Chronicle* (hereafter referred to as *ASC*) is the earliest extant example of an Anglo-Saxon/Old English chronological registry. Easter tables may well have furnished the material that was incorporated into the prefaces to Manuscripts A, D, E, and F and, perhaps, into some of the initial entries. Other sources from which the chroniclers gleaned information include Bede's *Historia Écclesiastica Gentis Anglorum* (*Ecclesiastical History of the English People*) (A.D. 731), various genealogies, regnal and episcopal lists, an epitome of world/ universal history, and early northern and West Saxon annals plus continental annals, most likely Frankish in content. All of the surviving manuscripts of the *ASC* were maintained in monasteries or other religious establishments and by scribes who tended to be more concerned with chronology than with literary form and presentation. The *Anglo-Saxon Chronicle*, then, is a collective title applied to a series of annals, a vernacular composite work comprised of seven extant manuscripts and two fragments.

Manuscript A: Corpus Christi College, Cambridge, MS 173

Known as the Parker Manuscript, after Matthew Parker, archbishop of Canterbury (1559–1575), whose private library housed the manuscript; also known as the *Winchester Chronicle*; probably begun at Winchester monastery; the earliest version of all the manuscripts; extends from 60 B.C. to A.D. 1070.

Manuscript B: British Library, MS Cotton Tiberius A.M.

Also known as one of the *Abingdon Chronicles*; contains the *Mercian Register* (902–924); some yearly numbers omitted by the scribe; extends from 60 B.C. to A.D. 977.

Manuscript C: British Library, MS Cotton Tiberius B.i

Also known as one of the *Abingdon Chronicles*; maintained at Abingdon and features events peculiar to this area; contains the *Mercian Register*; extends from 60 B.C. to A.D. 1056/1066.

Manuscript D: British Library, MS Cotton Tiberius B.iv

Known as the *Worcester Chronicle*; contains the *Mercian Register*; contains entries that focus on internal Scottish affairs, especially those dealing with St. Margaret of Scotland; extends from A.D. 1 to 1080.

Manuscript E: Bodleian Library, Oxford, MS Laud 636

Known as the Laud Manuscript after Archbishop William Laud of Canterbury; also known as the *Peterborough Chronicle*, after the monastery where it was maintained; longest-running version of all the manuscripts; contains some entries in Latin; extends from A.D. 1 to 1154.

Manuscript F: British Library, MS Cotton Domitian A.viii

Dual-language version (Old English and Latin); probably maintained at Canterbury; extends from A.D. 1 to 1058.

Manuscript G: British Library, MS Cotton Otho B.xi

Three leaves survived the fire of 1731; served as the basis for Abraham Wheloc's 1643 edition and, to that degree, has been preserved; is a copy of Manuscript A before it was subjected to alteration at Canterbury. The designation for this version is subject to disagreement. On one hand, noted scholars such as Plummer, G.N. Garmonsway, and the contributors to *Dictionary of Literary Biography* recognize it as a variation of Manuscript A. Equally reputable scholars such as Dorothy Whitelock and Janet Bately consider it to be an independent work and refer to it as G.

Manuscript H: British Library, MS Cotton Domitian A.ix

Single leaf; covers years 1113–1114.

Manuscript I: British Library, MS Cotton Caligula A.xv

Belonged to Christ Church, Canterbury; consists of Easter table with brief historical notations in the margin; dual-language (Old English and Latin); extends from A.D. 925 to 1268.

Following decades of conflict in which the seven-kingdom Heptarchy was remolded into the three kingdoms of Northumbria, Mercia, and Wessex, and years of bloody encroachment by Danish marauders, finally, during the reign of King Alfred, Britain gained some semblance of peace and stability. True, national unity was not accomplished until after Alfred's death and during the reign of Edgar (A.D. 959), who was the first king to be recognized as king of all England *Engla waldend*, and the Danes still raided occasionally. However, hostilities ceased long enough for efforts to be directed toward educational, intellectual, religious, and social endeavors. One such project was aimed at devising and maintaining a comprehensive, national history. The consensus among critics is that the first copy of the *ASC* was begun sometime during the reign of King Alfred (871–899). In order to construct a comprehensive registry of events, predictably the first compiler had to dispose of hundreds of years of past history before continuing with current affairs. Altogether, the *ASC* traces events from sixty years before the birth of Christ and the arrival of the Roman general Gaius Julius (Julius Caesar) to the last entry in Manuscript E, which records the death of King Stephen in A.D. 1154.

Coverage of actual Anglo-Saxon history does not begin until the entry for A.D. 449 that notes the coming of Hengest and Horsa at the invitation of Vortigern to fight against the Picts. With regard to historical events recorded in close proximity to the year in which they occurred and by contemporary, even eyewitness, record keepers, A.D. 890 seems to be the earliest point of reference. The first copy of the *ASC* was probably composed in the far south central region of England, at the monastery of Winchester in Wessex. Shortly thereafter various copies were produced and disseminated to other areas, such as Abingdon just a short distance to the north, near Oxford; Worcester to the west and north; and eventually York to the far north. Yet however convincingly critics argue that King Alfred provided the impetus for initiating a chronological account of national history and that the account originated in Wessex around A.D. 890, neither the exact date, location, nor compiler can be verified with certainty.

Apparently the scribes who selected the entries for the various versions were bound by no strict guidelines for determining which events were valuable enough to preserve for the sake of posterity. Understandably, they favored recounting Anglo-Saxon victories over the Danes; reporting the deaths of kings and archbishops; and recording catastrophic natural phenomena such as a two- to three-hour eclipse of the sun (A-538), the recurring appearances of a star called "comet" (E-678), a red cross in the moon or a circle around the sun (F-806), a severe famine (C-1005), or an earthquake (C-1048). However, they also included mundane, even trivial events: the dining in state of Archbishop Æthelnoth with Pope Benedict VIII (D-1022), the increase in the price of wheat to fifty-five pence (E-1039), the consecration of a tower at Peterborough (D-1059), or a trip to Rome by Earl Tostig and his wife (D-1061).

Most early *ASC* entries are annalistic in form, consisting of succinct one- or two-line statements of fact; later entries from the tenth through the twelfth centuries are longer and more detail oriented. Seldom does a scribe attempt to analyze or establish a relationship between events, but there are a few exceptions. The years 885, 892, and 895 (Manuscript A) are connected by a weak link. The compiler mentions that the Danish army whose activities he is once more going to report is the same army he has named in previous entries. To a limited extent, the composer of the Cynewulf-Cyneheard story (C-755) traces the cause-and-effect relationship of the events that expanded the feud. The reporter for 892 (Manuscript C) takes time to briefly explain why three Scots came from Ireland to King Alfred in a boat without any oars.

Regarding the scope of coverage, internal evidence substantiates that up to A.D. 891 all seven extant manuscripts derived from a common stock of events and exhibited a national flavor. Thereafter, the scribes observed no restrictions governing the range of coverage. After 891 national events were sometimes omitted, and, at their own discretion, individual compilers substituted news of international affairs or of local events peculiar to the area in which the manuscript was being maintained. Thus amid Anglo-Saxon happenings the scribes insert news from the international scene. The Romans cut out Pope Leo's tongue (C-799); Carloman, king of the Franks, was killed by a wild boar (A-882); and St. Margaret of Scotland married and converted the king from the path of error (D-1067). On the local level, an upper story collapsed in a meetinghouse in Calne, injuring or killing some English councilors (D-978). In 1083 Thurstan, abbot of Glastonbury, instigated a raid upon his own monks in which many who sought sanctuary in the church were killed or seriously wounded (Manuscript E). The *Mercian Register* (A.D. 902–924) that were incorporated into several versions of the *ASC* were localized records, concentrating explicitly upon events in Mercia.

Strangely enough, at one time or another, all of the copies of the *ASC* show signs of having erred in matching events to corresponding years. Generally, the discrepancies range from one to three years. Any of several explanations may account for these dating irregularities. Concerning the early entries, frequently no definitive sources were available to the scribes for verifying the accuracy of their data. Another cause may be chronological mechanical dislocation, otherwise interpreted as scribal blunder. Blank years in which no historical entries were made seem to have been the most serious culprit. In the process of recopying, entries were simply, though erroneously, moved up a yearly date or two or three. Further exacerbating the problem, some scribes deliberately tampered with the arrangement to eliminate inconsistencies they had detected. Yet a third explanation focuses on the confusion surrounding when a year actually began. In the absence of any type of official calendar and depending upon the inclination of the compiler, a year could just as conveniently begin at Christmas, as in the autumn on September 24 with the Caesarean indiction or on March 25 with the Annunciation.

Regardless of these inconsistencies, the composite *ASC* is important, not only because it offers the most detailed, accurate, and comprehensive coverage of Britain's early history, but also because it employs the Old English vernacular rather than the traditional Latin as the recording medium. Thus it constitutes the first historical prose document to be composed in Old English, and, according to Garmonsway, is one of only three histories (including a set of Irish annals and an early Russian chronicle) composed in a "native tongue in the whole of Europe before 1200" (xvi). Moreover, it preserves three hundred years of development in the Old English language as it evolved into Middle English, as well as differences in the various Old English dialects.

Even though the historical and linguistic value is of major importance, the *ASC* also has literary merit. It contains some excellent examples of historical narrative prose and a few poems. Manuscript A contains the most polished of the poetic entries, "The Battle of Brunanburgh" (937). This heroic, unrhymed, alliterative poem constitutes a celebration of the victory of the West Saxon King Æthelstan and his brother Edmund over a coalition of Norsemen, Scots, Irish, and Celtic Britons from Strathclyde under the leadership of Olaf Guthfritharson and Constantinus III (Scotland). Additional poems from Manuscript A composed in the traditional style, but of less aesthetic and literary interest, are "The Capture of the Five Boroughs" (942), "Edgar's Coronation" (973), and "King Edgar's Death" (975). Poems from other versions include "The Death of Alfred (the Son of Ethelred)" (1036) and "The Death of Edward (the Confessor)" (1065), both incorporated in Manuscript C. While it exhibits a narrative style that is reminiscent of Old Icelandic and Norse sagas, the entry for 755 describing the slaying of King Cynewulf of Wessex by Cyneheard may even be considered "the first English short story." Similarly, the entries dealing with William the Conqueror constitute "the beginnings of English biography" (Garmonsway xvi).

Since the *ASC* was basically a historical document, in most instances the record keepers were impersonal and objective when they recorded their observances, but sometimes emotions spilled over. For example, in 874 (Manuscript A) the writer is so outraged that he calls Ceolwulf "one foolish king's thane" because he has capitulated completely to the Danish interlopers and agrees to be at their service should they come again. For the year 959 (Manuscript D) the scribe verbally castigates King Edgar for dallying too much with heathen people and their customs. The entry of 979 in Manuscript D records the author's righteous indignation over the murder and disrespectful treatment of King Edward (St. Edward). The exasperated compiler of Manuscript C for the year 1011 boldly blames the needless suffering of the people upon the policy of misguided English leaders who repeatedly stall too long in paying tribute to the Danish army or, worse yet, refuse to stand up to the Danes at all. Filled with sermonizing and moralizing, the entry of 1087 (Manuscript E) resembles a minihomily, equating the suffering of the people with God's just punishment of their wickedness.

Most yearly entries record actual events or factual data. Occasionally, in the midst of historical affairs, and mainly before A.D. 809, an element of legend or myth creeps in. The royal houses of Bernicia, Deira, East Anglia, Essex, Kent, Mercia, and Wessex all trace their ancestry back to Woden, an ancient Norse god. Some regnal genealogies list as a progenitor Scyld Sceaf, the same Scyld Sceaf who is depicted as the legendary, mythical king of the Danes in the Old English heroic poem *Beowulf*. A few Anglo-Saxon royal houses even claim to be descendants of Methuselah, Seth, and Adam (Preface to A, 449; A, D, E, C, F, 855–858). In 448 John the Baptist is said to have revealed his head to a couple of monks in Jerusalem (Manuscript F). But the most startling and questionable of the entries derives from the year 793 (Manuscript D). The scribe notes that fiery dragons were seen flying over Northumbria. Also noteworthy is the fact that in spite of the popularity in later chronicles of the legendary Arthur, in none of the surviving manuscripts of the *ASC* is he even mentioned.

To search for additional representatives of the chronicle genre in Old English would be futile. If others were compiled, they have not been preserved. In the opinion of Mitchell and Robinson, the last few entries of Manuscript E of the

ASC signaled "the end of historical writing in English prose until the fifteenth century" (142). Yet during the centuries from 1200 to 1500 chronicles were still produced, and while many of these chronicles were composed in Latin, chronicles in the vernacular were maintained simultaneously. In the fifteenth century vernacular chronicles even proliferated.

Up through the time of Bede, Latin was the preferred language for scholarly writing, but the Danish invasion initiated a change in emphasis. During the next three centuries, the time in which the *ASC* was being compiled, prose writing in the vernacular gained precedence. Following the Norman Conquest, the last half of the twelfth century experienced the rise of Anglo-Latin chronicles. Consequently, the change in language used for historical documents came full circle back to Latin. The other surviving chronicle from the Anglo-Saxon period, which ended roughly in 1066 with the Norman Conquest, is in Latin, as are many later chronicles from the twelfth through the fifteenth centuries. Because most exhibit evidence that the compilers depended upon some version of the Old English *ASC*, they do not contribute significant new information. Their value is determined primarily by the degree to which they can verify the accuracy of the *ASC* entries and the quality of the later entries, the compiler's original observations.

The Chronicle of Æthelweard (tenth century), the earliest Latin chronicle from the Old English period, was contemporary with the *ASC* as well as being partially based upon the *ASC*. Compiled by Æthelweard, ealdorman of Wessex in the time of Æthelred the Unready, it closes with the entry for 959. This writer is probably the same Æthelweard mentioned in the *ASC* (C-994) as the government representative who was involved in the negotiations to secure a truce between King Æthelred and the Danes. Besides the *ASC*, Æthelweard availed himself of Bede's records and some other independent source. Because he was particularly interested in family history and genealogy, he provides information on the foreign marriages of the West Saxon royal house, information that is absent from the *ASC*. Unfortunately, in spite of his literary interests, Æthelweard's grasp of Latin and scholarly writing skills were less than adequate. His inaccuracies and ambiguities were serious enough to have earned the disapproval of critics from as early as William of Malmesbury's twelfth-century comments up to the present day. His "most valuable [historical] contribution" is the entry for 900 that confirms that Eadweard the Elder was crowned king on Whitsunday, substantiating the *ASC* reference to Alfred's death in October of 899 (Campbell xliii).

The majority of the better-known Latin chronicles are from the early Middle English period and contain material that closely resembles, if not duplicates, entries found in Manuscript E, perhaps D, and possibly even an archetype of the Old English *ASC*. The *Chronicon ex Chronica*, often called the *Chronicle of Florence* or the *Chronicle of Worcester*, probably was commissioned by Bishop Wulfstan. The early entries show evidence of the use of Bede, the chronicle of Marianus Scotus, and more than one version of the *ASC*. Due to the weakness of the evidence supporting Florence rather than John as the chronicler, the specific date and authorship of this chronicle are controversial. Indeed, if Florence was the initial record keeper, his contribution begins with the Creation and ends in 1117. A continuation by John of Worcester brings the chronicle up to 1141, and two additional hands continue the yearly notations up to the final entry in 1154. This particular chronicle is unique in that it is the first to include the full text of numerous documents that often reinforce the chronicler's own record keeping.

Simeon (Symeon) of Durham is often credited with having compiled the *Historia Regum* (twelfth century), a work based chiefly upon Bede's history and Florence's chronicle (from 848 to 1118). Furthermore, Simeon had at his disposal certain annals from the north containing eighth-century records of Northumbrian kings, records that have since been lost to scholars. Only in Simeon's *Historia* has the material from *Gesta Northanhumbrorum* been preserved. Like the author of the Florence chronicle, Simeon includes copies of the full text of various documents. Although Clark considers Durham's account to be "derivative and unpolished," she does admit that he provides some valuable information, such as his description of the 1070 conflict between the Scots and the Northumbrians, an episode the *ASC* omits entirely (xxx).

Other Latin chronicles are attributed to William of Malmesbury, Eadmer, Henry of Huntingdon, William of Newburg, Matthew Paris, and the monks at the Abbey of Waverley. William of Malmesbury, a noted historical scholar of the early twelfth century, probably used Manuscript E, perhaps D, or an archetype as a source for his chronicle of the English kings, *Gesta Regum Anglorum* (Plummer 2: xxxvii). Basically, his two-part work covers the years 449–1142. William was a highly educated and traveled cleric whose reporting is more impartial and open minded than that of fellow Latin chroniclers, yet he mentions supernatural occurrences and includes interesting or humorous anecdotes that have little or no historical value. On one hand, since William's chronicle is primarily a compilation of a wide variety of sources, many of which have been identified and some of which have not, it introduces few fresh historical details. On the other hand, it does provide excellent "commentary which enlarges and deepens our understanding" of some of the skimpy entries in the *ASC* (Clark xxiv).

Eadmer's six-volume *Historia Novorum in Anglia* (c. 1095–1123) not only includes a biography of Archbishop Anselm, but also provides a detailed account of contemporary national events up to 1122. Eadmer pays close attention to the relations between the church and the state, especially the circumstances that led up to the confrontation between Anselm and William II (Rufus). In the *Historia Anglorum*, composed sometime after 1125, Archdeacon Henry of Huntingdon closely follows the entries of Manuscript E or an archetype. Plummer believes that Huntingdon had in his possession a second version of the *ASC*, Manuscript C (2: lvii–lviii). Huntingdon's original entries are confined to the years 1129–1154 and resume approximately where Eadmer's entries stop. During the Middle

Ages his chronicle was exceptionally popular, and twenty-five medieval copies have survived.

Later in the century William of Newburg produced the *Historia Rerum Anglicarum*. According to *The Cambridge History of English Literature*, William authored the "best single commentary upon the history of the twelfth century" (Ward and Waller 1: 171). The *Historia* covers the years from the Norman Conquest to 1198 and is valuable today because the compiler used a biography of Richard I that has since been lost (Gransden, *Historical* 264). William was the only historian of his time to recognize and openly criticize Geoffrey of Monmouth's fictitious history of England. Another Latin chronicle, Roger Wendover's *Flores Historiarum*, begins with the Creation and ends in 1234. Wendover's work gained importance due to its association with Matthew Paris. Paris incorporated Wendover's chronicle into his own chronicle, the *Chronica Majora*, which runs from the Creation to 1259, the year in which Paris probably died. Paris's longer edition is the "most comprehensive history" produced in England up to that time (Gransden, *Historical* 359). In addition, Paris compiled shorter works: the *Historia Anglorum*, whose scope reaches from the Norman Conquest to 1253, the *Abbreviatio Chronicarum*, and his own history entitled *Flores Historiarum*. Paris (c. 1217–1259) was in an excellent position to obtain current news, and the scope of his work is indeed international. Unfortunately, the reputation of this chronicle as a reliable historical document is a bit tarnished. Paris included forged papal bulls to bolster his claims and periodically engaged in diatribes aimed at the vices and growing authority of the papacy and the Crown, especially of Henry III. During the thirteenth century the *Waverley Annals* were compiled by Cistercian monks assigned to the Abbey at Waverley. The scope of these annalistic entries extends from the Incarnation to 1291, but the chronicle is unfinished. Since the abbey was not founded until 1126, the entries from 1000 to 1121 are based on information borrowed from another source: the *ASC*. While the early entries demonstrate a close resemblance to Manuscript E, observations from 1157 onwards seem to be firsthand.

Before moving to the chronicles composed in Middle English, Geoffrey of Monmouth's Latin chronicle must be introduced. A mixture of fact and fiction, Geoffrey's *Historia Regum Britanniae* (c. 1136) was judged to be a legitimate source of historical data, and later chroniclers did not hesitate to borrow from him. The *Historia* contributed greatly to the acceptance of legendary and mythical Arthurian material into medieval accounts of English history. Divided into twelve books and spanning almost two thousand years, the *Historia* comprises a prose rendition of Britain's legendary history, including accounts of the reigns of King Lear as well as Arthur. Book 1 begins with the fall of Troy and the founding of an empire in Britain by Brutus, the grandson of Aeneas. Book 12 ends with the death of Cadwallader, the last of the kings of the Britons, in 689, and the flight of the remaining Britons into the rugged mountainous regions of southwestern Britain and Wales.

Serving the church first as a priest and later as the bishop of St. Asaph,

Geoffrey had access to a vast store of sources ranging from other chronicles to Celtic materials, ancient folktales, and Scandinavian and Carolingian accounts. For the most part, he supplemented material from Bede, Gildas, and especially from Nennius's *Historia Brittonum* with his imagination to create the earliest full account of the legendary King Arthur. At a tenuous time in Britain's history, Geoffrey's *Historia* served both a historical and a patriotic purpose. First, it provided a record of events for the 150-year gap in Britain's history following the departure of the Romans in 410. More important, it created for Britain a noble history that rivaled that of any medieval nation, cautioned against civil strife and moral decay that had unraveled many an ancient ruling government, and supplied a role model (Arthur) worthy of emulation.

With the demise of the Old English prose chronicle, a new type of vernacular chronicle gained prominence: the verse chronicle. Although the Middle English chroniclers were for the most part still preoccupied with reporting historical events, they began to pay more attention to literary presentation and critical delving into cause-and-effect relations. No longer tied strictly to the parameters of annalistic reporting, they focused more on detail, elaborate descriptions, and the development of individual styles. The earliest important verse chronicle in Middle English is Layamon's (Lawman's) *Brut* (c. 1205), a pseudohistorical chronicle. Composed in alliterative and rhymed verse, *Brut* consists of approximately 16,000 lines, making it "the longest poem in English apart from *The Faerie Queene*" (Bennett 68). Commencing with the fall of Troy and the founding of Britain by Brutus and continuing to 689 and the ultimate defeat of the Britons, *Brut* is the earliest extant manuscript in the English vernacular to focus on Arthur. Approximately one-third of the work consists of Arthurian legends. Because magic and the supernatural abound and the historicity of many events is questionable, the historical value of *Brut* is small. In the introduction to his translation of *Brut*, Bzdyl suggests that Layamon's chronicle is "a hodgepodge of everything Layamon happened to know about early British history" (5). Layamon's episodic approach prevents the work from being strictly categorized as a chronicle. So, too, does his style. The narrative incorporates extensive dialogue, and frequently the descriptions are highly elaborate: abundantly detailed, shockingly graphic, and overly dramatic.

Layamon, a parish priest from Areley Kings, located near Worcester and on the border between Wales and England, borrowed primarily from Wace's Anglo-Norman *Roman de Brut*, itself a translation of Geoffrey's *Historia*, Celtic lore, and his own fertile imagination. The criticisms most frequently lodged against Layamon's chronicle center on the repetitive pattern of events and the excessive relish with which he describes man's brutal mistreatment of man in the battle scenes. As for the repetitive nature, in lines 11156–11315 the surrenders of the kings of Ireland, Iceland, Orkney, Jutland, and Winetland are identical in many respects. As for the numerous slaughter scenes, two examples will suffice. Lines 10453–10468 note that men of learning are laid upon burning coals, suckling infants are drowned, and men, women, and children are indiscriminately put to the sword. In another instance, Arthur alone strikes such a blow that his sword is lodged in the teeth of one warrior. He then proceeds to decapitate a second warrior, and yet a third he cuts in half (ll. 10669–10673). Often considered a lay chronicle intended for the common people, *Brut* gained enough popularity to be translated into Anglo-Norman and Latin, and numerous copies of the manuscript in all three languages have survived. In his discussion of Middle English historical prose, Matheson claims that *Brut* was "the most popular secular work of the Middle Ages in England" (210).

Layamon's *Brut* in verse form should not be confused with *The Prose Brut*. The prose rendition is preserved in 172 manuscripts and is based chiefly on the Anglo-Norman prose *Brut*. The various manuscripts all begin with the founding of Albion and continue to 1272, the year in which Henry III died. In most, the coverage is extended via continuations to the mid-1400s, but the different versions do not end simultaneously. Printed by William Caxton under the title *The Chronicles of England, The Prose Brut* was the first chronicle to be printed in England.

Data on later medieval English chronicles and their authors are often sketchy and in some cases almost nonexistent. The most extensive accounts, which are usually confined to a few pages at most, are found in *The Cambridge History of English Literature*, E.D. Kennedy's *Chronicles and Other Historical Writing*, and *Dictionary of Literary Biography*. Not only is biographical information sparse, but some chronicles from the period have never been printed, and others have been edited and published only during the past decade. The authors can generally be determined, but occasionally even their identity is disputed. Skimpy records furnish estimated birth and death dates; the probable birthplace; ecclesiastical positions held, if any; and a list of works for most. For instance, in his edition of *A Summarie of English Chronicles* (1570), John Stow credits a *Chronicle* to Robert of Gloucester, but this fact is debatable. This chronicle is a composite work, and two versions have been preserved. The longer, rhyming work, composed sometime between 1290 and 1310, begins with the story of Brutus and ends in 1270. With some confidence this lengthy version can be attributed to Robert. A shorter version, often referred to as the *Short Chronicle*, ends in 1272. It was written by another hand and cannot logically be credited to the same man. In the same vein, internal evidence is too inconclusive to substantiate if Robert was a monk or a secular clerk. Thus the chronicle may have been a monastic record or a secular history compiled for a wealthy patron. In any case, the numerous surviving manuscripts confirm that this chronicle was popular and well known in its day.

In the longer version Robert offers specialized coverage of events from Gloucester and Oxford. Occasionally he excels in vivid description such as that of the student riot at Oxford in 1263 or the battle of Evesham in 1265, and especially of the death and dismemberment of Simon de Montfort. Regarding the Barons' War, the chronicle is sympathetic toward the barons rather than the king and offers the best contemporary coverage of this internal conflict. It includes specific dates and detailed lists of names of men who were members of various and sundry contingents. Robert gleaned his facts from a variety of sources: the chronicles of Geoffrey of Monmouth and Henry of Huntingdon, the *Life of St. Kenelm*, William of Malmesbury, the Winchester and Waverley annals, and the metrical *Lives of the Saints*.

Thomas (Bek) of Castleford composed a massive chronicle of approximately 40,000 lines that resembles other "Brut" chronicles. In line 290 the author even refers to his work as the "Boke of Brut." Beginning with the founding of Albion, *Castleford's Chronicle* continues up to 1327, when Edward III became king. This chronicle is important to history because Thomas includes one of the earliest vernacular accounts of King Lear. In addition, he focuses on northern events in Yorkshire during the reigns of Edward I and Edward II, the conflict between England and Scotland, and the struggle of Robert the Bruce for the Scottish throne. Only one manuscript of this particular chronicle exists. Rolf Kaiser's 1958 edition of *Medieval English* contains excerpts, but not until *Castleford's Chronicle; or, The Boke of Brut*, edited by Caroline Eckhardt, was published in 1996 by the Early English Text Society was a copy of the full text made available. A proposed third volume containing commentary, glossary, and bibliography has yet to be published.

In his two-part *Chronicle of England* (1338) Robert Mannyng of Brunne, a skillful storyteller, traces the history of mankind from the biblical Noah to the death of Edward I in 1307 and incorporates the Arthurian material. Primarily he draws from Bede, Wace's *Roman de Brut* based on Geoffrey of Monmouth's *Historia*, and Pierre de Langtoft's Anglo-Norman chronicle, likewise based on Geoffrey's *Historia*. Mannyng wrote for the common man (*comonalte*, 1, 123) and the uneducated (*lewed*, 1, 6). To hold the interest of his unlettered audience, Mannyng relied upon simple language, humor, and embellishment of stories like Godwin's choking on a piece of bread immediately after he falsely swears that he did not kill Alfred when, in reality, he did (I11335–1338), or William's tripping over a nail and falling end over end into the mire when he attempts to disembark upon English soil (II 1721–1743). In addition, Mannyng included political songs and some graphic descriptions such as those of the destruction of Troy, the 1263 riot in Oxford, and the 1265 battle of Evesham. He also tended to moralize, which is not surprising considering that he was a member of the Order of St. Gilbert in Lincolnshire and rose to the rank of canon. He equates the downfall of the Britons and the conquest of England by the Normans with God's judgment on sin and political irresponsibility. As for style, his efforts to adapt the alexandrine lines of Langtoft's version to the octosyllabic verse form were often rough. Nor were his attempts to maintain rhyme in every line totally successful. Notwithstanding, the resulting couplet rhyme seems to have served as the forerunner of the heroic couplet.

The *Orygynale Cronykil of Scotland* (c. 1420) was compiled by Andrew of Wyntoun, a Scottish, Augustinian canon. Divided into ten books (nine comprising the narrative), the chronicle begins with a history of the angels based on the Bible and moves forward. Unfortunately, Andrew's excessive patriotic fervor prevented him from maintaining objectivity and accuracy; thus the historical value of the early entries is minor. He dwells on marvels and miracles and tampers with the chronology and facts in order to create a genealogy for Scotland every bit as illustrious as that of England. His later entries are more valuable because they provide eyewitness information about a period of Scotland's history for which scholars have practically no historical documentation. Andrew's descriptions of the battles between Scotland and England, especially when Scottish forces were victorious, are the strongest literary feature. Excerpts of Andrew's chronicle can be found in Eyre-Todd's *Early Scottish Poetry*.

John Capgrave was a priest who later advanced to fill the position of prior provincial at the monastery at Lynn, a religious house maintained by the Augustinian Hermits, a mendicant order. Although he is not considered to be either an "outstanding theologian or historian," Capgrave was a learned man who composed numerous works in Latin: biblical commentaries and lives of saints (Seymour 206). Besides religious works, Capgrave composed works of a historical nature, mostly in Latin, a few in English: *Liber de Illustribus Henricis* (Latin), *The Life of St. Katherine* in English, and the *Abbreuiacion of Cronicles* (1462), a three-section prose chronicle in English that he may have dedicated to King Edward IV. The *Abbreuiacion* starts with the Creation and progresses through the reigns of the various Roman emperors and popes. While the scope of his coverage initially is universal, with the 1216 entry Capgrave begins to specialize, concentrating strictly on the kings of England and supplying valuable historical information on the reigns of Henry IV, Henry V, and Edward IV. Capgrave closely follows Martinus Polonus's *Chronicon Pontificum et Imperatorum* and Walsingham's *St. Albans Chronicle*, in many instances duplicating them word for word. The closing entry is for 1417. The *Abbreuiacion* has been preserved in only two manuscripts, one from the library collection of John Moore, bishop of Ely, and the other from the library of Matthew Parker, archbishop of Canterbury, the same collection that contained Manuscript A of the *ASC*.

John Hardyng and his late-fifteenth-century long verse chronicle composed in rhyme royal have been subjected to much harsh criticism. Yet the chronicle was popular in its time and influenced writers such as Malory, Spenser, and others. In his own lifetime Hardyng composed two versions of his chronicle. The longer version of 19,000 lines he presented to Henry VI in 1457; the shorter version of approximately 12,500 lines he presented to Edward IV in 1464. Like Andrew of Wyntoun, Hardyng failed to report objectively and accurately. His manipulation of facts and events to support his obsessive claim that the Scottish nation owed allegiance to England and his infamous reputation for forgery have all but nullified any historical value of the work. Hardyng's chronicle is dominated by two self-serving goals: one political, to forward the claims made by the documents he had previously forged and offered as substantiation, and the other personal, to appeal for remuneration for his bogus efforts. In spite of these weaknesses, Hardyng's account does have a few redeeming features. Like Robert of Gloucester, Hardyng incorporates lists of names, mostly of men who supported or opposed Henry VII's claim to the throne. As far as mythology and legend are concerned, this chronicle gives exposure to the story of Joseph of Arimathea, who supposedly first brought Christianity to England, and for the first time ever associates the story of Galahad's Quest for the Grail with the Arthurian material.

By the close of the fifteenth century the popularity of and demand for national chronicles had decreased. During the reign of the Tudors, chronicles were replaced by histories, but even the histories at times relied upon earlier chronicles. During the decline of national record keeping, civic chronicles, especially those centered on London, became popular. Most begin in 1189, when Richard I ascended to the throne, and basically consist of annalistic historical notes made on lists headed by the names of city officials: bailiffs, mayors, and sheriffs. The audience was usually restricted to merchants, aldermen, small business owners, and city officials, and the authors of most local chronicles were anonymous. One major town chronicle is *Gregory's Chronicle*, a London chronicle compiled by William Gregory, a skinner who later became mayor of London. Gregory's civic record ends in 1469 and incorporates ballads, weather news, and other interesting tidbits of local trivia. The *Chronicle* compiled by Richard Arnold covers London from 1189 to 1519. *Richard Hill's Chronicle* (from 1413 to 1536), the *Chronicle of the Grey Friars of London* (1556), and *Charles Wriothesley's Chronicle* (1559) all are based upon *Richard Arnold's Chronicle*. Robert Fabyan, a London alderman who was interested in preserving records, is credited with the second part of the *Great Chronicle of London* and the entirety of *The New Chronicles of England and France* (1504), an intermingling of national English and French accounts with local records from London. Even more specialized chronicles are the *First Battle of St. Albans* (1455), the *Chronicle of the Rebellion in Lincolnshire* (1470), and Warkworth's *Chronicle* covering the early years of Edward IV's reign (1461–1474). Perhaps the most unusual chronicle is John Rous's *English Roll Chronicle* that focuses on the earls of Warwick and incorporates biographical sketches and pen-and-ink portraits.

For those interested in the chronicle genre, an entry by N.F. Blake in the *Dictionary of the Middle* Ages offers a brief overview of chronicles. Another article, "The Chronicles of Medieval England and Scotland: Part I" (1990), by Antonia Gransden, first defines *chronicle*, then follows up with a brief general survey of chronicle writing in England. Though the secondary references are a bit outdated in the 1977 reprint of *The Beginnings of English Literature to Skelton, 1509*, W.L. Renwick and Harold Orton offer brief biographical sketches of the better-known chroniclers. Gransden's longer work, *Historical Writing in England: C. 550 to C. 1307*, published in 1974, offers comprehensive coverage of histories, chronicles, and biographies from Gildas and Nennius through William of Malmsbury and Matthew Paris to the local London chronicles. The time limits established by Gransden encompass the *ASC* and the Latin chronicles, but exclude all of the vernacular chronicles save one. Robert of Gloucester's chron-

icle receives several pages of detailed attention. In sharp contrast, *Brut* by Layamon is covered in two sentences and a footnote.

To cover the two-hundred-year gap between Gransden's study and the end of
chronicle writing, Lister M. Matheson's chapter entitled "Historical Prose" in
Middle English Prose: A Critical Guide to Major Authors and Genres (1984)
focuses on the fifteenth-century vernacular chronicles: Layamon's *Brut*; Mannyng's *Chronicle*, part 2; Capgrave's *Abbreuiacion of Cronicles*; and several
specialized London chronicles. Surveys of the Middle English chronicles include
Middle English Literature (1986) by J.A.W. Bennett. Bennett devotes one chapter to Layamon and a second chapter entitled "History in Verse" to the *Short
Chronicle*, Mannyng's *Chronicle*, and the *Chronicle* of Robert of Gloucester.
By far the most thorough study is *Chronicles and Other Historical Writing*
(1989), by E.D. Kennedy. He explores nine categories of historical writing in
medieval England, in particular the *ASC*, the *Brut* chronicles, town chronicles,
and Scottish chronicles. Kennedy includes an extensive bibliography of over
two hundred double-column pages.

Concerning the *Anglo-Saxon Chronicle* specifically, *Dictionary of Literary
Biography* contains a concise review by Jolyon Helterman entitled "The Anglo-
Saxon Chronicle." A 1969 reprint of John Earle's late-nineteenth-century study
and a survey of Anglo-Saxon literature by C.L. Wrenn both offer a single chapter on the *ASC*. Still the standard for *ASC* textual studies and detailed critical
analysis is Charles Plummer's two-volume revision of Earle's edition of the
Anglo-Saxon Chronicle. Plummer devotes one volume to the text of Manuscripts
A and E and a second volume to extensive notes and a lengthy critical analysis/
introduction. A.H. Smith's 1957 reprint of the *Parker Chronicle* has been around
since 1938 and is limited to the years A.D. 832–900. It emphasizes the earliest
Danish invasions and the reign of Alfred. The *Peterborough Chronicle, 1070–
1154*, edited by Cecily Clark (1958), focuses on the version and years of the
ASC that contribute most to our knowledge of the developments in the Middle
English language. A most ambitious undertaking, *The Anglo-Saxon Chronicle:
A Collaborative Edition* may become the definitive edition of Old English chronicles once it is completed. Under the auspices of Boydell and Brewer, between
twenty and twenty-five volumes have been proposed. Thus far, only six volumes
have been published: facsimiles of manuscripts F, A, B, D, and C, and *The
Annals of St. Neots*. Each volume includes extensive historical and linguistic
analyses.

Among translations of the *ASC* are those by G.N. Garmonsway, Anne Savage,
and Dorothy Whitelock. Garmonsway's translation for Everyman's Library,
which was first released in 1954 and reprinted in 1967 and 1990, is based on
Plummer's 1892–1899 revision of Earle's edition of the chronicles. Garmonsway's arrangement is somewhat confusing. Savage has produced a conflated,
modernized translation of all the versions of the *ASC*, complete with attractive
and "brief pictorial essays" that place the text in context (5). Still the most
popular translation is Whitelock's *The Anglo-Saxon Chronicle*, which incorpo-

rates all versions of the *ASC*, including the fragments G and H. In one column Whitelock presents the material that is considered to be the common stock for all the versions; in a second column she offers the material that is peculiar to only one or two versions. She omits entries made after the Norman Conquest if they make no significant historical contribution.

Before A. Campbell's Latin-English edition of *The Chronicle of Æthelweard* was published in 1962, the world of scholarship had access to the work via two difficult-to-procure nineteenth-century translations by J.A. Giles (1848) and J. Stevenson (1854). Campbell bases his translation on Henry Savile's 1596 version that appeared in *Rerum Anglicarum Scriptores post Bedam Praecipui*. Campbell includes an index of names that is helpful when comparing entries in this work with those from the *ASC*. *The Arthurian Material in the Chronicles* (1906) is Robert H. Fletcher's analysis of the influence of Geoffrey of Monmouth on later chroniclers. Though older, this study still offers comprehensive coverage of major chronicles by Henry of Huntingdon, Layamon, Robert of Gloucester, Thomas of Castleford, Mannyng, Capgrave, Hardyng, and Fabyan. In a later study published in 1946, Laura Keeler examines the less well known Latin chronicles from 1300 to 1500, chronicles that Fletcher omitted. She discusses thirty-two additional works containing Arthurian material that the writers borrowed mostly from Geoffrey of Monmouth.

Due to the paucity of critical editions and analyses, chronicles from the Middle Ages have not received extensive attention. Because F. Madden's 1847 edition of the verse *Brut* was not easily accessible, the Early English Text Society (EETS) produced two volumes of the full text (1963, 1978) edited by G.L. Brook and R.F. Leslie. A proposed third volume of introductory and commentary material is still unfinished. Because he was intent upon producing a "congenial, readable version," Donald G. Bzdyl's translation of the full text of the verse *Brut* by Layamon is in prose (21). *Layamon's Arthur: The Arthurian Section of Layamon's* Brut, translated and edited by W.R.J. Barron and S.C. Weinberg, offers a Middle/Modern English translation, but is limited to lines 9229–14297, the Arthurian material that is in greatest demand. This study contains a lengthy and informative introduction and commentary that relates passages from the *Brut* to Geoffrey of Monmouth's *Historia* and Wace's *Roman de Brut*. Friedrich W.D. Brie's two-volume edition (1906, 1908) published by the Early English Text Society has become the standard primary source of *The Prose Brut*. As with the three-volume series of the verse edition, the last volume with Brie's introduction and comments has never been printed, leaving readers with the text only.

The Metrical Chronicle of Robert of Gloucester, edited by W.A. Wright in two volumes for the Rolls Series in 1887, still serves as the standard primary source. Since the longer version lacks internal evidence establishing specific authorship, this point is highly controversial. In "Robert of Gloucester and the Antiquaries, 1550–1800" Anne Hudson scrutinizes the early history of this chronicle to determine the validity of attributing it to Robert of Gloucester. She begins her investigation with John Stow, who first claimed Robert of Gloucester as the author, and traces references forward, particularly through the sixteenth century. Regarding the short version, Ewald Zettl edited *An Anonymous Short English Metrical Chronicle* (1935) for the Early English Text Society.

In 1996 the Medieval and Renaissance Texts and Studies group was able to publish the first full-text edition of *Robert Mannyng of Brunne: The Chronicle*. Edited by Idelle Sullens, this version encompasses both parts 1 and 2 of Mannyng's *Chronicle* and includes a lengthy introduction, glossary, and side and endnotes. Because Robert Mannyng provides the only information about himself in his own works, Ruth Crosby's article "Robert Mannyng of Brunne: A New Biography" (1942) offers few new biographical details. However, Crosby has collected and collated into a single source all relevant references to Mannyng's dates of birth and death, locations where he lived and served, and what positions he held. In "Politics and Poetry in the Early Fourteenth Century: The Case of Robert Manning's *Chronicle*" (1988), Thorlac Turville-Petre reviews the same biographical details, emphasizing Mannyng's political agenda: freedom for the common man. Thea Summerfield offers a book-length comparative study of the chronicles of Pierre de Langtoft and Robert Mannyng in *The Matter of Kings' Lives* (1998). Summerfield compares and contrasts the influences on and motivations of the two men and how they structured their narrative strategy to reach a specific audience. She concludes that fear was Mannyng's chief motivation (198).

Peter J. Lucas's edition of *John Capgrave's Abbreuiacion of Cronicles* (1983) for the Early English Text Society includes a reliable version of the text, a glossary, commentary, and a lengthy introduction that reviews biographical data and analyzes the language and sources. Capgrave has received additional recent attention from the scholarly world. In *Augustiniana* (1979) J.C. Fredeman contributes a forty-page update on Capgrave's life, elaborating on the nature of Capgrave's religious training. Of the five writers who are discussed in volume 3 (1996) of the series *Authors of the Middle Ages*, John Capgrave is the last. Besides editing this volume, M.C. Seymour also contributes the informative chapter on Capgrave. Seymour combines familiar biographical information with a discussion of Capgrave's works, including appendices of lost works and patrons, as well as a bibliography of primary sources and other relevant secondary sources not named in his chapter.

As mentioned, Hardyng has received limited attention in survey studies of Middle English chronicles. In addition, volume 8 of *Arthurian Literature* contains a chapter entitled "John Hardyng and the Holy Grail." In this chapter E.D. Kennedy explores the origin, development, and ramifications of Hardyng's having incorporated the Joseph of Arimathea and Galahad and the Grail Quest stories into his chronicle. Finally in 1976 W.J. Johnson published in facsimile Hardyng's chronicle *The Chronicle from the Firste Begynnyng of Englande, 2 Parts*. The print is beautiful to behold, but not easily read due to the fussiness of the typeface. But at least a modern edition has made Hardyng's work accessible.

By its very nature, the chronicle was not created to entertain but to inform. Therein lies the difficulty in reaching large audiences or maintaining enthusiastic support. That the genre was able to survive centuries of conflict and change is somewhat amazing. That it has enjoyed one of the earliest, most continuous, and longest runs of use, at times extremely popular, at times all but unknown to the general populace, is almost beyond belief. Without the chronicles, little knowledge of English origins, factual or mythological, would be available to us today. The factual information the chronicles supply is abundant, invaluable, and frequently the sole extant source of particular facts. Since the earliest days mankind has been infatuated with leaving a record of his sojourn upon earth. During the Old and Middle English eras the chronicles served the purpose.

SELECTED BIBLIOGRAPHY

Barron, W.R.J., and S.C. Weinberg, eds. and trans. *Layamon's Arthur: The Arthurian Section of Layamon's* Brut *(Lines 9229–14297)*. Harlow: Longman, 1989.

Bately, Janet M., ed. *The Anglo-Saxon Chronicle: A Collaborative Edition*. Vol. 3. *MSA*. Cambridge: D.S. Brewer, 1986.

Bennett, J.A.W. *Middle English Literature*. Ed. Douglas Gray. Vol. 1, pt. 2, of *The Oxford History of English Literature*. Ed. John Buxton and Norman Davis. Oxford: Clarendon Press, 1986.

Blake, N.F. "Chronicles." *Dictionary of the Middle Ages*. Vol. 3. New York: Scribner, Ed. Joseph R. Strayer. 1983. 325–330.

Brie, Friedrich W.D., ed. *The Brut; or, The Chronicles of England*. 2 vols. EETS 131, 136. Oxford: Oxford University Press, 1960.

Brook, G.L., and R.F. Leslie, eds. *Layamon: Brut*. 2 vols. EETS 250, 277. London: Oxford University Press, 1963–1978.

Bzdyl, Donald G., trans. *Layamon's* Brut: *A History of the Britons*. Binghamton, NY: Medieval and Renaissance Texts and Studies, 1989.

Campbell, A., ed. *The Chronicle of Æthelweard*. London: Thomas Nelson, 1962.

Clark, Cecily, ed. *The Peterborough Chronicle, 1070–1154*. Oxford: Oxford University Press, 1958.

Crosby, Ruth. "Robert Mannyng of Brunne: A New Biography." *PMLA* 57.1 (1942): 15–28.

Earle, John A. "The Chronicles." *Anglo-Saxon Literature*. 1884. New York: AMS, 1969. 169–85.

Eckhardt, Caroline D., ed. *Castleford's Chronicle; or, The Boke of Brut*. 2 vols. EETS 305, 306. London: Oxford University Press, 1996.

Eyre-Todd, George, ed. *Early Scottish Poetry*. 1891. Westport, CT: Greenwood Press, 1971. 142–76.

Fletcher, Robert H. *The Arthurian Material in the Chronicles*. New York: Burt Franklin, 1958, 1966.

Fredeman, J.C. "The Life of John Capgrave, O.E.S.A." *Augustiana* 29 (1979): 197–237.

Garmonsway, G.N., trans. *The Anglo-Saxon Chronicle*. London: Dent, 1990.

Gransden, Antonia. "The Chronicles of Medieval England and Scotland: Part I." *Journal of Medieval History* 16 (1990): 129–150.

———. *Historical Writing in England: C. 550 to c. 1307.* Ithaca, NY: Cornell University Press, 1974.

Hardyng, John. *The Chronicle from the Firste Begynnyng of Englande, 2 Parts.* Norwood, NJ: W.J. Johnson, 1976.

Helterman, Jolyon. "The Anglo-Saxon Chronicle." *Old and Middle English Literature.* Vol. 146 of *Dictionary of Literary Biography.* Ed. Jeffrey Helterman, and Jerome Mitchell. Detroit: Gale Research, 1994. 61–66.

Hudson, Anne. "Robert of Gloucester and the Antiquaries, 1550–1800." *Notes and Queries* 16.9 (1969): 322–333.

Kaiser, Rolf. *Medieval English: An Old English and Middle English Anthology.* 3rd ed. Berlin: Rolf Kaiser, 1958. Excerpt 173.

Keeler, Laura. *Geoffrey of Monmouth and the Late Latin Chroniclers, 1300–1500.* Berkeley and Los Angeles: University of California Press, 1946.

Kennedy, E.D. *Chronicles and Other Historical Writing.* Vol. 8 of *A Manual of the Writings in Middle English, 1050–1500.* Ed. Albert E. Hartung. Hamden, CT: Archon Books, 1989.

———. "John Hardyng and the Holy Grail." *Arthurian Literature.* Ed. Richard Barber. Vol. 8. Cambridge: D.S. Brewer, 1989. 185–206.

Lucas, Peter J., ed. *John Capgrave's Abbreuiacion of Cronicles.* EETS 285. Oxford: Oxford University Press, 1983.

Matheson, Lister M. "Historical Prose." *Middle English Prose: A Critical Guide to Major Authors and Genres.* Ed. A.S.G. Edwards. New Brunswick, NJ: Rutgers University Press, 1984. 209–248.

Mitchell, Bruce, and Fred C. Robinson. *A Guide to Old English.* 5th ed. Oxford: Blackwell, 1992.

Plummer, Charles, ed. *Two of the Saxon Chronicles Parallel.* 2 vols. Oxford: Clarendon Press, 1892–1899.

Renwick, W.L., and Harold Orton. *The Beginnings of English Literature to Skelton, 1509.* St. Clair Shores, MI: Scholarly Press, 1977.

Savage, Anne, trans. *The Anglo-Saxon Chronicles.* New York: St. Martin's, 1983.

Seymour, M.C. "John Capgrave." *English Writers of the Late Middle Ages.* Ed. M.C. Seymour. Vol. 3 of *Authors of the Middle Ages.* Aldershot, Hants: Variorum, 1996. 197–256.

Smith, A.H., ed. *The Parker Chronicle, 832–900.* 3rd ed. London: Methuen, 1957.

Sullens, Idelle, ed. *Robert Mannyng of Brunne: The Chronicle.* Binghamton, NY: Medieval and Renaissance Texts and Studies, 1996.

Summerfield, Thea. *The Matter of Kings' Lives: The Design of Past and Present in the Early Fourteenth-Century Verse Chronicles by Pierre de Langtoft and Robert Mannyng.* Amsterdam and Atlanta, GA: Rodopi, 1998.

Turville-Petre, Thorlac. "Politics and Poetry in the Early Fourteenth Century: The Case of Robert Manning's *Chronicle.*" *Review of English Studies* 39 (1988): 1–28.

Ward, A.W., and A.R. Waller, eds. *The Cambridge History of English Literature.* 15 vols. Cambridge: Cambridge University Press, 1963–1965.

Whitelock, Dorothy, trans. *The Anglo-Saxon Chronicle: A Revised Translation.* Westport, CT: Greenwood Press, 1986.

Wrenn, C.L. "[Prose:] The Beginnings." A *Study of Old English Literature*. London: George G. Harrap, 1967. 195–205.

Wright, W.A., ed. *The Metrical Chronicle of Robert of Gloucester*. 2 vols. London: Rolls Series, 1887. 86.

Zettl, Ewald, ed. *An Anonymous Short English Metrical Chronicle*. EETS 196. London: Oxford University Press, 1935.

8

Debate Poetry

Robert Thomas Lambdin and Laura Cooner Lambdin

In medieval English literature the poems of the debate genre have lent themselves to various, although scarce, interpretations that range from allegorical readings to those responses dependent upon unraveling a work's historical contexts. Curiously, there is no complete survey presenting the diverse criticism of these poems. Moreover, a substantial gap exists in the recognition and criticism of the debate as it appears in Middle English literature. Regardless, debates serve to illustrate both sides of some sort of moral or philosophical instruction. Given this significant function of the Middle English debate, it seems necessary to recognize its importance in the canon of Middle English literature.

Before identifying and exploring various debates in major works of this period, it is first necessary to define the debate as it appears in Middle English literature and then to trace its literary background from classical literature through its appearance around 1200 in the Middle English poem *The Owl and the Nightingale*. Few genres of English literature have stimulated such cursory critical analysis. Indeed, one must study and synthesize several secondary sources in order to comprehend the components and evolution of the Middle English debate. C. Hugh Holman and William Harmon (132) state that in the debate two persons or objects (birds, conditions, feelings, and so on) argue a specific topic and refer it to a judge. Thomas Garbáty (555) adds that the *tensouns*, sardonic works of the twelfth-century Provençal troubadours that poked fun at contemporary love, initiated the caustic, satiric tensions that are the inherent quality of many debates. However, these descriptions must be amended to include the rhetorical dialectic of the debate that offers distinct theses and antitheses that are to be pondered and interpreted in order to persuade the debate's audience to select the best possible alternative provided. Thus the debate becomes a highly individualized teaching tool through which the audience, using interpretive and reasoning skills, must synthesize the points provided by the debaters to expose themselves to the moral or philosophic message of the debate. This genre, then, was a handy tool for the church to incorporate in explaining the dogmatic mysteries of its canon—ideas that depend upon the faith of the audience. The debate provided a valuable service among the schemata of church ethics.

These works, usually poems, begin by introducing the scene and the points to be argued, often by a dreamer or a coincidental observation by an "unknowing" narrator. The two combatants in turn offer particular theses and antitheses that are supported by proofs or points meant to strengthen their various arguments. The debaters speak alternatingly and, often by using sarcasm, attempt to refute the proofs provided by their opponent. Following several rounds of this verbal interplay the debate concludes, often without the announcement of a clear victor. It is up to the author to provide enough clues and evidence for the audience to decide for itself who or what wins the debate. Naturally, the social status of the audience weighs heavily in the listener's ability to choose a winner. For example, the tone and rhetoric of *The Owl and the Nightingale* work on several levels of interpretation toward a varied audience.

To more fully comprehend the role of the debate in Middle English literature, it is beneficial to trace the form from its apparent foundation in classical literature through its continental influences to its eventual integration into the works of the Middle English canon. Of seminal importance is J.H. Hanford's study, which traces the roots of the Middle English debate to the Latin *Eclogues* of Virgil. In the *Eclogues*, composed in 43 B.C., Hanford convincingly identifies the pastoral settings of Virgil's work as comparable to those of the medieval debate poems. Also, the *Eclogues* center upon shepherds who gather and participate in singing contests. The victor of these confrontations is the shepherd who most convincingly proves that his song is the best. The poems consist of sharp alternation of speeches between the debaters. These personal pastorals lend a format easily adaptable into a literary form whose function it is to illuminate conflicting points of view.

It is Hanford's contention, one reinforced by A.C. Baugh (54), that Virgil's pastoral poems are the root of the eighth-century work of Alcuin, the *Conflictus Veris et Hiemis* (The strife between spring and winter). The *Conflictus* closely mirrors the *Eclogues*; only the characters of the dialogue and the nature of their contest are different. More important, as Hanford (24) notes, the *Conflictus* makes use of the external form and framework of the eclogue, especially in relation to Virgil's seventh eclogue, which opens, as does the *Conflictus*, with a narrative introduction, passes to the song contest, and ends with more narrative. The judgment is then pronounced and the winner duly praised.

The debate form of the *Conflictus* continued in an outbreak of Latin debate poetry that spread up through what is now Germany. These debates, such as the *Carmen Nigelli Ermoldi Exulis* (written between 824 and 830), differ from the *Conflictus* and the *Eclogues* because they lack the pastoral setting and the sharp alternation of speeches of the earlier works. Also, they are, for the most part, purely academic in their elements.

The German derivation from the traditional form of the pastorals and the *Conflictus* established the basis for the next phase of the evolution of the debate form, the French *dit*. The *dit*, sometimes didactic or moralizing in its content, occurs popularly as a debate, often in dialogue form, and usually between personifications or spokesmen for religious themes. John Fox (xx) remarks that nearly a hundred of the oldest French poems, dating from about 1100, survive today. The popularity and function of the French *dit* are seen in *La Complaint d'outremers*, a debate of Routebouf, a twelfth century French author highly esteemed in the French court (Harvey and Heseltine 219). Brian Woledge (159) notes that this work is representative of an explosive stage in French poetry when the works emerge as rich and varied literature, admired and imitated throughout Western Europe.

With the Norman Conquest, England became closely associated with French influences. French became the language of the English court and the nobility; French works were composed in England, and copies of French literature were made available to English readers (Woledge xix). This influx, which lasted for some three hundred years, provides a strong background for the appearance of the Middle English debate poems, such as *The Owl and the Nightingale*, in England around the year 1200. Given this interaction between these two cultures, it is natural that the debate genre would be available to and used by Middle English writers.

Another movement occurring in England at this time which may account for the structural differences that are evident between the medieval English works and their continental ancestors. During the time that the French were taken with the *dit* and its derivation, the debate, England was experiencing the growth of Scholasticism. This movement was to become the predominant theological and philosophical teaching tool in England from 1100 to 1500. William T. Jackson finds that the eleventh and twelfth centuries in Europe were an age of intellectual reawakening that was reflected above all in the Scholastic movement. The chief feature of Scholasticism was its reliance upon human reasoning—especially on dialectic—in interpreting sacred and secular knowledge. Jackson continues that no orthodox thinker would have challenged the basic assumptions of Christian faith. This meant that rational investigation itself had to be based on rational inquiry into matters of faith; thus it became an indispensible element in comprehending Christian belief. The study of dialectic imposed upon the student certain rules of logical inquiry drawn from the works of Aristotle, such as the *Categories* and *Posterior Analytics*, then available, as well as the *Isagoge* of Porphyry and Boethius's *Commentaries*. Further, the study of dialectic also hinged upon the classification of concepts and the application of logical and metaphysical elements to determine a concept's validity. In this way faith was useful in guiding reasoning, while reason and dialectic became an integral part of the approach to an understanding of the truths of revelation. The relationship between faith and reason constituted the main part of the Scholastic movement, which reached its peak in the thirteenth century (405).

Paramount here is the premise that Scholasticism's main intent was to reconcile the works of Aristotle with the Scriptures and reason with faith (Drabble and Stringer 500). Since the clerics trained in this mode became the main authors of this period, the link with Aristotle and, especially, clerical instruction in the tools of rhetoric act as precursors to the debate tradition in England. This facet of Scholasticism, united with the popular French *dit*, provides a background that could be a direct link to the establishment of and continued fascination with the written debate in Middle English poetry. The attempt to reconcile reason with faith, as noted earlier, replicates the motive behind the use of the debate poems to convey moral teachings that explain the mysterious church dogma.

By the end of the twelfth century there is evidence of the coming together of several movements that will be prominent in the study of the debate. First, the debate had evolved into a popular form on the Continent, being especially prominent in France. At the same time there was a growing Scholastic regime where the works of the great classical writers were being translated and analyzed. These movements coincided with the establishment of universities in England. Consequently, these university curricula heavily emphasized the classics in their teaching of young clerics. Since the universities were the product of the church, it is only natural that their writings would be applied toward the dogmatic, didactic teachings in an attempt to reconcile reason with faith. Aristotle, whose "pagan" works closely mirrored Christian elements, was the ideal source in the medieval scholars' attempts to solidify the link between reason and logical truth and religious truth.

With the growth of the Scholastic movement came the evolution of the university. This is important in the establishment of the debate tradition because the clerics trained at these universities wrote the majority of the age's literary works. The establishment of the university in England coincided with the date of the first extant English debate, *The Owl and the Nightingale*. A.B. Cobban (99) explains that while the majority of European universities grew from the need of cathedral schools to fall into accord with an increasingly urbanized society, the great universities of England did not. In England monasticism was so dominant that the secular cathedrals tended to be less affluent and influential than those of the Continent. It was not until 1167 that there was evidence of several masters teaching together at Oxford, although evidence does exist that Oxford schools were able to attract scholars in the fields of law and theology, perhaps as early as 1094 (Cobban 99–100). Further, the French greatly influenced the initial growth of the university. The constitution of the Parisian system influenced the charter of Oxford. Cobban (101) concludes that "the dating of Oxford must clearly be placed in the twelfth century." Given the clerics' university curricula, which included a heavy stress on the learning of the classics, the French influence on the universities that trained the clerics, and the dating of the establishment of these English universities, there is a background that coincides nicely with the appearance of the debate form around 1200. Certainly this training can be seen to contribute to the secular subject matter of the debates, works that display the clerics' own human desires both to communicate with and entertain their audiences while teaching them a moral lesson.

Maurice de Wulf, remarking on the effect the classics had upon the curriculum of the Middle Ages university, holds that studies were based upon a clearly designated hierarchical plan with the "liberal arts at the base, philosophy at the centre, and theology at the top" (53). Here both rhetoric and dialectic become essential parts of this curriculum, "especially preponderant in the eleventh and twelfth centuries" (54), with dialectic, specifically, playing a major role in the twelfth-century university curriculum.

In the Scholastic method of education two philosophical methodologies are of great import. De Wulf writes that this Scholastic method "may signify certain more or less uniform systems which assist in the understanding of these system- izations (those which conform with the exigencies of methodology): definitions, distinctions, objections, the reduction of the reasoning to the syllogistic form, the accumulation of the arguments for or against a thesis" (8). The Scholastic method also was "a didactic or teaching method: such as the use of the com- mentary (*lectio*), or the methods of debate (*disputatio*)" (8). The *disputatio* was a kind of debate based upon an exchange between the master and the pupil, appearing during the twelfth century when the *logica nova* was introduced (Wulf 57). Further, these forms of instruction produced the two main types of medieval scholarly literature, the commentary and the question (Kristeller 31).

In Scholasticism the *quaestio*, an interrogatory exercise in logic, became uni- versal in medieval thought from the twelfth until the fifteenth century (Leff 93). Yet it neither originated then, nor was it peculiar to philosophy. Gordon Leff (93) claims that the *quaestio* was already in evidence by the tenth century among the codifiers of canon law. Both the canonists and the Scholastics were ruled by the same need to pursue the conflicting arguments, drawn from authority, in order to arrive at the truth. The overriding technique of the *quaestio* was the method of *pro* and *contra* and soon became associated with the legal procedure. Since the Scholastically educated clerics who were trained at these schools be- came the probable authors of the extant Middle English debates, it was only natural that they incorporate this form of give-and-take into their works.

At the university the clerics learned that in ancient Greece the art of speaking so as to persuade (rhetoric) was from the first linked to both ethics (the criteria for a good life) and literature (language used in order to please) (Drabble and Stringer 472). This system reduced the art of oration to a system capable of being taught (Harvey and Heseltine 362). For the church, the art of rhetoric presented an ideal form through which it could reconcile the mysterious dogma of its faith with the human element of reason—again a characteristic of the Scholastic movement. For other authors, such as Chaucer and the *Gawain* poet, the art of rhetoric provided a means through which their works endeared their audiences to thinking as a means of rationalizing a particular moral dilemma presented to them in written form.

Given this background of twelfth-century England, it seems evident that it is useless to look for an individual source for this mass of literature; the debate should be regarded as the outcome of many tendencies. It is the melding of these separate movements that accounts for the development and popularity of the Middle English debate poems that appear around 1200 and continue into the fifteenth century.

Since the genre of debate poems was such a popular mode in medieval English literature, it is not surprising that authors of this period would integrate variations of the debate into their works. It must be recalled that during this period mimesis was among the highest compliments one author could give another. To attempt to demonstrate that the debate appears throughout Middle English literature, common features between the debate poems proper and the debates in larger works need to be identified. It will be shown that some of the elements of classical oratory exist in the debate poems proper and will be used to analyze the works of other authors to reveal the literary debates that occur throughout the Middle English period. The historical background of the Scholastic movement and the growth of the university in England—institutions dedicated to the training and instructing of clerics—suggest that a distinct Aristotelian influence prevails in the writings of this age. When the popularity of the French *dit* at this time (one in which France was the cultural center of Europe and French the language of the English court and nobility) is considered, the schematic for the growth of the debate form seems to be complete. The fusing of these forces created a literary background favorable to the composition of Middle English debate literature. Since the debate form was pervasive in the early Middle Ages, it is no wonder that the debate poems proper and the elements of debate technique are common in the literature of the later Middle Ages.

THE OWL AND THE NIGHTINGALE

An early Middle English poem of 1,794 lines in octosyllabic couplets, *The Owl and the Nightingale* is the earliest extant example of the Middle English debate poem. Composed anonymously sometime after the death of Henry II in 1189, it is the debate between a grave owl and a gay nightingale over whose song is better. The ensuing proofs and refutations primarily explain the benefits of each bird to mankind. Drabble and Stringer (417) note the work's dependence upon Scholastic legalism concerning matters of serious contemporary interest: foreknowledge, music, confession, and papal missions. Indeed, *The Owl and the Nightingale* is a curious combination of literary constructions indicative of an author struggling with a new form. In the first twelve lines of *The Owl and the Nightingale* the poem's narrator describes events that occur one day as he walks in the woods and overhears the argument between an owl and a nightingale whose "plait was stif and starc and strong" ["strife was vigorous and hard and strong"] (l. 5). Unnoticed in this secluded pastoral setting, the narrator observes that the birds' discussion was strongly forensic:

> Þat aire worste þat hi wuste
> and hure and hure of oþeres songe.
> Hi holde plaiding suþe stronge. (10–12)
>
> [That all the worst that they knew
> and especially of the other's song.
> They held strife so strong.]

This section of the poem is similar to the exordium of classical oratory. Here the disputants are introduced and the tone of the birds' verbal combat is established. The idea that they held "plaiding suþe stronge" regarding each other's song foreshadows the bitter debate to follow.

Next, the observer comments upon the nightingale and introduces the points that will be debated. This poetic technique is like the narration of classical oratory. The nightingale's song is first complimented:

> Ho was þe gladur vor þe rise
> and sung a vele cunne wis.
> Bet þuȝte þe drern þat he were ishote
> of harpe and pipe þan of þrote. (19–22)
>
> [She was the gladder because of the bough
> and sang in many kinds of ways.
> Better seemed the sound of it was issued
> from a harp or pipe than from her throat.]

The narrator notes that the nightingale espies and verbally berates the owl, an act that initiates the conflict that will follow. The nightingale is particularly displeased with the owl's song:

> "Unwiȝt," ho sede, "awei þu flo!
> Me is þe wurs þat ich þe so.
> Iwis for þine vule lete
> wel oft ich mine songe forlete." (33–36)
>
> ["Monster," she said, "fly you away!
> I am the worse that I see you.
> Indeed for your foul voice
> Well often has my song interrupted."]

At first the owl is taken aback by the nightingale's allegations and defends her song:

"Hu þincþe nu bi mine songe?
Wenst þu þat ich ne cunne singe,
þeʒ ich ne cunne of writelinge?" (47–49)

["How think you now by my song?
Think you that I do not know how to sing
Though I know nothing of chattering?"]

The nightingale counters with a catalog of the owl's traits that the nightingale deems distasteful, mainly that the owl is "loþ al fuelkunne" ["hated by all birds"] (65). All fowls would rather drive the owl away than look at her, for "Þu art lodliche to biholde / and þu art loþ in monie volde" ["You are ugly to behold and you are horrible in many ways"] (71–72). Ultimately, because the owl "sittest adai and fliʒt aniʒt" ["sits during the day and flies by night"] (89), she is perceived by the other birds to be an evil monster. This speech exposes the proposition of the poem: whose song is best? In turn, the proposition is broken down into smaller partitions that the owl will be forced to refute throughout the debate: that she is ugly, hated by man, and evil, and that her song is worse than the nightingale's.

The nightingale continues, spurred by the owl's earlier comments about her song, and heaps an invective tirade of personal abuse on the owl. This infuriates the owl, who

luste þiderward
and hold hire eʒe noþerward,
and sa tosvolde and ibowle
also ho hadde one frogge isolʒe. (143–46)

[listened to all this
and turned her eyes northward,
and sat swollen and blown up
as if she had swallowed a frog.]

She calls for the nightingale to "fly up here" (150–152) and face the owl's wrath. The nightingale refuses to comply with the owl's request for physical combat, "No! þu havest wel scharpe clawe; / ne kepe ich noʒt þat þu me clawe" ["No! you have very sharp claws and I do not care to have you claw me"] (153–154), and bids the two to resolve their differences through an oral discussion. The owl at once agrees—with the understanding that they find a fair intermediary. The nightingale suggests Nicolas of Guildford to be the judge, for Nicolas is

"wis and war of worde,
he is of dome suþe gleu,
and him is loþ evrich unpeu.
He wot insiʒt in eche songe,
wo singet wel, wo singet wronge,

and he can schede vrom þe riȝte
þat woȝe, þat þuster from þe liȝte." (192–198)

["wise and aware of words,
he is of judgments so intelligent,
and he hates every vice.
He will understand in each song,
who sings well, who sings wrong,
And he can distinguish from the right
the wrong, the darkness from the light."]

The owl readily accepts Nicolas as judge, for while he at one time favored nightingales,

"Ich wot, he is nu suþe acoled;
nis he vor þe noȝt afoled,
þat he for þine olde love
me adun legge and þe buve;
ne schaltu nevre so him queme,
þat he for þe fals dome deme." (205–210)

["I know, he is now so cooled;
nor is he for you not fooled,
that he for his old love
put me down and you above;
nor shall you never please him so,
that he for a false judgment gives."]

Curiously, the debate then begins in earnest with Nicolas, the chosen judge, absent. Following the exordium and narration of the initial 214 lines, the initial partition of the debate's proposition is exposed (215–252) when the nightingale asks "Wi dostu þat unwiȝt is doþ" ["Why do you do what monsters do?" (217); she follows this with a strong invective speech strewn with allegations that the owl will be forced to refute:

"Þu singist aniȝt and noȝt adai,
and al þi song is wai la wai.
Þu miȝt mid þine songe afere
alle þat ihereþ þine ibere.
Þu schirchest and jollest to þine fere,
þat hit is grislich to ihere;
hit þincheþ boþe wise and snepe,
noȝt þat þu singe, ac þat þu wepe." (219–226)

["You sing at night and not the day,
and your song is always lamenting.
You might with your song frighten
All that hear your cry.

You screech and yell to your mate,
So that it is grisly to hear,
I think this is both wise and stupid,
Not that you sing, but that you weep."]

The nightingale concludes with an ad hominem reiteration that the owl is evil; in her eyes, there is nothing good about the owl.

The duration of the debate proper (1253–1617) consists of a sequence of alternating confirmations and refutations in which the debaters argue the allegations of the proposition. The nightingale must simply prove that her song is the more beneficial to mankind. The owl has a much harder task; she must disprove the charges forwarded by the nightingale that she is evil, universally hated, and ugly in addition to proving the main argument that her song is better. This section is filled with bitter rebuffs, satiric jests, and personal affronts.

The debate proper concludes with the nightingale claiming victory because she feels that the owl has made a *stultiloquium*, or a mistake in her argument: when the owl is confirming her worth to man, she mentions that her value extends even after she is dead. After her death she is hung as a scarecrow to frighten off other birds from the farmers' fields. The nightingale finds this crucifixion to be the owl's supreme shame and thus proclaims herself the instant winner of the debate by default. As the nightingale's allies fly down to congratulate her, the owl refuses to call her own army to fight because the two had agreed to be judged (1667–1716). Here the wren intervenes and tells the nightingale where Nicolas may be found.

At this point, while the debate is over, the poem is not. The editorial comment that encompasses the final lines of the poem (1749–1794) falls into the format of a miniature debate. Nicolas has earlier been lauded as a fair and wise man (189–198). The birds' bickering at the poem's conclusion narrates Nicolas's qualities and states the proposition: while Nicolas is a good and wise man, because of his bishops' misdeeds, he has but one house; why do the bishops not give Nicolas a larger place and more rent? The owl states proofs that support the good cleric, condemn the church officials, and attack the church: rich men err when they ignore Nicolas's talents and give rents to unfit men. This odd section concludes with the birds flying to Nicolas, where the owl plans to recount the bird's confirmations and refutations.

The Owl and the Nightingale is clearly the most scrutinized work in the genre of Middle English debate poems. Critics have analyzed almost every aspect of *The Owl and the Nightingale*: its author, didactic interpretations, and even the poem's victor. R.B. Palmer (320) sees the poem as an exploration of the process by which a text creates meaning. Given the twelfth-century background of the Middle English debate, it is perhaps better to say that the poem is an example of an author's struggle to imitate a popular form, such as the French *dit*. To the *dit* form the author of *The Owl and the Nightingale* (probably a cleric) adds Scholastic reasoning and integrates popular forms of literature into his work.

These include the *Proverbs of Alfred*, a work likely composed around 1150 (Drabble and Stringer 457), and the exempla moralized tales used by medieval preachers to illustrate morals and doctrines (Holman and Harmon 192). Both of these forms were highly popular around the ascribed date of the composition of *The Owl and the Nightingale*.

To determine the moral or philosophical lesson of the poem, a characteristic mandated by the definition of the debate poems, it is profitable to scrutinize how the birds fare in proving their arguments and refuting their opponent's allegations. According to the proposition, the nightingale must prove that her song is better than the owl's, or, at least, that her song does man the more good. Toward this end the nightingale confirms (435–450) that her song is blissful and makes men glad; the flowers and the trees approve of her song. In particular, the rose rises to greet her singing. Further, the nightingale posits,

> "Ich warni men to here gode,
> þat hi bon bliþe on hore mode,
> and bidde þat hi moten iseche
> þat ilke song þat evre is eche." (739–742)

> ["I warn men for their good,
> that they be happy in their spirit,
> and bid that they must seek
> that same song that ever is eternal."]

She is so confident that her song is better that she sarcastically challenges the owl:

> "Nu þu miȝt, hule, sitte and cling
> heramong nis no chateringe,
> ich graunti þat we go to dome
> tofore þe sulfe þe pope of Rome." (743–746)

> ["Now you may, owl, sit and cling
> herein is not any chattering,
> I grant that we go to judgment
> before himself the Pope of Rome."]

However, the nightingale's attempt to confirm her argument has gaps. Her song is only available when the weather is fair. Once the first indication of winter arises, she leaves because

> "Wan ich iso þat cumeþ þat harde,
> ich fare hom to mine erde
> and habbe boþe luve and þonc,
> þat ich her corn and hider swonk.

Wan min erende is ido,
sholde ich bileve? Nai, warto?" (459–464)

["When I see that hardship is coming,
I go home to my dwelling
and have both love and thanks,
that I came here and here endeavored.
When my mission is done,
should I remain? No, for what?"]

The nightingale feels that since her song is about life, not death, she does right by not staying overlong.

The owl in her speeches exposes other flaws or shortcomings in the nightingale's argument. Besides the truth that the nightingale flies away when the weather turns bad, the owl, in an invective refutation, announces that the nightingale fails to take her song to those who need it most:

"Þu neaver ne singst in Irlonde;
ne þu ne curnest noȝt in Scotlande;
hwi nultu fare to Norweie,
and singin men of Galeweie?" (907–910)

["You never sing in Ireland;
nor do you go to Scotland;
why will you not go to Norway,
and sing to the men of Galloway?"]

The nightingale is vehement in refusing to go where people are grim or wild because

"hi nute elles wat hi do;
hi nabbeþ neither win nor bor,
ac libbeþ also wilde dor" (1010–1012).

["they know not what they do;
they have not neither wine nor beer,
but live as wild deer"].

The basis of the nightingale's argument for refusing to travel north is that she feels that these "animals" would not appreciate her song; it would be a wasted effort.

Next, the owl steps up her attack on the nightingale with a depreciative refutation: she claims that the nightingale only sings in the summer, the time of lust:

"whan he ne recþ noȝt of clennesse,
al his poȝt is of golnesse;

vor none dor no leng nabideþ,
ac evrich upon oper rideþ." (491–494)

["when he cares nothing of cleanliness,
all his thoughts are on lustfulness;
for no animal longer waits not,
but each upon others ride."]

The owl's attack on the nightingale's sinful song continues, this time with invective sarcasm:

"vor wan þu sittes on þine rise,
þu draȝst men to fleses luste,
þat willeþ þines songes luste." (894–896)

["for when you sit on your branch,
you draw man to flesh's lust,
that will your songs listen to."]

and

"al þat þu singst is of golnesse
for nis on þe non holinesse;
ne wened na man for þi pipinge,
þat eni preost in chirche sing." (899–902)

["all that you sing is of wantonness
for there is in you no holiness;
nor believes no man that your piping,
that any priest in church will sing."]

Responding to the owl's allegation that the nightingale's song generates lust and cuckolding, the nightingale claims that it is not her fault if women interpret her song wrongly, for anything may be abused. The nightingale blames this abuse on the frail nature of women. The idea that her song generates lustful love is not her doing; adultery is a shame, and maybe husbands' poor treatment of their wives causes them to seek love and understanding elsewhere. Unfortunately, here the nightingale has refuted herself by admitting that her song is a contributing force to cuckolding couples.

In the poem the nightingale's proofs are easily countered and refuted by the owl; she is constantly forced to restructure her refutations against the owl's allegations. However, the nightingale does fare well in one instance. When the owl, in an ad hominem speech, tells the story of a nightingale sentenced to be drawn by horses because she has caused a man to be cuckolded, the nightingale answers convincingly and refutes the owl's story. It seems that King Henry judged the case, he found the knight guilty, and

"He let forbonne þene kniȝt,
þat hadde idon so muchel unriȝt,
ine so gode kinges londe,
vor riȝte niþe and for fule onde
let þane lutle fuȝel nime
and him fordeme lif and lime." (1093–1098)

["He had banished the knight,
that had done so much wrong,
in so good a king's land,
for right he loves and foul hates
that let that little fowl take the blame
and he was judged to lose life and limb."]

Thus the nightingale (in the tale, at least) wins the opportunity to continue singing her song. However, when the nightingale claims victory at the debate's conclusion, it is not because she has proven the owl's song to be of lower value than hers, but only because the owl has admitted that she is hated. Thus it appears that her claim is premature.

In the debate the owl has systematically refuted all of the nightingale's allegations. The owl feels that she is not ugly, but misunderstood. She compares herself favorably with the hawk:

"Ich habbe bile stif and stronge
and gode clivers scharp and long,
so hit bicumeþ to havekes cunne." (269–271)

["I have a bill stiff and strong
and good claws sharp and long,
as is so becoming for hawk's kin."]

In response to the intimation that she is evil because she flies at night, the owl tells the nightingale, "Þu liest!" ["You lie!"] (367). The owl comments that her eyesight may be just as good in the day as at night:

"Ne sholde he vor boþ his eȝe
so don, ȝif he þe bet niseȝe.
Ich mai ison so wel so on hare
þeȝ ich bi daie sitte and dare." (381–384)

["Nor should he for both his eyes
so do, if he the better not saw.
I may see as well as a hare
Though I by day sit and hide."]

The nightingale does not know enough about the owl's eyesight to give credence to her ad hominem refutation. In the same way, the nightingale has also claimed that the owl is evil because she can see the future. To this accusation the owl answers,

"Þat eni man beo falle in odwite,
wi schal he me his sor atwite?
Þah ich iseo his harm bivore,
ne comeþ hit noȝt of me þarvore." (1233–1236)

["That any man be fallen in disgrace,
why should he for me his grief blame?
Though I see his harm before,
it does not come from me therefore."]

Next, the owl refutes the nightingale's allegation that the owl does no good deeds, explaining that she "folȝi ban a ȝte manne/ and flo bi niȝte in horre banne" ["follow[s] then after man and fl[ies] by night in their troop"] (389–390). The owl replies that she, at the very least, keeps troops company at night. Also, the owl abides in the country throughout the year. The owl confirms that she is good and then sarcastically disparages the nightingale, who flies away when the weather turns cold. The nightingale has belittled the owl:

"Þu singest a winter wo la wo;
þu singest so doþ hen a snowe,
al þat ho singeþ, hit is for wowe." (412–414)

["You sing in the winter alas;
you sing as does a hen in snow,
all that you sing, it is of woe."]

To which the owl sardonically answers that she is available during the winter, a time when folk are lonely:

"wane riche and povre, more and lasse,
singeþ cundut niȝt and dai,
ich hom helpe what ich mai." (482–484)

["when rich and poor, more and less,
sing carols night and day,
I help them as I may."]

Further, the owl adds,

"Ich singe an eve a riȝte tome,
and soþþe won hit is bedtime,
þe þridde siþe ad middelniȝte;
and so ich mine song adiȝte,
wone ich iso arise vorre

oþer dairim oþer daisterre
Ich do god mid mine þrote
and warni men to hore note." (323–330)

["I sing in the evening at the right time,
and truly when it is bedtime,
thirdly, sing I at midnight;
and so my song makes ready,
when I see arise from afar
either dawn or morning star
I do good with my throat
And warn men to their needs."]

She sings at the right time (midnight) that prepares men for the coming of the new day. This speech refutes the nightingale's premise that the owl does no good with her song. The owl additionally refutes the nightingale's stance on women by announcing that wives truly do have problems—and when they do, they go to the owl for help because she sympathizes with them. The owl's final refutation concludes with her recapping her good deeds, especially,

"Ich do heom god mid mine deaþe,
warvore þe is wel unneaþe.
For þah þu ligge dead and clinge,
þi deþ nis nawt to none þinge." (1617–1620)

["I do them good in my death,
wherefore for you it is hard.
For there you lie dead and wither,
Your death is not good to nothing."]

On the basis of the convincing confirmations and refutations delineated by the owl, she must be construed as the winner of the debate; she has answered most wisely and consistently. This being so, the moral lesson should be clear. Thomas Garbáty (556) explains that the poem was probably written by a clerical judge and was directed toward inclusive courtly, popular, or religious audiences (967–970). The work's judicial overtones appeal to the courtly audience, a group that can grasp the pleading as it occurs throughout the poem. *The Owl and the Nightingale* would also be enjoyed by the masses; while the common folk might not grasp the legal jargon or the work's complicated format, they would enjoy the poem's quick wit and its use of exempla and the proverbs of Alfred. Of course, *The Owl and the Nightingale*'s religious overtones would morally account for the work's clerical interest. But the moral lesson of the poem may not be clearly identified from this perspective alone.

It is this premise that has befuddled critics. Kathryn Hume analyzes various interpretations that explain *The Owl and the Nightingale* as either religious, literary, or political allegory before she concludes that the work is a "burlesque-satire on human contentiousness" (108). Because Nicolas seems to be a cleric, Anne Baldwin (224) sees the poem as a religious debate, because clerics were legally permitted to deliver judgments only on ecclesiastical issues. Moreover, since the owl so convincingly wins the debate, the owl must merit some significance in the poem's meaning.

It could be that the poem depicts the struggles of the Jews in a Christian society where they are scorned, a point convincingly explored by Laura Cooner. At the proposed date of *The Owl and the Nightingale*'s composition, England fell prey to anti-Semitic feelings. Religious enthusiasm and economic hardships, both the products of the Crusades, increased Christian distrust of the Jews to the point of hatred. To save the depressed (both moral and financial) economy, both the church and the state were forced to quell the hostile attitude toward the Jews and, inevitably, to protect them. This stance is supported by J. Gottschalk (657), who finds that the poem was meant to give moral instruction to a mixed, popular audience; this would account for the poem being written in English, a language still considered vulgar at this time. As a Christian, Nicolas would be obligated to appeal to the masses to halt their campaign of hatred against the Jews. Certainly, the satiric references against certain church practices would also put the cleric in disfavor with his superiors.

Cooner's reading helps account for the author's use of two birds, rather than two humans, in his work. It does not prove, as Wells (21) believes, that Nicolas "wouldn't dare criticize his potential benefactors" and is, therefore, not the author. Instead, the work reemphasizes the goodness of Nicolas's character and may even gain him favor with the king for his attempt to halt the massacres of Jews by Christians (Cooner 30). Nicolas has little to lose by criticizing his potential benefactors; he has already been passed over for preference. Obviously, A.C. Baugh's statement that "so delightful a poem should be allowed to stand as an example of the bird fable, as a story told for its own sake, without our seeking to find a hidden meaning which isn't there" (155) falls short. It is, as Douglas Peterson (13) finds, hard to believe this 1,800-line Middle English poem was conceived only as "a story for its own sake." A poem that is so carefully constructed to analyze the nature of its two combatants probably exposes some aspects of the author's nature. If Nicolas could not receive preference from the bishops, his only recourse was to seek preference from the king—and at the same time present a scathing attack on the moral atrocities of the church.

THE THRUSH AND THE NIGHTINGALE

The Thrush and the Nightingale, a bird debate concerning the value of women, was probably written around 1272–1307, during the reign of Edward I. It is the second extant bird debate of the long tradition originated by *The Owl and the Nightingale* (c. 1200). *The Thrush and the Nightingale* consists of thirty-two six-line stanzas (*aabccb*). Lines 1, 2, 4, and 5 of each stanza contain four stresses; lines 3 and 6 contain three stresses. The poem is written in the South-west Midlands dialect and is quite short compared to *The Owl and the Night-ingale*. Despite this length differential, *The Thrush and the Nightingale* is structurally similar to *The Owl and the Nightingale*; it even shares a strong legal coloration with its predecessor (Hartung 721). This mimetic compliment pro-vides proof of the popularity of the debate form. Analyzing the poem structurally will show that *The Thrush and the Nightingale* contains many of the same rhetorical elements as *The Owl and the Nightingale*.

The Thrush and the Nightingale begins (1–12) with the glorification of a summer pastoral setting. In this land of blossoming trees and singing birds' glad refrains, the poem's wandering narrator happens across a debating thrush and nightingale. The female nightingale praises women, "That on hereth wimmen that hoe beth hende" (10) ["That women here on earth are good"], and their beneficent deeds. The male thrush adopts the misogynist perspective and shames women. After providing this background, the narrator announces "That strif ye mowen i-here" (12) ["their strife you may hear"]; he will now report on the conflict as he observes it.

In the next section of the debate (13–24), the birds announce their proposi-tions. The nightingale's stance will be in defense of women; she would "shilden hem from shome; / Of scathe hoe wole hem skere" (14–15) ["Shield them from shame and save them from injury"]. The antithesis of this proposal will be argued by the thrush, who "seyth by nighte and eke by day/ That hi beth fendes i-fere" (17–18) ["says that by day and also by night women keep the devil company"]. To this premise the thrush adds that men who believe in women are deceived and that the world would be a better place if women had never been created, for they "beswiketh euchan mon" (19) ["deceive every man"]. With this dialectic the narrative section concludes; the birds have drawn distinct battle lines for their polemic argument.

In the ensuing partition (25–48) of the debate's proposition, the two disputants restate their stances in more detail and clearly define the basis of their argument. The nightingale feels:

> "Hit is shome to blame levedy,
> For hi beth hende of corteisy;
> Ich rede that thou lete!" (25–27)

> ["It is a shame to blame the ladies
> For they are both good and courteous;
> I beg that you quit!"]

As proof, the nightingale argues that women cheer the angry, the noble, and the base. Also, she says that women were created as men's companions; both earth and man could not exist without them. Therefore, the nightingale is convinced that women

> "gladieth hem that beth wrothe,
> Bothe the heye and the lowe;
> Mid gome hi cunne him grete." (31–33)

> ["gladden those who are sad,
> Both the high and the low,
> With games they know how to greet them."]

The thrush follows the nightingale's speech by restating his stance that allows no praise for women; he views the entire sex as being false in thought, "For hi bet swikele and false of thohut,/ Also ich am ounderstonde" (38–39) ["For I affirm that they are false of thought and know that they will cheat"]. From the thrush's perspective, this implication, which mirrors the Pauline stance of the church, is the only true way to view women. They are not to be seen from the nightingale's perspective, as objects to be adored. The duration of the conflict (49–180) contains alternating speeches through which the thrush and the nightingale try to prove their propositions and refute the allegations forwarded by their opponent. The thrush posits his belief that all women are false, lustful, and responsible for the fall of man. To reinforce his stance, the thrush augments his argument with specific examples.

The nightingale presents her side of the debate through emotional, rather unsubstantiated proofs; in essence, her argument is artificial. Her theses, that women are kind, are good in bed, and make good companions are somewhat lacking and dependent upon ad hominem arguments; she even admits to women's inherent carnal lust. It is not until her final speech, when the nightingale reminds the thrush of the virtue of the Virgin Mary, the mother of Jesus, that the nightingale turns the flow of the debate in her favor.

In the poem's conclusion the thrush admits his error:

> "Nighttigale, I was woed,
> Other I couthe the luttel goed,
> With thee forto strive." (181–183)

> ["Nightingale, I was mad,
> Or else I thought of only a little good,
> With thee to strive."]

He thereby concedes the debate:

> "I suge that ich am overcome
> Thoru hire that bar that holy sone
> That soffrede wundes five." (184–186)

> ["I say that I am overcome
> By her that bore that holy son
> That suffered wounds five."]

He swears that he will never again tarnish the reputation of women, decides to leave at once, and flies away.

This conclusion has disturbed the poem's few critics. While the conclusion is obviously contrived, it does not merit this lack of critical interpretation. Josepha Gellinek-Schellekens (143–44) notes that the nightingale's success depends upon her "various conventional arguments," and the nightingale's argument that Mary was a woman would "hardly be one of her strongest." Kathryn Hume (35) characterizes the work as a feeble poem in which a more sensible poet would have the nightingale concede some of women's faults while "still holding out the example of the Virgin to defeat the thrush's total denigration of the sex." It seems that these critics may be too quick to believe the poem's seemingly obvious conclusion.

Since the general purpose of the debate was to dictate some moral or philosophical lesson, this must also be the case in *The Thrush and the Nightingale*. If the reader of the poem is to believe the poem's sudden conclusion, then the lesson would appear to be that since Mary was a woman, all women are elevated above men; but this does not fall into the traditional thinking of medieval England. As Eileen Power (10) notes, according to canon law, the fact that governed woman's position was not her personality but her sex, and by her sex she was inferior to man. Therefore, unless this poem is an early precursor to the feminist movement, there must be more to the moral lesson of the poem.

A careful reading of the poem may reveal this lesson. Throughout the debate (save the sudden conclusion), the thrush has presented his argument in much more convincing terms. The thrush initially claims that he could tell a hundred stories to support his argument (44) before he reports King Alexander's censure of women: "In the world nes non so crafty mon, / Ne non so riche of londe" (45–46) ["In the world there is not so crafty a man, / Nor none so rich in all the land"]. This example is indicative of the invective approach the thrush will use to argue his points. His consistent relation of concrete models or events seems to confirm the credibility of his argument.

The thrush "habbe with hem in bowre i-be" (62) ["has with them (women) in the bower been"], and often the ladies assented to his will—actions that are typical of their sex and will help to damn their souls. He follows this with the example of Adam "That wes oure furste man / That fonde hem wicke and ille" (71–72) ["That was our first man and found them [women] wicked and false"]. The thrush also testifies that Sir Gawain, the knight to whom Jesus Christ gave virtue, failed in his worldwide search to find a virtuous woman. To this he adds an exemplum about the Queen of Constantinople:

> "Foul wel hire semede fow and grene—
> How sore hit gone hire reue!
> Hoe fedde a crupel in hire bour
> And helede him with covetour:
> Loke war wimmen ben treue!" (116–20)

["Full well she liked green and sundry colors—
How she regretted it later!
Who fed a cripple in her bower
And held him and coveted him:
Look how women are true!"]

Contrary to those of the thrush, the nightingale's speeches contain no tangible evidence that support her premises. She chides her opponent in an ad hominem speech for attacking women who are not present and cannot defend themselves. The nightingale continues that women, when shielded in a bower, are safe from shame and the sweetest things for men (who delight in their charms). Here the nightingale has altered her proposition by adding an amendment: it is the shielded woman who is virtuous. The nightingale then argues that it is unfair to blame all women for the few who have gone astray (an admission of some failure) and reminds the thrush of the physical satisfaction women give their mates in carnal love. She then admonishes the thrush, again using an ad hominem approach to charge that the thrush will be banished for laying the blame on those who have such charm: "For hem thou shalt gon sory—/ Of londe ich wille the sende!" (82–83) ["For those accusations you shall be sorry—/ I will have you banished!"].

Through the majority of the debate the nightingale has presented proofs that she believes establish her proposition as valid: women are worthy of praise. However, she has provided no tangible evidence to confirm her statements, and her arguments are, therefore, unsubstantiated. Without any documentation or examples to heighten these premises, the nightingale must be perceived to be failing in her attempt to sway the audience of the debate to her side. The nightingale has even strengthened the thrush's argument by admitting to women's carnal lust, a position looked down upon by clerics of the church.

Contrarily, the thrush has provided logical, concrete proofs of his allegation that women are worthless and not to be trusted. His misogynistic views seem harsh, but they fall in line with the teachings of the church; the thrush's concrete examples of Adam and Gawain would probably confirm this perspective to the audience. Until line 156 of the debate it seems that the thrush is rhetorically crushing the nightingale. The poem then makes its dramatic shift. In lines 157–169 the thrush, for the first time, strays from his method of providing concrete examples to substantiate his position. Instead, he falls into the nightingale's approach of careless rhetoric:

"Among on houndret ne beth five,
Nouther of maidnes ne of wive,
That holdeth hem al clene,
That hi ne wercheth wo in londe,
Other bringeth men to shonde,
And that is wel i-sene." (160–65)

["Among a hundred there are not five,
Neither maidens or wives,
That keep themselves all clean,
That they do not bring woe to their land
Or bring men to harm,
And that is well known."]

The thrush's only proof of this assertion is that he knows this to be a certainty; he has clearly strayed from the distinct proofs in his earlier speeches. This is the first time that the thrush has admitted even a small portion of good in women, a shift that halts the thrush's momentum. Perhaps the poem's author is foreshadowing that startling reversal that immediately follows in the debate. The nightingale gives her first (and only) tangible proof for her initial stance that women are good by reminding the thrush of the one woman who forever changed the world, the Virgin Mary:

"a maide meke and milde!
Of hire sprong that holy bern
That boren wes in Bedleham,
And temeth al that is wilde.
Hoe ne weste of sunne ne of shame—
Marie wes ire righte name;
Crist hire i-shilde!" (171–77)

["a maid meek and mild!
Of her sprang that holy child,
that born was in Bethlehem,
and tames all that is wild.
She knew no sin nor shame—
Mary was her proper name;
Christ shield her!"]

Here the thrush concedes the debate.

It seems clear that until the poem's conclusion the thrush was well in control of the debate, and the proposition that he posits—that women are evil and responsible for the Fall of Man—is well defended. Yet the thrush quickly accepts his defeat when the nightingale introduces her proof of Mary, the one woman not tainted by sin; the thrush flies off to repent his former "false belief." This sudden shift could be indicative of the author's failure to resolve two traditional medieval beliefs: the Pauline doctrine that women are evil and its contradiction, that Mary, the mother of Jesus, is holy.

The stance of the thrush is indicative of the Pauline insistence that woman is the instrument of the devil, a thing at once inferior and evil. Power (16) states that this idea was predominant in the writings of Paul and the early Christian fathers and became the embodiment in the ethics and philosophy of monasticism. This attitude became so ingrained in the monastic mind that even matrimony could not surmount it. Yet the masses continued to ignore this teaching and married—with the blessing of the church upon their unions. While the monastic point of view was bound to intrude upon the thought and morals of society as a whole, without these sanctified unions civilization would cease to exist. Power (19) adds that the church, to alleviate this dilemma, established the doctrine of the woman's subjection, which was apt to be linked with the notion of her essential inferiority. Meanwhile, the cult of the Virgin grew at a steady pace at the end of the thirteenth century, a movement that eased the social conscience concerning matrimony. It is this movement that appears in *The Thrush and the Nightingale*.

When the poem's proofs are examined, the examples provided by the thrush (Adam, Gawain, Samson, and the teachings of Jesus) would all appeal to the common folk. This revelation serves the church nicely; not only would the commoners be exposed to the popular tenets that expound a moral platitude, they would also learn a valued church belief. Power (11) writes, "The common people went to church on Sundays and listened while the preachers told them in one breath that woman was the gate of hell and that Mary was the queen of Heaven." Given *The Thrush and the Nightingale*'s short length and straightforward argument, the poem would appeal to this lower class that could easily follow the poem's progress. Thus *The Thrush and the Nightingale* would provide a valuable tool of instruction at a time when the church held a fairly firm grip on its followers.

THE DEBATE OF THE BODY AND THE SOUL

The Debate of the Body and the Soul from the *Worcestershire Miscellany* is a prime example of the debate genre's popularity in fourteenth-century England. This debate concerning the effect of a corrupt body or soul on man's attempt at salvation is a variation of a theme found in works as early as the Old English Exeter Book (a manuscript copied about A.D. 940) and the Vercelli Book (c. 1000). *The Address of the Soul*, found in both of these manuscripts, is a monologue; *The Debate of the Body and the Soul*, written at the Cistercian Abbey of Saint Mary's Bordesley sometime after 1388, is a true debate. Strongly influenced by the *Conflictus Corporis et Animae* and the *Noctis sub Silentio, The Debate of the Body and the Soul* consists of sixty-two eight-verse stanzas, or 496 lines.

The Debate of the Body and the Soul begins (1–12) with the framing device prevalent in Middle English literature, the dream vision. In this section of the debate poem, again similar to an exordium, the narrator recounts the events that occurred one winter night as he lay "droupnyng to-fore þe day" (2) ["in a drowsy sleep before the day"] when "me þouȝt I seye a sely syȝt" (12) ["I thought I saw a marvelous sight"]. This setting, the antithesis of the gay pastoral settings of *The Owl and the Nightingale* and *The Thrush and the Nightingale*, atmospherically foreshadows the frightening debate about the grimly symbiotic relationship between a body and its soul. Next, the focus of the debate is introduced: lying on a bier is a "cumly kny3t" (5) ["handsome knight"] who "lytel seruyd God" (6) ["little served God"]; at the moment the narrator views the grisly corpse, the soul has just begun to leave the body.

The soul "so sorfullyche wiþ drery mode" (12) ["so sorrowful with a dreary heart"] eyes the dead body and initiates the debate's extended narration (13–176). The soul angrily berates the body as "fekul fieshe" ["treacherous flesh"] and "false blode" (14) ["false blood"] responsible for the damnation of both the soul and the body. The soul lists the body's hedonistic tendencies and its indulgence in several of the seven deadly sins, especially the dead knight's desire for worldly possessions, as reasons for their precarious position. To these the body counters with its allegations that the soul is responsible for their grief. While the body admits to having lived a life of pleasure, it claims that the soul irresponsibly failed to guide it toward a Christian life and has doomed them both to eternal damnation.

The poem's proposition is divulged when the soul tells the body to remember the body's foul physical acts when it suffers torment in the pit: "Of alle þat euer þu haste done ille / þat þu so ly3tlyche schalt be quyt?" (183–184) ["Of all that ever you have done ill / that you so lightly shall be requit?"]. The soul grimly acknowledges that on Judgment Day, when the two are reunited, they will be doomed to perpetual hell. The soul then attempts to define its stance: the knight is responsible for their lot because he has committed several of the seven deadly sins and failed to shrive himself after living a sinful life. The body will argue that it was not the first, nor will it be the last, human to indulge in such a life. If he is guilty, then it is the soul's fault for failing to steer him in a more righteous direction.

The debate concludes with a vivid display of the process of damnation. The torment of the soul is revealed when thousands of fiends lie upon the hapless soul, which is "in a pore plyte / Rufullych þolyd to and fro" (383–384) ["in a poor plight / Ruefully tormented to and fro"). The demons show the soul little mercy because it is God's will that the soul be plagued by the heinous crimes of monsters. Before the gates to hell are closed behind him, the soul cries:

> "Þu God þat wystest alle to-forne,
> Why schope þer me to wroþer-hele,
> To ben þus togged or to-torne,
> Or for to welden eny wele?
> Þo þat scholden have been i-lorne,
> Wel my3tyst þu suche wreche speke,
> Alas, why letyste þu us be borne,
> To 3euen þe foule fende so felle?" (449–456)

> ["You God that knows all before,
> Why shape you me to the destruction,
> To be thus pulled or torn apart,

Or for to enjoy any prosperity?
They that should have been lost,
Well might you such wretches warn.
Alas, why let you us be born,
To be given to the foul fiend so fierce?"]

From this vividly didactic conclusion, the moral lesson of the poem should be clear. It seems that the soul has paid the ultimate price for its neglect in not leading the body toward a life of salvation. However, it must be remembered that although the body's punishment has been deferred until Judgment Day, in no way is the body totally innocent. Thus the poem illustrates that salvation must be a joint effort between the body and soul of man, for mere penitence is not enough. An examination of the protagonists' arguments exposes this to be a Thomistic observation, that man is the central point of contact between the two great realms of "form" (the body) and "matter" (the soul). In medieval dogma the soul is credited with the function of thinking and willing, thus determining all behavior (Jones 250). The body can only depend upon the soul to guide it away from sin, for the body is simply a vessel for the soul.

In the debate the soul attempts to direct the blame of damnation on the body. Interestingly, these accusations initially take the form of the Old English *ubi sunt*, as in "The Wanderer," a lament for people or possessions now lost. Here the form is transmitted to the consequences of man's submission to the seven deadly sins. The soul asks the body, "Where ys now all þi grete pryde?" (22) ["Where now is all your great pride?"]. This, as well as all of the body's worldly possessions, has disappeared now that the body lies on its funeral bier. Next, avarice, the love of worldly possessions, is condemned when the soul asks, "Where ben alle þi worþi wedis?" (25) ["Where be all your worldly goods?"]. The irony of the soul's attack on greed is inescapable. After cataloging the body's rich acquisitions, the soul explicitly describes the body's only remaining possession: "Lo wreche, where now is þi bowre? / To morwe schal þu þer-in falle" (39–40) ["Lo, wretch, where now is your chamber? / Tomorrow shall you therein fall"]. The sin of gluttony is also decried as the soul criticizes the body's lack of judgment as the reason for their fate: "me þe þytte and þyne of helle / Wiþ þe glotenye hast þu geten" (47–48) ["me the pit and you hell / With your gluttony you have gotten"]. To this point the soul's words express its moral stance: the hedonistic life condemns man to a life of eternal torment in hell.

The soul's position subtly shifts to expound upon the ongoing evil that worldly possessions institute by belittling the men who envied the knight while the knight was alive and the men who entertained the knight solely that "Þey had of þe þat þey myȝt geton" (56) ["They had of you what they might get"]. These scamps had actually deceived the knight, wanting only his wealth and not his cameraderie. This broad implication of sin among the knight's companions serves to reinforce the moral lesson of the poem: this knight is not alone in his guilt. He and his friends were equally involved in revelry.

While the knight catered to his lecherous acquaintances, he overlooked the truly needy. Instead, the poor were mocked, their cries were passed over, and if they persisted in their call for alms, they were "strekun wiþa staf" (64) ["struck with a staff"]. The knight welcomed the rich and shunned the poor; obtusely obstinate, the soul blames the body for this unkindness, although the audience must realize from the previous points made that the soul is obviously at least equally at fault.

The judgment has now fallen into God's hands, and the soul reminds the body, "haste þu wreche lytel þonke" (72) ["have you wretch little thought"], an admonishment for the corrupt shell that "madeste hit so towhe, / Alle þi bose is sone astynte" (76–77) ["made it so difficult, / All your boasting is soon ended"]. The point of this attack is that the soul feels that the body is responsible for the soul's loss of bliss. While the two argue incessantly over whose fault their damnation actually is, the soul is the first to realize the horror of condemnation to perpetual torment. Certainly the soul should be the more impressed, since the body will no longer exist after the bier fire.

The soul notes the irony of the body's lust for wealth, for now "þu ne schalte neuer efte be blyþe" (86) ["nor shall you never after be blissful"]. In reality the knight will have to trade his jewel-encrusted palace for a seven-foot pit of clay. Further, the knight's wealth will be distributed to people he did not want to give it to. Thus the knight's "false ere" (97) ["false heir"] celebrates the knight's demise, as do the executors who stand to divide the estate. Still, the body will be oblivious to this pain once the soul is removed to hell.

The soul has bared several interesting elements in the debate. First, the soul, by angrily denouncing the habits of the body, is guilty of violating one of the seven deadly sins, an act for which it has just soundly berated the body. The soul's moral lapse negates many of the strong proofs that it presents in its speech; it has already forgotten its own preaching. Also, while the soul has presented many allegations, it has not provided any specific examples to verify its stance. These sweeping generalities serve to limit its attack to depict only the fate of all men who submit to temptation. If this is the case, then it is only natural that the soul should be more concerned with its own salvation than that of its human shell. Given its fate, the soul may be a bit envious of the life the knight led; since the soul was unable to stop the body from its life of wanton hedonism, it might as well have joined in the bacchanalia.

The dead knight questions the soul's allegations and offers proofs that he believes will stem the tide of the debate from turning against him. The knight, in an ad hominem stance, claims that no one is totally good. The knight names both "Samson" and "Sesar" as great mortal men who shared his fate, as well as their mothers, that "no man can now fynde one mote of hem" (131–132) ["no man can now find one bit of them"]. It seems that the body could have found two examples that are more apropos to his cause; Samson fell because he lusted after Delilah, and the pagan Octavius Caesar dared to call himself "Augustus," a title applied to gods or divine objects (Collins 3).

Regardless, the body continues to expound a sinful attitude toward life: since death is inevitable, the knight believes that man should do all he can to enjoy life to its fullest. He disputes the soul's condemnation of the body's accumulated wealth, saying that the money could only be stolen from him by death; further, others will profit when he is gone from the riches he accumulated. With this sordid logic the body attempts to establish proof of a rational motive behind his lifestyle. What he has failed to realize is that his statements expose his failure to grasp the spiralling effect his wealth will have on others. They, too, are now in a position where they will have to resist temptation.

The body further attempts to shift the blame for this troublesome situation to the soul, "for alle was hit þine owne gylte" (156) ["for all was it your own guilt"]. The body's proposition is supported by several interesting allegations: The knight believes that the soul "boþen schuldest þu fro schame have schylte" (160) ["both should you from shame have shielded"], for God created the soul

> "aftur hys schafte
> And ȝaf þe boþ wyt and skylle,
> And in þi lokyng alle was I lafte." (161–163)

> ["after his kind
> And gave you both wit and skill,
> And in your care all was I left.]

This ad hominem proof strongly favors the body's innocence because it did not know the difference between what was good and what was evil. The soul has accused the body of violating five of the seven deadly sins; at the same time the soul itself is guilty of violating two (anger and envy). The body, while admitting to its hedonistic tendencies, argues correctly that it was the soul's responsibility to guide him morally. The knight alleges that no overriding moral instruction has ever been provided by the soul.

The soul replies in an invective manner that the first time the body met evil, it was enthralled: "Wiþ þy tethe þe brydul þu lawht / And deduste alle þat I forbade." (195–196) ["With your teeth the bridle you bit / And did all that I forbade"]. This was the body's response despite the soul's claim that "Sor I chydde aȝen and faute, / And euer þu nome þyne owne rede" (199–200) ["Sorely I chided against and fought, / And ever you took your own counsel"]. The soul pleads that it spoke of the body's needs, "mas, matynse, or euensong" (202) ["mass, matins, or evensong"], but the body ignored the soul and allowed pride to rule. Then the soul laments, "Þow were mayster an I þi knave" (216) ["You were the master and I the knave"]. This passage seems to preach the Thomist belief in the rational faculty that distinguishes the free will in terms of "freedom from coercion." The will, as maintained by St. Thomas, can never be coerced or forced. By this Thomas does not deny that terror or pain sometimes causes man to do things that defeat his real ends instead of fulfilling them (Jones 251). In essence, the soul believes that the body willed to attain whatever it wanted simply as a means of fulfillment. Since the will of man, according to Thomas, naturally seeks whatever is desirable to it, it is up to the soul to control this "outer" part of his will. W.T. Jones (248) adds that in the basic Thomistic assumption it does seem that the part of man that is independent of the body and active in its own right will survive the corruption of the body called death. Here Thomas dictates that the rational faculty of the soul passes into theology and should seek fulfillment in terms of faith. Again, it is up to the body to distinguish what is "good" and what is "evil"; the soul can only provide the basis for faith. In terms of Thomistic dogma, the soul has presented valid proof in this speech.

The dead knight claims that he cannot be held accountable for actions that he did not know were wrong, and he questions:

> "Where was I by wode or by-way
> Sat or stode or dyd owht misse,
> Þat I was euer vndur þine eye?" (221–223)

> [Where was I by woods or by way
> Sat or stood or did anything amiss,
> That I was ever [not] under your eye?"]

All the soul had to do, the body claims, was place the idea of sin in his mind; then, at least, the body would not have repeated his sins. This and the body's other refutations, that the soul was sent by God to be aware of man's nature, and that man is an irrational beast not in control of his morality, all recall the Thomistic dogma.

To further complicate his refutation, the body promotes sloth. In stanza 33 the body claims that he would have been better off without reason, as are animals that lie about and bide their times until their deaths. The body concludes by adding a shocking codicil: "Ne þu scholdest not into hel depe, / Nere þe wythe þat alle was þyne" (255–256) ["Nor you should not go into hell deep / Were it not that all was for reason"). Without the ability to reason, the body admits, man would not have to worry about going to hell. Here the body has neglected the premise of the church in its Great Chain of Being that illustrates that reason in man is the attribute that links man to God. Without it, man would not be the highest of the corporeal subjects (Jones 242).

The soul continues with a depreciating attack upon the body's ignorance: It is horrible when the one you trust the most causes you most to suffer. It was up to the body to use its gift of reason to at least prepare itself for peace and dying; it is this lack of foresight that has purchased the pain and suffering for the soul. Next, the soul describes death as a fixed state; although the world continues, the dead corpse is blind, deaf, and dumb to the world's ongoing existence. The soul then states the bitter reality of the situation and scourges the body's worldly sins:

"Nis no leuedy so bryht of ble
Þat of þe were wel wone to lete,
Þat one day wolde now wiþe þe be
For alle þe golde þe euer get." (281–284)

["There is not any lady so bright of hue
That of you were well wont to esteem,
That one day would now with you be
For all the gold you ever had."]

This realistic condemnation makes way for the soul's attack on the body's pride and exposes in stark realism the truth of death: the rotting body is now ugly to see, ugly to kiss, and all of his friends will now flee from him.

In the body's next speech he tells the soul, "I was euer at þi hest" (294) ["I was ever at your command"] because the soul has the "myȝtis moste" (296) ["most might"]. This is a rhetorical error and a false argument; in his earlier refutation the body has claimed that the soul was nowhere to be seen and never told the body the differences between good and evil. Now the body scrambles his logic by claiming that he was following the lead of the soul. This argumentative shift continues in stanza 38 when the body argues that it was he who completely followed the soul's bidding and "Alle to þi counsayle moste I cleuer, / As he doþ þat non oþer dar" (303–304) ["All to your counsel must I adhere / As he that does nothing else dare"]. The body has placed himself in the role of a liar; if the soul guided him to damnation, as this refutation argues, then during his lifetime the body had to be aware of the soul. It must be recalled that in his earlier refutations the body has denied that he knew of the existence of his soul.

The soul detects this lapse and immediately brings this error to the body's attention:

"Þat þu louest me þu lyet,
And madist me an house of glasse.
I dude alle þat þe þouȝt swete,
And þu traytur euer wasse." (317–320)

["That you loved me you lied,
And made me a house of glass.
I did all that you thought sweet,
And you the traitor ever were."]

The soul refutes the body's weakness by exposing the body's moral lapses. Now that the body has admitted that it was aware of the soul, the soul can expound more concrete proofs that will tag the body the loser of the debate and at fault for their damnation. The soul maintains:

"I bade þe schryte take,
And leue þi synnus euer and o,

Done penance and faste and wake,
Þe fende sayde, 'schalte þu not so,
Þuჳ ჳonge þi ryote forsake,
To leuen longe in sorwe and wo
loy and myrthe I rede þu make,
And þenke to leue ჳytte ჳerys mo.' " (321–328)

["I bade you shrive take,
And leave your sins ever and all,
Do penence and fast and wake,
The devil said, 'Shall you do not so,
So young, the rioting forsake,
To live long in sorrow and in woe
Joy and mirth I advise you make,
And think to live yet years more.' "]

The body, which has admitted being aware of the soul, refused to shrive itself
or to do penance for its sins. Instead, the body listened to Satan and his promises
of happiness and a longer life, even though the soul had pleaded with the body
to abandon its promiscuous life of wantonness and to heed the consequences of
its indulgence in the seven deadly sins:

"And when I bid þe leue pryde,
Þine mony messe, þi semelyche schrowde,
Þis wrechyd worlde þe stode bysyde,
And bad þe be ful qweynte and proude,
Þi fiesche wiþ ryche robys schryde,
Noht as a begger in a cloute,
And on hye horse for to ryde,
Wiþ mekul meyny in and owte.
And when I bad þe erly to ryse,
And of me take goode kepe,
Þu seydest þu myჳtyst in no wyse,
For þe mery morne-slepe." (329–340)

["And when I bid you leave pride,
Your money much, your seemly dress,
This wretched world you stood beside,
And bade you be very eloquent and proud,
Your flesh with rich robes clothed,
Not as a beggar in a cloak,
And on high horses for to ride,
With large retinue in and out.
And when I bade you early to rise,
And of me take good keep,
You said you might in no way,
Because of the pleasant morning sleep."]

Certainly this is a denunciation of greed, pride, avarice, and sloth. The soul believes that it must be the body whose actions have condemned them to hell.

Now the body realizes his fault and, in his remorse, wishes that he had died as soon as he was born. The body rationalizes that this would never have allowed the body to learn of evil or yearn for anything worldly so that "ne payne suffurde and nowe I mote" (356) ["No pain suffered and now I must"]. The body realizes that he should have prayed:

> "Wheþer no seynt may byd owre ernde,
> To hym þat boaȝt vs wiþ hys blode,
> Þat we ne bene in þis fyre forbrende,
> Þrow hys mercy to done vs bote." (357–360)

> ["Whether no saint may make our petition,
> To him that bought us with his blood,
> That we not be in this fire burned up,
> Through his mercy to do us good."]

Then the soul offers a chilling revelation in the debate's conclusion:

> "Nay wreche, nay, now ys to late
> For to pray or for to preche.
> Now is ryȝt at þe ȝate,
> And þi tonge hath leyde þe speche." (361–364)

> ["Nay wretch, nay, now is too late
> For praying or preaching.
> Now we're right at the gate,
> And your tongue has lost its speech."]

The point here is clear: man must heed the advice of his soul, even if it is not terribly strong, and repent before he dies. Once the hour of death is reached, he has lost the faculty of speech and thus cannot repent. If the audience members allow themselves to be damned, then they will follow in the footsteps of this personified body and soul, for "suche ys Godes wrathe and wreche!" (366) ["such is God's wrath and will!"]. The soul concludes:

> "For helle-houndes here i ȝelle
> And feendes mo þan I may se,
> Þat cometh to feche me to hell.
> I may no way fle
> And þu schalt come in fleche and felle,
> At domys-day to wone wiþ me." (371–376)

> ["For hell-hounds hear I yell
> And devils more than I may see,
> That come to fetch me to hell.

I may in no way flee
And you shall come in flesh and skin,
At judgment day to live with me."]

This conclusion, which is not unlike the peroration of classical oratory, is of interest because it confesses that the body is not totally at fault for its damnation. Early in the debate the soul is guilty of violating two of the seven deadly sins, anger and envy, so, while its torment is excessive and startling, it is somewhat deserved.

When the narrator awakens from his fitful sleep, he displays what must be perceived as the appropriate response: "On euery here a drope stode / For sore aferde þer I lay" (476) ["On every hair a drop stood / for sore afraid there I lay"]. The narrator immediately prays to Jesus lest he be "borne away" and repeats the pedagogical lesson of the poem, crying for "Crystys mercy" (488) and God's "holy grace" (489).

The power of *The Debate of the Body and the Soul* is astounding in the moral lesson it presents, yet the poem has failed to rouse the interest of many scholars. J.D. Bruce traced the popularity of the theme of the poem from its roots in German literature. Tempe Allison continued Bruce's thematic study and located a version of *The Debate of the Body and the Soul* in the popular morality play *The Castle of Perseverance*.

Given the dualistic nature of the soul, the audience should realize that both the body and the soul are responsible for their damnation. The body has every obligation to atone for its hedonistic lifestyle. The soul could only suggest that the body heed the teachings of the church and repent; it could not make the body utter the necessary words of redemption. Yet the soul is not as innocent as it claims; it apparently had not exerted enough pressure to dissuade the body and is culpable of the sins itself. This makes the soul's descent into hell seem just and warranted.

These personified attributes of the soul present a curious and ironic twist to the poem. During the debate's conclusion the body tries to repent and is unable to speak; the soul never offers a disclaimer or seeks to atone for its sins. In essence, this provides yet another clear moral: The mere saying of words of repentance is not enough; in order to be truly penitent, the message must come from the sinner's inner soul. It is up to the sinner while on earth to place his total faith in Jesus and God and act accordingly, lest he face the same fate as the body and the soul.

It appears that the Middle English debates contain certain elements that show that the debate genre is a literary type that appears consistently throughout the literature of this period. The components of the debate are similar to those of classical rhetoric: exordium, narration, partition, proofs, refutations, and peroration. While not all of the debates contain each of these parts, they are structured in a way that seems mimetic of this tradition. These works were originally foremost concerned with the ideas of moral or didactic instruction, as exemplified by *The Owl and the Nightingale*, the twelfth-century work that is the earliest extant Middle English debate. The thirteenth-century debate *The Thrush and the Nightingale*, although very didactic in its theme, also presents a church-related misogynistic perspective of women, especially in their behavior in love. In this work the difference between love, lust, and procreation is touched upon, but the overall theme of the poem seems to be the glorification of the Virgin Mary. It is the debate of *The Thrush and the Nightingale* that exposes the church's reconciliation of the Virgin Mary's stature with the accepted Pauline dogma, a policy that condemns women.

The Debate of the Body and the Soul is a vigorous debate of the fourteenth century that challenges the conflicting roles of the body and the soul in their relationship to salvation; the gist of this debate is an intense moral lesson and dogmatic instruction. This debate highlights, in the grimmest of terms, the horror of the hedonistic life. Its resolution is accented by the grotesque image it presents of the soul in its torment as it is swept into the bowels of hell, an incident that vividly illustrates the moral of the debate. Members of the audience, by deciding for themselves which of the characters is victorious in the debate, would learn a valuable lesson in faith. Again, the debate would serve as propaganda for the church as it attempted to retain its iron grip on the common folk.

By the middle of the fourteenth century there was a discernible interest in the courtly love tradition and the folly of its conventions. Chaucer readily integrates this theme into a number of his works; often the debate form is the means through which this argument is produced. In *The Parliament of Fowls* the poet combines the dream vision and the debate to explore the differences between courtly love and spiritual love. The contrary nature of these attributes (joy and sorrow, ease and pain) presents a lesson on the dualistic nature of these emotions. The resolution of the debate is implied: the lower-class birds fly happily away, while the upper-class birds are forced to suffer a year of pining for their love.

These literary debates were all obviously reflective of the dogma of the church and would be popular enough to attract many levels of audiences. However, because of the lack of manuscripts, these works had limited accessibility. Only through oral renditions would the majority of the debate poems be available to the masses.

The vast number of debate poems proper show a remarkable similarity in their composition, a finding that seems to be missing in the sparse criticism of this genre. Myra Stokes (37) says that the dreamer of Langland's *Piers Plowman* occasionally falls into clearly defined debates; she also notes several debates in the works of Chaucer. In "The Nun's Priest's Tale" Stokes reveals that Chauntecleer and Pertelote debate at length on the nature of dreams: are they prophetic or merely psychosomatic? This question is disputed in earnest with the due citation of various authorities on both sides and concludes with Chauntecleer boldly announcing that not all dreams are prophetic, but some are.

Troilus and Criseyde is seen by Stokes to contain many debates; these occur in the passages in which one party exercises his powers of persuasion over another. Stokes finds that the debate that is nearest to the classical form is that of book 4, when Troilus argues that the couple should elope. Criseyde argues vehemently against this, for she is unwilling to submit to such an extreme measure. Troilus and Criseyde argue the merits of their own plans and decry the course advocated by the other. Criseyde wins the debate, not because Troilus is either convinced or beaten by her arguments, but simply because he perceives her to be so determined that he is unwilling to agitate her by continued futile resistance.

There is no doubt that the debate form is found again and again in literary works of the Middle English period; its popularity is not difficult to explain. The debate offered a versatile means of formulating conflicts and controversies of all types: theological, moral, political, social, and amorous. What is difficult to understand is the limited attention that the debate form has generated. It is obvious that the debate genre was prominent throughout the canon of Middle English literature, yet its role has been hardly recognized. David Zesmer does not mention the debate as a literary type in his listing of the "dominant types and verse forms employed by Middle English writers" (18). While his list is not intended to be exhaustive, it is typical. Margaret Drabble and Jenny Stringer's work does not contain an entry that even mentions the debate. Hardin Craig and Alastair Fowler have written two fine histories of English literature; however, both neglect the debate in their discourses. Unfortunately, these works are not the exception—they are the norm.

Nancy Reale astutely concludes that "debate literature has a place within Western European literary history that is at once important and difficult to define and delimit. How the idea of debate as a dialectical method of inquiry was understood at different historical moments can suggest much to modern readers about basic philosophical perspectives either actively employed or implicitly relied upon by writers" (144). She then adds that medieval "assumptions about the appropriateness of particular subjects for debate—and, indeed, the sustained use of some of these—can also reveal useful information about the social, philosophical, and aesthetic interests and concerns of various authors' milieux. Above all, a sustained look at a related body of work—in this case seen loosely as debate poetry—can afford the modern reader an opportunity to appreciate both the cultural continuities that were so highly valued during the Middle Ages and the ruptures, sometimes deliberate and sometimes not, that make clear how diverse were the many individual voices that are all too often and too simplistically grouped together as 'medieval' " (Reale 144).

The preponderance of debate poems of the Middle English period demonstrate that the debate is a major literary type that demands recognition. It is a genre that continually appears at critical times in Middle English literature. As Reale finds, "The debate poetry of the Middle Ages speaks to a wide range of practical and theoretical issues and reflects the ways in which medieval authors were able to avail themselves of a vast and complex literary heritage and to extract from it ideas, styles, formal frameworks, and points of view that could be renovated and reinterpreted through their own distinct voices" (144). It should have a verified position as an immensely valuable literary tool. So far, medieval debates present a wealth of critical potential this study has only skimmed.

SELECTED BIBLIOGRAPHY

Allison, Tempe Elizabeth. "On the '*Body and Soul*' Legend." *MLN* 43 (1927):102–6.

Baldwin, Anne W. "Henry II and *The Owl and the Nightingale*." *JEGP* 66 (1967): 207–229.

Baugh, A.C. "The Middle English Period." *A Literary History of England*. Ed A.C. Baugh, et al. New York: Oxford University Press, 1948.

Baugh, Nita Scudder, ed. *The Debate of the Body and the Soul. Medieval English Literature*. Ed. Thomas J. Garbáty. Lexington, MA: D.C. Heath, 1984. 603–619.

Bruce, J.D. "A Contribution to the Study of the *Body and Soul* Poems in English." *MLN* 5 (1890): 385–401.

Cobban, A.B. *The Medieval Universities: Their Development and Organization*. London: Methuen, 1975.

Coe, Richard. *Form and Substance: An Advanced Rhetoric*. New York: Wiley, 1981.

Collins, R.W. *A History of Medieval Civilization in Europe*. Boston: Ginn and Co., 1936.

Cooner, Laura E. "*The Owl and the Nightingale*: A Cleric's Unpopular Vision." Thesis. University of South Florida, 1988.

Craig, Hardin, ed. *A History of English Literature*. New York: Oxford University Press, 1967.

Drabble, Margaret, and Jenny Stringer. *The Oxford Companion to English Literature*. Oxford: Oxford University Press, 1987.

Engelhardt, George J. *Poetry of Chaucer*. Carbondale: Southern Illinois University Press, 1987.

Everett, Dorothy. *Essays on Middle English Literature*. Oxford: Clarendon Press, 1955.

Fowler, Alastair. *A History of English Literature*. Cambridge, MA: Harvard University Press, 1950.

Fox, John. *The Middle Ages*. New York: Barnes & Noble, 1974.

Garbáty, Thomas J., ed. *Medieval English Literature*. Lexington, MA: D.C. Heath, 1984.

Gellinek-Schellekens, Josepha E. *The Voice of the Nightingale in Middle English Poems and Bird Debates*. New York: Peter Lang, 1984.

Gottschalk, J. "*The Owl and the Nightingale*: Lay Preachers to a Lay Audience." *PQ* 45 (1966): 657–667.

Hanford, J.H. "Classical Eclogue and the Medieval Debate." *Romanic Review* 11 (1911): 16–31, 129–143.

Hartung, Albert E., ed. *A Manual of the Writings in Middle English, 1050–1500*. 10 vols. Vol. 3. New Haven, CT: Connecticut Academy of Arts and Sciences, 1972.

Harvey, Paul, and J.E. Heseltine, eds. *The Oxford Companion to French Literature*. Oxford: Oxford University Press, 1959.

Hoffman, Richard L. "The Influence of the Classics on Chaucer." *Companion to Chaucer Studies*. Ed. Beryl Rowland. 1968. Rev. ed. New York: Oxford University Press, 1979. 185–201.

Holman, C. Hugh, and William Harmon. *A Handbook to Literature*. 5th ed. New York: Macmillan, 1986.

Hume, Kathryn. *"The Owl and the Nightingale": The Poem and Its Critics*. Toronto: University of Toronto Press, 1975.

Jackson, William T.H. *European Writers: The Middle Ages and the Renaissance*. 2 vols. New York: Scribner's, 1983.

Jones, W.T. *The Medieval Mind*. 1952. New York: Harcourt, 1969.

Knowles, David. *The Evolution of Medieval Thought*. New York: Vintage Books, 1962.

Kristeller, Paul O. *Renaissance Thought: The Classic, Scholastic, and Humanist Strains*. New York: Harper & Row, 1955.

Leff, Gordon. *Medieval Thought: St. Augustine to Ockham*. 1958. Chicago: Quadrangle Books, 1959.

Murphy, James J., ed. *A Synoptic History of Classical Rhetoric*. Davis, CA: Hermagoras Press, 1983.

Palmer, R.B. "The Narrator in *The Owl and the Nightingale*: A Reader in the Text." *Chaucer Review* 22.4 (1988): 305–321.

Peterson, Douglas L. "*The Owl and the Nightingale* and the Christian Dialectic." *JEGP* (1956): 13–26.

Power, Eileen. *Medieval Women*. Cambridge: Cambridge University Press, 1975.

Reale, Nancy M. "Debate Poetry, Medieval European." *Encyclopedia of Medieval Literature*. Ed. Robert Thomas Lambdin and Laura Cooner Lambdin. Westport, CT: Greenwood Press, 2000. 130–146.

———. "Rhetorical Strategies in *The Owl and the Nightingale*." *PQ* 63.4 (1984): 417–29.

Stansburrough Cook, Albert, ed. *A Treatise against Miracle Plays. A Literary Middle English Reader*. Boston: Ginn and Co., 1915. 278–281.

Star, Jonathan, and Shahram Shiva, trans. *A Garden beyond Paradise: The Mystical Poetry of Rumi*. New York: Bantam, 1992.

Stokes, Myra. *Justice and Mercy in Piers Plowman: A Reading of the B Text Visio*. London: Croom Helm, 1984.

Stone, Brian, trans. *The Owl and the Nightingale, Cleanness, St. Erkenwald*. Harmondsworth: Penguin, 1971, reprinted 1977.

The Thrush and the Nightingale. Middle English Poetry. Ed. Lewis J. Owen and Nancy H. Owen. New York: Bobbs-Merrill, 1971. 272–281.

Tuetey, Charles Greville, trans. *Classical Arabic Poetry*. London: KPI, 1985.

Turville-Petre, Thorlac. *Alliterative Poetry of the Later Middle Ages: An Anthology*. Washington, DC: Catholic University of America Press, 1989.

Wells, John Edwin, ed. *The Owl and the Nightingale*. Boston: Heath, 1907.

Wilson, Peter Lamborn, and Nasrollah Pourjavady, trans. *The Drunken Universe: An Anthology of Persian Sufi Poetry*. Grand Rapids, MI: Phanes Press, 1987.

Woledge, Brian, ed. *The Penguin Book of French Verse*. 2 vols. Baltimore: Penguin, 1961.

Wulf, Maurice de. *The History of Mediaeval Philosophy*. London: Thomas Nelson and Sons, 1951.

Zesmer, David M. *Guide to English Literature*. 1961. New York: Barnes and Noble, 1966.

9
Medieval English Drama

Daniel Kline

DEFINITION AND CHARACTERISTICS

The study of medieval drama in England has traditionally focused on the three "M's": the mystery, morality, and miracle plays. The "mystery" plays, from the French *mystère* or "guild," include the great biblical "cycle" dramas of York, Chester, Towneley, and N-Town depicting Christian history from the Fall of the Angels to the final judgment of humanity. The "morality" plays, dramas like *The Castle of Perseverance*, *Wisdom*, and *Everyman*, teach moral and religious lessons through personified allegorical figures like the Virtues and Vices who struggle over the fate of the human soul. The "miracle" (or "saint") plays, like the Digby *Mary Magdalene*, the Croxton *Play of the Sacrament*, and St. George festivities, portray saints or other figures whose lives demonstrate the power of Christianity to convert the fallen or intercede in the lives of the faithful.

In this conventional view medieval drama has often been seen as an unsophisticated precursor to its more famous cousin, the theater of Shakespeare's time, and has usually suffered in the comparison. The perspective that drama in England evolved from the relatively rustic theater of the Middle Ages to the glory of Shakespeare and his contemporaries, convincingly put to rest by O.B. Hardison in *Christian Rite and Christian Drama in the Middle Ages*, still is embedded in the anthologies and course structure of many high-school and college classes. However, for many scholars, the salient terms for "medieval drama" have undergone a profound reassessment over the last two decades as our knowledge of the period has increased: What do we mean by "medieval," what counts as "drama," and what is the relationship between these forms of representation and the cultures in which they took shape? Such questions have unsettled any simplistic view of medieval drama and have brought new perspectives to the subject.

First, there is the question of historical era or "periodicity," as scholars put it: What counts as "medieval"? Traditionally speaking, the "medieval period" is considered to have ended, at least in England, in the late fifteenth or early sixteenth century with a series of profound historical and cultural changes: as early as the advent of the printing press (1470–1472) and the accession of Henry Tudor to the throne (1485), or as late as Henry VIII's break with the Roman Catholic church (1533) or Elizabeth I's ascent to the throne (1558). In other words, while the Middle Ages are commonly thought to have ended around 1500, the earliest version of *Everyman*, the quintessential morality play that represents the "medieval drama" in many college anthologies, is a print version from around 1525; the famous cycle plays were performed as late as the 1560s in Coventry and elsewhere; and the antiquarian manuscripts of the Chester cycle date from as late as the early seventeenth century. Clearly, "medieval" drama persisted after the Middle Ages are generally thought to have ended.

Second, there is the question of a typically "medieval" mode of production, an issue reinvigorated by modern productions of early English drama. Put on by local guilds, the ubiquitous trade and religious groups that provided social identity for the merchant and artisan classes in late medieval England, and produced once yearly in summertime on processional wagons and/or fixed platforms throughout town, the cycle plays combined religious ritual, social celebration, and civic spectacle. Performed in inn yards and town squares, the morality and saints' plays were rendered by small troupes of actors who plied their craft locally or traveled from town to town. Some plays, like *The Castle of Perseverance*, may have required a dedicated playing space, and others, like *Wisdom*, required large casts and elaborate special theatrical effects. Simply put, medieval drama encompassed a wide variety of production types that required anything from a few people in a traveling troupe to an entire town's dedicated and year-round production effort.

Third, there is the question of subject matter. While the great biblical dramas of York, Towneley, Chester, and N-Town are infused with both contemporary cultural concerns and social awareness, they depict Christian history in biblical episodes from the Fall of the Angels to the Last Judgment, including significant episodes from the Old Testament (particularly the Creation and the Fall of Humanity) and the New Testament (particularly the Nativity and the Passion of Christ). Unlike their sprawling, historically minded cyclic cousins, the morality plays are allegorical; characters depict abstract virtues and vices and are distinguished by their didactic impulse and religious subject matter. *Everyman* concerns the "final accounting" every person must make before God; *Mankind* details the perils of temptation for the human soul. Miracle plays appear to be a kind of hybrid in which the process of redemption is exemplified in a specific, often historical character; the Digby *Mary Magdalene*, a combination travelogue and miracle play, depicts the conversion and sanctification of a woman of ill repute into a biblical heroine. Beyond these, folk drama depicting Robin Hood or local saints was perhaps even more abundant than the cycle or morality plays.

Fourth, there is the question of the variety of medieval "dramatic" forms. Late medieval England reveled in a broad spectrum of theatrical representations: the preparation and pomp of a royal entry or the lord mayor's pageant in London; the sacred solemnity of the liturgy and the celebration of saints' days or religious processions; the annual rhythm of the church year with its sacred feasts and holy days; and a whole multitude of "ludi" or games, local carnivals and festivals, celebrations and competitions, and pageants and processions punctuating the flow of work and rest in towns and countryside. Simply put, the mystery, morality, and miracle plays are but three narrowly defined manifestations of what we know to be a wide variety of dramatic activity in late medieval and early modern England.

Fifth, there is the notion of cultural context; that is, what influence did local political, social, and cultural concerns have on the drama, what is the precise character of the communities in which these different dramatic forms arose, and what is the interrelationship of drama and community, of performance and community structure, identity, and economy? Why, for example, do the cycle plays seem to have taken hold in the north of England (York and Chester) while none appear in London, the ostensible financial and cultural center of the country? How (and why) does the drama of East Anglia differ from that in the Midlands or Cornwall? Medieval drama in England did not occur in a cultural vacuum but was integrally a part of the life of the community in its controversy as well as its commonality. Literary critics now also examine how specific local concerns, social movements, or other cultural practices impinge upon the drama.

Simply put, our understanding of medieval drama over the last twenty years has been reshaped in the academic turn toward cultural studies and literary theory. This reassessment has been so widespread that the generic designations traditionally given to these medieval plays have themselves been reevaluated.

THE EXAMPLE OF THE YORK CYCLE

Because they are social as well as aesthetic artifacts, the mystery plays offer fertile ground for the kind of broadly based cultural analysis I have been describing, and the York civic records provide an especially rich source of contemporary documentation surrounding the production of the York cycle. As we have it today, the manuscript of the York cycle contains forty-seven plays, though it is unlikely that this group of plays was ever performed exactly in this configuration; the manuscript itself evidences a number of revisions as particular pageants were added or fell into disfavor and guilds lost influence or gained economic power (Beadle). The earliest reference to a play performed in York comes from 1376, and the famous cycle was performed in various guises until the 1560s. Its origin is tied to the promulgation of the feast of Corpus Christi (1311), during which the consecrated Host was paraded through town in a solemn procession of clerical personages. It appears that in York the dramatic pageants displaced the eucharistic procession, and the process by which the cycle was produced is somewhat complex. The best evidence for understanding this process comes from two documents, the "Ordo Paginarum," the "order of pageants" from 1415, and the York "Register," a compilation of the individual guilds' play texts compiled sometime between 1463 and 1477. In short, the guilds sponsoring plays were required to maintain a play text and a pageant wagon and provide actors and costumes. Bad acting could elicit a fine, and the "Register" evidences some form of vetting in which the text of the play in the official "Register" was checked against performance.

The plays divide naturally between the Old Testament (plays I–XI) and New Testament (plays XII–XLVII) sections, and they might be further subdivided thematically as follows:

Manuscript Play Number	Title	Sponsoring Guild
Pageants I–VII: _Creation and Fall of Humanity_		
I	_The Fall of the Angels_	Barkers or Tanners
II	_The Creation_	Plasterers
III	_The Creation of Adam and Eve_	Cardmakers
IV	_Adam and Eve in Eden_	Fullers
V	_The Fall of Man_	Coopers
VI	_The Expulsion_	Armorers
VII	_Cain and Abel_	Glovers
Pageants VIII–XI: _The Old Covenant_		
VIII	_The Building of the Ark_	Shipwrights
IX	_The Flood_	Fishers and Mariners
X	_Abraham and Isaac_	Parchmentmakers and Bookbinders
XI	_Moses and Pharoah_	Hosiers
Pageants XII–XX: _Nativity and Childhood of Christ_		
XII	_The Annunciation and Visitation_	Spicers
XIII	_Joseph's Troubles about Mary_	Pewterers and Founders
XIV	_The Nativity_	Tilehatchers
XV	_The Shepherds_	Chandlers
XVI	_Herod/The Magi_	Masons/Goldsmiths
XVII	_The Purification_	Hatmakers, Masons, and Laborers
XVIII	_The Flight into Egypt_	Marshals
XIX	_The Slaughter of the Innocents_	Girdlers and Nailers
XX	_Christ and the Doctors_	Spurriers and Lorimers

Pageants XXI–XXIV: *Ministry of Christ*

XXI	*The Baptism*	Barbers
XXII	*The Temptation*	Smiths
XXIIA	*The Marriage at Cana*	Vintners
XXIII	*The Transfiguration*	Curriers
XXIIIA	*Jesus in the House of Simon the Leper*	Ironmongers
XXIV	*The Woman Taken in Adultery/The Raising of Lazarus*	Cappers

Pageants XXV–XXXVII: *Passion of Christ*

XXV	*The Entry into Jerusalem*	Skinners
XXVI	*The Conspiracy*	Cutlers
XXVII	*The Last Supper*	Bakers
XXVIII	*The Agony in the Garden and the Betrayal*	Cordwainers
XXIX	*Christ before Annas and Caiaphas*	Bowers and Fletchers
XXX	*Christ before Pilate I: Pilate's Wife's Dream*	Tapicers and Couchers
XXXI	*Christ before Herod*	Litsters
XXXII	*The Remorse of Judas*	Cooks and Waterleaders
XXXIII	*Christ before Pilate II: The Judgment*	Tilemakers
XXXIV	*The Road to Calvary*	Shearmen
XXXV	*The Crucifixion*	Pinners
XXXVI	*The Death of Christ*	Butchers
XXXVII	*The Harrowing of Hell*	Saddlers

Pageant XXXVIII–XLVII: *Resurrection and Judgment of Christ*

XXXVIII	*The Resurrection*	Carpenters
XXXIX	*Christ's Appearance to Mary Magdalene*	Winedrawers
XL	*The Supper at Emmaus*	Woolpackers and Woolbrokers
XLI	*The Incredulity of Thomas*	Scriveners
XLII	*The Ascension*	Tailors
XLIII	*Pentecost*	Potters
XLIV	*The Death of the Virgin*	Drapers
XLIVA	*The Funeral of the Virgin ("Fergus")*	
XLV	*The Assumption of the Virgin*	Weavers
XLVI	*The Coronation of the Virgin*	Hostelers

| XLVIA | *The Coronation of the Virgin* (late version) | Not assigned |
| XLVII | *The Last Judgment* | Mercers |

The entirety of the cycle drama, from before Creation to the Last Judgment, was called a "play," while the individual episodes were termed "pageants," and the individual episodes were produced and performed by separate civic groups, usually a trade or religious guild, which staged the pageant upon a "pageant wagon" at prearranged "stations" throughout the city (Twycross 39). In York stations were established at key points throughout town and were vendible commodities auctioned to the highest bidder, rather like skyboxes in a contemporary sports stadium. In effect, the clockwise processional route through the city followed the history of York's political struggles, religious investments, and economic exertions. Beginning in the westernmost section of town at the gates of the Holy Trinity Priory, the pageant wagons moved east on Micklegate across the river Ouse until they reached the center of town and then headed north along Coney Street, where they turned northeast at the Austin Friars' Common Hall. From the Common Hall the wagons then processed to the York Minster gates, where they probably turned to the southeast along Petergate and Collergate streets until they reached the Pavement, "an ancient broad space, the center of the city's commerce. From time out of mind it had been where traitors were executed, drunks pilloried, rogues whipped, kings and queens proclaimed, bulls baited" (Higgins 89). Put on by the Mercers, one of York's wealthiest and most prestigious guilds, the Last Judgment play was performed at the Pavement. In this final accounting of humanity, performed in the York city center by its most affluent guild, commercial interests, religious devotion, monetary concerns, social discipline, and political posturing all intersect and coalesce.

As civic celebration, religious commemoration, and economic investment, the York plays combined both piety and spectacle, and it is essential to read the plays on these different levels. One angle of entry into this metatextual aspect of the York cycle is the vocabulary of "work" in its multiple valences—the often-self-conscious language of making, production, labor, creation, toil, craft, effort, exertion and other such terms—for the religious work of individual pageants results in simultaneous cultural production. The plays stand as a monument to York's own efforts, their production as a reflection of the town's wealth, and their history as a testimony to the complicated interplay of spirituality and materiality. Stated simply, the York cycle displays a vernacular theology of work and reward in which the imitation of godly work yields divine blessing and sinful or false work results in condemnation.

As might be expected, the lexicon of work and reward dominates the first three plays of the York cycle: York I, The Fall of the Angels (Barkers), York II, The Creation (Plasterers), and York III, The Creation of Adam and Eve (Cardmakers). In York I Deus is a master craftsman, a "maker vnmade" (2, 9). The source of "lyfe and way vnto welth-wynnyng" (3), Deus creates "A place full of plenté to my plesyng at ply" (12). While "onely þe worthily warke of my [Deus's] wyll" (17), Lucifer confuses his status as a created being with God's eminence as creator (81). Because he pridefully aspires to the same status as God (91) and "wolde noght . . . worschip [the one] þat wroghte" him (135), Lucifer and his minions are cast out of heaven and into darkness. Speaking to the audience, in contrast, Deus intones that all who worship him shall dwell in heaven (137) and purposes, "Mankynde of moulde will I make" (141). The play ends with Deus dividing the night from the day—the work of the first day—and concludes with Deus's promise that "To all I sall wirke be þhe wysshyng" (157). For Deus, "my fyrste makyng" (145) is a "warke likes me right wele" (159).

York II continues the emphasis on Deus's "warkes" (27), and he calls all things into being through the next four days of creation. York III finds Deus surveying the created order:

> Thys werke is wroght now at my will,
>   Bu ȝet can I here no best see
> Þat acordys be kynde [nature] and skyll [reason],
>   And for my werke myght worschippe me. (13–16)

The intent of God's work is to foster worship from what is created. Work and worship are thus inextricably linked in the opening of the York cycle: God's work creates a world capable of worshipping him, and the work of humanity is to praise God and maintain the created order. God creates Adam and Eve "Eftyr my scape and my lyknes" (23) for two purposes: "To kepe þis warlde" (21) and "worschipe to me take" (24). Punning upon the term "skyll" or "reason" as both "rational faculty" and "basis of action," Deus answers Adam's query, "Qwate we sall do and whate to dewell?" (64):

> For þis skyl made I ȝow þis day,
>   My name to worschip ay-whare;
> Louys me, forþi, and louys me ay
>   For my makyng, I axe no mare. (65–68)

Work and worship are humanity's primary purposes, and both are an expression of love for God, even to the point that while Adam and Eve are in the Garden of Eden, their work is a form of loving worship of the one who created them. Unlike Lucifer, Adam and Eve recognize their position as created beings who owe God reverence as their maker, so the creation of humanity reestablishes the divine order disturbed by the Fall of the Angels, at least initially.

The importance of work shifts from the divine realm to the human in the balance of the Old Testament plays in the York cycle, while the relationship of work to worship also is transformed. The Fall of Man (York V) is depicted as a perversion of divine making. Satan's "trauayle were wele sette" to betray

God's work (19–20) and to promise Eve "worshippe and a gret wynnynge" (68) for eating the forbidden fruit. After tasting the prohibited morsel, Adam castigates his partner, "Þis werke, Eue, has þou wroght, / And made þis bad bargayne" (119–20). Work no longer leads to worship but to exchange, and hierarchy (figured as reciprocity) gives way to negotiation (figured as competition). When Dominus asks the primeval couple, "Þis werke hwy hast þou wrought?" (141), their work of sin results in the primordial division of labor into male production and female (re)production: for both Adam and Eve, "In erhte þan sall ye wete and swywnke, / And trauayle for youre foode" 161–62), while for Eve, "Trauell herto shalle þou ta, / Thy barnes to bere with mekill wa-" (VI.70–71). The divisive results of sinful work further divide the originary family when Cayme (Cain), the farmer, kills Abell, the hunter. The pious Abell's "warkes . . . / fulfille thy [God's] commandment" (VII.38–39); the verbally abusive Cayme "wille wyrke euen as I will" (53), and Abell's tithe ("teynde" or tenth, 58) seems foolish to his brother: "Ya, deuell, methynkeþ þat werke were waste, / That he vs gaffe geffe hym agayne / To se" (60–62). As a result of his failure to share the results of his labor either with God or with his family, Cayme's labor literally will be fruitless, for God's curse is that "Yff þou wolde tylll þe erthe so rounde / No frute to þe þer shalle be fonne" (109–10). Sinfulness is equated to nonproduction. Cayme, who hoards what he produces for himself alone, thinks it foolish to return to God what God has given him and is thus condemned to nonproductivity, while Abell's tithe—the return of at least a portion of what God has bestowed upon him—rehabilitates the fallenness of human labor and reestablishes the relationship of work and worship. Proper work—work that is spiritually directed and socially responsible—is a form of worship.

The redemptive potential of labor in the Old Testament sequence is extended most fully in York VIII, The Building of the Ark. In the opening stanzas Deus recapitulates the action from Creation to the dramatic present in terms of the good work of Creation over against the sinful work of humanity. Whereas Deus "wrought þis world so wyde" (1), including the entire natural order and the first couple, God must now "repente / My werke I wroght so wele and trewe" (17–18) because humanity "hays . . . wroght so woefully / And synne is nowe reynand so ryffe" (13–14). God purposes to "wirke þis werke I will al newe" (24) by flooding the earth and saving only Noah and his family. Much in the same way that Abell's tithe both rehabilitates labor and worships God, so Noah's work is salvific, and Noah is a colaborer with God in the preservation of humanity. Deus states, "I wyll þou wyrke withouwten weyne / A warke to saffe þiselfe wythall" (35–36), for

> A shippe I will haue wroght in hye;
> All-yf þou can litill skyll,
> Take it in hande, for helpe sall I. (46–48)

Then God, the master craftsman (150), gives Noah detailed instructions for building the ark (which double as handy stage directions), detailing the dimensions of the ship, the quantities of material, and the quality of workmanship (69–88), and Noah follows the instructions explicitly: "þus schall I wyrke . . . / Thurgh techyng of God, maistir myne" (103–4). Deus created humanity and the animals that Noah now will save through "þis werke" (148) of the ark.

The York Old Testament sequence consistently portrays godly figures as those who "work" after God's "will," those whose work is in response to God—Abell, Noah, and finally Abraham, "For als God comaunded so wirke will we, / Vntill his tales vs take hede" (X.127–28). The Abraham and Isaac play (York X) is an especially crucial play in the overall trajectory of the cycle, for it explicitly links specific Old Testament episodes to the life and death of Jesus in the New Testament plays. These connections are made through "typology" or "figural" correspondences. Isaac is thus a "type" of Christ, and the binding of Isaac in the Old Testament prefigures the Crucifixion of Jesus in the New Testament. With its emphasis on obedience, the Noah play foreshadows Jesus' Baptism, and its depiction of God's judgment prefigures the Last Judgment play. Thus the reinvocation of literary themes and verbal echoes and parallels in staging and costume provide a sense of internal coherence within the York cycle as a whole.

Nonetheless, even though the dramatic focus has shifted to New Testament events, the York cycle maintains its emphasis on the notion of "work" in its various forms and on the relationship of labor, making, and production either to reverence and worship or sin and evil. The New Testament portion of the York cycle begins with the Annunciation and Visitation (York XII), put on by the Spicers. The pageant opens with a long didactic speech by a "Doctour" who recalls "Howe man was made withouten mysse" (XII.2) and then recounts the Old Testament figures who foretold (Amos, David, Joel) or prefigured (Abraham and Isaac) the birth of Jesus from a "mayden full mylde" (22). Paralleling God's earlier work of creation, these "forme-faders" or former fathers (110) were witness to "þis werke grete" of how within Mary "one [was] to be knytte, / Godhed, maydenhed, and manne" (107–8).

As a transitional moment between the Old and New Testament portions of the York cycle, the Annunciation and Visitation focuses attention upon Mary's christological work in giving birth to Jesus. The play immediately following, Joseph's Troubles about Mary (York XIII), contrasts Elizabeth's acceptance of Mary's pregnancy with Joseph's skepticism. Enacting a favorite medieval trope, the conflict between youth and age—particularly the problems arising when older men marry younger women—the aged Joseph thinks himself cuckolded. In York XII Mary at first protests against the Angel's declaration that she is pregnant because she knows that she has not participated in any "werkis wilde / In chastité I haue ben ay [always]" (175–76). In York XIII the crotchety old Joseph, prefigured by henpecked Noah, adopts the language of work to describe his troubles:

Hir werkis me wyrkis my wonges to wete;
    I am begiled-how, wate I noȝt.
My ȝonge wife is with childe full grete
    Þat makes me nowe sorowe vnsoght. (41–44)

The York cycle represents Mary as an exemplary worker, though one whose "work" seems ambiguous at times. Joseph insists that Mary must have been intimate with another man, and that her inappropriate sexual "work" has worked to deceive him. Finally, an angel appears to Joseph in a dream and corrects Joseph's misconception, and Joseph and Mary journey to Bethlehem. More significant, however, is that Jesus' birth is not laborious for Mary—she suffers no travail at his delivery, thus reversing Eve's curse to suffer in childbirth. In the brief moment Joseph goes to find light for the cattle stall, Jesus' birth is simple, silent, and sudden. Joseph is surprised by the peacefulness of the birth, and Mary reconfirms the sinlessness of Jesus' conception and the simplicity of his birth before the Magi in York XVI, Herod/The Magi:

For I consayued my sone sartayne
    Wothouten miss of man in mynde,
And bare hym here withouten payne,
    Where women are wonte to by pynyd. (347–350)

Mary's uniquely virginal status has reversed the punishment meted out to women in childbirth as a result of Eve's sin, and unlike many births in the late medieval period, this birth is assured, uncomplicated, free of hazard for mother and baby.

In honor of Jesus' miraculous conception and prophesied birth, contemporary Yorkshire shepherds bring gifts to the divine cradle as do the biblical Magi, anachronistically brought together at the Nativity. More importantly for the theology of work, worship, and reward in the York cycle, however, the gift givers represent the entire range of laborers in York, while their gifts represent both the rustic and refined, the high and the low, of agricultural, craft, and mercantile production in the late medieval city. On one hand, the poverty-stricken medieval shepherds in York XV, The Shepherds, bring "a slyke [glossy] harnays / [and] A baren-broche by a belle of tynne" (102–3), "two cobill notis [hazel nuts] vppon a bande" (112), and "an horne spone" (124). On the other, the wealthy Magi bring the traditional "golde," "Insens," and "mirre" (XVI.319–342), costly gifts from "oure tresurry" (302), no doubt extravagantly prepared by the Goldsmiths who put on the Herod / The Magi pageant. The York cycle thus reinforces the notion that no work is either too extravagant or too lowly to be dedicated to God.

The theology of work and worship in the York cycle develops a further contrast between the two sets of gift givers in that the shepherds seek individual blessing from the infant savior, while the Magi more formally and publicly make their offering. As he presents his "harnys," I Pastor asks that "whenne ȝe shall welde all / Gud sonne, forgete noȝt me" (XV.105–6); II Pastor gives the simple hazel nuts and beseeches "whan ȝe sall be lorde in lande / . . . forgete me noght" (115–116); and with his hand-crafted spoon, III Pastor asks, "Nowe loke on me, my lorde dere" (120). In contrast to the simple gifts and individual—almost private—blessings of the shepherds, the Magi create a formidable public spectacle, with each offering his elaborate gifts in the midst of an equally ornate twelve-line "Hayll" lyric. I Rex asks that "þou marc us þi men and make vs in mynde" (XVI.313); II Rex declares "þat [Christ] shall saue vs of synne þat oure syris had" (324); and III Rex prophesies that "For our boote shall þou be bounden and bett" (334). The simple shift from the shepherds' "I" to the kings' "our" is evocative of York's social stratification based upon one's status as either "foreigner" or "freeman"—the former indicating an origin outside the *civitas* with few statutory rights and the latter indicating full citizenship from membership in a craft or religious guild.

The topos of the faithful worker or plowman is a commonplace in late medieval England. The allegorical dream vision *Piers Plowman* is built around the image. In the well-known morality play *Everyman* the protagonist is summoned by Death to make an "accounting" of his life, but his ledger of good works is empty. *Mankind*, another less well known and less reverent morality play, has at its heart the temptation of Mankind, representative of all humanity, to sloth. Nought, New Guise, and Nowadays tempt Mankind away from the "goode werkys" (25) proffered by Mercy, and under the guidance of Myscheff and Titivillus, they trick Mankind into believing that he is unable to plow the ground and plant his corn:

> Thys londe ys so harde yt makyth wnlusty and yrke.
> I xall sow my corn at winter and lett Gode werke.
> Alasse, my corn ys lost! Here ys a foull werke!
>   I se well by tyllynge lytyll xall I wyn.
> Here I gyff wppe my spade for now and for euer. (545–549)

Mankind's inability to be productive leads to accusations of sloth and unworthiness from Titivillus. The devilish trio put Mankind to trial, where he vows to take on a life of crime, but ultimately, in a speech directed at Mankind and the audience, Mercy convinces Mankind that he is not beyond redemption:

> Man onkyndé, whereuer þou be! Fall all þis world was not aprehensyble
>   To discharge þin orygynall offence, thraldam and captyuyte,
> Tyll Godys own welbelouyde son was obedience and passyble.
>   Euery droppe of hys bloode was schede to purge þin iniquite. (742–745)

As depicted in the Nativity sequence, Jesus, a product of both humanity and divinity, is God's greatest work; his purposeful labor is to redeem humanity; and much of the New Testament portion of the York cycle shows how Jesus' divine work collides with the satanic work of those who conspire against him in the events leading to the Crucifixion. As early as York XIX, The Slaughter of the Innocents, Herod's attempt to kill his infant rival is figured as decidedly unchivalric "werke" for Herod's knights: "To dede they must be brought, / Knave-childre, lesse and more" (185–86), and in return the knights are "worthy to haue rewarde" (254). The youthful Jesus in York XX, Christ and the Doctors, lectures the learned clerics in the meaning of the greatest commandment, and when Joseph and Mary arrive to take him back to Bethlehem, Jesus famously wonders at their distress at having left him behind in Jerusalem:

> Wherto shulde ȝe seke me soo?
>   Ofte tymes it hase ben tolde you till,
> My fadir werkis, for wele or woo,
>   Thus am I sent for to fulfill. (257–260)

The youthful Jesus' cryptic comment about his "father's work" points, of course, to God rather than to Joseph, and after this point Joseph disappears from the cycle as Jesus takes up his divine mission. Much in the same way, then, that Jesus works the will of his heavenly father, so too Jesus' disciples follow Jesus' example in their own spiritual vocation, as Johannes, John the Disciple, affirms in York XXIII, The Transfiguration: "Lorde, we will wirke thy will / Allway with trewe entent" (45–46), while Jesus' opponents are known by their "mysdedis" (York XXIV, The Woman Taken in Adultery/The Raising of Lazarus, 55).

According to the Gospels, Jesus' Passion begins when he journeys to Jerusalem; it is precisely in York XXV, The Entry into Jerusalem, that the city of York itself self-consciously becomes the stage upon which this prelude to salvation history is played out in civic celebration. On one hand, York XXV emulates the liturgical procession of Corpus Christi, in which the York clergy entered the city carrying the eucharistic Host. On the other, the play reflects the civic processional celebrations for which York was well known and with which, for example, York welcomed Henry VII in 1486. In the words of Martin Stevens,

The prescribed route of the royal entry processional was, interestingly, very much the same as that of the Corpus Christi play, and when, therefore, Jesus is greeted in the course of the Skinners' pageant with the accustomed royal entry ceremony as the King of Kings in the streets of York, the spectators saw him take possession of their city much as they had secular kings and queens. There was no more powerful a link to be found between present-day York and historic Jerusalem than this dramatic setting provided. (*Four Middle English Mystery Cycles* 52)

IV Burgensis, representing the people of Jerusalem to the York audience and the York civic hierarchy to itself, thus affirms, "Oure kyng is he—þat is no lesse — / Oure awne law to it cordis will" (225–226). In effect, the work of the cycle is to bring contemporary York into salvation history, and the civic contentiousness that marked York's internal politics is both reflected in the dramatized negotiations over Christ's fate in the cycle and subsumed in the communal effort to produce the Corpus Christi pageants. Immediately upon Jesus' arrival in town, however, the political forces of Pilate and Herod, in conjunction with the religious establishment, figured as Annas, Caiaphas, and Judas, conspire to eliminate this new rival to their power. Pilate tells Judas in decidedly monetary terms to "Bidde furthe thy bargayne" in betrayal of Jesus (York XXVI, The Conspiracy 227). In York XXVIII, The Agony in the Garden and the Betrayal, Jesus intones as he sweats "both watir and bloode" (50) that he might bypass his fate "if þou se it may noght, / Be it worthely wrought" (59–60). Finally, it is for his works that Jesus is condemned: "With dole vnto ded þei did hym / For his wise werkis þat he wroght þame" (York XL, The Supper at Emmaus, 61–62).

The worthy work of Jesus is, of course, his Passion, and the imagery of work, labor, and production reaches its ironic zenith in the well-known York Crucifixion play (York XXXV), scripted by the so-called York Realist. In a masterpiece of black comedy the four soldiers charged with crucifying Jesus busily and sweatily go about their gruesome task, boisterously cajoling one another to work harder and casually commenting upon the difficulties of their task. Jesus' body does not quite fit the cross, it seems ("Owe, þis werke is all vnmeete — / This boring must all be amende," 127–28), so as one soldier takes Jesus' right hand, the other his left, the third stretches out his arm, and the fourth holds his head still; the procedure is repeated for Jesus' legs; all the while the soldiers complain about their job and narrate its grisly details. It is for Jesus to call attention to the spiritual valence of their malicious work:

> What þei wirke wotte þai noght;
>   Therfore, my fadir, I craue,
> Latte neuere þer synnys be sought,
>   But see þer saules to saue. (261–264)

The contrast between "spiritual" and "physical" labor here is as striking as it is ironic. The soldiers going about the tedious, messy work of crucifying a prisoner are oblivious to the subject of their brutal ministrations; at the same time, their cruel exertions are necessary for the salvation of humanity; their own physically abusive labor ultimately yields their own salvation. Addressing his mother from the cross in the following play, The Death of Christ (York XXXVI), Jesus reminds her in words reminiscent of the Christ and the Doctors play:

> þou woman, do way thy wepyng,
>   For me may þou nothyng amend.

My fadirs wille to be werkyng,
   For mankynde my body I bende. (144–47)

Here the youthful Jesus' cryptic words in the temple are given their eschatological completion, for the body to which Mary gave birth without labor becomes the vehicle for the mightiest physical exertion and spiritual effort, the
crucifixion, death, and ultimately resurrection of Jesus. Of all the cycles, York,
recognizing Mary's colabor in the work of salvation, includes a series of plays
between the Ascension and the Last Judgment devoted to the Virgin. In York
XLV, The Assumption of the Virgin, Mary comforts the disciples by saying
that whoever prays to her will receive succor, for no matter

If he synke or swete in welte or in swoune.
   I schall sewe to my souerayne sone for to say me
      He schall graunte þame þer grace.
         Be it manne in his mourning
         Or wommane in childinge,
         All þes to be helpinge. (194–199)

Woman's work, embodied in childbearing, and men's labor, the grunt and sweat
of the fields, are both put under the purview of Mary's domestic mediation, for
she sits beside her son in heaven in intercession and wisdom. In a replication
of the Holy Family after the episode of Christ and the Doctors, Joseph has
disappeared from the scene while God the father, Mary, and Jesus form a re-
configured domestic unit—Mary, not Joseph, intervenes for all workers, male
and female, while Jesus looks to the spiritual lives of all persons.

Nonetheless, Jesus' work of salvation is both spiritual and material, for the
physical labor—the trauma of torture and exertion of execution—of Jesus' Passion enables his spiritual work in the balance of the cycle, particularly the Harrowing of Hell (York XXXVII), the Resurrection (York XXXVIII), and the Last
Judgment (York XLVII). Bringing the typological connections between the Old
and New Testament to completion, the Harrowing of Hell depicts Jesus storming
the gates of hell to redeem the faithful Old Testament figures who looked forward to the coming Savior or prophesied his advent. In the words of Jesus:

And so I schall þat steede restore
   For whilke þe feende fell for synne,
Þare schalle mankynde wonne euermore
   In blisse þat schalle neuere blynne.
All þat in werke my werkemen were,
   Owte of thare woo I wol þame wynne (13–18)

Whether Old Testament or New, in ancient Palestine or contemporary York,
faithful followers are known by their godly works, deeds, actions, and labor;
they are God's "workmen." The sign of Jesus' action to free the souls from

hell—"all thes dedis" (24)—is a symbolic light, presumably a torch. Adam and Eve, Isaiah, Symeon, John the Baptist, and Moses all testify to the coming of this light, and while the devil and his minions panic over the growing joy in hell ("Þis werke is werse þanne euere it was" [200], cries Belsabub), Jesus and Satan debate Jesus' legal right to set the prisoners free. Satan contends, "And here werkis þou all wrang" (264), but Jesus contends:

> I wirk noght wrang, þat shal pow witte,
>   If I my men fro woo will wynne.
> Mi prophetis playnly prechid it,
>   All þis note þat nowe begynne. (265–268)

The sanctification of human labor through Jesus' bodily Passion therefore translates into the criterion for the Last Judgment: those who honor God and perform good deeds have their evil doings overlooked, while those who ignore God and sin are judged according to their evil doing. Unlike many of the York New Testament plays, the Mercers' Last Judgment pageant begins with lengthy and magisterial disquisition by Deus, echoing the cycle's opening plays, who links this final apocalyptic moment of "doom" or judgment to the originary instant of sinless creation:

> First when I þis worlde hadde wroght—
>   Wode and wynde and wateris wan,
> And all-kynne thing þat now is oght—
>   Fulle wele meþoght þat I did þanne. (XLVII.1–4)

However, now grieving that he created the cosmos (8), Deus's opening speech recapitulates the theology of Creation, Jesus' work of salvation, and the necessity for judgment of human sin. The "blissid children" (75) are sent to the right side, to paradise, and to "life in lykinge schal ʒe lende" (368), while the evil are sent into damnation at God's left hand. The righteous are known by their works of mercy in feeding the hungry, clothing the naked, and comforting the oppressed (277–300), while the sinful never recognized the necessity for such works of compassion (301–8). The evil spirits (I Anima Mala and II Anima Mala) testify that "Oure wikkid werkis may we not hid, / But on our bakkis vs muste þem bere" (154–55), while the good spirits "Ne suffir vs neuere to fendis to be thrall" (111). In other words, even the afterlife is defined by work or its cessation. The sinful labor under the burden of their sins, while the redeemed are delivered from slavery and the thralldom imposed after the Fall of Humanity in the Garden of Eden.

In his final stanza—and in the final lines of the York cycle—Deus punctuates the necessity of physical work in the economy of salvation, for "All worldly wightis þat I haue wroght, / Aftir þer werkis haue nowe wonnyng" (374–75). In a single moment at the end of the final pageant of the York cycle, Deus's speech gestures at once toward the soul's final dispensation according to its spiritual deeds and toward York's physical environment as the townsfolk, like the souls in judgment, return to their "wonnyng" or dwellings.

HISTORY OF CRITICISM

Editions

Although it was preceded by important antiquarian-critics like Thomas Sharp, whose 1825 *A Dissertation on the Pageants or Dramatic Mysteries Anciently Performed at Coventry* is still an important source of information, the modern study of medieval drama could be said to begin with E.K. Chambers. Along with the textual work of W.W. Greg on the relationships between the cycle plays and the Early English Text Society's (EETS) initial critical editions of the York (Toulmin Smith), Towneley (England and Pollard), *Ludus Coventriae* (or N-Town [Block]), and Chester plays (author), E.K. Chambers sought to release medieval drama from the veil of obscurity and situate it in its historical context. Working under the evolutionary assumption that Latin liturgical drama moved from the sanctuary into the church courtyard and developed into the late medieval processional form of the mystery play, out of which came the glories of the Elizabethan stage, Chambers sought to identify the dramatic elements in liturgical and other manuscripts, which he then excerpted and published in *The Mediaeval Stage* (1903). Karl Young's encyclopedic *The Drama of the Medieval Church* (1933) likewise compiled dramatic records from a variety of sources. Although the legitimacy of Chamber's broadly anthropological method has been questioned recently, particularly his penchant for excising the "dramatic" elements from their manuscript contexts, *The Mediaeval Stage* still showcases a great wealth of material.

Since the Early English Text Society fostered the production of critical editions of three major cycles at the end of the nineteenth century by distinguished scholars—Lucy Toulmin Smith (York, 1885), George England and Alfred Pollard (Towneley, 1897), and Katherine S. Block (*Ludus Coventriae*)—new editions of all the major texts have been produced by Richard Beadle (York, 1982), R. M. Lumiansky and David Mills (Chester, 2 vols., 1974–1986), Stephen Spector (N-Town, 2 vols., 1991), and Martin Stevens and A.C. Cawley (Towneley, 2 vols., 1994). In addition, important editions of particular plays, groups of related plays, or individual manuscripts have come from Peter Meredith (the *Mary Play* and *Passion Play* from the N-Town manuscript); Hardin Craig (Coventry); A.C. Cawley (*The Wakefield Pageants in the Towneley Cycle*); Mark Eccles (Macro); Donald C. Baker, John L. Murphy, and Louis B. Hall, Jr. (Digby); and Norman Davis (noncycle plays and fragments). Students of medieval drama have also been well served by a series of anthologies, most notably David Bevington's *Medieval Drama* (1975), which catalogs Latin liturgical drama (*Quem Quaeritis*) and important continental texts, as well as a synthetic cycle and morality and saints' plays in English. Peter Happé's Penguin classic text *English Mystery Plays* (1975) provided an inexpensive classroom text but has unfortunately gone out of print. Oxford University Press produced a modernized version of select York plays edited by Beadle and Fergeson, and Blackwell's major anthology *English Medieval Drama* (1997) seeks to replace Bevington's aging edition.

In conjunction with updated primary texts, the study of medieval drama has benefited immensely by the sometimes-controversial project sponsored by the University of Toronto Centre for Research in Early English Drama, Records of Early English Drama (REED). The ambitious REED project's stated aim is "to locate, transcribe, and edit all surviving documentary evidence of drama, minstrelsy, and public ceremonial in England before 1642," including "the historical MSS that provide external evidence of drama, secular music, and other communal entertainment and ceremony from the Middle Ages until 1642, when the Puritans closed the London theatres" (REED Web site). Beginning with the publication of York in 1979 through Sussex in 2000, REED has published twenty studies, and another thirty are currently in the works. The massive REED volumes provide scholars worldwide with the documentary evidence once limited to English manuscript archives, facilitating the understanding of early English drama in its cultural context.

Monographs

What has made REED controversial for some scholars is the question of definition: What kind of external documentation should be granted the status of evidence? What is the dividing line between "entertainment" and "nonentertainment"? While older scholars confidently asserted such categorical differences, the division between the "dramatic" and "nondramatic" in medieval culture is not as clear cut as earlier critics may have assumed, in light of some recent studies. Building upon the textual foundation laid by Chambers and others, the work of three scholars stands out in the period before midcentury: H.C. Gardiner's discussion of the suppression of the mystery plays in the last quarter of the sixteenth century, A.P. Rossiter's discussion of "Gothic" drama and its characteristics, and F.M. Salter's intensive work on textual history and cultural context of the Chester cycle. In *Mysteries' End: An Investigation of the Last Days of the Medieval Religious Stage* (1946) Gardiner's primary contribution was to assert that the cycle drama was suppressed not because it was no longer popular but because it was viewed with suspicion as overly "Catholic" by Protestant authorities. Rossiter's *English Drama from Early Times to the Elizabethans* (1950) focused upon the seemingly incongruous juxtaposition of black and sometimes bawdy humor with the high moral and religious significance of the plays' content, a clash he termed the heart of medieval "Gothic" drama. In his study of the Chester plays, *Mediaeval Drama in Chester* (1955), F.M. Salter combined a historian's archival sensibility, a literary critic's aesthetic sense, a churchman's sense of religious piety, and a theater critic's sense of the dynamics of performance. He saw clearly that the Chester plays were complex cultural artifacts combining civic, religious, dramatic, and literary concerns. While the combination of burlesque content and pious intent of Rossiter's "Gothic" drama has served as the starting point for many later critics, Salter's extensive investigations into the relationship of the Chester cycle to the civic records set the tone for many later readings of not only the Chester cycle in particular but also of medieval drama in general.

Embracing a literary formalism that asserted the autonomy of the poetic text and the organic unity of literary productions, critics influenced by New Criticism through midcentury began to investigate the cycle plays not simply as scattered individual plays but as unified wholes with specific artistic effects and cultural purposes, and appreciation for medieval drama entered a new phase with studies by Rosemary Woolf and, in particular, V.A. Kolve. Woolf's *The English Mystery Plays* (1972) takes as its organizing principle a generic cycle of plays from before Creation to the Last Judgment, and in dividing the plays into discrete episodes, Prophets' Plays, for example, or Nativity Plays, she compares the English plays with one another and to selected continental plays to divine both the distinctiveness of the English material and the didactic emphases of the individual cycles. Kolve's *The Play Called Corpus Christi* (1966) is in many ways a pivotal study in the criticism of medieval drama, for Kolve broadened the critical focus to include culturally informed audience analysis. By reading the plays in light of non-dramatic religious texts, Kolve attempted to elucidate the essential religious contribution of the plays. The medieval theater, the "play," Kolve concluded, embodied a salvific "game": "The particular order that this game sought to create was not only aesthetic, but historically true: it sought to pattern human experience, to give to the history of men an order that would reveal its meaning" (20). The Corpus Christi drama transcended the simply didactic to create a mythic space within "real life" wherein an audience not only witnessed but also experienced the religious truths presented in the drama. More than any critic before or since, Kolve considered the generic form of the cycle plays as integral to their ultimate meaning.

Once Kolve had established the "cycle" as a generic form with specific characteristics, a conclusion that has recently been questioned, other critics set about defining and exploring the particular emphases of the different extant cycles. John Gardner (*The Construction of the Wakefield Cycle* [1974]) and Jeffrey Helterman (*Symbolic Action in the Plays of the Wakefield Master* [1981]) considered the plays of the Towneley manuscript generally attributed to the Wakefield Master, both scholars focusing on the Wakefield Master's role as reviser of the Towneley plays. For Gardner, the Wakefield Master brought unity to "a hodgepodge of literary texts" by "typologizing Old Testament figures" in "realism-based allegory" and depicting evil as satanic, while remaining true to the source materials and varying the dramatic rhythm of the episodes (133–35). For Helterman, the Wakefield Master's genius rests in his ability to bring a brisk realism to the typological figures in the plays he reworked and to dramatize through comedy "the absurd logic of Christianity [that] the joke can be true. The child *is* a lamb as the parody is transformed into a symbol" (15, emphasis Helterman's). Peter Travis's *Dramatic Design in the Chester Cycle* (1982) traces the Chester cycle's historical development and the dramatic emphases of its "paginae" or groups of plays, concluding that the cycle utilizes the twelve articles of the Apostles' Creed as an organizing principle. He writes that while "Chester is obviously more than a Creed play in disguise," this creedal impulse "intensifies Chester's consistent emphasis upon the need to recognize the power and authority of Christ's truth" (216). Clifford Davidson's *From Creation to Doom: The York Cycle of Mystery Plays* (1984) integrated medieval music and the visual arts (iconography, manuscript illumination, and stained glass) into a reading of the York cycle, tapping new sources of evidence to be considered in the study of medieval drama. These cycle-specific studies reached their zenith in Martin Stevens's finely nuanced *Four Middle English Mystery Cycles: Textual, Contextual, and Critical Interpretations* (1987). Considering the cycles in their historical and manuscript contexts, Stevens argued that each is a unified artistic product with a discernible theological center consonant with the cultural conditions of its composition and supposed performance.

Critical Anthologies

The study of early English drama, as many now choose to term the traditionally named "medieval drama," has also been furthered by a small number of landmark critical anthologies. The first of these, Jerome Taylor and Alan H. Nelson's *Medieval English Drama: Essays Critical and Contextual* (1972), took as its organizing principle the rejection of the view that all medieval drama is merely an unsophisticated precursor to the drama of the English Renaissance. Jerome Taylor remarks in the introductory essay that like Polonius in *Hamlet*, "Collectively and uncritically taken, modern scholarship similarly gives one the impression that medieval drama is a ritual-dramatical-tragical-comical mystery stretching upwards into the morality play; at the same time it seems to present medieval drama as a technically undramatic and disjointed thing . . . indivisible and unlimited" (2). Offering both reprinted and original articles, *Medieval English Drama* viewed the medieval dramas as artifacts of particular cultural moments and social pressures rather than simple religious rituals and featured eighteen studies, including those by Mary H. Marshall ("Aesthetic Values of the Liturgical Drama"), William L. Smoldon ("The Melodies of the Medieval Church Dramas and Their Significance"), Alan H. Nelson ("Some Configurations of Staging in Medieval English Drama"), and Hans-Jürgen Diller ("The Craftsmanship of the Wakefield Master"). The next year Stratford-upon-Avon Studies issued *Medieval Drama*, edited by Neville Denny (1973). Taking a formalist and thematic approach to the plays, *Medieval Drama* featured ten articles, including David Bevington's "Popular and Courtly Traditions on the Early Tudor Stage," Arnold Williams's "The Comic in the Cycles," and T.W. Craik's "Violence in the English Miracle Plays."

These important foundational anthologies of studies were followed in the 1980s and 1990s by a wealth of critical commentary and scholarly erudition that continued to call into question the historical boundary between the "medieval period" and the Renaissance. Clifford Davidson has collected a number of articles from *Comparative Drama*, one of the most important venues for critical work in medieval drama, and published two collections (1982 and 1991) on *The Drama of the Middle Ages: Comparative and Critical Essays*, and 1989 saw the publication of Marianne Briscoe and John Coldewey's important *Contexts for Early English Drama*. Two important collections have further subverted the artificial separation between the Middle Ages and the Renaissance and have embraced the new literary-theoretical paradigms of the last twenty-five years. John D. Cox and David Scott Kastan argue in the introduction to *A New History of Early English Drama* (1997) that new literary theories undermine the presuppositions that govern and categories that structure conventional literary study; as a result, "[l]iterary texts are now understood not merely as exclusive sources but as contested sites of meaning" (1), for "[d]rama is always radically collaborative, both on stage and in print, and this volume seeks to restore the collaborative sense of early English dramatic activity by focusing on the conditions and constraints of playmaking, networks of dependency, both discursive and institutional, that motivated and sustained it" (2). The twenty-five new articles in *A New History* are organized in a way that reflects new theoretical preoccupations: "Part I: Early English Drama and Physical Space" covers staging in church, university, household, street and marketplace, and theater; "Part II: Early English Drama and Social Space" looks at various cultural contexts, including religious, civic, domestic, court, literary, and popular cultures; "Part III: Early English Drama and Conditions of Performance and Publication" analyzes the conditions of touring, costuming, censorship, audiences, acting style, playwriting and revision, patronage, and manuscript and printing. Finally, the cultural-studies approach, which problematizes any easy division between "medieval" and "Renaissance" drama and recognizes the emergence of medieval English drama as a result of particular cultural forces rather than a gradual evolution from the liturgy, has been canonized, in effect, by *The Cambridge History of Medieval English Literature* (1999). In "From Ungodly Ludi to Sacred Play," Lawrence M. Clopper argues that in England "[i]t is the clergy's inability to control lay activities that allows an opening for dramatization of vernacular biblical texts, for drama appears in those cities and towns where the laity have political dominance or equality" (747). In other words, vernacular drama in medieval England is the result of a complex series of cultural negotiations in which the interests of the local church authorities are pitted against broader civic ambitions, and the didactic and reforming impulses of the clergy are filtered through the written texts underlying the drama and the innovations of play authors, players, and producers. A final collection worthy of mention is the outstanding *Cambridge Companion to Medieval English Theatre* (1994), a critical introduction to medieval theater in all its forms suitable for the introductory student.

Morality Plays

With the increased attention to the cycle drama in the last half of the twentieth century, other genres of medieval drama have likewise become objects of intense scholarly attention, not the least of which are the English morality plays. The year 1975 saw the publication of two important works, Stanley J. Kahrl's *Traditions of Medieval English Drama* and Robert A. Potter's *The English Morality Play: Origins, History, and Influence of a Dramatic Tradition*. Kahrl's approach is largely comparative, and he contrasts the major forms of fifteenth- and sixteenth-century playacting in terms of their staging, dramatic impulses, and characterological and thematic emphases. Potter's treatise examines "The Idea of the Morality Play," the title of his first chapter, from the medieval period through its manifestations in Tudor and Elizabethan forms, including continental plays and the "rediscovery" and modern appropriations of, particularly, *Everyman* since the eighteenth century. T.W. Craik's *The Tudor Interlude* (1967) was the first to acknowledge this form critically, and Glynne Wickham's *Early English Stages, 1300 to 1660*, volume 1 (1959) anticipates Kahrl and Potter. It is especially in the study of the morality-play tradition that the lines between "medieval" and "Renaissance" become blurred, and David Bevington's important work should be credited for initiating much of the current interest in the transitional period prior to the flowering of Elizabethan drama. His 1962 study *From Mankind to Marlowe* was the first major study to examine Tudor drama as it developed from school plays and the interlude form through the moralistic productions of Bale and Skelton into the complex dramaturgy of Marlowe.

New Approaches

The combination of new critical editions, increased attention to the historical and cultural contexts of the plays, and the incorporation of new critical methodologies has given rise to the current generation of theoretically sophisticated and historically grounded studies. Important works like Gail McMurry Gibson's *Theater of Devotion: East Anglian Drama and Society in the Late Middle Ages* (1989) examine performance in light of local customs, practices, and history. Others like Jody Enders's *Rhetoric and the Origins of Medieval Drama* (1992) or her *Medieval Theater of Cruelty: Rhetoric, Memory, Violence* (1999) examine drama through particular discursive traditions, like classical and medieval rhetoric and education, or specific social practices, like law and the penal system. Claire Sponsler looks at all types of textual production through a Foucauldian lens in *Drama and Resistance: Bodies, Goods, and Theatricality in Late Medieval England* (1997). In the course of twentieth-century scholarship, medieval drama has become less a transitional moment in intellectual or religious history and more the site where history is contested and created.

CONCLUSION

While critical analysis of medieval drama continues to focus upon the three "M's"—the mystery, morality, and miracle plays—the commonplace assumptions that governed that analysis in the last quarter-century have all undergone a radical reassessment in light of both the increased historical understanding of the place, role, and development of dramatic festivities in late medieval England and the growing theoretical sophistication of the practitioners of literary studies. Whereas earlier critics sought to define the generic characteristics of medieval drama in order to distinguish it from other forms of literature and to set about the work of analyzing its cultural characteristics and literary content, more recent critics have attempted to resituate the drama in its historical context in order to analyze the cultural work the drama does and to evaluate its discursive effects in the multifarious social context of late medieval England. No longer simply considered the predecessor to Elizabethan drama, medieval drama is recognized as a vital tradition of unique dramatic power.

SELECTED BIBLIOGRAPHY

Baker, Donald C., John L. Murphy, and Louis Brewer Hall Jr., eds. *The Late Medieval Religious Plays of Bodleian MSS Digby 133 and E Museo 160.* Published for the Early English Text Society. London: Oxford University Press, 1982.

Beadle, Richard, ed. *The Cambridge Companion to Medieval English Theatre.* Cambridge: Cambridge University Press, 1994.

Bevington, David. *From Mankind to Marlowe: Growth and Structure in the Popular Drama of Tudor England.* Cambridge: Harvard University Press, 1962.

———, ed. *Medieval Drama.* Boston: Houghton Mifflin, 1975.

Block, Katherine Salter, ed. *Ludus Coventri; or The Plaie Called Corpus Christi, Cotton ms. Vespasian D. VIII.* Published for the Early English Text Society by H. Milford. London: Oxford University Press, 1922.

Cawley, A.C., ed. *The Wakefield Pageants in the Towneley Cycle.* Manchester: Manchester University Press, 1958.

Centre for Research in Early English Drama. Records of Early English Drama (REED). Web site .<http://www.chass.utoronto.ca/~reed/reed.html>.

Chambers, E. K. *The English Folk-Play.* New York: Haskell House, 1996.

———. *The Mediaeval Stage.* London: Oxford University Press, 1903.

Craig, Hardin, ed. *Two Coventry Corpus Christi Plays: 1. The Shearmen and Taylors' Pageant.* Published for the Early English Text Society. London: Oxford University Press, 1957.

Craik, T. W. *The Tudor Interlude: Stage, Costume, and Acting.* Leicester: University Press, 1967.

Davidson, Clifford. *From Creation to Doom: The York Cycle of Mystery Plays.* New York: AMS, 1984.

Davis, Norman. *Non-cycle Plays and the Winchester Dialogues. Facsimiles of Plays and Fragments in Various Manuscripts and the Dialogues in Winchester College MS33*. Leeds: University of Leeds, 1979.

Eccles, Mark. *The Macro Plays: The Castle of Perseverance, Wisdom, Mankind*. Published for the Early English Text Society. London: Oxford University Press, 1969.

Enders, Jody. *The Medieval Theater of Cruelty: Rhetoric, Memory, Violence*. Ithaca, NY: Cornell University Press, 1999.

———. *Rhetoric and the Origins of Medieval Drama*. Ithaca, NY: Cornell University Press, 1992.

England, George. *The Towneley Plays. Re-edited from the Unique Ms. By George England, with Side-Notes and Introduction by Alfred W. Pollard, M.A.* Published for the Early English Text Society, London: K. Paul, Trench, Trübner & Co., 1907.

Gardiner, H. C. *Mysteries' End; An Investigation of the Last Days of the Medieval Religious Stage*. New Haven: Yale University Press, 1946.

Gardner, John. *The Construction of the Wakefield Cycle*. Carbondale: Southern Illinois University Press, 1974.

Gibson, Gail McMurray. *The Theater of Devotion: East Anglian Drama and Society in the Late Middle Ages*. Chicago: University of Chicago Press, 1989.

Greg, W. W. *A Bibliography of the English Printed Drama to the Restoration*. London: Bibliographical Society, 1962.

Happé, Peter, ed. *English Mystery Plays: A Selection*. Baltimore: Penguin Books, 1975.

Hardison, O. B. *Christian Rite and Christian Drama in the Middle Ages; Essays in the Origin and Early History of Modern Drama*. Baltimore: Johns Hopkins University Press, 1965.

Helterman, Jeffrey. *Symbolic Action in the Plays of the Wakefield Master*. Athens: University of Georgia Press, 1981.

Higgins, Anne. "The Theaters." In *A New History of Early English Drama*. Eds. John D. Cox and David Scott Kastan. New York: Columbia University Press, 1997. 83–94.

Kahrl, Stanley J. *Traditions of Medieval English Drama*. London: Hutchinson, 1974.

Kolve, V. A. *The Play Called Corpus Christi*. Stanford, CA: Stanford University Press, 1966.

Lumiansky, R. M., and David Mills, eds. *The Chester Mystery Cycle*. 2 vols. Published for the Early English Text Society. London: Oxford University Press, 1974–1986.

Meredith, Peter, ed. *The Mary Play: From the N. Town Manuscript*. London: Longman, 1987.

Potter, Robert A. *The English Morality Play: Origins, History, and Influence of a Dramatic Tradition*. Boston: Routledge & K. Paul, 1975.

Rossiter, A. P. *English Drama from Early Times to the Elizabethans; Its Background, Origins, and Developments*. New York: Barnes & Noble, 1950.

Salter, F. M. *Mediaeval Drama in Chester*. Toronto: University of Toronto Press, 1955.

Sponsler, Claire. *Drama and Resistance: Bodies, Goods and Theatricality in Late Medieval England*. Minneapolis: University of Minnesota Press, 1997.

Stevens, Martin. *Four Middle English Mystery Cycles: Textual, Contextual, and Critical Interpretations*. Princeton, NJ: Princeton University Press, 1987.

Stevens, Martin and A. C. Cawley. *The Towneley Plays*. 2 vols. Published for the Early English Text Society. London: Oxford University Press, 1994.

Travis, Peter. *Dramatic Design in the Chester Cycle*. Chicago: University of Chicago Press, 1982.

Twycross, Meg. "Introduction." In *Iconographic and Comparative Studies in Medieval Drama*. Ed. Clifford Davidson and John H. Stroupe. Kalamazoo, MI: Medieval Institute Publications, 1991.

Wickham, Glynne William Gladstone. *Early English Stages, 1300 to 1660*. New York: Columbia University Press, 1959.

Woolf, Rosemary. *The English Mystery Plays*. Berkeley: University of California Press, 1972.

Young, Karl. *The Drama of the Medieval Church*. Oxford: Clarendon Press, 1933.

10

Dream Vision

Kevin Marti

Many scholars of medieval literature today believe that among the literary genres of medieval Europe only romance surpassed the popularity of dream vision. Particularly well established is the popularity of dream vision in England; medieval English poets produced several dream visions whose status as major works of literature is beyond dispute. But in early scholarship texts now generally thought of primarily as dream visions were treated under a variety of other generic rubrics, and debate among critical camps espousing different rubrics dominated scholarship on some of these texts for years without producing much consensus. Much of the scholarship in recent decades, however, suggests that dream vision functions as a metagenre that subsumes and interrelates many other literary genres. Many texts viewed primarily as dream visions today have at earlier stages of their critical reception been regarded principally as examples of allegory, elegy, autobiography, debate, or other genres. Many of these texts have accumulated four or five different generic labels over time because the dream frame allows one text to incorporate the conventions of several different genres. Ironically, then, the importance of dream vision has perhaps made it harder to define than any other medieval literary genre, including romance. The role of dream vision as metagenre has contributed to the difficulty; it cannot be approached as an independent literary genre. Medieval romances, for example, appear to outnumber medieval dream visions, but scholars have long pretty much agreed on which texts to call romances and have generally acknowledged that the paradigmatic form shared by all romances is the quest. The form of most other medieval literary genres, like that of romance, is much more widely understood than that of dream vision.

The structural principle of dream vision, like that of romance, is the quest, a journey to the otherworld: romance entails a waking quest, dream vision a sleeping quest. But the form of the quest in both medieval romance and medieval dream vision derives in turn from a paradigm in ancient dream narrative. This paradigmatic textual form is constituted by a series of visions representing successive degrees or gradations of abstraction through which an initial material image transforms itself in stages into its immaterial, Platonic counterpart. The dreamer experiences an ascent to or vision of heaven in stages that figure simultaneously as the stages of an interior journey to the core of his own creativity. By visualizing more and more abstract representations of some earthly object or person, the dreamer manages to perceive its immaterial counterpart in the heavenly realm of Platonic form. The importance of these stages of abstraction in textual and other cultural form is rooted in ancient schemes for the return of the soul to God after death (*regressus animae*) and for the resurrection of the body. The fact that dream vision shares this quest paradigm with romance is just one example of the way dream form connects different genres.

The most important aspects of this formal paradigm, identified in general studies of the genre and/or in studies of individual dream visions, may be summarized briefly as follows: The prologue and epilogue of medieval dream poems are usually set in the waking life of the dreamer. The depiction of waking life in the prologue typically offers a kind of index to the structure and theme of the dream account that follows. The dream mirrors and transforms the real-life situation depicted in the prologue in the manner of what are today called day-residue dreams. The prologue reveals spiritual crisis in the dreamer's life, and normally also in his art, that results from his inexperience and from his limited, earthbound perception. The sequence of visions he experiences obliges him to correct his earthbound perspective in a way that transforms his poetry. The poem that reports the dream vision bears witness to this transformation; to the degree possible in mortal language it attempts to represent its subject from the perspective of the Platonic realm of forms. Dream vision is thus characteristically self-reflexive: the poem reports on a search for the generative nucleus of the poem itself. Reading a dream poem or hearing it recited, its audience processes the text in stages that parallel the stages of abstraction encountered by the dreamer. Within a given text the form of the dream frame usually appears more than once to create a linear sequence of dreams and/or a structure consisting of outer dreams and inner dreams (dreams within dreams). An important aspect of the self-consciousness or self-reflexivity of the best medieval dream poems is their exploration of their own origins in literary tradition through a pattern of allusions to earlier dream texts made possible by their common form.

The dreamer character in dream vision is typically obtuse and naïve, slow to understand what he sees and hears. As the poem begins, he is mired in a state of turmoil that limits his artistic powers, a state caused in part by his own flawed perception. His words and actions illustrate the literal-minded, mortal perspective that the vision is designed to correct. The figures of dreamer, narrator, and author overlap, but not entirely. The perspective of the dreamer is transformed, in the course of the poem, into the perspective of the narrator; typically a few autobiographical details identify both in part with the author. An authority figure appears within the dream to serve as the dreamer's guide, usually rendering in the form of didactic speech the message otherwise conveyed to the dreamer by way of visual imagery. The guide helps the dreamer resolve the problem from waking life revealed in the prologue and unblock his creativity by helping him understand what he sees in the dream. The speeches by the guide and the dialogue between dreamer and guide are the verbal, rational counterpart to the imagery of the dream.

The idealized landscape settings of dream texts, including prologue settings and dreamscapes, are remarkably consistent. The same archetype appears over and over with variations in an extensive tradition of dream poems; it also typically appears over and over within the separate visions contained within a single dream poem. Most of the landscape settings in dream vision feature either a walled garden with a well or fountain and/or a meadow with a stream or river. The landscapes are illuminated by bright light and are filled with a diverse assortment of flowers, trees, and birds. Often dream landscapes offer more abstract, dematerialized versions of prologue landscapes, such that the relationship between the settings of prologue and dream parallels the relationship between created matter and Platonic form or idea. Medieval English dream poems typically exhibit a tripartite structure in which the landscape imagery the waking dreamer sees in the prologue reappears transformed into more and more abstract versions of itself in the first and second dreamscapes. The slight variations among parallel elements in the three visions or scenes help us see each vision as a separate stage of abstraction in an inward journey.

The transformations the dreamer and readers see the idealized landscape undergo each time it reappears are accompanied by a semantic transformation associated with repeating key words (leitwords) as well as a transformation of the dreamer/narrator and other characters. Often leitwords mark off the boundaries of separate visions and other subdivisions of dream poems. Such key words gather new associations as they recur in different contexts; like the successive transformations of the idealized landscape, the successive semantic transformations associated with a repeating key word mark off stages of abstraction. Through wordplay, literal meaning gives way to more abstract or allegorical meaning associated with the same leitword. The character of the dreamer/narrator undergoes a transformation that likewise suggests stages of abstraction: he sometimes quotes the words he speaks as the dreamer during the dream, but at other times he speaks as the narrator who has had time to reflect on the completed dream, and at still other times he makes autobiographical references that identify him as the author. In stages the dreamer/narrator is transformed into a composite character, just as a sequence of transformations of setting produces a composite landscape and as a sequence of semantic transformations links multiple senses to the same leitword. A similar sequence of different associations resembling stages of abstraction transforms other characters in dream vision into composite characters like the dreamer/narrator. Because the theology of the Incarnation and of the Eucharist presupposes this same scheme of stages of abstraction, this characteristic pattern of reappearing landscapes, key words, dreamers/narrators, and other characters may be said to define a sacramental or incarnational poetics.

The features of the dream-frame (quest) paradigm outlined here are key to its metageneric role. They not only provide a general parallel to the form of romance (and *chanson d'aventure*, Davidoff 1988), they also provide a common framework for allegory, elegy, autobiography, debate, and other genres. Because medieval schemes of allegory presuppose the same stages of abstraction that structure dream vision, the dream journey figures as a pilgrimage from material (literal) reality through stages of greater and greater abstraction corresponding with higher and higher levels of allegory. Elegiac or autobiographical material introduced as part of the dreamer's waking experience in the prologue (including any revelation of occasional purpose) may serve as the literal level of such an allegorical scheme. The dialogue through which the guide helps the dreamer acquire a less earthbound perspective shares with the literary genre of debate a counterpoint of earthbound and spiritual perspectives based on the same scheme; this dialogue also reflects influence from the literary genre of the *ars poetica*. Because the stages of abstraction in dream vision also underlie the metaphor of pilgrimage, what scholars think of as a paradigm for dream vision underlies many texts structured according to the metaphor of pilgrimage not usually thought of as dream poems, including Geoffrey Chaucer's *Canterbury Tales*.

PROMINENT EXAMPLES OF THE GENRE

Judging by the volume of scholarship dedicated to each, six late-fourteenth-century texts rank among the most prominent dream visions in medieval English: William Langland's *Piers Plowman*, the anonymous *Pearl*, and Geoffrey Chaucer's four dream visions, in about that order of importance. Chaucer's major dream visions are *The Book of the Duchess*, *The House of Fame*, *The Parliament of Fowls*, and the Prologue to *The Legend of Good Women*, probably written in that order. *Piers Plowman* and *Pearl*, the most important medieval English dream visions, both represent the fourteenth-century revival of alliterative poetry in the west Midlands; four minor alliterative dream visions from this same tradition survive, all anonymous: *Winner and Waster*, *The Parliament of the Three Ages*, *Mum and the Sothsegger*, and *Death and Life*. Other fourteenth-century English dream visions include John Gower's *Confessio Amantis* and accounts of the title characters' dreams in Chaucer's *Troilus and Criseyde* and of Chauntecleer's dream in Chaucer's "Nun's Priest's Tale." Fifteenth-century imitators of Chaucer in Scotland and England produced several dream visions, prominent among which are *Kingis Quair*, attributed to King James I of Scotland, and John Lydgate's *Temple of Glass*. Guillaume de Deguileville's *Pèlerinage de l'âme* circulated in the fifteenth century with some adaptations as the Middle English *Pilgrimage of the Soul*. The anonymous

Dream of the Rood is sometimes cited as an Old English example of the dream-vision genre.

Because dream vision is a self-referential, cumulative tradition, medieval English dream visions allude to ancient Hebrew and Greek dream visions available in Latin translation as well as to earlier medieval dream poems in Latin, French, and Italian. Among the dream poems produced outside of medieval England, those most relevant to medieval English dream vision include: the books of Ezekiel and Daniel in the Old Testament; the Apocalypse of St. John in the New Testament; the Dream of Er that concludes Plato's *Republic*; the Dream of Scipio that concludes Cicero's *Republic* and Macrobius's *Commentary on the Dream of Scipio*; Alain de l'Isle's *Complaint of Nature*; the *Romance of the Rose* of Guillaume de Lorris and Jean de Meun; Guillaume de Machaut's *Dit des quatre sieges* and *Dit dou vergier*; Froissart's *Paradys d'amours*; and Dante's *Divine Comedy*.

SURVEY OF SCHOLARSHIP ON MEDIEVAL ENGLISH DREAM VISION

This chapter briefly surveys major trends within the voluminous scholarship relevant to medieval English dream vision, most of which is a subset of scholarship on the six texts discussed at greatest length here: *Piers Plowman*, *Pearl*, and Chaucer's *Book of the Duchess, House of Fame, Parliament of Fowls*, and Prologue to *The Legend of Good Women*. Because bibliographies do not classify most of these relevant publications as studies of genre or of dream vision, they can be hard to find. This overview brings together representative studies that shed light on each of the features that help classify these texts as dream visions. Many of the studies listed here discuss other English dream poems as well. Most editions, translations, concordances, and bibliographies have not been included. In this survey and in the bibliography that follows, an initial section devoted to general studies of the genre (the survey considers only monographs) is followed by separate sections devoted to scholarship on the six dream poems cited earlier. Space does not permit treatment within this chapter of all sources included in the bibliography. A separate listing of general studies related to Chaucer's dream visions has been inserted after the section on *Pearl* in the bibliography.

Monographs about Medieval Dream Vision

Because monographs that compare several medieval dream visions have played such a central role in defining the genre, this survey begins by briefly reviewing such book-length studies, more or less in order of publication. The scope of these studies varies; they include general books on medieval dream vision as well as books that focus on one historical period (high or late medieval), language (English), or author (Chaucer; see also the listing of general studies related to Chaucer's dream visions). Some such studies define and name a subgenre of dream-vision literature (e.g., high medieval philosophical dream vision, apocalypse, Boethian apocalypse). Although the defining characteristics of dream vision have been brought to scholarly attention mostly by way of these comparative, full-length studies, the more specialized studies of individual texts discussed later have both contributed to and drawn from the conclusions of these monographs.

Several books published between 1967 and 1976 identified many characteristics still used to define dream vision. The first, by Constance B. Hieatt, introduces many of these characteristics as features that make medieval dream visions resemble real dreams, particularly as psychoanalysis understands dreams (1967). For Hieatt, the tendency of people and places to blend and fuse in medieval dream vision is consistent with the "compression of many ideas into a few symbols" that Freud termed "condensation." This compression or condensation, which underlies Jung's theory of the "collective unconscious," has its roots in Neoplatonic notions of the "world mind" that underlie medieval dream vision. For example, the roles of Seys and Alcyone within the short waking narrative of the prologue of *Duchess* mirror the roles of the knight and the deceased duchess in the longer dream narrative; one pair of characters blends or fuses with the other such that the prologue narrative reverses and condenses the main narrative. Not only do places and characters fuse as if in a dream, characters move about as if in a dream and sometimes vanish altogether. The dreams-within-dreams and other abrupt shifts in focus in *Piers* are consistent with dream psychology. The early chapters of Hieatt's work define the form of dream vision in light of medieval authorities on dream interpretation; two later chapters treat the relationship between dream vision and the genres of elegy and allegory. Other dream poems discussed include *Pearl, Three Ages, Winner,* and those by Chaucer.

In a somewhat related approach based on C.G. Jung's notion of archetypes, Paul Piehler finds that medieval "visionary allegory" helps readers undergo a process resembling modern psychotherapy (1971). The basic content of such allegory derives mostly from the symbolism in classical and preclassical myth. Medieval allegory analyzes such "seminal images" into symbolic, allegorical, and rational elements; dialogue, also classical in origin, controls and rationally explicates the symbols. The quest of each dreamer is for a principle of authority, a goddess (*potentia*) in a sacred setting (*locus animae*): "Typically, a medieval allegory enacts the transformation of some bare personification or other static or unstructured image into a full visionary potentia in its appropriate locus" (15). The meanings of *potentia*, like those of *imago* in Latin and *eidolon* in Greek, include "mental image," "spirit," "idea," or "concept"; Piehler's *potentia* is a representation of Platonic form. The vision of a *potentia* in a *locus*, the defining form of dream vision, reflects the Platonic tradition of the ascent of the soul as transmitted by the *Consolation*. Piehler also traces this form in *Complaint, Romance, Comedy,* and *Pearl*, as well as Jean de Hautville's *Architrenius*.

James Winny's readable introduction to Chaucer's dream visions, like most other general treatments of this subject, says little about the Prologue to the *Legend* (1973). He finds great consistency of form among Chaucer's first three dream visions, all of which share with most other dream visions a slow-witted dreamer/narrator and a guide who resembles the moral teacher in the kind of dream Macrobius calls *oraculum*. Some features shared by these three texts are not common to all dream visions, including their respectful treatment of dream lore and their common departure from the aristocratic ideal established by de Lorris. Winny writes: "The poetic unity of Chaucer's writing is nowhere more apparent than in the persistence of certain basic circumstances and central figures throughout the early poems, and at last as structural elements of the *Tales*. The Narrator . . . is the most conspicuous of these common features" (149). Despite any apparent disjuncture among the parts of any one of Chaucer's dream visions, all share the same basic form; their form somewhat resembles that of his *Tales*, which features the Host as *oraculum*.

A.C. Spearing, in the most influential of the earliest studies, draws on earlier tradition to focus mostly on medieval English dream poems (1976). Like scholars before him, he maintains that authors of dream poems were "conscious of writing in an ancient tradition, going back to scriptural and classical sources, to which they felt a need to establish the relationship of their own poetic visions"; that the ascent of the dreamer has its basis in the Platonic ascent of the soul; and that the dreamlike fluidity of allegorical characters is consistent with psychoanalytic understanding of dream condensation. The heavenly setting of dream vision, a "universal psychic archetype," stays constant, an ideal Mediterranean landscape. Nonetheless, "there is some doubt whether the dream-poem can properly be considered an independent literary genre" or "distinct literary kind" (2). Long chapters on Chaucer's dream visions, *Piers*, and *Pearl* are followed by a lengthy treatment of fifteenth-century dream poems.

During a hiatus between this early group of monographs and the group of monographs that appeared in the late 1980s, two monographs of some importance appeared: Peter Dinzelbacher discusses visions of religious ecstasy and their appearance in literature as background for the dream visions of Chaucer and Langland (1981); and B.A. Windeatt brings together for the first time translations of the chief sources of Chaucer's four dream visions, including works of Machaut, Froissart, Alain, and Boccaccio (1982).

For the most part the group of monographs on dream vision that appeared in the late 1980s confirms the characteristics of the genre defined by earlier studies, but most of the studies in this later group define a subgenre of dream vision by finding detailed formal parallels within a subset of the texts earlier studies termed dream visions or dream poems. Thus Michael D. Cherniss (1987) labels *Complaint, Romance, Confessio, Parliament, Pearl, Duchess, Kingis Quair*, and Robert Henryson's *Testament of Cresseid* as "Boethian apocalypse," a genre of literary visions influenced by the *Consolation of Philosophy*; the Middle English examples are his main focus. Applying a kind of practical criticism, Cherniss argues that elegiac and allegorical approaches have blinded critics to the overriding genre of these texts, a genre based on Boethius's notion of philosophy as an ascent from the corporeal to the incorporeal (22). He compares the way *Complaint* and *Pearl* develop from seminal images compressed into the prologue of each (155).

Kathryn L. Lynch, whose book has been the most influential of those published in the late 1980s, identifies another subgenre of dream vision she terms "the philosophical vision poem in the High Middle Ages"; the twelfth and thirteenth centuries are "the Age of the Dream Vision" (1988). Texts in this subgenre share a common structure based on the contemporary notion of stages of abstraction, stages one encounters by using "faculties of reason and imagination to ascend through and beyond naturally obtained knowledge, rising from image to divine significance" (16). This spiritual or perceptual ascent, based on a literary tradition of such ascents she traces to Plato's *Dream of Er*, takes the form of an inner journey whose tripartite form reflects the three stages of cognition. This subgenre reflects the high medieval synthesis of natural philosophy and received theology. The poems of this subgenre, like the philosophy of the twelfth and thirteenth centuries, synthesize Platonic and Aristotelian traditions by accommodating natural philosophy to a realist framework: "The philosophical vision poem in the High Middle Ages had as one of its governing ideas or purposes the defense of a philosophically realist paradigm within a framework of continuous change" (15–16). An understanding of the Scholastic paradigm of the stages of abstraction clarifies the special generic status of dream vision; in some poems influenced by several genres dream vision is the "true, overriding genre" (164). Separate chapters on *Complaint, Romance, Purgatorio*, and *Confessio* trace decreasing trust in the role of poetry as vehicle of truth.

The definition of "late medieval dream vision" in J. Stephen Russell's study of the English tradition probably excludes many texts generally termed dream visions even as it hints at a metageneric status: late medieval dream vision exists "in the space between the literary categories of apocalypse and narrative dream" (1988, 21). Like apocalypse, late medieval dream vision shows readers the Platonic world of forms as the Christian afterlife (82–83). In these texts, Plato's forms are Christianized as "extramental universals," a basic concept of natural philosophy (109), but the external form shared by *Duchess, Pearl*, and *House* also contains an internal dynamic derived from nominalism. These three "deconstructive dream visions" draw on this common form to express distrust of language and of the knowability of reality. Early chapters trace the origins of the genre to Augustine, Macrobius, *Romance*, and other dream authorities, and an epilogue touches on *Mum* and *Temple*.

Drawing on medieval literary theory, Robert Edwards argues that Chaucer's first three dream visions are performative texts that join mimetic representation to aesthetic speculation (1989). As philosophical explorations of their own creation, these self-referential texts not only reflect but also contribute to medieval aesthetic theory. The narrator stands at the point where mimesis and rhetoric converge. Approaching poetic form, like Kathryn Lynch, by way of cognitive structure, Edwards discusses imagination and memory in *Duchess* and *House* and intellect in *Parliament*.

Roberta L. Payne considers only medieval English dream visions in which she perceives the influence of Dante: separate chapters consider *Pearl*, *House*, *Parliament*, and Criseyde's dream of the eagle in *Troilus*, and the conclusion briefly discusses *Temple* and *Kingis* (1989). *Pearl* most closely reflects the structure of the *Commedia*; the pearl maiden is a synthesis of Mathilda and Beatrice, and both *Pearl* and *Purgatorio* feature a similar moment when the female guide is suddenly discovered to be far away. Like the *Commedia, House* is an *ars poetica* structured by a "trip backward to the source of poetic inspiration and fame" (72); Chaucer's Eagle is a synthesis of Virgil, Beatrice, and divine illumination (73). Like the Eagle, Africanus in *Parliament* helps the dreamer "learn about ascending qualities of love, beginning from the most human and terrestrial and moving progressively upwards" (103). These dream visions share this paradigm of ascent with the *Commedia*.

Studies of Individual Dream Poems

The review of scholarship for each of the following six dream poems first discusses the genres and sources whose influence scholars have detected in the poem and then describes the studies related to each of the features of dream form in the poem, including studies of structure, spatial form, wordplay, transformational or sacramental symbolism, the dreamer/narrator, and the guide.

Piers Plowman

Studies of *Piers* as apocalypse prepare for an understanding of *Piers* as dream vision. The scholarly roots of Cherniss's general rubric "Boethian apocalypse" (1987) can be traced to Morton Bloomfield's rather hesitant identification of *Piers* as a "fourteenth-century apocalypse" (1962). Apocalyptic tradition includes depictions of the end of time, in various media, derived from St. John's Apocalypse and related eschatological material, and Bloomfield brings together much apocalyptic material relevant to *Piers*. He recognizes a confluence of three main genres in *Piers*: allegorical dream narrative; dialogue, *consolatio*, or debate; and encyclopedic or Menippean satire. Bloomfield shows how apocalyptic tradition is incorporated within a scheme for stages of perfection that serves as the defining form of *Piers*. This scheme for individual and social perfection, which underlies the Three Lives (Dowel, Dobet, Dobest), resembles that of monastic philosophers who model their conception of the ideal monastery after the New Jerusalem. Langland's antifraternalism is consistent with such a monastic scheme. Bloomfield's stages of perfection anticipate the stages of abstraction Kathryn Lynch identifies as the defining form of all dream vision.

Several later studies of apocalyptic tradition in *Piers* likewise bear on the status of the poem as dream vision. Ruth Ames confirms influence from the Apocalypse of John (1970). Robert Adams finds a parallel between Need and the Noonday Devil who is the immediate precursor of Antichrist, among other apocalyptic influences (1978, 1985). Mary Carruthers traces a temporal progression based on the "plot" of Christian history in apocalyptic tradition (1982). E. Talbot Donaldson discovers in B XIX–XX stylistic parallels with the biblical Apocalypse that include a disjointed time sequence and the convergence of different levels of allegory (1983). Douglas Bertz draws from apocalyptic tradition to show how the inner dream of the Tree of Charity serves as a vision of the future (1985), and Richard Emmerson identifies the dream-within-a-dream structure as an apocalyptic motif based on Apocalypse 4:1–2 and 17:3 (1993).

Dream vision and allegory are so interdependent that the two terms appear together in various rubrics for a hybrid genre discerned in *Piers* ("allegorical dream narrative," Bloomfield 1962; "visionary allegory," Piehler 1971, Aers 1975; "dream-allegory," Cali 1971; "allegorical visions," Barney 1988). Most of the defining features and representative texts cited for this hybrid genre are familiar from more general studies of dream vision. The same form, the stages of abstraction, underlies both dream vision and allegory. Different levels of allegory correspond with different degrees of abstraction and different stages of the sleep cycle, perceived by the dreamer as stages of a Platonic ascent to heaven. A figure gathers new associations by reappearing in a succession of dreams; for example, Piers the plowman comes to be associated in the course of the poem with St. Peter, Christ, and the Good Samaritan. The approach to allegory in *Piers* taken by D.W. Robertson, Jr., and Bernard F. Hüppe concerns itself less with the relation of allegory to dream vision than the studies just cited (1951).

Although areas of scholarly disagreement regarding the structure of *Piers* remain, the following observations, generally supported by the representative studies cited, are consistent with the paradigmatic stages of abstraction: that despite complaints that the text is disjointed or chaotic, it has a discernible form (Wells 1929; cf. Muscatine 1972); that the basic form of each of the three texts (A, B, and C) is a series or progression of dreams representing stages of increasingly spiritual perception (Gerould 1948, Kirk 1972, Wittig 1972, Kaske 1974, Clopper 1985, Kaulbach 1987 and 1993, Weldon 1987, K. Lynch 1988); that B has ten dreams, including two inner dreams (Frank 1951; cf. Gerould 1948); that inner dreams represent a later stage of ascent or perception than the dreams that contain them (Kaulbach 1987); that inner dreams are therefore prophetic (Alford 1988), sometimes representing events that take place later in an "outer dream"; that larger textual or thematic structures are condensed or emphasized within key substructures (first *passus*, Bloomfield 1962, Salter 1962, Kaske 1974; last two *passus*, Higgs 1993; Latin quotations, Alford 1977 and 1988); that while levels of allegory are sometimes mixed, there is a general pattern of progression from literal to allegorical levels as the poem proceeds (Clopper 1985, 1988); and that the form of the text is tripartite at various different levels of organization (Wells 1929, Clopper 1979, Weldon 1987).

In *Piers* the way new meanings cluster around the same repeating word is related to the tendency for reappearing dream characters and figures to assume composite identities (Spearing 1963). Thus in dream visions wordplay, like allegory, is "sacramental" (Schmidt 1983) and "incarnational" (Chessell 1971) because words and allegorical figures enact what they signify: to signify a sacramental transformation, the words and figures undergo that transformation themselves. Where through punning repetition literal associations give way to more spiritual ones, wordplay reveals the stages of abstraction within the form of language itself. Mary Clemente Davlin explains that in the case of the name of Piers, this clustering of associations through wordplay is consistent with the doctrine of the Whole Christ, the mystical body of Christ in which all believers are embodied (1972; cf. Jennings 1978). The form of the text derives in part from wordplay, which occurs most where dreams and individual *passus* begin and end. The role of wordplay in underscoring major themes in *Piers* has long been recognized, though some of the first instances of wordplay cited have not been widely accepted (Hüppe 1950). Patterns of repeated words in B are intensified in C (Spearing 1963, Schmidt 1987), and intertextual puns link A, B, and C texts (Tristram 1983).

In *Piers* the role of the dreamer/narrator is consistent with other characteristic features of the dream frame. By way of puns on Will, the more literal author, narrator, and dreamer merge with each other (see Kane 1965) and with the more abstract allegorical concept of the human will or *voluntas*. Just as later visions offer a more abstract version of earlier visions, the figure of Will acquires a more abstract sense in the course of the poem. The dreamer is obtuse, but his earthly perspective becomes more spiritual by the end of the poem (Wittig 1975; cf. Holleran 1966). The central experience of the poem takes place in his mind, whose development the reader follows (Higgs 1974). His characterization, however, is fuller than that of other medieval dream narrators (Arn 1981). For David Mills, Will represents the limitations of earthbound men, and Will and Piers combined are Langland (1969). Miceal F. Vaughan takes the first lines of the poem to be a confession whereby dreamer converts to narrator (1991). David Lawton notes how intersecting discourses create contradictions in Will (1987). The dreamer's guide is Holy Church, whose long speech in the first *passus* previews the form of the whole text on a small scale more meticulously than does its structural counterpart in most other dream poems, the representation of the dreamer's waking life featured in the prologue (e.g., in *Complaint*, Cherniss 1987, 155). Unlike other dream guides, she completely disappears from the poem after her initial appearance (see Jennings 1978).

Pearl

Several studies discuss apocalyptic features in *Pearl*, which include a paraphrase of Apocalypse 21:10–22:5, describing a vision of the heavenly Jerusalem, in lines 973–1080. The early debate between proponents of allegory and elegy as genre classifications for *Pearl* (summary in Eldredge 1975; early allegorical readings include Fletcher 1921, Madaleva 1925, Robertson 1950, and Hamilton

1955) distracted attention from apocalyptic features *Pearl* shares with other dream visions, as did early scholars' low estimation of this paraphrase passage (cf. Field 1986). Thomas C. Niemann attempts to place in perspective the influence of other genres on *Pearl* by showing that the dream in *Pearl* resembles visits to the Christian otherworld in apocalyptic literature; he notes parallels with the *Vision of Tundale* and the *Comedy* (1974). Muriel A. Whitaker finds influence from illuminated Apocalypse manuscripts of the period; the *Pearl* dreamer resembles the figure of John in these illuminations (1981). Sarah Stanbury discusses the perception of space in *Pearl* and illuminated Apocalypses (1991). Theodore Bogdanos focuses on the problem of representing the ineffable in apocalyptic tradition (1983). Building on the various meanings of "form" in *Pearl*, which include "genre" and "iconographic image," Sandra Pierson Prior considers parallels with apocalyptic tradition in church iconography and elsewhere (1996; cf. Nolan 1977). Kevin Marti observes that the pearl maidens appear to possess the characteristics of the resurrected body even though the general resurrection has not yet occurred within the time frame of the poem, so the poem appears to grant a vision of the end of time (1993). Since both Boethius and St. John record dream experiences, these studies of *Pearl* as apocalypse are prepared for by earlier studies of *Pearl* as consolation. John Conley finds parallels to Boethius's *Consolation* in theme, situation, roles, and treatment (1955), and other scholars provide further support for this claim (Watts 1963, Bishop 1968, Wimsatt 1970, Means 1972).

While the relationship between allegory and dream frame in *Pearl* appears to resemble that in *Piers*, it has received less scholarly attention, but Jane Chance argues that the three levels of medieval exegesis above the *sensus literalis* explain the three main divisions of the poem (1991), a scheme consistent with the stages of increasing abstraction characteristic of dream allegory elsewhere. Some such allegorical scheme is supported by studies that trace how the earthly imagery of the prologue (first stanza group) reemerges in increasingly abstract representations in the two dream landscapes. In such a scheme the waking dreamer contemplates images while awake whose increasingly abstract Platonic counterparts he then dreams about. As with *Piers*, studies of *Pearl* term this pattern of figuration "sacramental" and "incarnational" (in *Pearl* also "transformational"; Kean 1967, Bishop 1968, Gatta 1974, Stiller 1982, Schotter 1984, Spearing 1987); this approach can be traced to Robert Max Garrett's application of eucharistic doctrine to the poem (1918; cf. Gatta 1974, Phillips 1985). As with the figure of Piers, the clustering of different associations around the symbol of the pearl as the poem progresses has been compared to the embodiment of different believers within "the whole Christ" (Mahl 1966; cf. Davlin 1972). Louis Blenkner argues that transformations of the imagery of the waking setting within the two dream landscapes reflect the dreamer's three-stage mystical ascent. The three landscapes represent separate stages in the evolution of light imagery, jewel imagery, vegetation imagery, and the symbolism of the pearl. These three stages reflect the traditional tripartite division of human sources of knowledge (sense, intellect, and inspiration) and also the corresponding three stages (without, within, above) of the ascent of the soul to God (1968, 1971). Clopper argues similarly that *Pearl* incorporates elements of consolation into a scheme for meditation that involves reading the created world as a kind of text in order better to comprehend the spiritual world; the scheme reflects Bonaventure's version of Augustine's theory of vision (1992). Within some such scheme the paraphrase of the parable of the vineyard at the center of the *Pearl* text previews the climactic vision of heavenly Jerusalem, much as inner dreams in *Piers* and the *Comedy* preview later visions.

Some such scheme of increasing abstraction finds support among studies of spatial form in *Pearl*, whose observations include the following: The dreamer begins the poem with an earthbound sense of space and is taught by the pearl maiden to understand space from a heavenly perspective (Clark and Wasserman 1979). Circular form in text and landscape contributes to the incarnational art (Nelson 1973). The "incarnate" form of *Pearl*, based on the relationship traditionally perceived between body and heart, resembles the form of many other medieval texts and of Gothic cathedrals (Marti 1991). The notion of the body of Christ as temple at several different levels—heavenly Jerusalem, earthly Jerusalem, church as a whole, body of one Christian, heart of one Christian—helps clarify the relationship between the dead maiden's body and the heavenly Jerusalem in *Pearl*; the lost female body incorporated into the city serves as a framework for such transformational symbolism (Stanbury 1994). All of the landscapes are presented as constructs of the narrator's visionary, and visual, imagination (Stanbury 1991). *Pearl* shares formal similarities with the *Visio* of *Piers* (Russell 1980).

Studies of wordplay in *Pearl* have drawn some of the same conclusions as studies of wordplay in *Piers*, again conclusions generally consistent with seeing the stages of abstraction as the basic form. As with *Piers*, most of the wordplay in *Pearl* results when the same words and phrases repeat themselves at the boundaries of the most important structural units: in *Pearl* the beginning and end of stanzas and stanza groups, and the beginning, middle, and end of the whole text. As with *Piers*, it is claimed that the play of meaning in these leitwords provides the thematic structure of the entire poem (Macrae-Gibson 1968). These repeating words change meaning as first the dreamer, then the maiden, uses them (Milroy 1971): that is, as the poem progresses, an initial earthbound meaning for a word comes to be replaced by a supernatural significance (Wilson 1971). Such wordplay exploits both lexical and syntactic ambiguity, such that the wordplay appears to be built into the language (Donner 1988, 1989). As in *Piers*, wordplay in *Pearl* contributes to the sacramental or incarnational nature of the symbolism. In both poems the repeating words thus provide a kind of precis of the sequence of transformations underlying the stages of the dreamer's inner journey.

The dreamer, typically, is self-absorbed and slow to acquire the spiritual perspective his guide attempts to reveal during their long dialogue or debate; the form of his poem, however, shows his mastery as poet/narrator of the *ars poetica* spoken by his guide. Two recent studies discuss the dreamer's evolution in terms of the male construction of self in relation to a female other (Astell 1990, Aers 1993). Like the figure of Piers, the figure of the pearl guide is transformed in stages into a composite. The role of this one-year-old guide instructing her father in some ways inverts that of the authoritative guide of other dream visions.

Chaucer's Dream Visions

Chaucer's *Duchess, House, Parliament*, and *Legend* Prologue all share several features identified earlier as defining characteristics of dream vision. The basic form, generally tripartite, is an inner journey that figures as an ascent to heaven; the dreamer ascends to the Logos by way of an interior quest for the principle of his own creativity. The dream narratives are framed by accounts of the dreamer's waking experience featured in the prologue and usually also in the epilogue. Instructed by an authoritative guide during the dream, the naïve and obtuse dreamer comes to a better understanding of a problem from waking life introduced in the prologue, albeit slowly and with great difficulty. Imagery introduced in the prologue is transformed into dream imagery. As with *Piers* and *Pearl*, early scholarship approached what scholars now call Chaucer's dream visions primarily as examples of other genres. Chaucer's dream visions also share features with each other that are not as consistently found in other dream visions: the dreamer's inexperience in love is emphasized; dream lore is usually treated respectfully; the dream narrative grows out of the narrative contained in a book the dreamer reads before he falls asleep; the dream, in turn, inspires the dreamer to write something after he awakens.

Several studies contribute to an understanding of more than one of these four poems as dream visions. Donald R. Howard discusses the representation of time and space in these poems in a study of heavenly journeys in the apotheosis tradition (1975). Carrie Esther Hammil sets *House, Parliament*, and the Epilogue to *Troilus* within the literary tradition of the celestial journey (1980). Howard Schless considers influences from Dante (1984), Robert W. Hanning influence from Ovid (1986).

In these four texts, as in *Piers* and *Pearl*, dreamer, narrator, and author form a composite character like the composite figures of Piers and of the pearl. Old French love visions that provide a partial model for the narrators of Chaucer's dream visions include *Romance* and several of Machaut's writings (David 1976, 9–26; Calin 1987; Finlayson 1990). Some studies of Chaucer's dream visions question the possibility of coherence through a narrative presence, of organic unity (Jordan 1967, Donner 1973, Payne 1973, Lawton 1985, Anderson 1992; cf. Gellrich 1985). Studies of the fragmentation of the narrating subject are related to studies of nominalist influence in Chaucer's dream visions (Peck 1978, Sklute 1984).

The Book of the Duchess

Genres whose elements scholars claim to have found in *Duchess* include elegy, French love vision (*dit amoreux*), apocalypse, and consolation (genres also associated with *Pearl*), or combinations thereof; as elsewhere, scholars often define genre by identifying sources. In the elegiac reading *Duchess* commemorates the death of Blanche, wife of John of Gaunt, duke of Lancaster (Tisdale 1973, Butterfield 1991). Readings of *Duchess* as *dit amoreux* pay particular attention to influence from the *Romance* and the love visions of Machaut (Lawlor 1956, Pelen 1976–77, Nolan 1981, Palmer 1981, Butterfield 1991, Palmer 1998). Cherniss argues that influence from elegy and French love vision has kept scholars from seeing that *Duchess* is a Boethian apocalypse (1987; cf. Rambuss 1990). In fact, the dream-vision metagenre accommodates and interrelates all of these genres because so many major representatives of these genres share the basic form of the dream frame. Of all the genre classifications proposed for *Duchess*, that of consolation (linked to elegy in early studies) has preoccupied scholars the most; in this reading consolation is offered to the grieving Black Knight, who represents John of Gaunt. For A.J. Minnis, the poem's status as a consolation is the "central crux of criticism of *Duchess*" (1995, 135; see Lawlor 1956 and other early studies cited by Robertson in Rowland 1979, 406–407, in addition to Robertson 1965, Tisdale 1973, Phillips 1981, Rambuss 1990, Thundy 1995; cf. Walker 1981).

The text of *Duchess* exhibits structural similarities with other dream texts, including tripartite organization (Boitani 1986; cf. Shippey 1996). Andrew Lynch perceives in *Duchess* what Charles Muscatine refers to as "Gothic form," a "linear series of discrete episodes" (1986), and Helen Phillips identifies "juxtaposition" as the structural principle of the text (1981); this un-Aristotelian, linear sequence of abruptly or loosely joined episodes is a hallmark of dream vision (cf. Jordan 1974). According to Judith Neaman, the form of *Duchess* reflects medieval belief that the brain has three parts that involve themselves sequentially in perception (1980; cf. Schless 1984 and Hardman 1994 on memory in *Duchess*); the sequenced divisions of brain and text resemble the familiar stages of abstraction. Medieval understanding of the relationship between brain structure and melancholia, says Neaman, accounts for the "customary stupidity" of the dreamer/narrator, who is the subject of several studies (Kittredge 1915, Kreuzer 1951, Manning 1956, Kiser 1983).

The House of Fame

Early studies discuss *House* in relation to some of the same genres and sources, including earlier dream poems, that receive attention in the scholarship on other English dream visions. Paul G. Ruggiers argues for Boethian influence, finding a principle of unity in the theme of earthly mutability (1953). Wolfgang Clemen identifies *House* as an *ars poetica* in the form of an "allegorical or heavenward journey" (1963); its function as an art of poetry is central to several other major studies as well (Bennett 1968, Delany 1972, Kean 1972). Bringing together important currents of early scholarship, Wilbur Owen Sypherd declares *House* a love vision, with Boethian roots, in the French tradition, but denies influence from the *Commedia* (1965; cf. Leyerle 1971). In an allegorical reading based on medieval exegesis, on the other hand, B.G. Koonce finds a *Commedia*-like movement from hell through purgatory to paradise, as well as parallels with the biblical Apocalypse (1966).

More recent studies again find, among other sources, influence from the authors of several dream poems. For Laurence K. Shook, *House* is an *ars poetica* posing as an *ars amatoria*, in the tradition of Ovid and Guillaume de Lorris; the love theme is subordinate to the subject of poetry itself (1979). J.A.W. Bennett (1968) and Piero Boitani (1984) see a parallel with Dante's attempt to valorize the vernacular. Martin Irvine detects influence from Macrobius and Boethius (1985; cf. Tisdale 1973); John M. Fyler finds allusion to Macrobius's definition of the phantasm (1986). According to Robert Boenig, material is adapted from the biblical Apocalypse in a way that negates Bede's commentary on it, and the text is deliberately left unfinished, a failed apocalypse (1985). Kathryn Lynch argues similarly that *House* is a parody or inversion of classical literary visions (1995).

Despite Nevill Coghill's early claim that *House* lacks unity (1967), the stages of abstraction of the inner journey and of Platonic ascent—the familiar structure of dream vision—are more firmly established in scholarship on *House* than in that on Chaucer's other dream visions. Joseph E. Grennen traces influence from the literature of mystical ascent and celestial vision, including direct influence from Chalcidius's commentary on and translation of Plato's *Timaeus* (1984). Steven F. Kruger describes the dreamer's journey as simultaneously inward/self-reflexive and outward/upward, toward the realm of "eternal phenomena" and "abstract ideas" (1993). The words that take on the shape of their speakers after ascending to heaven in lines 1074–1082 bring to mind the resurrection (Minnis 1995, 198), aligning the resurrection of the body with this Platonic scheme for the reversion of the soul. The unfinished state of the text, if deliberate, is consistent with a reading of *House* as a parodic, chaotic version of the *regressus animae*.

The division of *House* into three books is consistent with the tripartite form of many other dream visions in that each book appears to correspond with a different stage of abstraction. For Ruggiers, each book represents a stage in a Boethian progression of increasingly universal conceptions of Fame: from Love to Order to Wisdom (1953). Similarly, Elizabeth Buckmaster sees a progression in attention to memory, intelligence, and foresight and to past, present, and future (1986); and John Finlayson finds a progression in the narrator's perception from vision to hearing to a more direct revelation that nonetheless confuses visual and aural perception (1986). Kathryn Lynch notes that the structure of *House* is informed by medieval understanding of the tripartite mind (1995). Several scholars have discussed *House* as an art of memory or as an attempt to exemplify a mnemonic system to help the medieval memory (Rowland 1975, 1981, 1993; Buckmaster 1986; Carruthers 1986, 1990).

The narrator is characteristically obtuse (Bevington 1961, Grennen 1984), but in the prologue a discussion of the confusions of modern dream theory (probably reflecting Chaucer's appreciation for it) serves as a variant on the usual description of the dreamer's own confusion (Kathryn Lynch 1995). The eagle guide is sometimes compared to Dante's eagle (Leyerle 1971; Minnis 1995, 201–203); for John M. Steadman, the eagle is a contemplative symbol that brings a new vision of the art of poetry (1960).

The Parliament of Fowls

The summary of the *Dream of Scipio* in the prologue is one of several features that align *Parliament* with the dream tradition of Cicero, Boethius, and Macrobius (Bennett 1957, 24–61, and 1979; Dubbs and Malarkey 1978; Gilbert 1978; Baker 1979; Arthur 1987; Cherniss 1987, 119–47) as well as the *Romance* and *Complaint* (Baker 1979, Pelen 1979, Quilligan 1981). Features influenced by the *Comedy* include the mottos on the gate of the garden (overview in Minnis 1995, 289). R.W. Frank reads *Parliament* as a satire of the love-vision genre (1956).

Typically, some early studies identify elements of other genres in *Parliament*, especially allegory. Some scholars have perceived here, as in *Duchess*, allegorical references to members of royalty (overview in Baker 1979, 430–431). Dorothy Bethurum discusses the psychology of love as depicted through the allegory of the garden of love (1955). Beginning with R.C. Goffin (1936), *Parliament* has also been interpreted as an allegory in which the narrator must choose between true and false felicity (overview in Baker 1979, 433; cf. Owen 1953), but Maureen Quilligan argues that *Parliament* is deliberately unallegorical (1981). *Parliament* also reflects the genre of debate, and its use of eschatological lore (von Kreisler 1971) may suggest apocalyptic influence.

The attempt to find structural unity among discordant elements has, as with many other dream visions, drawn scholarly attention. According to Bertrand H. Bronson's seminal study, contradiction—man's contradictory attitudes toward love—is the main theme (1935). Winny attributes the sense of disharmony and inconclusiveness to a stress between comic style and the conventions of love vision (1973, 113–143). Baker perceives a "development by link and parallel rather than by straight narrative" that is typical of love vision (1979, 430), and Jordan likewise finds discontinuity and acentricity rather than any organic model of unity (1977; cf. Kelley 1979, Sklute 1981). Like *Duchess* and *House*, *Parliament* appears to have a tripartite structure (Frank 1956, Boitani 1986). The prologue, like those of many dream visions, provides unity by introducing the main themes (Gilbert 1978, Mucchetti 1978).

The naïve dreamer/narrator of *Parliament* resembles that of other dream visions, especially those by Chaucer (see especially Owen 1953; Bethurum 1959; Clemen 1963, 126–28; Cherniss 1987, 119–47). The guide is Africanus, whom the dreamer first encounters awake while reading the *Dream of Scipio* in the prologue. Like the eagle guide in *House* and the eagle in *Purgatory*, Africanus brings the dreamer to a gate; his role also resembles that of Dante's Virgil (Baker 1979, 432).

Prologue to The Legend of Good Women

The *Legend* Prologue, composed later than Chaucer's other dream visions, has long been viewed as a transitional work between major phases of Chaucer's development (Frank 1972, Payne 1975). Because of its transitional nature and early scholarly preoccupation with its occasional status (overview in Fisher 1979), its resemblance to other dream visions has received relatively little attention. According to Cherniss, the Prologue is a self-contained dream poem that serves as a travesty of Boethian vision; in it he identifies typical elements of the genre (1986). In establishing the influence from Old French marguerite poetry by Machaut, Deschamps, and Froissart, and from Machaut's *Jugement dou Roy de Navarre*, a *dit amoreux*, early studies established channels for influence from the same authors' dream poems (Minnis 1995, 348–350; cf. Estrich 1939, Meecham-Jones 1996); another possible source is the *Purgatorio*. Like many other dream visions, the Prologue has been discussed as an *ars poetica* (Peck 1986).

Studies of the two versions of the Prologue, F and G, also bear on its status as dream vision. F has been thought closer to the French sources than G, which suggests that G is a revision of F; the existence of two prologues was first taken as evidence that the poem is occasional. The fact that there are two versions underscores the transitional status of the Prologue: Robert O. Payne argues that G represents a later stage of Chaucer's spiritual-artistic development (1973, 1975; cf. Delany 1994, 34–43); William A. Quinn claims that F is a script for a performance, while G is to be read as an independent text (1994).

The dreamer/narrator of the Prologue, like those in Chaucer's other dream poems, is a lover, but he is even more closely identified with the author than the others (Payne 1975, Cherniss 1986); he resembles the narrators of *Purgatory* (Kiser 1987) and of Jean de Meun's continuation of the *Romance* (Knopp 1973). Cherniss argues that Chaucer splits the Boethian guide into two figures, Cupid and Alceste; Kiser perceives in Alceste's role as guide a parallel with the role of Beatrice.

As suggested near the beginning of this chapter, a hallmark of the dream vision genre is its ability to sustain a broad pattern of convergence among a huge number of texts produced over a vast span of time. This feature enabled medieval writers to incorporate thousands of years of literary tradition within a single dream poem, so that a reader makes sense of the text by negotiating its dense texture of allusion to earlier literary dreams. A consequence of this feature of the genre that scholars have not sufficiently appreciated is the extensive pattern of correspondences it creates among publications focused on isolated aspects of individual dream poems, publications whose shared concerns are often overlooked. By showing which studies of individual dream texts relate to which defining features of dream vision, this chapter attempts to facilitate broader application of a body of knowledge mostly acquired through narrowly focused research.

SELECTED BIBLIOGRAPHY

General Studies of Medieval Dream Vision and Related Subjects

Bridges, Margaret. "The Sense of an Ending: The Case of the Dream-Vision." *Dutch Quarterly Review of Anglo-American Letters* 14 (1984): 81–96.

Cherniss, Michael D. *Boethian Apocalypse: Studies in Middle English Vision Poetry.* Norman, OK: Pilgrim, 1987.

Davidoff, Judith M. "Dream Vision Framing Fictions." *Beginning Well: Framing Fictions in Late Middle English Poetry.* London: Associated University Presses, 1988. 60–80.

Dinzelbacher, Peter. *Vision und Visionsliteratur im Mittelalter.* Monographien zur Geschichte des Mittelalters 23. Stuttgart: Hiersemann, 1981.

Edwards, Robert. *The Dream of Chaucer: Representation and Reflection in the Early Narratives.* Durham, NC: Duke University Press, 1989.

Erickson, Carolly. *The Medieval Vision: Essays in History and Perception.* New York: Oxford University Press, 1976.

Hieatt, Constance B. "Un Autre Fourme: Guillaume de Machaut and the Dream Vision Form." *Chaucer Review* 14 (1980): 97–115.

———. *The Realism of Dream Visions: The Poetic Exploitation of the Dream-Experience in Chaucer and His Contemporaries.* De Proprietatibus Litterarum, Series Practica 2. The Hague: Mouton, 1967.

Kruger, Steven F. *Dreaming in the Middle Ages.* Cambridge Studies in Medieval Literature 14. Cambridge: Cambridge University Press, 1992.

Lynch, Kathryn C. *The High Medieval Dream Vision: Poetry, Philosophy, and Literary Form.* Stanford, CA: Stanford University Press, 1988.

Means, Michael H. *The Consolatio Genre in Medieval English Literature.* University of Florida Humanities Monographs 36. Gainesville: University of Florida Press, 1972.

Miller, Jacqueline T. "Dream Visions of *Auctorit.*" *Poetic License: Authority and Authorship in Medieval and Renaissance Contexts.* New York: Oxford University Press, 1986. 34–72.

Nolan, Barbara. *The Gothic Visionary Perspective.* Princeton, NJ: Princeton University Press, 1977.

Payne, Roberta L. *The Influence of Dante on Medieval English Dream Visions.* American University Studies II, Romance Languages and Literature 63. New York: Lang, 1989.

Piehler, Paul. *The Visionary Landscape: A Study in Medieval Allegory.* London: Arnold, 1971.

Quinn, William A., ed. *Chaucer's Dream Visions and Shorter Poems.* Garland Reference

Library of the Humanities, Basic Readings in Chaucer and His Time, Series 2105. New York: Garland, 1999.

Russell, J. Stephen. *The English Dream Vision: Anatomy of a Form*. Columbus: Ohio State University Press, 1988.

———. "Meaningless Dreams and Meaningful Poems: The Form of the Medieval Dream Vision." *Massachusetts Studies in English* 7 (1980): 20–32.

Spearing, A.C. *Medieval Dream-Poetry*. Cambridge: Cambridge University Press, 1976.

Windeatt, B.A., ed. and trans. *Chaucer's Dream Poetry: Sources and Analogues*. Woodbridge, Eng.: Brewer; Totowa, NJ: Rowman, 1982.

Winny, James. *Chaucer's Dream-Poems*. New York: Barnes, 1973.

Piers Plowman

Adams, Robert. "The Nature of Need in *Piers Plowman* XX." *Traditio* 34 (1978): 273–301.

———. "Some Versions of Apocalypse: Learned and Popular Eschatology in *Piers Plowman*." *The Popular Literature of Medieval England*. Ed. Thomas J. Heffernan. Knoxville: University of Tennessee Press, 1985. 194–236.

Aers, David. *Piers Plowman and Christian Allegory*. London: Arnold, 1975.

Alford, John A. "The Design of the Poem." *A Companion to "Piers Plowman."* Ed. John A. Alford. Berkeley: University of California Press, 1988. 29–65.

———. "The Role of the Quotations in *Piers Plowman*." *Speculum* 52 (1977): 80–99.

Ames, Ruth M. *The Fulfillment of the Scriptures: Abraham, Moses, and Piers*. Evanston, IL: Northwestern University Press, 1970.

Arn, Mary-Jo. "Langland's Characterization of Will in the B-Text." *Dutch Quarterly Review of Anglo-American Letters* 11 (1981): 287–301.

Barney, Stephen A. "Allegorical Visions." *A Companion to "Piers Plowman."* Ed. John A. Alford. Berkeley: University of California Press, 1988. 117–133.

Bertz, Douglas. "Prophecy and Apocalypse in Langland's *Piers Plowman*, B-Text, Passus XVI to XIX." *JEGP* 84 (1985): 313–328.

Bishop, Ian. "Relatives at the Court of Heaven: Contrasted Treatments of an Idea in *Piers Plowman* and *Pearl*." *Medieval Literature and Antiquities: Studies in Honour of Basil Cottle*. Ed. Kevin Kiernan. Cambridge: Brewer, 1987. 111–118.

Bloomfield, Morton W. *"Piers Plowman" as a Fourteenth-Century Apocalypse*. New Brunswick, NJ: Rutgers University Press, 1962.

Bowers, John M. *The Crisis of Will in "Piers Plowman."* Washington, DC: Catholic University of America Press, 1986.

Cali, Pietro. *Allegory and Vision in Dante and Langland*. Cork: Cork University Press, 1971.

Carruthers, Mary. "Imaginatif, Memoria, and 'The Need for Critical Theory' in *Piers Plowman* Studies." *Yearbook of Langland Studies* 9 (1995): 103–114.

———. "Time, Apocalypse and the Plot of *Piers Plowman*." *Acts of Interpretation: The Text in Its Contexts, 700–1600: Essays on Medieval and Renaissance Literature in Honor of E. Talbot Donaldson*. Eds. Mary J. Carruthers and Elizabeth D. Kirk. Norman, OK: Pilgrim, 1982.

Chessell, Del. "The Word Made Flesh: The Poetry of Langland." *Critical Review* 14 (1971): 109–124.

Clopper, Lawrence M. "The Contemplative Matrix of *Piers Plowman* B." *Modern Language Quarterly* 46 (1985): 3–28.

———. "Langland's Markings for the Structure of *Piers Plowman*." *Modern Philology* 85 (1988): 245–255.

———. "Langland's Trinitarian Analogies as Key to Meaning and Structure." *Medievalia et Humanistica* 9 (1979): 87–110.

———. "The Life of the Dreamer, the Dreams of the Wanderer in *Piers Plowman*." *Studies in Philology* 86 (1989): 261–285.

Davlin, Mary Clemente. *A Game of Heuene: Word Play and the Meaning of "Piers Plowman" B*. Cambridge: Brewer, 1989.

———. "*Petrus, id est, Christus*: Piers the Plowman as 'The Whole Christ.' " *Chaucer Review* 6 (1972): 280–292.

Donaldson, E. Talbot. "Apocalyptic Style in *Piers Plowman* B XIX–XX." *Leeds Studies in English* 14 (1983): 74–81.

Economou, George D. "The Vision's Aftermath in *Piers Plowman*: The Poetics of the Middle English Dream-Vision." *Genre* 18 (1985): 313–321.

Emmerson, Richard K. " 'Covetise to Konne,' 'Goddes Pryvetee,' and Will's Ambiguous Dream Experience in *Piers Plowman*." *"Suche Werkis to Werche": Essays on "Piers Plowman" in Honor of David C. Fowler*. Ed. Miceal F. Vaughan. East Lansing, MI: Colleagues, 1993. 89–121.

———. "Introduction: The Apocalypse in Medieval Culture." *The Apocalypse in the Middle Ages*. Ed. Richard K. Emmerson and Bernard McGinn. Ithaca, NY: Cornell University Press, 1992. 293–332.

Frank, Robert W., Jr. "The Number of Visions in *Piers Plowman*." *Modern Language Notes* 66 (1951): 309–312.

Gerould, Gordon Hall. "The Structural Integrity of *Piers Plowman* B." *Studies in Philology* 45 (1948): 60–75.

Higgs, Elton D. "Conscience, Piers, and the Dreamer in the Structure of *Piers Plowman* B." *"Suche Werkis to Werche": Essays on "Piers Plowman" in Honor of David C. Fowler*. Ed. Miceal F. Vaughan. East Lansing, MI: Colleagues, 1993. 123–146.

———. "The Path to Involvement: The Centrality of the Dreamer in *Piers Plowman*." *Tulane Studies in English* 21 (1974): 1–34.

Holleran, J.V. "The Role of the Dreamer in *Piers Plowman*." *Annuale Mediaevale* 7 (1966): 33–50.

Hüppe, Bernard F. "*Petrus id est Christus*: Word Play in *Piers Plowman*, the B-Text." *ELH* 17 (1950): 163–190.

Jennings, Margaret. "Piers Plowman and Holychurch." *Viator* 9 (1978): 367–374.

Kane, George. *The Autobiographical Fallacy in Chaucer and Langland Studies*. The Chambers Memorial Lecture delivered at University College, London, 2 March 1965. London: University College: Lewis, 1965.

Kaske, R.E. "Holy Church's Speech and the Structure of *Piers Plowman*." *Chaucer and Middle English Studies in Honour of Rossell Hope Robbins*. Ed. Beryl Rowland. London: Allen, 1974. 320–327.

Kaulbach, Ernest N. *Imaginative Prophecy in the B-Text of "Piers Plowman."* Piers Plowman Studies 8. Cambridge: Brewer, 1993.

———. "The 'Vis Imaginativa Secundum Avicennam' and the Naturally Prophetic Powers of Ymaginatif in the B-Text of *Piers Plowman*." *JEGP* 86 (1987): 496–514.

Kerby-Fulton, Kathryn. " 'Who Has Written This Book?': Visionary Autobiography in

Langland's C-Text." *The Medieval Mystical Tradition in England: Exeter Symposium V.* Ed. Marion Glasscoe. Cambridge: Brewer, 1992. 101–116.

Kirk, Elizabeth D. *The Dream Thought of "Piers Plowman."* Yale Studies in English 178. New Haven, CT: Yale University Press, 1972.

Kruger, Steven F. "Mirrors and the Trajectory of Vision in *Piers Plowman.*" *Speculum* 66 (1991): 74–95.

Lawlor, John. *"Piers Plowman": An Essay in Criticism.* London: Arnold, 1962.

Lawton, David. "The Subject of *Piers Plowman.*" *Yearbook of Langland Studies* 1 (1987): 1–30.

Mann, Jill. *Langland and Allegory.* The Morton W. Bloomfield Lectures on Medieval English Literature 2. Kalamazoo, MI: Medieval Institute, 1992.

Mills, David. "The Role of the Dreamer in *Piers Plowman.*" *"Piers Plowman": Critical Approaches.* Ed. S.S. Hussey. London: Methuen, 1969. 180–202.

Muscatine, Charles. "*Piers Plowman*: The Poetry of Crisis." *Poetry and Crisis in the Age of Chaucer.* University of Notre Dame, Ward-Phillips Lectures in English Language and Literature 4. Notre Dame, IN: University of Notre Dame Press, 1972. 71–109.

Robertson, D.W., Jr., and Bernard F. Hüppe. *"Piers Plowman" and Scriptural Tradition.* Princeton, NJ: Princeton University Press, 1951.

Salter, Elizabeth. *Piers Plowman; An Introduction.* Oxford: Blackwell, 1962.

Schmidt, A.V.C. *The Clerkly Maker: Langland's Poetic Art.* Piers Plowman Studies 4. Cambridge: Brewer; Wolfeboro, NH: Boydell, 1987.

———. "The Inner Dreams in *Piers Plowman.*" *Medium Ævum* 55 (1986): 24–40.

———. "Lele Wordes and Bele Paroles: Some Aspects of Langland's Word-Play." *Review of English Studies* 34 (1983): 137–150.

Spearing, A.C. "Verbal Repetition in *Piers Plowman* B and C." *JEGP* 62 (1963): 722–737.

Thompson, Claud A. "Structural, Figurative, and Thematic Trinities in *Piers Plowman.*" *Mosaic* 9 (1976): 105–114.

Tristram, Hildegard L.C. "Intertextuelle Puns in *Piers Plowman.*" *Neuphilologische Mitteilungen* 84 (1983): 182–191.

Vaughan, Miceal F. " 'Til I Gan Awake': The Conversion of Dreamer into Narrator in *Piers Plowman* B." *Yearbook of Langland Studies* 5 (1991): 175–192.

Weldon, James F.G. "*Ordinatio* and Genre in MS CCC 201: A Mediaeval Reading of the B-Text of *Piers Plowman.*" *Florilegium* 12 (1993): 159–175.

———. "The Structure of Dream Visions in *Piers Plowman.*" *Mediaeval Studies* 49 (1987): 254–281.

Wells, Henry W. "The Construction of *Piers Plowman.*" *PMLA* 44 (1929): 123–149. Rpt. in *Middle English Survey: Critical Essays.* Ed. Edward Vasta. Notre Dame, IN: University of Notre Dame Press, 1965. 147–168.

Wittig, Joseph S. "The Dramatic and Rhetorical Development of Long Will's Pilgrimage." *Neuphilologische Mitteilungen* 76 (1975): 52–76.

———. "*Piers Plowman* B, Passus IX–XII: Elements in the Design of the Inward Journey." *Traditio* 28 (1972): 211–280.

Pearl

Aers, David. "The Self Mourning: Reflections on *Pearl.*" *Speculum* 68 (1993): 54–73.

Astell, Ann. "Mourning and Marriage in St. Bernard's *Sermones* and in *Pearl.*" *The Song of Songs in the Middle Ages.* Ithaca, NY: Cornell University Press, 1990. 119–135.

Bishop, Ian. *"Pearl" in Its Setting: A Critical Study of the Structure and Meaning of the Middle English Poem.* Oxford: Blackwell, 1968.

Blenkner, Louis. "The Pattern of Traditional Images in *Pearl.*" *Studies in Philology* 68 (1971): 26–49.

———. "The Theological Structure of *Pearl.*" *Traditio* 24 (1968): 43–75. Rpt. in *The Middle English "Pearl": Critical Essays.* Ed. John Conley. Notre Dame, IN: University of Notre Dame Press, 1970. 220–271.

Bogdanos, Theodore. *"Pearl": Image of the Ineffable: A Study in Medieval Poetic Symbolism.* University Park: Pennsylvania State University Press, 1983.

Chance, Jane. "Allegory and Structure in *Pearl*: The Four Senses of the *Ars Praedicandi* and Fourteenth-Century Homiletic Poetry." *Text and Matter: New Critical Perspectives of the "Pearl"-Poet.* Ed. Robert J. Blanch, Miriam Youngerman Miller, and Julian N. Wasserman. Troy, NY: Whitston, 1991. 31–59.

Clark, S.L., and Julian N. Wasserman. "The Spatial Argument of *Pearl*: Perspectives on a Venerable Bead." *Interpretations* 11 (1979): 1–12.

Clopper, Lawrence M. "*Pearl*: The Consolation of Scripture." *Viator* 23 (1992): 231–245.

Conley, John. "*Pearl* and a Lost Tradition." *JEGP* 54 (1955): 332–347. Rpt. in *The Middle English "Pearl": Critical Essays.* Ed. John Conley. Notre Dame, IN: University of Notre Dame Press, 1970. 50–72.

Donner, Morton. "A Grammatical Perspective on Word Play in *Pearl.*" *Chaucer Review* 22 (1988): 322–331.

———. "Word Play and Word Form in *Pearl.*" *Chaucer Review* 24 (1989): 166–182.

Eldredge, Laurence. "The State of *Pearl* Studies since 1933." *Viator* 6 (1975): 171–194.

Field, Rosalind. "The Heavenly Jerusalem in *Pearl.*" *Modern Language Review* 81 (1986): 7–17.

Finlayson, John. "*Pearl*: Landscape and Vision." *Studies in Philology* 71 (1974): 314–343.

Fletcher, Jefferson B. "The Allegory of the *Pearl.*" *JEGP* 20 (1921): 1–21.

Garrett, Robert Max. *"The Pearl*: An Interpretation." *University of Washington Publications in English* 4 (1918): 1–45. Also pub. separately: Seattle: University of Washington, 1918.

Gatta, John, Jr. "Transformation Symbolism and the Liturgy of the Mass in *Pearl.*" *Modern Philology* 71 (1974): 243–256.

Hamilton, Marie Padgett. "The Meaning of the Middle English *Pearl.*" *PMLA* 70 (1955): 805–824.

———. "Notes on *Pearl.*" *JEGP* 57 (1958): 177–191.

Hieatt, Constance B. "*Pearl* and the Dream-Vision Tradition." *Studia Neophilologica* 37 (1965): 139–145. Rpt. in *The Realism of Dream Visions.* The Hague: Mouton, 1967. 61–67.

Johnson, Lynn Staley. "*Pearl.*" *The Voice of the "Gawain"-Poet.* Madison: University of Wisconsin Press, 1984. 144–210.

Johnson, Wendell Stacy. "The Imagery and Diction of *The Pearl*: Toward an Interpretation." *ELH* 20 (1953): 161–180. Rpt. in *Middle English Survey: Critical Essays* Ed. Edward Vasta. Notre Dame IN: University of Notre Dame Press, 1965. 93–

115. Also rpt. in *The Middle English "Pearl": Critical Essays*. Ed. John Conley. Notre Dame, IN: University of Notre Dame Press, 1970. 27–49.

Kean, P.M. *"The Pearl": An Interpretation*. London: Routledge, 1967.

Macrae-Gibson, O.D. *"Pearl*: The Link-Words and the Thematic Structure." *Neophilologus* 52 (1968): 54–64. Rpt. in *The Middle English "Pearl": Critical Essays*. Ed. John Conley. Notre Dame, IN: University of Notre Dame Press, 1970. 203–19.

Madeleva, M. *"Pearl": A Study in Spiritual Dryness*. 1925. New York: Phaeton, 1968.

Mahl, Mary R. "The Pearl as the Church." *English Record* 17 (1966): 27–29.

Marti, Kevin. *Body, Heart, and Text in the "Pearl"-Poet*. Studies in Mediaeval Literature 12. Lewiston, NY: Mellen, 1991.

———. "Traditional Characteristics of the Resurrected Body in *Pearl." Viator* 24 (1993): 311–335.

Milroy, James. *"Pearl*: The Verbal Texture and the Linguistic Theme." *Neophilologus* 55 (1971): 195–208.

Nelson, Cary. *"Pearl*: The Circle as Figural Space." *The Incarnate Word: Literature as Verbal Space*. Urbana: University of Illinois Press, 1973. 25–49.

Niemann, Thomas C. *"Pearl* and the Christian Other World." *Genre* 7 (1974): 213–232.

Phillips, Heather. "The Eucharistic Allusions of *Pearl." Mediaeval Studies* 47 (1985): 474–486.

Pilch, Herbert. "The Middle English *Pearl*: Its Relation to the *Roman de la Rose*." Trans. Heide Hyprath. *The Middle English "Pearl": Critical Essays*. Ed. John Conley. Notre Dame, IN: University of Notre Dame Press, 1970. 163–184. Rpt. of "Das mittelenglische *Perlengedicht*: Sein Verhältnis zum Rosenroman." *Neuphilologische Mitteilungen* 65 (1964): 427–446.

Prior, Sandra Pierson. *"The Lombe* and *His Meyny Schene*: Signs of God in *Pearl* and the Apocalypse." *The Fayre Formez of the Pearl Poet*. East Lansing: Michigan State University Press, 1996. 21–66.

Rhodes, Jim. "The Dreamer Redeemed: Exile and the Kingdom in the Middle English *Pearl." Studies in the Age of Chaucer* 16 (1994): 119–142.

Robertson, D.W., Jr. "The Pearl as Symbol." *Modern Language Notes* 65 (1950): 155–161. Rpt. in *The Middle English "Pearl": Critical Essays*. Ed. John Conley. Notre Dame, IN: University of Notre Dame Press, 1970. 18–26.

Schotter, Anne Howland. "Vernacular Style and the Word of God: The Incarnational Art of *Pearl." Ineffability: Naming the Unnamable from Dante to Beckett*. Ed. Peter S. Hawkins and Anne Howland Schotter. New York: AMS, 1984. 23–34.

Spearing, A.C. *"Pearl." The Gawain-Poet: A Critical Study*. Cambridge: Cambridge University Press, 1970. 96–170.

———. *Readings in Medieval Poetry*. Cambridge: Cambridge University Press, 1987.

Stanbury, Sarah. "The Body and the City in *Pearl." Representations* 48 (1994): 30–47.

———. "Gazing toward Jerusalem: Space and Perception in *Pearl." Seeing the "Gawain"-Poet: Description and the Act of Perception*. Middle Ages Series. Philadelphia: University of Pennsylvania Press, 1991. 12–41. Rpt. of "Visions of Space: Acts of Perception in *Pearl* and in Some Late Medieval Illustrated Apocalypses." *Mediaevalia* 10 (1988): 133–158.

Stiller, Nikki. "The Transformation of the Physical in the Middle English *Pearl." English Studies* 63 (1982): 402–409.

Watts, V.E. *"Pearl* as a *Consolatio." Medium Ævum* 32 (1963): 34–36.

Whitaker, Muriel A. "*Pearl* and Some Illustrated Apocalypse Manuscripts." *Viator* 12 (1981): 183–196.

Wilson, Edward. "Word Play and the Interpretation of *Pearl.*" *Medium Ævum* 40 (1971): 116–134.

Wimsatt, James I. *Allegory and Mirror: Tradition and Structure in Middle English Literature.* Pegasus Backgrounds in English Literature. New York: Pegasus, 1970. 117–136.

Wood, Ann Douglas. "The *Pearl*-Dreamer and the 'Hyne' in the Vineyard Parable." *Philological Quarterly* 52 (1973): 9–19.

Studies Not Previously Listed That Contribute to Studies on Chaucer's Dream Visions

Anderson, J.J. "The Narrators in the *Book of the Duchess* and the *Parlement of Foules.*" *Chaucer Review* 26 (1992): 219–235.

Bethurum, Dorothy. "Chaucer's Point of View in the Love Poems." *PMLA* 74 (1959): 511–520.

Boitani, Piero. "Old Books Brought to Life in Dreams: The *Book of the Duchess*, the *House of Fame*, the *Parliament of Fowls.*" *The Cambridge Chaucer Companion.* Ed. Piero Boitani and Jill Mann. Cambridge: Cambridge University Press, 1986. 39–57.

Burlin, Robert B. *Chaucerian Fiction.* Princeton, NJ: Princeton University Press, 1977.

Calin, William. "Machaut's Legacy: The Chaucerian Inheritance Reconsidered." *Studies in the Literary Imagination* 20 (1987): 9–22.

Carruthers, Mary J. *The Book of Memory: A Study of Memory in Mediaeval Culture.* Cambridge Studies in Medieval Literature 10. Cambridge: Cambridge University Press, 1990.

Clemen, Wolfgang. *Chaucer's Early Poetry.* Trans. C.A.M. Sym. London: Methuen, 1963.

Coghill, Nevill. *The Poet Chaucer.* Oxford Paperbacks. 2nd ed. London: Oxford University Press, 1967.

David, Alfred. *The Strumpet Muse: Art and Morals in Chaucer's Poetry.* Bloomington: Indiana University Press, 1976.

Donner, Morton. "Chaucer and His Narrators: The Poet's Place in His Poems." *Western Humanities Review* 27 (1973): 189–195.

Ferster, Judith. *Chaucer on Interpretation.* Cambridge: Cambridge University Press, 1985.

Finlayson, John. "The *Roman de la Rose* and Chaucer's Narrators." *Chaucer Review* 24 (1990): 187–210.

Fyler, John M. *Chaucer and Ovid.* New Haven, CT: Yale University Press, 1979. 98–115.

Gellrich, Jesse. *The Idea of the Book in the Middle Ages: Language Theory, Mythology, and Fiction.* Ithaca, NY: Cornell University Press, 1985.

Hale, David G. "Dreams, Stress, and Interpretation in Chaucer and His Contemporaries." *Journal of the Rocky Mountain Medieval and Renaissance Association* 9 (1988): 47–61.

Hammil, Carrie Esther. "Chaucer and the Dream of Harmony." *The Celestial Journey and the Harmony of the Spheres in English Literature, 1300–1700.* Fort Worth: Texas Christian University Press, 1980. 39–74.

Hanning, Robert W. "Chaucer's First Ovid: Metamorphosis in *The Book of the Duchess* and *The House of Fame.*" *Chaucer and the Craft of Fiction.* Ed. Leigh A. Arrathoon. Rochester, MI: Solaris, 1986. 121–163.

Hieatt, Constance B. "The Dreams of Troilus, Criseyde, and Chauntecleer: Chaucer's Manipulation of the Categories of Macrobius *et al.*" *English Studies in Canada* 14 (1988): 400–414.

Howard, Donald R. "Flying through Space: Chaucer and Milton." *Milton and the Line of Vision.* Ed. Joseph Wittreich, Jr. Madison: University of Wisconsin Press, 1975. 3–23.

Hum, Sue. "Knowledge, Belief, and Lack of Agency: The Dreams of Geoffrey, Troilus, Criseyde, and Chauntecleer." *Style* 31 (1997): 500–522.

Hüppe, Bernard F., and D.W. Robertson, Jr. *Fruyt and Chaf: Studies in Chaucer's Allegories.* Princeton, NJ: Princeton University Press, 1963.

Jordan, Robert. *Chaucer and the Shape of Creation.* Cambridge, MA: Harvard University Press, 1967.

Kean, P.M. *Chaucer and the Making of English Poetry.* vol. 1. *Love Vision and Debate.* London: Routledge, 1972.

Kittredge, G.L. *Chaucer and His Poetry.* Cambridge, MA: Harvard University Press, 1915.

Kolve, V.A. *Chaucer and the Imagery of Narrative: The First Five Canterbury Tales.* Stanford, CA: Stanford University Press, 1984.

Larson, Charles. "The Squire's Tale: Chaucer's Evolution from the Dream Vision." *Revue des langues vivantes* 43 (1977): 598–607.

Lawton, David. *Chaucer's Narrators.* Cambridge: Brewer, 1985.

Muscatine, Charles. *Chaucer and the French Tradition: A Study in Style and Meaning.* Berkeley: University of California Press, 1957.

Payne, Robert O. *The Key of Remembrance: A Study of Chaucer's Poetics.* 1963. Westport, CT: Greenwood Press, 1973.

Peck, Russell A. "Chaucer and the Nominalist Questions." *Speculum* 53 (1978): 745–760.

Peden, Alison M. "Macrobius and Mediaeval Dream Literature." *Medium Ævum* 54 (1985): 59–73.

Pratt, R.A. "Some Latin Sources of the Nonnes Preest on Dreams." *Speculum* 52 (1977): 538–570.

Robertson, D.W. *A Preface to Chaucer: Studies in Medieval Perspectives.* Princeton, NJ: Princeton University Press, 1962.

Rowland, Beryl, ed. *Companion to Chaucer Studies.* Rev. ed. New York: Oxford University Press, 1979.

Ryan, Marcella. "Chaucer's Dream-Vision Poems and the Theory of Spatial Form." *Parergon: Bulletin of the Australian and New Zealand Association for Medieval and Renaissance Studies* 11 (1993): 79–90.

———. "The Concept of Textual Unity in Chaucer's Dream-Visions." *AUMLA: Journal of the Australasian Universities Language and Literature Association* 74 (1990): 25–33.

Scanlon, Larry. *Narrative, Authority, and Power: The Medieval Exemplum and the Chau-*

cerian Tradition. Cambridge Studies in Medieval Literature 20. Cambridge: Cambridge University Press, 1994.

Schless, Howard H. *Chaucer and Dante: A Revaluation.* Norman, OK: Pilgrim, 1984.

Sklute, Larry. *Virtue of Necessity: Inconclusiveness and Narrative Form in Chaucer's Poetry.* Columbus: Ohio State University Press, 1984.

Spearing, A.C. *The Medieval Poet as Voyeur: Looking and Listening in Medieval Love-Narratives.* Cambridge: Cambridge University Press, 1993.

Wallace, David. "Chaucer's Continental Inheritance: The Early Poems and *Troilus and Criseyde.*" *The Cambridge Chaucer Companion.* Ed. Piero Boitani and Jill Mann. Cambridge: Cambridge University Press, 1986. 19–37.

Wetherbee, Winthrop. "Latin Structure and Vernacular Space: Gower, Chaucer, and the Boethian Tradition." *Chaucer and Gower: Difference, Mutuality, Exchange.* Ed. R.F. Yeager. Victoria, British Columbia: University of Victoria, 1991. 7–35.

The Book of the Duchess

Baker, Donald C. "The Dreamer Again in *The Book of the Duchess.*" *PMLA* 70 (1955): 279–282.

Butterfield, Ardis. "Lyric and Elegy in *The Book of the Duchess.*" *Medium Ævum* 60 (1991): 33–60.

Cherniss, Michael D. "The Boethian Dialogue in Chaucer's *Book of the Duchess.*" *JEGP* 68 (1969): 655–665.

Donnelly, Colleen. "Challenging the Conventions of Dream Vision in *The Book of the Duchess.*" *Philological Quarterly* 66 (1987): 421–435.

Hardman, Phillipa. "*The Book of the Duchess* as a Memorial Monument." *Chaucer Review* 28 (1994): 205–215. Rpt. in *Chaucer's Dream Visions and Shorter Poems.* Ed. William A. Quinn. New York: Garland, 1999. 183–96.

Heinrichs, Katherine. "Love and Hell: The Denizens of Hades in the Love Poems of the Middle Ages." *Neophilologus* 73 (1989): 593–604.

Jordan, Robert M. "The Compositional Structure of *The Book of the Duchess.*" *Chaucer Review* 9 (1974): 99–117.

Kiser, Lisa J. "Sleep, Dreams, and Poetry in Chaucer's *Book of the Duchess.*" *Papers on Language and Literature* 19 (1983): 3–12.

Kreuzer, James R. "The Dreamer in *The Book of the Duchess.*" *PMLA* 66 (1951): 543–547.

Lawlor, John. "The Pattern of Consolation in *The Book of the Duchess.*" *Speculum* 31 (1956): 626–648. Rpt. in *Chaucer Criticism: "Troilus and Criseyde" and the Minor Poems.* Ed. Richard J. Schoeck and Jerome Taylor. Notre Dame, IN: University of Notre Dame Press, 1961. 232–260.

Lynch, Andrew. " 'Taking Keep' of the *Book of the Duchess.*" *Medieval English Religious and Ethical Literature: Essays in Honour of G.H. Russell.* Ed. Gregory Kratzmann and James Simpson. Cambridge: Brewer, 1986. 167–178.

Lynch, Kathryn L. "The *Book of the Duchess* as a Philosophical Vision: The Argument of Form." *Genre* 21 (1988): 279–305.

Manning, Stephen. "That Dreamer Once More." *PMLA* 71 (1956): 540–541.

Minnis, A.J. *Shorter Poems.* Oxford: Clarendon Press, 1995.

Neaman, Judith S. "Brain Physiology and Poetics in *The Book of the Duchess.*" *Res publica litterarum* 3 (1980): 101–113.

Nolan, Barbara. "The Art of Expropriation: Chaucer's Narrator in *The Book of the Duchess*." *New Perspectives in Chaucer Criticism*. Ed. Donald Rose. Norman, OK: Pilgrim, 1981. 203–222.

Palmer, R. Barton. "*The Book of the Duchess* and *Fonteinne amoureuse*: Chaucer and Machaut Reconsidered." *Canadian Review of Comparative Literature* 7 (1981): 380–393.

———. "Rereading Guillaume de Machaut's Vision of Love: Chaucer's *Book of the Duchess* as Bricolage." *Second Thoughts: A Focus on Rereading*. Ed. David Galef. Detroit: Wayne State University Press, 1998. 133–146.

Pelen, M.M. "Machaut's Court of Love Narratives and Chaucer's *Book of the Duchess*." *Chaucer Review* 11 (1976–1977): 128–155.

Phillips, Helen. "Structure and Consolation in the *Book of the Duchess*." *Chaucer Review* 16 (1981): 107–118.

Rambuss, Richard. " 'Processe of Tyme': History, Consolation, and Apocalypse in *The Book of the Duchess*." *Exemplaria* 2 (1990): 659–683.

Robertson, D.W., Jr. "*The Book of the Duchess*." *Companion to Chaucer Studies*. Ed. Beryl Rowland. Rev. ed. New York: Oxford University Press, 1979. 403–413.

———. "The Historical Setting of Chaucer's *Book of the Duchess*." *Mediaeval Studies in Honor of Urban Tigner Holmes, Jr*. Ed. John Mahoney and John Esten Keller. Chapel Hill: University of North Carolina Press, 1965. 169–195.

Shippey, T.A. "Chaucer's Arithmetical Mentality and *The Book of the Duchess*." *Chaucer Review* 31 (1996): 184–200.

Thundy, Zacharias P. "The Dreame of Chaucer: Boethian Consolation or Political Celebration?" *Carmina Philosophiae: Journal of the International Boethius Society* 4 (1995): 91–109.

Tisdale, Charles P. "Boethian 'Hert-Huntyng': The Elegiac Pattern of *The Book of the Duchess*." *American Benedictine Review* 24 (1973): 365–380.

Walker, Denis. "Narrative Inclusiveness and Consolatory Dialectic in the *Book of the Duchess*." *Chaucer Review* 18 (1983): 1–17.

Wimsatt, James. "*The Book of the Duchess*: Secular Elegy or Religious Vision?" *Signs and Symbols in Chaucer's Poetry*. Ed. John P. Hermann and John J. Burke, Jr. University: University of Alabama Press, 1981. 113–129.

———. *Chaucer and the French Love Poets: The Literary Background of "The Book of the Duchess."* Chapel Hill: University of North Carolina Press, 1968.

The House of Fame

Bennett, J.A.W. *Chaucer's "Book of Fame": An Exposition of "The House of Fame."* Oxford: Clarendon Press, 1968.

Bevington, David M. "The Obtuse Narrator in Chaucer's *House of Fame*." *Speculum* 36 (1961): 288–298.

Boenig, Robert. "Chaucer's *House of Fame*, the Apocalypse, and Bede." *American Benedictine Review* 36 (1985): 263–277.

Boitani, Piero. *Chaucer and the Imaginary World of Fame*. Chaucer Studies 10. Cambridge: Brewer; Totowa, NJ: Barnes, 1984.

Buckmaster, Elizabeth. "Meditation and Memory in Chaucer's *House of Fame*." *Modern Language Studies* 16 (1986): 279–287.

Carruthers, Mary J. "Italy, *Ars Memorativa*, and Fame's House." *Studies in the Age of Chaucer*, Proceedings Ser. 2 (1986): 179–188.

David, Alfred. "Literary Satire in *The House of Fame*." *PMLA* 75 (1960): 153–159.

Delany, Sheila. *Chaucer's "House of Fame": The Poetics of Skeptical Fideism*. Chicago: University of Chicago Press, 1972.

Doob, Penelope Reed. *The Idea of the Labyrinth from Classical Antiquity through the Middle Ages*. Ithaca, NY: Cornell University Press, 1990.

Finlayson, John. "Seeing, Hearing, and Knowing in *The House of Fame*." *Studia Neophilologica* 58 (1986): 47–57.

Fyler, John M. " ' 'Cloude,'—and Al That Y of Spak': 'The House of Fame,' v. 978." *Neuphilologische Mitteilungen* 87 (1986): 565–568.

Grennen, Joseph E. "Chaucer and Chalcidius: The Platonic Origins of *The Hous of Fame*." *Viator* 15 (1984): 237–262.

Irvine, Martin. "Medieval Grammatical Theory and Chaucer's *House of Fame*." *Speculum* 60 (1985): 850–876.

Koonce, B.G. *Chaucer and the Tradition of Fame: Symbolism in "The House of Fame."* Princeton, NJ: Princeton University Press, 1966.

Kruger, Steven F. "Imagination and the Complex Movement of Chaucer's *House of Fame*." *Chaucer Review* 28 (1993): 117–134.

Leyerle, John. "Chaucer's Windy Eagle." *University of Toronto Quarterly* 40 (1971): 247–265.

Lynch, Kathryn C. "The Logic of the Dream Vision in Chaucer's *House of Fame*." *Literary Nominalism and the Theory of Rereading Late Medieval Texts: A New Research Paradigm*. Mediaeval Studies 5. Ed. Richard J. Utz. Lewiston, NY: Mellen, 1995. 179–203.

Rowland, Beryl. "The Artificial Memory, Chaucer, and Modern Scholars." *Poetica* 37 (1993): 1–14.

———. "The Art of Memory and the Art of Poetry in *The House of Fame*." *University of Ottawa Quarterly* 51 (1981): 162–171.

———. "Bishop Bradwardine, the Artificial Memory, and the *House of Fame*." *Chaucer at Albany*. Ed. Rossell Hope Robbins. New York: Franklin, 1975. 41–62.

Ruggiers, Paul G. "The Unity of Chaucer's *House of Fame*." *Studies in Philology* 50 (1953): 16–29.

Shook, Laurence K. "The *House of Fame*." *Companion to Chaucer Studies*. Ed. Beryl Rowland. Rev. ed. New York: Oxford University Press, 1979. 414–427.

Steadman, John M. "Chaucer's Eagle: A Contemplative Symbol." *PMLA* 75 (1960): 153–158.

Sypherd, Wilbur Owen. *Studies in Chaucer's "Hous of Fame."* 1907. New York: Haskell, 1965.

Tisdale, Charles P.R. "*The House of Fame*: Virgilian Reason and Boethian Wisdom." *Comparative Literature* 25 (1973): 247–261.

The Parliament of Fowls

Arthur, Ross G. "Chaucer's Use of *The Dream of Scipio* in *The Parliament of Fowls*." *American Benedictine Review* 38 (1987): 29–49.

Baker, Donald C. "*The Parliament of Fowls*." *Companion to Chaucer Studies*. Ed. Beryl Rowland. Rev. ed., New York: Oxford University Press, 1979. 428–45.

Bennett, J.A.W. *"The Parlement of Foules": An Interpretation.* Oxford: Clarendon Press, 1957.

———. "Some Second Thoughts on *The Parlement of Foules*." *Chaucerian Problems and Perspectives: Essays Presented to Paul E. Beichner, C.S.C.* Ed. Edward Vasta and Zacharias P. Thundy. Notre Dame, IN: University of Notre Dame Press, 1979. 132–146.

Bethurum, Dorothy. "The Center of the *Parlement of Foules*." *Essays in Honor of Walter Clyde Curry.* Foreword by Hardin Craig. Nashville: Vanderbilt University Press, 1954. 39–50.

———. "Chaucer's Point of View as Narrator in the Love Poems." *PMLA* 74 (1959): 511–520.

Bronson, Bertrand H. "In Appreciation of Chaucer's *Parlement of Foules*." *University of California Publications in English* 3 (1935): 193–224.

Dubbs, Kathleen E., and Stoddard Malarkey. "The Frame of Chaucer's *Parlement*." *Chaucer Review* 13 (1978): 16–24.

Everett, Dorothy. "Chaucer's Love Visions, with Particular Reference to *The Parlement of Foules*." *Essays on Middle English Literature.* Ed. Patricia Kean. Oxford: Clarendon Press, 1955. 97–114.

Frank, R.W., Jr. "Structure and Meaning in *The Parlement of Foules*." *PMLA* 71 (1956): 530–539.

Gilbert, A.J. "The Influence of Boethius on the *Parlement of Foulys*." *Medium Ævum* 47 (1978): 292–303.

Goffin, R.C. "Heaven and Earth in *The Parlement of Foules*." *Modern Language Review* 31 (1936): 493–499.

Hewitt, Kathleen. " 'Ther It Was First': Dream Poetics in *The Parliament of Fowls*." *Chaucer Review* 24 (1989): 20–28.

Jordan, Robert M. "The Question of Unity and *The Parlement of Foules*." *English Studies in Canada* 3 (1977): 373–385.

Kelley, Michael P. "Antithesis as the Principle of Design in *The Parlement of Foules*." *Chaucer Review* 14 (1979): 61–73.

Mucchetti, Emil A. "The Structural Importance of the Proem and the *Somnium Scipionis* to the Unity of *The Parliament of Fowls*." *Publications of the Arkansas Philological Association* 4 (1978): 1–10.

Owen, Charles A., Jr. "The Role of the Narrator in *The Parlement of Foules*." *College English* 14 (1953): 264–269.

Pelen, Marc M. "Form and Meaning of the Old French Love Vision: The Fableau dou Dieu d'Amors and Chaucer's *Parliament of Fowls*." *Journal of Medieval and Renaissance Studies* 9 (1979): 277–305.

Piehler, Paul. "Myth, Allegory, and Vision in *The Parliament of Foules*: A Study in Chaucerian Problem Solving." *Allegoresis: The Craft of Allegory in Medieval Literature.* Ed. J. Stephen Russell. Garland Reference Library of the Humanities 664. New York: Garland, 1988. 187–214.

Quilligan, Maureen. "Allegory, Allegoresis, and the Deallegorization of Language: The *Roman de la Rose*, the *De Planctu Naturae*, and *The Parlement of Foules*." *Allegory, Myth, and Symbol.* Ed. Morton W. Bloomfield. Cambridge, MA: Harvard University Press, 1981. 164–186.

Sklute, Larry M. "The Inconclusive Form of *The Parliament of Fowls*." *Chaucer Review* 16 (1981): 119–128.

von Kreisler, Nicolai. "The *Locus Amoenus* and Eschatological Lore in *The Parliament of Fowls*." *Philological Quarterly* 50 (1971): 16–22.

Prologue to *The Legend of Good Women*

Baker, Donald C. "Dreamer and Critic: The Poet in *The Legend of Good Women*." *University of Colorado Studies in Language and Literature* 9 (1963): 4–18.

Cherniss, Michael D. "Chaucer's Last Dream Vision: The *Prologue* to *The Legend of Good Women*." *Chaucer Review* 20 (1986): 183–199.

Delany, Sheila. *The Naked Text: Chaucer's "Legend of Good Women."* Berkeley: University of California Press, 1994.

Estrich, Robert M. "Chaucer's Prologue to *The Legend of Good Women* and Machaut's *Le Jugement dou Roy de Navarre*." *Studies in Philology* 36 (1939): 26–29.

Fisher, John H. "*The Legend of Good Women*." *Companion to Chaucer Studies*. Ed. Beryl Rowland. Rev. ed. New York: Oxford University Press, 1979. 464–476.

Frank, Robert Worth, Jr. *Chaucer and "The Legend of Good Women."* Cambridge, MA: Harvard University Press, 1972.

Kiser, Lisa J. "*The Legend of Good Women*: Chaucer's *Purgatorio*." *ELH* 54 (1987): 741–760.

———. *Telling Classical Tales: Chaucer and the "Legend of Good Women."* Ithaca, NY: Cornell University Press, 1983.

Knopp, Sherron. "Chaucer and Jean de Meun as Self-Conscious Narrators: The Prologue to *The Legend of Good Women* and the *Roman de la Rose*." *Comitatus* 4 (1973): 25–39.

Meecham-Jones, Simon. " 'Myn Erthly God': Paradigm and Parody in the Prologue to *The Legend of Good Women*." *Myth and Its Legacy in European Literature*. Durham Modern Languages Series GM6. Ed. Neil Thomas and Françoise Le Saux. Durham: University of Durham, 1996.

Payne, Robert O. "Making His Own Myth: The Prologue to Chaucer's *Legend of Good Women*." *Chaucer Review* 9 (1975): 197–211.

Peck, R.A. "Chaucerian Poetics and the Prologue to *The Legend of Good Women*." *Chaucer in the Eighties*. Ed. Julian N. Wasserman and Robert J. Blanch. Syracuse, NY: Syracuse University Press, 1986. 39–55.

Percival, Florence. *Chaucer's Legendary Good Women*. Cambridge Studies in Medieval Literature 38. Cambridge: Cambridge University Press, 1998.

Quinn, William A. *Chaucer's "Rehersynges": The Performability of "The Legend of Good Women."* Washington, DC: Catholic University of America Press, 1994.

Rowe, Donald W. *Through Nature to Eternity: Chaucer's "Legend of Good Women."* Lincoln: University of Nebraska Press, 1988.

Selected Editions

Chaucer, Geoffrey. *The Riverside Chaucer*. Ed. Larry D. Benson. 3rd ed. Boston: Houghton Mifflin, 1987.

Fischer, Steven R. *The Complete Medieval Dreambook: A Multilingual, Alphabetical "Somnia Danielis" Collation*. Bern: Lang, 1982.

Langland, William. *"Piers Plowman": A Parallel-Text Edition of the A, B, C, and Z Versions*. Ed. A.V.C. Schmidt. 1 vol. to date. London: Longman, 1995– .

———. *"Piers Plowman": The Three Versions*. Gen. ed. George Kane. 3 vols. London: Athlone; Berkeley: University of California Press, 1988–1997.

———. *The Vision of Piers Plowman: A Critical Edition of the B-Text Based on Trinity College Cambridge MS B.15.17*. Ed. A.V.C. Schmidt. Everyman Library. 2nd ed. London: Dent; Rutland, VT: Tuttle, 1995.

"Pearl" and "Cleanness." Ed. William Vantuono. Vol. 1 of *The "Pearl" Poems: An Omnibus Edition*. The Renaissance Imagination 5. New York: Garland, 1984.

"Pearl": An Edition with Verse Translation. Ed. and trans. William Vantuono. Notre Dame, IN: University of Notre Dame Press, 1995.

"The Pilgrimage of the Soul": A Critical Edition of the Middle English Dream Vision. Ed. Rosemarie Potz McGerr. New York: Garland, 1990.

The Poems of the Pearl Manuscript. Ed. Malcolm Andrew and Ronald Waldron. Rev. ed. Exeter Medieval English Texts and Studies. Exeter: University of Exeter Press, 1987.

11
Epic and Heroic Poetry

John Michael Crafton

BRIEF OVERVIEW

The two terms *epic* and *heroic* have been used almost synonymously, and for many medieval texts this equation is not inappropriate; however, most scholars are careful to make a distinction and to demonstrate that a text may be epic but not heroic and vice versa. A survey of the literature relevant to these two terms in both Old and Middle English creates, potentially at least, a dizzyingly complex picture, so for the sake of clarity, we will first provide a brief but clear definition and description of both epic and heroic, then a survey of some of the more important texts of Old and Middle English that represent each mode, and finally a brief critical history of the term.

In its earliest incarnations the heroic seems to grow from very specific places, deeds, and people. It could be argued, as Michael Alexander does in *Old English Literature*, that "this poetry comes first in any history of Old English literature because most other Old English verse grows out of it in vocabulary and form, and also, since the medium is itself conservative, in its view of the world—even when the metaphysics of the later world-view are quite different" (38). In short, much of what we consider Old English literature, including the epic, could be said to grow out of the heroic. The term *heroic poetry* refers to a more narrow set of formal characteristics than does the term *epic* and to a more narrow ideological range and audience response. In the briefest definition, heroic poetry is composed to commemorate the deeds, usually martial, of one or more heroes whose accomplishments represent the supreme values of a community and inspire the listeners either to emulate or to admire these heroes. Furthermore, these fundamental values, especially in times of military conflict, are steadfast valor and complete loyalty and are expressed in a highly stylized manner designed to achieve something of an anthemlike, war-chant effect on the audience. This functionality is exemplified most clearly in this famous stanza from the *Chanson de Roland* (in Dorothy Sayers's translation):

> Look to it now! Let each man stoutly smite!
> No shameful songs be sung for our despite!
> Paynims are wrong, Christians are in the right.
> Ill tales of me shall no man tell, say I! (79: 1009–1012)

That the *Chanson* could achieve its function in the battlefield is suggested by the legend that William the Conqueror had the French epic sung to his soldiers during the Battle of Hastings. The simplicity of the message, moreover, is communicated well in the simplicity of a four-beat line in Old French. Likewise, Anglo-Saxon heroic poetry uses a four-stress line to pound out its anthemic message.

Another very important part of the world view of the heroic poem, which is implied in the quotation just given, is the significant role of heroic poetry itself. The poem and the poet are, in fact, necessary components of the heroic world. This fact doubtless comes from the oral culture of heroic poetry, according to which culture if an event is not recorded in song, it is not remembered; if it is not remembered, it ceases to exist.

Beowulf provides a very good example of this self-referential valuing of the role of the heroic poet. After Beowulf's defeat of Grendel, the thanes of Hrothgar follow the blood spoor of Grendel and become so flushed with victory that one "thane / of the king's household, a carrier of tales" begins to create a new poem about Beowulf and his success against Grendel, "rehearsing Beowulf's / triumphs and feats in well-fashioned lines" (Heaney translation 59). In this example the entire cycle of the heroic poem can be seen. Having heard heroic songs, Beowulf performs a heroic deed. When the hero has performed a heroic deed, a heroic song is composed commemorating it and urging others to perform similar deeds.

A more complex genre, the *epic* might be best defined by three perspectives: one, formal characteristics; two, ideology and social connection; and three, audience reception or reader response. Formally, an epic is a long narrative poem commemorating the exploits of one or more heroes of national significance in an elevated or grand style that includes elaborate descriptions of battles, armaments, adventures, and monsters, as well as elaborate speeches, catalogs, similes, allusions, digressions, and epithets. Furthermore, these exploits often involve divine or otherworldly beings and journeys to ends of the known world and beyond. The term *epic*, then, denotes a certain level of subject matter (deeds of supremely national significance) and style (nonconversational, memorializing verse). Both the subject and the style are summed up in Northrop Frye's discussion of the epic hero and imagery as high mimetic mode, a term that he develops to emphasize the fact that there is some verisimilitudinous dimension to the epic, but not so much as to be considered domestic nor so little as to be considered mythological. Another formal trait associated with epic is its inclusiveness or encyclopedic quality. In general, this trait is understood as the epic's tendency to contain the history, religion, and wisdom of an ancient people; not too surprisingly, the epic also contains within it other literary genres, such as lyric, elegy, proverbs and aphorisms, and even at times satire or mock epic, thus sowing the seeds of its own deconstruction.

A most fundamental defining condition of the epic concerns its composition, whether oral or written. The oral or folk or primary epic is said to have been composed over time as the tale passed from singer to singer in the oral-formulaic tradition, first persuasively argued by Milman Parry in Homeric scholarship. These epics, of which *Beowulf* may be one, are characterized by a higher degree of repetition, less explicit historical references, elliptical allusiveness, and a lesser degree of self-reflection or interpretation or allegoresis. The literary or secondary epic, a term made famous in C.S. Lewis's *A Preface to* Paradise Lost, refers to epics that are written in imitation of the primary epics. All of those texts considered heroic or epic in Old and Middle English come to us in a written form, but it is not the consensus that all of these were composed thus. The most obvious case is, of course, *Beowulf*, which for a long time was considered to be composed of strung-together folktales from northern Europe with a composition date of the mid-eighth century in Mercia. The only surviving copy of *Beowulf*, however, is preserved in a written manuscript dating to the early eleventh century, thus suggesting to some a later composition. While more scholars seem to be accepting the later date of composition, that fact does not preclude the influence of the oral-formulaic method of composition.

The second perspective of the epic is its sociopolitical nexus. The epics of Old and Middle English represent the point of view of the aristocracy; the epic subject matter is ancient, in a distant land, and thus divorced from contemporary space and time in order to be rendered in such a way as to represent the highest ideals of a conservative. This distancing in space and time is also accompanied by a singular dialect, what Bakhtin referred to as monoglossia, the single dialect of power and authority. The language and its composition are designed to elevate the discourse above discursiveness and again approach the monumental.

Finally, the manner in which the text is received is considered to be one of the most important of the defining traits of the epic. The overall performance of the epic, the sense of its grandeur, of its almost sacred and ritualistic quality, is what is truly the sine qua non of the epic and what may be in fact the most difficult trait to describe. Put simply, the epic was to be heard or read in a mood of solemnity approaching that of a religious or political ritual, a disjunction the medieval world perhaps did not know. In speech-act theory the term often invoked here is the performative. That is, for an epic to happen or occur, the language has to be such that the listener or reader is moved to perceive that listening to or reading an epic results in something more than the comprehension of a story; rather, it is a participation in the memorializing of the highest values of the culture and an awareness that in keeping the epic alive, the culture survives.

OLD ENGLISH TEXTS

The heroic tradition is exemplified throughout the corpus of Anglo-Saxon poetry, and this field of representation ranges from very short fragments to the full scale in *Beowulf*. Perhaps the easiest way to organize the discussion of this rather large body of poetry is to divide it into three groups: secular, Christian, and *Beowulf*.

Widsith is one of the oldest, if not the oldest, of the secular heroic poems. In it the speaker, a scop who may be advertising for a new patron, tells a simple story of accompanying a young woman to meet her husband-to-be, Eormanric, and retelling his many journeys and boasting about his many connections in the Germanic world. His list comprises a veritable who's who of the ancient Germanic world, including names both legendary and historic, such as Hrothgar, Hama, and Offa. The poem ends with the assertions that the only lasting glory available to the earl is in the singer's song, the implication being that the listening earl (or king, since we do not know who the intended audience was) should support Widsith. *The Fight at Finnsburg* is interesting as one of the shortest of all the heroic poems in the corpus. It is a fragment found only in George Hickes's *Linguarum Veterum Septentrionalium Thesaurus Grammatico-Criticus et Archaeologicus* (Oxford, 1705). The larger story of which this fragment is a part is told a bit more completely in *Beowulf*. As best as we can understand in the fragment, the Dane Hnaef is under attack by Finn in the fragment and awakens his thanes in typical heroic style:

> "Soon shall be the cough of birds,
> Hoar wolf's howl, hard wood-talk
> Shield's answer to shaft.
>   . . .
> Awake! On your feet! Who fights for me?
> Hold your lindens right, hitch up your courage,
> Think bravely, be with me at the doors!" (7–9, 13–15)

Waldere is another good fragmentary example of secular heroic verse. Of this pre-Christian poem, also set in ancient Germania, we have only two brief sections. The poem must have recounted some part of the legendary story of Walter of Aquitaine and his wife and Hildegund of Burgundy, the full story of which is preserved in a ninth-century Latin prose epic, *Waltharius*. The extant lines refer to a time after Walter and Hildegund have escaped the court of Attila the Hun. On their way home they are attacked by the wicked king of the Franks, Gunthere. This poem is furthermore noteworthy in having a strong woman's voice. In the first section Hildeguth urges Waldere to fight:

Right hand of Attila, let not your royal strength
droop now, nor your daring—now that the day has come
when, son of Ælfhere, you shall surely either
give over living or a long doom
have among after-men, one or other. (Alexander, *Earliest* 38)

Two late examples of heroic verse in Old English are *The Battle of Brun-anburgh* and *The Battle of Maldon*. In each case, we know very well the date of the historical referent, as both are listed in the *Anglo-Saxon Chronicle*. In the case of *Brunanburgh*, the action in the poem refers to a battle won by Æthel-stan's army of Wessex in 937, and in the case of *Maldon*, the battle is one lost by Æthelred's forces in the year 991 under Earl Byrhtnoth. Both are excellent examples of the Anglo-Saxon relatively short heroic poem, but although (per-haps because) *The Battle of Maldon* represents a loss, a glorious failure, it is generally preferred to *Brunanburgh*. Indeed, *Maldon* is much more developed than the other poem. It develops the battle scene incrementally and creates a great deal of suspense in doing so. This poem exemplifies in exceeding clarity the heroic mode of defending to the death a very localized, ostensibly very small piece of land. Byrhtnoth and his followers, thanes of Æthelred, do their best to defend the eastern shore from Scandanavian invaders, but the heroes all die, and in one of the most quoted passages from the poem, Byrhtwold, an elder warrior, speaks:

Courage shall grow keener, clearer the will,
the heart fiercer, as our force faileth.
. . .
Though I am white with winters I will not away,
for I think to lodge me alongside my dear one,
lay me down by my lord's right hand. (Alexander, *Earliest* 111)

Christian poetry in Anglo-Saxon is likewise infused throughout by the heroic idiom. Even from the earliest Christian poem, *Cædmon's Hymn*, which Bede recorded in his Latin history, *Historia Ecclesiastica Gentis Anglorum* (*Ecclesi-astical History of the English People*) (731), God is described as the "glory father" and protector. More explicitly in what is perhaps the most famous of the Anglo-Saxon Christian poems, *The Dream of the Rood*, the poet represents the Crucifixion as a physically active and heroic act. So it is no surprise that heroic and epic conventions are used for retelling the lives of saints and the narratives of the Bible.

Christian poetry is sometimes divided into the Cædmonian and Cynewulfian schools, but aside from *Cædmon's Hymn* and the four poems signed by Cyne-wulf in runes (*The Fates of the Apostles, Juliana, Elene, Christ II*), scholars do not make any serious claims of authorship. The Cædmonian poems are those found in the Junius Manuscript and consist of Old Testament narratives (two

Genesis poems, *Genesis A* dating from about 700 and *Genesis B* from around 850, *Exodus*, and *Daniel*) and a group of poems collectively called *Christ and Satan*. The later Cynewulfian poems, in addition to those already mentioned, include various saints' lives told in heroic meter, in particular, *Guthlac, Juliana, Judith, Elene*, and *Andreas*, preserved in the Exeter Book. Perhaps a better way of organizing this poetry is suggested in Stanley Greenfield and Daniel Calder's extremely useful *New Critical History of Old English Literature*, that is, to group the poems by subject matter: Old Testament narrative, Christ as hero, and saint as hero.

In the poetry retelling Old Testament narratives, the familiar biblical characters appear as warriors. For example, Abraham in *Genesis A* is described as the war leader particularly as he delivers Lot from Sodom and Gomorrah: "Abraham gave battle as ransom for his nephew, in no wise twisted gold; he slew and slaughtered the foe in fight; the Lord of heaven struck to aid him" (Gordon 99). In *Genesis B*, which some scholars claim to be a major influence on Milton's heroic portrayal of Satan in *Paradise Lost*, the characters of God and Satan are presented as rival warriors. In *Exodus* Moses is, of course, the warrior of the chosen people. The following passage describes Moses' people getting ready to meet Pharoah's army:

Then they told [counted] off twelve tribes, brave in heart, in the van to meet the dread onslaught; their might was roused up. In each were fifty companies chosen of warriors. That was a warlike multitude; the leaders of the host received no weaklings into that number, who by reason of youth could not yet guard with their hands under the shield the breast-net of men against the wily foe, or who had not suffered grievous hurt of the over the edge of the target, the mark of a wound, warfare of the spear. (Gordon 116)

Finally, one of the most interesting poems of Old Testament narratives, which comes at the end of the *Beowulf* manuscript, is *Judith*. Judith, who cut off the head of Holofernes, is very much the Germanic woman warrior. As medieval scholars Brzezinski and Evitt state in their recent book *Minding the Body*: "The poem casts Judith as a warrior, a role normally filled by men. Yet it does not suggest that its heroine's exploits are unusual for a woman—perhaps because the Anglo-Saxons were not wholly unfamiliar with women warriors" (36).

Poems that might be grouped under the Christ-as-hero subject heading include *The Dream of the Rood*, mentioned earlier, *Christ I* (Advent), *Christ II* (Ascension), by Cynewulf, and *Christ III* (Last Judgment), and *Christ and Satan*. *Christ and Satan* is divided into three parts: the Fall of the Rebel Angels, the Harrowing of Hell, and the Temptation in the Wilderness, in this achronological order. Christ appears heroic in various forms and for various reasons, simply being coeternal with the Creator being no small part of those reasons. In this aspect Christ is the victorious creator, as in the first lyric of *Christ I*: "O true, victory-bright One, reveal now your own might / through your mysterious skill, and let wall / remain upright against wall" (Gordon 197). Of course, one of the most popular of heroic modes for the figure of Christ is the Harrowing of Hell. In the second part of *Christ and Satan* we learn the effect of Christ's entry before he actually appears by listening to the words of Satan: "This is terrible, now that this storm, the Prince with His host, the Lord of angels, has come" (Gordon 131). Typical of heroic verse, the description of the hero often begins with the response of those who are about to meet the hero in battle. Once Christ arrives, the narrator gives very clear heroic descriptions: "The God by His might entered hell to the sons of men; He was minded to bring forth many thousands of men up to His home. Then came a sound of angels, a noise at dawn. The Lord Himself had laid low the fiend; the struggle was yet to be seen at daybreak; then the dread strength was made manifest" (Gordon 131). The other more overt heroic role for Christ is as judge in the Last Judgment. Here again he wars with Satan and not only all of his angelic followers but the humans who have erroneously followed Satan as well. In the iconography of the Last Judgment Christ bears a sword, and in the Anglo-Saxon poet's hands it is indeed a battle sword: "He shall swing the victor-sword with His right hand, so that the devils shall fall into the deep pit, the host of the sinful into the dark flame, the fated souls under the face of the earth, the multitude of the corrupt into the abode of fiends, those damned to destruction in the house of torment, the devil's hall of death." (Gordon 161). It often strikes a modern reader as odd that Christ and his apostles would be figured in Anglo-Saxon poetry as a war leader and a band of thanes, but the logic of representing the most cherished values in heroic poetry could lead only to this conclusion. However, we must stress that while these heroic modes appear worldly, to be sure, they are used to depict a warrior against the worldly, a battle continued in the saints' lives.

The saint's legend was certainly one of the more popular genres of later Anglo-Saxon literature and in poetic form almost invariably took on a heroic cast. The clearest examples of the saint as hero are *Juliana, Elene, Andreas, Guthlac,* and the *Fates of the Apostles.* The one with the closest parallels to a heroic narrative is *Andreas.* The overall plot is suggestive of *Beowulf.* In *Andreas* we find the Apostle Matthew captured, blinded, and about to be eaten by the Mermedonians, cannibals from Ethiopia. Andrew is summoned by God to rescue Matthew and thus has to enter the strange territory, purge it of cannibalism, convert everyone to Christianity, and perform the odd miracle here and there. The poem opens with a very clear heroic formula: "Lo! we have heard in distant days of twelve glorious heroes, servants of the Lord, under the stars. Their majesty failed not in fight when banners clashed together" (Gordon 181). Later, after Andrew has rescued Matthew, he faces the leader of the pagans in battle, and the narrative picks up pace:

Then a sign was given to the men of the city; men brave in battle leaped up amid the shouting of the host, and warriors pressed to the gates, bold under banners, with a great troop to the conflict, with spears and with shields. Then the Lord of hosts spoke a word,

God strong in might said to His servant: "Andrew, thou shalt do bravely; hide not from the throng, but make thy mind steadfast against trials." (Gordon 201)

This passage is interesting not only because of the very clear war imagery, but also because of the fact that God takes an active role in spurring on the apostle warrior. The narrative moves very quickly, accomplishing these deeds and ending with the summary statement "The saint cast down the heathen temples, destroyed idolatry, and overthrew false belief. That was sore for Satan to suffer" (Gordon 216).

Of the total corpus of Anglo-Saxon heroic poetry, or indeed of all Old Germanic poetry, *Beowulf* stands out as the greatest exemplar of the epic, J.R.R. Tolkien's famous lecture to the contrary notwithstanding (see Tolkien's "*Beowulf*: The Monsters and the Critics"). Not only is it the longest of the poems, but the development of the characters, the speeches, the interwoven tales of other heroes, the variety and development of the monsters, and wisdom lore all combine to produce one of the best examples in the English tradition of a heroic epic. Some of the analogues to parts of the plot of *Beowulf*, as they were first usefully collected and discussed in the classic edition of the poem by Klaeber (1922), date back to prehistory. The one clear historical reference in the poem is to King Hygelac's death while raiding in the Netherlands in 524, as recorded by the historian Gregory of Tours. (Using this reference, George Clark has produced an amusing speculative chronology for Beowulf's life.) The events of the poem, set in Scandinavia, quite clearly are pre-Christian, and the dating of the poem itself, not the poem's events, is subject to much debate. For much of the twentieth century the assumption was that the poem was composed, most likely in an oral-formulaic mode, in East Anglian dialect in the seventh century, whereas the sole surviving manuscript, Cotton Vitellius A.xv in the British Library, dates from about the year 1000 from Wessex (see Magoun). However, Kevin Kiernan, who leads a research team that is producing some of the most interesting contemporary work on the manuscript, argues for a later date of composition, closer to the 1000 date of the manuscript.

Beowulf is heroic throughout, though not that much text is taken up in describing battle scenes; rather, the bulk of the poem is devoted to conveying the heroic code or ethos. The poem opens with a reference to the founding father of the Spear-Danes, Scyld Schefing, and describes his mysterious birth, victorious life, and glorious funeral by sea burial, all of which functions to provide at the beginning of the poem a paradigmatic narrative example of the code of the hero. As the narrator states at the end of this section, "Þæt wæs god cyning" (that was a good king). This heroic mode continues through the description of the coming of Beowulf to relieve Hrothgar's court of Grendel and then of Beowulf's facing the threat of Grendel's mother to the end of the poem as Beowulf goes to meet his certain death in the final battle with the dragon. Perhaps the clearest statement in the poem of the heroic ethos is Beowulf's statement to

Hrothgar upon the discovery of the death of the latter's favorite companion Æshere:

> Wise sir, do not grieve. It is always better
> to avenge dear ones than to indulge in mourning.
> For every one of us, living in this world
> means waiting for our end. Let whoever can
> win glory before death. When a warrior is gone,
> that will be his best and only bulwark.

This, then, is the Germanic hero's complete dedication to valor and glory in battle. Beowulf's battle skills are extended to mythical or superhuman dimensions since he can defeat Grendel without weapons, swim underwater for a day to reach Grendel's mother's lair, and go unflinchingly as an aged king to fight the dragon by himself after all his noble retainers, save only Wiglaf, have fled in fear. We also see Beowulf exemplify the heroic traits of loyalty and generosity. He receives much treasure for cleansing Heorot, the Hall of the Danes, of the monsters, but all of that treasure he in turn gives to others, especially to his king.

One of the common traits of the epic is its inclusive or encyclopedic quality; that is, the epic, especially when considered as a preliterate repository of a people's collective wisdom, often includes as much as possible that is worthy of being remembered. So there is much wisdom literature in *Beowulf* that appears as histories of the Swedes, the Danes, and the Frisians and simply as advice, such as that spoken to Beowulf by Hrothgar, full of sententiae regarding the dangers of pride and of old age. Epics are also inclusive of other literary genres, and *Beowulf* is no exception here. The two parts of *Beowulf* correspond to the two dominant modes of epic, romance and tragic, again to use terminology from Northrop Frye. Accordingly, the first half of the poem traces the arc of the young hero, ending in a romance or Odyssean fashion with a homecoming. The second half of the epic is tragic or Iliadic, ending with the death and burial of Beowulf and the prediction of a rather bleak future for the Geats. Likewise, in the first part of the poem the digressions are more the stuff of legend, such as Sigemund the dragon slayer, whereas in the second half the digressions tend more toward the historical, such as the account of Hygelac's raids on the Frisians and the death of Ongeantheow the Swede. The lyrical style of the epic falls into two dominant modes, the romantic sublime in the first half, as in the description of the lair of Grendel's mother, and the elegiac in the second half, as exemplified in the so-called lay of the lone survivor.

As is clear from this brief summary, there is a binary structure organizing much of the poem. While the binaryism in *Beowulf* is most obvious in the plot structure of youth and age, prince and king, it is also evident in the organization of characters and imagery. Grendel and his mother represent the binaries male and female and youth and age. They also represent cold, wet, and exile opposing the hall of Heorot signifying warmth, dryness, and community. Although it is clear that *Beowulf* takes advantage of a binary organization (youth and age, birth and death, light and dark, warm and cold, valor and cowardice, pride and humility, loyalty and kin killing), there is likewise something of a triune organization. When Beowulf approaches the land of Hrothgar, he is met by three verbal challenges (the guard of the coast, Wulfgar, and Unferth). Also, the three monsters that Beowulf faces are three that some critics have related to three stages in the hero's life, or three archetypal phases of life.

Beowulf, then, is the supreme example of the epic; however, the longer heroic poems, particularly of saints or of Christ, may be considered epics as well. There was certainly a tradition of Latin epics that were focused on biblical narrative and saints' lives. Smithson argues that *Juliana, Andreas*, and *Christ* should all be read as epics that were written with both *Beowulf* and the *Aeneid* in mind. In each of these hagiographic verse narratives there is clearly an attitude of the heroic, holding up the saint as an individual who is fighting (even if the fighting is enduring torture) for a new nation, the nation of Christianity.

MIDDLE ENGLISH TEXTS

By the thirteenth century, when English, albeit in a much changed form, was again emerging as the language for narrative verse after its displacement by Anglo-Norman French imposed by the Norman Conquest, the heroic and the epic had undergone a radical transformation. Some scholars have argued that it died completely and had to wait on the Renaissance, not the late Middle Ages, for reanimation. Most would agree, however, that the heroic mode resurfaced, but in the softened form of the verse narrative that dominates this period, the romance; therefore, we should survey briefly the expression of the epic and heroic in the poetry of the romance.

The subject matter of the romances is traditionally organized into the three "matters," and in all of these matters the primary or foundational subject is the life and adventures of a military hero. In "the Matter of France" the subject is Charlemagne and his paladins, particularly Roland; in "the Matter of Rome" (which includes more texts about ancient Greece and Asia Minor than Rome) it is Alexander the Great and the heroes of Troy and Thebes; and in "the Matter of Britain" (which generally refers only to Arthurian stories, but we shall include other English subjects in this category) and "the Matter of England it is, of course, Arthur and knights, although we may also link King Horn, Havelok the Dane, Guy of Warwick, Æthelstan, and other native heroes in this mix. While there are obvious exceptions to this generalization, such as Robin Hood and Sir Orfeo, to mention only two, narratives of military or war heroes do account for an overwhelming majority of the romances.

The romance, whether considered as a mode or genre (see Barron), is generally regarded as an amalgamation of the Latin epic (particularly of the Virgilian mode), the *chanson de geste*, Provençal lyric, the chronicle, a dash of

Augustinian Neoplatonic Christianity, and, of course, the influence of a greatly changing structure of economic and power relations. The result is a narrative that focuses less on the local event and place and less on the deeds of the body than on the universal in events and on the modes of the mind or soul. A classic comparison to illuminate this difference is often made between *Beowulf* and *Sir Gawain and the Green Knight*. While both verse narratives are well wrought, skillfully organized, and focused on the growth of a particular individual, in *Beowulf* it seems rather important that we travel from a kingdom in Sweden to a kingdom in Denmark in order to fight a particular foe to save a particular king. The geopolitics of the poem, the diplomatic relations of the Frisians and the Swedes to the Geats, are very important and are emphasized from first to last. Furthermore, while Beowulf is tested in various ways, his battles, all three of them, are fundamentally physical battles. Sir Gawain, on the other hand, travels to the wilderness, but its only importance is to symbolize universal wilderness—it is the place where he ends up finding his challenger the Green Knight. It really could be anywhere. The battles, finally, are battles of the soul. The narrator tells us that Sir Gawain fights boars, bears, wild men of the woods, giants, and dragons on his way to find the Green Chapel, but these fights are all dispatched in a single summarizing stanza. The real battle takes place in the bedroom as Sir Gawain fights off the temptations offered by the Lady of the Castle. The difference, then, between heroic poetry and the poetry of the romance hero is quite pronounced, but the former can be perceived in the latter, particularly in earlier poems and poems from the north and west of England.

By most accounts Layamon's *Brut* (c. 1205) is either the earliest of the romances or the last of the Anglo-Saxon epics. Based upon the Anglo-Norman Wace's *Roman de Brut* (c. 1155) (which was itself based on Geoffrey of Monmouth's *Historia Regum Britanniae* [c. 1136]), it is an ambitious history in alliterative verse of the Britons from the legendary Trojan who founded the race, Brutus, to the last of Arthur's successors, Cadwallader. The heart of the poem is the Arthuriad; in fact, the 16,000 lines of the poem can be divided roughly into three parts: part one, the history leading up to Arthur; part two, Arthur's history; and part three, the history after Arthur. While it is not written in Anglo-Saxon, its dialect is closer to Anglo-Saxon than most other poems of the post-1100 period. One finds Anglo-Saxon pronouns and inflectional endings still reflecting the grammar of the earlier language. The poem also represents the spirit of Anglo-Saxon poetry; it is marked by alliteration, heavy stresses, paraphrasis, and the solidity of the heroic world.

Indeed, Arthur has much more in common with Beowulf, ironically enough, than the descriptions of Arthur in the later romances. His story here is replete with battles of tremendous force and unrelenting cruelty, with much blood being spilled and thousands of dead and wounded knights littering the landscape. His armor is said to be made by Widia, a descendant of Weland, who provided armor for Beowulf; thus the Teutonic Vulcan forges weaponry for the greatest Celtic enemy of the Germanic invaders in literary history. Although the plot of the Arthuriad in *Brut* is episodic in structure, it is as straightforwardly heroic as is *Beowulf*. Arthur purges England of evil in battle after battle, and at each battle he readies the knights, dons his armor, and flies into battle with unsentimental ruthlessness. At the battle of Bath, for example, after dividing his army into five groups for the attack on the Saxons who are holding Bath, he ceremoniously puts on his armor, each piece of which is described and named, then leads the fight against the leader of the Saxons, Earl Borel. With Ron, his spear, Arthur charges straight at the earl and "smote Borel the earl right through the breast" (658). As soon as Arthur realizes his achievement, he calls out in a style straight out of the *Chanson de Roland*:

> "The foremost hath met his fate!   Now the Lord help us
> And the heavenly Queen,   who gave birth to the Lord!"
> Then cried Arthur,   noblest of kings:
> "Now at them, now at them!   The foremost is done for!" (Loomis and Wil-
> lard 660–663)

The style of Layamon's *Brut* is expansive, and its elaborate descriptions of battle scenes and the lists that accompany them could be said to create a sense of epic amplitude. This amplitude is likewise conveyed in the dynastic coverage of the poem, that is, in covering the history of the Britons from the founder to the last king. While this plot feature does violate the classic norm of classical epic plots, *in medias res*, it does still produce the grand sweep of epic scope and scale. Finally, the characters, particularly Arthur, do appear rather larger than life, to occupy, as it were, a plane of reality between mortal and immortal.

The verse romances between Layamon and the close of the period exemplify the heroic spirit with increasingly less text devoted to martial encounters and more devoted to adventures of various sorts or spiritual struggles. In fact, most of the romances focus on the entire life of the hero and the adventures therein. That is, the development of the hero, the life of the hero as a young man, so to speak, becomes an expected part of the plot; therefore, we must learn about the hero's mysterious beginning and precocious youth, the high noon of his adventures (generally episodic in nature), and, frequently, the death of the hero, or at least some passing reference to the life the hero led after the adventures. In all cases these heroic adventures represent the sum of the values of courtesy that must be read as an idealization of the values of the new aristocracy.

This biographical or dynastic aspect of these heroic romances and the episodic nature of the plot structure clearly mark a departure from the typical form of the epic with its tight focus on an event; on the other hand, there still remain these epic traits: amplitude, a hero of national or ethnic importance, and a design to effect in the audience a sense of pride and a desire to emulate the higher qualities of the hero. The biographical romances that are the most noteworthy for comparison with the heroic epic tradition are the English narratives of *King Horn* (c. 1225), *Havelok the Dane* (c. 1290), *Guy of Warwick* (c. 1300), *Ath-*

elstan (c. 1355), *Sir Tristrem* (c. 1290), *Richard Coer de Lyon* (c. 1300), and *Sir Perceval of Galles* (c. 1300), and to the list we should add one romance from "the Matter of Rome," *Kyng Alisaunder* (c. 1300).

The romances that more closely approxmiate the heroic mode are those that concentrate on a key event or events. The urtext of "the Matter of France," the *Chanson de Roland*, provides the primary example here. The Middle English *Song of Roland* (c. 1400) treats the incident of Roland's defeat at Roncevaux very late in the history of the romances, indicating that this style of heroic romance clearly had lasting appeal. Other episodes of Charlemagne's adventures are told in the romances called the *Ferumbras* group (*The Sowdone of Babylone* and *Sir Ferumbras*) and the *Otuel* group (*Roland and Vermague, The Sege of Melayne, Duke Rowland and Sir Otuell of Spayne, Otuel and Roland,* and *Otuel*), all from the latter part of the fourteenth century. These romances focus on single events in the battle vita of Charlemagne or his knights. In "the Matter of Britain" perhaps the most significant single event is the last battle of Arthur and his resulting death. The justly famous alliterative *Morte d'Arthur* and the stanzaic *Morte Arthure* render these events in a tragic heroic mode that becomes the inspiration in part for Malory's ambitious *Le Morte d'Arthur*. As for "the Matter of Rome," the tales of Thebes and Troy could be considered to be about events, but as they were Englished in *The Gest Historiale of the Destruction of Troy* (c. 1360), *The Seege of Troye* (c. 1225), and the *Laud Troy Book* (c. 1400), the tales turn into long series of battles, and as a result the poems lose that quality of epic concentration. The two tales were translated again by John Lydgate in the early fifteenth century as the *Troy Book* and *The Siege of Thebes* (c. 1420); both of these are episodic battle narratives.

The greatest writer of this period, Chaucer, ventured into the heroic romance in his "Knight's Tale" and *Troilus and Criseyde*. Both of these poems would fall, strictly speaking, in "the Matter of Rome"; "The Knight's Tale" is taken from the Siege of Thebes stories and *Troilus* obviously from the Troy legend. Importantly, both of these narratives focus more on the spiritual worthiness of the heroes than their physical worthiness. In *Troilus* we are told that Troilus is one of the best soldiers of Troy, next only to Hector, and as a result of his falling in love with Criseyde he fought more bravely than ever before:

> And yet was he wherso men wente or riden
> Founde oon the beste, and lengest tyme abyden
> Ther peril was, an dide ek such travayle
> In armes, that to thenke it was mervayle. (I.473–476)

Yet we learn that his valor comes not from a desire to save his city, at this point, but rather to impress Criseyde. Likewise, in "The Knight's Tale," Arcite and Palamon fight more bravely than anyone in the poem, except for Theseus, and the tournament battle is described in language that recalls the alliterative heroic narratives of previous years:

Ther shyveren shaftes upon sheeldes thikke;
He feeleth thurgh the herte-spoon the prikke;
Up spryngen speres tweny foot on highte;
Out goone the swerdes as the silver brightes. (I.2605–2608)

Again, however, the heroes are not fighting to save a people, but to settle a dispute over the claim of the lover. In both cases, furthermore, the goal of the narrative is to evoke lamentation. It is the grief over the death of Arcite and the loss of Criseyde that provides the emotional force of the poems.

While there have been some attempts to read *The Canterbury Tales* as influenced by the Western epic tradition and attempts to read *The Canterbury Tales* as a unified work, few scholars have suggested that *The Canterbury Tales* be considered an epic. Richard Neuse, however, has recently made a case for that position. He argues, as have others, that Dante radically transformed the nature of the epic genre and that Chaucer is simply following this tradition by continuing this process of transformation. The figure of Chaucer the pilgrim/narrator is analogous to Dante the pilgrim/poet, and tale telling as a form of spiritual pilgrimage is the epic theme. Furthermore, Neuse argues, Chaucer is able to catch up an entire epoch in his masterwork in a way that would work for the time. Truly, Chaucer's work is encyclopedic; it includes a description of a wide variety of social types and occupations and an even wider variety of literary styles and genres. As John H. Fisher has argued, Chaucer seems to have Virgil's wheel of three styles in mind in arranging the styles in Fragment I. The three styles are, of course, high, middle, and low, with the high style referring strictly to the style of epics.

The other two candidates for epic poets of the late fifteenth century are the *Pearl* poet and William Langland. One may claim to take all of the *Pearl* poet's works together as a whole in order to argue for epic reach, but no one has made this case persuasively. *Cleanness* (or *Purity*) is certainly a poem of epiclike dilation and espouses a theme that is at the core of Christian beliefs, but of all the poems in the manuscript, it is the one that has had the least effect on its audience. *Sir Gawain and the Green Knight* and *Pearl* are the two poems that are most influential. Langland's *Piers Plowman*, on the other hand, was championed nearly fifty years ago in Tillyard's *The English Epic and Its Background* (1954). After a survey of the literature of the period, Tillyard claims that the dream-vision allegory captured the fundamental ground of being for English people at this time in an appropriately solemn way and in an appropriately epic scale and scope. (Langland is discussed more later.)

CRITICAL HISTORY OF THE GENRE

This historical survey of the criticism of the genre concentrates on the twentieth century. If we were to write a complete critical history of epic and heroic poetry, we would have to begin with Aristotle's comments on Homer in the

Rhetoric and the structure of plots and characters that he takes from that study and his study of tragedy; then it would move on to the rhetorical tradition in the later Greek and Roman worlds, particularly in Horace, Cicero, and Quintilian and in the poetry textbooks that grew out of the *ars rhetorica* tradition and the practice of teaching Virgil. The Virgilian and Ovidian traditions are then carried forward into the Middle Ages with comments in the allegorical traditions as well as simple statements by Isidore of Seville in his *Etymologiae* on the nature of the hero, the *sapientia et fortitudo* formula, and the appropriateness of biblical narratives as epics. It would be important to survey the late medieval texts by John of Salisbury, Geoffrey Vinsauf, Matthew of Vendome, Brunetto Latini, Thomas Aquinas, Dante, and Boccaccio, to name a few who have commented on the structure of poems. This full history would have to spend a good deal of time on Renaissance writers such as Castiglione, Machiavelli, Sir Philip Sidney, Joseph Caesar, and Castelvetro, all of whom it may be said attempted to reclaim the classical epic as an expression of the elite, an elite that emerging aristocratic power was anxious to emulate. This Renaissance reappropriation, it would have to be pointed out, finds its antithesis in the romantic rereadings of the epic by Wordsworth, Schiller, Schlegel, and Herder, who read the epic as expressions of the folk in contradiction to the artificial art of the aristocratic and learned writers of the day.

Our concentration on the twentieth century, however, must begin with W.P. Ker's 1908 masterwork *Epic and Romance*. It is still readily recognized as the starting place for any serious introduction to this question of genre as it relates, especially, to the literature of northern Europe in the Middle Ages. Ker's book is a thorough survey of the poetry of this period, grounded in historical settings, and thus to a certain extent continues the late romantic reading of heroic poetry and epic as an expression of history. Furthermore, Ker's programmatic positioning of epic versus romance, a positioning still viable in the late twentieth century, though then termed epic versus novel, is very influentially expressed, as it often is in such lapidary statements as the following: "Whatever epic may mean it implies some weight and solidity; Romance means nothing if it does not convey something of mystery and fantasy" (4). This general critical trend is furthered and more developed in the specialized works of H.M. Chadwick, *The Heroic Age* (1912), C.M. Bowra's two books *Heroic Poetry* (1952) and *From Virgil to Milton* (1945), and E.M.W. Tillyard's *The English Epic and Its Background* (1954). With each successive text the historical specificity of heroic and epic is made less important as the heroic and epic are essentialized so that the term becomes transhistorical, so that heroic becomes a term to describe literature that reflects a particular shape of society at any given time in any given society and epic is broadened to include such obviously epic texts as Milton's *Paradise Lost* and, in the case of Tillyard, Langland's *Piers Plowman* and Shakespeare's history plays taken as a group from *Richard II* through *Richard III*.

It would seem that in early-twentieth-century criticism the tendency was to

collapse the romantic historical grounding with something of the idealizing quality of the neoclassical. This idealizing appeared as the writers worked to isolate
key forms of the genre, a methodology influenced no doubt by the philosophies
of form prevalent during this period and one that would emerge as one of the
most influential modes of criticism in Anglo-American studies, formalism or
New Criticism. For example, Tillyard develops five essential traits of the epic
and then uses them to size up a candidate in line for the title of epic. In looking
at Langland he says, "The first question that meets us when we begin to examine
the claims of *Piers Plowman* to be epic is the fundamental one of whether
Langland was poet enough to command one of the great literary forms" (154).
Thus we can see that epic form takes on a priori reality or is just a fact like the
height of a mountain. The only question that remains is how well the poem
climbs the mountain. Tillyard attempts to persuade us that Langland's poem has
climbed the mountain by arguing for three points: one, his metrical gift is un-
questioned; two, he could speak for a great body of the nation, an "epic quality
which no one would deny" (157); three, that the vast accumulation of detail in
this very long poem adds up to something more than just the accretion of detail.

Finally, it must be said that this essentializing mode of criticism invariably
produces something of a ranking of genres. Tillyard says, "I have said so much
on this topic to try to show how difficult it is for the ordinary reader to get a
fair view of Langland and hence to judge whether he really earns the high title
of epic writer" (154). The "high title" is given only to the elite, lifting them
from history. This same critical habit of mind of developing the essential into
the elite is more famously demonstrated in T.S. Eliot's critical essays, such as
Tradition and the Individual Talent.

There were several important critical texts on epic and the heroic produced
in the middle of the twentieth century. Probably nowhere is this critical paradigm
more powerfully and more influentially expressed than in Eric Auerbach's *Mimesis* (1946; trans. 1953). In his chapter on the *Chanson de Roland* Auerbach
comments on the medieval heroic epic in terms of its relentless use of parataxis
as high style. Auerbach's method throughout the book is founded upon a close
analysis of style; each chapter in *Mimesis* begins with a long quotation in the
original language and is followed by an even longer close analysis. He reads
this representation of reality in terms of rigidity, rigidity of morality and of
politics, brought about by the decline of the classical world, particularly the
Roman world, and by Christianity's response to this development by the use of
figural representation, allegory. An important point for Auerbach is that heroic
poetry during this period was history; it was kept alive in the songs of the bards.
R.W. Southern's *The Making of the Middle Ages* contains a very important
chapter on the epic, "From Epic to Romance," in which he likewise connects
the rigidity of the medieval epic to early conditions of medieval Christianity, a
posture of defense, a posture that influences not only theology but art and architecture as well. Just as Romanesque art seemed to demand rigid construction,
so did the structure of the native heroic poem. With the advent of twelfth-century

spirituality, such as the emotional spirituality of the Cistercians, and particularly that of Bernard of Clairvaux, and the development of logic in the new universities, the romance develops concomitantly with the meditation techniques that are designed to understand the essential or universal nature of emotional states of being by concentrating on particular historical moments in the life of Christ or Mary. C.S. Lewis's great work on Milton, *A Preface to* Paradise Lost (1942), comments very economically on what he terms the primary and secondary epic, epic of the folk (generally the heroic epic) and the epic of the literati (which has a greater chance of not being heroic), and in this text Lewis, like Auerbach and Tillyard, reads the style of the text carefully to render an entire world view from that style.

The early-twentieth-century fascination with form took another route as well in the emergence of a critical methodology that would come to be recognized as structuralism, exemplified in some very significant texts for the history of medieval epic. Certainly Northrop Frye, although following a more Jungian approach to form, produced perhaps the most influential text on genre theory of the century in his *Anatomy of Criticism* (1957). Not only did this book enliven an interest in Aristotelian poetics, myth, and archetypes, but also it stimulated much rethinking about the borders between epic, romance, and novel by deessentializing these terms and rewriting the structure of the epic along the lines of heroic mode, mythoi, image, and rhetoric. Although Frye does offer a history of narrative—tracing in a somewhat Viconian manner how the dominance of myth gradually gives way to realism and showing how the image, for example, of the god and the thunderbolt metamorphoses into the king and the scepter, the knight and the lance, the land baron and the cane, and finally the farmer and the pitchfork—his history has less to do with history than it does with narrative. Similarly, in *The Nature of Narrative* (1966) Scholes and Kellogg provide something of a structuralist account of the history of narrative from the oral epic tradition to the novel. According to the authors, oral-formulaic epics rely extensively on mythoi, and the changes in narrative involve a split into two groups: one of narratives relying on idealizations and another of narratives relying on empirical reality. These categories are divided again, but, the authors claim, all the divisions are reunited in the development of the novel.

Structuralism took root most deeply in Russian soil, and its effect on midcentury criticism in English was indirect, particularly in the work of René Wellek, Roman Jacobson, and Tzvetan Todorov. One of the most influential theoretical critics of recent history to write on the epic grew out of this tradition. Mikhail Bakhtin's *The Dialogic Imagination*, along with his work on the carnivalesque, became very important in medieval and Renaissance scholarship. Bakhtin contrasts the epic with the novel and argues for the epic's remoteness in time and space, unity of cultural norms, and singularity of language, its monoglossia. Thus the epic becomes in Bakhtin's hands the truly monumentalized, distant text, which Bakhtin then uses as the starting point in his history of the development of the novel and of the decline of aristocratic politics, which are marked in texts of heteroglossia, novelization, dialogism, and the various forms of Rabelaisian humor and the carnivalesque in general.

Another very important school of criticism for understanding the epic that evolved in the early to mid-twentieth century was less interested in describing the forms and their functions than it was in accounting for the generation and the reception of them. This school we might call the anthropological school of the epic, and the headmaster of this school has to be Milman Parry. Parry and his followers, such as Albert Lord and F.P. Magoun, worked likewise from a mode of describing how the epic was produced in an oral-formulaic manner and thus based their analyses on fieldwork in Yugoslavia on extant oral epics. Parry and Lord were primarily concerned with Homer, but Magoun and many others applied their insights about the nature of oral narratives to work on *Beowulf* and other medieval epics. The primary revelation, of course, is that the poems were composed by accumulation and by reliance on formulae of scene construction and patterns of repetitions. John Miles Foley's *The Theory of Oral Composition* details this history very well and provides an excellent bibliography.

In the final decades of the twentieth century, while there was still something of the dialectic between conceptions of the epic as a song of the folk versus a closed monument to the past, the polarity of this debate and other polarities surrounding the theory of the epic were challenged in recent criticism. The collection *Epic and Epoch: Essays on the Interpretation and History of a Genre* (1994), edited by Steven M. Oberhelman, Van Kelly, and Richard J. Golsan, and the very fine volume of articles entitled *Epic Traditions in the Contemporary World: The Poetics of Community* (1999), edited by Margaret Beissinger, Jane Tylus, and Susanne Wofford, both make great strides toward redefining the genre in terms of form as well as audience, or, in other words, moving the borders of the genre and redefining the old categories of the reception of the epic. One feature that is demonstrated well in *Epic Traditions* is the role of grief and lamentation in the epics. The authors of the chapters on this subject, in particular Robert Greene, Sheila Murnaghan, and Elaine Fantham, contend that through the evocation of grief the solemnity of the primary epic is achieved. By closely attending to the role of the affective in epic and the function of lamentation, the authors argue for a radical reassessment of the feminine element in these poems that are generally understood as predominantly masculine. Furthermore, in Greene's chapter the role of Dante in the history of the epic is read as transformational, as is the case in Richard Neuse's *Chaucer's Dante*. What some of the recent work on epic is accomplishing is the merging of the oral-formulaic tradition and the speech-act or pragmatic theory of criticism. Richard P. Martin's *The Language of Heroes* (1989) demonstrates this point quite persuasively. In David Quint's *Epic and Empire: Politics and Generic Form from Virgil to Milton* (1993) the binary of triumph and victory is reworked to argue for a binary history of the epic, a history for political winners, after Virgil, and political losers, after Tasso. In Quint's last chapter, an essay on Ossian, he demonstrates how the desire in the nineteenth century to found a national identity on an original epic, even if it is the story of a heroic loss in the face of an invading foreign force, was so strong that medieval epics, even great forgeries, were fought over. One final text relevant to medieval secondary epic is Ann Astell's *Job, Boethius, and Epic Truth* (1994), in which Astell argues that the forms of the classical epic were rejected by medieval epicists so as to better render the "truth" or matter of the epic. In her view, the Book of Job and Boethius's *Consolation of Philosophy* provide a new path to see the dichotomy of epic and romance collapsed as romance is reread as a secondary epic; "the formal discontinuity that has led most literary historians to deny the very existence of secondary (i.e., imitative) epic in the Middle Ages actually demonstrates the conscious continuation of heroic poetry, not in its false (and therefore rejected) letter, however, but in its underlying, allegorical truth—a truth revealed most clearly in the paired books of Job and Boethius and the writings patterned (albeit diversely) after them" (x–xi).

In summary, then, it would seem that the trend in most recent theoretical treatments of the epic and of medieval long poems is to destabilize the old dichotomies of epic and romance and of the near and remote as defining categories. The epic is now being defined much less by specific formal traits and much more by the affective dimension of what it accomplishes for a community.

SELECTED BIBLIOGRAPHY

Alexander, Michael, trans. *The Earliest English Poems*. London: Penguin, 1966.

———. *Old English Literature*. London: Macmillan, 1983.

Astell, Ann. *Job, Boethius, and Epic Truth*. Ithaca, NY: Cornell University Press, 1994.

Auerbach, Eric. *Mimesis: The Representation of Reality in Western Literature*. Trans. Willard R. Trask. Princeton, NJ: Princeton University Press, 1953.

Bakhtin, Mikhail. *The Dialogic Imagination: Four Essays*. Ed. Michael Holquist. Austin: University of Texas Press, 1981.

Barron, W.R.J. *English Medieval Romance*. New York: Longman, 1987.

Beissinger, Margaret, Jane Tylus, and Susanne Wofford, eds. *Epic Traditions in the Contemporary World: The Poetics of Community*. Berkeley: University of California Press, 1999.

Beowulf. Trans. Seamus Heaney. New York: Farrar, 2000.

Bowra, C.M. *From Virgil to Milton*. New York: St. Martin's Press, 1945.

———. *Heroic Poetry*. London: Macmillan, 1952.

Brzezinski, Monica, and Regula Meyer Evitt. *Minding the Body: Women and Literature in the Middle Ages, 800–1500*. New York: Twayne, 1997.

Chadwick, H.M. *The Heroic Age*. Westport, CT: Greenwood Press, 1974.

Clark, George. *Beowulf*. Boston: Twayne, 1990.

Curtius, Ernst Robert. *European Literature and the Latin Middle Ages*. Trans. Willard R. Trask. New York: Harper, 1963.

Fisher, John H. "The Three Styles of Fragment I of *The Canterbury Tales*." *Chaucer Review* 8 (1973): 119–127.

Foley, John Miles. *The Theory of Oral Composition: History and Methodology*. Bloomington: Indiana University Press, 1988.

Frye, Northrop. *Anatomy of Criticism*. Princeton, NJ: Princeton University Press, 1957.

Gordon, R.K. *Anglo-Saxon Poetry*. London: Dent, 1926.

Greenfield, Stanley B., and Daniel G. Calder. *A New Critical History of Old English Literature*. New York: New York University Press, 1986.

Ker, W.P. *Epic and Romance: Essays on Medieval Literature*. 1908. New York: Dover, 1957.

Kiernan, Kevin. *Beowulf and the Beowulf Manuscripts*. New Brunswick, NJ: Rutgers University Press, 1981.

Klaeber, Friedrich, ed. *Beowulf and The Fight at Finnsburg*. Boston: Heath, 1922.

Lawrence, William W. *Beowulf and Epic Tradition*. New York: Hafner, 1961.

Lewis, C.S. *A Preface to* Paradise Lost. New York: Oxford University Press, 1961.

Loomis, Roger Sherman, and Rudolph Willard. *Medieval English Verse and Prose*. New York: Appleton-Century-Crofts, 1948.

Magoun, Francis P., Jr. *Béowulf and Judith*. Cambridge, MA: Department of English, Harvard University, 1959.

Martin, Richard P. *The Language of Heroes: Speech and Performance in the* Iliad. Ithaca, NY: Cornell University Press, 1989.

Mason, Eugene, trans. *Arthurian Chronicles/Wace and Layamon*. London: Dent, 1976.

Neuse, Richard. *Chaucer's Dante: Allegory and Epic Theater in* The Canterbury Tales. Berkeley: University of California Press, 1991.

Nichols, Stephen G., Jr. "The Spirit of Truth: Epic Modes in Medieval Literature." *New Literary History* 1 (Spring 1970): 365–386.

Oberhelman, Steven M., Van Kelly, and Richard J. Golsan, eds. *Epic and Epoch: Essays on the Interpretation and History of a Genre*. Lubbock: Texas Tech University Press, 1994.

Quint, David. *Epic and Empire: Politics and Generic Form from Virgil to Milton*. Princeton, NJ: Princeton University Press, 1993.

Scholes, Robert, and Robert Kellogg. *The Nature of Narrative*. London: Oxford University Press, 1966.

Smithson, George Arnold. *The Old English Christian Epic*. New York: Phaeton, 1971.

The Song of Roland. Trans. Dorothy L. Sayers. London: Penguin, 1957.

Southern, R.W. *The Making of the Middle Ages*. New Haven, CT: Yale University Press, 1953.

Tillyard, E.M.W. *The English Epic and Its Background*. London: Chatto and Windus, 1954.

Tolkien, J.R.R. "*Beowulf*: The Monsters and the Critics." *Proceedings of the British Academy* 22 (1936): 245–295.

12

The Epic Genre and Medieval Epics

Richard McDonald

If you are reading this chapter, then you are interested in epic poetry, meaning that you and I have something in common. We find something in epic stories worthy of our attention and consideration. As twenty-first-century readers, often we look back on the literature of the past and find ways to group different varieties of writing under generic headings. Why we make generic demarcations is probably the stuff of another study, but at the outset of this chapter two questions oblige us to become theoretical about our appreciation of the epic or epic poetry (poetry being the vehicle of most epics). The first is, "Did medieval writers and readers of epics see 'epic literature' the same way we do?" A second, related question would be, "If our perceptions are different, how do our differing beliefs about 'the epic' influence what we see as the 'medieval epic'?"

You will come to recognize as this chapter proceeds that ideas about epic literature vary from scholar to scholar. Commentators have traditionally recognized the difficulty of defining and listing all the characteristics of an epic, mainly because epics, although often similar, differ significantly in terms of what generic conventions they include. After discussing some distinctly medieval problems with solidifying a description of "the epic," I will include a list of conventions that epics tend to employ and finally provide a list and brief synopsis of specific works that might qualify as medieval epics.

THE "EPIC" AND THE MEDIEVAL WRITER/READER

Probably one of the central obstacles to achieving an acceptable and useful definition of the medieval epic is that "epic," as Ann W. Astell points out, was not a word used by medieval writers (17). The *Oxford English Dictionary* establishes the first use of the term "epic" in English in 1589.

Of course, medieval writers did have an idea about what epics were, but they did not use the term "epic" to denote that type of writing, and then (as now) the idea of what an epic was often differed from place to place, time to time, and individual to individual. In fact, we may have more agreement today about what an epic is (and that is not all that much agreement) than medieval writers had. Medieval writers did not have direct access to Aristotle's *Poetics*, which contains one of the earliest discussions of epics. They knew Latin and were often familiar with the *Aeneid*, and they had heard of Homer and his epics either from Virgil or other Latin commentators or imitators. Because much of the commentary on literature of the medieval period concerned the reading of religious texts, medieval commentators often discussed the heroic characteristics of Bible stories (like those of Job or Jonah) and related them to their under-standing of Homer's or Virgil's epics. Astell argues that the Book of Job and Boethius's secular philosophical work *The Consolation of Philosophy* were lik-ened to classical epics because they presented truth about the world in a similar manner (3). Although today's reader may not see much epic action in these two works, struggles to understand good and defeat evil were accepted as epic battles in their own right. According to Astell, medieval writers' interest in the alle-gorical value of epic works (allegory being a sustained multilevel interpretation of the literal occurrences in a text) led to a partial identification of "epic" with allegory. From Latin writers like Seneca and Macrobius, medieval writers knew about the moral and spiritual interpretations of epic events by Greek commen-tators, and they saw epics as containing the moral beliefs of Greek society, although these beliefs were sometimes encoded within a morally confusing lit-eral story (Astell 8–9). Throughout history, excerpts from epics have been used to teach students proper conduct (or morality). Greek commentators made use of the actions of epic characters as examples of how one should or should not act in particular circumstances, and that technique was employed later by Roman teachers and writers. The practice continued for many centuries throughout Eu-rope, even into the Renaissance and beyond.

It may be that medieval writers' lack of direct knowledge of Homer's heroic poetry made possible what would have been a difficult alteration in the concept of epic/heroic poetry. Although there are a fair number of "heroic" poems con-cerning warrior heroes in medieval writing, there also are a large number of spiritual "heroes" presented in various saints' lives written during the period, and the distinction between these two types of heroes may have been less clear to a medieval audience that in many ways equated the biblical Job with Achilles or Aeneas. Dennis Krantz points out in his *Mocking Epic* that medieval writers of "epics" often subtly cast aspersions on actively aggressive and violent char-acters and saw the adherents to more Christian ideals of heroism (like patience and persistence) as the more truly heroic individuals (1–2). Hrotsvit of Gander-sheim, a tenth-century Saxon, Benedictine nun, wrote an epic about Otto the Great (*Carmen de Gestis Oddonis Imperatoris*) that emphasizes Otto's Christian qualities as an epic hero/ruler, and the Old Saxon *Heliand* is an adaptation of the New Testament Gospels in which Christ is treated as a Germanic chieftain.

The question then arises, "Does any definition of medieval epic need to be substantially different from a classical definition of epic?" I believe that a broad definition of epic can be posited that incorporates aspects of many different literary eras and that this definition can be applied to the "heroic" poetry of the medieval period in productive ways, even though the term "epic" is one we are essentially inserting into medieval discourse. The writers of medieval epics were readers of Roman/Latin epics and understood the genre as it functions in the *Aeneid*. Additionally, they believed that there was a type of heroic poetry that purported to exhibit the defining moral values of the society for which it was created. They saw heroic poems as important stories containing moral exemplars and nonexemplars. The fact that the moral codes may have changed from one type of "heroic" poetry to another does not necessarily hamper the creation of generic heroic/epic conventions that different poets use toward different ends.

THE CONVENTIONS OF HEROIC/EPIC POETRY

One reason that superimposing the term "epic" on a medieval audience does not disturb me is that an epic is never merely a heroic poem; it is a long narrative heroic poem, and once one reads a number of long narrative heroic poems, it becomes clear that there are many things that "epics" tend to have in common. For me, an acceptable definition of the epic would be the following: An epic is a long narrative poem concerning events important to the history or mythology of a nation or race of people, featuring a hero or heroes of high position within that society whose valorous deeds represent characteristics viewed as beneficial by her/his society. The action of the poem covers a large portion of the hero's world and includes his/her interaction with supernatural forces or deities. Within the course of the story there are events that are common, such as the arming of the hero, the explanation of a person's or inanimate object's ancestry, an emphasis on the importance of religious observances and/or prophecies and omens, a far-ranging journey, references or allusions to legendary stories from that or previous societies, a presentation of how that society's gods interact, a descent into the underworld, and encyclopedic allusions to the types of learning valued by that society. The story is created either orally, for oral presentation, or in writing, with the intention that it will be read (oral or literary epic). The grandeur of the story is achieved through the frequent use of an elevated style, elaborate and often-allusive similes (epic similes), formal speeches by the characters, authorial commentary, invocation of the gods or muses to aid the poet's presentation of the material, and all-inclusive lists of people or things involved in a part of the story (epic catalog). Humor is scarce in an epic and is of the dark or wry variety; the poem begins with the action already started (*in medias res*) and requires a main character of wrath or guile to resolve the conflict that is often stated as a question at the outset of the poem (epic question).

A list of epic conventions might look something like this:

- Long narrative poem
- Hero of high position/characters of high position
- Nationally or historically important episodes
- Events and persons of legendary significance
- A vast setting—a nation or the world
- Deeds of valor and courage
- A world-changing event
- Gods and demigods (supernatural forces)
- The arming of the warrior/hero
- Ancestry of men and inanimate objects
- Allusions to stories, science, history, or cultural beliefs
- Topical digressions
- Epic similes
- Epic epithets or kennings
- Religious observances
- Lives of the gods
- Prophecies/omens
- Descent into the underworld
- Elevated and majestic language and imagery
- Oral or literary formulation
- Begins in the middle, *in medias res*
- Epic question
- Wrath or guile
- Invocations
- Formal speeches and boasts
- Epic catalogs
- Dark humor; wry wit

Undoubtedly you have heard the word "epic" used in contemporary, casual conversation. It is often used as an adjective for words such as "huge," "vast," or "monumental." In today's parlance, if we call something epic, it means that it is large and important, and although that usage is not entirely true to the nature of what "epic" means, there is something about the largeness and importance of epics that makes these two characteristics integral to understanding the term. In his introduction to *Epics of the Western World* Arthur Hutson acknowledges the difficulty of ever offering an acceptable definition for the term "epic," but he conjectures, "Any attempt at a definition must use words like grand, noble, universal" (7). He adds, "The epic poet must tell of people, their actions and emotions, in such a way that his story expresses everything about his world. The materials of the epic poet are the ideals, customs, traditions, mythology and—basic to all these—the moral values of a whole society" (Hutson 7). To be able to include all that is important to one's society within one's poem would certainly make that poem vast and important. The problem with any specific definition of the epic—such as my definition earlier or the list of epic conventions—is that often epics just happen. The maker of *Beowulf* was not trying to create an epic; he was trying to tell a heroic story. In the course of his telling he created a poem that is very much an epic, but he probably had no list of conventions he was trying to include. As a result, all epics share certain conventions from my list, but different epics make use of various conventions to differing degrees. In order to understand exactly what epics include and do, let us look at the conventions individually and how they manifest themselves in particular epics.

THE CONVENTIONS APPLIED

Long Narrative Poem

Epics tend to be quite long—*Beowulf*, a relatively short epic, is 3,182 lines long. (The *Iliad* has more than 15,000 lines.) There is no minimum length for an epic, but the importance of its subject matter and the development of its story generally require thousands of lines. Because the story introduces numerous specific events and people important to the poem's audience and develops these characters and events for a purpose, we call the epic a narrative. Although the epic could be presented in prose, it is more likely to be a specifically poetic invention, reflecting the poetic conventions that a particular society believes convey grandeur and seriousness. For the audience of *Beowulf*, that poetic form was alliterative verse, each line consisting of two half-lines of poetry; *Chanson de Roland* is written in laisses of varying numbers of lines using rhyme and/or assonance, and Homer wrote both the *Iliad* and the *Odyssey* using dactylic hexameter.

Characters/Hero(es) of High Position

The epic very rarely focuses on the common man or even the plight of common men. In general, epics involve some special individual performing feats that benefit his own and future generations, so even when that individual may have been born into a nonnoble family, there is something about them that makes him/her better able to achieve the purpose of the epic than the common person. A saint, for example, might be a character in an epic story, but that saint may have had a relatively unimpressive upbringing by peasant parents. Nevertheless, there is something noble about the lineage of many epic heroes, and there is often something mysterious about their birth. All epic heroes exhibit character traits seen as beneficial within the poet's society. One interesting problem with epic heroes is that although they are examples of what is best within a particular society, epic heroes often have traits that would be recognized as faults as well. The epic hero is seldom completely perfect (Webber 2). Roland (*Chanson de Roland*) is exceedingly courageous and strong, but too proud. Dante the Pilgrim (*Commedia*) also is too proud, and it is Achilles' unquenchable wrath that is the driving force of the *Iliad*.

Nationally or Historically Important Episodes

The epic deals with a story that is so important that its effects are felt by later generations. Typically the epic deals with events that occurred many years before the life of the poet; sometimes the events constitute the very earliest history of a society. Because these events greatly precede the writing of the epic, the events in part or whole are known by members of the poet's audience. The poem is intended to present these events in some particular way that pieces together numerous accepted stories about some historical occurrence with some episodes of the poet's own invention. *Chanson de Roland* is loosely based upon the defeat of Charlemagne's rear guard as his army returned from Spain to France, Dante's *Commedia* tries to make clear what a wayward soul needs to do to achieve union with God, and the *Aeneid* recounts some of the most important myths concerning the founding of Rome.

Events and Persons of Legendary Significance

It is important to remember that there is usually some historic basis for the events of an epic. Even the *Commedia* recounts attitudes and events that might be known to Dante's audience, although his journey to heaven might come as a surprise to them. Generally, the event that inspires the epic has generated multiple stories of which a particular epic is only one version. In the case of the *Commedia*, Dante includes many lesser and more verifiable stories about individual saints and sinners as part of his explanation of how to receive eternal salvation, and he uses the many societal beliefs about Virgil's power as a white magician to further his plot. Often, the characters and events of an epic are so well known that numerous disparate versions of their story exist by the time the poet writes, and some of what his/her writing does is solidify one particular version of an individual's character or the chronology of an event.

A Vast Setting—a Nation or the World

An epic depicts an important event in the history of a society, and as such, it requires a large setting. If the story is limited to a single battlefield, the idea of vastness is still present through the inclusion of the sheer numbers of combatants who come from diverse areas of the world. *Roland* not only depicts Charlemagne's forces at war with Spain, it includes combatants from the Middle East and Africa as well. The *Commedia* includes all of hell, part of earth, and all of heaven as its setting. Beowulf crosses the sea to aid Hrothgar, and the poem includes recurrent references to many of the principal Scandinavian tribes.

Deeds of Valor and Courage

The heroes of an epic must behave in a way that the poet's audience would believe is courageous. For some cultures, the hero must be a barbarous warrior before the enemy (Diomedes in the *Iliad*), or simultaneously pious and warriorlike (Archbishop Turpin in *Roland*), or desirous of fame and fearless (Beowulf battling Grendel); however, a religious audience could expect and accept a more passive hero (such as Dante persevering through the trials of hell) or a character fearlessly welcoming threats of violence and martyrdom (like Andreas in the Anglo-Saxon story of St. Andrew, *Andreas*).

A World-changing Event

In addition to being important to the history of a people, the event should be perceived (at least from the perspective of the poet's audience) as a significant milestone in the life of the world. Although Charlemagne's triumph over the pagans and the subsequent trial of Ganelon restores justice in the world, the defeat of Roland signifies the real threat to Christendom that the Saracens pose. Beowulf's triumphs, even his triumphant death, may say one thing about the strength of one Anglo-Saxon character, but the poem's ending makes clear that his death portends an authentic change in the world that his people are left to inhabit.

Gods and Demigods

The presence of supernatural beings or forces is integral to the appeal of the epic in at least three ways. First, the epic often partakes of elements of the culture's religious heritage. Second, supernatural allies and adversaries can be used to showcase any of the hero's powers that exceed humans' capacity to test. Third, the unexplainable can be attributed to the workings of divine characters. The early Greek and Roman epics presented their gods in stereotypical characterizations appropriate to each god. In later epics a hero such as Roland or Beowulf is endowed with abilities beyond the potential of normal men. Roland kills thousands of men during his final battle and has the strength to repeatedly cleave through not only a man and his armor, but the man's horse as well. Beowulf's own phenomenal and inexplicable hand strength allows him to grapple with and defeat the supernatural Grendel. Although *wyrd* (or fate) in Beowulf is not specifically a god, it has volition attributed to it in phrases such as "Wyrd (fate) often saves an undoomed man when his courage is strong" (572b–573).

The Arming of the Hero

Because epics traditionally involve a warrior hero, the arming of that hero, especially before his most important battle, is an important recurrent element in epics. Achilles (after Patroclus has died and lost Achilles' armor) must wait before going into battle so that his mother can secure ornately decorated armor from Hephaestus. Aeneas receives a similar gift from his goddess mother. In *Roland* armor is important and is well made, but its description does not compare to Aeneas's or Achilles'. The emphasis on armor is reversed in *Beowulf* in that the hero has exquisite armor that he fortuitously takes off, along with Nægling, his sword, before battling the enchanted monster Grendel (Fitt XI). But even in more passive, Christian epics the hero must be armed: Dante must gird himself with the reed of true contrition before he can ascend Mount Purgatory (*Purgatorio* I).

Ancestry of Men and Inanimate Objects

Since much of the action of an epic involves individuals fighting for their beliefs or honor, knowing what and whom one is fighting against becomes especially important. Homer often allows his heroes to make speeches before fighting, declaring their lineage, making themselves more real to the audience, and possibly allowing listeners to identify with them as ancestors. The *Roland* poet allows less talking between combatants, but he makes clear the lineage of the French knights and specifies the home region and the ancestry of the Saracen knights, who are often descendants of devils. Dante, too, discusses ancestry in his *Commedia*, and in the course of the epic we find different members of the same family populating different regions of the afterlife. Just as men have histories so do swords, armor, and other inanimate objects in epics. When Beowulf leaves his sword, Nægling, behind while tracking Grendel's mother, he borrows Unferth's sword, Hrunting, before descending into the mere. His comments about Hrunting, upon receiving it and returning it, make clear that Beowulf knew of its reputation (Fitts XXI and XXII). Named and magical weapons and armor are common in epic and romance literature. Often the importance of an object's ancestry blends with the importance of a man's ancestry because the previous owner of the object is extolled in the same breath that the object is.

Allusions to Stories, Science, History, or Cultural Beliefs

Especially during the Middle Ages, epic or grand heroic stories were often encyclopedic in nature. Because the genre dealt with the most significant topics a culture had to offer, the allusions within that story were also far-reaching, recognizing the grandeur of elements of that society mentioned only in passing. In the course of writing about good kingship (and fealty) as part of *Beowulf*, the poet alludes to traditional characters who serve as examples of good or bad kingship. Modthrytha the evil princess who kills men for looking at her is re-formed by her marriage to Offa, although the story is mentioned only briefly (Fitt XXVII). As mentioned earlier, the *Roland* poet often refers to Saracens as demons or the offspring of demons by using short cryptic allusions to their heritage. The audience would be expected to have enough knowledge from these short descriptions to cipher out the importance of the allusive references. Dante likes to include references to contemporary science in his work. In Canto II of *Paradiso* he alludes to an experiment using mirrors that he hopes will make clear how light remains at a consistent level of brightness while decreasing in size as it is seen from a distance. (Dante's allusions were sometimes so intricate and involved that his own sons were unable to make sense of them.)

Topical Digressions

Often the allusions within an epic are for a specific purpose, but not always. Many times in the course of a simile or while allowing a character to speak for herself/himself, the poet includes information that may be more digressive than allusive. Many of Dante's historical allusions to people and events in Florence's history go far enough afield to be no longer allusive but digressive. The whole phenomenon of the epic simile is one that encourages digression. If the information calls to mind an applicable parallel in some other story, then it is allusive, but when it does not, it is digressive. Not all digressions are bad. Although they may add little that actually advances the story, they help us better understand some aspects of the culture that the epic depicts or for which the epic was written. Adrien Bonjour in *The Digressions in Beowulf* points out that there are numerous moments when the poet strays from advancing the action of his story, but critics disagree as to whether or not the details the poet includes in these "digressions" have as little value as the term digression implies.

Epic Similes

Epic similes often contain digressive or allusive material, and their presence in an epic is one of the indicators of the poet's attempt to achieve an elevated style. These sustained and often-lengthy comparisons between someone or something in the poem and some observable detail of the outside world add beauty and grandeur to the poem. Dante inserts scientific allusions into his similes, like this one concerning his inability to understand the true nature of god: "As the geometer his mind applies / To square the circle, nor for all his wit / Finds the right formula, howe'er he tries" (Sayers and Reynolds, *Paradiso* XXXIII 133–35). However, Homer holds the crown for extended elaborate similes, such as one in the *Iliad* when Aias retreats under attack by enemy soldiers: "Even as a tawny lion is driven from the fold of the kine by dogs and country folk, that suffer him not to seize the fattest of the herd, watching the whole night through, but he in his lust for flesh goeth straight on, yet accomplisheth naught thereby, for thick darts fly to meet him, hurled by the bold hands, and blazing brands withal, before which he quaileth, how eager soever he be, and at dawn he departeth with a sullen heart" (Murray 521).

Epic Epithets or Kennings

If the epic simile is the granddaddy of poetic expressions, the epic epithet is its great-grandchild. Epithets are typically short compound tag words that are attached to a person, a group of people, or an inanimate object. Homer's "flowing-haired Achaeans" is an epithet for the Greeks. The recurrence of "white-armed" in descriptions of women and goddesses is an epithet revealing the desirability of that characteristic in Greek women. An epithet like "bulwark of the Achaeans" refers to a big strong Greek warrior (such as Aias) and recognizes characteristics that an individual warrior has and the value of these characteristics. Related to the epithet is the Anglo-Saxon poetic technique of the kenning, a metaphoric word compound used to poetically describe someone or something. The sea becomes "the whale-road," anguish upon a warrior's death becomes "war-sorrow," a warrior becomes a "shield-bearer," and a sword becomes a "battle-friend."

Religious Observances

Even in the most martial heroic poems there are references or allusions to religious rites and practices. The epic story concerns a world-changing event, and so not only will the warlike capacities of the society be called upon for help, but the religious powers as well. Hector implores his mother and all the older women of Troy to pray for the success of the Trojan forces (*Iliad*). More than once Apollo is said to answer the prayer of archers in the *Iliad*, making clear the efficacy of religious observances in some instances. Religious observances offer an alternative to the precarious violence that leaves death in its wake. With no clear solution to their Grendel problems in sight, Hrothgar's people return to the religious rites of their ancestors in hopes that some divine deliverance from the monster is possible (*Beowulf* Fitt II).

Lives of the Gods

Often epics will show interaction between the supernatural beings who are mentioned in the story. A council of the gods or a depiction of the way that the gods act apart from humans is a common occurrence in classical epics. Although the gods and supernatural beings are frequently mentioned in medieval epics, only Dante's description of the petty way that demons of different sorts interact in hell is comparable to the sometimes-sad, often-comic presentation of the gods as self-interested, vain beings in classical literature.

Prophecies and Omens

Because of the importance of supernatural forces in an epic, the natural world sometimes sends coded messages for the epic hero(es) or some type of priest to interpret. The flight of certain birds can be a sign of good or evil. Often it is what the birds do that determines how the omen is interpreted, and often an omen will be ignored even though it is read correctly by a seer. Hector has no use for the prophecies of his Trojan seer Polydamas, even though he accepts that they may be correct. Aeneas is a hero of prophecy and destiny. Throughout the *Aeneid* Aeneas and his followers fulfill the intricate prophecies created by Virgil to establish Romans as the descendants of the people of Troy and Augustus as the direct descendant of Aeneas. Prophecies about Dante's eventual expulsion from Florence abound in his *Commedia*, and the death of Beowulf serves as a prophetic omen presaging the destruction of the Geatish nation.

Descent into the Underworld

Not all epics have a literal descent into the underworld, but for most epics, critics are able to identify some specific event where the hero is forced to descend to face evil or the unknown. Aeneas descends, golden bough in hand, into the underworld to speak with the soul of his dead father (*Aeneid* Book VI); Dante spends one-third of the *Commedia* touring hell; and Beowulf after his battle with Grendel must descend through the mere to face Grendel's mother in a cavern filled with evil imagery (Fitts XXII and XXIII). Even in a story like *Roland*, wherein almost all the action in which the hero is involved occurs on the battlefield, one could speculate that fighting the demonlike Saracens in a valley at the base of a mountain pass is much like a descent into hell. Bravely facing and even pursuing adversity is one of the valorous traits of even the more passive epic heroes.

Elevated and Majestic Language and Imagery

The fact that epic stories are frequently told through poetry ensures that the language will differ from normal conversational patterns, but the idea that the tone and style of an epic are consistently elevated holds true for very few poems. Often there is a mix of high, middle, and some low style, but the importance of an epic story means that it can readily sustain grand, elevated language about the important deeds of its heroes. Because the content is significant and serious, the tone can be formal and serious, and the style must be elaborate to do justice to the depiction of the action. Epic similes lend themselves to this usage, as do the long formal speeches of one hero to another or authorial commentary about the significance of some episode. Terms like "grand," "majestic," "noble," "dignified," "aristocratic," "decorous," "ornate," "elegant," and "elaborate" seem more appropriate when they are used in describing epic poetry than anywhere else. One example of this grandeur should suffice; nowhere has the half-hearted reader been more beautifully or carefully rebuked than by Dante in *Paradiso* II:

> O you that follow in light cockle-shells,
> For the song's sake, my ship that sails before,
> Carving her course and singing as she sails,
> Turn back and seek the safety of the shore;
> Tempt not the deep, lest, losing unawares
> Me and yourselves, you come to port no more.
> Oceans as yet undared my vessel dares;
> Apollo steers, Minerva lends the breeze,
> And the nine Muses point me to the bears. (Sayers and Reynolds 1–9)

Even in translation, the imagery and the careful choice of words create an overwhelming sense of beauty and propriety for these lines.

Oral or Literary Formulation

Whether an epic was initially composed orally or written down is often one of the first concerns of an epic scholar. The different demands of each type of composition pose different obstacles and opportunities for their practitioners; even so, how certain epics were composed still serves as a topic for lively debate. It is widely accepted that the *Iliad* and *Odyssey* are the products of oral formulation. With remarkable memory the oral poet creates discrete segments of a story and learns the basic outline of their events; he/she then recounts individual sections of the work for a group's entertainment, relying on memory and improvisational skills. Elements typical to orally formulated poems are repetition, formulaic phrases, epithets and/or kennings, and variations on stock speeches. With so much to remember, the oral poet would fit the specific events of a particular epic into formulae he/she used regardless of the poem. Epics that are composed in writing (literary epics) allow the poet the luxury of crafting individual words and lines to present very particular meanings. They allow the writer to include a denser variety of subject matter, and because they require no memorization, even seemingly repetitive features can convey important variations upon one another. The *Aeneid, Commedia*, and numerous lives of kings and saints are literary creations. Although literary epics allow for more detail and specifics of thought on the part of the poet, the liveliness of orally formulated poems has kept them popular and equally well loved. Scholars debate whether *Roland* and *Beowulf* are literary or oral epics, but for me they have more in common with the oral works of Homer than any literary creations.

Begins *in Medias Res*

An epic is rarely ever the attempt to tell a story from start to finish. Usually the text begins at some critical juncture of the story as a whole, and when necessary, allusions and flashbacks to earlier scenes are used to clarify the plot. Because epics tend to depict real or legendary events from a culture's past, there is often little need for the author to clarify what has happened before his/her story opens. This often poses a problem for readers from other cultures and later generations in that the basic story that the epic draws upon may be unknown to the reader. Often introductory matter in an edition of an epic will make clear some of the basic story that the writer's contemporary readers might be expected to know. The *Iliad* starts well into the ninth year of a ten-year war and the *Odyssey* after Odysseus has already been stranded for years on Calypso's island. When the poet begins presenting the main story of *Beowulf*, Beowulf is already a great warrior, and Grendel has been ravaging Hrothgar's hall for some time. Even in *Roland* the treacherous Ganelon only decides to betray Roland and Charlemagne because of events that occurred before *Roland* begins.

Epic Question

Often epics begin with a question or statement posed during the invocation. The answer or response to the epic question constitutes the text's plot. A.T. Murray begins his translation of the *Odyssey* with the epic question "Tell me, Muse, of the man of many devices, driven far astray after he had sacked the sacred citadel of Troy" (13). *Beowulf* begins by calling the reader's attention to past stories about the glory of Danes (and Geats), and *Roland* begins abruptly with a statement about how no power stands against Charlemagne except Saragossa, and implies that it too will fall as a result of Roland's prowess. At the beginning of an epic the topic can be made clear because there is no intention to surprise the reader. The poet seeks merely to recount an important cultural story/fact.

Wrath or Guile

Traditionally, epics depict a great war, and this war will be won through strength or intelligence or some combination of these characteristics. This is probably true for all epics, but the emphasis on wrath (Achilles) or guile (Odysseus) comes directly from the earliest epics. If it is fair to say that we resolve all our most difficult problems through "brains" or "brawn," then the wrath or guile distinction can be useful, but in many epics there is a character who employs both intelligence and strength. Additionally, in some Christian epics, ideas like "wrath" or "guile" are actually evils, even though a character (such as Dante) has strength of mind, faith, and intelligence. In *Roland*, Roland is a hero of strength, and possibly his sidekick Oliver is a hero of guile (or intelligence): Roland acts; Oliver thinks.

Invocations of the Muses/Gods

Because epics retell such grand, far-reaching, important events, the writer is often obliged to appeal for divine help. Epics that follow the classical model (and even many Christian epics do this) tend to invoke one or more of the Muses. Sometimes invoked all at once or without being specifically named, the Muses and their specific provinces are Calliope (epic poetry), Clio (history), Erato (love poetry), Euterpe (music), Melpomene (tragedy), Polyhymnia (sacred poetry), Terpsichore (song and dance), Thalia (comedy), and Urania (astronomy). At the opening of the epic there is usually an invocation, and these can and do recur at moments of high drama. The invocation is used by the poet to point to important information that he/she claims requires divine assistance to recount accurately. In cases where classical gods are not used, often an appeal to some deity (general or specific) makes clear that the poet needs supernatural help to retell such an important story.

Formal Speeches and Boasts

Epic characters often interact with each other verbally as well as physically. They frequently give long formal speeches during which they recount information important to the plot. These speeches can serve as flashbacks (as when Odysseus recounts his travels to the Phaeacians in the *Odyssey* Books IX–XII), or they can present information essential for the characters and readers to understand the present situation (as does Sordello's speech regarding the rules of the mountain in *Purgatorio* VII). One especially prevalent type of "speech," epic boasts or epic taunts, can be found in a wide variety of epics. Owing to the often-antagonistic interaction between characters in epic literature, the warring between characters can take on verbal as well as physical forms. Fredrick Goldin translates a typical epic boast/taunt by Roland thus:

> "Oliver, Companion, Brother,
> that traitor Ganelon has sworn our deaths:
> it is treason, it cannot stay hidden,
> the emperor will take his terrible revenge,
> no man has seen the like of it.

I will fight here with Durendal, this sword,
and you, my companion, with Haltclere—
we've fought with them before in many lands!
how many battles have we won with these two!
Let no one sing a bad song of our swords." (1456–1465)

Epic Catalogs

Epics include large numbers of people and things from different important places in the world as it is known to the epic's author. The large scale of the epic necessitates the inclusion of long lists of people, gifts, armor, ships, or other materials important to the story. The most infamous of epic catalogs is the catalog of ships in the *Iliad*, wherein Homer goes on for pages and pages about where the Greek ships came from and how many men were on them. Shorter catalogs are more common (and easier reading), such as the catalog of treasure and armor presented in *Beowulf* (Fitt XXXVIII).

Dark Humor/Wry Wit

Epics deal with serious subjects and on the whole contain little comedy, but there are moments of dry or wry comedy in most epics. Although humor, for me, tends to depend upon the way one perceives a certain scene, I find moments of comedy in every epic. I believe that the long-winded reminiscences of the aging warrior Nestor are sometimes humorous (*Iliad*), and medieval epics offer some forms of dark humor in battle scenes. It is a bit funny in *Roland* when Roland needs to remind Oliver to draw his sword, and Oliver replies that he has been too busy killing pagans with anything at hand to have time to draw his sword (1360–1366). Additionally, I find the word choice in *Beowulf* often humorous when the anguish of battle is discussed. When sea monsters hope to eat the swimming Beowulf, he serves them sword instead (559–561); when Grendel first realizes the true strength of Beowulf, the narrator tells us that never before had Grendel received a greeting like Beowulf's (756–757)—who eventually rips his arm off.

MEDIEVAL POEMS THAT CONTAIN EPIC QUALITIES

Now that we have established a list of conventions one can look for in epics, let us briefly consider a few of the many medieval heroic poems/epics to which one could apply these conventions. Remember, there are many types of stories (particularly romances, saints' lives, and lives of kings) that will adhere to a significant number of these conventions, even though they might not be categorized as epics.

Guida M. Jackson's *Encyclopedia of Traditional Epics* and *Encyclopedia of Literary Epics* are two useful books for anyone researching basic story lines or concepts as they relate to works that might be considered epics. Jackson's reference works were extremely influential in my formulation of the following long, yet incomplete, list of European medieval heroic stories. The works listed here have been identified by various scholars as containing a significant number of epic qualities, although many are not by definition "epics." Not all of these works are readily available in English translation, and for some of them we only have a fragment of the original text.

Sixth Century
- Arthurian Legend
- *Gododdin*
- *Hengerdd*

Seventh Century
- *Battle of Ros na Rig*
- *Cattle Raid of Cooley*
- *Cattle Raid of Froech*
- *Fight at Finnsburgh*
- *Hexaemeron*
- *Hildebrandslied*
- *Voyage of Bran, Son of Febral*
- *Widsith*

Eighth Century
- *Beowulf*
- *Bricriu's Feast*
- *Adventure of Conle*
- *Fate of the Sons of Usnech*
- Fenian (Finn) Cycle
- *Pursuit of Diarmaid and Grainne*
- *Siaburcharput Conchulainn*
- *Tain Bo Cuailnge*
- *Tochmarch Ferb*
- *Waldere*
- *Wolfdietrich*
- *Wooing of Etain*

Ninth Century
- *Andreas*
- *Deor*
- *Doon De Mayence*
- *Poetic Edda*

- *Grimnismal*
- *Hamdismal*
- *Havamal*
- *Heledd*
- *Heliand*
- *Judith*
- *Waltharius*

Tenth Century

- *Armes Prydein*
- *Battle of Brunanburgh*
- *Battle of Maldon*
- *Gesta Oddonis*
- *Primordia*
- *Reynard the Fox*
- Vercelli Book

Eleventh Century

- *Chanson de Roland*
- *Culwhich and Olwen*
- *Faereyinga Saga*
- *Mabinogion*
- *Ruolieb*

Twelfth Century

- *Alexandreis*
- *Anticlaudianus*
- *Amis et Amiles*
- *Architrenius*
- *Lay of Atli*
- *Book of Leinster*
- *Book of the Dun Cow*
- *Poema del Cid*
- *Destruction of Da Derga's Hostel*
- *Eneit*
- *Erec*
- *Erec et Enide*
- *Floire et Blancheflor*
- *Le Fresne*
- *Guigemar*
- *Saga of the Jomsvikings*

- *Konig Rother*
- *Lanval*
- *Morkinskinna*
- *Nibelungenlied*
- *Perceval*
- *Renaus*
- *Rolandslied*
- *Roman de Renart*
- *Roman de Thebes*
- *Roman de Troie*
- *Tristan and Iseult*
- *Tristrant und Isalde*
- *Tuatha de Danann*
- *Willehalm*
- *Ynglinga Tal*

Thirteenth Century

- *Aspremont*
- *Aucassin et Nicolette*
- *The Brut*
- *Commedia*
- *Egil's Saga*
- *Enfance Ogier*
- *Engelhard*
- *Fostbraeda Saga*
- *Gundrunlied*
- *Huon de Bordeaux*
- *Interrogation of the Old Men*
- *Iwein*
- *Karl*
- *Die Krone*
- *Kudrun*
- *Laxdaela Saga*
- *Mocedades de Rodrigo*
- *Njal's Saga*
- *Olaf's Saga Helga*
- *Olaf's Saga Tryggvasinar*
- *Orkneyinga Saga*

- *Parzival*
- *Roman de la Rose*
- *Titurel*
- *Tristan*
- *Der Torjanerkreig*
- *Vafthrudnismal*
- *Volsunga Saga*
- *Yngling Saga*

Fourteenth Century

- *Africa*
- *The Bruce*
- *Fiery Vuk*
- *Filostrata*
- *Grettis Saga*
- *Hrolf's Saga Kraka*
- *Karlmeinet*
- "The Knight's Tale"
- *Oguzname*
- *Piers Plowman*
- *Sir Gawain and the Green Knight*
- *Teseida*
- *Troilus and Criseyde*

Fifteenth Century

- *Tale of Gamelyn*
- *Orlando Inamorato*
- *Valentin und Namelos*
- *Valentin und Orson*

SIX MEDIEVAL EPICS IN BRIEF

Now let us take a quick look at six different medieval texts that I believe clearly fulfill the role of an epic.

Beowulf

Composed sometime in or before the ninth century, *Beowulf* is an important work of Anglo-Saxon (or Old English) literature. The central hero, Beowulf (a thane of the Geatish king Hygelac), sails from Sweden to Denmark to rid the Danish king Hrothgar of an evil monster who is marauding Hrothgar's mead hall. Beowulf is tested verbally in the Scylding (Danish) court and is then allowed to fight Grendel, a monster from the race of Cain. Beowulf grapples with Grendel and tears his arm off, and Grendel escapes back to his mother's lair at the bottom of a mere and dies. The next evening the court has been celebrating because of the death of Grendel and Beowulf has been rewarded, but Grendel's mother appears and kills another of Hrothgar's valuable thanes. Again Beowulf is called upon to destroy a monster. He descends into the mere and kills Grendel's mother with a sword forged by the giants (which melts in her toxic blood). Hrothgar again rewards Beowulf, and Beowulf and his men sail back home. Upon his return home we see how Beowulf reveres his king and queen, Hygelac and Hygd. Years pass during which there is warfare that results in Beowulf assuming kingship of the Geats. When Beowulf is an old man, a dragon is awakened from its sleep on an enchanted treasure and begins to ravage Beowulf's people and mead hall. Beowulf resolves to destroy the monster no matter what. He and twelve retainers march to the dragon's lair, and he attempts single combat with the monster. The dragon's fiery breath and tough skin make this a difficult battle, and all but one of his men run for fear of the dragon. Wiglaf alone runs to help his lord successfully slay the magical creature, and Beowulf dies as a result of his wounds, presaging the end of the Geatish nation.

Il Commedia

Dante's *Commedia*, called the *Divine Comedy* by some critics, is a tale of one sinner's journey through hell, purgatory, and heaven. Dante serves as an everyman figure of sorts witnessing the despair, pain, hope, and ecstacy of the dead as they exist in hell, purgatory, and heaven. In *Inferno* (hell) he meets and talks with nonrepentant sinners, guilty of a wide variety of crimes for which they will suffer eternally and never see God. The punishments are often fitted to the crime, as in the punishment for soothsayers, who try to peer too far ahead into the future and are damned to spend eternity walking along in pain with their heads facing backwards. Through the intervention of Beatrice (a woman who served as Dante's inspiration, but who died young), Virgil (who was greatly admired by Dante for his *Aeneid* and for living the life of a virtuous pagan) guides Dante through hell explaining some of its architecture and rules and vouching for Dante's authority to visit the infernal realm to many of the classical beasts and devils that inhabit the nether region.

In *Purgatorio* (purgatory) Dante and Virgil watch sinners do proper penance for their sins as they ascend the mountain of penance, and they grow to understand the forgiving nature of God as they discuss the nature of the mountain with various sinners. Torment and punishment are welcomed by the sinners in purgatory because as soon as a sinner fully pays for her/his sins, she/he may enter heaven. Sins in purgatory are fittingly remitted by the sinners suffering appropriate consequences for their sins: gluttons are starved; the slothful must run.

In *Paradiso* (paradise), Dante leaves Virgil behind (only those who believed in Christ enter heaven). Beatrice serves as Dante's guide as he meets the saints who inhabit the different levels of heaven and are united with the godhead. He speaks with numerous famous saints who espoused different virtues in life and learns how different virtues fit into the overall picture of holiness and godliness. As he ascends higher and higher in heaven, he slowly adjusts to the divine light and beauty of each realm in preparation for seeing God and the union of saints in the empyrean. Upon seeing God, Dante is struck by the inadequacy of language and the human mind to comprehend the godhead. The *Commedia* in many ways is an attempt to explain the most important journeys of medieval Christian life (the journey of the soul toward heaven) to the average Christian.

Chanson de Roland

Chanson de Roland is a medieval story of bravery, chivalry, and justice. Roland, who is the most powerful of Charlemagne's elite knights (the twelve peers), is betrayed (along with 20,000 French troops and the other peers) by his traitorous father-in-law Ganelon. Charlemagne has been tricked by Ganelon and the Saracens (Muslims, in this case in Spain) to leave off conquering Spain and return to France. His troops are delighted to be able to return home. The dangerous job of guarding Charlemagne's army's retreat falls to Roland and his friends along with their troops. Once Charles has crossed over the Pyrenees Mountains, the pagans launch an aggressive attack, eventually sending more than 300,000 men against Roland's 20,000 Franks. Oliver, Roland's closest friend and the second most powerful of the twelve peers, advises him to blow his horn to recall Charlemagne, but Roland refuses. Roland resolves to fight the pagans to the last man and defeat them. The Franks miraculously hold their own against the greater number of Saracens, but both armies' numbers eventually dwindle down. In the end, Roland blows the horn so that Charles can return to avenge the valiant French against the pagans, and Roland dies as a result of broken blood vessels caused by so forceful a blow on the horn. Charles returns to find all his rear guard dead, and he defeats all of the pagans in Spain and an additional 1,500,000 reinforcements that arrive from Arabia. When the war is over, Ganelon is tried for Roland's death and treason to Charlemagne. Ganelon enlists the help of a powerful knight to win his trial by combat, but Charlemagne's weaker knight defeats him, with the help of God, restoring justice to France.

Arthurian Cycle

We do not need to look far to find heroic stories in Arthurian legend. Many of the stories of Arthur and his knights' adventures adhere to numerous epic conventions, and the overall story of Arthur's rise to power, betrayal, and death play out in extended fashion probably all of the conventions associated with epic stories: Arthur has an obscure birth, rises to kingship quickly and assuredly, leads his people admirably, fights valiantly, and governs and manages his knights effectively, and his death forebodes a return to disorder for his country. Various medieval sources recount different aspects of the tale, although the most complete and best-known versions would have to be the fifteenth-century alliterative *Morte d'Arthur* and Malory's *Le Morte d'Arthur*.

In addition to Arthur's personal story, the stories of his principal knights often approach epic status. Some of the stories of Lancelot are epic romances. *Sir Gawain and the Green Knight* seems only less than epical in its lack of a world-changing event, and some critics find the poem's inherent questioning of the chivalric order an event that could change the nature of knighthood and kingship.

El Cid (Poema Del Cid, Cantar de Mio Cid)

El Cid is a Spanish epic of some 3,735 lines recounting the exploits of Rodrigo Díaz de Vivai (the Cid, an Arabic title for lord). The poem is made up of three principal parts. In the first section, King Alfonso of Spain sends the Cid to collect tribute from the king of Seville. The Cid is attacked by Count Ordonez of Castile, but defeats this traitor to Alfonso. The Cid's success earns him the envy of other Spanish nobles who misrepresent his actions to King Alfonso. As a result, the Cid is exiled from Alfonso's court, but he and a loyal band of men begin battling Alfonso's enemies and sending him tribute as they defeat them.

In section two, the Cid successfully defeats the king of Seville and sends King Alfonso precious gifts. Alfonso recognizes the Cid's devotion and ends his banishment. The king even arranges for a marriage between two Spanish nobles, Fernando and Diego Gonzalo, and the Cid's two daughters.

In section three, we see that the Cid's new sons-in-law are actually cowards in battle, although the Cid's forces protect them. Fernando and Diego abuse and then abandon the Cid's daughters (their wives), and the Cid and his loyal followers exact revenge for the girls' mistreatment. The fate of the miscreant sons-in-law is decided by a trial by combat in which two of the Cid's men easily defeat them, and Fernando and Diego are disgraced. The story shows the strength of the Spanish court and how truly brave men (the Cid and his followers) bring order to that war-stricken nation.

Nibelungenlied

The *Nibelungenlied* is a Middle High German poem depicting stories revolving around the life and death of the Germanic hero Siegfried. This thirteenth-century epic was sometimes later referred to as the *Kriemhild*, a title that reflects the centrality of Siegfried's wife, Kriemhild, to the entire story. Before the story opens, Siegfried was a hero who had defeated the Nibelung kings. He wins the treasure of the Nibelungs and uses a magic cloak of darkness (invisibility) to slay the dragon Fafnir. As a result of slaying the dragon, Siegfried's skin has been made impenetrable except on his back, where a leaf kept his skin from being exposed to the dragon's blood.

Siegfried leaves his kingdom, with his father, Siegmund, in charge, and seeks the hand of Kriemhild, the beautiful Burgundian princess. Kriemhild has sworn to marry no man, but Siegfried hopes to win her by securing the support of her brothers, Gunther, Gernot, and Giselher. Hagen, King Gunther's retainer, knows some of the stories of Siegfried and makes the brothers aware of the value of an alliance with him. Siegfried fights and defeats the enemies of the Burgundians and helps Gunther win the hand of Queen Brunhild of Iceland. Brunhild has incredible strength and puts all her suitors to death who cannot defeat her in a contest. With Siegfried's invisible help Gunther throws a stone, leaps, and throws a javelin farther than any other man (or Brunhild) and wins Brunhild as his bride. On their wedding night Brunhild tries Gunther's strength and ends up tying him up in her girdle. The next night Gunther has Siegfried subdue Brunhild, and once Brunhild loses her virginity, her great strength dissipates.

Because Gunther wanted to impress Brunhild, he initally introduced Siegfried as his vassal. Once Kriemhild (now Siegfried's wife) and Brunhild meet, they argue about whose husband is more important and powerful. Eventually Kriemhild reveals that it was Siegfried who first slept with Brunhild, and this revelation results in Hagen secretly vowing revenge against Siegfried. Kriemhild is tricked into stitching a cross onto the spot on Siegfried's tunic where his skin is vulnerable, supposedly so Hagen will know how best to protect Siegfried. Gunther and Hagen take Siegfried hunting one day, and while he is not looking, Hagen stabs Siegfried with a spear in his one vulnerable spot.

After Siegfried's death Hagen eventually convinces Gunther to have Kriemhild bring the treasure of the Nibelungs to Burgundy, and Hagen takes it from her and sinks it to the bottom of the Rhine. When King Etzel of Hungary seeks the hand of the widowed Kriemhild in marriage, she agrees only if he will help her avenge Siegfried's death. The last section of the epic deals with the death of Kriemhild's brothers and their retainers after they accept an invitation to visit her in Hungary. Many Burgundians die, and Kriemhild eventually burns down the hall in which the Burgundians are trapped. She tries to force Hagen to return her treasure, but he refuses, so she beheads both Gunther and Hagen. In the end one of her own allies, Hildenbrand, kills and dismembers her for having caused the death of so many men.

CONCLUSION

Memorizing the conventions of medieval epics as listed and recognizing the examples noted as members of the genre will certainly enhance your understanding. It is also especially important to remember that the purpose of epic poetry is to define the moral values of a particular culture through the wise actions of its highborn hero. Medieval epics are less warlike and more spiritual than Greek heroic poetry, primarily because of the huge influence of the Christian church on all aspects of medieval literature. Weighty topics of great significance imparted in language noble and sincere allowed little room for the humor present in other medieval genres such as fabliaux or ballad. While our own modern perceptions color our reading and understanding of the entire epic genre, the sincerity of the discourse encourages contemporary readers to believe that they have gained some perspective of the medieval writer's worldview.

SELECTED BIBLIOGRAPHY

The Alliterative Morte Arthure: A Critical Edition. Ed. Valerie Krishna. New York: B. Franklin, 1976.

The Alliterative Morte Arthure: A New Verse Translation. Trans. Valerie Krishna. Washington, DC: University Press of America, 1983.

Andreas. Trans. Charles W. Kennedy. *The Poems of Cynewulf.* New York: Peter Smith, 1949. 211–263.

Aristotle. *The Poetics.* Trans. W. Hamilton Fyfe. Loeb Classical Library. Cambridge, MA: Harvard University Press, 1991.

Astell, Ann W. *Job, Boethius, and Epic Truth.* Ithaca, NY: Cornell University Press, 1994.

Beowulf. Trans. Howell D. Chickering, Jr. Garden City, NY: Anchor Books, 1989.

Boethius. *The Consolation of Philosophy.* Trans. Richard Green. New York: Macmillan, 1985.

Bonjour, Adrien. *The Digressions in Beowulf.* Oxford: Blackwell, 1965.

Dante. *The Divine Comedy 1: Hell.* Trans. Dorothy L. Sayers. New York: Penguin, 1949.

———. *The Divine Comedy 2: Purgatory.* Trans. Dorothy L. Sayers. New York: Penguin, 1955.

———. *The Divine Comedy 3: Paradise.* Trans. Dorothy L. Sayers and Barbara Reynolds. New York: Penguin, 1962.

"Epic." *The Compact Edition of the Oxford English Dictionary.* Vol. 1. 1987.

The Heliand: The Saxon Gospel. Trans. G. Ronald Murphy. New York: Oxford University Press, 1992.

Homer. *The Iliad.* Trans. A.T. Murray. Loeb Classical Library. vols. 1 and 2. Cambridge, MA: Harvard University Press, 1999.

Homer. *The Odyssey.* Trans A.T. Murray. Loeb Classical Library. Vols. 1 and 2. Cambridge, MA: Harvard University Press, 1995.

Hrotsvit of Gandersheim. *Hrotsvit of Gandersheim: A Florilegium of Her Works.* Ed. Katharina Wilson. Cambridge: D.S. Brewer, 1998.

Hutson, Arthur E. Introduction. *Epics of the Western World.* Philadelphia: Lippincott, 1954.

Jackson, Guida M. *Encyclopedia of Literary Epics.* Santa Barbara, CA: ABC-CLIO, 1996.

———. *Encyclopedia of Traditional Epics.* Santa Barbara, CA: ABC-CLIO, 1994.

Krantz, Dennis. *Mocking Epic: Waltharius, Alexandreis, and the Problem of Christian Heroism.* Madrid: J. Porrúa Turanzas, 1980.

Lacy, Norris J., ed. *The New Arthurian Encyclopedia.* New York: Garland, 1986.

Malory, Thomas. *Le Morte d'Arthur.* Ed. Janet Cowen. 2 vols. New York: Penguin, 1986.

The Nibelungenlied. Trans. A.T. Hatto. Penguin: London, 1969.

The Poem of My Cid. Trans. Peter Such and John Hodgkinson. Warminster, UK: Aris and Phillips, 1987.

Sir Gawain and the Green Knight. Trans. Marie Borroff. New York: Norton, 1967.

The Song of Roland. Trans. Fredrick Goldin. New York: Norton, 1978.

Virgil. *Aeneid VII–XII, the Minor Poems.* Trans. H. Rushton Fairclough. Loeb Classical Library. Cambridge, MA: Harvard University Press, 1999.

———. *Eclogues, Georgics, Aeneid I–VI.* Trans. H. Rushton Fairclough. Loeb Classical Library. Cambridge, MA: Harvard University Press, 1999.

Webber, Ruth House. "Towards the Morphology of the Romance Epic." *Romance Epic: Essays on a Medieval Literary Genre.* Kalamazoo, MI: Medieval Institute Publications, 1987. 1–9.

13

The Fabliau

Marie Nelson and Richard Thomson

What is a fabliau? "A verse tale meant for laughter." Raymond Eichmann, writing an introduction to John DuVal's English translations of twenty fourteenth-century French fabliaux, considers attempts to make Joseph Bédier's identification in *Les Fabliaux* of fabliaux as "contes à rire en vers" more specific. He finds that Per Nykrog's restriction to the narration of one episode and its immediate results, Knud Togeby's categorization system, with its dependence on level, length, and attitude, Thomas D. Cooke's argument for fulfillment of a reader/listener's expectations, Willem Noomen's expectation of octosyllabic couplets, human protagonists, and independent status, and Mary Jane Stearns Schenck's identification of arrival, departure, interrogation, communication, deception, misdeed, recognition, retaliation, and resolution as basic fabliau components might well exclude a number of stories that should be considered members of the genre (*Fabliaux Fair and Foul* v–viii). Thus Eichmann's survey, though it does not cause him to accept all of Bédier's contributions to fabliau studies (he rejects, for example, his predecessor's assumption that fabliaux are mere jokes), leads him to the conclusion that Bédier's single phrase still provides the best answer to the define-the-genre question. A fabliau is a verse tale intended to amuse.

Consideration of restrictions included in other definitions may, however, serve to draw attention to certain distinguishing features of the genre. We propose to examine this possibility by turning to definitions found in M.H. Abrams's *Glossary of Literary Terms*; Sylvan Barnet, Morton Berman, and William Burto's *Dictionary of Literary Terms*; Harry Shaw's *Concise Dictionary of Literary Terms*; and William Flint Thrall, Addison Hibbard, and C. Hugh Holman's *Handbook to Literature*, that is, to the work of lexicographers whose purpose was to define terms needed by readers of English literature.

M.H. Abrams adds a number of details to the basic Bédier definition. "The fabliau," Abrams says, "was a medieval form: a short comic or satiric tale in verse dealing realistically with middle-class or lower-class characters and delighting in the ribald and the obscene" (*Glossary* 58). Abrams includes Chaucer's "The Miller's Tale," often taken as the prototype fabliau, as an example in his short definition paragraph. Chaucer's "The Merchant's Tale," another story widely recognized as a fabliau (Larry D. Benson and Theodore M. Andersson include Latin, Italian, German, and French analogues in *The Literary Context of Chaucer's Fabliaux*) would not, if we take Abrams's apparent restriction of fabliaux characters to those belonging to the middle or lower classes, fit within the boundaries established by his definition. "The Merchant's Tale" 's candidate for cuckoldry is a sixty-year-old knight who, refusing to listen to good advice, marries a young bride who deceives him by making love with a squire in a pear tree.

Barnet, Berman, and Burto also cite "The Miller's Tale" as a readily recognizable example of the fabliau genre. Their definition of "fabliau" is "an earthy, humorous medieval tale, in verse or prose, usually satirizing the clergy and middle-class life, and often obscene" (*Dictionary of Literary Terms* 41). This definition, with its focus on men of the church, would readily admit to the fabliau canon the tales of trickery told by Chaucer's Friar and Summoner. The summoner of "The Friar's Tale," a man so obtuse that he does not recognize a green yeoman who actually identifies himself as the devil, persists in a course of action that leads to his own damnation, while the equally persistent friar of "The Summoner's Tale" most decidedly earns the "gift"—a fart—that his angered parishioner gives him. The Friar-Summoner pair of tales, then, are as closely related as the prototype "The Miller's Tale" and its immediately following response, "The Reeve's Tale." The Miller tells a tale that ridicules a carpenter, and the Reeve of Chaucer's *Canterbury Tales*, who is a carpenter and thus sees himself as the target of the Miller's tale, responds by telling his story of a miller's jealously guarded young wife and her lover.

Harry Shaw says that fabliaux are "frequently ribald" and "*conventionally* told in eight-syllable verse that satirize[s] the faults of clergymen and women" (*Concise Dictionary* 110, emphasis mine, to draw attention to Shaw's hesitance to make hard-and-fast distinctions). He lists as fabliau examples "stories by the Friar, the Miller, the Reeve, the Cook, the Manciple, etc." Shaw's "etc." can perhaps be taken to mean something like "and the list goes on." We wonder, however, if his list should be as long as it is. The Cook, readers of *The Canterbury Tales* will remember, barely got started with his tale. He was too drunk to continue what only promises to be a story about an energetic apprentice who serves a master who has a wife who "swyve[s] for hir sustenance" (*Riverside Chaucer*, "The Cook's Tale," 1.4422). "The Cook's Tale" "example," then, will not be discussed here. "The Manciple's Tale," which Shaw also cites, will, however, receive attention. The presence of the animal character of "The Manciple's Tale"—a white crow punished by being turned black—might lead to its placement in the fable rather than the fabliau genre, but its focus on the genre-defining husband-wife-lover triangle should justify its consideration here as a fabliau.

Here too the less-than-serious "moral" with which the Manciple concludes his tale (he goes on at length about his mother's instruction about talking too much) may make his tale appropriate for discussion as at least a borderline example. Indeed, consideration of a certain "moral" distinction may serve to strengthen our definition of the fabliau in terms of its basic intention and characterizing features by adding a sense of what it is not. Thrall, Hibbard, and Holman, who include "The Manciple's Tale" in their list of fabliau examples, distinguish fabliaux from fables in this way: "Although fabliaux often had ostensible 'morals' appended to them, they lack the serious intention of the fable, and they differ from the fable too in always having human beings as characters and in always maintaining a realistic tone and manner" (*Handbook to Literature* 197).

Another question that has a certain relevance to the fable-fabliau distinction may lead to further understanding of the essential nature of the English fabliau: Where did the English fabliaux come from? Robert Hellman and Richard O'Gorman explain in a brief afterword to *Fabliaux: Ribald Tales from the Old French* that the word "fabliau" itself is a diminutive form of the word "fable," and that it was invented by fabliaux composers of the Old French period. They next trace the fabliau's origins back to the fable of classical antiquity, which, like their etymological explication, contributes little to the task of definition. But Hellman and O'Gorman then turn their attention to the contrasting ways in which fable and fabliau accomplish their individual storytelling purposes, and the question of fabliaux origins becomes relevant to the task of definition.

(1) The fable, like the parable of the New Testament, is a tale with a moral purpose. The fabliau, on the other hand, exploits the story for its own sake, being intended solely to amuse the listener. Except for some very early examples, it illustrates no moral precept and has no didactic purpose whatsoever. It is, in fact, perhaps the first distinct genre in Western literature of which this may be said. (2) The fable traditionally uses animal characters. The fabliau, with few exceptions, is concerned with ordinary people. (3) The fable may be either in prose or verse. The fabliaux always are in verse, all but one in octosyllabic rhymed couplets. (4) The fable is serious in purpose, if not always in content. The most essential characteristic of the fabliau, on the other hand, is that it is always a humorous tale.

The fabliau is, in short, a brief tale in verse written to amuse, with characters, action, and scenes drawn from real life, and with few supernatural or marvelous elements. Or, in the even more succinct definition of the medievalist Joseph Bédier, it is "un conte à rire en vers" (182).

Hellman and O'Gorman would seem to conclude, as Eichmann concluded, that Bédier's brief definition served its purpose well enough, and perhaps served it better than more specific definitions could. It may nevertheless still be useful, since the purpose here is to extend our understanding of the English fabliau, to extend Hellman and O'Gorman's brief exploration of French-English fabliau connections. Let us begin by noting the characterizing features of the French fabliau as Charles Muscatine presents them in *Chaucer and the French Tradition*. Muscatine's features include (1) a remarkable preoccupation with the animal facts of life; (2) a blunt economy of plan and procedure; (3) a spare setting; (4) prosaic language; (5) a representative collection of characters—peasants and bourgeois, clerks, priests, nuns, jongleurs, and miscellaneous rascals, along with a few knights and ladies; (6) formulaic description of characters; and (7) dramatically conceived dialogue (59–65).

Turning to John Hines's *Fabliau in English*, we see that Hines presents the defining features of English fabliaux much as Muscatine describes those features with respect to the French tradition. Hines's consideration of the language of Chaucer's fabliaux, however, presents a particularly valuable extension of interpretive possibility. Demonstrating that the language of Chaucer's fabliaux is far from "prosaic" (to pluck Muscatine's adjective out of context) and using the term "marked language" rather than "obscenity," Hines points out that the marked language of the English fabliaux, like that of French fabliaux, provides multiple opportunities for wordplay. As Hines demonstrates—first with a short list of words that name body parts and excretions, and then through explication of individual tales—fabliau composers demonstrate a remarkable flexibility in their use of words that carry double meanings, and in their frequent reliance on the sound similarities of relatively "innocent" words to project less innocent meanings. Here we might recommend to the reader of fabliaux who finds amusement in wordplay (there is, after all, no stipulation in Bédier's definition about the kind of amusement we may expect to enjoy) Thomas W. Ross's *Chaucer's Bawdy*, an altogether different kind of dictionary from those referred to at the beginning of this chapter. Our next question, however, has to do with the amusement fabliaux provided to audiences of Chaucer's time.

Who listened to and enjoyed the fabliaux? Hellman and O'Gorman claim a wider audience for the fabliaux than the earlier studies of Bédier and Per Nykrog (cited by Eichmann, viii–ix) would suggest:

Composed for and enjoyed by all social classes, the fabliaux were recited or read at every occasion which brought people together in the courts of France and England, both great and small; in the taverns of the bustling cities and commercial centers; in the homes of the prosperous burghers of the town and of the country squires, both of whom were eager to imitate the style of life of their betters. It is conceivable that fabliaux were told at formal ceremonies in court and castle as comic relief after the recitation of a battle epic or a chivalric romance. They may have been recited on the steps of a church or on a busy street corner at market time, or during one of the important fairs. They may even—God forbid—have been heard in the rectory or the cloister. (184–85)

Hellman and O'Gorman's "all social classes" and "every occasion" do have the ring of overstatement. Nevertheless, their position is closer to Eichmann's re-

jection of Bédier's (qualified) categorization of the fabliaux audience as bourgeois and Nykrog's assumption that only educated, or upper-class, listeners
could truly enjoy the parody of courtly love to be seen in the fabliaux than their
language might suggest. Nor is it far from Charles Muscatine's conclusion about
the wide, general audience for the "verse tale[s] meant for laughter," since Muscatine, though he introduces the genre in a chapter titled "The Bourgeois Tradition," makes it clear that in doing so, he has no intention to limit the fabliaux
audience to the bourgeoisie.

Who told these stories? This question, like other questions of origin, leads
our literary lexicographers back to the fabliau's French past. Thrall, Hibbard,
and Holman point to the apparent origins of the genre with their reference to
the "jongleur, who spread the fabliaux widely throughout France" (*Handbook*
197), then add that though the jongleur was primarily a performer of poems
composed by others, he sometimes supplied nonmusical forms of entertaining
like juggling and tumbling (252). Eichmann, in his development of the teller-
tale relationship, not only credits the jongleurs with a wider range of talents,
but with a higher degree of originality. As Eichmann reads the historical record,
these multitalented performers were not just accomplished jugglers and acrobats.
Their skills also included those of the animal trainer, dancer, actor, and fire-
eater. Taking calls for attention like "My lords, if you will linger here / A little
while and lend an ear" as evidence, Eichmann lays the groundwork for consideration of the skills of the jongleur in oral composition, that is, in presenting a
story not as a recitation of a text already written down but as a story in the
process of creation as the teller tells it.

But this is our question: Who told these stories in English? Hines's answer,
which does not take Melissa M. Furrow's publication of *Ten Fifteenth-Century
Comic Poems* into account, is " 'Dame Sirith' is the only extant Middle English
fabliau by an author other than Chaucer" (*The Fabliau in English* 43). "Dame
Sirith," with its story of an old woman who tricks a young married woman into
yielding to a clerk who pleads his desperate love, is certainly ribald enough to
fall into the fabliau tradition. This story tells how Dame Sirith, acting on behalf
of the lover (who will pay her for her services) feeds her dog mustard to make
him cry, then convinces the young wife that the dog is her daughter who has
been turned into a dog because she would not show mercy to her lover. The
trick succeeds, and the young wife yields.

Hines cites the manuscript Digby 86 as his "Sirith" source, dating this written
version of the story between 1272 and 1283. In 1484 William Caxton published
a very similar story in his *Fables of Alfonce and Poge*. This story appears in
P.M. Zall's *Hundred Merry Tales and Other English Jestbooks of the Fifteenth
and Sixteenth Centuries* under the heading "The eleventh fable is of an old harlot
or bawd" (33–35). The Alfonce and Poge story is essentially the same as the
story cited by Hines and included in Benson and Andersson's *Literary Context
of Chaucer's Fabliaux* as "the earliest fabliau in English and the only surviving
example of the genre before Chaucer" (372). Except for the transformed daugh-

ter, who in the Alfonce and Poge fable is a cat who eats bread covered with mustard, cries, and becomes the means whereby the young wife is frightened into surrendering to the importunities of the lover, the characters in both the Digby manuscript and Caxton versions of the story are the same—husband, young wife, and would-be lover (the fabliau triangle) plus the old bawd who has come to be known as Dame Sirith and the transformed "daughter." Are these two stories simply different versions of a single story, the work, originally, of the only English author of fabliaux besides Chaucer? Perhaps, but this does not seem likely in an age of oral composition.

Further exploration points to other non-Chaucerian fabliaux that must be considered. Melissa Furrow, making no claim that all ten of the Middle English poems she edits in *Ten Fifteenth-Century Comic Poems* are fabliaux, or even that all are complete poems, asserts that several "must be, according to any definition of the term, [fabliaux]" (xv). "Sir Corneus," a story of a chastity-testing horn, and "The Boy and the Mantle," another chastity-testing story drawn from Arthurian tradition, to name just two of those included in Furrow's collection, would certainly fit within the fabliau genre as it has been defined here, as would "The Tale of the Basin."

In "The Tale of the Basin" we hear a story about a lusty priest named Sir John (a typical fabliau figure) who pursues a wife (who seems closer to what the young Alisoun of Bath must have been than to the Alisoun we meet in "The Miller's Tale") who deceives a husband (who is typically foolish). This priest is caught by the magic of a "basin" (a chamber pot) that he cannot let go of. The wife, called upon to help, finds her hands stuck too, as does a chambermaid who also responds to a summons for help, and a carter, who strikes the chambermaid (his "speciall") with a shovel. The four are released when the husband's parson brother undoes the spell, and the husband's formerly scolding wife mends her ways.

"The Lady Prioress," which Furrow points out is similar to the first tale of the ninth day of Boccaccio's *Decameron*, would also seem to fit into the fabliau genre. Interestingly enough, this story presents the success of a woman, not a man of the church, in playing a trick that takes its origins from a promise of sexual pleasure. Here the characters are a Lady Prioress and her three suitors: a knight who boasts of successes he never achieved (like killing a giant); a parson (whose services are called upon to say a prayer for the knight, who is only to pretend to be dead); and a successful merchant (who has a record of past adventures that his wife must not know about). Promising her sexual favors as the reward if they successfully carry out their assigned tasks, the Lady Prioress persuades the knight to play dead, the parson to say the prayers required for the corpse's entry into heaven, and the merchant to play the role of a devil. The merchant successfully plays his role. The parson is frightened half to death. Then the knight, apparently rising from the dead in fear of the devil, frightens the merchant into headlong flight. Each having failed in his own way, all three are denied the Lady's love, and the merchant pays an additional penalty as well.

He must pay twenty marks to keep the Lady Prioress from telling his wife about the night's adventure, and thus she gains a sizeable endowment for her convent.

The story of the Lady Prioress may not fit the expectations established by our reading of Chaucer's fabliaux and their French and Italian counterparts. A woman is its central figure. She engages in deception, but the deception is not the typical deception of a husband. She has no husband. She leads her suitors (all three of them) to expect that she will satisfy their sexual needs, but has no intention of satisfying those needs. She makes a financial profit, but does not do so in ways made familiar by the "General Prologue" description of the Pardoner of *The Canterbury Tales*, by the Pardoner's personal prologue, or by the Friar and Summoner exchanges. Instead of using the church for her own financial gain, the Lady Prioress uses her personal attractiveness (she is described as a lovely daughter of a lord) to gain support for an institution of the church. But as a tale of trickery involving promises of sexual pleasure, and as a tale told in Middle English verse with an intention to entertain, this story deserves, as Furrow suggests, to be included in our fabliau canon, as do two other stories Furrow includes in her collection, "Dane Hew, Munk of Leicestre" and "The Friars of Berwick."

The character who plays the title role in "Dane Hew, Munk of Leicestre" is almost immediately introduced as a proper fabliau monk. Dane Hew is "yung and lusty / and to fair women he had a fansy" (ll. 7–8). The triangle we find here, however, is a bit unusual. The wife is a "woman fair and good" who has been happily married to her tradesman husband for seven years. But Dane Hew loves the wife and will go out of his mind, he tells her, if he cannot have her. She replies that she already has "many a shrewd fit / Of [her] husband every day" (164), but when he persists, she agrees, for a payment of twenty nobles, to let Dane Hew come when her husband is out of town. She then tells her husband, a tailor, about the agreement she has made. He protests, but agrees to the woman's plan to get the money while still remaining "a good woman."

The plan develops: the wife locks her husband in a chest; the monk arrives at five o'clock in the morning as agreed. Having determined that the husband is out of town, he swiftly embraces the wife. She, however, demands the money first. He throws it in her lap. She asks leave to put the money away before they begin. She opens the chest, her husband leaps out and hits the monk on the head, and the monk falls down dead. The wife berates her husband for his hasty action, and he turns to her for solution of their problem. They will wait until evening and then take the monk to his abbey and stand him up against a wall.

As the story develops, the abbot of his monastery, angry because he cannot find Dane Hew, is led to the standing corpse by his man and angrily addresses him. Hitting Dane Hew's dead body on the head, he vows, "I will giue thee such a stroke vpon thy head, / That I shall make thee to fall down dead" (155–156). The abbot suits his action to the word and the monk falls down—dead. Aghast, the abbot promises his man forty shillings if he can save his honor. The abbot's man, knowing of Dane Hew's lust for the tailor's wife, says that the best thing to do is take him to their home and stand him by the door. The plan is carried out.

The tailor and his wife are faced again with the unsolved problem of what to do with the body of Dane Hew, and the wife's new solution is to lay him in a corner until morning, then put him in a sack and throw him into the dammed-up water behind the mill. The husband starts to carry out the plan, but sees two thieves who, upon seeing him, think that he is the miller and break into a run, dropping the sack they are carrying to the ground. The tailor-husband picks up the thieves' sack, sees that it is full of bacon they have presumably stolen from the miller, and carries it home to his wife. The thieves pick up the tailor's monk-laden sack and take it to the home of one of the thieves. The thief's wife (it is wives who think of solutions here), upon discovering what is in the sack, tells the two thieves to take Dane Hew to the mill and hang him up there like a slab of bacon. They follow her instructions.

The miller's wife, going to fetch some bacon, sees "the false munk, by cocks bones / That hath been so lecherous many a day / and with mens wiues vsed to play" (261–263). (Everyone, it seems, knows Dane Hew for what he is—or was.) The miller, like the other husbands, relies on his wife for a solution to their problem. She does not fail to provide one. The abbot has a farmyard close by, where he keeps horses. They will mount Dane Hew on one of the horses and send him charging back to his abbey. The plan will work out, the miller's wife says, because the abbot rides a mare every morning, which will attract the stallion on which the dead monk is mounted. The plan works. The stallion races to the abbey, the abbot's men come to his defense against the mounted monk, and Dane Hew is killed a fourth time—and finally buried.

"The Friars of Berwick" introduces two traveling men of the church, both of whom are skilled at flattering women, as its action begins. Robert, who is young, is "verry heft of blude" (41) ("very hot of blood"). In this context we can read this as "very ready for action." The other man, Allane, is old.

As they approach Berwick, Allane is tired and wishes to find lodging. Coming to a good hostelry outside of Berwick, the two friars take their ease and are served ale, wine, and cheese by the fair wife of Symone Lawrear, who is away from home. Knowing that their abbey will be closed before they can get there—they hear the prayer bell ring—they also ask for a night's lodging. The wife, having said already that her husband is not at home, refuses their request. When they persist, she gives them permission to stay, but only if they will sleep in a loft at the end of the hall. The two friars accept the offer of limited hospitality happily enough, but Friar Robert hopes to have some sport.

He finds it. Watching from above in their loft, the friars discover that the wife is preparing for a tryst with her rich suitor, Friar John. Friar John comes, and he and the wife begin their play. Above, Friar Allane is content to take his rest, but Friar Robert is curious. He makes a hole in the floor through which he can watch the wife and her lover. Then, when she is ready to serve the sump-tuous meal she has prepared, a knock is heard at the gate. Symone has returned.

Friar John, aghast, fears that he will lose his testicles if the husband finds him there. Symone's wife, whose name is Alesoun, determines to hide her suitor in a trough she uses to store baking supplies and orders her maidservant to hide all the signs of her preparation for a feast. Meanwhile, her husband continues to knock at the gate. Pretending not to recognize his voice, she tells him to go away, saying that her husband is not at home and she cannot take in any lodgers. (The irony of the repeated reluctance to permit anyone to enter while her husband is away is of course a bit heavy here.) At last the wife lets her husband in, serves him ale and wine and cheese, and refuses his invitation to join him at his meal. She would rather be in bed.

At this point Friar Robert chooses to announce his presence with a cough. Questioned, the wife explains the presence of Friars Allane and Robert, and the hospitable husband insists that they join him at his meal. He only wishes that he had better food to offer them. Friar Robert says that he has magic that will provide the best food in the country and Gascon wine as well. The wife, watching his performance, knows that he has seen her preparations for the feast with Sir John. The "magic" rites completed, Friar Robert orders the wife to go to the cupboard to fetch the feast he has watched her prepare. She obeys, afraid not to, lest her deception be revealed.

Symone and the two traveling friars feast upon the food prepared for Friar John. Then Symone, full of curiosity, wants to know how Friar Robert worked his magic. He has a servant, Robert says. "Let me see him," Symone says. "Oh no, he is too ugly," Friar Robert replies. "The sight would drive you out of your mind." "Well, let him be in a tolerable form," Symone says. "Let him be a friar, clothed in white as you are." Friar Robert says no, that would disgrace his order. If he is to appear, it must be as a gray friar.

Symone seizes a cudgel to protect himself. Friar Robert orders him not to strike until he tells him to, then approaches the trough where Alesoun has hidden her suitor, Friar John. Friar Robert, having set up his escape, now orders Friar John to pull his cowl down over his face and run for the door. Friar John runs, Friar Robert tells Symone to strike boldly, and he strikes so hard he loses his balance and falls down and breaks his head. Friar John loses his footing and falls into a mire under the stairs. Nevertheless, he escapes, and the narrator rather doubts that Friar John will ever want to come back again. The story ends with this graceless escape, a promise of the injured husband's recovery, and an observation that Alesoun did not get everything she wanted.

The anonymous author or authors of the Dame Sirith story or stories, then, were not the only tellers of fabliaux besides Chaucer. Furrow's publication of *Ten Fifteenth-Century Comic Poems* (1985) would seem to suggest that there could have been a fairly rich hoard of Middle English fabliaux, and I hope that the extended summaries of the action of "Dane Hew" and "The Friars of Berwick" presented have begun to suggest the possibilities for variation and combination inherent in the husband-wife-lover and culpable-man-of-the-church themes. What we do not see in the non-Chaucerian fabliaux, however, is the narrative richness he achieves by assigning specific tales to individual tellers.

Our question now becomes: Who tells the fabliaux of *The Canterbury Tales*? The Miller and the Reeve, the Merchant and the Shipman, the Friar and the Summoner, and maybe the Manciple. These tellers have already been introduced as part of the definition process. The question of why Chaucer assigns particular stories to particular tellers lies outside the parameters of this chapter, but we can easily see that the pilgrims just named show themselves to be well qualified to respond to the "solaas" part of the challenge the Host extends in the "General Prologue" to *The Canterbury Tales*. Others may tell "tales of best sentence" (798). The tellers of fabliaux are to provide the best entertainment. To entertain, to bring pleasure to their fellow pilgrims—this is the mission of the tellers of the *Canterbury Tales* fabliaux, and for the most part, as the links between the tales show, they succeed.

As the Miller ends his tale, Chaucer the narrator or stage manager steps forward to say that "Diverse folk diversely they seyde / But for the moore part they loughe and pleyde" (3857–3858), and thus the Miller, drunk as he confessed himself to be as he began his story, fulfills his function as storyteller. Oswald the Reeve, one of the pilgrims, is not pleased. Therefore he may have intended that his story not be pleasing to the Miller. The Miller knows Oswald is a carpenter, and just as recognizably a target as the miller who plays a role in "The Reeve's Tale."

This could be one of the reasons for the continuing success of the Miller-Reeve exchange. Readers of our time, if we do not necessarily take pleasure in seeing a character "put down" by the telling of a tale, may well find a certain enjoyment in exercising our ability to see the skill with which a particular tit-for-tat exchange is carried out. With the Miller-Reeve exchange we see before us not just two natural rivals ready to get all the profit they can take, by fair means or foul, but two men engaged in a contest to determine who can tell the best story, a contest that may, incidentally, enable a winner to humiliate an adversary. What we may also see is a man behind the scene, one man who demonstrates his remarkable skill in the handling of fabliau plot elements. Who tells the better tale, Chaucer's Miller or his Reeve? It would be difficult to find an animal sexuality to compare with that of Alisoun's "body gent and smal" in "The Reeve's Tale," or to find a freshness to compare to her "newe pere-jonette tree" appeal anywhere in *The Canterbury Tales*. Nor can we expect to see the skill with which Chaucer, speaking through his Miller, brings the climax of young Nicholas's seduction of Alisoun.

The second of Chaucer's Canterbury fabliaux, perhaps because a number of modern readers are put off by what they see as the Reeve's revenge motive, has not been as highly regarded as "The Miller's Tale." Reading it as a fabliau in its own right, however, can show that the Reeve was a pretty artful storyteller too. The "litel ire" attributed to the Reeve may actually be, as Hines suggests, just a bit of anger, not an emotion continually seething within an unhappy man.

In any case it does not keep the Reeve from telling a story that has its own narrative complexity.

There is, to be sure, a degree of irony in the pride the Reeve's miller is shown to take in his high-born wife (who is the daughter of a supposedly celibate priest) and in the daughter whose value he must ensure by his own vigilance. He may not lock her in a chest at night, as the miller of a thirteenth-century fabliau that Benson and Andersson present as "The "Reeve's Tale" 's closest analogue does (100–115), but the miller's intention to protect his prized "possession" is nevertheless clearly visible and is in fact pointed to by the use of marked fabliau language. With the appearance of two young scholars from Oxford who have come to get their grain ground, we may, if we know the sexual implication of the verb "grind" to which Thomas Ross gives attention (98), be alerted to the possibility of fun to come.

The Reeve's "game" (his word for the story he will tell) does not depend on just a conventional husband-wife-lover situation. Here we see instead the development of a context that depends on a double triangle of relationships, one in which a single character, the miller who is the husband of one vulnerable female and the father of another, becomes a doubly vulnerable fabliau target. The man who is an expert in the art of the "heavy thumb" will be tricked by two young men he is sure he can get the better of, and who are equally determined not to be cheated. One additional character is introduced as a member of the miller's family, an infant child who sleeps in a cradle at the foot of the bed of the miller and his wife, and the stage is set for a game of "trick the trickster."

In round one of this contest, the students watch the grinding of their grain, with one standing above the hopper and one below to watch the ground grain come out. The miller is unable to steal ground grain, or flour.

Round two: the miller releases the students' horse, who runs after mares in the field. Here, as Hines points out, Chaucer develops a linguistic continuity with "The Miller's Tale." The two tales share a field of animal imagery, and the horse becomes an embodiment of male lust as Symkin the miller releases him, knowing that there are mares in the field close by. This particular animal metaphor will find expression again when John, one of the two young men, is said to "priken hard" when he entices the miller's wife into his bed.

Round three: darkness falls, and the students are unable to return to their college. They pay for a capon (a castrated, fattened male chicken) and other victuals that Malyne, the daughter, is sent to fetch, and thus Symkin would seem to enjoy a further profit. Having eaten and drunk to satiety, he falls asleep.

Round four: Aleyn, one of the two clerks, kept awake by the miller's snoring and farting, enters the bed of the daughter. Both enjoy their play.

Round five, and this begins the action of the "musical-beds" game: John tricks the wife into coming into his bed by moving the cradle so that she will mistake his bed for that of her husband. She says that she has not had such good sex for years.

Aleyn goes out to piss. (There is no reluctance to use four-letter words here.)

Going by the location of the moved cradle (it is still very dark), he returns to the wrong bed, the miller's bed, which he thinks is the one he shares with John, exulting in his success with Symkin's daughter. The miller, awakened by Aleyn, strikes the first blow. Mayhem follows, and the final blow is struck by the wife, who mistakes her husband's bald head for that of one of the students.

With Malyne the daughter's gift to Aleyn of a cake made from the flour the miller stole (in gratitude for pleasure experienced), the story ends and the losses of Symkin the miller can be added up. They include his expected payment for grinding the scholars' grain, the stolen flour, and the "swyving" (to use the marked Middle English term) of his wife and daughter. The dishonest miller has himself been tricked. The Reeve's "A gylour shal hymself bigyled be" (4321) draws attention to this nugget of fabliau wisdom, which, despite a tendency to read "The Reeve's Tale" in dark contrast to "The Miller's Tale," seems to distance the teller from his tale, which can, after all, be properly placed in an English set of "verse tales meant for laughter."

With "The Shipman's Tale," the next fabliau to be considered here, we again find an extended contest of wits involving the profit motive along with a drive toward sexual pleasure that admits no obstacles. The sex-for-money, money-for-sex exchanges of "The Shipman's Tale" can, we think, be visualized after giving attention to a series of verbal exchanges. First there is a conversation between the wife and the visiting monk. The merchant's wife complains, "Though husbands should be / Hardy and wise, and riche, and therto free [generous] / And buxom unto his wyf and fressh abedde" (176–177), her successful merchant husband to her shows a serious lack of generosity. His stinginess has led to her present predicament: she has had to borrow one hundred francs to pay back a debt she assumed because of her need to keep up the appearances expected of the wife of a presumably prosperous man, and the one hundred francs have to be paid back next Sunday. The first deal is struck. The monk will loan her one hundred francs, and in exchange she will do whatever he wants her to do. Off she goes, jolly as a magpie, to order the preparation of a dinner that will be a pleasure for all. Ross (120) notes that though the Modern English form has lost all suggestion of sex, Chaucer's "joly" was almost always associated with play between the sexes.

The next extended conversational exchange is between the wife and the husband. She complains that he neglects their guest. He complains about the demands of the life of a merchant and says that he must prepare now to go on a business trip to Flanders. The next exchange of money comes when the monk asks his merchant friend for a loan of one hundred francs before he goes. The request is readily granted, but the merchant says that he will need to have the loan repaid. The reason, as the merchant presents it, is a fairly straightforward extension of an agricultural metaphor: money is the merchant's "plough." The sexual meaning, at this stage of the narration, simply serves as part of the marked-language background.

Off goes the merchant. Back comes the monk, and the wife pays the monk's loan to her back with a night of sexual pleasure.

Meeting the monk later in Paris, the merchant speaks of his need to take out a loan for a further enterprise. The monk, of course, would be glad to help, but it just so happens that he left the one hundred francs earlier loaned to him by the merchant with the merchant's wife.

Back home in Seint-Denys again, his business deals completed, the merchant briefly chides his wife about his embarrassment at not knowing that the monk had returned the money he had loaned him to her. The husband, full of the pleasure of his recent business success, does not pursue the subject further. And what of the hundred francs? Where are they now? The wife thought that they were just given to her out of friendship, so she has now spent the money on clothes to honor her husband. The hundred francs accounted for, "The Shipman's Tale" ends with its teller's own play with the word "taillynge."

With the Shipman's contribution to the *Canterbury Tales* sequence, a story referred to by folklorists as "the lover's gift regained," we see two prominent fabliau features brought into play. We have the basic fabliau triangle, which leads to a story of a husband tricked by his wife and her lover; and we have a man of the church who plays a key role in the action. The lover of the "Shipman's Tale" is a monk. Also, most notably in the Shipman's concluding wish for "Taillynge ynough unto our lyves ende" (1623), we have a fabliau pun that brings together the dominant concerns of this fabliau: financial gain and sexual pleasure.

John McGalliard, having drawn attention in "Characterization in Chaucer's Shipman's Tale" to the multiple versions in which this fabliau survives, and having charted its diffusion from ancient India to the twentieth-century American Midwest, summarizes the story as "told by Fred Rollins, originally from Maine, now living in Texas, as a joke." Two suburban couples are friends and neighbors, sharing cookouts, bridge, and camping trips. One husband gets interested in the wife of the other and asks if he can "come over" and "just talk." The wife asks for a present "or something," "if you come." She needs to slip-cover the sofa, "and money doesn't grow on trees with old tightwad Whitcomb [her husband] there." It is agreed that $100 is about right for a good slipcover. Two weeks later the friend telephones, offers to stop by with the money, and suggests that "we could talk awhile." He does and they do. Coming home that evening, Whitcomb asks his wife, "Was Bill here this afternoon?" "Yes . . . ," she replies, and the husband answers, "That's OK then. He borrowed $100 yesterday and said he'd drop it off here with you this afternoon."

As McGalliard summarizes the Chaucer story, the wife, who seems to be given to verbal as well as monetary extravagance, scolds, bullies, and browbeats her husband. Turning to "The Shipman's Tale," we can hear her do this. Going to summon her merchant husband to dinner, she knocks on his counting-room door and says

> "Peter! it am I,"
> Quod she, "what, sire, how longe wol ye faste?
> How longe tyme wol ye rekene and caste
> Your sommes, and youre bookes, and youre thynges?
> The devel have part on alle swiche rekenynges!
> Ye have ynough, pardee, of Goddes sone;
> Com doun to-day, and lat youre bagges stonde.
> Ne be ye nat ashamed that daun John
> Shal fasting al this day alenge goon?
> What! lat us heere a messe, and go we dine." (214–223)

Her husband replies to this summons to dinner with an account of the difficulties of the "chapman," or merchant. The language of this text is heavy with business terms: "marchant," "chapman," "chapmanhede," "marchandise," "ware," "tresor," "hord," "acountes," "silver," "purs," "bond," "faire," "creaunce," "chevysaunce," "chaffare," "reconysance," "contour," "contourdore," "counterhous," and "counterbord," to list a few. Also, "bisynesse," an ancestor of the Modern English word "business," is involved in Peter, the husband's, reply:

> "Wyf," quod this man, "litel kanstow devyne
> The curious bisynesse that we have.
> For of us chapmen, also God me save,
> And by that lord that clepid is Seint Yve,
> Scarsly amonges twelve tweye shul thryve
> Continuelly, lastynge unto our age." (224–229)

Though "bisy," as Ross points out (44), can be associated with sexual intercourse, the word "bisynesse" as the husband uses it here seems to have no other meaning than the one we attach to its descendant, "business." The same limitation would seem to apply when the husband says that he has to go out into the "queynte world" to make a living, but we can expect, since this tale is a fabliau, that words like "taille," used by the wife when she says, "I am your wyf; score it upon my taille," will have more than just a "keep-the-accounts-straight" meaning.

The wife of "The Shipman's Tale" is cast in essentially the same fabliau triangle role that we have seen the wives of "The Miller's Tale" and "The Reeve's Tale" play, but she does it in a more active way. Alisoun is persuaded to deceive her carpenter husband in "The Miller's Tale," and the wife of "The Reeve's Tale," though she offers little resistance when she finds herself in the wrong bed, does not plan to get into that bed. The wife of "The Shipman's Tale" tells the visiting monk her sad story of a husband ungenerous with money and too concerned with business to have time for pleasure, and it is her complaint that leads to their sex-for-money, money-for-sex agreement.

As "The Shipman's Tale" draws to a close, we see the wife facing, or perhaps we should say "not facing," a possibility that her husband may find reason for making a complaint himself. At this point she encourages her successful husband to remember that they have reason to "laughe and pleye" and makes this promise of further pleasure to come: "Ye shal my joly body have to wedde" (423). As Joseph Allen Hornsby (46) notes, many fourteenth-century records of debt litigation show that a debtor found guilty of owing money offered his body as a pledge that he would satisfy his creditor. Here, especially since the wife follows her pledge with a refusal to pay in any other way than the way she proposes to pay it (she says to her husband, "I wol nat paye yow but a-bedde"), it is clear that double meanings are intended. Sex? Money? For the wife of "The Shipman's Tale," both are clearly commodities for exchange, and she is happy to extend credit.

In "The Miller's Tale" we saw an old husband cheated of his rights as a husband. In "The Reeve's Tale" we saw a husband cheated of profit from his business, of his proprietary right as a husband, and of a possible rise in social status to be gained by marrying a virgin daughter upward. In "The Shipman's Tale" the husband is cheated of his right to sole enjoyment of his wife's sexual favors and of the money he loaned his friend as well, but here we see no fall from the rafters, no concluding scene of bedlam. All the trickery is carried off with what seems to be a joyful willingness to continue to play the fabliau game as the wife encourages her husband, whose business trip has after all been successful, to score her debts to him upon her "tail."

We know from their "General Prologue" descriptions what the Miller looks like right down to the wart on his nose, and what the Reeve looks like right down to his skinny legs, but we have no comparable mental portraits for the Shipman and the Merchant. We know simply that the Shipman is "a good felawe" (395), and the Merchant is a "worthy man" (279). The "Prologue" narrator does not happen to know the names of either pilgrim, and neither phrase communicates anything more than conventional approval of congeniality and business success.

The Merchant's introductory remarks, however, reveal his lack of contentment with his own marital status. He has been unhappily married for two months and has thus gained the authority to give advice on marriage. Compared to the experience on which the Wife of Bath bases her claim to authority, the Merchant's claim seems slim indeed, but, combined with the "Epilogue" to his tale in which the Host complains about his wife, the Merchant's short sharing of personal experience does serve a continuity-establishing purpose. With his "Prologue" and "Epilogue" to "The Merchant's Tale," Chaucer provides what can be read as a framing narrative for a story about an abused husband.

"But," as Chaucer might say, "to the point." "The Merchant's Tale" is a richly elaborated development of the basic fabliau triangle. First of all, the Merchant starts a bit further back in his story than the Miller, Reeve, and Shipman do. He begins before the marriage of the old husband to the young wife, back in the narrative space where there might have been time to prevent the inevitable cuckolding. This provides an opportunity to develop the foolishness of Januarie, a sixty-year-old man who believes that "wedlok is so esy and so clene, / that in this world it is a paradys" (1264–1265); who considers "a wyf [to be] the fruyt of [a husband's tresor]" (1270); who thinks that no one can be expected to be as "buxom" ("obedient") or as ready to look after the welfare of a husband as a wife (1287–1289); and who can value a wife as a gift of God worth more than gifts of Fortune like "londes, rentes, pasture, or commune, Or moebles" (1313–1314), which is to say worth more than any real-estate property or any movable goods a man could possibly possess. Nor does the Merchant's husband-to-be hesitate to cite biblical examples in support of his thesis that women can help men prosper. Furthermore, he is confident of his ability not only to make a wise decision—in this case a decision to marry—but to choose a suitable wife.

Januarie has a friend, Justinus, who gives him good advice based on his own experience. Justinus's neighbors all think well of his "steadfast" and "obedient" wife, but, with the homely metaphor "I woot best where wryngeth me my sho" (1553) ("I know best where my shoe pinches me"), he warns Januarie, saying that even a young man would have a difficult time keeping the kind of wife he proposes to marry in line. The Merchant's old knight, of course, does not listen. This is a fabliau. He calls upon Placebo, another friend who will tell him only what he wants to hear, and, thinking that he will achieve a state of paradise on earth, marries a young woman whose name, appropriately enough, is May.

Two fabliau characters are in place. Enter Damyan. The Merchant narrator, seeing in advance how the story he tells will unfold before his very eyes, warns Januarie,

> "O Januarie, dronken in plesaunce
> In mariage, se how thy Damyan,
> Thyn owene squier and thy borne man,
> Entendeth for to do thee vileynye.
> God graunte thee thyn hoomly fo t'espye!
> For in this world nys worse pestilence
> Than hoomly foo al day in thy presence." (1788–1794)

The triangle is complete. The story of deception from within Januarie's own household has only to play itself out.

There is an exchange of notes—from Damyan to May, and from May to Damyan. Januarie has a garden made, an enclosure in which he and he alone will enjoy the beautiful May, because only he will have a key. Then catastrophe befalls the foolish husband. Januarie is struck physically blind. (It has, of course, been clear from the beginning, especially to an audience wise in the ways of fabliaux, that he is blind to the world of relationships between men and women.) May gives Damyan a second key to the garden of sexual pleasure, and the two plan to deceive the blind Januarie in his own garden. At this point Pluto, an old husband from classical legend, appears, ready to inform Januarie. Immediately the not-so-captive-or-obedient Persephone appears at Pluto's side, ready to provide May with a suitable explanation for what Januarie will see.

Now we see May lusting, she says, for the fresh sweet pears growing on a tree in the garden, and persuading Januarie to let her climb the tree. She uses his back to begin her ascent. Damyan, according to their prearranged plan, is waiting in the tree. They proceed to satisfy their desire. Then Pluto, true to his word, acts on Januarie's behalf and restores his sight. Januarie sees what is going on. When he cries out that he can see, May claims credit for the restoration of his sight. There could be no better remedy for blindness, she claims, having been provided with this defense by Persephone, than to provide a vision of a struggle with a man in a tree.

"Strugle," Januarie cries out, "ye, algate in it wente. . . . He swyved thee, I saugh it with myne yen" (2376–2378). But May, still aided by Persephone, has an answer to Januarie's "I saw you do it with my own eyes." Since Januarie's sight has just this minute been restored, it cannot be expected that his vision would be perfect. He could have some "glymsyng," or glimmerings. His situation is comparable to that of a man just awakened from sleep who cannot be sure that what he "sees" is really an accurate perception. Januarie accepts May's explanation of what has happened, and so the story closes, with the Merchant himself apparently able to accept the deception of Januarie with good grace and with an encouragement to his fellow pilgrims to be happy.

The Merchant, concerned as he may be with his own marital difficulties, has kept his storytelling obligation in mind. He has told a story intended to entertain, to provide "solaas," not a story intended to provide "sentence," or wisdom about the ways of women. That his listener the Host cannot quite let it go at that does not affect the spirit of the tale as Chaucer assigns it to the Merchant to tell.

With "The Merchant's Tale" we have just seen a knight play a role in the kind of story that our introductory survey of definitions would lead us to expect to be populated by middle- or lower-class characters, and the assignment of peripheral roles to two characters from the classical pantheon of gods as well. In "The Manciple's Tale" the god Phebus assumes the role of husband. The second character the Manciple introduces is a white crow, possessed, like Phebus, of remarkable talents. This crow can sing like a nightingale and is able to tell tales about what it sees. With the introduction of the third character, a much-loved wife, jealousy, a quality conventionally associated with the fabliau husband, is attributed to the god Phebus. Here too it can be said that the Manciple, who observes that it does not pay to be too suspicious about wives, nor does it pay to try too hard to please them, would seem to be taking a fabliau narrator's stance.

It does not take the Manciple long to introduce the topic of the vulnerability of the married man. Having introduced the bird and the bride (interestingly enough, a *Chaucer Glossary* definition indicates that "bryd" can be used as a term of endearment) in precisely parallel sentences, "Now hadde this Phebus in his hous a crowe" (130) and "Now hadde this Phebus in his hous a wife" (139), the Manciple observes that the essential nature of neither bird nor woman can be changed by caging it or her. Cat and she-wolf parallels follow. The well-fed cat will escape its comfortable confinement to hunt a mouse, the she-wolf to hunt a mate. Then, despite the overt sexual attribution of the third example, the Manciple claims that he is providing parallels just to the natural behavior of men. What he is saying has nothing to do with the natural behavior of women.

The stage is set for the entry of the designated lover, and the Manciple, despite his denial that he intends to tell this kind of story, proceeds. He rapidly regrets his use of the kind of language that fabliaux depend on. Having spoken of Phebus's wife's "lemman," he immediately apologizes and asks forgiveness for his "knavyssh speche" (205). The Manciple nevertheless continues to use words like "wenche" and "lemman," and the suggestion seems to be that though a high-born woman who acts amiss may be called a "lady" while a poor woman who acts in the same way is a "wenche" or a "lemman," the difference is not as great as the language used to refer to women of the different social levels would suggest.

To continue the story, the lover comes while Phebus is gone. The crow observes "hire werk" (their "work" being the sexual activity of the wife and her lover) and calls out "Cokkow! Cokkow! Cokkow!" when Phebus returns. Then, with words like "swyve" and "lecherye," the crow directly reports what it has seen. Phebus, overcome by anger, kills his wife. Overcome by remorse (the language here turns to the apostrophe of high style), he then turns upon the crow, pulls out all its feathers, and deprives it of song and speech. This is a story of how crows came to be black and incapable of meaningful utterance, and it concludes with what could have been a straightforward statement of pithy wisdom of the kind we associate with fable—do not tell everything you know—if the Manciple had not delivered this advice, given to him by his mother when he was a boy, at such great length. His tale ends with no less than ten of her quoted directions to "my sone" and with final instruction to "Kepe well thy tonge and thenk upon the crowe" (362).

With the two tales to be presented in conclusion here, "The Friar's Tale" and "The Summoner's Tale," we turn to fabliaux that rely for their appeal on satire of activities of men of the church. The Friar does give attention to the topic of sexual transgression as he begins his tale, and we learn that "lecchours" (1310) are the sinners who must pay the biggest fines, and that the summoner of his tale employs "wenches" (1355), with the word apparently referring to prostitutes since these women enable him to extract money from the men that "lay by hem" (1358). But "The Friar's Tale" does not, like the tales told by the Miller, the Reeve, the Merchant, the Shipman, and the Manciple, rely on acts of adultery for its narrative center. It focuses instead on the activities of a man of the church who is determined to make a profit by making others pay for committing what is, in this particular fabliau context, the sin of adultery.

The Friar openly announces his fabliau intention in the "Prologue" to his tale: he will tell "a game" of a summoner. In proposing to tell a story that will provide information about the activities of a certain summoner, the Friar asserts his freedom to speak as openly as he pleases. Friars are not under the jurisdiction of the church officials whom summoners answer to, he says. The pilgrim Summoner loudly objects to this, saying that "wommen of the styves" ("styves" were brothels licensed by the church) are similarly exempt. But the "game" begins.

The summoner of "The Friar's Tale" is a thief. He steals half of what should go to his employer, the archdeacon. He is also a "baude," a pimp. He employs a number of informants (including the previously named wenches) in his pursuit of a profitable business. The target figure of the Friar's tale, then, is a man of the church who uses the services of prostitute informants to pursue his own mercenary purposes. He is not a man who would seem to be susceptible to the wiles of women. The only woman in the story the Friar tells is an old "rebekke" (fiddle, woman) who, upon the summoner's demand to pay what he says is a long-overdue debt for cuckolding her husband, asserts that she does not owe this debt, that she has never been summoned to answer to this charge, and that, furthermore, she never was unfaithful to her husband.

Here, in a tale that must be considered a masterpiece of irony, a summoner whose official function is to call sinners to the judgment of an ecclesiastical court is condemned to eternal damnation when he persists in persecuting an old woman until she at last cries out in anger. "The devel . . . so fecche hym ere he dye" (1628) ("May the devil take him before he dies"). With these words she curses the summoner, thus giving the devil the justification he requires to carry her persecutor off to hell. The green yeoman the summoner meets as he goes on his rounds is more scrupulous in his administration of justice than the man who pledges his loyalty to him. He requires a genuine curse to carry the summoner off to hell while he is still alive. The summoner's intended victim's curse may include a condition, a loophole that could permit his escape. The words "but he wol hym repente" ("unless he will repent") immediately follow the old woman's seriously intended curse. But the foolish man refuses to repent. Still hoping to gain the only valuable property she has, he continues to threaten punishment if she will not give him a new pan in payment for forgiveness of a crime she has not committed. Thus the summoner earns for himself the punishment with which he has so assiduously threatened others. Justice is served an unjust man, a man of the church who uses every trick available to him to make a profit.

He should have known better. This is a reaction we can hardly help expressing. The green yeoman tells him that he is a "feende" and that his "dwellynge is in helle" (1448). Questioned about his shape, which seems very much like that of the summoner, the green yeoman goes on about his ability to change his shape as he pleases. The summoner then claims to be a yeoman himself (he is ashamed to be a summoner) and swears that he will be a brother to the man he has just met even if he is "the devel Sathanas" (1526). But the "brother" to whom he promises to be loyal is the devil. Any listener can see that. It is no wonder that the pilgrim Summoner, having just listened to a tale that paints him—or his double—as a man so steeped in corruption that he cannot recognize the devil when he sees him, stands up in his stirrups and demands to be heard. He will be heard. The Host allows it. As the Summoner begins his tale, he establishes its setting more precisely than his rival the Friar did. The Friar began with a very general reference to "my contree." The Summoner's setting, presented in more characteristic fabliau style, is a "mersshy contree called Holdernesse . . . in Yorkshire." Both places are immediately identified as settings for sanctimonious malpractice. The Friar's summoner's territory was dominated by an avaricious archdeacon, while the Summoner's friar's more limited territory (a "lymytour" like this friar is licensed to beg only within a prescribed area) is a place where he alone is allowed to sell "trentals" (prayers for souls in purgatory). As for the sincerity with which the friar sells forgiveness, the Summoner says that his central character immediately purges the names of contributors from his slate. So much for details of setting and characterization of the Summoner's target figure with reference to his site of operation.

The central action of the tale takes place within the confines of a domestic scene, the home of an ailing man named Thomas. Here the friar immediately makes himself at home, driving the cat from its favorite resting place. Pretending to be a conscientious man of the church, he tells how he "tendrely [gropes] a conscience" (the verb will take on a literal meaning as the story approaches its climax) and displays his appetite by placing an extravagant dinner order. All he wants, he says, is the liver of a capon, a shivver of soft bread, and a roasted pig's head. Then, having been told by Thomas's wife that he is "as angry as a pissemyre" despite all her efforts to make him comfortable, the friar launches into an extended account of the virtuous practices of his group of friars. Here he gives particular attention to the poverty they live in and their abstinence. Then, turning his attention to Thomas's sin, he tells how twenty thousand men lost their lives because they struggled with their lovers and their wives, how Seneca unjustly sentenced men to death in anger, how the angry Cambises killed the son of a knight simply to demonstrate his own skill as an archer and his right to do as he pleased, and how Cyrus of Persia destroyed a river because a horse of his had drowned in that river, all of which is supposed to persuade Thomas to repent his anger.

The friar's sermon does not move Thomas, who has already confessed to his own curate, to contrition. The friar nevertheless proceeds to ask for a gift for his order, pleading the friars' poverty. This request intensifies Thomas's anger. The sick man, the Summoner says,

> wax wel ny wood for ire;
> He wolde that the frere had been on-fire
> With his false dissymulacioun (2121–2123).

What Hines finds to be the truly fabliau part of "The Summoner's Tale" follows. Thomas promises to make a gift to the friar's convent if he will follow his directions exactly. The friar follows these directions. He reaches down behind the sick man's back and "grope[s] wel bihynde." There he finds underneath the man's "buttok" a "thyng" that he has hidden in "pryvetee." Each of the words quoted here, even the word "thyng" (thing), is a marked word, one that signals its use as part of the fabliau tradition. The gift, the "thyng" the friar finds as he gropes, is a fart that the ailing patient releases from his "clifte" (the cleft of his buttocks) that is as loud as any fart that any horse drawing a cart ever released. The friar, the man who preached the sermon on anger, is of course enraged.

This is not quite the end of the story. The Summoner's friar, to his further humiliation, must take the gift Thomas gives him back to be shared with his brothers, and then, in a complex ceremony that involves the turning of a twelve-spoked wheel, equal distribution of a follow-up gift—a second fart—must be achieved. Thus the friar of "The Summoner's Tale," who really had no intention to follow through on his claim of dedication to a share-and-share-alike philosophy, is forced to share a gift he did not want.

It can, however, be said that "The Summoner's Tale"—like "The Friar's Tale" that immediately precedes it, and like Chaucer's other fabliaux and still others that have come down to us in Middle and later English—fulfills its fabliau purpose. It can also be observed that the Summoner, like the other Canterbury Pilgrims who tell tales to entertain, fulfills his obligation to the group. It can perhaps be said that stories like the ones we have just considered may provide a degree of "sentence" along with the "solaas" that would seem to have been their primary reason for survival. At least we can say that by surviving they give us something to think about. Looking at what we laugh at may tell us a good deal about the value systems we live by and the fears we face.

SELECTED BIBLIOGRAPHY

Abrams, M.H. *A Glossary of Literary Terms*. 3rd ed. New York: Holt, Rinehart and Winston, 1971.

Barnet, Sylvan, Morton Berman, and William Burto. *A Dictionary of Literary Terms*. Boston: Little, Brown, 1960.

Bédier, Joseph. *Les Fabliaux: Etudes de littérature populaire et d'histoire littéraire du moyen âge*. 6th ed. Paris: Champion, 1964.

Benson, Larry D., and Theodore M. Andersson. *The Literary Context of Chaucer's Fabliaux*. Indianapolis: Bobbs-Merrill, 1971.

Chaucer, Geoffrey. *The Riverside Chaucer*. Ed. Larry D. Benson. 3rd ed. Boston: Houghton Mifflin, 1987.

Coggeshall, John M. "Chaucer in the Ozarks: A New Look at the Sources." *Southern Folklore Quarterly* 45 (1981): 41–60.

Cooke, Thomas D. *The Old French and Chaucerian Fabliaux: A Study of Their Comic Climax*. Columbia: University of Missouri Press, 1978.

Davis, Norman, Douglas Gray, Patricia Ingham, and Anne Wallace-Hadill. *A Chaucer Glossary*. Oxford: Clarendon Press, 1979.

Eichmann, Raymond. Introduction. *Fabliaux Fair and Foul*. Translations by John DuVal with introductions and notes by Raymond Eichmann. Medieval and Renaissance Texts and Studies. Binghamton, NY: Center for Early Medieval and Renaissance Studies, 1992.

Furrow, Melissa M., ed. *Ten Fifteenth-Century Comic Poems*. New York: Garland, 1985.

Hellman, Robert, and Richard O'Gorman, trans. *Fabliaux: Ribald Tales from the Old French*. New York: Thomas Y. Crowell, 1966.

Hines, John. *The Fabliau in English*. London and New York: Longman, 1993.

Hornsby, Joseph Allen. *Chaucer and the Law*. Norman, OK: Pilgrim Books, 1988.

McGalliard, John C. "Characterization in Chaucer's Shipman's Tale." *PQ* 54 (1975): 1–18.

Muscatine, Charles. *Chaucer and the French Tradition: A Study in Style and Meaning*. Berkeley: University of California Press, 1957.

Noomen, Willem. *Nouveau Recueil Complet des Fabliaux*. 3 vols. Assen: Van Gorum, 1983–1986.

Nykrog, Per. *Les Fabliaux*. Geneve: Droz, 1973.

Ross, Thomas W. *Chaucer's Bawdy*. New York: E.P. Dutton, 1972.

Schenck, Mary Jane Stearns. *The Fabliaux: Tales of Wit and Deception*. Philadelphia: J. Benjamins, 1987.

Shaw, Harry. *Concise Dictionary of Literary Terms*. New York: McGraw-Hill, 1976.

Thrall, William Flint, Addison Hibbard, and C. Hugh Holman. *A Handbook to Literature*. New York: Odyssey Press, 1960.

Togeby, Knud. *Structure Immanente de la Langue Française*. Paris: Larousse, 1965.

Zall, P.M., ed. *A Hundred Merry Tales and Other English Jestbooks of the Fifteenth and Sixteenth Centuries*. Lincoln: University of Nebraska Press, 1963.

14

Hagiographic, Homiletic, and Didactic Literature

John H. Brinegar

DEFINITIONS AND BACKGROUND

Upon first consideration, the phrase "hagiographic and didactic literature" may seem somewhat vague; what kinds of writing does it properly include? The word "hagiographic" suggests that saints' lives and legends must form a large part of this category, but it also has a wider significance. Strictly defined, hagiography is the study of saints and their worship, and so the numerous saints' lives in Old and Middle English are the basic matter of this genre. There are a number of works, however, that are not strictly saints' lives but that have much in common with their subject matter and literary characteristics. For example, section V of John Edwin Wells's *A Manual of the Writings in Middle English, 1050–1500* (1916), "Saints' Legends," also includes legends of Adam and Eve, of the cross, of Jesus and Mary, and of the afterlife. In order to include these other categories, we will define hagiography as instructive literature about saints and other exemplary religious figures.

The meaning of "hagiographic" is now clear, but we still need to define "didactic" literature. Some scholars, such as D. W. Robertson, would argue that all medieval literature is essentially didactic, but this position is unhelpful when one is trying to separate works into categories. A more useful description of didactic literature might be that it is literature that explicitly aims to instruct the reader. Such a definition excludes most allegorical works, which may be instructive but are not explicitly so. Didactic literature can then be further divided into religious and secular categories, based on the matter of instruction. Religious didactic literature comprises a variety of texts, including but not limited to homilies and sermons, biblical translations and commentaries, and works of general religious instruction such as penitentials and treatises on vices and virtues. Secular didactic literature also varies widely, including collections of proverbial wisdom, works of philosophical instruction, and medical and scientific treatises.

Works on science, medicine, and philosophy are all accurately described as didactic; they are certainly intended to instruct their audience. This chapter confines itself to religious didactic works, however, for the following reasons. Saints' lives and legends were one of the most popular genres of medieval English literature and hence deserve detailed treatment. Certain categories of religious didactic literature, such as homilies and biblical translations, are closely involved with hagiographic writing and make good companions to it. Discussion of these genres leads naturally to consideration of works of general religious instruction, both for secular priests and lay folk and for those in religious orders. Nonreligious didactic literature is difficult to fit smoothly into this sequence. Hence, in the interest of presenting a well-organized discussion within a brief space, secular didactic literature has been omitted.

We will begin our overview of the backgrounds of didactic literature with hagiography. The development of Latin hagiography sheds a great deal of light on the features of medieval English saints' lives. During Christianity's early centuries, certain churches kept lists of Christian martyrs in order to commemorate the anniversaries of their martyrdoms; when these lists were expanded to include the place of each saint's martyrdom, they became known as martyrologies. During the liturgies in which the martyrs were commemorated, it became customary to read accounts of their sufferings and deaths. The material contained in these accounts was initially drawn from official court records of the martyrs' trials and from eyewitness reports, but partially or wholly fictional details were later added to this factual information. Early medieval martyrologies added much of this material to the rather terse lists of names and places for each date.

In addition to the martyrologies, early Christianity gave rise to somewhat longer works concerning individual saints, such as the *Martyrdom of Saint Polycarp* and Athanasius's *Life of Saint Antony*. Not all of the subjects of these works were martyrs in the strictest sense: Antony, the founder of Christian monasticism, died a natural death, but his asceticism was considered a form of martyrdom. Three fourth-century saints' lives are particularly important because they establish conventions that persist in medieval English hagiography. The first of these is the aforementioned *Life of Saint Antony*; the others are Jerome's *Life of Paul* and Sulpicius Severus's *Life of Martin*.

The *Life of Saint Antony* was written by Athanasius around 357. Although it was originally composed in Greek, it was soon translated into Latin, and its influence was enormous. The *Life* is a true biography, a birth-to-death narrative of Antony's life. In fairly short order it chronicles his youth, his first call to an ascetic life, his solitude in the desert, and how he came to be the teacher of a group of monks. A lengthy address to the monks follows, after which the *Life* places great emphasis on Antony's prophecies and miracles. It ends with his death, followed by an exhortation to read the *Life* to monks and also to pagans. This epilogue reveals Athanasius's purpose in writing about Antony: he wishes to provide a model for those already trying to lead an ascetic Christian life and to challenge unbelievers to abandon their false gods. This dual function of encouragement and exhortation becomes standard in medieval hagiography, although in Christian Europe the saint's life calls slack Christians to self-exertion rather than calling pagans to conversion.

The *Life of Saint Antony* also incorporates much sensational detail. Antony is frequently tempted by demons and discusses them at length in his address to the monks; this material, along with the stories of his miracles, renders the text quite vivid. This tendency toward the fantastic is even more apparent in Jerome's *Life of Paul*. In this text Antony travels into the desert seeking the holy hermit Paul. On his way he meets both a satyr and a centaur; when he finds Paul, the two of them eat bread that a raven brings to them; and when Paul dies, two lions come to help Antony bury him. Sulpicius Severus's *Life of Martin* continues this trend toward sensationalism, but ties the amazing occurrences more firmly to the central holy figure. Martin, bishop of Tours, is clearly a wonder-worker; much of the text is devoted to accounts of his miracles, with little attention to their chronology. The description of fantastic occurrences, usually associated either with temptations or miracles, also becomes a standard feature of medieval saints' lives. For example, the Old English prose *Guthlac* describes Guthlac's struggles against demons in terms that recall Antony's temptations in the desert.

Eventually a desire arose for hagiographic compilations that were more detailed than the martyrologies. The earliest extant example of such a compilation, dating from the early fourth century, is Eusebius of Caesarea's *On the Martyrs of Palestine*, which describes the last Roman persecution in that province. Works like Gregory of Tours's *Glory of the Martyrs* and *Glory of the Confessors* and the *Dialogues* of Gregory the Great followed in the early medieval period. These collections are at best loosely organized. *Glory of the Confessors* tells the stories of several Gaulish saints, but has no further order; Gregory's *Dialogues* have even less order, except for book 2, which is devoted entirely to the life of Benedict of Nursia. The *Dialogues* were translated into Old English in the ninth century by Wærferth, bishop of Worcester. Later medieval hagiographic collections took a more organized form, arranging the stories of saints by their dates in the calendar. Such collections are called legendaries, or sometimes passionaries. By far the most famous medieval legendary was the *Legenda Aurea*, or *Golden Legend*, of the thirteenth-century Dominican Jacobus de Voragine. This work was a source for many Middle English saints' lives and was translated into Middle English at least twice.

Having discussed the background of English vernacular hagiography in detail, we will move on to other genres of religious didactic literature. Homilies are, in the strictest sense, explications of the pericope, or gospel lesson read at mass, in which the homilist explains the meaning of the gospel reading and how Christians can apply it to their lives. In the homilies of the church fathers, such as Augustine and Gregory the Great, the passage is usually explained allegorically; that is, its literal content is interpreted as a symbol of some item of Christian faith. The term "homily" is also used more loosely to describe any speech on Christian doctrine intended to instruct the faithful, even if it does not explain the pericope. For example, a homily for the feast day of a saint might be a brief account of the saint's life, followed by an exhortation to the congregation to practice similar virtues in their own lives. This exhortation or instruction in Christian behavior is common to all homilies, whether they meet the strict definition or not.

Biblical translation and commentary is another prevalent genre of didactic literature in medieval English literature. It has roots in the early Christian period; in the fourth century Jerome produced the Vulgate, a translation of the Greek Bible into Latin, which became the standard Bible of the medieval period. The Vulgate arose out of the need for an accurate version of the Bible in a language the faithful could understand; this need was felt again by the Anglo-Saxons and became a source of controversy in fourteenth-century England when John Wyclif began to translate the New Testament. Jerome and other patristic authors like Augustine also wrote commentaries on the various books of the Bible. These commentaries included allegorical explanations of biblical episodes; for example, several psalms were interpreted as prophecies of Christ. Works like Jerome's *Hebrew Questions in Genesis* also explained the meaning of various biblical names. Later medieval authors compiled bits of these patristic works into their own commentaries; while these commentaries were not generally translated into English, they do influence Middle English biblical poems like *Cursor Mundi*.

Works of religious instruction for both lay folk and priests form another important didactic genre. There are a number of patristic texts setting forth the proper qualities and duties of priests. One excellent example is Gregory the Great's *Pastoral Care*, which describes the character and obligations of a bishop. Book 1 explains what sorts of people are and are not suited to be bishops, book 2 discusses how bishops should interact with those in their care, book 3 addresses their duties of preaching and teaching, and book 4 cautions them to examine their consciences carefully. King Alfred translated *Pastoral Care* in the ninth century; we will examine his version of this and other works later. One common kind of instructive work meant for lay folk is the penitential. Penitentials are books of questions for confessors to ask of those coming to confession, along with lists of penances for various sins. They are particularly pertinent to our topic, since Anglo-Saxon missionaries were instrumental in introducing the idea of such books to the Continent. Like all the works in this category, the penitentials aim to increase lay people's involvement with the Christian faith by educating them in its elements. Works of general religious instruction increased in number dramatically after the Fourth Lateran Council in 1215, at which annual confession was made obligatory for all Christians and bishops were instructed to be more attentive to their teaching duties. In order to fulfill these precepts, both priests and their flocks needed education, and a variety of works on the basic elements of Christianity were produced in Latin and vernacular languages.

In addition to works instructing priests and lay folk, there are also several works of instruction for those in religious orders. The most important of these are the various sets of rules governing the lives and activities of the members of each order. The earliest rules, such as those of Pachomius and Basil, were loosely organized collections of precepts for monastic life. These were followed in the sixth century by the foundational text of Western monasticism, *The Rule of Saint Benedict*. This text lays out a systematic plan for the maintenance of a religious community. It begins with several chapters praising the ascetic life and then moves to a detailed outline of the order of divine service. This is followed by regulations on the elections of officers, the hours for manual labor, reading, and sleep, and other such practical matters; this last part of the *Rule* also includes punishments for infractions of the various precepts. *The Rule of Saint Benedict* influenced all subsequent rules for religious life; its importance cannot be overstated. As various other religious orders arose, they composed rules to address their particular situations and goals; these rules were written in Latin, but vernacular translations became necessary in order to accommodate members of the orders who were not literate in Latin. Some vernacular rules also seem to have been written for particular groups; we will examine one of these, *Ancrene Riwle*, later. In addition to rules, many other instructive treatises were intended for persons in religious life. Unsurprisingly, a number of these are works in praise of virginity. One such work, *Hali Meiðhad*, has some affinities with *Ancrene Riwle* and will be discussed along with it.

REPRESENTATIVE EXAMPLES

Numerous saints' lives survive in Old and Middle English, both in compilations and as independent works. Perhaps the best-known Old English saints' lives are those that make up Ælfric's *Lives of Saints*. Ælfric, abbot of Eynsham, is widely considered the greatest of Anglo-Saxon prose writers, and his reputation is largely due to the three series of homilies that he wrote between 989 and 1002. *Lives of Saints* is the third of these series and consists of thirty-three homilies, of which most, but not all, tell the story of the life, passion, and miracles of a saint. These homilies would have been preached on the days of the saints whose lives they chronicled, as instruction and example for the lay folk. The homily for August 5, on the life of St. Oswald, is worth discussing in detail as a good example of Ælfric's hagiographic style.

Oswald was king of Northumbria from 633 to 641. Ælfric's homily follows a fairly conventional hagiographic outline, first chronicling important events in his life, then moving on to describe his death in some detail, and concluding with accounts of a number of his miracles. It begins with Oswald's youth and exile in Scotland, where he receives baptism; upon the death of his uncle, he returns to fight a Welsh invasion. He raises a cross to God's honor before the battle and is victorious. The cross later heals many sick people; even the moss growing on it has healing powers. Afterward Oswald summons the Scottish bishop Aidan to Northumbria to give his people Christian instruction. One day Oswald breaks up a silver dish to give as alms to poor people, and Aidan blesses the hand with which he does so; Ælfric says that the hand remains uncorrupted to the present day. Oswald does many other pious works: he endows a church and stands sponsor to Cynegils, king of the West Saxons, at his baptism.

This account of Oswald's life ends with a description of his death. Oswald is slain in battle while defending his people from invasion by the heathen Mercians. When he sees that his death is near, he prays for God's mercy on his soul and those of his warriors. Penda, king of the Mercians, orders that Oswald's head and right arm be cut off and put on a stake as a trophy. Later Oswald's brother Oswy rescues his head and arm and takes them to the church at Lindisfarne.

After describing Oswald's pious end, Ælfric relates several miracles associated with his relics. After his death his niece takes his bones to the monastery of Bardney. The monks will not accept the bones at first, until they begin to shine with a heavenly light. Many sick people are healed by the bones and even by dirt taken from the place where water used to wash them was poured out. Dirt from the place where Oswald was slain also has healing powers: a sick horse and a paralyzed girl are both healed by lying on that spot. A house burns down completely, except for a post on which hangs a cloth containing dust from the site of Oswald's death. Oswald's fame spreads to Ireland and the Frankish realms, and an Irishman is healed by his relics.

Ælfric has painted a careful picture of a holy life in this homily. Oswald is baptized at an early age, showing his piety, and he invokes God's aid when he is fighting against his enemies. He brings in a wise and holy Christian teacher for the instruction of his people, and he gives alms freely. He promotes the faith at home by endowing a church and abroad by sponsoring Cynegils at his baptism. In short, he is the model of a Christian king who can defend his people's lives in this world and help prepare them for their life in the world to come. His death is particularly fitting for the life he has led. He is martyred while resisting the invasion of a heathen king, who serves as his antithesis; we are told that Penda knew nothing about Christ, and all his people were unbaptized. Oswald's last act in life is a prayer for mercy, not only for himself but for his people. Every detail of Oswald's life, up to and including his death, demonstrates his eager and ready service of God.

Ælfric also demonstrates Oswald's sanctity through the miracles associated with him. Not only do his bones have wondrous curative powers, but even water that has touched them or dust from the spot where he died can work miracles. Further removed from his physical presence, even the moss that grows on the cross Oswald erected can heal people. By emphasizing the miraculous power of things only tenuously connected to Oswald himself, Ælfric emphasizes the extreme degree of Oswald's holiness; this desire to show that a particular saint is not merely holy, but possesses extraordinary virtues, extends at least as far back as Sulpicius Severus's *Life of Martin*.

Ælfric took almost all of his information about Oswald from Bede's *Historia Ecclesiastica Gentis Anglorum* (*Ecclesiastical History of the English People*), rearranging and adapting it to produce a conventional hagiographic legend. Most of Ælfric's saints' lives are translations or adaptations of Latin sources, and this is also true of what is perhaps the best-known Old English saint's life not written by Ælfric, the prose *Guthlac*. This text is a somewhat free translation of Felix of Crowland's eighth-century *Vita Sancti Guthlaci*, which also inspired *Guthlac B*, one of two Old English poems about the saint found in the Exeter Book. The prose *Guthlac* was probably intended for private devotional reading and hence is considerably longer than Ælfric's saints' lives, which were meant to be delivered as homilies. Despite this difference in length, the prose *Guthlac* follows the familiar hagiographic pattern.

At Guthlac's birth he is marked with a miraculous sign from heaven. He leads a virtuous childhood, but then becomes a fierce raider, pillaging many villages. After nine years of this he has a vision of the vanity of worldly success and leaves his war band to become a monk. He spends two years in the monastery and then decides to become a hermit in the East Anglian fens. There he leads an ascetic life and is greatly tormented by devils. The account of Guthlac's tribulations is heavily influenced by Athanasius's *Life of Antony* in its great emphasis on the devils' horrible appearances and the violence with which they afflict the saint. They drag him through brambles, beat him with iron whips, and try to carry him to hell. Finally they depart in the forms of various beasts. The narrative then turns to Guthlac's miracles. The beasts and birds obey him, and he is able to find lost objects. He is able to heal many grievous injuries, and he knows the thoughts and deeds of those who come to visit him. He also makes prophecies concerning his successor in eremitical life and the ascension of the exiled King Æthelbald to the throne of Mercia.

After fifteen years as a hermit Guthlac dies on Easter Wednesday. Upon his death a heavenly light shines from his hut, and a sweet fragrance fills the area. Twelve months after his burial his body is disinterred for removal to a more fitting tomb and is found to be uncorrupted. The narrative concludes with two posthumous miracles. Guthlac appears to Æthelbald to assure him that he will return from exile to rule Mercia, and a blind man regains his sight by the application of salt that Guthlac had consecrated.

In the prose *Guthlac*, as in Ælfric's life of Oswald, we see the sequence of the holy life, pious death, and posthumous miracles, but the types of events presented are somewhat different. Guthlac's saintly destiny is apparent from his birth; even though he falls away from Christian virtue as a young man, he returns to the service of Christ as an anchorite. This temporary pursuit of worldly affairs is not uncommon in saints' lives and helps emphasize the superiority of spiritual goals to earthly ones. Also, Guthlac dies a natural death rather than being martyred. This kind of death is typical of the classical saints' lives; both Paul and

Antony die as old men, praising God and looking forward to the glories of heaven. Finally, most of Guthlac's miracles occur while he is still living. This helps to show the spiritual advancement he has gained through asceticism.

Guthlac is very much the same kind of saint as both Paul and Antony, an anchorite striving for self-perfection in the wilderness, and so the story of his life can closely parallel theirs. Medieval hagiographers drew such close parallels between their subjects and those of the famous early saints' lives in order to show that the later saints were truly holy. How better to emphasize Guthlac's sanctity than to make his story very like that of Antony, the founder of Christian asceticism? Oswald, on the other hand, has a very different position in life. He is a king and hence cannot escape worldly entanglements. Nonetheless, Ælfric arranges his life according to the traditional pattern in order to show that he too is a model of Christian virtue. Oswald's activity as a king allows few opportunities for miracles during his lifetime, but Ælfric takes care to include several posthumous miracles. Even though Oswald lives an active life, these miracles show that he is just as saintly as the contemplative Guthlac.

One other Old English prose work, the *Old English Martyrology*, deserves mention here. This martyrology draws on a wide variety of sources for its accounts of saints' lives, some of which are fairly detailed. One important source was Bede's Latin martyrology, which enjoyed an immense circulation and influenced the form of martyrologies throughout the medieval period. While none of the entries in the *Old English Martyrology* are as detailed as Ælfric's lives, the work is still an important part of Old English hagiographic writing.

In addition to prose saints' lives, there are six Old English works that may be described as hagiographic poems because they describe the acts of a holy man or woman. These are *Guthlac A* and *B*, Cynewulf's *Elene, Juliana*, and *Fates of the Apostles*, and *Andreas*. *Guthlac A* describes the saint's heroic resistance to temptation and torment by devils. Despite the subject matter, there is probably no direct relationship between this poem and Felix's *Vita*. *Guthlac B*, however, does depend on Felix's work; it describes Guthlac's death in detail, incorporating a long dialogue between him and his servant Beccel. *Elene* is an account of the discovery of the true cross by Helena, the mother of Emperor Constantine, and of the conversion to Christianity of Judas, a Jew who assists her. *Juliana* is the story of a fourth-century Christian convert who demands that her suitor also convert; in punishment she is thrown into prison, where she fights with a devil. Afterwards she undergoes various horrific tortures and is finally beheaded. *Fates of the Apostles* is a list of the twelve apostles, including the locations of their missions and the manner of their deaths. *Andreas*, a considerably longer poem than the other five, describes the capture of Matthew by the cannibalistic Mermedonians, his rescue by the apostle Andrew, and the subsequent conversion of the Mermedonians. Of all these poems, only *Juliana* is hagiography in the strictest sense, since it deals with the suffering and death of a martyr; the five others can loosely be called saints' lives, though, because they present the exemplary and inspiring acts of particularly holy Christians.

Turning to Middle English literature, we find an abundance of saints' lives. Among the earliest of these is a group of three lives of St. Katherine, St. Margaret, and St. Juliana, dating from the late twelfth century. In several manuscripts these lives are found together with an allegorical work called *Sawles Warde* and a treatise on virginity called *Hali Meiðhad*. Because of this, and because of their close linguistic similarities, these five texts are commonly referred to as the Katherine Group. The saints' lives of the Katherine Group are similar in many respects. All three are stories of young virgin martyrs, contain sensational descriptions of devils and torments, and strongly promote chastity. Katherine argues against Emperor Maxentius's enforced idol worship; he engages fifty philosophers to argue against her. She refutes their objections to Christianity, and in the end they convert. In a rage Maxentius orders them all to be burnt, and Katherine urges them to remain steadfast. Maxentius then woos Katherine, who says that she is already the virgin bride of Christ. She is sentenced to be tortured on a horrible, mangling wheel that is miraculously destroyed, and she is finally beheaded. Margaret is tortured by an official whom she has refused to marry, preferring to remain a virgin. Afterwards she is placed in prison, where a demon in the shape of a dragon swallows her up; she makes the sign of the cross, and the dragon bursts asunder. Another demon appears in order to tempt her, but she casts him under her foot and forces him to submit. She is then tortured with fire and water before being beheaded. Juliana's story was summarized in the discussion on Old English hagiographic verse. The Middle English version is similar, with a few noteworthy additions. For example, Juliana's fight with the devil Belial is very comical. She thrashes him soundly and finally drags him through the marketplace, where the merchants pelt him with stones. In the now-familiar pattern she is tortured on the wheel, threatened with fire, covered in boiling pitch, and finally beheaded.

The lives of these saints exhibit the underlying pattern of an early Christian martyrdom narrative: the saint refuses to renounce Christian principles, is tortured by authorities, and dies praising God. They also show the kinds of legendary material that became firmly affixed to such narratives by the medieval period. The detailed descriptions of bizarre tortures and fights against devils have no basis in factual report but help to give saints' lives the enormous popularity they enjoyed in the medieval period. The Katherine Group's saints' lives also seem to be intended for a particular audience. Their common emphasis on the excellence of virginity, an emphasis not found to such a degree in other versions of these saints' lives, suggests an audience of women who had taken religious vows; their association with *Hali Meiðhad*, and to a lesser extent with the *Ancrene Riwle*, supports this suggestion.

Having looked at the Katherine Group's lives in some detail, we will briefly consider some saints' lives found in later Middle English works. Two of Chaucer's *Canterbury Tales* could be called saints' lives: "The Second Nun's Tale" is a life of St. Cecilia, and "The Prioress's Tale" tells how the murder of a small boy by Jews was discovered and avenged through the intervention of the Virgin

Mary. Both of these tales exhibit some typical hagiographic features. "The Second Nun's Tale" follows the same pattern as the lives of the Katherine Group: a young virgin is to be married, desires a chaste life, and is condemned, tortured, and finally martyred by Roman officials. Since it is not strictly a saint's life or legend, but rather the story of a miracle of the Virgin Mary, "The Prioress's Tale" follows a rather different narrative pattern. However, the attention given to the details of the boy's murder and to the punishment of his murderers reflects the sensationalism common in hagiographic writing.

The monk John Lydgate, perhaps the most prolific English writer of the fifteenth century, also wrote several saints' lives. The most ambitious of these is his *Life of Saints Edmund and Fremund*, a poem almost half again as long as *Sir Gawain and the Green Knight*. *Life* narrates the life of the Anglo-Saxon St. Edmund in great detail. His story has a long tradition in English, beginning with Ælfric; since Lydgate was a monk of Bury Saint Edmunds, an abbey whose patron was Edmund, it is especially fitting that he should write such a life.

In addition to individual lives of saints, there are Middle English hagiographic compilations as well. The most popular of these is the *South English Legendary* (*SEL*), which exists in various versions in fifty-one manuscripts ranging from the thirteenth to the late fifteenth centuries. *SEL* is a true legendary, following the liturgical calendar, although the order of material varies from manuscript to manuscript, and later manuscripts have more saints' legends than earlier ones. The types of legend also vary widely, from romanticized stories of early martyrs to lives of contemporary saints like Thomas Becket. The inclusion of native English saints like Becket or St. Kenelm gives *SEL* much of its interest, as it becomes a sort of impressionistic history of the English church.

As mentioned earlier, Jacobus de Voragine's *Legenda Aurea* was easily the most popular legendary of the later medieval period and was translated into English twice during the fifteenth century. The earlier translation was in existence by 1438 and derives from a French version of the *Legenda Aurea* rather than directly from the Latin. As with *SEL*, different manuscripts of this legendary contain different saints' legends according to the needs and preferences of local audiences; this is a reminder that vernacular hagiography was instructive as well as entertaining. Several manuscripts also include a number of added lives of English saints, further demonstrating the adaptation of the legendary for local use. In 1483 William Caxton, best known as the printer of Malory's *Morte d'Arthur*, made another translation of the *Legenda Aurea* drawing on French, English, and Latin texts. Caxton orders his version of the legendary differently from the earlier translation, separating material on feasts of the church like Easter and Pentecost from the lives of saints. In the preface to his translation, called the *Golden Legend*, he says that the reasons for a new English version were to include material not found in the previous version and to reorder the legendary. Caxton seems to have wanted to produce a text that would be easy to use and would contain enough material to suit any user's needs; in short, a kind of standard legendary. This aim was largely successful, for the *Golden*

Legend was very popular and was reprinted several times until 1527. It is the last substantial Middle English hagiographic work and makes a fitting close to our examination of hagiography.

Religious didactic literature falls into several categories besides saints' lives. One category with a long-standing vernacular tradition is the homily. As mentioned previously, a homily is properly an explication of the gospel lesson for a particular day's mass, although not all homilies fit this definition. As we have seen, some are really saints' lives, and many others address general Christian themes such as the need to prepare for the Day of Judgment. A monastic congregation could understand a Latin homily, but a lay congregation would require one in the vernacular; hence homilies appear in English very early on. Because the gospel would be read in Latin, vernacular homilies tend to include a summary of the passage that they interpret. There are several notable homiliaries, or collections of homilies, in Old English. In addition to *Lives of Saints*, Ælfric wrote two series of homilies intended to be preached throughout the church year, which are now known as *Catholic Homilies*. The two series provided some variety; one could be preached in one year and another in the next. Wulfstan, archbishop of York and a contemporary of Ælfric, also wrote a number of homilies, including *Sermo Lupi ad Anglos*. There are also two somewhat earlier collections of homilies, both probably written in the late tenth century; both are named after the locations of the manuscripts in which they are found. The eighteen Blickling Homilies cover a range of topics, including saints' lives and such feasts as the Annunciation of Mary, while the twenty-three Vercelli Homilies mostly address penitential themes and issues related to Judgment Day.

The Day of Judgment is a common theme in Old English homilies. Indeed, this is the subject of one of the best-known homilies of this time, Wulfstan's *Sermo Lupi ad Anglos*, or *Sermon of Wolf to the English*. Wulfstan begins this homily by saying that the world is swiftly drawing to a close and will therefore grow worse in preparation for the reign of the Antichrist. The English have been exceedingly sinful and must return to God's law if they wish deliverance from their present evils. He then details all the sins the English have committed, such as enslaving people and refusing to give alms, and all the punishments they now suffer, such as plague, famine, and foreign invasion. People have rebelled against their earthly lords and their heavenly Lord and have broken faith with one another. The English have suffered greatly from Danish raids as a manifestation of God's wrath. Wulfstan then goes into another catalog of the sins of the English, which culminates in the statement that they now prefer evil deeds to good ones. Finally, he refers to Gildas's *De Excidio Brittanniae*, which describes how the Britons were overcome by the Anglo-Saxons in punishment for their sins, and says that the English are now much worse than the Britons were. He concludes with an exhortation to return to God's law and be ever mindful of the impending judgment.

Sermo Lupi is typical of homilies that are not based on any particular gospel passage. Wulfstan circles around his basic theme of impending doom, constantly returning to the sins of the English and their urgent need to repent. Time after time he repeats that the sins of the English themselves have brought on their present troubles. His message is simple and frequently restated: return to God before it is too late. Homilies that explain the hidden significance of biblical imagery have to proceed in a more structured and linear way, but those concerned with general subjects frequently adopt this kind of loose, recursive organization to drive home a simple point.

Collections of Middle English homilies survive as well. One of the most curious of these is *The Ormulum*, so titled by its author, Orm. *The Ormulum*, written in the late twelfth century, is a series of verse homilies that first present the gospel pericope in an expanded form and then expound upon its meaning. The verse is unrelentingly regular and is often filled out with conventional tags; it does not make entertaining reading. As a result, scholars' prime interest in the work has been linguistic. Orm uses a special spelling system to indicate vowel length, and this provides significant information about the dialect of *The Ormulum*. The marking of vowel length, along with the extreme regularity of the verse, also suggests that these homilies may have been intended for use by a non-English-speaking priest who had an English-speaking congregation. The priest could have intoned the homilies intelligibly, aided by meter and orthography. Despite *The Ormulum*'s lack of literary merit, its aim is the same as that of more engaging homiliaries: to present the gospel stories clearly and give simple yet pertinent interpretations of them. In this respect it is an entirely typical work.

Turning to a later example, the English sermons of John Wyclif are decidedly atypical in their sharp criticism of the fourteenth-century church. Among other things, Wyclif anticipates Martin Luther's condemnation of the sale of pardons and indulgences and also his questioning of papal primacy. Formally, however, the homilies are quite traditional, presenting a summary of the gospel in English and proceeding to interpret it, albeit according to Wyclif's unorthodox views. This basic method of vernacular religious instruction remains essentially unchanged even when it is used to spread dissenting opinions.

Wyclif also began the process of translating the Bible into Middle English, but he did not live to see it completed. Biblical translations and commentaries, and literature influenced by them, are another genre with a long history in English. King Alfred translated the first fifty psalms into Old English prose in the ninth century, and the remainder were put into Old English verse in the tenth century. The Gospels were translated into Old English in the mid-tenth century, and Ælfric translated large portions of Genesis and Numbers. Some of Ælfric's homilies are also summaries of biblical material; for example, homilies XVIII and XXV from *Lives of Saints* are paraphrases from the books of the Maccabees. Ælfric's translation of Genesis was incorporated into the so-called Old English *Heptateuch*, a translation of and commentary on the first seven books of the Old Testament; scholars formerly thought that Ælfric had written the entire work, but this opinion is not now held. Ælfric wrote a preface to his Genesis translation in which he expresses grave misgivings about putting the Scriptures into the vernacular. He was concerned that foolish people would read the work and think that they could act as Old Testament patriarchs did. For example, since Abraham had two wives, some reader might think that he himself could practice polygamy. Ælfric was also concerned that uneducated people would only see the literal meaning of the biblical text and would miss its deeper spiritual significance. To combat this, he talks at length in the Preface to Genesis about how to interpret the Bible spiritually; in this respect the Preface falls squarely into the prevailing Western trend of biblical commentary.

Several Old English poems are also biblical translations. *Genesis, Exodus, Daniel*, and *Judith* all render portions of their biblical namesakes into Old English verse. *Azarias* also translates a portion of the Book of Daniel. The poems *Christ I, II*, and *III* and *Christ and Satan* do not translate much biblical material on the life of Christ, but are to some extent commentaries on events like the Nativity, the Crucifixion, and the Ascension; thus they fit into this category as well.

The tradition of biblical translation and commentary continues in Middle English. *The Ormulum* belongs in this genre, as well as among the homiliaries, because of its basic pattern of biblical paraphrase followed by explication. Another early Middle English example of the genre is the late-thirteenth-century poem *Cursor Mundi*. This monumental work describes the history of salvation from Creation to Doomsday in almost 30,000 lines, incorporating material from a wide variety of commentaries and other exegetical sources. The resulting combination of scriptural stories and commentary lore is a very thorough example of the medieval view of biblical history. Another example of Middle English poetic biblical history is the somewhat earlier *Genesis and Exodus*, which paraphrases these books and incorporates some commentary.

Individual books of the Bible were also translated into Middle English. The Psalms were a particularly popular choice for translation; they exist in several vernacular versions, including one by the fourteenth-century mystic Richard Rolle. The only complete Middle English translation of the Bible is the aforementioned work of John Wyclif and his followers, completed around 1395. This is the first translation of the Bible into English and exists in over 170 manuscripts in at least two states of revision. Those portions written earlier are somewhat stiff, but the later ones show real grace and fluidity. A related text is a version of the Gospels accompanied by substantial commentaries, referred to as the "Glossed Gospels." These may be the work of John Purvey, one of Wyclif's principal followers.

The translation of the Bible into English is an obvious means of religious instruction. Some of the earliest prose works in English concern religious instruction; the translations done by King Alfred and his circle of assistants are good examples, especially his translation of Gregory's *Pastoral Care*. In general, it is a faithful and accurate rendering of Gregory's work into Old English. In Alfred's famous preface to the translation he laments the decay of learning in

England, noting that very few people are literate in Latin, and announces his intent to translate books that everyone should know into English. Alfred obviously intended *Pastoral Care* as instruction for clergy who could not read Latin, and some of the other translations made under his auspices have a religious instructive purpose as well. Wærferth's translation of Gregory's *Dialogues* has already been noted, and the Old English version of Bede's *Historia Ecclesiastica Gentis Anglorum* (*Ecclesiastical History of the English People*) brought the examples of earlier English holy men and women to a broader audience.

Two of Alfred's other translations also teach Christian lessons. His version of Augustine's *Soliloquies* is a treatise on the immortality of the soul and its reward or punishment in the afterlife according to its merits; he has taken a work that retained much Neoplatonic doctrine and made it a thoroughly orthodox Christian text. This process is even more apparent in his translation of Boethius's *Consolation of Philosophy*. Here he takes a complex philosophical inquiry into providence, free will, and the meaning of misfortune and converts it into an exhortation to trust in God above all worldly attractions. Alfred's project of translation produced few texts, but their instructive purpose is clear.

A later Old English text is a more typical example of religious instruction aimed at priests. Wulfstan, whose *Sermo Lupi* was previously discussed, also wrote a brief work, *Canons of Edgar*, aimed at improving the conduct of secular clergy. It is a series of short rules stating what priests may and may not properly do and reflects the concerns of the tenth-century monastic reforms now applied to secular clergy.

As noted, Anglo-Saxon missionaries were essential in the spread of penitentials, so it is not surprising to find penitentials in Old English. These do not differ from the Latin penitentials previously mentioned. After the Fourth Lateran Council, there was a great increase in vernacular penitential material; much of this material took the form of treatises on the seven deadly sins and their opposing virtues. Three of the most notable Middle English texts of this sort are Robert Mannyng's *Handlynge Synne*, Dan Michel's *Ayenbite of Inwit*, and Chaucer's "Parson's Tale," all dating from the fourteenth century. In addition to addressing the seven deadly sins, *Handlynge Synne* discusses the Ten Commandments, the seven sacraments, the twelve points of confession, and the twelve graces derived from it. Clearly it is a compendium of basic Christian instruction. The *Ayenbite of Inwit* contains even more material: the Ten Commandments, the articles of the Apostle's Creed, the seven deadly sins, sins of the tongue, instructions in dying a Christian death, the seven petitions of the Lord's Prayer, and the seven gifts of the Holy Spirit. Although it is not of much literary merit, it is a very good example of vernacular religious instruction. "The Parson's Tale" is a detailed instruction on penitence in three parts. The first part discusses contrition; the second, confession, the seven deadly sins, and their opposed virtues; and the third, satisfaction or, in other words, penance. Between them, these three texts demonstrate the typical concerns of Middle English religious instruction of lay folk.

Because of its sheer popularity, one other Middle English poem should be included here. *The Prick of Conscience* survives in more manuscripts than any other Middle English poem, giving it a fair claim to be the most popular English verse work of the Middle Ages. It describes the wretchedness of earthly life and then moves on to discuss the four final things: Death, Purgatory, Heaven, and Hell. In its emphasis on the need to prepare for death, *The Prick of Conscience* is a good example of the *ars moriendi*, or the art of dying, a common kind of instructive work that tells the reader how to achieve a devout Christian death.

Works of instruction for those in religious orders form the last genre of our survey. The most common of these works in English are the rules of the various orders. Æthelwold, bishop of Winchester, translated *The Rule of Saint Benedict* into Old English in the tenth century. He made two versions: one for monks and one for nuns. Various Middle English versions of the Benedictine rule exist, along with translations of the rules of St. Augustine, St. Francis, and St. Clare. All of these translations represent some degree of local adaptation of their original source. The best-known and most studied vernacular English rule is, however, *Ancrene Riwle*, sometimes called *Ancrene Wisse*. This thirteenth-century text is a rule originally composed for three sisters who wished to become religious hermitesses; it was later adapted for use by men as well and was translated into both French and Latin. It is divided into eight sections. The first describes the prayers the sisters are to say; the second, third, and fourth deal with guarding against temptations that enter through the senses. The fifth and sixth parts address confession and penance, while the seventh concerns love and the eighth governs domestic conduct. *Ancrene Riwle* contains some of the best early Middle English prose; the passage in part 7 in which Christ is compared to a knight wooing and defending the soul has been particularly praised.

Another instructive work presumably intended for those in religious orders is *Hali Meiðhad*, a short treatise in praise of virginity. The text describes virgins as spiritual warriors overcoming the devil and sharply dissuades young women from marrying. It depicts the trials of pregnancy in great detail and says that all pleasures of marriage end in sorrow. While the author never explicitly says that he is addressing nuns, his condemnation of marriage makes his audience clear. As noted previously, *Hali Meiðhad* is one of the texts of the Katherine Group and shares many linguistic features with its other members.

CRITICAL SURVEY AND BIBLIOGRAPHY

A critical survey of studies of Old and Middle English could easily become vast; this one will perforce be selective. For Old English scholarship before 1972, see Stanley B. Greenfield and Fred C. Robinson, *A Bibliography of Publications on Old English Literature to the End of 1972* (1980); for earlier scholarship on Middle English works, see the appropriate volumes and editions of Wells's *A Manual of the Writings in Middle English, 1050–1500* (*MWME*). Several more recent works are excellent introductions to scholarship on the subject. Paul Szarmach's anthology *Holy Men and Holy Women: Old English Prose Saints' Lives and Their Contexts* contains numerous splendid articles; while none are especially introductory, the collection as a whole gives a very thorough picture of current studies in Old English hagiography. Michael Lapidge's article on the topic in *The Cambridge Companion to Old English Literature* is a better general introduction and would be beneficial as an initial reading. D.G. Scragg's "The Corpus of Vernacular Homilies and Prose Saints' Lives before Ælfric," though not recent, is an important study of early hagiographic texts. With regard to Middle English saints' lives, Julia Boffey's "Middle English Lives" is a very good overview. Renate Blumenfeld-Kosinski and Timea Szell's *Images of Sainthood in Medieval Europe*, while its focus is broader than English literature, contains much interesting material. Manfred Görlach's *Studies in Middle English Saints' Legends* is also very worthwhile. A more specific study is Klaus Jankofsky's *The South English Legendary: A Critical Assessment*. Scholarship on the Katherine Group's lives has broadened from an earlier interest in linguistic issues to a variety of topics; Jocelyn Wogan-Browne's "Saints' Lives and the Female Reader" is an example of the rising interest in women's issues in hagiography. Feminist critiques of Middle English saints' lives have become fairly common. For earlier scholarship on Middle English hagiography, see "V. Saints' Legends" in *MWME*, volume 2.

Both Old English homilies and Wycliffite writings have seen continuous scholarly activity. John Pope's edition of Ælfric's homilies is a monument of scholarly excellence, and more recently D.G. Scragg's edition of *The Vercelli Homilies* has been outstanding as well. Malcolm Godden has edited the second series of *Catholic Homilies*, but scholars must still rely on Thorpe's 1844 edition for the first. Godden's completion of Peter Clemoes's edition of the first series would be a boon. Source studies have always been a focus of work on the homilies, and articles like Joyce Hill's 1996 work on Ælfric's sources show that the tradition is still productive. Janet Bately's bibliography of source studies on the anonymous homilies is particularly valuable. For a general introduction to Old English homilies, chapter 3 of *A New Critical History of Old English Literature*, "Ælfric, Wulfstan, and Other Late Prose," by Daniel Calder, is useful. Scragg's article "The Homilies of the Blickling Manuscript" is a very good examination of a particular group. For Middle English sermons, Siegfried Wenzel's "Medieval Sermons" is a superlative introduction; for Wyclif particularly, Anthony Kenny's *Wyclif in His Times*, although fairly specific, is very useful. For early studies on Wyclif, see "III. Wyclyf and His Followers," in *MWME*, volume 2. Thomas Heffernan's "Sermon Literature" and Ann Hudson's "Wycliffite Prose" deserve mention as well. While scholars continue to study *The Ormulum*, their studies are almost invariably linguistic, and this focus is unlikely to change.

Work on Old English biblical translations and commentaries largely centers on the Psalms and psalter glosses; Sarah Larratt Keefer's book is a judicious study of these. Bright and Ramsay's edition of the Old English prose Psalms is still standard, but untrustworthy; publication of Patrick O'Neill's edition is eagerly awaited. Source studies have been and continue to be a primary focus of scholarship on the Old English psalms. For studies of Ælfric's biblical translations, Peter Clemoes's article in *Continuations and Beginnings* is still an excellent introduction. Janet Bately's article on Old English prose in *The Cambridge Companion to Old English Literature* and Daniel Calder's chapter on Ælfric previously noted are also important. Richard Marsden's 1991 article is a notable recent study. Apart from Wyclif's work, the Middle English biblical translations considered in this chapter have attracted comparatively little scholarly attention recently; for earlier work on *Cursor Mundi*, see "XX. Works of Religious and Philosophical Instruction" in *MWME*, volume 7, and for *Exodus and Genesis*, see "IV. Translations and Paraphrases of the Bible, and Commentaries," *MWME*, volume 2. *Cursor Mundi* has been thoroughly edited over the past twenty years, but has not been much studied; scholarship has been mostly linguistic or textual. Sarah Horrall's 1985 article on the manuscripts of *Cursor Mundi* is fairly typical. *Genesis and Exodus* has fared even worse. Donna Minkova's 1992 article on verse structure is the only substantial criticism on the poem in the last fifteen years. Though its literary merit is not great, the text represents an opportunity for further scholarly inquiry.

The Alfredian translations are the focus of lively criticism. Earlier scholarship tended toward source studies; while these are still a strong element, more recent criticism examines the translations in their historical context. *Studies in Earlier Old English Prose*, edited by Paul Szarmach, contains several perceptive articles on various Alfredian texts. The best book on Alfred's translation of Boethius remains Kurt Otten's *König Alfreds Boethius*; though F. Ann Payne's *King Alfred and Boethius* raises some interesting points, it is generally unconvincing. Joseph Wittig's 1983 article is of vital importance to discussion of Alfred's use of other Latin sources in his translation. For a general overview, Janet Bately's 1988 article on early Old English prose is valuable. As for Middle English instructive works, earlier scholarship again focused on sources, as well as identifying the authors; see "XX. Works of Religious and Philosophical Instruction" in *MWME*, volume 7. These trends continue, but recent criticism has also focused on the relations between the texts and their social environment. *Handlynge Synne* has received some attention of various sorts, including a good edition. Work on *The Prick of Conscience* is sparser and tends to be linguistically oriented. *The Ayenbite of Inwit* seems to be receiving no critical attention at present, making it fertile ground for inquiry. Judith Shaw's 1985 article on popular books of instruction is a useful but brief look at the ecclesiastical reforms that helped create these texts.

Turning to works of instruction for religious orders, *Ancrene Riwle* has enjoyed steady critical attention. For early works, see "VI. Instructions for Religious" in *MWME*, volume 2, or Geoffrey Shepherd's edition of parts 6 and 7. Shepherd's edition also provides the best introduction to the text. It lists several editions of separate manuscripts, of which J.R.R. Tolkien's is the standard. Early criticism was largely linguistically oriented. More recently scholars have taken a variety of approaches to the text. Elizabeth Robertson's work is a good example of a feminist perspective. Roger Dahood's 1997 article provides a useful summation of the current state of scholarship on the text. *Hali Meiðhad* has received much less attention. Bella Millett's edition gives a good discussion, but most scholarship is again linguistic or limited to brief notes on sources.

SELECTED BIBLIOGRAPHY

Hagiography

Editions

Ælfric. *Lives of Three English Saints*. Rev. ed. Ed. G.I. Needham. Exeter: University of Exeter, 1976.

Ælfric's Lives of Saints. Ed. Walter W. Skeat. EETS 76, 82, 94, 114. London, 1881–1900.

Das altenglische Martyrologium. Ed. Günter Kotzor. Bayerische Akademie der Wissenschaften, Philos.-hist. Klasse, Neue Folge 88, 1–2. Munich: Bayerische Akademie der Wissenschaften, 1981.

Se Liflade ant te Passiun of Seinte Iulienne. Ed. S.R.T.O. d'Ardenne. EETS 248. London: Oxford University Press, 1961.

Seinte Katerine. Ed. S.R.T.O. d'Ardenne and E.J. Dobson. EETS SS 7. London: Oxford University Press, 1981.

Seinte Marherete, Meiden ant Martyr. Ed. F.M. Mack. EETS 193. London: Oxford University Press, 1934.

The South English Legendary. Ed. C. D'Evelyn and A.J. Mill. EETS 235, 236, 244. London: Oxford University Press, 1956–1959.

Studies

Blumenfeld-Kosinski, Renate, and Timea Szell, eds. *Images of Sainthood in Medieval Europe*. Ithaca, NY: Cornell University Press, 1991.

Boffey, Julia. "Middle English Lives." *The Cambridge History of Medieval English Literature*. Ed. David Wallace. Cambridge: Cambridge University Press, 1999. 610–634.

Gaïffier, Baudouin de. "Le Martyrologe en vieil anglais du IXe siècle." *Analecta Bollandiana* 104. 1–2 (1985): 163–166.

Görlach, Manfred. *Studies in Middle English Saints' Legends*. Heidelberg: Carl Winter Universitätsverlag, 1998.

Jankofsky, Klaus P., ed. *The South English Legendary: A Critical Assessment*. Tübingen: Francke, 1992.

Jankowski, Eileen S. "Reception of Chaucer's *Second Nun's Tale*: Osbern Bokenham's *Lyf of S. Cycyle*." *Chaucer Review* 30.3 (1996): 306–318.

Lapidge, Michael. "The Saintly Life in Anglo-Saxon England." *The Cambridge Companion to Old English Literature*. Ed. Malcolm Godden and Michael Lapidge. Cambridge: Cambridge University Press, 1991. 243–263.

Nicholls, Alex. "The Corpus of Prose Saints' Lives and Hagiographic Pieces in Old

English and Its Manuscript Distribution." *Reading Medieval Studies* 19 (1993): 72–96; 20 (1994): 51–87.

Price, Jocelyn. "The Liflade of Seinte Iuliene and Hagiographic Convention." *Medievalia et Humanistica* 14 (1986): 37–58.

Sadlek, Gregory M. "Laughter, Game, and Ambiguous Comedy in the South English Legendary." *Studia Neophilologica* 64.1 (1992): 45–54.

Scragg, D.G. "The Corpus of Vernacular Homilies and Prose Saints' Lives before Ælfric." *Anglo-Saxon England* 8 (1979): 223–277.

Szarmach, Paul E., ed *Holy Men and Holy Women: Old English Prose Saints' Lives and Their Contexts*. Albany: State University of New York Press, 1991.

Wogan-Browne, Jocelyn. "Saints' Lives and the Female Reader." *Forum for Modern Language Studies* 27.4 (1991): 314–332.

Homilies

Editions

Ælfric's Catholic Homilies: The Second Series. Ed. Malcolm Godden. EETS SS 5. London: Oxford University Press, 1979.

The Blickling Homilies of the Tenth Century. Ed. Richard Morris. EETS 58, 63, 73. London: *Oxford University Press*, 1874–1880.

Homilies of Ælfric: A Supplementary Collection. Ed. John C. Pope. EETS 259, 260. London: Oxford University Press, 1967–1968.

The Homilies of the Anglo-Saxon Church: The First Part, Containing the Sermones Catholici or Homilies of Ælfric. Ed. B. Thorpe. 2 vols. London: Ælfric Society, 1844–1846.

The Homilies of Wulfstan. Ed. Dorothy Bethurum. Oxford: Clarendon Press, 1957.

The Ormulum. Ed. R.M. Holt. Oxford, 1878.

Sermo Lupi ad Anglos. Ed. Dorothy Whitelock. 3rd ed. Exeter: University of Exeter, 1976.

The Vercelli Homilies and Related Texts. Ed. D.G. Scragg. EETS 300. Oxford: Oxford University Press, 1992.

Studies

Bately, Janet, comp. *Anonymous Old English Homilies: A Preliminary Bibliography of Source Studies*. Binghamton, NY: COMERS, 1993.

Calder, Daniel. "Ælfric, Wulfstan, and Other Late Prose." *A New Critical History of Old English Literature*. Stanley B. Greenfield and Daniel G. Calder. New York: New York University Press, 1986. 68–106.

Godden, Malcolm. "Apocalypse and Invasion in Late Anglo-Saxon England." *From Anglo-Saxon to Early Middle English*. Ed. Malcolm Godden, Douglas Gray, and Terry Hoad. Oxford: Clarendon Press, 1994. 130–162.

Heffernan, Thomas J. "Sermon Literature." *Middle English Prose: A Critical Guide to Major Authors and Genres*. Ed. A.S.G. Edwards. New Brunswick, NJ: Rutgers University Press, 1984. 177–207.

Hill, Joyce. "Ælfric's Sources Reconsidered: Some Case Studies from the Catholic Homilies." *Studies in English Language and Literature: "Doubt Wisely."* Ed. M.J. Toswell and E.M. Tyler. London: Routledge, 1996. 362–386.

Hudson, Anne. "Wycliffite Prose." *Middle English Prose: A Critical Guide to Major Authors and Genres*. Ed. A.S.G. Edwards. New Brunswick, NJ: Rutgers University Press, 1984. 249–270.

Kenny, Anthony, ed. *Wyclif in His Times*. Oxford: Clarendon Press, 1986.

Scragg, D.G. "The Homilies of the Blickling Manuscript." *Learning and Literature in Anglo-Saxon England*. Ed. Michael Lapidge and Helmut Gneuss. Cambridge: Cambridge University Press, 1985. 299–316.

Wenzel, Siegfried. "Medieval Sermons." *A Companion to Piers Plowman*. Ed. John A. Alford. Berkeley: University of California Press, 1988. 155–172.

Biblical Translations and Commentaries

Editions

Liber Psalmorum: The West-Saxon Psalms. Ed. James W. Bright and Robert L. Ramsay. Boston: Heath, 1907.

The Old English Version of the Gospels. Ed. R.M. Liuzza. EETS 314. Oxford: Oxford University Press, 1994–2000.

The Old English Version of the Heptateuch, Ælfric's Treatise on the Old and New Testament, and His Preface to Genesis. Ed. S.J. Crawford. EETS 160. London: Oxford University Press, 1922.

The Southern Version of Cursor Mundi, I: Lines 1–9228. Ed. Sarah M. Horrall. Ottawa: University of Ottawa Press, 1986.

The Southern Version of Cursor Mundi, III: Lines 12713–17082. Ed. Henry J. Stauffenberg. Ottawa: University of Ottawa Press, 1985.

The Southern Version of Cursor Mundi, IV: Lines 17289–21346. Ed. Peter H.J. Mous. Ottawa: University of Ottawa Press, 1986.

Studies

Bately, Janet. "Lexical Evidence for the Authorship of the Prose Psalms in the Paris Psalter." *Anglo-Saxon England* 10 (1992): 69–95.

———. "The Nature of Old English Prose." *The Cambridge Companion to Old English Literature*. Ed. Malcolm Godden and Michael Lapidge. Cambridge: Cambridge University Press, 1991. 71–87.

Clemoes, Peter. "Ælfric." *Continuations and Beginnings: Studies in Old English Literature*. Ed. E.G. Stanley. London: Thomas Nelson and Sons, 1966. 176–209.

Horrall, Sarah M. "The Manuscripts of *Cursor Mundi*." *TEXT: Transactions of the Society for Textual Scholarship* 2 (1985): 69–82.

Keefer, Sarah Larratt. *Psalm-Poem and Psalter-Glosses*. New York: Peter Lang, 1991.

Lindstrom, Bengt. "Some Textual Notes on the ME Genesis and Exodus." *English Studies* 77.6 (1996): 513–516.

Marsden, Richard. "Ælfric as Translator: The Old English Prose Genesis." *Anglia* 109. 3–4 (1991): 319–358.

Minkova, Donka. "Verse Structure in the Middle English Genesis and Exodus." *JEGP* 91.2 (1992): 157–178.

O'Neill, Patrick P. "The Old English Introductions to the Prose Psalm and the Paris Psalter: Sources, Structure, and Composition." *Studies in Philology* 78.5 (1981): 20–38.

Works of Religious Instruction

Editions

Bischof Wærferths von Worcester Übersetzung der Dialoge Gregors des Grossen. Ed. Hans Hecht. 2 vols. Bibliothek der ags Prosa 5. Leipzig: Wigland, 1900–1907.

Dan Michel's Ayenbite of Inwyt. Ed. Richard Morris. EETS 23. London, 1866. Rev. P. Gradon. 1965.

King Alfred's Version of Saint Augustine's Soliloquies. Ed. Thomas A. Carnicelli. Cambridge, MA: Harvard University Press, 1969.

King Alfred's Old English Version of Boethius "De Consolatione Philosophiae." Ed. Walter J. Sedgefield. Oxford: Clarendon Press, 1899.

King Alfred's West-Saxon Version of Gregory's "Pastoral Care." Ed. Henry Sweet. EETS 45, 50. London, 1871–1872.

The Pricke of Conscience. Ed. Richard Morris. Berlin, 1863.

Robert Mannynge of Brunne. *"Handlynge Synne."* Ed. Idelle Sullens. Binghamton, NY: Medieval and Renaissance Texts and Studies, 1983.

Wulfstan's Canons of Edgar. Ed. Roger Fowler. EETS 266. London: Oxford University Press, 1972.

Studies

Bately, Janet. "Old English Prose before and during the Reign of Alfred." *Anglo-Saxon England* 17 (1988): 93–138.

Bradbury, Nancy Mason. "Popular Festive Forms and Beliefs in Robert Mannyng's *Handlyng Synne." Bakhtin and Medieval Voices.* Ed. Thomas J. Farrell. Gainesville: University Press of Florida, 1995. 158–179.

Frantzen, Allen J. *King Alfred.* Boston: Twayne, 1986.

Ho, Cynthia. "Dichotomize and Conquer: 'Womman Handlyng' in Handlyng Synne." *Philological Quarterly* 72.4 (1993): 383–401.

Otten, Kurt. *König Alfreds Boethius.* Tübingen: Niemeyer, 1964.

Payne, F. Anne. *King Alfred and Boethius: An Analysis of the Old English Version of the "Consolation of Philosophy."* Madison: University of Wisconsin Press, 1968.

Shaw, Judith. "The Influence of Canonical and Episcopal Reform on Popular Books of Instruction." *The Popular Literature of Medieval England.* Ed. Thomas J. Heffernan. Knoxville: University of Tennessee Press, 1985.

Szarmach, Paul, ed. *Studies in Earlier Old English Prose.* Albany: State University of New York Press, 1985.

Wittig, Joseph S. "King Alfred's Boethius and Its Latin Sources: A Reconsideration." *Anglo-Saxon England* 11 (1983): 157–98.

Works of Instruction for Religious Orders

Editions

"Ancrene Wisse" Edited from MS Corpus Christi College Cambridge 402. Ed. J.R.R. Tolkien. EETS 249. London: Oxford University Press, 1962.

Ancrene Wisse: Parts Six and Seven. Ed. Geoffrey Shepherd. London: Thomas Nelson and Sons, 1959.

Die ags Prosabearbeitungen der Benediktinerregel. Ed. Arnold Schröer. Bibliothek der ags Prosa 2. Kassel, 1885–1888. 2nd ed. Rpt. with an appendix by H. Gneuss. Darmstadt: Wissenschaftliche Buchgesellschaft, 1964.

Hali Meiðhad. Ed. Bella Millett. EETS 284. London: Oxford University Press, 1982.

Studies

Barratt, Alexandra. "The Five Wits and Their Structural Significance in Part II of *Ancrene Wisse.*" *Medium Ævum* 56.1 (1987): 12–24.

Dahood, Roger. "The Current State of Ancrene Wisse Group Studies." *Medieval English Studies Newsletter* 36 (June 1997): 6–14.

———. "Design in Part I of Ancrene Riwle." *Medium Ævum* 56.1 (1987): 1–11.

Fletcher, Alan J. "The Dancing Virgins of *Hali Meidhad.*" *Notes and Queries* 40(238).4 (December 1993): 437–439.

Innes-Parker, Catherine. "The Lady and the King: Ancrene Wisse's Parable of the Royal Wooing Re-Examined." *English Studies* 75.6 (1994): 509–522.

Millett, Bella. "Ancrene Wisse and the Conditions of Confession." *English Studies* 80.3 (1999): 193–214.

———. "*Hali Meiðhad, Sawles Warde,* and the Continuity of English Prose." *Five Hundred Years of Words and Sounds: A Festschrift for Eric Dobson.* Ed. E.G. Stanley and Douglas Gray. Cambridge: D.S. Brewer, 1983. 100–108.

Robertson, Elizabeth. " 'An Anchorhold of Her Own': Female Ancoritic Literature in Thirteenth-Century England." *Equally in God's Image: Women in the Middle Ages.* Ed. Julia Bolton Holloway, Constance S. Wright, and Joan Bechtold. New York: Peter Lang, 1990. 170–183.

Savage, Anne. "The Translation of the Feminine: Untranslatable Dimensions of the Anchoritic Works." *The Medieval Translator, IV.* Ed. Roger Ellis and Ruth Evans. Binghamton, NY: Medieval and Renaissance Texts and Studies, 1994. 181–199.

Smith, Lesley, and Jane H.M. Taylor, eds. *Women, the Book, and the Godly: Selected Proceedings of the St. Hilda's Conference, 1993.* Cambridge: D.S. Brewer, 1995.

15
Lyric Poetry

Sigrid King

In the lyric form in English there are two distinct linguistic classes, the Germanic and the Celtic. Most prevalent in English studies are the Germanic works, which tend to fall into two time frames: the Old English or Anglo-Saxon period, which began with the North Germanic invasion of Britain in the fifth century, and the Middle English period, which followed the Norman Conquest of 1066. The Old English works are distinguished by their use of alliteration and the kenning, a rhetorical device that is formulaic in its dissemination of novel ways of expounding common objects (e.g., the "sea" is the "swan's road," the sky is "dove's lane"). The poems depend little upon rhyme, so alliteration is the key element of these works, binding them together with the aid of a caesura. The alliterative sound is usually repeated three times in a segment (Wilhelm 337–338).

The lyric poetry of the Middle English period has much more of a lilt to it; gone is the imposed harshness of alliteration, replaced by a love of ambiguity and a fondness for puns. This technique is similar to that seen in the ballads, which tend to be more folk oriented and sometimes reflect the tragic spirit of the love crazed in a way very different from medieval romances (Wilhelm 338). Regardless, the lyrics can be seen to mirror the history of English literature. Holman notes that some passages of *Beowulf* have lyrical qualities, and *Deor's Lament* is for all intents a lyric poem. The sheer bulk of extant anonymous lyrics demonstrates the popularity of this genre. By 1310 there was a collated collection of some forty different lyrics. By 1400 even Geoffrey Chaucer had written his share of lyrics, particularly influenced by the French prototypes (Wilhelm 283).

Defining the term "lyric" has always been difficult. Studying this genre from its etymological roots in the Greek word *lyra*, a stringed musical instrument, helps us to perceive that lyrics, on their most basic level, must have songlike qualities that help distinguish this form of poetry from narrative and dramatic poetry. Middle English poets do not appear to have used the term "lyrics," instead calling their works "songs." It is not until the sixteenth century that we find the term "lyric" used by Elizabethan literary critics. The Middle English lyric poems are usually short and tend to express strong feeling, although not necessarily the emotion of the lyricist. Some longer lyrics have narrative cores, and critics have differed over their inclusion in the lyric genre. In general, though, the Middle English lyric can be distinguished from the Middle English narrative poem in that its central concern is not to narrate an event so much as to express an emotion or idea.

The Middle English lyric became a mainstay between the twelfth and the early sixteenth centuries, although the lyrics flourish mainly in the thirteenth through the fifteenth centuries. The earliest lyrics, composed shortly after the Norman Conquest of 1066, were shorter and were frequently accompanied by musical notations, indicating that they were intended to be sung or danced. This demonstrates a typical progression where the written poems would be rooted in the music of the wandering minstrels and bards. These early lyrics are usually anonymous and based on oral culture that is not part of the courtly tradition. It was not until the late fourteenth century, when the Continental French lyric modes, including the popular ballade, were introduced, that lyrics began to move more toward a written tradition in England. By the end of the fourteenth century we see a distinct change in style and content of the lyric as it became more complex in nature and more easily attributable to a specific poet. Today there are several hundred extant Middle English lyrics. There are at least four important sources for the Middle English lyric: Anglo-Saxon verse, Latin Christian and secular traditions, French verse, and the European minstrel tradition.

Anglo-Saxon verse is rooted in the scop, a reciter who accompanied himself on a musical instrument, such as a lute, while singing heroic narrative poetry with a four-beat line, frequent alliteration, and a caesura. Too, the form of this time relied upon the occasional use of stanzaic form, meter (the two stressed syllables in the short line), and rhyme technique, which became the norm in Middle English lyric poetry as early as the twelfth century. The Anglo-Saxon elegies "The Wanderer" and "The Ruin" contain some metrical similarities to Middle English lyrics.

The Middle English lyric demonstrates certain elements of style, such as aureation, allegory, wordplay, and vibrant language, and certain elements of sound, such as repetition, rhyme, and alliteration. In terms of style, the medieval lyric is sometimes marked by "aureation," extreme stylistic ornamentation. The majority of Middle English lyric poems were religious verses sung in Latin, praising the Virgin Mary. Aureate verse particularly makes use of alliteration and assonance and coins new words.

Another source for the Middle English lyric is the Latin Christian tradition, particularly the devotional writings, sermons, the Scriptures, liturgy, the Psalms, commentaries, and hymns. Many of these writings, although prose, had an important impact on the content, imagery, and language of Middle English lyrics. Rosemary Woolf traced the English religious lyric directly back to the Latin devotional movement, as practiced by St. Anselm, archbishop of Canterbury (1033–1109), St. Bernard of Clairvaux (1090–1153), and St. Francis of Assisi (1181–1226). The devotional movement emphasized the meditation on Christ's Passion and the Virgin's joys and sorrows. Many of the Latin hymns fall under the category of the *planctus Mariae*, or the complaint of Mary at the site of Christ's crucifixion, a theme that appears in the Middle English lyric. In addition to the influential content, Latin hymns contain regular meter, rhyme, and stanza form as far back as the fourth century, and several Middle English stanza forms resemble Latin stanzas.

In the latter half of the medieval period the lyric, while still influenced by the Latin hymn in terms of content and expression, became more based on the poet's original designs for meter and form. The early existence of works of this type is known because their popularity was readily questioned by the elders of the church. Indeed, Robert Mannyng cites an example where a group of carolers disturbed a priest during mass. The priest cursed them that they might not stop their singing and dancing for a year. What the priest did not know was that his daughter was among the singers, and when her brother tried to force her from the ring, he pulled off her arm. Unmoved, the carolers stood nonstop, without food and drink, for an entire year. This showed that the early clerics believed that lyrics could only lead to discord.

In addition to the Latin Christian tradition, there are Latin secular traditions that occasionally appear in the Middle English lyric; they cover a wide range of topics, from the profane to the topical and satirical. Most prominent is the satire on women, which first appears in Middle English around the twelfth century. While the debate about women was based initially on religious doctrine, it became incorporated into courtly literature. The second element from the Latin secular tradition is the drinking song, sung by wandering scholars, which can be found in the Latin of the anonymous *Carmina Burana*, a thirteenth-century manuscript from the Bavarian Benediktbeuren monastery.

As noted, a third major source for the Middle English lyric is the French lyric, which began to appear in England after the Norman Conquest in 1066. This tradition developed from yearly May dances; early French lyrics were called *caroles*, during which dancers moved in a circle and responded to a singer's verses with jointly sung refrains. The syllabics and end-rhyme of French poetry were important influences on the Middle English lyric. French genres frequently found in Middle English poetry include the *chanson d'aventure* and the *pastourelle*, and French forms include the ballade, the rondel, the carol, the burden, and the envoy. For more detailed descriptions of these elements, see the discussion of form later in this chapter.

Another important element of French lyric influence was the courtly love idea, in which a man serves a distant or unattainable woman and suffers mental and physical anguish until his desire to win her is fulfilled. The French poet Jean Froissart, who came to England and enjoyed the patronage of Queen Philippa from 1361 to 1369, is a recognized influence on the lyrics of Geoffrey Chaucer. Froissart's 199 lyrics include *pastourelles, chansons royales,* ballades, and *rondeaux,* many of which express the courtly love ideas that clearly influenced lyrics like Chaucer's "Complaint to His Lady." In some Middle English lyrics the secular worship of the courtly lady is transformed into the worship of the Virgin Mary.

A fourth important source for the Middle English lyric was the music of the wandering minstrels, variously called the troubadours (from Provence), the trouvères (from northern France), or the minnesingers (from Germany), who traveled through Europe from the ninth to the thirteenth centuries. The second half of the twelfth century was the golden age of the troubadours. The music of the troubadours and trouvères developed from the French May dances described earlier. These singers would either accompany themselves with an instrument, sing unaccompanied, or be accompanied by an assistant, or juglar. The lyrics of the troubadours were written for entertainment of the aristocracy (*chanson courtoise*), but they contained elements of the seasonal folk dances, particularly in their frequent allusions to spring. Troubadour poetry emphasized technique, utilizing more than eight hundred different meters. Forms created by the troubadours include the ballade (dance song) and the *pastourelle,* although none wrote in English. Their poetry was intended for the aristocracy, and the aristocracy in England up through the thirteenth century, when the troubadours disappeared, still spoke French. Their influence in England was facilitated by the marriage of Eleanor of Guienne (daughter of William of Poitou, "the father of the troubadours") to the English Henry II. During her reign from 1154 to 1206, French troubadours came to perform at the English court. Troubadour lyrics frequently focused on the difficulties of love and contrasted the speaker's sadness with the promise of new life inherent in spring, a subject that is echoed in Middle English lyrics.

Thus it is clear that lyrics were more public than private; they frequently contained a nature motif. Also, they demonstrated certain elements of style and sound and frequently appeared in recognizable forms. In many ways the lyrics are more conventional than individual. While the lyrics generally are not expressions of individual "selves," Rosemary Woolf argued that the poets were aware of their public role, of being watched as she put it. The persona in most Middle English lyrics is usually an easily recognized biblical or historical figure. The majority of the lyrics are anonymous; during this period it was not important to know who wrote them, although this would change by the fourteenth century when the works were signed by the likes of Chaucer, Thomas Hoccleve, William Dunbar, John Lydgate, and Robert Henryson.

Middle English lyrics usually begin with or contain some specific reference to a pastoral scene, a carryover from the troubadour songs. They could be simply a joyous celebration of the changing of the seasons, such as *Sumer Is I-Cumen*

In. Other times nature serves merely as a symbolic motif, as seen in *Alysoun*, which begins with the setting "Bitweene Merch and Averil, / When spray biginneth to springe." Conversely, the same imagery of spring may be used in a religious lyric celebrating the Virgin Mary.

Lyric style of this period is also characterized as allegory and could appear in the form of a riddle, as in *I Syng of a Myden*, or as a joke, as in the poem in which the speaker lay all night by a rose, which he dared not steal, and yet he bore the "flour" away (i.e., he deflowered the "rose"). This allegory is made more ambiguous by the frequent association of the rose image with the Virgin Mary. Symbolism and metaphor are related elements that frequently occur in Middle English poems. For example, April frequently appears in poems as a symbol of new life or regeneration. The many levels of meaning may lead to the use of irony and paradox, both of which are at work in the devotional *Now Gooth Sunne under Wode*, in which the wood represents both the cross of Christ and a forest. Lyrics also frequently employ puns, such as the word "makeles" in *I Syng of a Myden*, where it means both matchless and mateless.

In the Middle English lyric the language varies from colloquial and occasionally crude to courtly and polished. In *Farewele! Advent, Christmas Is Come*, a boisterous Christmas carol by James Ryman, for example, the speaker complains about the food and drink, noting the "stinking fishe not worthe a louse." The words of a lyric may be shockingly realistic or gently euphemistic, as is much of the courtly language introduced into the love lyric around the end of the fourteenth century. Macaronic verse (verse combining two or more languages) clearly demonstrates the comingling of French, Latin, and English and the variety of sources for the Middle English lyric. The combination of Latin with English for religious poems adds a dignity and seriousness to a lyric like Ryman's fifteenth-century Nativity poem *Angelus Inquit Pastoribus* in lines 3 and 4: "Upon a night an aungell bright / *Pastoribus apparuit*" (appeared to the shepherds). In comic verse the combination of languages can create a nonsense effect for satire.

Middle English lyrics also used certain elements of sound, especially repetition, which may occur in single words, in lines, as a verse for a song, or as incremental repetition. This is a throwback to the Anglo-Saxon use of alliteration. As a type of repetition, parallelism (or anaphora) is a common technique, as demonstrated in the poem "Wanne Mine Eyhnen Misten," where the speaker describes what happens when he dies in a series of "when . . . then" statements detailing the body's decay. Alliteration is another important sound element, as in the first line of the complaint against blacksmiths, describing them as "Swartesmekyd smethes, smateryd wyth smoke." Assonance is also used for emphasis, as in the line from *Alysoun* describing "hire browe broune." End rhyme is also very common in Middle English lyrics, and a kind of slant-rhyme sometimes appears. In addition to displaying certain characteristics of style and sound, the Middle English lyric also appears in recognizable forms.

In early Middle English lyrics meter, which varies widely, seems to be determined by counting the number of stressed accents rather than the number of syllables, another holdover from Old English poetry, as is the caesura, or pause, that sometimes appears. In Middle English lyrics it is not uncommon to find four stressed accents in a line, regardless of the number of syllables present. The emphasis on counting stresses only was eventually replaced by the conventional "foot" measure, based on the model of classical prosody. Line breaks in poems tend to occur when the speaker would pause for a breath. Stanza forms vary from the simple pairs of rhyming couplets or quatrains of alternating rhymes to more complex stanza forms, such as rhyme royal or ballade. In longer lyrics stanza breaks may be marked by a change in speaker or a repetition of a line.

It is clear from the amount of extant manuscripts that the ballade, the rondel, the carol, and the rhyme royal were among the most popular types of lyric. The traditional form of the ballade is three octave stanzas, rhyming *ababbcbc*, with an optional envoy rhymed *bcbc*. The envoy (from the French *envoi*) is a conventional address to a patron or person of importance that repeats the refrain line and consists of four lines usually rhyming *bcbc*. Ballade stanza length can vary from seven to ten lines, and the line length can vary. Another element of the ballade is the refrain, which contains the motif of the poem and occurs after each stanza. An example of the ballade is Chaucer's "Balade de Bon Conseyl." Another frequent form, the rondel, which is a variant of the *rondeau*, may have been introduced as a stanza form by Chaucer from the French. While fourteen lines are most common, the length of the poem can vary from seven to fourteen lines. A two-line refrain occurs throughout the poem and frequently appears at the very end. The most common rhyme scheme is *ABbaab ABabba AB*, containing only two rhymes with the capitalized rhymes as repeated words. An example is Chaucer's Saint Valentine roundel in *The Parliament of Fowls*, which begins, "Now welcome somer, with thy sonne softe."

The carol, which appeared in the late fourteenth century, is now thought of as a religious lyric, but it was originally defined primarily by its form rather than by its content, so it may also be secular. It includes a regular stanza form and a burden after each stanza, which functions as a refrain but is also found at the beginning of the poem. The most common rhyme scheme for the stanza is *aaab*, with the last line rhyming with the burden's *bb* scheme. Originally, carols were not associated with Christmas and only came to have that connection later in the medieval period. Christmas religious carols focus on the Nativity; one example is *Lullay, Lullay, Litel Child*, which has a four-line stanza rhyming *aaab* and a burden rhyming *ab*. In this carol the speaker is mankind and the lyric is addressed to Christ. Some five hundred or so Middle English carols remain, less than one hundred of which are secular. In Middle English the word "carol" is used to mean "ring-dance," and the carol is intended to be sung as an accompaniment to dancing. The word is probably a derivative of the French *carole*, a ring-dance that can be traced back several centuries earlier. The rhyme royal is a fourth popular form during this period; it consists of a seven-line iambic pentameter stanza with the rhyme *ababbcc*. This was the form favored by Chaucer, William Dunbar, Thomas Hoccleve, and John Lydgate.

The imagery of nature, the public purpose, and the elements of style, sound, and form all appear in the two most frequently cited types of Middle English lyric: the secular and sacred. Ironically, the Franciscans occasionally used the secular lyric in sermons and noted down favorite secular lyrics in the margins of sacred texts. Priests also used preexisting secular lyrics and wrote religious words for them so that their congregations would remember their message. Many of the early secular lyrics seem to have been recorded in fragments, especially the popular lyrics (the *chansons populaires*). There are also courtly lyrics (*chansons courtoises*), which appear in complete form later in the period.

In general, the purposes of the secular and sacred lyrics may be described as Raymond Oliver classified them: to celebrate (an occasion or season), to persuade (for religious or courtship purposes), or to define (a widely accepted position or doctrine, or a state of being). Most medieval lyrics are religious, rather than secular, at a ratio of four to one. The reasons for this are obvious, since most copying of manuscripts was done by religious orders, and in most cases secular lyrics served no practical purpose for the religious orders and thus were less likely to be preserved. In fact, many of the religious lyrics exist in multiple manuscripts, but secular lyrics are usually found only in one. In some cases, such as the songs that celebrate ancient holidays, the nature of the lyric was one of pagan influences and thus was inappropriate for monastic copying.

Many of the religious lyrics are practical in nature and were composed in English as a way of instructing the illiterate populace in religious belief. The lyric may have been used as part of religious ceremony, outside the Latin liturgy, as part of religious drama, as part of church festivals, or in private devotional practices. Approximately 10 percent of Middle English lyrics are translations, including poems by William Herebert, James Ryman, and John Lydgate. In the church service itself, poems used in preaching can be found in collections of Latin sermons (such as the Franciscan preaching book *Fasciculus Morum*, which is written in Latin but includes English lyrics). Some of these use mnemonic devices to help the congregation remember a point of religious doctrine.

Religious lyrics were also used in hymns during the services. Because sacred lyrics use a wide variety of forms, they can best be described by content rather than form. Rosemary Woolf designated four popular categories: poems on Christ's Passion, poems on death, poems on the Virgin and her joys, and poems on the compassion of the Blessed Virgin. Poems on Christ's Passion are designed to create in the mind of the layperson a visual image of Christ suffering in his human form and to evoke through that image strong feelings of compassion and love. The earliest important collection of these poems is found in John of Grimestone's preaching book. The speaking voice in the poems on the Passion can be that of a mediator exhorting the reader to see Christ crucified or of Christ himself urging the reader to "Loke man to my back hou yt ys ybeten, / Loke to my sydyn wat blod it havyn iletyn." These Passion poems have a connection with the secular complaint tradition, in which the speaker complains of his treatment by his beloved or laments the state of the world or his own particular state. In some of the Passion poems Christ is analogous to a lover-knight with whom the speaker is in love. Couched in the terms of the love poem, these lyrics express the idea that the love of Christ is the ultimate love, for which one speaker says, "I sygh and sob both day and nyght for one so fayre of hew"—that "one" being Christ.

A second type of sacred poem is the poem on death. These poems attempt to create an image in the mind of the reader of the appearance of a dying person and the reality of physical decay in order to provoke a response of fear. The fear caused by these "signs of death," or *proprietates mortis*, is intended to bring the reader/listener to salvation. These poems are related to the penitential movement, which emphasized the fear of death to move Christians to repentance and a more religious life. A good example is the fifteenth-century poem in which the speaker explains that he now must "leeve liif that lyvest in welthe." In the persona of a wealthy man who has now died, the speaker says, "I was ful fair, now am I foul." His fair flesh "bigynneth forto stynke," and "wormis" find him as their "mete" and their "drinke." Other less graphic poems appeal to the reader through well-known imagery of the wheel of Fortuna or the Dance of Death, in which people of all social ranks eventually join the dance.

Other death poems take the form of apostrophes to death, as in James Ryman's *O Cruell Deth Paynfull and Smert*, in which the speaker asks, "Why art thou so cruell to man / Of hym no man grisly to make?" Also in this category may be included the poem of contempt of the world or the *contemptus mundi* tradition, which expresses the Middle English anxiety about the transitory nature of this world. This type of complaint frequently uses the *ubi sunt* topos, which sets up a series of parallel "where are" clauses that demonstrate how all material things pass away. An example of this tradition is the late-thirteenth-century "Where beth they, beforen us weren, / Houndes ladden and havekes beren, / And hadden feld and wode?" which conjures up images of the lords and ladies enjoying the material pleasures during life but suffering the pangs of hell for their enjoyment of comforts. Poems on death also frequently use natural images of winter and sunset to emphasize change.

The third type of religious poetry, poems on the Virgin and her joys, includes poems that praise the Virgin (frequently using secular traditions), poems that celebrate the Virgin's five joys (the Annunciation, the Nativity, the Epiphany, her Death, her Assumption), and poems that, like lullabies, picture the Virgin with the Christ child. Poems that praise the Virgin frequently focus on her beauty in ways that are evocative of French love lyrics, using traditional metaphors, such as the rose and the lily, as in the fifteenth-century carol that has as its burden "Ther is no rose of swych vertu / As is the rose that bare Jesu." Poems on the compassion of the Blessed Virgin frequently place Mary at the site of the cross: "They leyde hym dede me before, / Me thouth or sorw my lyfe was lore." The *planctus Mariae*, the complaint of Mary, shows how her own suffering has brought her to an understanding of and compassion for others. At other times she is described weeping over the Christ child as she foresees his death. A well-known example is the poem written around 1400 that begins with the speaker's description of Mary's appearance to him "In a tabernacle of a toure / As I stode musing on the mone." Mary proceeds to describe her role as mother both of Christ and of mankind.

Although there are fewer secular lyrics, they demonstrate the same interesting variety seen in the sacred poems. Most of the secular lyrics occur after the 1370s, when English was more frequently used at court, but there are some scattered early secular lyrics. The earlier lyrics focus more on daily celebrations or activities, such as drinking songs. These early secular lyrics are usually shorter and more straightforward than the later secular lyrics, which are sometimes called "art lyrics" for their intricate artistry. There are approximately three hundred of the later courtly love lyrics, which celebrate (or satirize) the beauty of a woman, plead a lover's case, or complain against a beloved's hard-heartedness or fickleness. Chaucer is the first great Middle English court poet, and he and those who followed in his footsteps used the conventional rhetoric of the aristocratic tradition. Most of these court poems were written for entertainment purposes, as opposed to the sacred poems, which were written for more practical purposes. Chaucer's *Parliament of Fowls* is an example of this genre. Most critics agree that the remaining secular lyrics must be a very small percentage of what once existed. Among the earlier secular lyrics are political poems and poems of social commentary. Many other secular poems are also taken from French genres, such as the *reverdie*, the *pastourelle*, the *chanson d'aventure*, and the *alba*.

The political poems were written primarily between 1250 and 1350. One of the first political lyrics was the satiric "Richard, that thou be ever trichard [deceiver]," written about 1265, which celebrates Simon de Montfort's defeat and capture of Richard, earl of Cornwall, in 1264. Another interesting political lyric serves as a warning to "be ware and be no fool" and to "Thenke apon the ax, and of the stool [execution block]" that were "scharp" and "hard" in "The iiii yere of kyng Richard." John Audelay's early-fifteenth-century poem beginning, "It is the best, erely and late, / Uche mon kepe his owne state," is an interesting poem in which the speaker urges others to stay in their own estate.

The poem of social commentary frequently takes the form of a satire. A well-known example is the satire against the blacksmiths, "Swarte-smekyd smethes, smateryd wyth smoke," in which the speaker complains about the noise and fumes created by these men, whom he says "Dryve me to deth wyth den [din] of here dyntes [blows]." A very popular target for satire was the friar, whose corruption is pointed out in the lyric in which the narrator notes that though he has "yved now fourty yers," he has never seen "fatter men about the neres [kidneys] . . . than are these frers." A third frequent subject for satire was the role of women, as reflected in poems about the *querelle des femmes*, such as *Notbrowne Mayde*, which debates the merits of women. Another type of social poem is the poem on the power of money. An example is the fourteenth-century lyric *Sir Peny*, which describes how "In erth there ys a lityll thyng / That reynes as a grete kyng." That little thing is "Sir Peny." The power of money is also illustrated by a Harleian manuscript poem that relays the difficult life of the poor farmer who is forced to pay heavy taxes.

The *reverdie* is one of the genres borrowed from French sources for the later court poetry. *Reverdie* literally means "greening again" or song of spring; thus it is a lyric celebrating new life that comes with the return of spring. In some cases the *reverdie* occurs only as the opening for another type of poem. A well-known example of the *reverdie* is the opening lines of *Sumer Is I-Cumen In*. The *pastourelle* is another secular genre that comes from French sources. This lyric takes the form of a dialogue in which a rural woman, usually a shepherdess, is wooed by an aristocratic man. The man is frequently a poet, who may be successful or unsuccessful in his suit. The dialogue may be broken off by the appearance of a male relative of the woman. As this genre developed, it contributed to the later Elizabethan pastoral lyric. A similar genre from French sources is the *chanson d'aventure* (song of love-adventure). This lyric is usually a poem about knightly love in which the speaker travels into the country during the springtime and encounters a lady, with whom he carries on a wooing dialogue. An interesting example of this genre that uses readers' expectations to provide a surprise ending is "Nou Sprinkes the Sprai."

The *alba* originated in the French vernacular verse of the twelfth century. The *alba*, or dawn song, is sung by a lover whose secret tryst with a beloved is interrupted by the rising of the sun, which signals the end of their meeting. As Gale Sigal pointed out, the word *alba* means "white" in the Old Provençal, which is associated with the brightness of dawn. The *alba*, unlike some of the other traditional French forms, provides an opportunity for a female speaker, although the poet is usually male. The first Middle English *alba* is found in Chaucer's longer narrative poem *Troilus and Criseyde*. According to Sigal, the *alba*'s characteristics are its theme of separation, its use of dialogue, a refrain containing the word *alba*, and the use of a watchman figure.

Most of the poets who wrote the various types of secular and religious lyrics remain anonymous. In some cases the anonymity is a result of loss of information about the writers, but more often the authors of the earlier lyrics remain unknown because these lyrics were not written in a culture that expected poetic expressions of an individual's emotions and ideas. In the early part of the period most of the lyricists were friars or monks, but as the years progressed, more and more lay people, such as professional scriveners and minstrels, began writing.

The twelfth-century St. Godric (d. 1170) is the earliest known Middle English lyricist; at various times he was a merchant, religious pilgrim, and hermit near Durham. Three hymns are attributed to him, including the devotional *Sainte Marye Virgine*, which is addressed to the Virgin Mary, asking her to receive him, defend him, and cleanse him from sin so that he can be brought to God. Mary reportedly appeared to Godric and "taught him words and music." His second fragment of verse is a four-line hymn that came to him in a vision of his deceased sister. The third lyric, *Cantus Sancto Nicholao*, is the result of a vision in which St. Nicholas appeared. Godric's lyrics are written in roughly four-stress lines. Another early lyricist may have been King Canute (d. 1035), whose *Song of Canute* was recorded by Thomas of Ely around 1167 in his *Liber Eliensis*. According to this source, the four lyric lines were composed by King Canute while listening to monks singing along the banks of the river Ouse. The lyric describes King Canute overhearing the monks' voices and ordering his knights to row nearer the land so that "here we thes muneches saeng."

Reflecting the educational level of churchmen, from 60 to 90 percent of the thirteenth- and early-fourteenth-century lyrics were written by the Franciscan friars, sometimes as direct translations of Latin verse, at other times as devotionals or tools for preaching. The Franciscan movement developed in southern Europe in the late twelfth and early thirteenth centuries and focused on a devotional emphasis within an Augustinian theology. Middle English lyrics began to appear in significant numbers around 1240, approximately twenty years after the beginnings of the Franciscan friars in England, whose movements among the common folk would have exposed them to secular lyrics. Some of the better-known friars during this period were Thomas of Hales (c. 1275), William Herebert (d. 1333), and John Grimestone (c. 1372). Thomas of Hales's *Love Song* to Jesus (thirteenth century) is one of the first Middle English devotionals and combines the secular with the sacred through the image of Christ as a lover. This lyric, intended to be sung by a nun, praises virginity and love for Christ. The poem asks, in *ubi sunt* format, "Hwer is Paris and Heleyne / That weren so bryht and feyre on bleo [appearance]?" Thomas contrasts the mutability of secular love with the permanance and power of the love of Christ.

The work of Herebert, a fourteenth-century Franciscan, survives in seventeen lyrics, most of which are paraphrases of Latin hymns. His "What ys he, thys lordling, that cometh vrom the vyht?" is a paraphrase of Isaiah 63:1–7. John Grimestone, a Norfolk Franciscan, compiled a preaching book around 1372 that contains almost 250 lyric pieces. Preaching books, which were Latin prose manuals with alphabetical lists of sermon topics, frequently included both secular and religious lyrics interspersed with the prose entries. The number of English lyrics included in Grimestone's book is unusual for this period. Richard Rolle of Hampole (c. 1290–1349) was also a poet in the mystical tradition. Born in Yorkshire, Rolle was briefly a student at Oxford and then at nineteen became a hermit, continuing to travel for a while and finally dying at Hampole. Rolle expressed his belief in *The Form of Perfect Living* (c. 1342) that it is sinful to "syng" and "lufe" secular songs; thus he wrote religious lyrics that focus on God's love and the Crucifixion of Christ. Rolle expresses these ideas through his own mystical experience and through instructions for women in religious orders, such as his manual *The Boke Maad of Rycharde Hampole to an Ankeresse*, intended for the nun Margaret Kirkby.

Geoffrey Chaucer (c. 1344–1400), although better known for his narrative poetry, was also a skillful lyric poet. Critical response to his lyric poetry has been negligible until the recent revival of interest in the last decade and a half. In his study of Chaucer's lyrics Jay Ruud argues that although Chaucer's earlier lyrics were more conventional, over time they became more individual expressions and merit reevaluation. Chaucer probably introduced ballades, rondels, and the rhyme-royal stanza into English. Only about twenty-two of his lyrics remain, including the well-known *To Rosemounde, Truth*, "Complaint to His Purse," and *Lak of Stedfastnesse*, although there are at least twelve lyrical segments in his longer works, such as "Hyd, Absolon, Thy Gilte Tresses Clere" in the prologue to *The Legend of Good Women*. Ruud argued that a handful of Chaucer's poems "qualify him as one of the great lyric poets in the English language." Julia Boffey has noted that in addition to introducing the French forms, Chaucer also influenced the development of the Middle English lyric through his presentation of general situations, rhetorical strategies, and rhymes that were imitated by later lyric poets.

Thomas Hoccleve (c. 1369–1426) wrote thirty-eight poems altogether, including both lyrics and longer poetic works, from 1402 to 1422. His lyrics cover a range of topics, from his experiences during his thirty-five years as a clerk in the Privy Seal office to humorous requests for money and hymns to the Virgin. The four lyrics for which he is particularly well known are *How to Die, Mother of God, The Letter of Cupid*, and *Prologue and a Miracle of the Blessed Virgin*. The satirical poem that begins, "Of my lady well me rejoise I may!" turns upside down the conventions of female beauty in lines such as "Hir comly body shape as a footbal, / And she singeth full like a papejay." Hoccleve suffered from mental illness around 1416 but appears to have recovered over the next five years. Hoccleve's admiration for Chaucer is inscribed in the now-famous lines "O Maister dere, and Fader reverent! / My Maister Chaucer, floure of eloquence."

John Lydgate (c. 1370–1450), once considered one of the most important fifteenth-century poets during his lifetime and for 150 years after his death, has suffered adverse criticism of his work and has only recently come under reappraisal. Born around Suffolk, he became a Benedictine monk and spent most of his life at the abbey of Bury Saint Edmunds. About 150,000 of his verse lines are still in existence. Some of his most effective are his poems on the Passion, which conjure up clear visual images of Christ's suffering, including *The Dolerous Pyte of Crystes Passioun*, a poem using the Christ/knight analogy. In this lyric Christ says, "I schal be your Trusty champioun." In a ballade Lydgate uses the *ubi sunt* motif in a series of questions about famous historical figures; each stanza ends with the line "All stand on chaunge as a midsomer rose."

John Audelay (early 1400s) wrote fifty-five extant poems, twenty-five of which are carols, in one manuscript dated 1426. Audelay was a blind priest in Shropshire whose poems contain some personal references in their mention of his blindness and his name. His *O Ihesu Crist Hongyng on Cros* is an example of the lyrics on the Passion, and his *Lady! Helpe, Jesu! Mercy* is an example of a poem about the fear of death. Most of his lyrics are penitential in nature and use a variety of meters and verse forms.

Charles d'Orléans (1394–1465) was French, the nephew of King Charles VI of France and a prisoner in England from 1415 to 1440 after his capture at Agincourt. He is well known for his ballades and rondels and for his *vers de société*. He wrote a series of love poems, including *For Dedy Liif, My Livy Deth I Wite*, a ballade that explores the paradoxical nature of his "living death" as the result of the death of his love, and the humorous *My Ghostly Fader, I Me Confess*, which is written in the form of a confession based on a kiss he "stale" (stole) and now vows to "restore." He, like Chaucer and William Dunbar, is considered a court poet.

James Ryman (late 1400s) was a Franciscan who has been credited with writing 166 lyrics, some of which are Latin hymn translations and 119 of which are carols. Ryman is believed to have penned a quarter of all carols written up to 1550. Ryman's work covers a wide range from the folksy *Farewele! Advent, Christmas Is Come* (noted earlier for its complaint about the fish) to his serious lyrics on religious subjects.

Robert Henryson (1420s or 1430s–c. 1505) is considered the most important of the "Scottish Chaucerians" in the late fifteenth century. Little is known about his life, although his death is mentioned in William Dunbar's *Lament for the Makars*, and some city records indicate that he was a schoolmaster in Dunfermline's Benedictine abbey school. His name is attached to several lyrics, including the interesting *Robene and Makyne*, described as a "pastoral ballad" written in Middle Scots. He is also known for *The Moral Fables, The Testament of Cresseid*, and *Orpheus and Eurydice*.

William Dunbar (1465?–1530) was a well-known "Scottish Chaucerian" who wrote approximately eighty shorter poems, both religious and secular. Quite a few of his secular poems are based on his association with the court of the Scottish James IV, from whom he received a pension between 1500 and 1513. Dunbar received B.A. and M.A. degrees from the University of St. Andrews and around 1504 took religious orders. Among his most frequently anthologized lyrics are the aureate *Hale! Sterne Superne, Hale! In Eterne*, and the allegorical *Done Is a Battell on the Dragon Blak!* Dunbar acknowledged Chaucer and Lydgate as his models. He is particularly known for his satires and allegories. Arthur K. Moore argued that Dunbar, as the last of the Middle English lyric poets, serves as a transition to the Renaissance lyricists.

As the preceding discussion makes apparent, the best-known Middle English lyricists were men. The two best-known Middle English women writers, Julian of Norwich and Margery Kempe, wrote in prose, and two other well-known medieval women writers, Christine de Pisan and Marie de France, wrote in French and had their works translated into English during this period. However, a study of Middle English women's writing by Alexandra Barratt argues that there were women lyricists during this period. Barratt discusses the fifteenth-century Juliana Berners, whose verse translation of *The Book of Hunting* is more practical than lyrical. More interestingly, in chapter 16 Barratt argues that there is good reason to believe that some anonymous fifteenth-century poems were written by women. In three cases poems are specifically ascribed to women: *A Hymn to Venus* is credited to Queen Elizabeth (wife of Edward IV), and two hymns to the Virgin are attributed to "an holy anchoress of Mansfield" and to Eleanor Percy, duchess of Buckingham. In addition to these attributions, there are other poems that Barratt felt may have been written by women because of their treatment of the topic and their tone, including two poems previously attributed to Chaucer, *The Assembly of Ladies* and *The Floure and the Leaf.*

Middle English lyrics appear in a variety of places. Among the most common sources are the collections of sermons, the miscellanies, compilations of devotional materials, and books of hymns. These collections were compiled by scribes or friars who usually were not the authors of the lyrics. The most famous manuscript that includes Middle English lyrics is the British Library Harley manuscript, which contains thirty-two lyrics, twenty-four of a religious nature and eight that are secular. The Harley manuscript, which includes lyrics (and prose) in English, French, and Latin, was copied at the Herefordshire priory between approximately 1250 and 1340. The anonymous lyrics are in several different dialects. To get a sense of what is contained in the Harley manuscript, see G.L. Brook's edition of *The Harley Lyrics* (1956) or N.R. Ker's *Facsimile of British Museum MS. Harley 2253* (1965).

Other important collections (of a religious nature) are found in John of Grimestone's preaching book mentioned earlier and the late-fourteenth-century Vernon Manuscript. Lyrics also appear in some of the mystery plays, such as the lullaby *Lulla, Lulla* lyric that appears in the Coventry Nativity play and poems in the Towneley shepherd and Nativity plays addressed to the Christ child. The drinking song of Noah's wife and her gossips in the Noah play is another popular example of a dramatic use of secular lyric.

Early critical response to the Middle English lyric was limited because the Middle English lyric was considered less sophisticated and worthy than its continental contemporaries. Among the earliest studies were Felix E. Schelling's *The English Lyric* (1913) and Edward Bliss Reed's *English Lyrical Poetry: From Its Origins to the Present Time* (1914). In the 1930s Carleton Brown's *English Lyrics of the XIIIth Century* and Richard L. Greene's *The Early English Carols* were among the first scholarly collections. *The Index of Middle English Verse*, compiled by Carleton Brown and R.H. Robbins (1943), provided a list of manuscripts, which has since been updated. Other important early collections include G.L. Brook's *The Harley Lyrics: The Middle English Lyrics of MS Harley 2253* (1948), Arthur K. Moore's *The Secular Lyric in Middle English* (1951, reprinted 1970), and R.H. Robbins's *Secular Lyrics of the XIVth and XVth Centuries* (1952).

Other anthologies followed these early editions, including R.T. Davies's *Medieval English Lyrics: A Critical Anthology* (1964), Robert D. Stevick's *One Hundred Middle English Lyrics* (1964, revised and reissued in 1994), and Lewis and Nancy Owen's *Middle English Poetry: An Anthology* (1971). In 1982 George Pace and Alfred David edited the variorum edition of Chaucer's *Minor Poems*.

Critical appreciation of the sacred Middle English lyric began to escalate after the publication of Stephen Manning's *Wisdom and Number: Toward a Critical Appraisal of the Middle English Religious Lyric* (1962). Other works that examine the lyric in its religious context include Rosemary Woolf's *The English Religious Lyric in the Middle Ages* (1968), Sarah Appleton Weber's *Theology and Poetry in the Middle English Lyric* (1969), Douglas Gray's *Themes and Images in the Medieval English Religious Lyric* (1972), David L. Jeffrey's *The Early English Lyric and Franciscan Spirituality* (1975), Patrick Diehl's *The Medieval European Religious Lyric: An Ars Poetica* (1985), and Siegfried Wenzel's *Preachers, Poets, and the Early English Lyric* (1986).

Other useful critical appraisals of the lyric appear in books and articles. Among the books are Raymond Oliver's *Poems without Names* (1970), Edmund Reiss's *The Art of the Middle English Lyric* (1972), Lois Ebin's edited collection of articles *Vernacular Poetics in the Middle Ages* (1984), Daniel J. Ransom's *Poets at Play: Irony and Parody in the Harley Lyrics* (1985), Douglas Gray's edited and completed version of J.A.W. Bennett's *Middle English Literature* (1986), Alasdair MacDonald's valuable introduction to the Middle English lyric in *Companion to Early Middle English Literature* (1988), and Robert R. Edwards's *Ratio and Invention: A Study of Medieval Lyric and Narrative* (1989). Interesting articles include Rossell Hope Robbins's "The Middle English Court Love Lyric" (1980), John Scattergood's "Social and Political Issues in Chaucer: An Approach to Lak of Stedfastnesse," and John Stephens's "The Uses of Personae and the Art of Obliqueness in Some Chaucer Lyrics."

SELECTED BIBLIOGRAPHY

Barratt, Alexandra, ed. *Women's Writing in Middle English*. London and New York: Longman, 1992.

Boffey, Julia. "The Reputation and Circulation of Chaucer's Lyrics in the Fifteenth Century." *Chaucer Review* 28.1 (1993), 23–39.

Cornell, Christine. " 'Purtreture' and 'Holsom Stories': John Lydgate's Accommodation of Image and Text in Three Religious Lyrics." *Florilegium* 10 (1988–1991): 167–178.

Figg, Kristen Mossler. *The Short Lyric Poems of Jean Froissart*. New York: Garland, 1994.

Fries, Maureen. "(Almost) without a Song: Criseyde and Lyric in Chaucer's *Troilus*." *Chaucer Yearbook* 1 (1992): 47–63.

McClellan, William. "Radical Theology or Parody in a Marian Lyric of Ms Harley 2253." *Voices in Translation: The Authority of "Olde Bookes" in Medieval Literature*. Ed. Deborah M. Sinnreich-Levi and Gale Sigal. New York: AMS, 1992. 157–68.

Moore, Arthur K. *The Secular Lyric in Middle English*. Lexington: University of Kentucky Press, 1951.

Oliver, Raymond. *Poems without Names; The English Lyric, 1200–1500*. Berkeley: University of California Press, 1970.

Pickering, O.S. "Newly Discovered Secular Lyrics from Later Thirteenth-Century Cheshire." *Review of English Studies* 43 (1992): 157–180.

Reiss, Edmund. "The Middle English Lyric." *Old and Middle English Literature*. Ed. Jeffrey Helterman and Jerome Mitchell. Vol. 146 of *Dictionary of Literary Biography*. Detroit: Gale, 1994. 392–399.

Ruud, Jay. *"Many a Song and Many a Leccherous Lay"; Tradition and Individuality in Chaucer's Lyric Poetry*. New York: Garland, 1992.

Sigal, Gale. *Erotic Dawn-Songs of the Middle Ages: Voicing the Lyric Lady*. Gainesville: University Press of Florida, 1996.

Stevick, Robert D., ed. *One Hundred Middle English Lyrics*. Rev. ed. Urbana: University of Illinois Press, 1994.

Wilhelm, James J., ed. and trans. *Medieval Song*. New York: Dutton, 1971.

Wimsatt, James. *Chaucer and His French Contemporaries: Natural Music in the Fourteenth Century*. Toronto: University of Toronto Press, 1991.

Woolf, Rosemary. *The English Religious Lyric in the Middle Ages*. Oxford: Clarendon, 1968.

16

The Middle English Parody/ Burlesque

Keith P. Taylor

During the final decades of the fourteenth century three poems appeared that scholars perpetually have considered to be among the finest examples of the romance genre ever to have been composed in English. Two of these—"The Knight's Tale" (c. 1380) and *Troilus and Criseyde* (c. 1385)—belong to Chaucer; the third is the anonymous alliterative masterpiece *Sir Gawain and the Green Knight* (c. 1390–1400). But at virtually the same moment that the romance tradition reaches its apex in England, we see the rise of a body of poetry that gently—and humorously—takes the romance tradition to task. Though much poetry of this type, to which we refer collectively as Middle English "parody/burlesque" literature, is preserved in manuscripts dating from the very end of the fourteenth century through the middle of the fifteenth century, we should not take this fact to indicate that poetry of this sort did not exist in England—or in English—prior to that time. The parody is, after all, among the oldest of the literary genres. It exists almost by convention wherever there is a vogue to be burlesqued. If we take tradition to be our guide, then the sheer volume of romance literature produced in England from the time of the Norman Conquest until the end of the fourteenth century ought to suggest that any number of poems parodying this tradition once circulated throughout the island via the oral tradition, only to vanish without ever having had the good fortune simply to have been written down.

It is not at all difficult to account for the virtual absence of English parody/ burlesque literature in manuscripts prior to the end of the fourteenth century, particularly when we consider that for several centuries following the Norman Conquest, the readership of England was comprised almost exclusively of persons who did not regularly speak English. Given this state of affairs, it is hardly surprising that virtually all of the parodic literature that has survived in pre-fourteenth-century manuscripts is composed either in French (the language of the English noble caste) or, in the case of the ubiquitous liturgical and hagiographic parodies of the period, in Latin (the universal language of the clergy). During the fourteenth century, however, the constitution of the medieval English readership was irrevocably altered by a series of historical phenomena, most notably the rise of the English middle class and the adoption of the London dialect of English as the official language, first of Parliament (1362) and then of the schools (1385). As more and more members of the English middle class became both literate and able to afford the sorts of codices that had once been available only to those in the very highest echelons of the English aristocracy, we begin to find preserved in manuscripts, probably not merely by coincidence, a series of poems parodying the romance that appear to have been composed with the interests of a distinctly middle-class audience in mind, the very kinds of poems that in earlier days might easily have been lost to posterity. Among the most important poems of this sort are *The Tournament of Tottenham* (c. 1400–1440) and *The Wedding of Sir Gawain and Dame Ragnell* (c. 1450), both anonymous. However, it is to the satiric genius of Geoffrey Chaucer, himself a privileged member of the English middle class, that Middle English parody/burlesque literature undoubtedly owes its greatest debt. In his hands the courtly conventions of the romance tradition, conventions with which Chaucer over and over again demonstrates his intimate familiarity, simultaneously receive their most artistic and most irreverent treatments. His numerous contributions to the parody/burlesque genre, most notably "The Tale of Sir Thopas" (c. 1390) and "Complaint to His Purse" (c. 1400), stand today as some of the finest parodies ever composed, not merely in English, but in any language.

Of course, the single greatest barrier to any but the most cursory discussion of the Middle English parody/burlesque is that our own cultural vantage point, which is now some six centuries removed from that of Chaucer and his contemporaries, sometimes renders the humor of the earliest English parodies difficult for us to understand or appreciate. It is easy enough to say, for example, that the Middle English parody/burlesque is everything that the Middle English romance is not. Yet if one is not already reasonably well acquainted with the literary conventions that once governed the romance tradition in both France and England, then the later Middle English poems that purport to lampoon this tradition have all the humorous impact of a punch line taken out of context. This being the case, it seems important that we pause at the outset of this glance into the workings of Middle English parody/burlesque literature, if only long enough to construct a working definition of the genre as it generally appears in Middle English. This is difficult to do except via reference to the poetry of romance tradition, at which, as I have mentioned earlier, the greatest portion of Middle English satire is directed.

The Middle English romance can be described most succinctly as a courtly literature composed primarily for a courtly audience. As such, it is predominately a literature of courtly manners and "ideals," and the poetry of this genre extols by convention the aristocratic virtues of chivalric knighthood, courtly love, courteous kingship, and the unattainable quest. By contrast, the vast majority of Middle English parody/burlesque literature, including the texts that we will consider in this chapter, pokes fun at the courtly conventions of the romance tradition, normally either by treating in the elevated style typical of the romance a series of subjects and characters that could best be described as "common" or by burlesquing those characters who had come to exemplify the aristocratic ideals at the thematic locus of the English romance—Arthur and Gawain, for example. Obviously, poetry of this sort seldom sets its sights on a single aspect of the romance tradition; however, for the sake of simplicity, I have structured this necessarily quick look at the Middle English parody/burlesque as though this were the case. In the paragraphs that follow, we will consider one at a time and in some detail a series of the most important conventions of the romance tradition as they appear in the very best Middle English poetry of that genre; we will then turn our attention to the poem in Middle English that scholars generally have taken to contain the single most effective satire of this convention. Proceeding in this fashion, let us begin, as Chaucer himself does in the "General Prologue" to his *Canterbury Tales*, by glancing at the conventions surrounding those "parfit, gentil knight[s]" who, for better or worse, most often find themselves cast as the heroes of the Middle English romances.

As Wim Tigges has noted, we find at the heart of virtually every romance "a single hero of aristocratic birth or aspiration and chivalric nurture (usually a knight), who undertakes an adventure (in the form of one or more tests and/or quests), the successful achievement of which leads to the favour of the hero's feudal lord, his lady, and/or his God" (129). Though Chaucer's knight is not himself the hero of a romance per se, the description of him with which Chaucer heads the portraits of his Canterbury pilgrims reads like a veritable compendium of the attributes customarily ascribed to the hero of a romance. As such, it comprises what is arguably the single most concise account of the conventions surrounding the romance hero in the corpus of Middle English poetry. We know by virtue of his rank, for example, that Chaucer's knight is indeed a member of the noble estate; but more than this, Chaucer's narrator tells us that his knight is a "worthy man"—a man of integrity—who prizes above all else the cardinal virtues of "chivalrie / Trouthe and honour, fredom and curteisie" (*Canterbury Tales* [*CT*] I.43, 45–46). During the course of his career, we learn, this knight has undergone a series of adventures that have taken him to the boundaries of the Christian world and beyond. He has campaigned in Alexandria, Prussia, Lithuania, Russia, Spain, and Turkey (*CT* I.51–66); he has been a member of "many a noble armee" (*CT* I.60); and he has participated in no fewer than "mortal batailles . . . fiftene" (*CT* I.61) with such great success that "Ful ofte tyme he hadde the borde bigonne / Aboven alle naciouns" (*CT* I.51–52). Like the typical romance hero, Chaucer's knight is certainly a dynamic man of action.

Yet though he has proven himself "ful worthy . . . in his lordes werre" (*CT* I.47), Chaucer's narrator seems to imply that this knight is more to be revered for the purity of his heart than for his performance on the battlefield. Perhaps our best evidence to this effect is to be found in the intimation of Chaucer's narrator that this knight had "foughten for oure feith at Tramyssene / In lystes thries, and ay slayn his foo" (*CT* I.62–63). Benson has pointed out that "lystes," or "formal duels" "between champions of opposing Christian and Moslem armies were fought as late as the seventeenth century" (801), and he rightly observes that "since no Christian army is known to have attacked Tlemcen during the fourteenth century," some critics have taken this statement to mean that "the knight [probably] was [in Tlemcen] as a mercenary serving the Arabs" (801).

Historically speaking, this reading is wholly sound; however, given the laudatory tone that pervades the description of the knight, I think that it is equally reasonable to presume that Chaucer's allusion here to a duel between two opposing champions, particularly champions of different religious backgrounds, would have recalled to the imagination of the medieval audience those trials by combat that often figure into the medieval romances. We must remember that at least insofar as the medieval romancers were concerned, the outcome of such a trial had very little to do with the military skill or strength of the combatants involved; rather, convention held that the results of these trials were determined by God, who awarded victory to the champion whom he deemed to be more pure of heart. In pointing out as he does that this knight had participated in three such duels and "ay slayn his foo," Chaucer's narrator simultaneously implies that this knight had thrice submitted himself to the judgment of God and that, in every case, he had been "honoured for his worthynesse" (*CT* I.50).

It is the shortcoming of many a romance hero that he ultimately shows himself to lack either *sapientia* (wisdom) or *fortitudo* (strength). Chaucer's narrator, however, suggests that this is not at all the case with his knight, who appears to owe his "sovergne prys" (*CT* I.67) to the fact that he lacks neither of these qualities, that he is "worthy" as well as "wys" (*CT* I.68). In addition, he is possessed of courtesy and humility, two qualities in which the romance heroes themselves are sometimes sadly lacking. Despite his obvious military prowess, this knight is "of his port as meeke as is a mayde" (*CT* I.69). He is likewise loath to abuse the authority of his position; Chaucer's narrator says of the knight that "He nevere yet no vileynye ne sayde / In al his lyf unto no manere wight" (*CT* I.70–71). The knight cares little for appearances. He arrives "to doon his pilgrymage" riding a horse that the narrator of *The Canterbury Tales* describes only as "goode" (*CT* I.74) and wearing a coarse tunic "al bismotered with his habergeon" (*CT* I.75–76). In short, Chaucer's portrait of his knight, characterized as it is by strength, wisdom, purity, courtesy, and humility, is also in many ways a portrait of the ideal romance hero. In fact, one could easily make the case that Chaucer's knight is more aptly suited to be the hero of a romance than many of the heroes of the romance tradition itself.

The conventional romance hero exemplified by Chaucer's knight finds its parodic counterpart in the guise of Sir Thopas, the subject of a mock romance that Chaucer the pilgrim tells in response to Harry Bailey's request for a "tale of myrthe" (*CT* VII.706) to lighten the spirits of the pilgrims, which have been understandably dampened by the Prioress's somber tale of a miracle of the Virgin. Chaucer begins his parody of the romance hero with an appeal to the members of his audience for their attention. He proceeds to place "The Tale of Sir Thopas" superficially within the confines of the romance tradition by announcing in the most formulaic of terms that he intends to recite a poem full "Of myrthe and of solas, / Al of a knight was fair and gent / In bataille and in tourneyment" (*CT* VII.714–716). Yet in the moment that he names the purported hero of the tale, "sire Thopas" (*CT* VII.717), Chaucer belies any narrative expectations that the members of his audience might have held for his poem to this point. The word "thopas," literally translated, means "topaz," and this precious stone had long garnered the praise of the medieval lapidarists for its numerous exceptional qualities, most notably its ability to promote chastity. This is a "knightly" virtue, to be sure. The topaz, however, was also held to possess peculiar reflective properties; as E.S. Kooper has pointed out, "in the Middle Ages the topaz was credited with the property of reflecting images as if it were a hollow mirror, i.e. upside down" (147). By naming the hero of this poem as he does, Chaucer tacitly attributes to Sir Thopas each of the qualities customarily associated with the topaz. In this fashion Chaucer winks to his audience; he hints to them that in the tale that is to follow, Sir Thopas, for all his heroic intent, will reflect the conventions of the romance tradition as if he were himself a funhouse.

Indeed, the actions and demeanor of Sir Thopas ultimately show him to be the distorted inverse of all that the members of the medieval audience had come to expect from the heroes of their romances. Thopas, it turns out, hails from Flanders (*CT* VII.719), a region that, during the fourteenth century, was recognized as a center of commerce. By virtue of Sir Thopas's ties to Flanders, Chaucer's audience immediately would have recognized Sir Thopas to be a member of the mercantile class. As if this were not enough to suggest to his audience that Sir Thopas is wholly unfit for the duties of knighthood, Chaucer goes on to point out, more specifically, that Thopas was born in "Poperyng" (*CT* VII.720), "a Flemish town noted for its cloth . . . and its pears" (Benson 918). Considering that during the Middle Ages cloth production was held to be a distinctly feminine occupation (it is, in fact, the profession of Alisoun of Bath) and that pears are likewise feminine in shape, there is no escaping the connotation of Chaucer's reference here. By casting Sir Thopas not merely as a resident, but as the prince of Poperyng "As it was Goddes grace" (*CT* VII.723), Chaucer implies that Thopas is an effeminate man and thus ill suited to trials of the sort to which the romance heroes are subjected on a regular basis.

Chaucer emphasizes these points—Sir Thopas's less-than-noble birth and his femininity—throughout his description of this would-be knight. He calls our attention, for example, to Sir Thopas's most prominent physical features, taking special care to mention his face "Whyte . . . as payndemayn"; his "lippes red as rose"; his "rode" (a term meaning "complexion" and applied almost exclusively to women) "lyk scarlet in grayn"; and his "semely nose" (*CT* VII.725–729). We often find features of this sort cataloged in the poetry of the romance tradition, but almost never in reference to a man. Rather, what we have in Chaucer's physical description of Sir Thopas is a list of those traits most commonly attributed to the ideal courtly woman; in fact, the narrator of *The Canterbury Tales* mentions several of these features in conjunction with the Prioress (*CT* I.118–162), who apparently does what she can to create the impression that she is a woman of precisely this sort. Even Sir Thopas's horse speaks to his effeminate demeanor. During the second fit of the poem we discover that Thopas's steed of choice is an "ambler," a type of horse with a slow, easy gait that made it a favorite of woman; this is indeed the very kind of horse upon which Alisoun of Bath has chosen to make her way to Canterbury (*CT* I.69).

Sir Thopas is likewise hopelessly out of touch with the courtly fashions of his day. Though long hair (for men, at least) had been out of style for some time by the late fourteenth century, Chaucer tells us that Thopas has allowed his hair and beard to grow to the point that both "to his girdle raughte adoun" (*CT* VII.731). Similarly, Thopas's attire—Chaucer mentions specifically his Cordovan leather shoes, his brown hose from Bruges, and his silk robe (*CT* VII.732–734)—is not merely rich; it is both gaudy and unsuited to the most simple of knightly pursuits. This is of no consequence, however, for Thopas apparently dedicates very little of his time to the tournament or quest. Yet he is not altogether untalented: Chaucer calls Thopas "a good archere" and notes that "Of wrastlyng was ther noon his peer / Ther any ram shal stonde" (*CT* VII.738–740). Pastimes such as these, however, were hardly the province of the aristocratic caste to which Sir Thopas so gallantly aspires. Thopas is, after all, not the first character in *The Canterbury Tales* whom Chaucer has recognized for his ability to wrestle well; that honor falls to the miller, the Chaucerian personification of all that is ignoble.

Chaucer continues in this vein throughout "The Tale of Sir Thopas," availing himself of every opportunity to burlesque the prospective hero of his mock romance. Whereas the romance heroes often are afforded ample opportunity to demonstrate their skill in combat against the likes of dragons, forest trolls, bulls, bears, and boars (as is the case with Sir Gawain in *Sir Gawain and the Green Knight* 720–722), Sir Thopas has no such luck. Chaucer merely sends his knight pricking "thurgh a fair forest" populated by "many a wilde best / Ye, bothe bukke and hare" (*CT* VII.754–756). In retrospect, one realizes that this is probably in Sir Thopas's own best interests, for when Thopas finally finds himself confronted by a reasonably formidable adversary, Sir Olifaunt, he responds by threatening to meet the giant the next day, when he is in possession of his armor, so that he may deliver a punishing blow to Sir Olifaunt's stomach (*CT* VII.817–826). It is also probably just as well for Sir Thopas that Harry Bailey abruptly brings his story to an end before he is able to keep his date with destiny. In the mock arming sequence that comprises the better part of the second fit of the poem, Sir Thopas outfits himself with no less than "an aketoun, / And over that

an haubergeoun / For percynge of his herte: / And over that a fyn hawberk"
(*CT* VII.860–863), the combined weight of which could have served only to
hinder a man of Sir Thopas's "sydes smale" in combat (*CT* VII.736). To make
matters worse, we learn that Thopas intends to carry with him into battle, among
other things, an ornamental sword complete with a "shethe of yvory" (*CT*
VII.876); a helmet of "latoun" (*CT* VII.877), a soft metal that would not have
protected Sir Thopas from even the most perfunctory blow to his head; and a
spear of "fyn ciprees" (*CT* VII.881), which, unlike ash (the material from which
spears were normally constructed), would have bent and broken under pressure.
Armed in this fashion, Sir Thopas hardly would have been a match for the bucks
and hares that populate Sir Olifaunt's forest, much less for Sir Olifaunt himself.

For these reasons and others too numerous to mention here, it is difficult to
understate the irony inherent in Chaucer's suggestion that above even the most
famous of heroes of the romance tradition, it is Sir Thopas who "bereth the
flour / Of roial chivalry" (*CT* VII.901–902). Yet there is at least one convention
of the romance that emerges from "The Tale of Sir Thopas" relatively unscathed.
Early in the poem Sir Thopas finds himself smitten at the thought of the fair
maiden, an "elf-queene" (*CT* VII.787–790), whom he pledges to love despite
the fact that she is tragically out of his reach (albeit, in Sir Thopas's case,
because she exists only in his imagination). It is via this episode of "The Tale
of Sir Thopas" that Chaucer alludes to the sort of relationship between a knight
and his lady that had long been a commonplace of the medieval romance. In
the romance tradition such relationships are governed by the rules of "courtly
love" and usually begin when a knight beholds from afar a woman who, by
virtue of her beauty alone, renders him "astoned" (*Troilus* I.274). Because this
woman is for some reason unapproachable (typically she is promised to another),
this knight has little choice but to undergo a period of suffering on her behalf,
at the completion of which he pledges his troth to this woman and resolves that
he will demonstrate the depth of his love for her as best he can by becoming
her chaste and faithful servant. It is the hope of this knight that eventually his
selfless dedication to this lady will inspire her to take pity on him and return
his love for her, though when courtly love takes a turn for the carnal (as in the
cases of Troilus and Criseyde and Lancelot and Guinevere, for example), it too
often does so with tragic results.

During his initial period of suffering the courtly lover is wont to compose
verses in which he simultaneously laments the anguish of his unrequited love,
deifies her who is the cause of his distress, and petitions a power higher than
himself to reverse the unfortunate circumstances of his plight. Many such lyric
poems, generically termed "love complaints," have survived to us from the Middle Ages; among the most noteworthy of these are the anonymous fifteenth-
century "Complaint to a Pitiless Mistress" (MS British Library Sloane 1212)
and Chaucer's own "Complaint unto Pity" and "Complaint to His Lady." Love
complaints are likewise a staple of the medieval romance, and the "Canticus
Troili" ["Song of Troilus"] that appears early in Book I of Chaucer's *Troilus*

and Criseyde exemplifies lyric poetry of this sort as it tends to appear within the context of the romance tradition.

In the initial stanzas of the "Canticus Troili," Troilus struggles to make sense of his feelings for Criseyde, which he describes in almost completely Petrarchan terms. He characterizes the "torment and adversite" he experiences at the thought of Criseyde as something to be savored rather than shunned, as a drink, one draught of which has inspired perpetual thirst (*Troilus* I.404–406). He calls his love for her a "quick dethe," a "swete harm so quente," and a "wondre maladie"; but finding himself unwilling to forsake the person whom he knows to be the source of his "illness," Troilus cannot understand the basis for what he calls his "waillynge and [his] pleynte" (*Troilus* I.407–413). Thus scorched by "owen lust" and this conflagration of opposites that plagues him, Troilus concedes that in his current emotional state, he is destined to be "possed to and fro / Al stereless withinne a boot . . . / Amydde the see, bitwixen windes two, / That in contrarie stonden evere mo" (*Troilus* I.415–418). It is therefore in the concluding stanzas of his song that Troilus "with pitous vois" appeals to the God of Love, asking only that he "beth to him benigne" (*Troilus* I.431). In return, Troilus pledges his spirit to love and all else that he possesses to Criseyde, assenting ever to honor them both by doing service to the "goddesse or womman" for whom love has led him "ay [to] lyve and sterve" (*Troilus* I.425–427).

Although the setting of *Troilus and Criseyde* is decidedly pagan, it is important to notice that the purgative process that Troilus undergoes during the course of the "Canticus Troili" is distinctly Christian in origin. In the initial stanzas of the "Canticus Troili," Chaucer positions Troilus as a man tormented by the consequences of his sins against love. Conversely, in the final stanzas of the poem Troilus seeks absolution for these sins, first by confessing them to the God of Love; then by repenting of them; and finally by demonstrating the depth of his contrition by agreeing to perform the penance necessary to absolve him of his guilt. Allusions such as these to the rituals of the Christian faith are a conventional component of the medieval love complaint; indeed, they appear almost as if to signify what the medieval poets took to be the sacrosanct nature of courtly love itself.

However, in the poem that many scholars believe to have been his last, Chaucer parodies the lover's complaint by assuming the persona of the scorned courtly lover only that he might pledge his troth to the least noble of "mistresses"—his purse. Chaucer begins his "Complaint to His Purse" by declaring his purse to be his "lady dere" (2); in so doing, he shows the persona of his poem to be the inverse of the conventional courtly lover, who under normal circumstances would be only too eager to eschew the worldly comforts epitomized by the image of the purse in deference to the selfless pursuit of his lady. He follows this statement with a series of puns that take their humor from the multiple meanings of "hevy" and "lyght" in Middle English. Applied to objects, of course, these terms almost always designate weight. However, these terms could likewise be used to describe a person's countenance, and in this context the term "lyght" would mean "happy" or "cheerful," while the term "hevy" would denote sadness or sobriety. By playing as he does upon the several possible readings of the terms "hevy" and "lyght" in the initial stanza of the "Complaint to His Purse," Chaucer manages at the outset of his poem to reverse the entire paradigm of the love complaint. Understood from a purely literal standpoint, the first lines of Chaucer's poem apologize to his mistress for her cheerfulness (3), ask her to look upon her lover with "hevy cher" (i.e., "sternly") (4), and beg her in what will develop into the poem's refrain to become "hevy ageyn" (7).

For the remainder of his "Complaint to His Purse," Chaucer works to consecrate the ties that bind a poet to his purse by burlesquing the central precept of the courtly love tradition, the concept of courtly love as sacrament. He does this primarily by applying to his purse a series of formulaic epithets that, rhetorically speaking, cause his purse to undergo a gradual apotheosis. Chaucer begins this process in the second stanza of his poem by lauding the figurative complexion of his purse, which he says glows in its "hevynesse" with a "colour lyk the sonne bryght / That of yelownesse hadde never pere" (10–11). Having successfully placed the beauty of his purse on a par with that of the natural world by means of a contrived Petrarchan conceit, Chaucer proceeds to lift up his purse to the heavenly sphere. He concludes the second stanza of his complaint by addressing his purse in conspicuously Marian terminology, calling it his "lyf," his "hertes stere," and the "Quene of comfort" (12–13), and finally raises his purse in the third stanza of the poem to the Christlike position of his "lyves lyght / and saveour" (15–16). Thus it is within the space of seven lines that Chaucer manages to elevate this least sacred of concerns—the pursuit of material gain signified by his purse—to a position normally reserved by the courtly lover for the lady whom he serves: that of his goddess. Finding that he is in no position to redress the unbearable lightness of his purse, Chaucer prays in the envoy of his poem to a power far greater than himself—the "conqueror of Brutes Albyon" (22)—that he might "Have mynde upon [his] supplicacion" (26) and rectify the circumstances that are the cause of his "lady's" suffering— not to mention, of course, his own.

Often in the romance tradition the predicament of the loyal knight turned courtly lover is complicated by the fact that he discovers himself to be but one of many men competing to gain the attention of the woman to whom he has secretly sworn his allegiance. When it at last becomes apparent to them that their fervent prayers to God (or the God of Love) have gone unanswered, these men tend to take matters into their own hands and agree to participate in a tournament, each of them hoping to prove himself most worthy of this lady's affection by besting her potential paramours in combat. The narrative pattern to which the medieval romancers adhere as they report the goings-on at these tournaments is as conventional to the romance tradition as the concept of the tournament itself. Such reports typically begin with a recapitulation of the names (and, when necessary, the lineages) of the knights who are about to do battle.

Following this, we normally see a detailed account of the arming and heraldry of the combatants involved in the tournament, which is almost always described in superlative terms. These tournament knights tend to wear the most brilliant of armor and carry the most elaborate of shields and banners sporting their coats of arms. They sit astride the most valiant of war-horses and carry the most daunting of weapons. In this fashion, we learn that these competing knights are both the best trained and (potentially) most noble of warriors.

After vowing in turn that their performance on the field will bring honor to their lords and the ladies they would serve, these knights take their positions on the field, and a blow-by-blow account of the tournament itself ensues. During the course of the contest untold numbers of lances and shields are splintered, and men routinely deal one another such grievous buffets that they fall together with their horses to the earth (this is almost always the case in Malory). However, in tournaments of this nature the measure of a knight's worth does not lie merely in the number of men he manages to best; it lies instead in his willingness to fight not only valiantly, but honorably. Invariably the knights who are proclaimed the victors of these tournaments are those who refuse to attack an opponent when they hold an unfair advantage over him. They are the knights who are unwilling to deliver a second blow when the first was sufficient to render their adversary harmless, who give their own horses to the knight whose horse they inadvertently have slain, who seek not to add insult to their rivals' injuries. In the romance tradition only a man of this caliber, a man whose righteousness has attracted the very attention of God, can find the strength necessary to overcome each of his competitors and emerge from the tournament victorious.

It is difficult to imagine an assembly of men less likely ever to participate in combat of this sort than the group of peasant lads and "trewe drynkers" (18) vying for the hand of "Tyb, þe dere" in *The Tournament of Tottenham*. However, by describing the misguided exploits of these rustic "bachelors" precisely as though he were detailing the proceedings of a chivalric contest, the anonymous fifteenth-century author of the poem systematically burlesques the dignified rites of the tournament proper. *The Tournament of Tottenham* is very much a study in contrasts, and much of the poem's humor stems from the incongruous gravity with which the poet recounts the details of a "tournament" that ultimately devolves into little more than a country brawl. The initial lines of the poem, for example, are almost epic in tone; the author of *The Tournament of Tottenham* promises his audience a story of "kene conquerours" and "fele fyʒtyng-folk" (1–2). He immediately undercuts this promise by proclaiming the subject matter of his poem to be the "Tournament of Tottenham" (3). The poet's juxtaposition here of the terms "Tournament" and "Tottenham" probably would have both surprised and amused the members of his late-fourteenth/early-fifteenth-century audience, who would have understood Tottenham to be a rural province of England populated primarily by members of the peasant class. For this reason Tottenham would have been among the least likely of settings for a "tournament" in any conventional sense of the word.

The impetus for the contest itself would have seemed equally absurd to the medieval audience of the poem. Its members certainly would have chuckled at the notion that so "hardy" a group of men would be willing—much less required—to submit to the hardships of battle solely in order to determine who among them is "best worthy" (26) to wed a woman who, strictly speaking, is not worth a great deal in the first place. Even Tyb's father seems unable to believe that this is the case; to the man who "berys hym best in þe turnament" he promises, not only the hand of his daughter, but a modest assortment of farm animals, including his own "spottyd sowe" (46–54). That Tyb's father would so generously endow his daughter after her potential suitors have already agreed to compete against one another on her behalf would seem to suggest that, at least in the eyes of her father, Tyb is not herself a dowry.

Tyb may be no Guinevere, but the men contending for her attention are hardly Lancelots themselves. Having spent a full week preparing their clothes for the tournament, this rabble returns to the tournament field with all the pomp and circumstance of a barbarian horde. The poet tells us that they come to do battle "armed . . . in mattis" (59) and "schepe-skins" (64). In place of helmets they sport "Gode blake bollys" designed "to kepe þer pollys . . . / For batryng of battis" [protect their noggins against the battering of bats] (60–63). The greatest part of their heraldry is the "blak hat" that each wears "insted of a crest" (65). These men take harrows for their breastplates (see Cooke, "Provenance" 115); they carry flails rather than lances; and they arrive at the tournament astride mares rather than war-horses (66–72). Thus ridiculously arrayed, these men clearly would not have been able to fight or defend themselves with anything akin to what the poet suggests is the "mekyl fors" they show on the field (69), and for the poet to refer to this throng of peasants as a "gret cumpany" (74) is obviously nothing short of preposterous.

The vows that these men exchange as they prepare to do battle likewise are bereft of nobility. Harry promises, for example, that he "schal not lefe behende" in the contest (91); in other words, he promises nothing more than to participate actively in the tournament. Dawkin swears to "mete with Tomkyn, / His flayl hym refe" [to meet with Tomkin and deprive him of his flail]—not as impressive a feat, one presumes, as wresting a lance from a well-trained knight (98–99). Hud boasts to Tyb of his "clere" coat of arms, upon which he proudly displays "a reddyl and a rake / Poudred with a brenand drake, / And iii cantell of a cake in ycha cornare" [a sieve and a rake decorated by a burning dragon and three slices of cake in each corner] (105–109). Terry boldly proclaims his intention to cheat in the contest; he declares that in the heat of battle he will simply withdraw from the field, "take Tyb by þe hand and hur away lede" (121). But once the tournament itself gets under way, these men rapidly discover what already is only too clear to the audience of the poem: for all their well-laid plans, they are simply incapable of staging an organized chivalric contest. Within the space of an afternoon (a proper tournament would have taken days to complete), Tyb's suitors find their "weapons" in pieces and their mares too tired to run, and their so-called tournament develops into a rustic wrestling match from which no one escapes entirely unscathed.

One gets the distinct impression that the Tournament of Tottenham would have gone on indefinitely had it not been for the women of the parish, who abruptly bring an end to the contest when they arrive at the end of the day to claim the exhausted combatants. These men competing for Tyb's hand, it turns out, are even less worthy to marry her than their modest performance on the battlefield might have otherwise indicated, for nearly all of them are already "trouth-plyȝt" [engaged or married] to other women. Perkin the Potter appears to be the notable exception to this rule; consequently, he is "graunt[ed] . . . þer þe gre" [awarded the prize] (208), and he celebrates his victory with Tyb in the least "courtly" fashion imaginable: by spending the night with her. Apparently the two have quite an evening. The poet tells us that Perkin "So wele hys nedys has . . . sped / Þat dere Tyb he has wed" [So well achieved his desires that he has wed dear Tyb] (213–214), and the poet moves quickly to an account of Tyb's wedding feast, at which the many "pryse folk" who fought (and lost) at the Tournament of Tottenham dine "Euery v and v [on] a cokenay" (227).

The poet's use of the term "cokenay" here conventionally has been difficult for editors of the poem to gloss. Probably the most satisfactory reading of the term to date is that proposed by Cooke, who argues that "cokenay" most likely means " 'cock's egg,' alluding to a popular belief that unusually small or misshapen eggs were laid by cocks." Cooke concludes that in saying that the wedding party dined on "rich fare, namely one poor egg to every five," "the poet is exhibiting his characteristic irony." However, there may be another level to the poet's satire here. As Cooke points out, the term "cokenay" was routinely applied during the Middle Ages (as it is in "The Reeve's Tale" at line I.2408) "to men thought to have small or misshapen testes, and hence to any man thought to lack virility" ("Provenance" 116). By concluding his poem as he does, with Tyb's unsuccessful suitors partaking of so dubious a delicacy at a feast celebrating the tangible evidence of Perkin's victory over them, the poet seems to imply that the lack of courtesy and "gentilesse" that characterizes the behavior of Tottenham's "bachelery" is not the greatest of their shortcomings.

But whereas *The Tournament of Tottenham* is content merely to satirize the ceremonial pageantry of chivalric knighthood, *The Wedding of Sir Gawain and Dame Ragnell* (one of several fifteenth-century analogues to Chaucer's "Wife of Bath's Tale") burlesques the values and precepts at the thematic epicenter of the romance tradition: the code of chivalry itself. The poem accomplishes this by offering its audience a strikingly irreverent look at the conduct of two icons of the English romance, Arthur and Gawain. The nature of the satire in *The Wedding of Sir Gawain and Dame Ragnell* is not at all difficult to appreciate, provided that one comes to the poem fully cognizant of the fact that by the mid-fifteenth century Arthur and Gawain were no longer considered by default to be paragons of chivalric virtue. It is fairly obvious why this is true in Arthur's case. Historically speaking (and a medieval English audience would have understood the tenets of what we call the Arthurian myth to have been rooted in history), Arthur's preoccupation with his reputation had led him to make a series of rash decisions that were held to have contributed in no small measure to the dissolution of the Round Table and the eventual collapse of Camelot. Even the *Gawain* poet speaks to these facets of Arthur's persona: when the Green Knight questions the reputation of his court, Arthur, we are told, "wex as wroth as wynde" (*Sir Gawain and the Green Knight* 321) and, without thinking, agrees to participate in the contest that Morgan le Fay has designed only to dishonor him. While the English romancers tend to downplay these less attractive attributes of Arthur's character, the author of *The Wedding of Sir Gawain and Dame Ragnell* constantly alludes to them, particularly in the opening sequence of the poem. In the formulaic preface to his tale, for example, he rehearses the reputation of Arthur via a series of thinly veiled invectives. Though he initially calls Arthur a king "curteys and royalle" (6), he is equally quick to point out that "of alle knyghtod [Arthur] bare away the honour" (8). This statement can be taken in either of two ways. Figuratively, it is a compliment: the poet is telling us that Arthur was routinely considered to be "the most honorable of knights." But literally what these words say is that Arthur himself took the honor out of knighthood. As if to provide an explanation for his unusually harsh assessment of Arthur's kingship, the poet points out that "In his contrey was nothyng butt chyvalry" (10). The poet's use of the word "chivalry" here is particularly telling, for in Middle English this term can refer either to the ceremonial rites of knighthood or to the code of conduct that a knight was sworn to uphold. Early in the romance tradition there was indeed "nothing but chivalry" in Arthur's court; he and his knights were renowned for their courtesy, their bravery, and their humility. However, a mid-fifteenth-century audience would have understood that one of Arthur's great failings will turn out to be his preoccupation with the appearance of his court, his reluctance to acknowledge (until it is too late) that his knights' behavior often belies their noble reputation. The knights of the Round Table eventually are more widely recognized for their dishonesty and treachery than for their courtesy, and the author of *The Wedding of Sir Gawain and Dame Ragnell* is quite right to suggest that by the time Camelot falls, there is "nothing but chivalry" in Arthur's country; nothing remaining of a once-great code but the rituals of knighthood themselves.

Arthur's behavior in The *Wedding of Sir Gawain and Dame Ragnell* is the antithesis of what we would expect from a man whom the poet previously has described as "curteys and royalle." During the poem's initial hunting sequence Arthur becomes suddenly (and inexplicably) "ferce and felle" as he pursues the deer he has wounded (46). Immediately thereafter Arthur happens upon Sir Gromer Somer Jour, who accuses the king of having "done [him] wrong many a yere"; specifically he berates Arthur for having "gevyn [his] landes in certayn, / Withe greatt wrong vnto Sir Gawen" (55–59). Sir Gromer Somer affords Arthur the opportunity to respond to these accusations, and, interestingly enough, Arthur does not deny them. Instead, he merely asks to know the name of his assailant. When Sir Gromer Somer proposes to kill Arthur for his misdeeds, the great king is reduced to begging for mercy. In exchange for his life, Arthur promises to grant Sir Gromer Somer whatever he desires and reminds the knight in the fashion of Sir Thopas that it would be dishonorable for him "to sle [the king] in venere," the knight being "armyd" and Arthur "clothyd butt in grene" (80–83).

Sir Gromer Somer finally relents, on the condition that Arthur will promise to return alone and unarmed to their meeting place in one year, bringing with him the answer to the question that will save his life: "What is it that women most desire?" Arthur agrees, and Sir Gromer Somer releases him, admonishing him to "kepe alle thyng in close" [keep the proceedings between them a secret] (111). Arthur promises to do so, vowing that Sir Gromer Somer shall never find him an "Vntrewe knyghte" (116). However, upon his return to Carlisle, the king immediately discloses the terms of his arrangement with Sir Gromer Somer to Gawain, even though Arthur himself acknowledges that in so doing, he is "forswore" (148).

The Arthur we meet in *The Wedding of Sir Gawain and Dame Ragnell* is, in short, nothing more than a grossly misshapen caricature of the courteous king whose noble exploits are at the heart of the English romance tradition. He is unjust, cowardly, dishonest, and all too willing to forsake the chivalric code of behavior in the moment he finds that it is in his own best interests to do so. But Gawain's conduct in *The Wedding of Sir Gawain and Dame Ragnell* is as surprisingly gallant as Arthur's is absurdly unbecoming. In order to understand precisely why this is the case, we must first remember that within the literature of the Arthurian tradition, the evolution of Sir Gawain's character is such that he eventually is stripped of the bravery, courtesy, loyalty, and humility for which he long had been renowned. Whereas the Gawain of the early continental romances—Chrétien's *Erec*, for example—is a man who "ranks first among the knights of the Round Table [and whose] courtesy acts as a foil to the crudity and churlishness of Kay" (Roger Loomis 160), Gawain's name comes by the thirteenth-century to be synonymous with disloyalty. John Mathews notes, for example, that in the prose *Tristan* Gawain is depicted as a man obsessed by thoughts of revenge "against King Pellinore and his family, whom [Gawain and his brothers] blame for the deaths of their father, King Lot, and their mother, Morgause; and that of Gawain alone for Lancelot and his kin, for the death of his brothers Gareth and Gaheries" (163). In the course of pursuing this revenge, Mathews points out, Gawain becomes the partner-in-arms of Modred in a feud that ultimately divides the Round Table. Gawain himself murders Pellinore and assists in the murders of Pellinore's sons (164). His actions throughout the text show him to be discourteous in every way; indeed, he "displays a lustful desire for every woman he sees and is not above fatally wounding an unarmed escort in order to have his way" (165).

This treatment of Gawain extends far beyond the prose *Tristan*. A.L. Morton carefully traces what he calls the gradual degradation of Gawain's character through the later French romances, particularly those treating the Grail Quest. In the process he is able to show that although Gawain "originally [was] the hero of the Grail Quest, he is deposed in favour of Lancelot, of Percival . . . and finally by Galahad" (17). Morton suggests that ultimately Gawain's character undergoes this sort of decline "because Gawain was a primitive figure, with the character of the pre-feudal age still strong upon him"; for this reason, Morton argues, "he came to seem by Church and feudal standards as morally unacceptable," and since Gawain "was no longer regarded as an especially edifying character," he was allowed by the romancers "to resume his old amoral nature." As evidence of Gawain's corruption in the later French romances, Morton points to a number of episodes from Malory's *Morte d'Arthur* that, taken together, are illustrative of Gawain's declining moral conduct. Among these he includes "the killing of Lamorak and his gross breach of faith in seducing Ettarde after he had promised to win her for Pelleas," noting that Gawain's actions in these romances "could not possibly be squared with the code of chivalrous behaviour: he is depicted as rash, passionate, and bloody-minded, so that even his own brother condemns him" (18).

If we bear in mind that by the fifteenth century Gawain had acquired an utterly ignominious reputation, then the portrait of him that we find in *The Wedding of Sir Gawain and Dame Ragnell* becomes absolutely fraught with irony. Gawain's well-known predilection for treacherous behavior, for example, renders moot his suggestion to Arthur that he is "nott that man that wold [the king] dishonour, / Nother by euyn ne by moron" (150–51); quite the contrary, in the Arthurian tradition Gawain is the single person most likely to dishonor his uncle at any given moment. Under normal circumstances Gawain would like nothing more than to see Arthur humiliated or destroyed, so the idea that he would agree to aid Arthur in his quest for the answer to Sir Gromer Somer's question is ludicrous. Gawain's predisposition to lecherous conduct with beautiful women makes it difficult for one to imagine that he would so readily consent to marry Dame Ragnell, a woman whom Arthur describes as "the fowlyst lady, / That euere [he] sawe sertenly" (336–337). In the unlikely event that he were forced to marry such a woman, Gawain certainly would not have afforded her the courtesy he shows Dame Ragnell by agreeing to marry her in public.

There are those critics who would argue that *The Wedding of Sir Gawain and Dame Ragnell* is much more a burlesque of Arthur than of Gawain, that Gawain's conduct in the poem squares very nicely with his depiction in the English romances, most notably *Sir Gawain and the Green Knight*. Scholars who hold this opinion (and there are many of them) would see nothing at all strange about the moment in *The Wedding of Sir Gawain and Dame Ragnell* when Arthur declares that "Of all knyghtes [Gawain bears] the flowre" (373). In the isolated context provided for it by the narrative of the poem, this statement is admittedly appropriate; Gawain has just agreed to marry Dame Ragnell, and Arthur is offering his nephew a well-deserved compliment for his bravery, his humility, and his selfless devotion to his lord. But I think that we would be wrong to ignore the broader satiric implications that Arthur's statement here probably would have held for a medieval English audience. For them, the outcome of the story of Arthur had already been fixed by history, and in the final analysis Arthur had shown himself to be a very poor judge of character where Sir Gawain had been concerned. He had often placed his trust in Gawain, and in virtually every case his nephew had betrayed him. For this reason, the irony inherent in Arthur's suggestion that of all his knights, it is Gawain who "bears the flower" would not have been lost on the original audience of the poem. It should not be lost on us either.

Scholarship touching medieval parody/burlesque literature in English is surprisingly sparse. There are few book-length studies specifically of the genre itself, and those books that have been written tend to concentrate primarily on the parody/burlesque in Latin. Still, the body of scholarly work treating the medieval Latin parody in particular is invaluable for the insight that it offers into the workings of the Middle English parody itself. In this regard, Lehmann's *Die Parodie im Mittelalter* (1922; 2nd ed. 1963) and, more recently, Bayless's *Parody in the Middle Ages* (1996) are especially noteworthy. Similarly, Gravdal's *Vilain and* Courtois: *Transgressive Parody in French Literature of the Twelfth and Thirteenth Centuries* (1989) does much to clarify the form and function of the genre in the literature of the medieval European tradition as a whole. Though Dane's *Parody: Critical Concepts versus Literary Practices, Aristophanes to Sterne* (1988) does not deal exclusively with the literature of the Middle Ages, it likewise is essential reading; students of the medieval parody will be especially interested in Dane's chapter on Lehmann, in which Dane questions the definition of "parody" adopted by Lehmann as the basis of his seminal text.

Concerning the Middle English parody in particular, Kitchin's chapter on the "Mediaeval Burlesque" in his *Survey of Burlesque and Parody in English* (1931), though it is now somewhat dated, serves as a concise, general introduction to the various incarnations of the parody/burlesque both in Latin and in the vernacular. The prefatory and explanatory material that Garbáty provides for the texts he anthologizes in his *Medieval English Literature* (1984) is also incredibly helpful. From a critical standpoint, however, the single best introduction to parody/burlesque literature in Middle English is undoubtedly that by Wim Tigges in *Companion to Middle English Romance* (1990). In his chapter "Romance and Parody" Tigges provides a succinct yet thorough history of the scholarly debate concerning the aesthetic principles of the medieval parody/burlesque and surveys a broad range of such poetry both in Middle English and Middle Scots so as to draw our attention to their distinctly metatextual elements. His work, which goes far beyond the scope of this chapter, is certainly not to be missed.

Insofar as the individual Middle English parodies themselves are concerned, it is unsurprising to find that those by Chaucer, particularly his "Tale of Sir Thopas," have garnered by far the greatest amount of critical attention. Interestingly, "Sir Thopas" was not considered by Chaucer's earliest critics to have been a burlesque at all. In fact, as Dane notes in his 1985 article "Genre and Authority: The Eighteenth-Century Creation of Chaucerian Burlesque," the poem generally was held to have been, in the words of Thomas Wharton, "a grave heroic narrative." Dane traces the generic transformation that "Sir Thopas" undergoes at the hands of the late-eighteenth-century critics in order to demonstrate that "*Sir-Thopas-the-Burlesque* is better characterized as an eighteenth-century creation rather than an eighteenth-century discovery" (345).

By the early twentieth century this reading of Chaucer's "Sir Thopas" as a parody/critique of the romance tradition had become well established, and in the types of source and analogue studies typical of that period, scholars began working to identify the romance in particular that Chaucer had intended to burlesque. As Laura Loomis notes, Charles Strong (1908) was among the first to recognize in "Sir Thopas" a series of references to the *Speculum Guy de Warwick*; Loomis herself goes on to identify the version of *Guy of Warwick* found in the Auchinleck Manuscript as the direct manuscript source for "The Tale of Sir Thopas." Scholars since that time (see Brewer 1966, Fisher 1977, and L. Benson 1987) have universally acknowledged Chaucer's indebtedness to the Auchinleck *Guy* for the "phrasings and details and even incidents of his burlesque" (L. Loomis 111). In more recent years scholars have returned to the text of the poem itself in order to elucidate the many parodic features of *"Sir Thopas"* that critics heretofore have overlooked. Tschann (1985), for example, has noticed that "in more than half of the manuscripts which preserve *Sir Thopas* . . . the method of indicating the verse form for this tale differs from that used for any other of the tales" (2). She points out that in manuscript "the [overly elaborate] layout of *Sir Thopas* does more than indicate the verse form; it comments upon it" (3) by "call[ing] attention to the skill of a poet who is so good at being bad" (7). This being the case, she concludes that "we modern readers of the printed tale miss some of the fun" of "Sir Thopas" (10). Both C. David Benson (1983) and Kooper (1984) have noted a series of (sometimes-ironic) connections between "The Tale of Sir Thopas" and its counterpart in *The Canterbury Tales*, "The Tale of the Melibee." Benson considers the "link between *Thopas* and *Melibee*" in order to demonstrate that each tale is designed to "explor[e] the relationship between the way a tale is told and its ultimate significance" (68), and Kooper posits that just as "Sir Thopas" inverts the image of the romance hero, "The Tale of the Melibee," is an ironic inversion of "The Tale of Sir Thopas" itself (152). Cullen (1974) has noted a series of "sexual and phallic references" in "Sir Thopas." Among the most interesting of these concerns the carbuncle that decorates Sir Thopas's shield, which she reads as "his defense against 'soft sore,' the common term for a venereal disease in Chaucer's day."

Aside from the sort of general commentary on "Complaint to His Purse" that one finds in virtually every major edition of Chaucer's works, scholars have had little to say about the poem. In 1967 Ferris attempted (quite successfully) to date the poem more accurately via reference to the historical documents con-

cerning Chaucer's "final annuity." Ludlum (1976) was among the first to notice
the "heavenly word-play" in the poem, the formulaic references to the Virgin
Mary that appear in its second stanza, and Ruud (1983) has offered further
support in favor of Donaldson's reading of "toune" in line 17 of Chaucer's
"Purse" as "state of being" rather than as a city (London, for instance). The
most recently published article concerning "The Complaint to His Purse" seeks
to contextualize the poem in terms of what Paul Strohm (1992) calls "the fab-
rication of the Lancastrian claim."

There are, however, a number of studies that consider the satiric elements of
other of Chaucer's poems, most specifically "The Miller's Tale," which is more
properly considered a fabliau than a burlesque. In this regard, Coffman (1952)
has argued that "The Miller's Tale" contains a Chaucerian burlesque of "the
Seven Liberal Arts." Kaske (1962), for example, pointed to Chaucer's parody
of the "*Canticum Canticorum* in the *Miller's Tale*," and Gellrich (1974) has
noted that throughout "The Miller's Tale," "the songs of characters sound con-
cordant with sacred tunes, but are rather discordant in intention" (186). Though
"The Miller's Tale" does contain a series of parodic elements, it is interesting
to note that critics have not always been able to agree upon precisely what
literary genre Chaucer is burlesquing here. Harder (1956) and Prior (1986) both
have argued that Chaucer may have written "The Miller's Tale" as a parodic
commentary upon the mystery plays, either to showcase what Harder calls the
"uncouthness" of the mystery plays (193) or in order to teach his audience that
"clerks who rewrite salvation history may burn (here, if not in hell)" (Prior 73).
Nearly all critics now accept that at least at one level, "The Miller's Tale" does
function as a parody of the medieval mystery cycles. In addition, however,
Miller (1970) has argued that the poem functions as a parodic "complaint against
the estates, conducted however from an anti-authoritarian point of view" (147),
and Jordan (1984) has seen "The Miller's Tale" as a burlesque of the fairy tale.

Much of the critical commentary concerning both *The Tournament of Tottenham* and *The Wedding of Sir Gawain and Dame Ragnell* appears in the editions
of these poems that have surfaced from time to time during the twentieth century. The most significant recent work on *The Tournament of Tottenham* is
undoubtedly that by Cooke (1988), who has done much to resolve a number of
the cruces generated by the intrinsic lexical difficulties of the poet's northern
dialect. Also of note are articles by Jones (1951) and Harris (1997), who endeavor to make better sense of the nature of the burlesque in *The Tournament
of Tottenham* by comparing the rituals of rustic tournaments to the events detailed in the poem; Zaerr and Baldassarre (1990), who consider the role that
music plays in *The Tournament of Tottenham*; and Wright (1997), who revisits
the long-standing critical question as to the nature of the poem's burlesque.
Similarly, scholars such as Shenk (1981), Field (1982), Glasser (1984), and
Aguirre (1993) have mined *The Wedding of Sir Gawain and Dame Ragnell* for
the value it obviously holds as an analogue to Chaucer and Malory, but of late,
only Garbáty ("Rhyme," 1984) has dwelt for long on the significance of the

poem as a burlesque in its own right. For this reason, both *The Tournament of Tottenham* and *The Wedding of Sir Gawain and Dame Ragnell* remain especially fertile ground for new scholarship.

SELECTED BIBLIOGRAPHY

Aguirre, Manuel. "The Riddle of Sovereignty." *Modern Language Review* 88.2 (1993): 273–282.

Bayless, Martha. *Parody in the Middle Ages: The Latin Tradition.* Ann Arbor: University of Michigan Press, 1996.

Benson, C. David. "Their Telling Difference: Chaucer the Pilgrim and His Two Contrasting Tales." *Chaucer Review* 18 (1983): 61–76.

Benson, Larry D., ed. *The Riverside Chaucer.* 3rd ed. Boston: Houghton Mifflin, 1987.

Brewer, D.S. "The Relationship of Chaucer to the English and European Traditions." *Chaucer and Chaucerians: Critical Studies in Middle English Literature.* Ed. D.S. Brewer. University: University of Alabama Press, 1966. 1–38.

Busby, Keith. *Gauvain in Old French Literature.* Amsterdam: Rodopi, 1980.

Coffman, George R. "The Miller's Tale, 3187–3215: Chaucer and the Seven Liberal Arts in Burlesque Vein." *MLN* 67 (1952): 329–331.

Cooke, W.G. "The Tournament of Tottenham: An Alliterative Poem and an Exeter Performance." *Records of Early English Drama Newsletter* 11.2 (1986): 1–3.

———. "*The Tournament of Tottenham*: Provenance, Text, and Lexicography." *English Studies* 69.2 (1988): 113–116.

Cullen, Dolores. "Chaucer's *The Tale of Sir Thopas.*" *Explicator* 32 (1974): item 35.

Dane, Joseph A. "Genre and Authority: The Eighteenth-Century Creation of Chaucerian Burlesque." *Huntington Library Quarterly* 48 (1985): 345–362.

———. *Parody: Critical Concepts versus Literary Practices, Aristophanes to Sterne.* Norman: University of Oklahoma Press, 1988.

Dannenbaum, Susan. "*The Wedding of Sir Gawain and Dame Ragnell*, Line 48." *Explicator* 40 (1982): 3–4.

Ferris, Sumner. "The Date of Chaucer's Final Annuity and of the 'Complaint to His Empty Purse.' " *Modern Philology* 65 (1967): 45–52.

Field, P.J.C. "Malory and *The Wedding of Sir Gawain and Dame Ragnell*." *Archiv* 219.2 (1982): 374–381.

Fisher, John H., ed. *The Complete Poetry and Prose of Geoffrey Chaucer.* New York: Holt, Rinehart and Winston, 1977.

French, W.H. and C.B. Hale, eds. *Middle English Metrical Romances.* New York: Prentice-Hall, 1930. New York: Russell & Russell, 1964.

Garbáty, Thomas J., ed. *Medieval English Literature.* Lexington, MA: D.C. Heath, 1984.

———. "Rhyme, Romance, Ballad, Burlesque, and the Confluence of Form." *Fifteenth-Century Studies: Recent Essays.* Ed. Robert F. Yeager. Hamden, CT: Archon, 1984. 283–301.

Gellrich, Jesse M. "The Parody of Medieval Music in the *Miller's Tale*." *Journal of English and Germanic Philology* 73 (1974): 176–188.

Glasser, Marc. " 'He Nedes Moste Hire Wedde': The Forced Marriage in the *Wife of Bath's Tale* and Its Middle English Analogues." *Neuphilologische Mitteilungen* 85.2 (1984): 239–241.

Gravdal, Kathryn. Vilain *and* Courtois: *Transgressive Parody in French Literature of the Twelfth and Thirteenth Centuries.* Lincoln: University of Nebraska Press, 1989.

Harder, Kelsie B. "Chaucer's Use of the Mystery Plays in the *Miller's Tale*." *Modern Language Quarterly* 17 (1956): 193–198.

Harris, A. Leslie. "Tournaments and The Tournament of Tottenham." *FCS* 23 (1997): 81–92.

Hartwell, David G. "The Wedding of Sir Gawain and Dame Ragnell: An Edition." Diss. Columbia University, 1973. Ann Arbor: UMI, 1973. 7328216.

Jones, George F. "The Tournaments of Tottenham and Lappenhausen." *PMLA* 66 (1951): 1123–1140.

Jordan, Tracey. "Fairy Tale and Fabliau: Chaucer's *The Miller's Tale*." *SSF* 21 (1984): 87–93.

Kaske, R.E. "The *Canticum Canticorum* in the *Miller's Tale*." *Studies in Philology* 59 (1962): 479–500.

Kitchin, George. "Mediaeval Burlesque." *A Survey of Burlesque and Parody in English.* 1931. New York: Russell & Russell, 1967. 1–37.

Kooper, E.S. "Inverted Images in Chaucer's *Tale of Sir Thopas*." *Studia Neophilologica* 56 (1984): 147–154.

Lehmann, Paul. *Die Parodie im Mittelalter: Mit 24 ausgewählten parodistischen Texten.* 2nd ed. Stuttgart: A. Hiersemann, 1963.

Loomis, Laura H. "Chaucer and the Auchinleck MS: 'Thopas' and 'Guy of Warwick.' " *Essays and Studies in Honor of Carleton Brown.* London: H. Milford, Oxford University Press, 1940. 111–128.

Loomis, Roger S. *The Development of Arthurian Romance.* New York: Norton, 1970.

Ludlum, Chas. D. "Heavenly Word-Play in Chaucer's 'Complaint to His Purse.' " *Notes and Queries* 23 (1976): 391–392.

Mathews, John. *Gawain: Knight of the Goddess.* Wellingborough: Aquarian Press, 1990.

Miller, Robert P. "*The Miller's Tale* as Complaint." *Chaucer Review* 5 (1970): 147–160.

Morton, A.L. "The Matter of Britain: The Arthurian Cycle and the Development of Feudal Society." *Zeitschrift für Anglistik und Amerikanistik* 8 (1960): 5–28.

Nykrog, Per. "Courtliness and the Townspeople: The Fabliaux as a Courtly Burlesque." *The Humor of the Fabliaux.* Ed. Thomas D. Cooke and Benjamin L. Honeycutt. Columbia: University of Missouri Press, 1974. 59–73.

Prior, Sandra Pierson. "Parodying Typology and the Mystery Plays in the Miller's Tale." *Journal of Medieval and Renaissance Studies* 16 (1986): 57–73.

Robinson, F.N., ed. *The Complete Works of Geoffrey Chaucer.* 2nd. ed. Boston: Houghton Mifflin, 1957.

Ruud, Jay. "Chaucer's 'Complaint to His Purse.' " *Explicator* 41 (1983): 5–6.

Sands, Donald, ed. *Middle English Verse Romances.* New York: Holt, Rinehart and Winston, 1966.

Shenk, Robert. "The Liberation of the 'Loathly Lady' of Medieval Romance." *Journal of the Rocky Mountain Medieval and Renaissance Association* 2 (1981): 69–77.

Skeat, W.W., ed. *The Complete Works of Geoffrey Chaucer.* 7 vols. Oxford, 1894–1900.

Strohm, Paul. *Hochon's Arrow: The Social Imagination of Fourteenth-Century Texts.* Princeton: Princeton University Press, 1992.

Sumner, Laura, ed. *The Weddynge of Sir Gawen and Dame Ragnell.* Northampton, MA: Smith College, 1924.

Tigges, Wim. "Romance and Parody." *Companion to Middle English Romance*. Ed. Henk Aertsen and Alasdair A. MacDonald. Amsterdam: VU University Press, 1990. 129–151.

Tschann, Judith. "The Layout of *Sir Thopas* in the Ellesmere, Hengwrt, Cambridge Dd.4.24, and Cambridge Gg.4.27 Manuscripts." *Chaucer Review* 20 (1985): 1–13.

Whiting, B.J. "The Wife of Bath's Tale." *Sources and Analogues of Chaucer's Canterbury Tales*. Ed. W.F. Bryan and Germaine Dempster. New York: Humanities Press, 1958. 242–264.

Wright, Glenn. "Parody, Satire, and Genre in *The Tournament of Tottenham* (1400–1440)." *FCS* 23 (1997): 152–170.

Zaerr, Linda Marie, and Joseph A. Baldassarre. "*The Tournament of Tottenham:* Music as an Enhancement to Prosody." *FCS* 16 (1990): 239–252.

17
Riddles

Michelle Igarashi

LOCATION, DEFINITION, AND CHARACTERICTICS

There are ninety-five extant Old English riddles. They appear in the Exeter Book, MS 3501 in the Library of the Dean and Chapter of Exeter Cathedral, circa 965, believed to be the earliest codex of Old English literature. It was donated by Leofric (d. 1072) when he moved the episcopal see from Crediton to Exeter in 1046, and was recorded as "i micel englisc boc be gehwilcu[m] þingu[m] on leoðwisan geworht" ("a large English book about various things written in verse").

There are seventeen gatherings in the Exeter Book, most in regular quaternions and with approximately twenty-two lines of text. The first and second sets of riddles, 1–59 and 30b and 60, appear in gatherings 13 (folios 98–105) and 14 (106–111), respectively. There are gaps after folios 105 and 111 that account for missing lines at the end of Riddle 20 and Riddle 40. The third set of riddles appears in gatherings 16 and 17 and concludes the Exeter Book itself.

Today we have only five single folios in the last gathering. John Pope discovered that a folio was missing in gathering 16 in the middle of Riddle 69 (after the word "gesceapo" in line 4). This lacuna prevents the accurate count of riddles and makes it impossible to tell if one or more folios are missing from the beginning of gathering 17. As most gatherings are quaternions, as mentioned earlier, up to three folios may be missing from the end of the book (in addition to the one at the beginning of the gathering). Bernard Muir conjectures that these missing folios may have contained a final six riddles, thus bringing the total to one hundred, the standard number set by Symphosius, who is considered by many to be the "father" of Western riddling.

As with most riddles, Anglo-Saxon enigmata are often viewed in terms of metaphor. Aristotle made the first connection between metaphors and riddles in general: "Good riddles do, in general, provide us with satisfactory metaphors: for metaphors imply riddles, and therefore a good riddle can furnish a good metaphor" (*Rhetoric* 170). Furthermore, as Ruth Wehlau asserts, "Metaphor is the intrusion of the concrete into the mind. In the world of language, . . . it is metaphor that brings the physical or sensory into our thoughts. At the same time, metaphor reveals the concrete grounding to most of our concepts. Metaphor is in fact a point of contact between an inner and outer world, between the accessible and familiar experience of our bodies in the world and the symbolic concepts that are the requirement of language" (1).

The Anglo-Saxons utilized metaphors throughout their poetry with such devices as the kenning, for example, the often-mentioned "hwælweg" or "whale-road," and descriptive word compounds such as "banhus," "bone-house," or "breostcofa," "breast-box." Johan Huizinga contends that "when the poet says 'speech-thorn' for 'tongue,' 'floor of the hall of winds' for 'earth' and 'tree-wolf' for 'wind,' . . . he is sending his hearers poetic riddles which are tacitly solved" (133–134). Indeed, such words are riddlelike because they ask the reader to break down the metaphor, envision the literal image, then transform it once again into a symbol that reveals the "actual" picture desired.

Thus it is not surprising that the Anglo-Saxons created at least ninety-five elaborate metaphors or riddles. These works offer a glimpse into everyday Anglo-Saxon existence not presented in other poetic genres. In the enigmata we see animals such as badgers, oysters, hens, and even the lowly gnat; home-used objects like bellows, plows, and rakes; Christian items and concepts, for example, the chalice, chrismal, and Creation; elements of nature such as storms, the sun, and the moon; and such miscellanea as recipes for parchment making and, concealed in double entendres, dough and butter.

This is not to say that one may consider a riddle and thereby view a direct reflection of an entire people. Indeed, one must keep in mind that enigmata are a literary form and therefore have authors, individuals with unique perspectives, approaches, and sensibilities, who do not necessarily represent the entire culture. Still, when riddles are considered in conjunction with each other and with other genres, the differences between individual authors are diminished, especially in the case of the Old English riddles, where we cannot assign authorship, and there is no discernible difference in style and tone between various riddles. These poems illustrate how the Anglo-Saxons saw themselves through the veil of poetry and deliberate puzzling. Therefore, while the Old English riddlers work to subvert understanding and twist meaning, the scholar, by unraveling the language and images hidden beneath these conundrums, can put together a literary Anglo-Saxon world.

All riddles, whether literary, *Kunsträtsel*, or folk, *Volksrätsel*, in origin, reveal a culture's traditions, norms, and mores. Every clue—each phrase, each line, often each word—carries cultural information that the intended riddlee as well as outsiders, be they from another class or even another time period, must consider in order to "get" the riddle. The need for such careful consideration requires the reader or audience member to understand both the riddler and the world behind his/her words, for behind every riddle is a person, and each riddle is told in relation to the effect of its subject upon humankind.

The Old English riddlers included neither titles nor solutions in their works. These omissions have caused heated debates among critics attempting to find definitive solutions for each poem, for instance, Riddle 4:

> Ic sceal þragbysig   þegne minum,
> hringan hæfted,   hyran georne,
> mind bed brecan,   breahtme cyþan
> þæt me halswriþan   hlaford sealde.
> Oft mec slæpwerigne   secg oðþe meowle
> gretan eode;   ic him gromheortum
> winterceald oncweþe.   Wearm lim
> gebundenne bæg   hwilum bersteð,
> se þeah biþ on þonce   þegne minum,
> medwisum men,   me þæt sylfe,
> þær wiht wite,   ond wordum min
> on sped mæge   spel gesecgan.

(I, fettered with rings, must, long busy, quickly obey my thane, break my rest, and loudly proclaim that my lord gave me a halter. A man or a maiden has often called on me sleep-weary. I, winter cold, answered them, hostile-minded. Sometimes a warm limb bursts [the] bound ring. That [one] is, however, acceptable to my thane, [a] foolish man, and likewise to me, if I know anything, and may say my answer with words successfully.) Craig Williamson discusses the various solutions posed by scholars:

> The most likely solutions to the riddle, "bell" and "millstone," were put forth by Dietrich.
> . . . Holthausen . . . first solved the riddle as "lock," but later . . . accepted *Handmühle*.
> Erhardt-Siebold accepts "handmill" and argues that the "ring" is the journal-box or socket
> in which a pivot (the "warm limb") turns. . . . Recently, Shook . . . solved the riddle as
> "feðer" of "Penna," taking the "ring" to be the reinforced nib wound about with thread
> and the breaking of the "ring" to be (somewhat illogically) the breaking of the nib. (Old
> English Riddles 142)

One should keep in mind several facts concerning these riddles. First, no titles are provided for any work in the Exeter Book. Indeed, no titles are given for any of the poems in the four extant manuscripts: Cotton Vitellius A. xv, Vercelli, Junius II, and of course, the Exeter Book. Second, the poetic qualities of the riddles are in no way diminished by the lack of identifying labels. Third, titles have attention-limiting as well as freeing qualities. When one approaches a titled work, one's focus has already been directed by the author. One knows from which position or direction one must experience the piece. Therefore, returning to the riddles, the absence of guiding labels allows one the freedom to study the works from different angles, considering different dimensions and weighing one possibility against another, and simultaneously forces the contemplation of meter and style and indeed of the poem as form.

Moreover, the absence of titles also allows one to ponder possible connections within the manuscript itself. Scholars have argued over the various boundary possibilities between works. Where do the riddles begin and end? Are works clearly assignable to other genres such as the *Husband's Message* really the beginning of riddles? Had the Exeter Book compiler chosen to include titles or solutions, such demarcations would have answered these questions. His silence, though, opens the door to other considerations.

While the Old English riddles do not include solutions, the Latin riddles of Symphosius, Aldhelm, Eusebius, and Tatwine, which many scholars consider to be the sources and analogues of the Exeter Book ones, do. As mentioned earlier, Symphosius (c. fifth century) is credited with being the first literary riddler in Western Europe (Taylor, *Literary Riddle* 52) and introduced the one-hundred-riddle series that most subsequent Latin riddlers followed. Little, however, is known about his background, and what information we do have must be inferred from the prologue to his riddle collection, where he writes that while attending the festival of Saturn, he is called to take his turn at entertaining fellow party-goers. Not having brought any material with him, he makes up the riddles that followed.

Symphosius influenced the work of many subsequent Anglo-Latin riddlers, for example, Aldhelm (d. 709). He developed his elaborate Latin style while under tutelage at the abbey of Malmesbury that was founded by the Irish scholar Maildubh. Aldhelm's one hundred enigmata are found in the middle of his prose *De Metris et Aenigmatibus ac Pedum Regulis*, a three-part text that includes a dialogue between a master and a student on the forms of the hexameter line, a cluster of one hundred riddles demonstrating the use of this metrical form, and a discussion on feet of two, three, and four syllables that may compose a hexameter.

These riddles ostensibly serve to demonstrate the various meters discussed in the preceding prose. Indeed, Aldhelm appears to have initiated the use of Anglo-Latin riddles for Christian didacticism, which all subsequent Anglo-Latin as well as a few of the Old English riddlers apparently kept in mind. Moreover, as with Symphosius, many of Aldhelm's riddled items have academic connections, for example, the alphabet, writing tablets, pen, and bookcase, or invite clustering or categorization, such as animals: dog, peacock, camel; elements of nature: earth, wind, clouds; and man-made metal objects: cauldron, sieve, shield, and dagger.

Next came Tatwine (d. 734), a Mercian who, after serving as a priest of a monastery in Breedon-on-the-Hill, became the archbishop of Canterbury in 731 and wrote forty riddles with Christian aesthetics akin to Aldhelm's. Tatwine also authored an *Ars Grammatica* based on Donatus and other authorities that demonstrates the pervasive concern of scholars with the poor quality of Latin literacy and the difficulty of teaching Latin grammar as a foreign language.

Eusebius (d. 747) is assumed to be Hwætberht, abbot of Wearmouth, a contemporary of Bede. Eusebius's enigmata are widely believed to have been written as a sixty-riddle conclusion to Tatwine's collection of forty. The two series, united, equal the one-hundred-riddle total of Aldhelm's and Symphosius's collections. Indeed, Eusebius's work directly follows Tatwine's in the manuscripts that house them. Moreover, Eusebius, unlike the other three Latin riddlers, does not include a prologue to outline his inspiration for composition. This omission supports the hypothesis that he composed his riddles as a continuation to Tatwine's.

The Anglo-Latin riddles were used to teach the Latin language and poetic form and are pure literary productions. As teaching tools, they neglect the "game" qualities of the genre, the immediacy of presentation and the riddlee's search for *the* answer; thus the surprise-defeating inclusion of solutions at the beginning of each work. The Old English enigmata, however, many of which probably existed in an oral form, maintain the basic interrogative nature of riddles. Even if title omissions were due to a general disinterest in them, the fact that the genre requests an audience to come up with an answer manipulates the dynamic by which the text is experienced and makes the Old English riddles a unique poetic form. The absence of a solution dictates the folk or oral quality of these works—the inclusion of images, ideas, and objects fundamental to a culture and therefore readily recognizable—while the Anglo-Latin enigmata did not have to do that and thus could focus on the manipulation of language. For clarification of these points, let us compare riddle 61, *Ancora*, "anchor," by Symphosius to the Exeter Book's Riddle 16 generally solved the same way:

> Mucro mihi geminus ferro coniungitur uno.
> Cum uento luctor, cum gurgite pugno profundo.
> Scrutor aquas medias, ipsas quoque mordeo terras.

(My twin points are united by one piece of iron. I wrestle with the wind, I fight with [the] deep, raging current. I probe the water's midst, I also bite [the] earth itself.)

> Oft ic sceal wiþ wæge winnan   ond wiþ winde feohtan,
> somod wið þam sæcce,   þonne ic secan gewite
> eorþan yþum þeaht;   me biþ se eþel fremde.
> Ic beom strong þæs gewinnes,   gif ic stille weorþe;
> gif me þæs tosæleð,   hi beoð swiþran þonne ic,
> ond mec slitende   sona flymað,
> willað oþfergan   þæt ic friþian sceal.
> Ic him þæt forstonde,   gif min steort þolað
> ond mec stiþne wiþ   stanas moton
> fæste gehabban.   Frige hwæt ic hatte.

(Often I must struggle against waves and fight against [the] wind, contend with them together, when I go to seek [the] earth covered by waves; the land is foreign to me. I am strong in [the] fight, if I be still; if [it] so fails me, they are more powerful than I, and tearing me soon put [me] to flight, they will bear away that [which] I must protect. I hinder them [from] that, if my tail endures, and [the] rocks must hold fast against me. Ask what I am called.)

The Latin and Old English versions are both examples of prosopopoeia. This first-person voice highlights the dire plight of the objects as they speak of their suffering. Symphosius, however, plays with language, while the Old English riddler generally concentrates on a straight description. In line 1, Symphosius works with numbers: the object has twin points, "mucro . . . geminus," which merge into one. The Old English does not mention numbers at all; when the object itself is finally mentioned in line 8, he refers to it as a "steort," a "tail." While Symphosius begins with a description of the object itself, the Old English riddler immediately plunges into a battle. Both riddled objects fight specifically against the wind and waves; the Anglo-Saxon, however, makes note that the object battles forces united against it. This explains the situation of the Old English riddler, which helps narrow solution possibilities, thereby aiding the reader in guessing the object's identity. Furthermore, there is no question of the Latin anchor's success. It simply enters the water, pierces the earth, and holds firm. The Old English anchor, on the other hand, is less sure of its success and contemplates for six lines (2b–7) the tragic result should it fail, as the foe could overpower it or the rocks holding it may slip. Moreover, the ship's location is "fremde," "foreign," to it; its inhabitants are lost and alone. The burden lies completely on the riddler. As the anchor says in line 7, they "willað opfergean þæt ic friþian sceal" ("will bear away that [which] I must protect"). It has made a vow to protect its *comitatus* or "kin," the ultimate pledge for an Anglo-Saxon warrior. This inclusion contextualizes the riddle within the Anglo-Saxon heroic ideal, thereby adding an additional clue to the speaker's identity.

In line 2, Symphosius emphasizes the plight of the anchor by repeating the preposition "cum," "with"; it must battle against both wind and current. The Old English also uses this formula and includes "wiþ," "against," twice in line 1 in a phrase almost identical in meaning to the Latin: "Oft ic sceal wiþ wæge winnan ond wiþ winde feohtan" ("Often I must struggle against waves and fight against [the] wind"). The major difference between the Latin and the Old English is the position of the phrase. Symphosius begins his poem with the riddled object itself, while the Old English riddler starts with a description of the object's circumstance. This difference points out the literariness of the Latin; because Symphosius's audience is already aware of his solution before entering the riddle, the object can speak of itself from the poem's onset. Anglo-Saxon audiences, however, must first discover the object's setting to situate themselves and thus limit possible solutions. They are therefore not ready for the object itself until line 8, when the riddler has significantly immersed the audience in the object's world. Therefore, unlike Symphosius, who utilizes the riddle form to demonstrate his command of language through a description of an identified anchor, the Anglo-Saxon riddler creates a narrative to lead his audience to a solution: the object is a water-bound warrior who attempts to protect its kin. Its importance is made clear by the information describing the direness of the sailors' condition and thus the necessity that the speaker remain steadfast.

EXAMPLES

For a sample of Old English riddling, consider Riddle 57, generally solved as swallows:

> Ðeos lyft byreð   lytle wihte
> ofer beorghleoþa.   Þa sind blace swiþe,
> swearte salopade.   Sanges rope
> heapum ferað,   hlude cirmað,
> tredað bearonæssas,   hwilum burgsalo
> niþþa bearna.   Nemnað hy sylfe.

(This air bears little creatures over mountain slopes. They are exceedingly black, swart, dark-coated. Strong of song, in flocks [they] go, loudly cry, [they] tread [the] woody promontories, sometimes [the] city houses of [the] children of men. Name them yourself.)

The first four lines are straightforward descriptions of birds. Then lines 5b through 6a, which describe their habitat, "hwilum burgsalo / niþþa bearna" ("sometimes [the] city houses of [the] children of men"), position the birds and thus the entire enigma within the realm of man. Such referencing is imperative to a riddle's success, for it only works when solvers can locate the object within their world. As the final half-line imparts, the riddler's goal is for riddlees to solve the enigma themselves. Indeed, several criteria must be met by a riddle in order for this to happen: first, the work must lead riddlees to a general answer; second, clues must be tied to common understanding, information from a shared knowledge base; third, the riddler must select words that both reveal and deceive concurrently. With literary riddles, such as those of the Exeter Book, the riddler's work is further complicated because he/she must anticipate a larger, more diverse audience than an author in a strictly oral setting. Moreover, the riddler's physical absence from the riddle moment removes the possibility of clues revealed through facial expressions, mannerisms, or verbal inflections. Thus textuality increases the importance of references to general human conditions and circumstances in these riddles.

A subgenre of riddles is the double entendre, in which the "actual" solution is hidden by a more obvious lewd one. The following, Riddle 44, is an often-quoted Old English illustration:

Wrætlic hongað   bi weres þeo,
frean under sceate.   Foran is þyrel.
Bið stiþ ond heard,   stede hafað godne;
þonne se esne   his agen hrægl
ofer cneo hefeð,   wile þæt cuþe hol
mid his hangellan   heafde gretan
þæt he efenlang ær   oft gefylde.

(A wondrous [thing] hangs by a man's thigh, under the lord's garment. In front is [a] hole. Both stiff and hard, [it] has [a] good firmness; when a man pulls up his own garment over his knees, [he] desires to visit with [the] head of his hanging [thing] that equally long, known hole that he often filled before.)

Although the riddler leads the audience to solve this conundrum as a penis, the "real" answer is a key. The enigma is carefully constructed to mislead the riddlee. The first half of the enigma illustrates the object itself. The initial line and a half, "Wrætlic hongað bi weres þeo, / frean under sceate" ("A wondrous [thing] hangs by a man's thigh, under the lord's garment"), immediately positions the object against the upper part of a man's leg, beneath his garment. Thus from the onset the riddlee is led to think of a body part. Of course, a key hanging on a chain at a man's waist also fits this description. The raunchy image is reinforced by the next half-line, "Foran is þyrel" (In front is [a] hole). Here the riddlee's attention is narrowed to a specific part of the object, to the front of a hanging thing that is situated under a male's clothing. As there are not many physical body parts that match this description, the solver's conclusion appears to be confirmed. Few would think of the top of medieval keys, which did include holes and hung from a man's belt. The next full line ends the description of the item and neatly divides the riddle in half: "Bið stiþ on heard, stede hafað godne" (Both stiff and hard, [it] has [a] good firmness). This line completes the description in the riddlee's imagination, particularly since the riddler offers an evaluative description of its firmness: "good." A key is useful indeed.

In the second part of the riddle the poser elaborates on why the object is so "good." Line 4 explains how the man accesses the object: "se esne his agen hrægl / ofer cneo hefeð" ("a man pulls up his own garment over his knees"). "Þonne" ("when") this happens, the man desires to use the object, to put it in a "hol" ("hole") that he has "ær oft gefylde" ("often before filled"). That is a "god" thing.

Within the space of seven lines the riddler creates a simultaneous description of two apparently dissimilar objects. The poser skillfully constructs his poem with binary phrases that hide the true game. In order for it to work successfully, receptees must be convinced of a single solution from the outset, and their belief must be maintained and reinforced throughout the telling. This builds anticipation in the poser, whose joy mounts until the riddlee blurts out the purported answer, thereby allowing the riddler to reveal the "true" answer. Thus the real joke is not the riddle itself, but the exposure of the riddlee's lewd thoughts.

THE LITERARY HISTORY OF THE OLD ENGLISH RIDDLE GENRE

Benjamin Thorpe's *Codex Exoniensis*, published in 1842, is the first modern edition of the riddles. It is useful for the neophyte Old English scholar because Thorpe offers side-by-side translations of the manuscript in half-lines with additions clearly marked by italics. As Robert Chambers points out, the major shortcoming of Thorpe's edition is his failure to transcribe single letters and fragmented or even whole words surrounding lacunae when there was not enough text to make sense of a section. Also, while he indicates missing segments with asterisks, he never indicates how much text has been lost. This reluctance to work through difficulties is especially frustrating for the riddle scholar, as Thorpe often does not attempt to translate enigmata that he found particularly difficult. He writes, "Though [the riddles] have baffled me, yet, as they will now be in the hands of the Public, a hope may reasonably be entertained, that one more competent will undertake their interpretation, and with a more favourable result. Of some I have deemed it advisable to give merely the Saxon text, unaccompanied by an effort at translation" (10). Still, one must acknowledge that Thorpe was the first to attempt any translation of the Exeter Book riddles. Christian W.M. Grein worked from Thorpe's book and in 1857 and 1858 published his two-volume *Bibliothek der angelsächsischen Poesie*. He gallantly attempted to fill in the gaps left by Thorpe, but as he used only Thorpe's edition, he was ignorant of the manuscript's actual words and of the letters that Thorpe had omitted. This, in turn, caused Grein to make egregious errors. Scholars did not return to the Exeter Book manuscript itself till 1933, when Chambers, along with Max Förster and Robin Flower, published a complete photographic facsimile copy of the Exeter Book that clearly delineated various scribal markings and breaks and included an extensive introduction to the codex. Their work directed attention away from Thorpe's edition because it made the original text widely accessible to all.

As the genre invites, scholars also labor to find definitive answers to the Old English enigmata. Franz Dietrich attempted to solve all of the riddles in two articles: "Die Rätsel des Exeterbuchs: Würdigung, Lösung, und Herstellung" and "Die Rätsel des Exeterbuchs: Verfasser, weitere Lösungen." His solutions are based on meticulous scrutiny of the manuscript, and many remain unchallenged to this day. On the basis of the original ascription of Latin sources by Thorpe, Adolph Ebert and August Prehn, in 1877 and 1883, respectively, tried to connect every Old English riddle with a Latin source. While both overstated correlations (Prehn grossly), their work spawned discussions on and interest in sources and analogues throughout the field. Frederick Tupper's 1910 *The Riddles of the Exeter Book* was the first edition based on the British Museum's transcript of the manuscript and reintroduced long-neglected passages from the riddles formerly deemed too damaged for study. The books of A.J. Wyatt in 1912 and Moritz Trautmann in 1915 were the only critical editions of the entire riddle sequence for most of the twentieth century till Craig Williamson edited *The Old English Riddles of the Exeter Book* in 1977 and Bernard Muir *The Exeter Anthology of Old English Poetry* in 1994, the only version of the text that considers the original manuscript as well as all previous editions.

In 1936 George Philip Krapp and Elliott Van Kirk Dobbie edited what is still considered the authoritative version of the Exeter Book. The editors followed the facsimile edition of Chambers, Förster, and Flower. Krapp and Dobbie included a lengthy introduction to the history of the codex and a brief discussion of the riddles in their introduction and notes. While this edition of the Exeter Book remains the primary edition of the codex, Muir's 1994 work, mentioned earlier, divided into two volumes, one with the text itself and the other dedicated to commentary, is more thorough and useful for those interested in an extensive discussion of the codex, an up-to-date bibliography, and a brief historical commentary on the various poems that comprise the manuscript. Richard Gameson's article "The Origin of the Exeter Book of Old English Poetry" provides a nice companion to Muir's work because Gameson presents a compelling and methodical argument against the widely accepted assumption that the Exeter Book was produced by the Exeter monks themselves. Instead, Gameson asserts that Leofric bestowed the codex, already completed, on Exeter Cathedral when he moved the episcopal see there.

In terms of reference material, Michael J.B. Allen's *Sources and Analogues of Old English Poetry I* and *II* offer detailed listings of proposed Latin, Germanic, and Celtic sources and analogues to the riddles. The only drawback is that all works are presented in Modern English translations, intended for ease of reference. This limitation, however, prevents scholars from considering the included texts in their original form. In 1981 Donald Fry attempted to compile every solution ever offered by scholars in "*Exeter Book* Riddle Solutions." This listing of solver and answer is extremely informative as a guide and is accurate considering the scope of his project but does not include discussion of proposed solutions. Still, it is an invaluable tool for one undertaking the study of the canon of Exeter Book riddles.

While critics generally agree that one person compiled the poems that comprise the Exeter Book, there is great disagreement as to authorship. In 1857 Heinrich Leo was the first scholar who attempted to identify an author of the riddles. By forcing runic names out of what he believed to be the first riddle, *Wulf and Eadwacer*, he argued that one could ascertain the author's name, Cynewulf. Franz Dietrich agreed and added that the *lupus* of Riddle 90 is a reference to the second half of the author's name, Cynewulf, and that Riddle 95's answer, "Wandering Minstrel," alludes to his occupation. By the late 1880s Leo's conjecture was disproved by Henry Bradley, who asserted that *Wulf and Eadwacer* was not a riddle at all, but was closer in theme and structure to *Deor* and *The Wife's Lament*. Eduard Sievers successfully deconstructed Leo's reading of runes and contended that the riddles predated Cynewulf. August Madert, in a book that significantly quieted those continuing to argue for Cynewulfian authorship, compared the language of the riddles to that of undisputed poems of Cynewulf and demonstrated the irreconcilable differences between them.

Twentieth-century scholars likewise have been stumped to prove authorship of any kind. Even more tenuous are the arguments made for the unity of the riddles in sections or as a single, unified whole. Frederick Tupper details the various arguments made, from those of Dietrich, who believed that a different author wrote the second series of riddles, 61–95, to Georg Herzfeld, who contended that all ninety-five riddles were composed by a single author. Yet the evidence for any kind of authorship is so tenuous that all theories so far that attempt to identify authorship are easily and commonsensically disproved. For example, Dietrich's position is based on three assumptions: (1) relationships between riddled subjects, (2) use of Latin sources, and (3) agreement in treatment. The first point depends upon finding a specific answer to every riddle, a task doomed to failure because there is no way to confirm the rightness of the answer beyond a doubt. The second does not point to definite authorship, as different riddles use Latin sources in different ways. The third is also problematic because Christian riddles are treated quite differently from secular ones, and moreover, within each of these two categories, treatment differs depending on a multitude of variables including sources, analogues, topics, and rhyme scheme.

Three nineteenth-century scholars put forth the major premises for twentieth-century discussions of the Latinity of the Exeter Book riddles. In 1842 Benjamin Thorpe wrote that the Exeter Book riddles are "too essentially Anglo-Saxon to justify the belief that they are other than original productions" (*Codex Exoniensis* x). He did not bother to explain what he meant by "too essentially Anglo-Saxon," as if to say that the case was so obvious that it did not warrant a more detailed explanation. Thus began the great debate among scholars as to the possibility or impossibility of Anglo-Latin sources and their influence on the Old English.

In 1877 Adolph Ebert was the first to outline connections between Anglo-Latin riddlers and the Exeter Book ones. He demonstrated that the Old English riddlers borrowed from Tatwine and Eusebius, who borrowed from Aldhelm, who borrowed from Symphosius. August Prehn's much-debated 1883 work *Komposition und Quellen der Rätsel des Exeterbuches* turned the discussion of sources into a debate on indebtedness. He found Latin sources, sometimes in combination, for example, a joining of a riddle by Tatwine with one by Aldhelm, for almost every Exeter Book riddle. While Prehn's technique is shaky at best, his work is important for the questions it raises about the originality, artistry, and skill of the Old English riddlers/translators. Were they merely copying Old English verses already in existence, making minor emendations along the way? How much poetic and literary skill could one attribute to them? What value did the Anglo-Saxons place upon originality? How much do we? Do we as readers, separated from the manuscript by centuries, judge the text anachronistically?

These questions are still debated today. In 1977 Craig Williamson continued the discussion while reminding scholars of several possible pitfalls:

[E]ven when the Latin and Old English solutions are the same, it is dangerous to generalize about Latin sources since (1) Latin and Old English riddle-writers may have used the same general sources like Isidore's *Etymologiae* or Pliny's *Historia Naturalis* in the composing of their riddles; (2) the riddle-writers may have had independent but similar human perceptions about certain riddle-creatures; and (3) at least in certain cases of the Anglo-Saxons like Tatwine and Eusebius and perhaps in the case of Aldhelm—except where riddles are directly translated from the Latin, it is impossible to tell if the motif in the Old English riddle came from Latin or vice versa. (*Old English Riddles* 20)

This recognition of a Latin source followed by an immediate downplaying of its importance occurs throughout modern Old English scholarship, for instance in the work of Seth Lerer, who argues that the Anglo-Saxons developed the riddle as a genre to such an extent that Latin sources need not be included in studies of the Exeter Book (*Literacy and Power* 123). Agop Hacikyan agrees: "These riddles, which are borrowed or translated from Latin, are not all sheer imitations. During the process of translation the poets subject their lines to English thought and sentiment and enliven the passages with a poetic faculty in which their models are lacking" (29). The reluctance to investigate the Latin and Anglo-Latin background of the riddles appears to be based on an assumption that to recognize the Latin as a model or source would require us to look down on the achievements of vernacular writers. This view, however, is based on two anachronistic notions: first, a modern definition of "originality," according to which all ideas from their very inception must be new and different from what has come before, as opposed to "originality" in the sense of elaborating on an existing idea; second, the assumption that the Anglo-Saxons valued this "originality" as much as we do now. Still, as even the naysayers concede that to some degree translations and borrowings have taken place, the consideration of the sources should not be avoided. The debate must continue.

Riddles are found in most cultures. One reason for this genre's popularity may be its ability to create a sense of community between the riddle and its riddlees, be they in a group or alone. While riddlees are engaged in the contemplation of an enigma, they must search for mental images that enable them to comprehend, ascertain, and meld the twofold, metaphoric and literal renderings of a riddle. Author-provided solutions are not necessary if the goal is not to come up with a "correct" answer but rather to experience language and images that in sequential accumulation lead one to a mental image that could only be reached by those initiated into the riddler's world.

It is certainly ironic that a genre that is ambiguous and confusing by nature should provide us a glimpse into the literary culture from which the works arose. Then again, perhaps that was the riddlers' ultimate game. While they pull audiences through their text, posers simultaneously include "blocks" that hinder progress. Therefore, enigmata are based on self-contradiction, as demonstrated in the following lines from Riddle 40:

Flinte ic eom heardre   þe þis fyr drifeþ,
of þissum strongan   style heardan,
hnescre ic eom micle   halsrefeþre,
seo her on winde   wæweð on lyfte. (78–81)

(I am harder [than] flint that forces this fire from this strong hard steel, I am much softer [than] the feathers of a down pillow, she [that] on [the] wind blows aloft.) In Old English enigmata contrary images often appear in a phrase, indeed sometimes in a single line, thereby playing with the audience's sensibility and its mental image of the riddled item. Such proximity creates a pattern of interwoven duality that demonstrates the complexity of language, of the Anglo-Saxon literary consciousness, and of the world around us.

SELECTED BIBLIOGRAPHY

Abbott, H.H., trans. *The Riddles of the Exeter Book.* Cambridge: Golden Head Press, 1968.

Abrahams, Roger D. "The Literary Study of the Riddle." *Texas Studies in Language and Literature* 14.1 (1972): 909–929.

Aldhelm. *Aldhelm: The Poetic Works.* Trans. Michael Lapidge and James L. Rosier. Cambridge: D.S. Brewer, 1985.

Allen, Michael J.B., Comp. *Sources and Analogues of Old English Poetry.* 2 vols. Cambridge: D.S. Brewer, 1976–1983.

Anderson, James. "*Deor, Wulf and Eadwacer,* and *The Soul's Address*: How and Where the Old English *Exeter Book* Riddles Begin." *The Old English Elegies: New Essays in Criticism and Research.* Ed. Martin Green. Rutherford, NJ: Fairleigh Dickinson University Press, 1983. 204–230.

———. "Strange, Sad Voices: The Portraits of Germanic Women in the Old English *Exeter Book.*" Diss. University of Kansas, 1978.

———. *Two Literary Riddles in the Exeter Book.* Norman: University of Oklahoma Press, 1986.

Aristotle. *Poetics.* Trans. Ingram Bywater. New York: Modern Library, 1954. 218–266.

———. *Rhetoric.* Trans. Rhys Roberts. New York: Modern Library, 1954. 19–217.

Assman, Bruno, ed. *Bibliothek der angelsächsischen Poesie.* Vol. 3.1. Leipzig: Georg H. Wigand, 1898.

Blaumer, D.G. "The Early Literary Riddle." *Folklore* 78 (1967): 49–58.

Baum, Paull, trans. *Anglo-Saxon Riddles of the Exeter Book.* Durham, NC: Duke University Press, 1963.

Ben-Amos, Dan. "Solutions to Riddles." *Journal of American Folklore* 89: 249–254.

du Bois, Elizabeth Hickman, ed. *The Hundred Riddles of Symphosius.* Woodstock, VT: Elm Tree Press, 1912.

Bradley, Henry. "Review of Morley, *English Writers.*" *Academy* 33.2 (1888): 197–198.

Cameron, M.I. "Aldhelm as Naturalist: A Re-Examination of Some of His Enigmata." *Peritia* 4 (1985): 117–133.

Chambers, Robert, Max Förster, and Robin Flower, eds. *The Exeter Book of Old English Poetry.* London: Percy Lund, 1933.

Cohen, Shlomith. "Connecting through Riddles; or, The Riddle of Connecting." *Untying the Knot: On Riddles and Other Enigmatic Modes.* Ed. Galit Hasan-Rokem and David Shulman. Oxford: Oxford University Press, 1996. 294–315.

Crossley-Holland, Kevin, trans. *The Exeter Riddle Book.* London: Folio Society, 1978.

———, trans. *"Storm" and Other Old English Riddles.* London: Macmillan, 1970.

Davis, Adam. "*Agon* and *Gnomon*: Forms and Functions of the Anglo-Saxon Riddles." *De Gustibus: Essays for Alain Renoir.* Ed. John Miles Foley, J. Chris Womack, Whitney Womack. New York: Garland, 1992. 110–150.

Dietrich, Franz. "Die Rätsel des Exeterbuchs: Verfasser, weitere Lösungen." *Zeitschrift für deutsches Altertum und deutsche Literatur* 11 (1865): 448–490.

———. "Die Rätsel des Exeterbuchs: Würdigung, Lösung, und Herstellung." *ZDA* 11 (1859): 448–490.

Ebert, Adolph. "Die Rätselpoesie der Angelsachsen." *Berichte über die Verhandlungen der Sächsischen Gesellschaft der Wissenschaften zu Leipzig* 29 (1877): 20–56.

Erhardt-Siebold, Erika von. *Die lateinischen Rätsel der Angelsachsen.* Heidelberg: Carl Winters Universitätsbuchhandlung, 1925.

Fry, Donald. "*Exeter Book* Riddle Solutions." *Old English Newsletter* 15.1 (1981): 22–33.

Gameson, Richard. "The Origin of the *Exeter Book* of Old English Poetry." *Anglo-Saxon England* 25 (1996): 135–185.

Glory, Frederich, ed. *Corpus Christianorum.* Vol. 133. Turnhout: Brepolis, 1989.

Green, Thomas, and W.J. Pepicello. "The Folk Riddle: A Redefinition of Terms." *Western Folklore* 38 (1979): 3–20.

Grein, Christian W.M., ed. *Bibliothek der angelsächsischen Poesie.* 2 vols. Göttingen: Georg H. Wigand, 1857–1858.

Hacikyan, Agop. *A Linguistic and Literary Analysis of Old English Riddles.* Montreal: Maria Casalini, 1966.

Hasan-Rokem, Galit, and David Shulman, eds. *Untying the Knot: On Riddles and Other Enigmatic Modes.* Oxford: Oxford University Press, 1996.

Herzfeld, Georg. *Die Räthsel des Exeterbuches und ihr Verfasser.* Acta Germanica, vol. 2.1. Berlin: Mayer and Müller, 1890.

Holthausen, Ferdinand. "Das altenglische Reimlied." *Festchrift für Lorenz Morsbach.* Ed. Ferdinand Holthausen and H. Spies. Halle: Max Niemeyer, 1913. 190–200.

———. "Review of Komposition und Quellen des Exeterbuches von August Prehn." *Anglia* 7 (1884): 120–129.

Huizinga, Johan. *Homo Ludens: A Study of the Play-Element in Culture.* Boston: Beacon, 1955.

Jacobs, Nicolas. "The Old English 'Book-Moth' Riddle Reconsidered." *Notes and Queries* 35 (1988): 290–292.

Jember, Gregory. "Literal and Metaphorical: Clues to Reading the Old English Riddles." *Studies in English Literature* 65 (1988): 47–56.

———. "Prolegomena to a Study of the Old English Riddles." *Journal of the Faculty of Liberal Arts, Saga University* 19 (1987): 155–178.

Krapp, George Philip, and Elliott Van Kirk Dobbie, eds. *The Exeter Book.* New York: Columbia University Press, 1936.

Lapidge, Michael. *Anglo-Latin Literature, 900–1066.* London: Hambledon Press, 1993.

Leo, Heinrich. *Quae de se ipso Cynerulfus poeta Anglosaxonicus tradiderit.* Halle: Herrigs Archiv, 1857.

Lerer, Seth. *Literacy and Power in Anglo-Saxon Literature.* Lincoln: University of Nebraska Press, 1991.

———. "The Riddle and the Book: *Exeter Book* Riddle 42 in Its Contexts." *Papers on Language and Literature* 25.1 (1989): 3–18.

Mackie, W.S., ed. *The Exeter Book.* Part II. London: Humphrey Milford, Oxford University Press, 1934.

Madert, August. *Die Sprache der altenglischen Rätsel des Exeterbuches und die Cynewulffrage.* Marburg: Buchdr. H. Bauer, 1900.

Maranda, Elli Köngas. "Riddles and Riddling." *Journal of American Folklore* 89 (1976): 127–137.

Muir, Bernard J., ed. *The Exeter Anthology of Old English Poetry.* 2 vols. Exeter: University of Exeter Press, 1994.

Nelson, Marie. "Four Social Functions of the *Exeter Book* Riddles." *Neophilologus* 75.3 (1991): 445–450.

———. "The Rhetoric of the *Exeter Book* Riddles." *Speculum* 49.3 (1974): 421–440.

Orchard, Andy. *The Poetic Art of Aldhelm.* Cambridge: Cambridge University Press, 1994.

Pepicello, W.J., and Thomas A. Green. *The Language of Riddles: New Perspectives.* Columbus: Ohio State University Press, 1984.

Pinsker, Hans, and Waltraud Ziegler, eds. and trans. *Die altenglischen Rätsel des Exeterbuchs.* Heidelberg: Carl Winter, 1985.

Pitman, James Hall, ed. and trans. *The Riddles of Aldhelm.* New Haven, CT: Yale University Press, 1970.

Pope, John. "The Text of a Damaged Passage in the *Exeter Book: Advent, (Christ I)."* *Anglo-Saxon England* 9 (1981): 137–156.

Prehn, August. *Komposition und Quellen der Rätsel des Exeterbuches.* Paderborn: Ferdinand Schöningh, 1883.

Robinson, Fred C. "Artful Ambiguities in the Old English 'Book-Moth' Riddle." *Anglo-Saxon Poetry: Essays in Appreciation for John C. McGalliard.* Ed. Lewis Nicholson and Dolores Warwick Frese. Notre Dame, IN: University of Notre Dame Press, 1975. 355–362.

Shook, Laurence K. "Riddles Relating to the Anglo-Saxon Scriptorium." *Essays in Honour of Anton Charles Pagis.* Ed. J. Reginald O'Donnell. Toronto: Pontifical Institute of Mediaeval Studies, 1974. 215–236.

Sievers, Eduard. "Zu Cynewulf." *Anglia* 13 (1891): 1–25.

Sisam, Kenneth. "The Exeter Book of Old English Poetry." *Review of English Studies* 10 (1934): 338–342.

Stanley, E.G. "Heroic Aspects of the *Exeter Book* Riddles." *Prosody and Poetics in the Early Middle Ages: Essays in Honour of C.B. Hieatt.* Ed. M.J. Toswell. Toronto: University of Toronto Press, 1995. 197–218.

Stewart, Ann Harleman. "Double Entendre in the Old English Riddles." *Lore and Language* 3.8 (1983): 39–52.

Stork, Nancy Porter. *Through a Gloss Darkly: Aldhelm's Riddles in the British Library MS Royal 12.C.xxiii.* Toronto: Pontifical Institute of Mediaeval Studies, 1990.

Tanke, John. "*Wonfeax wale*: Ideology and Figuration in the Sexual Riddles of the *Exeter Book.*" *Class and Gender in Early English Literature.* Ed. Britton J. Harwood and Gillian R. Overing. Bloomington: Indiana University Press, 1994. 21–42.

Taylor, Archer. *English Riddles from Oral Tradition.* Berkeley: University of California Press, 1959.

———. *The Literary Riddle before 1600.* Berkeley: University of California Press, 1948.

Thorpe, Benjamin, ed. *Codex Exoniensis: A Collection of Anglo-Saxon Poetry.* London: Society of Antiquaries of London, 1842.

Trautmann, Moritz. *Die altenglischen Rätsel.* Heidelberg: C. Winter, 1915.

———. "Alte und neue Antworten auf altenglische Rätsel." *Bonner Beiträge zur Anglistik* 19 (1905): 167–215.

Tupper, Frederick. "The Cynewulfian Runes of the First Riddle." *Modern Language Notes* 25.8 (1910): 235–241.

———. "Originals and Analogues of the *Exeter Book* Riddles." *Modern Language Notes* 18.4 (1903): 97–106.

———, ed. *The Riddles of the Exeter Book.* Boston: Ginn & Co., 1910.

Walker-Pelkey, Faye. " 'Frige hwæt ic hatte': *The Wife's Lament* as Riddle." *PLL* 28.3 (1992): 242–266.

Wehlau, Ruth. *The Riddle of Creation.* New York: Peter Lang, 1997.

Whitman, Frank Herbert. "The Influence of the Latin and the Popular Riddle Traditions on the Old English Riddles of the *Exeter Book.*" Diss. Madison: University of Wisconsin, 1968.

Williams, Edith Whitehurst. "Annals of the Poor: Folk Life in Old English Riddles." *Medieval Perspectives* 3.2 (1988): 67–82.

Williamson, Craig, trans. *A Feast of Creatures: Anglo-Saxon Riddle-Songs.* Philadelphia: University of Pennsylvania Press, 1982.

———, ed. *The Old English Riddles of the Exeter Book.* Chapel Hill: University of North Carolina Press, 1977.

Wülker, Richard, ed. *Bibliothek der angelsächsischen Poesie.* 3 vols. Kassel: Georg H. Wigand, 1883–1898.

Wyatt, Alfred J., ed. *Old English Riddles.* 1912. Norwood, PA: Norwood Editions, 1973.

18

Romance

Carolyn Craft

One of the most denotatively perplexing of medieval genres, *romance* refers to an extended narrative, usually involving more than one episode, including a quest, adventure, or test undertaken by a knight or someone of noble but sometimes initially unknown parentage. The knight usually quests alone or accompanied by his squire or a damsel. Often marvels or the supernatural are involved, and the presentation is idealized, with good and evil usually clearly demarcated: there are good knights and bad knights, good kings and bad ones (good knights, such as Lancelot, and good kings, such as Arthur, may, however, do bad deeds that carry disastrous consequences). Sometimes the knight may not perceive this distinction except in retrospect; for example, Perceval, about to make love to a woman, crosses himself and only then discovers that she is a demon, or Gawain in *Sir Gawain and the Green Knight*, having retained the magic girdle given him by his host's wife, realizes a day later that he has violated his knightly honor and oath to his host by his failure to exchange all his winnings the final day. Arthur, who fathers Mordred through incest and adultery, and Lancelot, who commits treason and adultery with Guinevere the queen, are prime examples of retrospective realization: in these situations the reader or audience sometimes sees moral distinctions before the protagonist does. At other times supernatural voice or vision is necessary to reveal the good or evil; nevertheless, the distinctions are idealistically heightened so that there is little, if any, moral ambiguity. This good/evil dichotomy relates to the general tendency toward stereotypic presentation of characters and situations, so that romance also denotes a method of presentation involving a number of frequent motifs such as the distressed damsel, the evil challenger, the fair unknown, the knight of unusual prowess, the power of love that enables overcoming otherwise-insurmountable obstacles, or the enchantment that must be removed by a feat performable only by the hero. Usually romance contains a strong, even if only implicit, confidence that good will ultimately triumph, or at least that loss will bring compensation; for instance, Arthur's death may be "redeemed" by the "Breton hope" that he has gone to Avalon for the healing of his wounds and that he will one day come again to rule, or it may be "redeemed" by hints of union in heaven with a chastened and forgiven Guinevere after her death. One may wonder if Malory's Arthur would not regard that as, at best, a Pyrrhic victory, but Lancelot as the priest who celebrates Guinevere's requiem sees Arthur's and Guinevere's joint tomb as just and fitting, even as "righting" past wrongs. As Edward E. Foster, author of "Simplicity, Complexity, and Morality in Four Medieval Romances," observes, "Romance represents ideas or ideals, defines heroes who embody those ideals, and celebrates the success of those heroes" (401).

Not only does the term *romance* refer to a type of extended narrative and a hyperbolic approach to its subject matter, but also it sometimes attempts to delineate subject matter. Jean Bodel, a thirteenth-century French poet, claimed that medieval romance concerned one of three subject matters: "the Matter of Greece and Rome" (Alexander legends and stories of the Trojan War and its consequences), "the Matter of France" (Charlemagne legends), and "the Matter of Britain" (Arthurian legends). Later commentators added "the Matter of England" (native English or Germanic heroes), giving four received categories; still later "miscellaneous" had to be added because the four matters excluded many recognized romances. Before Bodel, and sometimes afterwards as well, romance meant any vernacular translation of a Latin work, or, somewhat later, anything in Old French. Old French was the language in which the first romances (in the sense of genre) were composed, orally or in writing, at first in several types of verse in the twelfth and thirteenth centuries, but increasingly as time went on, in prose as well.

Like their Old French antecedents, most Middle English romances are courtly, but the popular, the religious, and the learned traditions developed romances as well. Indeed, the very first English romances are more popular than courtly or learned, for example, *King Horn* (about 1225) and *Havelok* (late thirteenth century). Frequently the medieval church responded to the popularity of romance by developing its own romances or romantic hagiographies; for instance, at least one of the versions of the Amis and Amiloun story and some of the Christianized Grail legends were attempts at providing more wholesome entertainment than the adulterous and violent heroes of courtly romance. As Kathryn Hume states in "Structure and Perspective: Romance and Hagiographic Features in the Amicus and Amelius Story," "The fundamental form of the story is not hagiographic but secular . . . it stems from the combination of two folktales, and . . . it celebrates an extraordinary friendship rather than holiness of life" (90). She shows that the later hagiographic versions depart from the purpose of the original version: "The hagiography concludes with a lengthy description of a holy war in which the friends die, and an account of a miracle involving their tombs. The romance ends with reassertion of social and family order" (93). Hume's article shows how the tripartite structures of romance and hagiography are different because in romance "the unifying factor is an earthly goal of a specific and often material nature," whereas in hagiography "it is a life pattern" (92). Romance at times served an instructive or didactic purpose, but a very different one from hagiography. In fact, the courtly chivalric romance may have focused on education in social or courtly values; for example, in Old French, romance was often a vehicle for teaching *fin amour*, and in Middle English, for teaching feudal and social duties. Usually entertainment was an important focus for this genre; entertainment even seemed so central to the genre that critical awareness of the romances' didactic function as a significant expression and a shaper of culture, especially courtly culture, is relatively recent. Foster shows that "the teaching function is integral to its narrative mode as a celebration of shared values" (401).

Because the list of narratives included under romance and the features of romance vary from critic to critic, and because in the received "canon" of romances almost everything described earlier except the narrative basis of romance has exceptions, any definition of romance is flawed. John Finlayson, in "Definitions of Middle English Romance," proposes a way out of this dilemma by imposing a set of criteria and denying romance genre to anything that fails to meet his criteria, which means that most hitherto-named romances except Arthurian ones are denied that appellation. In distinguishing the *chanson de geste* hero from the *romance* hero, Finlayson argues

that heroic literature *reflects* in a heightened manner rather than creates the system of values it expresses, whereas the *romance*, at least in its greatest period in France, creates a code and expresses values not generally current in society. . . . The basic definition of *romance*, therefore, is that it is a tale in which a knight achieves great feats of arms, almost solely for his own *los et pris* [praise and worth] in a series of adventures which have no social, political, or religious motivation and little or no connection with medieval actuality. (55)

The situation and values are different "in the *chanson de geste* [where] the group is dominant" (Finlayson 54).

While many of Finlayson's observations are apt, it might be more useful to recognize the medieval appellations and the overlapping fluidity of the various genres. Often critics bemoan the heterogeneous use of the term, but one of the strengths of romance as a genre may be its very ambiguity. In a world in which few writers composed original plots, and if they did, they frequently concealed that fact (e.g., Malory's episode of the healing of Sir Urry), variations on a basic narrative are the means of creative expression: no wonder there are works that are hybrids, part romance and part something else (e.g., part chronicle, epic, hagiography, exemplum, or romance parody). The amorphous qualities of the label *romance* are signs of its strength and vitality, of its ability to attract writers and audiences ever ready for another "spin" on an old story, and of sufficient interpretive ambiguity to serve various didactic purposes.

One way to define romance is by contrast, by stating what it is not. Romance is not history, though there may be some history buried in the story or some pseudohistory presented in the narrative. It is not a saint's life, although there may be hybrid forms involving romance and hagiographic features. Unlike romance, epic does not divorce the hero from his court and society; its "historic" or pseudohistoric deeds generally appear more realistic or credible than do those of romance. Although romance may have some very risqué behaviors, it is not fabliau. Indeed, Mark E. Amster shows in "Literary Theory and the Genres of Middle English Literature" that fabliau can become a parody of romance—for instance, in Chaucer's "Miller's Tale" (395). Amster continues,

> Like the author of *Sir Gawain*, like any successful writer, Chaucer was keenly aware of the kinds of texts he created. He recognized intuitively what made sense in a specific text, what elements at the heart of an historical genre like the romance or fabliaux could be manipulated, intensified, or transformed. Those manipulations and intensities make up our experience of Chaucer's texts, experiences which derive from each specific kind of text and which readers must actualize in terms of their own repertoire of texts, readings, experiences, and genre possibilities. (395–396)

Amster cautions, "Many of the genre distinctions made by the medievals themselves were based on surface features" (390). He observes, "Generic description and interpretation are the actions of perceivers, and therefore must be developed out of the ways we perceive and respond to texts" (391), so that it is possible for a given text to have different generic properties depending upon the perceivers—one of whom is the author.

Multigeneric properties become even more likely as different ages and cultures interact with the narrative. Paul Strohm's "Middle English Narrative Genres" provides "A Taxonomy of Middle English Narrative Terms" (379–382) that states that "romaunce" began as a description of language but then began to describe the contents of texts in romance language; this content represented "accounts of the deeds of a single hero, with emphasis not only on martial but also on amatory and fanciful episodes" (381). Strohm's taxonomy is quite useful, but its application is, as he demonstrates, problematic because "fourteenth-century authors could choose among these terms with some confidence in the significations and expectations they would evoke. This co-ordinated system of terms had essentially broken down by the fifteenth century" (384). Indeed, Strohm asserts that it is through the violation of traditional "rules" of genre that "authors persistently modify received traditions in order that they may retain their challenge for new audiences in new social and historical situations" (387). Nevertheless, a good list of Middle English works one may wish to consider as romances, while discarding some as being within the romance tradition but not themselves romances, is found in Helaine Newstead's article "Romances: General" in *A Manual of the Writings in Middle English, 1050–1500* (1:13–16). It is probably unnecessary to point out that narrative remains primary in romance, so poetic romance is not lyric—either in the sense of a short poem expressing a single emotion or in the sense of a stanzaic poem with repetitive musical setting.

Several early English romances illustrate the idealism, the courtly often blended with the popular, the didacticism, the doubling of plot motifs, and the entertainment value of romance. *King Horn*, the earliest extant English romance, from the early thirteenth century, uses the same plot, but not the courtly presentation and values, of *Horn et Rimenild*, by Thomas, an Anglo-Norman poet of the late twelfth century. *King Horn* tells the story of a king's son, Horn, whose father was murdered by Saracen pirates. Horn himself is cast into a boat with a loyal and a treacherous companion, Athulf and Fikenild; they go ashore in Westnesse, where the king's daughter, Rymenild, wants to marry Horn. The tale continues and Horn is banished a second time, finds another king's daughter available for marriage (though he declines her), avenges his own father's death, and disguises himself to rescue Rymenild from a proposed marriage. Many adventures follow, but eventually, after Horn settles affairs of two kingdoms and rewards his followers, Rymenild and Horn return to Horn's patrimony as king and queen. The romance involves a double exile and return motif. Horn is first exiled from his own patrimony, then from the land of his future bride; subsequently he vindicates himself in both countries; presumably he and the faithful Rymenild live harmoniously ever after. The narration involves *double-ment*: what happens once happens again; what happens in one place happens in another, suggesting the static and idealized nature of the world of romance. *King Horn* is simply told in somewhat irregularly stressed lines with simple rhyme. Fidelity, love, and martial skill are valued, while the world order seems to support eventual justice. While kings and knights are the subject matter and courts the setting, the romance is, as stated earlier, far more popular than courtly in tradition and attitude. The hero struggles through adventure after adventure against incredible odds in order to gain the woman he loves, to avenge his father's death, and to regain his patrimony. Several warning dreams, several disguises (as a "mere" knight, a beggar, and later as a harper), forced castle entries, a special ring, and other motifs support the idealistic presentation. Another romance, *Horn Child*, and a ballad, *Ballad of Hind Horn*, survive. They illustrate the variations, retelling, and recycling of plots and motifs that typify medieval romance.

Composed only slightly later, another romance, *Floris and Blauncheflur*, uses a plot found in many European versions, some courtly, others popular in tradition. The English version has the idealistic and sentimental emphasis found in courtly tradition rather than the action-oriented emphasis of the popular tradition. True love of a king's son and a captive triumphs as Floris seeks Blauncheflur in a Babylonian harem: not only does the determination of each not to survive without the other win their pardon from the emir after they are found together, but also the emir is converted from concubinage into monogamous marriage to Blauncheflur's friend. This courtly romance does not fit into any of the traditional "matters," and in the thirteenth-century English version its hero is a naïve, even childlike, faithful lover who will sacrifice everything for love. In addition to the courtly versions, there is a popular version that "is shorter (of inferior literary quality) and resembles a *chanson de geste* in its neglect of sentiment to stress physical prowess and stirring incident, e.g., Flores wins his lady by force of arms," according to Lillian Herlands Hornstein's "Miscellaneous Romances" in *A Manual of the Writings in Midde English, 1050–1500* (1:146).

Havelok is a late-thirteenth-century "Matter of England" romance involving unknown parentage, the king mark that attests to his identity, and a princess displaced from her patrimony by being married to Havelok, who is a servant in her deceased father's castle and who does not know his own true identity. By the end of the romance Havelok has not only obtained his deceased father's throne, Denmark, but has also gained his wife's deceased father's throne, England, by, in both cases, removing the earl who had assumed kingship. Again, despite its setting and characters, this romance comes from popular tradition; attempts have been made to validate it historically, and the town of Grimsby's official seal is related to the story. The historic and geographic detail, whether actual or invented, that chronicle and *chanson de geste* are noted for is not always absent in romance, but usually such detail supports idealized or supernatural action rather than heroic but more possible action. In *Havelok* the king mark on Havelok's shoulder and a supernatural light coming out of Havelok's mouth show supernatural intervention to prevent the future hero's being killed shortly after birth. The plot of *Havelok* is found in Gaimar's Anglo-Norman poem *Estoire des Engles* and in *Lai d'Haveloc*, both of which indicate its romance antecedents. *Havelok*'s values are even less courtly than those of *King Horn*; as Charles W. Dunn writes in *A Manual of the Writings in Middle English, 1050–1500*, "Though Horn . . . may disguise himself as a beggar, Havelok does not masquerade when he serves as a scullion; and the romancer portrays his hero's experiences with the gusto of one who himself relishes life in the kitchen and the fish-market," so that Dunn deems it "one of the freshest, most timeless, and most appealing of the early Middle English romances" (1:24–25).

The thirteenth-century romance *Bevis of Hampton*, based on an originally Anglo-Norman plot, became popular in several versions. Again, the story begins with a hero whose father was murdered and who himself was almost killed but was instead exiled shortly after his birth. Bevis is loved by a Saracen princess, Josian, who is willing to convert to Christianity out of love for Bevis. Twice she is forced to marry against her will (yet her virginity is preserved), once she is abducted, and later she must disguise herself as a palmer. Bevis must fight against evil several times to remove usurpers; finally, the romance ends in the hero's and heroine's holy deaths. This is a popular tale of the power of faithful love to remove obstacles and to conquer evil, as well as of the rightness of

Christianity and the evilness of anything else. Amplification or doubling by using the same episode in several situations, for instance, removing the usurper, contributes to the length of this poem and becomes a frequent romance technique. *Guy of Warwick*, even more popular in England than *Bevis*, also illustrates a mixture of Christian Crusader themes, dragon slaying, and pilgrimage motifs that produce a Christian hero—one who never succumbs to infidel women but who deserts his pregnant wife in order to do penance for his former fighting, then kills a giant in order to save a friend, and ultimately dies a hermit; his wife buries him. Here the claims of marital love are less significant or pressing than those of religious obligation and friendship. Adventure and feeling, rather than any internal logic, govern the episodes; Charles W. Dunn, writing in "Romances Derived from English Legends" in *A Manual of the Writings in Middle English, 1050–1500*, says, "Appropriately, Chaucer in the tale of *Sir Thopas* parodies Guy more completely than any other romance" (1:31).

In addition to *King Horn, Floris and Blauncheflur, Havelok, Guy of Warwick*, and *Bevis of Hampton*, Helaine Newstead lists three other thirteenth-century English romances ("Romances: General" 1:13–16). In Newstead's list of eight romances before 1300, four are "Matter of England" (*King Horn, Havelok, Guy of Warwick*, and *Bevis of Hampton*), two are "Matter of Britain" (*Arthour and Merlin* and *Sir Tristrem*), and two are "miscellaneous romances," one of these being based on Byzantine and Greek legends (*Floris and Blauncheflur*) and one being didactic (*Amis and Amiloun*). *Arthour and Merlin* (its earliest manuscript is fourteenth century, but Newstead dates the work as thirteenth) narrates both Merlin's and Arthur's births and rise to power, based mostly upon chronicle tradition but incorporating some Vulgate Cycle material concerning Arthur's many battles after he has been crowned king of England (Newstead 1:47, 1:13). *Sir Tristrem* tells of its hero's birth and childhood, the killing of the Irish king, Tristrem's return in disguise to Ireland for his own healing, his return yet again to get Ysonde as bride for King Mark, Tristrem's drinking the magic love potion with Ysonde, their adultery, the tricked trial by ordeal that "proves" Ysonde's innocence, Tristrem's exile, his marriage to the other Ysonde, and his knightly adventures; it ends abruptly without a conclusion.

Amis and Amiloun (late thirteenth century, previously discussed for its romance and hagiographical versions) recounts a story of faithful sworn male friendship so close that Amiloun takes Amis's place in a trial by combat when Amis is guilty; concurrently, Amis must sleep chastely (as attested by a sword between them) with his friend's wife. Later Amiloun becomes a leprous outcast because he fought wrongfully for Amis; finally Amis and his wife discover Amiloun's identity and, acting on divine command, restore him to health by bathing him with their children's blood. True to the eventual optimism of most romance, the children's lives are preserved, and the romance ends with the triumph of what the romance identifies as good. *Amis and Amiloun* probably will not appeal to the modern reader as much as *Arthour and Merlin* and *Sir Tristrem* will, but its plot was internationally popular. In addition to its theme of friendship tested, Lillian Herlands Hornstein, in "Miscellaneous Romances" in A *Manual of the Writings in Middle English, 1050–1500*, lists "the wooing princess, jealous seneschal, judicial combat, separating sword, faithful servitor, recognition token" motifs (1:169), to which should be added the voice-from-heaven (which appears twice) and child-sacrifice motifs. Hornstein lists the romance as "of didactic intent" but remarks that its theme "glorifies friendship at the expense of honor and family, [and] blurs moral distinctions" (1:167, 1:169). It is an interesting romance where justice does not prevail, virtue is not rewarded, and a voice from heaven counsels murder of innocent children; nevertheless, the romance is didactic, emphasizing in its courtly versions the supreme importance of true friendship and ending in divinely bestowed reward for all the friends, but emphasizing in its hagiographic versions the sanctity of its heroes. Of course, to the medieval mind, the murder of children on divine command had good biblical precedent in Abraham's willingness to sacrifice Isaac.

The fourteenth century brought the flowering of Middle English romance: Helaine Newstead lists nineteen romances between 1300 and 1350, thirty-eight (counting "Chaucer's tales" as one and "Gower's tales" as another) from 1350 to 1400, while the fifteenth century, except for Sir Thomas Malory's work, represents an increasingly worn-out tradition of forty-three romances (counting Lydgate's *Troy-Book* and his *Seige of Thebes*, as well as Malory's *Morte d'Arthur*, each as one); she also lists eleven early-sixteenth-century romances, none of them distinguished and several of them hagiographic (Newstead, "Romances: General" 1:13–16). Her list includes works many other critics would not list as romances, for example, the fourteenth-century alliterative *Morte d'Arthur*. This great poem has often been considered an epic, but William Matthews, in *The Tragedy of Arthur: A Study of the Alliterative "Morte Arthur,"* has made a strong case for considering the poem a tragedy: it certainly lacks the idealism, the love motive, and the optimistic eventual triumph of good often found in romance, although Arthur is given a hero's burial at Glastonbury, where Guinevere subsequently joins him in the tomb. Newstead herself writes in "Arthurian Legends" in *A Manual of the Writings in Middle English, 1050–1500* of the idea that *Morte d'Arthur* is an epic or a tragedy, "Both views . . . are compatible" (1:45). The work's primary Arthurian source is Wace's *Le Roman de Brut*, a courtly adaptation, translation, and development of Geoffrey of Monmouth's *Historia Regum Britanniae*, a "history" that contains the first extant account of King Arthur's "life" from birth to death; it is this chronicle tradition and, in England, the epic-tragic alliterative *Morte* that provide the impetus for much of later Arthurian romance. Part of the vitality of the romance tradition was that many streams—chronicle, epic, tale, ballad, legend, saint's life, even debate—led into and out of it, resulting in a rich tradition expressive of various medieval ideals, values, and motifs but not susceptible to easy delineation: to be true to this vital impulse, categories must remain fluid. Aside from this alliterative version's intrinsic literary merit, which is great, the work is important for its influence on Malory: again, epic or tragedy feeds into romance. This does not mean, however, that medieval writers lacked a sense of genre, as the previously referenced article by Paul Strohm has shown (379–388). Another example of the fluidity of genre is romance that becomes encompassed within a larger work, especially when the larger genre is not romance; prime examples here are the framed tales of John Gower's *Confessio Amantis* and Geoffrey Chaucer's *Canterbury Tales*, both works of the last half of the fourteenth century.

This flowering of romance in fourteenth-century England is supported by works in all of the great "matters" of romance, though "the Matter of England" has few representatives; however, *Gamelyn*'s twenty-five surviving manuscripts attest to the popularity of this folk romance, a popularity probably not shared by *William of Palerne* and *Athelston*, each of which survives in only one manuscript. The fourteenth century also produced a few miscellaneous romances and the extant Breton lays. *Richard Coer de Lyon*, an early-fourteenth-century romance outside the great "matters," survives in seven independent but incomplete manuscripts, two of which "amplify the fabulous materials," while the other five "are relatively historical," according to Hornstein ("Miscellaneous Romances" 1:159). Richard has a troubled background: his mother always left at the consecration of the Mass; one day she is detained but flies through the ceiling of the church clutching her daughter and dropping John, her youngest son. Subsequently, King Henry, Richard's father, will not attend Mass at all. Shortly thereafter Richard inherits the throne and becomes a larger-than-life Crusader who dines on Saracens and offers Saladin's ambassadors baked heads of their compatriots to eat, but such immorality is "justified" by the enemies' religion and by divine assistance when Saladin gives Richard a magical horse, as well as by the closing benediction's implication that Richard died in God's favor. Indeed, the romance acclaims Richard as the bravest of British kings. Chivalric romance also becomes a vehicle for relating miracle and punishment. In *The Siege of Jerusalem* (alliterative) and in *Titus and Vespatian* (couplets), two very popular romances (Hornstein, "Miscellaneous Romances," lists eight and eleven manuscripts, respectively, as well as one in prose [1:160–163]), the vernicle heals both Titus and Vespasian, who convert to Christianity and destroy Jerusalem and many Jews. These Jews are depicted not only as Christ-killers but also, prompted by a famine, as stubborn (refusing to surrender during a seige) and sometimes even as resorting to cannibalism. While many of the moral values in these romances are repugnant today, these romances are uncomplicated and even idealistic in their belief that defending Christianity justifies any means and that Christians are simply "right," while Jews are simply "wrong."

Exactly what a Breton lay is, especially one in English, is hard to determine, but the extant English ones are fourteenth century and illustrate again the fluidity both of lays as genre and of romance as genre in general. Indeed, Mortimer J. Donovan, in a chapter on the Breton lays in A *Manual of the Writings in Middle English, 1050–1500*, states that without a prologue identifying a given poem as a Breton lay, Breton lays "are difficult to distinguish from other short romances" (1:134). *Sir Launfal* and, less closely, *Lay le Freine* have antecedents in twelfth-century lays by Marie de France, although the immediate source of the former is the *Lay of Graelen*. Three other lays, *Emaré, Sir Gowther*, and *The Erle of Tolous*, claim a Breton lay source; other lays, for example, *Sir Orfeo* and *Sir Degaré*, in Donovan's list are less connected to extant lays, though Brittany provides the setting for *Sir Degaré*, and *Sir Orfeo*'s prologue (in some manuscripts) discusses lays, nevertheless, *Sir Orfeo* may be based on a now-lost French lay. *Emaré* is the story of a princess so beautiful that her father seeks her love; when she rejects him, he sets her adrift at sea. The story continues with her being rescued by a steward, marrying the steward's king, producing a male heir, and again being set adrift, together with the infant son, Segramour, by the evil offices of the queen mother, who intercepts two letters and substitutes others so that all think that the king has commanded setting his wife adrift. Emaré again comes ashore, this time in Rome; again she is rescued. Meanwhile, her husband has discovered his mother's treachery and, thinking Emaré and their son dead, has come to Rome to pray. Eventually, Segramour, the son, is able to work reconciliation between husband and wife and between the wife and her incestuously motivated father, who has come to Rome as an act of penance. The patient-Constance type of story does have one unusual detail—a special robe, described at great length, that depicts famous lovers from romance and makes Emaré appear supernatural, whether good or evil, because of her unusually striking beauty. This robe also provides the opportunity for the queen mother's treachery because she can support accusing Emaré of being a devil by pointing to the robe. Nevertheless, Donovan states, "If *Emaré* did not mention its source in a Breton lay, it would hardly be distinguishable from other romances associated with minstrels 'who walk far and wide' and write in tail-rime stanzas" (1:137).

Lay le Freine is a female version of the motif of the hero with unknown parentage; like Arthur, Havelok, and others, Freine is raised in ignorance of her true parentage. Unlike Arthur, Havelok, and other male heroes, this patient-Griselda type of woman has no personal light or ability that leads to discovery of identity. Instead, she has a very special robe and ring that were left with her when she was abandoned; that is, the token is humanly rather than divinely bestowed. As Donovan observes, the poem "builds on the motifs of the twin birth, the child separated from its parents and reunited, and the husband with two wives. The story materials are, therefore, not specifically Breton" (1:135). *Sir Orfeo*, which may have been written by the author of *Lay le Freine* (see Donovan 1:133–136), retells Ovid's and Boethius's story of Eurydice's abduction and Orpheus's mourning, leaving his throne, and searching for his wife. This story has, however, a happy ending, as the romance reader might expect, when Orfeo finds her in the Kingdom of Fairies, obtains her release, returns with Heurodis to his kingdom, finds his steward-regent faithful, is restored to his throne, and lives happily with his wife and queen.

Lay le Freine and *Sir Orfeo* represent the best literature among the extant so-called Breton lays except for Geoffrey Chaucer's "Franklin's Tale" and "Wife of Bath's Tale." The former, a very complex story of marital fidelity, a love triangle (at least from the perspective of the squire who plots to violate the marriage), an illusion wrought by a magician in support of the squire, and an ethical conflict between jesting oath and vowed relationship, may parody Breton lay tradition rather than straightforwardly use that tradition. In the latter tale, the bold Wife of Bath as teller identifies with an old hag who gains a young knight and, in the process, proclaims the "virtues" of female domination to a knight who needed that lesson because he had violated a woman. In both of Chaucer's lays the romance features exist primarily to delineate the character of the tale teller, that is, the Franklin and the Wife of Bath, but secondarily to entertain and instruct both the company of pilgrims and the reader. Removing cruel rocks from the coast and transforming an ugly hag reflect the idealism of the world of romance in which "anything can happen," to the dismay or delight of the protagonist, but also where, in parody, the moral or didactic concerns are undercut by improbability and much of the purpose is sheer appreciation and entertainment.

"The Matter of France" did not transfer into English with the brilliance with which "the Matter of Britain" transferred into continental vernaculars. Indeed, H.M. Smyser, author of the "Charlemagne Legends" chapter in A *Manual of the Writings in Middle English, 1050–1500*, states, "Viewed in the large, the cycle of Charlemagne differs from the similarly great cycle of Arthur perhaps most importantly in being more commonly and lastingly infused with the spirit of patriotism. Though Arthur was successively a figure of British, Anglo-Norman, and English national feeling, he and his court came to represent cosmopolitan Christian chivalry" (1:80). There are Charlemagne romances in English, but many "consist of translations, adaptations, and compendia," according to Smyser; he continues, "The best of the lot, the ebullient *Taill of Rauf Coilyear*, is only nominally a Charlemagne romance" (1:80). From the *chanson de geste* tradition there are a few Fierabras romances; Fierabras is the Saracen champion whom Oliver (who fought for Charlemagne against the Saracens) defeats, both militarily and religiously (Fierabras asks for baptism) in single combat. Another romance hero is Otuel, a Saracen who is baptized and fights for Christianity; the number of extant versions would suggest that Otuel was more popular than Oliver, perhaps because a converted Saracen sounded more exotic. Frequently these Charlemagne romances, some of which are popular rather than courtly, focus on the Christian motif rather than on the French patriotic one, but their connection to the French king apparently undercut their popularity in England. Related to the Charlemagne stories are a fourteenth-century and two fifteenth-century legends of Godfrey of Bouillon, an eleventh-century duke who became king of Jerusalem. Godfrey was subsequently declared one of the Nine Worthies and given legendary supernatural ancestry (Godfrey's putative ancestor, Charlemagne, is supplemented by swan-knight and swan-maiden and even by swan-children). Like many of the Charlemagne romances, the Godfrey ones often have religious motivation; indeed, R.M. Lumiansky states in "Legends of Godfrey of Bouillon" in *A Manual of the Writings in Middle English, 1050–1500* that "the simple religious theme and the lengthy elementary instruction given Enyas in arms [in *Chevalere Assigne*, the earliest of these romances] permit the speculation that the poem may have been prepared as instruction for boys of about Enyas' age (line 243)" (1:103). Indeed, so unromantic (in spite of swan-people and other supernatural elements) are these romances as a whole that Finlayson says, "The 'Charlemagne romances' are best considered as largely heroic works" (169).

"The Matter of Greece and Rome" fared only a little better in English than did "the Matter of France." The *Gest Historiale of the Destruction of Troy*, a late-fourteenth-century poem written in alliterative long lines, is an artistic treatment of the Trojan War viewed as a historical event; the work is, however, more chronicle than romance both because of its rapid narration and its seeming "historical" realism. The earlier *The Seege of Troye* R.M. Lumiansky classifies as a "minstrel romance," albeit a brief one, in his chapter "Legends of Troy" in *A Manual of the Writings in Middle English, 1050–1500* (1:117). *The Laud Troy-Book* of about 1400 Lumiansky classifies as "a Hector-romance" (1: 117), but it is important more for keeping the legend alive than for literary merit. Lydgate's *Troy-Book*, some Scottish fragments, *The Prose Siege of Troy*, and Caxton's translation *The Recuyell of the Historyes of Troy* from the fifteenth century contribute to the growing body of Troy literature. Geoffrey Chaucer's prior *Troilus and Criseyde* remains the Middle English work of highest literary merit with a matter-of-antiquity plot; it tells of Troilus's and Criseyde's love, of her betrayal of that love after her father betrays their country, and of Troilus's discovery of that betrayal. *Troilus* illustrates how epic and chronicle tradition blend into romance when told with sustained psychological insight into character, with careful plotting and foreshadowing, and with heightened emotion, but the cynicism with which the story is told and the tragedy of its ending make it, strictly speaking, not romance, but another example of generic ambiguity or fluidity. Regardless, it is certainly one of the highlights of Middle English literature and of the Chaucer canon.

In the fifteenth century Robert Henryson's *Testament of Cresseid* develops the aftermath of Chaucer's story in a poem that is, in the words of Florence H. Ridley's "Middle Scots Writers" in *A Manual of the Writings in Middle English, 1050–1500*, "almost a pastiche of literary conventions" (4: 978). Ridley states that it "has been variously interpreted as a study of sin, punishment, and regeneration transcending courtly love; a study of blasphemy against courtly love; an exercise in irony, Cresseid being punished merely for errors of judgment in choosing sexual partners; as a questioning of theological order in which Henryson attacks divine justice unmediated by mercy; as a medieval tragedy illustrating the turn of Fortune's wheel which brings the heroine from high to low, and more recently as an allegory depicting the interplay of appetite, moral virtue, and intellect" (4:978). The poem's focus on the downfallen Cresseid shows how quickly romance can become buried in didacticism, an ever-present tendency, as *Amis and Amiloun* and hagiographic romances also illustrate.

Lydgate's *Siege of Thebes* and *The Prose Siege of Thebes*, both fifteenth century, are the principal romances other than Chaucer's "Knight's Tale" (*The Canterbury Tales*) that deal with Thebes. Indeed, Lydgate presents his poem, consisting of a prologue and three parts, as a sequel to *The Canterbury Tales*. The prologue depicts Lydgate as arriving in Canterbury and being invited to have dinner with Chaucer's pilgrims and to accompany them on the journey back home, provided he tells a tale. The tale begins with Jocasta's pregnancy and the prediction that that son, Oedipus, will kill his father. It is told with much Christian interpolation and clear didactic intent (e.g., moralizing against the evils of pride, covetousness, and war); even though it has some similarity to Chaucer's "Knight's Tale," it is more epic than romance in its scope and detail. Alain Renoir and C. David Benson's "John Lydgate" in *A Manual of the Writings in Middle English 1050–1500*, summarizes the poem (6:1901–1904). Here again, Chaucer triumphs, presenting a story of sworn brotherhood undercut by love at first sight, and a story of seeming justice but also divine caprice. John Kevin Newman, author of *The Classical Epic Tradition*, comments:

On the surface, it ["The Knight's Tale"] is a romance, in which one knight dies for love, and where ultimately the true love of another knight wins through to perfect happiness. . . . But, behind all the external show, there lurk certain grim and ineluctable truths. Men are the instruments or, even worse, the playthings of the gods, who have no sense at all of morality in the human meaning of the word. For men, the horrible truth is that they are frail and they putrefy, and their passions are so irrational as to lead them on against their judgment to their own destruction. (366)

This romantic surface has many ambiguities that render it ultimately, for Newman, an epic in the Callimachean, Virgilian tradition: this tradition uses lyric technique, carefully chosen detail, style with emotional appeal, authorial persona, and language that both "inhibit[s] stereotyped reactions" and "avoid[s] the confident statement and large generalization." This "new epic" tradition becomes "a deliberate means of criticizing by implication the assumptions of the myths the poet handles" and yields a "criticism, which verges on the comic parody, . . . and prevents a passive acquiescence on the part of the reader in a world of guarantees" (Newman 20). Others find in "The Knight's Tale" a romance of idealistic and courtly love that reveals the triumph of worshipful love over conquesting love, of Venus over Mars, but while the reader may conclude that Palamon eventually weds Emilye, Chaucer ends the tale before such a consummation.

Chaucer's romances or quasi-romances are often found at the fringes of the genre: that is part of Chaucer's genius, that he is able to rework a tradition to suit new purposes. One of the purposes to which he puts romance in *The Can-*

terbury Tales is revelation of the character of the tale teller himself or herself. Of course, Chaucer uses other genres, such as saint's tale, fabliau, and beast fable, as well as penitential manual, for that purpose, but the romances tend both to hide and to reveal the tale teller at one and the same time. For instance, Chaucer the pilgrim tells a stupid, singsong "tale of Sir Thopas," but in doing so, he shows this observant introducer of the pilgrims in the "General Prologue" to be a careful observer of literary production as well: "Sir Thopas" is a wonderful parody of English romances such as *Guy of Warwick*. Chaucer knows that literary popularity and literary merit do not always coincide, but then Chaucer the poet parodies Chaucer the pilgrim's parody by permitting this pilgrim to be interrupted by a Host who knows how to interrupt, to flatter, to insult, but not to create. The Wife of Bath's tale of rape in an Arthurian fairyland becomes a tale of transformation revealing the Wife's strong desire to be other than she is, in spite of all the proud self-assertion of her own prologue. This Breton lay is wonderfully romantic in its wish-fulfillment motif and its "happily-ever-after" resolution. "The Man of Law's Tale," the romantic and pseudohagiographic tale of Custance, shows, according to Joseph Hornsby's chapter in *Chaucer's Pilgrims: An Historical Guide to the Pilgrims in* The Canterbury Tales, "a glimpse of the common lawyer's mindset. Part of that mindset is a confidence in the crucial role law and lawyers play in society, a confidence that over the centuries grew into an arrogance" (132). The tale about Griselda with its praise of her patience and obedience suits its pilgrim teller, the Clerk, not only because it comes from Petrarch's translation into Latin of Boccaccio's final *Decameron* tale, an appropriate source for clerics and scholars, but also because it prepares for the Clerk's antifeminist song in his epilogue. Bert Dillon, also writing in *Chaucer's Pilgrims*, shows how this tale reveals, together with its own prologue and epilogue as well as the "General Prologue" description, the pilgrim Clerk as "certainly admirable, but not without foibles; he may be ideal, but he certainly is not perfect" (114). The tale is romantic in its depiction of Griselda's loyal love and its "rags-to-riches"-and-back-to-rags-and-then-again-to-riches motif, but Griselda's self-effacement, reinforced by other marriage tales in *The Canterbury Tales*, may lead to its being read as parody; romantic idealism can easily, especially in the hands of a great writer, undercut itself.

John Gower's *Confessio Amantis* is a fourteenth-century collection of 133 tales, some of them romances, in a framing device. Although Gower stays closer to his sources than does Chaucer, Gower's use of romance is no more straightforward than Chaucer's: Chaucer's many pilgrim narrators, described in the "General Prologue" and sometimes interacting with each other along the pilgrimage, provide many angles from which to see the stories both as revelations of various tellers and as attacks on various pilgrims (fabliaux are used in this way even more than romance and saints' legends are) or at least as replies to other tales and pilgrims. Again, romance proves a remarkably plastic genre, ready to be molded by great writers into satire, criticism, irony, and even parody. Most of the tales in *Confessio Amantis* illustrate one of the seven deadly sins or a virtue that is its opposite and achieve interpretive ambiguity because this "confession" is to a priest of Venus—not of Christ—who uses the tales to instruct the "penitent" or aged lover, Amans, in the "sins" that are violations of courtly love or Christian precept and in the "virtues" that are their opposites. In the words of John H. Fisher and his colleagues, authors of the "John Gower" chapter in *A Manual of the Writings in Middle English, 1050–1500*, "The gods of love [i.e., Venus and Cupid] traditionally represent amoral or even immoral love, and are antagonistic to reason and divine order. Yet here we find them advocating reason and law. Their priest, Genius, gives advice not only on courtly love, but also on lawful married love, and on ascetic love. Thus he is no mere representative of the carnal, but of the divine forces of unity" (7:2209). In this way the romances, as well as many of the other tales, juxtapose or even super-impose two sets of values, courtly and Christian. In *Narrative, Authority, and Power: The Medieval Exemplum and the Chaucerian Tradition*, Larry Scanlon shows that Gower's purpose is not pious; indeed, the poem is anticlerical, sus-picious of lay as well as clerical authority, and critical of romance: "Gower's objection to romance is that it insufficiently recognizes its own contingencies" (268). According to Scanlon, Gower undercuts

the negational and utopian gestures which the romance characteristically employs. In the transgressive erotic relationships that define romance, *gentilesse* displays itself most em-phatically in the impossible pursuit of a love it cannot have. That is to say, romance makes *gentilesse* knowable precisely by the magnitude of its failure, by its incapacity to bend historical necessity to its own control. The adventurous, competitive spirit that drives the romance hero toward his forbidden love can never finish until it confronts the chivalric community that both gives that spirit meaning and forbids its full expression, and either the hero or the community, or both, are destroyed. Gower will defuse the dilemma by insisting on the radical contingency of both erotic desire and the ideological limits which constrain it. (269)

Significantly, the book (8) that deals with what one would expect to be the sin of lechery or lust deals with incest, using a retelling of the Greek/Byzantine romance of Apollonius of Tyre as the major exemplum. It also comes just after the book that departs from the motif of the seven deadly sins by considering the education of a king (book 7). An incestuous king becomes as much an example of misrule as of lechery. Here and elsewhere in Gower, romance be-comes a vehicle of political critique. Scanlon writes, "Gower's explicit engage-ment with the political was no less important in the establishment of the Chaucerian tradition than Chaucer's reappropriation and redefinition of clerical tradition. As the fifteenth century put the tradition in place, it gave the tradition Chaucer's name, and made him its authoritative source. In so doing, however, they drew just as heavily on the more explicitly political models of authority developed by Gower" (297).

The showcase of English romance in both the fourteenth and fifteenth centuries is certainly in "the Matter of Britain." Here again the intimate relationship among chronicle, epic, and romance traditions is apparent, as well as the use of romance for didactic, moralistic, social, and political instruction, or for commentary or satire. Helaine Newstead, in the chapter entitled "Arthurian Legends" in *A Manual of the Writings in Middle English, 1050–1500*, divides these romances into eight categories by principal characters (the Holy Grail, her sixth division, being almost a character): "The Whole Life of Arthur," "Merlin and the Youth of Arthur," "Lancelot and the Last Years of Arthur," "Gawain," "Perceval," "The Holy Grail," "Tristram," and "Arthur of Little Britain" (1:38–79). Layamon's *Brut*, the alliterative *Morte d'Arthur*, and Malory's *Morte d'Arthur* provide the most important whole-life portrayals of Arthur and stem from the "historical" tradition of Geoffrey of Monmouth's Latin *Historia Regum Britanniae* (c. 1136) and its courtly adaptation into the Old French *Le Roman de Brut* (1155) by Wace, who adds to the basic plot the Round Table and explicit Breton hope of Arthur's return. Both these works and Layamon's *Brut* are chronicles purporting to tell the history of Britain by focusing on its monarchs. As discussed previously, the alliterative *Morte Arthure* is more epic or tragedy than romance; that leaves Malory's fifteenth-century prose as the principal Middle English romance of Arthur's entire life. One of Malory's great inspirations for his work is the Vulgate Cycle, a series of Old French prose romances that incorporate a Grail history, a Merlin, a Lancelot, a Grail Quest, and a death-of-Arthur romance.

Malory's work may be a series of eight separate romances (see Eugène Vinaver, *The Works of Sir Thomas Malory* 1:xxv–lvi), or it may be a long, extended romance of interlocking parts (see Lumiansky, *Malory's Originality;* for another analysis, into five parts, see Benson). Certainly there are sequence and connection among the romances or parts, as well as themes and motifs extending through the various parts or romances, but where authorial purpose and emphasis lie is debatable. Thus, again, romance is a multivalent genre, and the dividing line between a sequence of romances and one long romance of many parts is not clear. Regardless, Malory's *Morte d'Arthur* provides a story of Arthur from before his conception until after his death, with major emphasis on the establishment of Arthur's kingdom; his war against the emperor Lucius; the knightly careers of Gawain, Lancelot, Gareth, and Tristram; the Grail Quest; and the final dissolution of Arthur's kingdom. Malory departs from the chronology of the alliterative *Morte d'Arthur*, one of his many sources, so that the war against the emperor Lucius occurs relatively early in Arthur's career, not just prior to his final battle. Arthur is thus, throughout much of Malory, a king whose knights engage in their own quests—a frequent romance feature. Charles Moorman shows in *The Book of Kyng Arthur* that three great themes of failure unite Malory's narrative: the failure in love (shown especially in the adultery of Lancelot and Guinevere), the failure in chivalry (shown especially in the quarrel between the houses of Pellinore and of Lot, a quarrel that persists in spite of the sworn brotherhood of the Round Table), and the failure in religion (shown especially in the failure of the Grail Quest undertaken by all 150 Round Table knights but achieved by only 3). All of these failures are presented in romance manner as departures from an explicit ideal, an ideal to which all the knights subscribe each year at Pentecost. The Round Table is the great ideal: early iconography of Jesus' final supper with his disciples before his crucifixion presents a round table, and roundness often represents eternity. Malory's Arthur begins as a Christ figure, complete with hidden parentage (though no virgin birth), who establishes his kingship through removing the sword from the stone at the great feasts representing Jesus Christ's life from nativity through resurrection; he removes the sword from the stone one final time at Pentecost. Arthur falls, however, as does Lancelot (or Lancelot Galahad, as he was named), the next almost Christ figure. Galahad, son of Lancelot and Elaine, succeeds in truly representing Christ throughout his appearances in the narrative: such idealism is one of the signs of romance. Malory's work has psychological depth in its characterization, especially as Lancelot's divided loyalties, to religion, to king, and to queen, develop. It also nostalgically looks backward from chivalry's disintegration in Malory's fifteenth century to its twelfth-century flowering, to Arthur's kingdom, as flawed as it is glorious. *Morte d'Arthur* remains the high point of Middle English prose romance and of fifteenth-century romance (see Wilson, "Malory and Caxton," in *A Manual of the Writings in Middle English, 1050–1500*).

   Arthour and Merlin, The Prose Merlin, and *Lovelich's Merlin* are the principal Middle English romances of Merlin. Newstead, in "Arthurian Legends" in *A Manual of the Writings in Middle English, 1050–1500*, does not consider any of these of high literary merit but finds *The Prose Merlin* significant because it is a pre-Malory English Arthurian prose work (1:49). Lancelot's story is found in the stanzaic *Morte d'Arthur,* in Malory, in the Scottish *Lancelot of the Laik,* and in two ballads. The stanzaic version of about 1400 was an important influence on Malory but is also important for its literary merit: good, fast-paced narration with clear direction. The narrative is full of misunderstandings: the maid of Astolat who wrongly concludes that Lancelot loves her, the queen who wrongly concludes from something Gawain said that Lancelot has betrayed her love, and the court that deems the queen guilty of murder. The maiden's letter and Lancelot's defense of the queen in trial by combat correct these last two misperceptions, but Agravain and Mordred, brother and half brother to Gawain, betray not only Lancelot and Guinevere but King Arthur himself. Again Lancelot must rescue the queen, this time from burning, but tragedy ensues as Arthur pursues and Gawain fights Lancelot, as Mordred usurps the throne, and Arthur and Mordred kill each other. Misunderstanding has prepared the way for evil-willed betrayal, but after another betrayal as Bedivere twice fails to follow Arthur's command about Excalibur, Arthur's sword, the tragic ending of king and kingdom yields to hope as Guinevere becomes a nun, later to be united with Arthur in the grave; after Lancelot becomes a hermit-priest and guardian of Arthur's grave, he dies with visionary testimony to his salvation. *Doublement,* focus on individual knights and king rather than on kingdom itself, characters typed as primarily good (though Lancelot and Guinevere are adulterous, they have many redeeming features and are ultimately redeemed) or primarily evil, and the "happily-ever-after" ending—even though "after" here is after death—create a romantic vision of great but forbidden love bending to a higher love.

Newstead points out that church influence on the French prose *Gawain* denigrated his character, but only in the stanzaic version and in Malory is the English Gawain denigrated (1:53). For Malory, Gawain is an ever-vengeful knight who never understands Arthur's great Pentecostal oath necessitating mercy to anyone who asks it, who never understands that the Grail Quest is a spiritual quest to be undertaken only by those who are shriven, and who causes the final denouement by insisting on avenging the death of his brothers, Gaheris and Gareth, an insistence that pits Arthur against Lancelot in a war in France and provides the opportunity for Mordred's treasonous usurpation. Newstead lists twelve Gawain works in Middle English, but not all of them are romances (e.g., the ballad *The Marriage of Sir Gawaine*), and several of them are inferior derivatives of that paragon of English Gawain romances, *Sir Gawain and the Green Knight* (1:53–54). This Gawain romance does not attempt a whole life: it focuses on two New Year's Day feasts and the intervening year in a wonderful combination of folklore motifs—the beheading game, the vegetation myth, the arming and testing of the hero, the exchange of winnings. Plot and place details become number symbolic, for example, two feasts, two parts of the beheading game, two courts, three temptations, four parts, four seasons. The poem's opening and closing stanzas' almost universal scope contrasts with particularity of incident and knight within, while the stanzaic pattern and the alliterative pattern complicate the verse, and reality and illusion (as knightly loyalty is genuinely tested at the initial beheading scene by an illusory Green Knight, i.e., Bercilak in disguise) exist in marvelous tension. Ultimately these tensions are united in the paradoxical conclusion that mark of shame and badge of honor are one and the same as Gawain retains the green girdle to remind him of his act of deception in withholding that winning and as Arthur's court wears the green girdle to remind them that Gawain was faithful in all else. The vegetation myth of life, death, and rebirth; the rise and fall of civilizations yielding to rebirth of others; and the Christian proclamation of life, death, and spiritual rebirth unite with the year-and-a-day time scheme in a great natural, civilizational, and spiritual cycle—an idealistic, romance portrayal of how the individual can fit into the great scheme of things.

Several other Gawain romances deserve brief mention. *Ywain and Gawain* is an artistic reworking of the story in Chrétien's *Yvain*. The romance has many supernatural trappings, such as a ring with which Ywain becomes invisible and a lion tamed by being rescued, but it also explores issues of knightly honor and love as Ywain's divided loyalties to knightly quest and to the woman he married come into conflict. After a broken commitment to his wife results in Ywain's being banished, disguise almost results in Round Table knight harming Round

Table knight as Gawain and Ywain fight; the romance ends in double reconciliation, between Gawain and Ywain, who recognize each other, and between Ywain and his wife, who recognizes her need of a knightly champion as well as a husband, so that Ywain's two roles unite. Here the doubling of incident and motif juxtaposes the knightly world and the amatory world as disguise and conflict occur in parallel forms in both. *The Wedding of Sir Gawain and Dame Ragnell* is a late-fifteenth-century romance about a loathly lady who is transformed; a more artistic treatment of this motif is Chaucer's "Wife of Bath's Tale."

There is only one romance focusing on Perceval in Middle English literature, the early-fourteenth-century *Sir Perceval of Galles*. Using some of the same plot as Chrétien's *Le Conte du Graal* (1180), this romance tells of Perceval's childhood, his setting out to become a knight of Arthur's court, his slaying of the Red Knight who repeatedly stole Arthur's goblets, his rescue of the lady Lufamour from Saracens who attack her castle, his knighting, his marriage to Lufamour, his yearlong quest to find his mother, his eventual reunion with her, and his return with her to Lufamour. Later Perceval is slain in the Holy Land after many successful battles there. Unlike Chrétien's unfinished work, this poem has a happy ending as Perceval is reunited with his mother and dies a holy death. The Middle English romance glories in supernatural marvels and the exploits of its hero but does not mention the Grail. It is more important for its relationship to other Perceval and Grail stories than for its literary merit.

The early history of the Grail is found in *Joseph of Arimathie*, a mid-fourteenth-century fragment that is significant because it is, in Newstead's words, "probably the earliest extant alliterative poem" (1:74). It and Henry Lovelich's *The History of the Holy Grail* used the French Vulgate Cycle's *Lestoire del Saint Graal* as their source—the Grail is a Christian cup, not simply a large serving platter (as in Chrétien)—but from a literary point of view, both of these works lack distinction. The most important Grail romance in Middle English is the sixth section of Malory's *Morte d'Arthur*. Malory uses the Vulgate Cycle's *Les Aventures ou La Queste del Saint Graal* as his principal source. In both Malory and the Vulgate Grail Quest, there are three achievers: Galahad, Perceval, and Bors; the story abounds in marvels and clearly delineated good and evil (though, as mentioned previously, occasionally that delineation is revealed in retrospect) and ends happily for the achievers (the others' failure is also fortunate in that it is portrayed as just).

Sir Tristrem, of the late thirteenth century, is the only English Tristram version except that within Malory's work. This version is close enough to that of Thomas, a twelfth-century Anglo-Norman poet, that it is useful in reconstructing lost portions of Thomas even though *Sir Tristrem*'s damaged manuscript ends without conclusion. *Sir Tristrem* is marred by distracting versification and its overcondensation of its source. Malory's version in the fifth section of *Morte d'Arthur*, too, ends without conclusion, as Malory recounts only about two-thirds of the Tristram plot, although Tristram's death is reported later in *Morte d'Arthur.* The Tristram story becomes for Malory a comparison that reiterates ideas from Malory's main Arthur/Lancelot plot: two kings, Arthur and Mark; two knights who betray them, Lancelot and Tristram; two queens, Guinevere and Isolde, who betray their husbands. There is, however, a big difference in that Mark is a traitor himself, a coward, and a bad king, while Arthur is quite the opposite, honorable, courageous, and a good king. This contrast of Lancelot and Tristram both serves Malory's thematic purposes and illustrates romance's use of character types and sharply drawn moral distinctions.

A Manual of the Writings in Middle English, 1050–1500 contains important descriptions of romances, some background information and commentary, and a bibliography listing manuscripts, printed texts, editions, and critical material. Middle English romances occupy the whole of volume 1, published in 1967 (see the following six bibliography entries: Donovan, Dunn, Hornstein, Lumiansky, Newstead, and Smyser), with material on Malory and Caxton (see Wilson), Gower (see Fisher et al.), Lydgate (see Renoir and Benson), and Middle Scots writers (see Ridley) in later volumes of the manual. Joanne A.Rice's *Middle English Romance: An Annotated Bibliography, 1955–1985* is a useful supplement to *A Manual*. Other useful supplementary information for "the Matter of Britain" is in the annual periodical *Bulletin Bibliographique de la Société Internationale Arthurienne* (also known as *Bibliographical Bulletin of the International Arthurian Society*), and for all romances the annual *MLA Bibliography* provides references. James P. Carley's "England," in *Medieval Arthurian Literature: A Guide to Recent Research* provides a very useful discussion of the critical literature and a bibliography of bibliographies (including bibliographic articles and surveys), editions and translations, and critical studies. *Motif-Index of the English Metrical Romances* by Gerald Bordman and *Motif-Index of Folk-Literature*, edited by Stith Thompson, are invaluable guides to recurring motifs in romance. An increasingly important source for texts, bibliographic information, and criticism is, of course, the Internet. Argos Limited Area Search of the Ancient and Medieval Internet, housed at the University of Evansville, is a peer-reviewed search engine that tries to ensure active links. The Labyrinth: Resources for Medieval Studies, housed at Georgetown University, is the primary medieval Web site, with text, image, and archival databases, and with links to other Web sites, including the University of Virginia's E-text site and the University of Michigan's Corpus of Middle English Verse and Prose, a site for selecting and searching within texts. (Currently the Labyrinth is being revamped for the new millennium and the University of Virginia is moving the E-text site; consult a general search engine to find these sites.)

   The following bibliographical suggestions emphasize studies that focus on genre and newer studies that are not mentioned in *A Manual of the Writings in Middle English, 1050–1500. The Popular Literature of Medieval England* in Tennessee Studies in Literature, volume 28, collects thirteen articles on various aspects of medieval popular culture, examining who "the people" are and discussing folkloric sources, among other topics. Its article "Romance" by Edmund

Reiss is especially apropos. Lee C. Ramsey's *Chivalric Romances: Popular Literature in Medieval England* is a more extended treatment that focuses on motifs, types, and conventions. *Writing Aloud: Storytelling in Late Medieval England*, by Nancy Mason Bradbury, focuses on five medieval romances (*The Tale of Gamelyn, Havelok the Dane, The Seege of Troye, Kyng Alisaunder*, and *Troilus and Criseyde*), on the wide variation within what were called "metrical romances," and on the performative aspects that gave rise to these variations. She states, "The romances are the products (and are also among the producers) of the slow but great transition from the predominance of oral to written storytelling traditions in late medieval England. Thus, it is important not to treat them as monolithic in terms either of their audiences or of their historical means of transmission" (21). *Companion to Middle English Romance*, edited by Henk Aertsen and Alasdair A. MacDonald, contains commissioned articles offering various critical approaches, for instance, articles about French background, narrative mode, psychology, and women; the *Companion*'s "Romance and Parody" by Wim Tigges is especially perceptive about stylistic and thematic romance conventions. Tigges concludes that "Chaucer was the first and the last intellectual in whose own time 'good' romances were still being composed and enjoyed. . . . He was therefore one of the few authors who could afford to criticise the genre which for him, entertaining as it may have been, had little or nothing to offer in the way of conveying his individual poetic spirit" (149–150). John Stevens's *Medieval Romance: Themes and Approaches* distinguishes experience from genre and provides an excellent extended analysis of various idealisms found in medieval romance. *The Arthur of the English: The Arthurian Legend in Medieval English Life and Literature*, edited by W.R.J. Barron, the second volume in the series Arthurian Literature in the Middle Ages, contains eight chapters, five of which are directly focused on romance (its tradition; the dynastic, chivalric, and folk romances; and Malory), as well as three other chapters and two interchapters that provide additional background. The book contains extensive bibliographical references and is the best place for initiating study of "the Matter of Britain" in English.

P.J.C. Field, in *Romance and Chronicle: A Study of Malory's Prose Style*, studies "the way in which Malory's style contributes to the meaning of the *Morte d'Arthur* as a whole" and observes, "Malory's style is unusually interesting in combining a strong demand for emotional response with a quite exceptional degree of self-effacement by the author within the story" (2, 5). In analyzing style, narration, description, dialogue, and the narrator's role, Field sheds light on some linguistic as well as emotional distinctions between romance and chronicle. *Irony in the Medieval Romance* by D.H. Green concerns signs and methods of irony as it interacts with chivalric and love motives; verbal, narrative, dramatic, and structural irony; and irony of values and reasons for irony in medieval romance. He observes that "there is no logical contradiction in poets [*sic*] applying irony to an ideal of courtliness (or of chivalry or love) which they are in process of propagating, for they make use of irony not to undermine or destroy that ideal, but to define it more clearly and to reach agreement on the detailed choices and decisions with which it confronts society" (324–325). Piero Boitani's *English Medieval Narrative in the Thirteenth and Fourteenth Centuries* considers technique in a different light by looking closely at religious and comic traditions, dream, and vision. Boitani defines the world of romance and studies narrative collections, Gower, and especially Chaucer. Chronicle and its relationship to romance are also investigated by Rosalind Field's article "Romance as History, History as Romance" in *Romance in Medieval England*, edited by Maldwyn Mills, Jennifer Fellows, and Carol M. Meale. Field concludes, in part, "History will continue to appeal (to the popular mind, we may say defensively) in terms of romance stereotype and mythic patterning; and romance will continue to provide a view of history which is acceptable and comprehensible. . . . The longevity of the historical myth created by the Anglo-Norman writers and preserved as 'tradition' by Middle English writers is impressive" (173).

SELECTED BIBLIOGRAPHY

Amster, Mark E. "Literary Theory and the Genres of Middle English Literature." *Genre* 13 (1980): 389–396.

Barron, W.R.J., ed. *The Arthur of the English: The Arthurian Legend in Medieval English Life and Literature.* Arthurian Literature in the Middle Ages 2. Cardiff: University of Wales Press, 1999.

Benson, Larry D. *Malory's Morte Darthur.* Cambridge, MA: Harvard University Press, 1976.

Boitani, Piero. *English Medieval Narrative in the Thirteenth and Fourteenth Centuries.* Trans. Joan Krakover Hall. New York: Cambridge University Press, 1982.

Bordman, Gerald. *Motif-Index of the English Metrical Romances.* FF Communications No. 190. Ed. for the Folklore Fellows by Reidar Th. Christiansen et al. Helsinki: Suomalainen Tiedeakatemia, Academia Scientiarum Fennica, 1963.

Bradbury, Nancy Mason. *Writing Aloud: Storytelling in Late Medieval England.* Urbana: University of Illinois Press, 1998.

Carley, James P. "England." *Medieval Arthurian Literature: A Guide to Recent Research.* Ed. Norris J. Lacy. New York: Garland, 1996. 1–82.

Dillon, Bert. "A Clerk Ther Was of Oxenford Also." *Chaucer's Pilgrims: An Historical Guide to the Pilgrims in* The Canterbury Tales. Ed. Laura C. Lambdin and Robert T. Lambdin. Westport, CT: Greenwood Press, 1996. 108–115.

Donovan, Mortimer J. "Breton Lays." *A Manual of the Writings in Middle English, 1050–1500.* Gen. ed. J. Burke Severs. New Haven: Connecticut Academy of Arts and Sciences, 1967. 1:133–143, 292–297.

Dunn, Charles W. "Romances Derived from English Legends." *A Manual of the Writings in Middle English, 1050–1500.* Gen. ed. J. Burke Severs. New Haven: Connecticut Academy of Arts and Sciences, 1967. 1:17–37, 206–224.

Field, P.J.C. *Romance and Chronicle: A Study of Malory's Prose Style.* Bloomington: Indiana University Press, 1971.

Field, Rosalind. "Romance as History, History as Romance." *Romance in Medieval England.* Ed. Maldwyn Mills, Jennifer Fellows, and Carol M. Meale. Cambridge: D.S. Brewer, 1991. 163–173.

Finlayson, John. "Definitions of Middle English Romance." Parts 1 and 2. *Chaucer Review* 15 (1980): 44–62, 168–181.

Fisher, John H., R. Wayne Hamm, Peter G. Beidler, and Robert F. Yeager. "John Gower." *A Manual of the Writings in Middle English, 1050–1500*. Gen. ed. Albert E. Hartung. New Haven: Connecticut Academy of Arts and Sciences, 1986. 7: 2195–2210, 2399–2418.

Foster, Edward E. "Simplicity, Complexity, and Morality in Four Medieval Romances." *Chaucer Review* 31 (1997): 401–419.

Green, D.H. *Irony in the Medieval Romance*. New York: Cambridge University Press, 1979.

Hornsby, Joseph. "A Sergeant of the Lawe, War and Wyse." *Chaucer's Pilgrims: An Historical Guide to the Pilgrims in* The Canterbury Tales. Ed. Laura C. Lambdin and Robert T. Lambdin. Westport, CT: Greenwood Press, 1996. 116–134.

Hornstein, Lillian Herlands. "Eustace-Constance-Florence-Griselda Legends" and "Miscellaneous Romances." *A Manual of the Writings in Middle English, 1050–1500*. Gen. ed. J. Burke Severs. New Haven: Connecticut Academy of Arts and Sciences, 1967. 1:120–132, 278–291; 1:144–172, 298–332.

Hume, Kathryn. "Structure and Perspective: Romance and Hagiographic Features in the Amicus and Amelius Story." *JEGP* 69 (1970): 59–107.

Lumiansky, R.M. "Legends of Alexander the Great," "Legends of Godfrey of Bouillon," "Legends of Thebes," and "Legends of Troy." *A Manual of the Writings in Middle English, 1050–1500*. Gen. ed. J. Burke Severs. New Haven: Connecticut Academy of Arts and Sciences, 1967. 1:104–113, 268–273; 1:101–103, 267–268; 1:119, 277; 1:114–118, 274–277.

———, ed. *Malory's Originality: A Critical Study of Le Morte Darthur*. Baltimore: Johns Hopkins Press, 1964.

Matthews, William. *The Tragedy of Arthur: A Study of the Alliterative "Morte Arthure."* Berkeley: University of California Press, 1960.

Moorman, Charles. *The Book of Kyng Arthur: The Unity of Malory's Morte Darthur*. Lexington: University of Kentucky Press, 1965.

Newman, John Kevin. *The Classical Epic Tradition*. Wisconsin Studies in Classics. Gen. eds. Barbara Hughes Fowler and Warren G. Moon. Madison: University of Wisconsin Press, 1986.

Newstead, Helaine. "Arthurian Legends" and "Romances: General." *A Manual of the Writings in Middle English, 1050–1500*. Gen. ed. J. Burke Severs. New Haven: Connecticut Academy of Arts and Sciences, 1967. 1:38–79, 224–256; 1:9–16, 199–205.

Ramsey, Lee C. *Chivalric Romances: Popular Literature in Medieval England*. Bloomington: Indiana University Press, 1983.

Reiss, Edmund. "Romance." *The Popular Literature of Medieval England*. Ed. Thomas J. Heffernan. Tennessee Studies in Literature, 28. Knoxville: University of Tennessee Press, 1985. 108–130.

Renoir, Alain, and C. David Benson. "John Lydgate." *A Manual of the Writings in Middle English, 1050–1500*. Gen. ed. Albert E. Hartung. New Haven: Connecticut Academy of Arts and Sciences, 1980. 6:1809–1920, 2071–2175.

Rice, Joanne A. *Middle English Romance: An Annotated Bibliography, 1955–1985*. New York: Garland Publishing, 1987.

Ridley, Florence H. "Middle Scots Writers." *A Manual of the Writings in Middle English,*

1050–1500. Gen. ed. Albert E. Hartung. New Haven: Connecticut Academy of Arts and Sciences, 1973. 4:961–1060, 1123–1284.

Scanlon, Larry. *Narrative, Authority, and Power: The Medieval Exemplum and the Chaucerian Tradition.* Cambridge: Cambridge University Press, 1994.

Smyser, H.M. "Charlemagne Legends." *A Manual of the Writings in Middle English, 1050–1500.* Gen. ed. J. Burke Severs. New Haven: Connecticut Academy of Arts and Sciences, 1967. 1:80–100, 256–266.

Stevens, John. *Medieval Romance: Themes and Approaches.* New York: Norton, 1973.

Strohm, Paul. "Middle English Narrative Genres." *Genre* 13 (1980): 379–388.

Thompson, Stith, ed. *Motif-Index of Folk-Literature: A Classification of Narrative Elements in Folktales, Ballads, Myths, Fables, Mediaeval Romances, Exempla, Fabliaux, Jest-Books, and Local Legends.* Rev. and enl. ed. 6 vols. Bloomington: Indiana University Press, 1966.

Tigges, Wim. "Romance and Parody." *Companion to Middle English Romance.* Ed. Henk Aertsen and Alasdair A. MacDonald. Amsterdam: VU University Press, 1990. 129–151.

Vinaver, Eugène, ed. *The Works of Sir Thomas Malory.* 2nd ed. 3 vols. Oxford: Clarendon Press, 1967. 3rd ed. rev. P.J.C. Field. New York: Oxford, University Press, 1990.

Wilson, Robert H. "Malory and Caxton." *A Manual of the Writings in Middle English, 1050–1500.* Gen ed. Albert E. Hartung. New Haven: Connecticut Academy of Arts and Sciences, 1972. 3:757–807, 909–951.

19

Visions of the Afterlife

Ed Eleazar

Belief in a life beyond the grave is a common theme throughout many of the world's major religions and has been such for at least the last six thousand years. The earliest written texts of which we have any knowledge, such as the epic of *Gilgamesh*, assume that eternal life is available to mortals in a realm beyond this present reality. Even in our own millennium, characterized as it has been by the ascent of rational, empirical thought and skepticism, belief in life eternal has persisted, fueling many elements of popular culture such as UFO abduction tales, blockbuster movies (*Ghost, What Dreams May Come*), and best-selling books (*Talking to Heaven, Embraced by the Light*). Belief in existence beyond the grave runs so deep in American culture that one of our major universities has even begun a long-term experiment to test its possibility (Japenga 18–19). Is it any wonder, then, that during the Middle Ages—the "Age of Faith"—that stories purporting to be visions of the world to come, told by men and women who had actually visited it in the spirit and returned, would become one of the most popular literary genres?

For the Christian church, the Revelation of St. John the Divine (especially chapters 20–22) represents the canonical locus classicus of all vision literature. However, many other early, noncanonical texts were also available to writers of the Old and Middle English periods, the most influential being the Apocalypse of Paul and the Apocalypse of St. Peter, both of which appeared roughly between the mid-second or early third centuries (MacRae and Murdock 257; Brashler and Bullard 373). Given the extensive history of otherworld visitations between 100 and 1500 A.D., it seems most prudent to restrict our discussion solely to the development of this genre in the Old and Middle English periods. Students desiring further discussion of the materials available to medieval authors should consult the studies of E.J. Becker, Howard R. Patch, A.B. van Os, and Carol Zaleski cited in the Selected Bibliography for this chapter. Our purpose here will be to provide a brief overview of a widely and wildly popular medieval literary genre that has just lately come to be recognized as a fertile field for study.

DEFINING THE GENRE

Classifying the various sorts of afterlife visions has caused modern scholars some trouble, particularly since these tales appear in such a wide variety of forms. English texts currently classified or dealt with as "otherworld visions" or "tales of the afterlife" were originally classified by John Wells in *A Manual of the Writings in Middle English* under a variety of categories, such as "Visits to the Underworld," "Homilies and Legends," and "Pious Tales." Even the more recent *Manual* edited by J. Burke Severs and Albert E. Hartung (1967–present), which devotes an entire chapter to "Legends of the After-Life" (Foster 452–457), places at least one text regarding the nature of purgatory in its chapter on "Dialogue, Debates, and Catechisms" (Utley 698–700). For the purposes of our investigations, we will follow the most recent definition as outlined by Robert Easting (" 'Send' " 186–187) and others, that is, to view any text whose major purpose is to describe a personal experience in the afterlife as being an otherworldly "vision."

This means that the genre includes tales that fall under no fewer than four major headings: (1) the *imram*, a tale like *The Voyage of St. Brendan* or *The Voyage of Bran*, in which the main characters and a group of followers go on real-time journeys through the physical world in search of the Earthly Paradise; (2) visions arising from altered states of reality, usually involving a person's falling into a near-death-like trance; (3) tales involving one person's entrance into an actual, temporal site long regarded as an entrance to the otherworld; and (4) tales involving the return of the dead to deliver a message to those still among the living. The *imram* never gained wide popularity as a form during either the Old or Middle English periods, and as a result, the surviving English visions are primarily tales either of men who have had an altered-state experience or of the return of the dead.

Descriptions of trancelike visions are by far the more frequent motif for English otherworld tales, and the vast majority of these grow out of visits to and sojourns through St. Patrick's Purgatory at Lough Derg, Ireland. In the early twelfth century the Canons Regular of St. Augustine had a priory on Saints' Island in the middle of Lough Derg, a massive lake covering more than 2,200 acres in south central Ireland, twenty-five miles north of the city of Limerick. Through this priory the Augustinians controlled access to Station Island, on which there was a cave generally believed to be an entrance into purgatory, one blessed by St. Patrick himself ("St. Patrick's Purgatory," *New Catholic Encyclopedia*). In 1150 an English knight named Owen made a pilgrimage to this "purgatory," and an account of his visions was written down by a Cistercian monk, H[enry] of Sawtry, in a tract entitled *Tractatus de Purgatorio Sancti Patricii* (*St. Patrick's* xvii). This Latin text was widely disseminated throughout Europe after 1180 and inspired other pilgrims to request entry to the purgatory, thereby encouraging other written accounts of visions vouchsafed to men who had spent three days and nights in the Station Island cave as required by the Augustinian monks.

An almost equal number of tales in Old and Middle English do not involve an actual visit to St. Patrick's Purgatory, but do involve an altered state of perception not unlike those of the pilgrims who underwent sensory deprivation and hunger in the Station Island cave. This second sort of vision is frequently vouchsafed to a monk, but does occur to laymen as well. In this subgenre the visionary enters a near-death trance so closely resembling death that friends and neighbors think that the person has actually died. The body is described as being cold on one side, but slightly warm on the other, implying that some life still resides in the corpse. While the visionary's community assembles to pray over his body, either for a night or sometimes for two to three days, the visionary's soul goes on a tour through the otherworld. When the vision is over, the dead man awakes, much to the surprise of family and friends, and lives an exemplary life ever after.

But whether they are engendered by three days without food and water in a dark cave or in the semiconsciousness of a catatonic fit, all afterlife tales share several structural elements that make them recognizably members of a particular genre. Each begins with (1) a description of the soul of the visionary exiting the body, followed immediately by (2) a judgment as to this person's fitness for entering heaven. This judgment scene, usually replete with graphic depictions of hideous demons arguing with the Virgin and/or Christ for control of the visionary's soul, is followed by (3) the introduction of a spirit guide for the visionary, either an angel or a saint, who directs him on (4) a journey through the various levels of hell, purgatory, or heaven. The descriptions of hell in particular become quite memorable, due to the extremely sadistic nature of the imagery; they are, however, also quite formulaic. Hell is chaotic in the extreme, since it has traditionally been described as the epitome of chaos, being as far removed from the glory and order of God as one can possibly be. The atmosphere there is characterized by unbearable, hideous noise—wailing, crying, cursing, the growling and shouting of demons. A variety of horrible smells cloud the air and choke the visionary's lungs—usually burning sulfur or rotten and scorched flesh. The visionary's eyes are frequently dimmed or partially blinded except to those sights that harrow up the soul and freeze the blood, and routinely, the tortures he encounters in hell involve a sort of poetic justice. For example, folk whose primary sin on earth was lying might have their tongues cut out repeatedly or be forced to drink molten metals such as lead, silver, or brass. Folks whose primary sin in life was pride of appearance are often horribly disfigured and forced to parade themselves before laughing demons; adulterers are strung up on wheels by their genitalia and slow-roasted over lightless flames.

Through all this, the spirit guide prompts the visionary forward, explains the chaos, and clarifies its deeper meaning to the visionary's life as well as the life of his community.

A fifth element found in many otherworld tales is the personal test the visionary must pass. Since upon exiting the body most visionaries are deemed worthy of suffering hell's pains, they often have to cross a "test bridge," usually over a river full of damned souls floating downward toward the depths of hell. Of course, the bridge the dreamer has to cross is very narrow, a physical representation of Jesus' image of the "way that leads to life eternal" (Matthew 7: 14), and often the trial it presents is apparently insurmountable, since the bridge may be razor sharp, superheated, or blocked by some immovable obstacle. Most visionaries make it over this bridge, but some fall into the river, from whence they must be rescued, usually by the spirit guide. In other tales the test may not be a bridge at all, but may take the form of a visionary's being tortured along with the damned, in which case the spirit guide serves as the voice of God, explaining the necessity of each torture and how it cleanses the visionary's soul, making him fit to enter heaven.

These horrible events, though, are usually not part of a journey through the profoundest hell but instead a side trip into an anteroom of hell where souls go to be purged. After the visionary has passed his tests here, the spirit guide leads him down into the bowels of the earth where he will see the true hell, the abode of Satan and his angels. After this, he exits the underworld and finds a wall separating the place of purgation and hell from two other sites, the paradise of the not-so-good and heaven itself. His journey may or may not conclude with a vision of heaven, but he will certainly scale the wall and be granted a full vision of paradise, where he will meet those who lived well on earth but were not clean enough to proceed directly to the throne of God. In this paradise all is order and light, and the souls dwelling there have their every physical need attended to. The air is filled with sweet fragrances; the land burgeons with blossoming fruit trees. It is the exact reverse of all that the visionary has encountered in the world below, an experience not altogether unlike an everlasting picnic in the country.

After this experience of the paradisiacal realms, our visionary usually returns—quite reluctantly—to his body, but even though he may carry a physical reminder of his experience on his body, he seldom tells others about what he saw on the other side. He does, though, usually manage to describe the vision to an amanuensis sometime before dying so that the story may be preserved for the faithful.

Each of these elements appears routinely in tales of the afterlife—so much so that we might wonder whether the more sophisticated members of a medieval audience might come to regard the entire genre as a collection of "old wive's tales." But given the almost universal popularity of these pieces, it seems highly unlikely that such was the case. Instead, it seems far more likely that this formulaic quality resulted from audience expectations—if a visionary were to deviate widely from any of these essential details, his story would be suspect, since the nature of the world to come was generally viewed as being immutable.

PROMINENT EXAMPLES

The most important otherworld visions of the Old English period are those of Fursey and Drycthelm, both of which Bede retells in his *Ecclesiastical History of the English People* (c. 731 A.D.), which originally circulated in Latin, but was translated into English in the late ninth century. Both stories—Fursey's in book 3, chapter 19; Drycthelm's in book 5, chapter 12—describe visions of hell, purgatory, and heaven, though Drycthelm's is by far the more detailed. These two tales represent a major step in the development of the doctrine of purgatory, being the earliest to describe a specific locale in which souls are cleansed before they are allowed into heaven (Le Goff, *Birth* 112).

Bede's theological forebears did not create a specific geography of the afterlife that would help the faithful visualize the stages a soul must pass through on its way to glory. St. Augustine of Hippo had discussed the nature of purgatory in his *Commentary on the Psalms, Enchiridion*, and *City of God*, but he did little more than speculate about the need for purgation after death and the necessity of the living to say prayers for the dead who dwelled in some amorphous state of purgation (Le Goff, *Birth* 62–68). Pope Gregory III (late sixth century) described a four-part afterlife in his *Moralia in Job* and *The Dialogues* and also employed exempla in the latter text about souls from purgatory who had returned to the abode of the living to achieve expiation of some sin or the stories of men who had actually had a vision of hell. Neither theologian seems to have presented a full description of exactly where these realms lay, though two of the visions in Gregory's *Dialogues* clearly describe the River of Souls and a test bridge over which the visionary must walk in order to achieve paradise (Le Goff, *Birth* 88–95). Bede's versions of Fursey's and Drycthelm's visions replicate Gregory's four-part afterlife and Gregory's focus on the need for the living to do almsdeeds for those in the otherworld, but they also localize heaven, purgatory, and hell more explicitly.

Bede's description of Fursey's vision is set within a larger discussion of this holy man's mission to East Anglia during the reign of Sigbert in A.D. 633, a story Bede apparently drew from a brief biography that circulated throughout England in the eighth century, *Vita Virtutesque Fursei Abbatis Latiniacensis* (Gardiner, *Visions* 241–242). Fursey was an Irish noble of whom Sigbert had heard amazing reports and whom he had invited to East Anglia to teach. Early in his mission to England Fursey becomes gravely ill and slips into a visionary state in which he hears the voice of God admonishing him to work diligently, for he knows not the day or hour in which the Lord shall return. As a result, Fursey sets out to build a monastery, which he does eventually establish at "Cnobheresburg," now Burgh Castle near Yarmouth (Bede, *History* 343). Later in life he again is taken deathly ill and enters a trance in which his soul leaves the body for the span of an evening. In this trance he receives a vision of heaven in which he hears angelic choirs singing. He recuperates, but three days later relapses and gains a full vision of heaven from which he is held back by horrific demons who accuse him of idle words, bad actions, and sinful thoughts—each one of which they have recorded in a book. He is granted solace, though, by saints and angels who appear and tell him of the joys of heaven that he will one day enjoy.

The bulk of Bede's retelling, though, focuses on a second revelation Fursey has immediately after this vision of heaven, one in which Fursey is carried to a great height by an angel guide and sees below a gloomy valley with four fires in the air. These fires turn out to be the fires of Falsehood, Covetousness, Discord, and Cruelty, which become one great ball of flames. As this massive fireball begins to move toward him, he asks his angel guide to protect him, and the angel tells him that this fire will not harm him since Fursey is a righteous man. This flame is a cleansing fire of atonement for those who lived impure lives on earth. Then three angels descend to split the flames so that Fursey may pass through, and as he does, demons pluck the soul of a man out of the fire and thrust him against Fursey, burning Fursey's arm and jaw. Fursey recognizes the man as someone he had known on earth, someone from whom he had accepted a gift of clothing, but a man who had died in mortal sin. The angel guide tells Fursey he has received this burn because he accepted the man's gift from his friend's deathbed and has thus deserved a share in the man's punishment. After Fursey returns to his body, he discovers that he has a livid scar on his shoulder and jaw to remind him of his experiences in the otherworld.

Bede ends the tale by claiming that he once met an older monk at the convent in Jarrow, a devout old man who, in his youth, had met Fursey in East Anglia. This last man claimed to have spoken with Fursey alone on a bitterly cold day, yet as Fursey recounted the vision, the old monk noticed that Fursey was sweating heavily, despite being clad in only a thin tunic. Such were the terrors his memories gave him, the old man said (Bede, *History* 171–175 ; Gardiner, *Visions* 51–55). Admittedly, this tale does present a weak vision of the topography of the otherworld, but it does include an intimation of the existence of heaven (the angel guide and protectors, Fursey's first vision), a purgatory (the four fires), and a hell (the gloomy valley). It does not, however, provide a complete vision of the process by which souls are shuttled from this world to their final home in the next.

Bede's version of Drycthelm's vision is more fully developed and unified than is his tale of Fursey, and it contains an even more fully developed description of a place of purgation. The tale begins in A.D. 699, when Drycthelm, a citizen of Cunningham in Northumbria, apparently dies and is about to be buried. To his wife's and neighbors' surprise, he rises up on his deathbed, very much alive and horribly shaken by his experience. He goes immediately to a local church, where he prays until sunrise. Not many days thereafter, Drycthelm leaves married life behind forever and enters a monastery at Melrose, where he lives out a life of exemplary piety for the remainder of his days. Although it is obvious that he has had some strange experience in the Land of Death, he never relates his tale to anyone whom he does not feel is in need of spiritual reform or of assurance of the world to come. However, Bede tells us that he has somehow obtained an exact record of Drycthelm's vision and quotes the man's tale at length.

Drycthelm describes leaving his body and being met instantaneously by a handsome young man in a white robe who serves as his spirit guide throughout the rest of his journey. The first place they pass through is a deep valley surrounded by a wall of flame on one side and a wall of ice and snow on the other. Drycthelm describes watching deformed and tormented souls broiling on the flaming side for as long as they could stand it, then jumping over the valley into the region of ice and snow. When these poor spirits had stood about as much freezing as they could, they would then leap back into the fiery region. From this valley Drycthelm's guide takes him down a long path into a Stygian night so dark Drycthelm can see only by the light reflected from the angel's robe. They pass by a large, open furnace that belches thick, sulfurous smoke, and as they watch, they see the souls of men flying up and out of the pit like sparks, reaching a high point and then falling back into the flames, where they are tortured by wicked spirits. The noise from this pit is intolerable, and it is impossible to separate the wailings of humans from the laughter of demons.

Suddenly Drycthelm sees a bright light approaching him, and as he exits through it, he finds himself on top of a wall, looking over into a flowery plain from which emanates an indescribably lovely smell. He sees beautiful people in white there singing bright hymns, and he assumes that he is seeing heaven. At this point his guide asks him if he understands all he has seen. Drycthelm says that he does not, and the guide explains the vision to him. The valley separating the lands of fire and frost is a place where "souls are tried and punished who have delayed to confess and amend their wicked ways. . . . Because they confessed and were penitent, although only at death, they will all be admitted into the Kingdom of Heaven on the Day of Judgment. But many are helped by prayers, alms, and fasting of the living, and especially by the offering of Masses, and are therefore set free before the Day of Judgment" (Bede, *History* 292–293). The fiery pit is the pit of hell, and the fair land he sees is not heaven, but a place like the Earthly Paradise where those unworthy of immediate entry into heaven dwell before they are accepted into heaven. Drycthelm is not yet good enough to see heaven, so he must return to his body at that time (Bede, *History* 171–175).

Both these earliest English visions of the otherworld are much more specific about a place of purgation than are the exempla found in Gregory's *Dialogues*. Drycthelm's vision in particular seems focused primarily on various spiritual states in the otherworld for believers who either experienced deathbed conversions or who were good but were guilty of venial sins. In this tale we never see heaven, and the pit of hell consumes only a paragraph or two of space. Bede also emphasizes that the living may perform certain deeds that will relieve the "not-so-bad" dead of their purgatorial pains and hasten their entry into heaven. Quite clearly these two tales represent a period in which there was a great deal of pressure, possibly from popular sources, to soften the older, harsher concept of there being nothing less than everlasting doom in hell for those whose lives were only marginally bad.

In the early Middle English period (eleventh–thirteenth centuries) afterlife visions became even more highly focused on the nature of purgatory and punishment. Two major works that were widely disseminated survive from this period: the vision of Knight Owen in *St. Patrick's Purgatory* (c. 1153) and *The Vision of Tundale* (c. 1149). Two other tales are discussed frequently by modern scholars, *The Vision of the Monk of Eynsham* (c. 1196) and *The Vision of Thurcill* (c. 1206), but neither of these was translated into English until after 1482, so their influence probably was not widespread outside academic circles other than possibly in sermons. The first of the two Englished Latin tales, the story of *Owayne Miles* (the Knight Owen) in *St. Patrick's Purgatory*, was known largely through a tract by that name, as well as through the chronicles of Roger of Wendover and Vincent of Beauvais. This vision differs somewhat from all the others in that it does not begin with a man who slips into a catatonic state to receive his vision, but instead with Sir Owen's pilgrimage into St. Patrick's Purgatory at Lough Derg.

A vicious man in need of spiritual cleansing, Owen travels on a pilgrimage from England to Lough Derg, Ireland, where he requests permission from the Augustinians who guard the purgatory to be allowed to spend time in the cave. They agree, warning him that at first he will be attacked by demons, but if he stands firm against them, he will be granted a vision of the saved and the damned as they exist in the world to come. He enters the purgatory, is attacked as warned, but remains firm, and the demons lead him to a plain where he sees naked men and women nailed into the ground with hot iron rods. Demons try to nail Owen to the ground also but cannot since he remains firm in his faith. The demons drag him along further, showing him a variety of horrid sights: men and women hung on hooks over a brimstone fire, suspended from red-hot wheels by nails, immersed in boiling metals, blown away by whirlwinds, and immersed in stinking, ice-cold rivers. Of course, he thinks that he is viewing hell, but the demons tell him that he is not and lead him down into a pit toward another stinking river of burning pitch filled with souls, over which is suspended a narrow, slippery bridge. The demons tell Owen that he must cross the bridge, and he does so—painfully.

After negotiating the bridge safely, Owen leaves the devils behind and comes to a high wall adorned with precious stones. Here he is met by a procession of monks, abbots, priests, and bishops who welcome him into their midst with exceptionally harmonious singing, providing a dramatic contrast to all the noise and chaos he has just encountered in the underworld. Two bishops serve as his spirit guides through this paradise where there is every sort of flower, a multitude of trees burgeoning with fruit, sweet, pleasant smells, and great comfort. This setting is, of course, quite similar to the plain that Drycthelm finds beyond the wall he encounters after his underworld journey, and as in Drycthelm's vision, this is not heaven, but a holding tank for the "not-quite-so-good." According to the holy men who lead Owen, it is the place where go those who have not "þat dygnyte / To come before [God's] mageste" (ll. 600–602, Easting, *St. Patrick's* 70). The bishops tell Owen to look up at a mountain growing from the center of the garden and to view heaven from afar, for as wonderful a place as this paradise is, it is not anything like the true heaven where God dwells. They then set Owen back on the right path to the hall from which he began his journey, and he returns to this world, thereafter living a pure life (*St. Patrick's* 3–75; Gardiner, *Visions* 135–48).

A second influential tale of the early Middle English period is *The Vision of Tundale*, which, like the story of Sir Owen, is the vision of a sinful man in need of spiritual reconditioning. Tundale's story was first set down in Latin by an Irish monk living in Bavaria, and this text, generally known as the *Visio Tnugdali*, was later translated into a host of European vernaculars, among them Dutch, German, French, and Middle English (Gardiner, *Visions* 252–253). In this tale Tundale, an Irishman living in the city of Cashel, goes to the home of a faithful friend to dun him over a debt of three horses, which the man has no means of repaying. Tundale becomes extremely angry and goes home, where he has a stroke and apparently dies. Two or three days later he revives and begins living a new life, one characterized by giving to the poor, rather than by calling in debts.

In retelling his vision, Tundale first describes his soul's exiting the body to be attacked by a host of demons gnashing their teeth and tearing their faces with their claws. They call him all sorts of horrible names and charge him with horrible sins they claim make him worthy to be led into hell. However, God sends an angel to lead Tundale out of this onslaught and through nine levels of hell, each division being for a separate loathly sin—one each for murderers, traitors, the proud, the greedy, thieves, gluttons, fornicators, those who multiply sin, and the hell of Satan. The punishments at each level are fairly predictable. The stench of burning sulfur and the noise of anguish and torment reign over all, just as in the earlier tales, but some innovative thinking does peek through upon occasion. In Tundale's version of hell murderers are cooked down to a broth in a large frying pan, traitors are pushed over a mountain by demons brandishing red-hot pitchforks, and the proud seethe in a river of burning sulfur. Tundale himself has to undergo several tortures. Most notably, he has to cross a long, narrow bridge studded with iron nails while leading a wild cow, this in recompense for his having stolen a cow on earth. He is threatened on this crossing by a multitude of towering beasts not unlike the horses he demanded of his friend, who block his path and seek to devour him. In other related horrors he sees a gigantic beast that swallows the souls of the greedy. He sees gluttons dissected by demons and their bodies magically reformed to undergo this punishment repeatedly. Fornicators are immersed in a frozen swamp where they are repeatedly impregnated by a foul beast that rules over that land.

After passing through these levels and viewing Satan on his throne, Tundale and his guide exit the underworld to find a high wall before which stands a multitude of hunger-racked people enduring a cold, driving rain. These are, of course, the "not-very-bad" who cannot yet make it into paradise, particularly those who were not generous to the poor and thus have to live outside paradise for many years before being allowed in. After viewing this, Tundale and his guide traverse the wall and visit the same field of joy (paradise) for the "not-very-good" with its Fountain and Tree of Life that both Drycthelm and Owen saw. But unlike Owen, Tundale is allowed a vision of heaven with its nine orders of angels (obviously balancing the nine circles of hell) and the glory of various saints, including St. Patrick (*Vision of Tundale* 81–154; Gardiner, *Visions* 149–195).

These two visions present, clearly, a particularized topography of the afterlife, one that is fourfold, as in Gregory's *Dialogues* and in Drycthelm's vision. The visionary in each of these early Middle English visions travels, first through a hellish realm that turns out to be a place for the "not-so-good," which is an appropriate starting place for the murderous knight Owen and the greedy Tundale to enter. Both visionaries have their lives threatened by demons, are forced over a test bridge, see the deepest hell, and enter the paradise of the "not-so-good" before returning to their bodies. What is missing from both tales is an emphasis on the suffrages that the living can provide for souls in purgatory. Both tales' intent seems to be largely to describe the system by which souls are punished and purgated in the world to come, and thereby to scare readers and listeners into right living so that they might immediately enter paradise.

The later Middle English period (fourteenth and fifteenth centuries) saw an increase in the number of English visions, among them *The Vision of William of Stranton* (*St. Patrick's* 78–117), *The Vision of Edmund Leversedge*, and the English translation of *The Vision of the Monk of Eynsham*. Each of these represents an otherworld very similar to those described by the Knight Owen in *St. Patrick's Purgatory* or Tundale's *Vision*. Other visions of the otherworld entered England through *The Liber Celestis of St. Bridget of Sweden* (234–236; 256–263; 429–433), new translations of *St. Patrick's Purgatory (Owayne Miles)*, and Guillaume de Deguilleville's *Le Pèlerinage de l'áme*, to name just a few. The major difference between these later texts and the earlier ones discussed here involves an increasing use of criticism of the ecclesiastical hierarchy, which, as Wiesje F. Nijenhuis notes, first creeps in *The Vision of the Monk of Eynsham* (*Vision of Edmund Leversedge* 20).

Two later texts, both from the late fourteenth or early fifteenth centuries, contrast heavily with these earlier texts—primarily in emphasis, since both focus only on the nature of purgatory. These are *The Gast of Gy* (c. 1380) and *A Revelation of Purgatory* (1422). Both are examples of the type of vision in which a dead person returns to the living to describe exactly what they are experiencing in the afterlife.

The Gast of Gy is the earlier and by far the more widely disseminated or influential text. It is an English translation of a Latin text generally entitled *De Spiritu Guidonis*, which survives in no fewer than seventy-five manuscript copies. The tale is set in Alés en Garde in southern France on St. John's Day 1323 and Epiphany 1324. It begins when a local woman, the widow of Gy de Thurno (or de Corvo), a local burgess, comes to the local Dominican priory and asks its leader, Jean Gobi, to perform an exorcism at her home. She has been tormented for several days by what she thinks is either the ghost of her former husband or a demon making a horrendous racket in one section of her house.

Gobi takes three of his brethren and more than two hundred of the local citizens and goes to Guy's home to sing the Office of the Dead. The subsequent text of *De Spiritu Guidonis* gives an itemized description of the elements of the Mass this particular group used, including the "Vidi Aquam," "Veni, Creator Spiritus," "Asperges Me," and instead of "Lauds," "The Seven Psalms with the Litany." When they get to the "Agnus Dei," Guy makes himself known, and he and the prior have an extended question-and-answer session in the ghost's old bedroom, where, Gy says, he and his wife committed a sin that he was unable to do penance for before he died. During this question-and-answer period, or dialogue and debate, the prior tests the ghost's origin and determines much about the nature of purgatory.

However, Gy's ghost describes very little about the nature of the underworld. He claims that purgatory is not a part of hell, but a place in the middle of the earth. He describes nothing more graphic about the pains of purgatory than the fact that he suffers a sudden changing from hot to cold (as in Drycthelm's vision) and that the invisible flame he is wrapped in during the dialogue is hotter than all the houses on earth on fire at once (*Yorkshire Writers* 1: 328). Gy and the prior spend much more time discussing the importance of the elements in the mass sung at the beginning of the tale, especially the use of "The Seven Psalms with the Litany" and their effect on reducing the pains those in purgatory experience because of the various sins they have committed (*Yorkshire Writers* 1: 317). They also debate the efficacy of masses said for particular souls, the power of prayers such as the *Summe Sacerdos* to help those in purgatory, the ability of preachers with "dry souls" to say the Mass effectively, and a host of other doctrinal points. In the process Gy also describes how his soul was attacked by demons upon its exit from the body, how the Virgin came and claimed his soul for purgatory instead of hell, and how at present he is suffering on this earth in a "particular purgatory" assigned to his spirit alone. His suffering at the site of his last, unexpiated sin will not only free his own soul but will also keep his wife from having to enter purgatory as well. At night, he claims, he is placed in a "common purgatory" with all other souls judged unworthy as yet to behold the Beatific Vision of God in his glory.

As their St. John's Day discussion winds down, the friars and the ghost decide to meet again at the same spot on Epiphany. When they do meet again, the ghost tells them that their prayers have helped him greatly and that he is now going on to heaven, in a shorter amount of time than he was originally doomed to spend in purgation. He tells all goodbye and moves on to heaven, never to be heard from again (*Yorkshire Writers* 1: 292–333).

As Francis Lee Utley has pointed out, the original impetus for writing this tale may have been to gain Pope John XXII's sanction for a local legend (700), but very soon thereafter members of the Papal Curia recognized its possible utility and sent copies to their colleagues outside Avignon. The tale entered England (c. 1325) first as a copy of Gobi's letter sent by John Rosse, bishop of Carlisle, to Walter Reynolds, archbishop of Canterbury (Langlois 542). By the end of the fourteenth century there were four separate English translations—in prose, couplet, and quatrain versions—surviving in ten manuscript copies. This popularity was replicated throughout Western Europe, with *De Spiritu Guidonis* being translated into French, Catalan, Italian, German, Dutch, Swedish, Welsh, and Irish, thereby equaling the popularity of older tales such as *St. Patrick's Purgatory* or *The Vision of Tundale*.

Though less popular, *A Revelation of Purgatory* does provide a more graphic description of the afterlife than does *The Gast of Gy*. The tale recounts a series of dreams a religious woman has beginning on the evening of St. Lawrence's Day 1422. The first dream comes to her between eight and ten P.M., when she feels that she has been physically rapt into purgatory. She awakes and goes to pray, but falls asleep around eleven o'clock and has a second dream in which she is met by the spirit of Margaret, a religious woman she had known before. In this second dream Margaret asks for the dreamer and others to pray for her soul—particularly to read the "Miserere," the "Veni Creator Spiritus," and the "Salue Sancta Parens." Margaret and the dreamer discuss in a question-and-answer pattern similar to the dialogue found in *Gast* the efficacy of these prayers and exactly how they help the souls in purgatory (*Revelation* 62–64).

Next evening, she has a third dream in which she sees all the various pains of purgatory, organized as three great fires in which are found numerous graphic tortures. She sees Margaret wearing a long gown filled with hooks and red-hot fire, being cut to ribbons by a cat and dog, having her lips sheared from her face (for lying and backbiting), having to eat snakes (for her gluttony), bathing in venom, being gnawed by the Worm of Conscience, and so forth. After many such horrible pains being administered to Margaret and others, the Virgin calls for Margaret to be released by the grace of Jesus from the hideous fiends. They release her, and the Virgin leads her over a "stronge bridge" at the end of which is a "whiter chapel," where she is washed, a mass is sung, and then she enters into heaven through a golden gate (*Revelation* 85–86).

As several critics have noted, both *Gast* and *A Revelation* seem focused less on scaring the faithful into living sinless lives than on encouraging prayers for the dead (Duffy 372–373; Keiser, "Progress" 82–83). Indeed, the text of *De Spiritu Guidonis* from which the English *Gast of Gy* is taken states explicitly in its preamble that the story concerns a miracle being transmitted not to frighten listeners, but to strengthen their faith, since it is by the consolation of things written that we have any faith at all (*Gast* 1). Both texts explain fully how prayers of the living help those in purgatory, and both make little mention of either heaven or hell. When Gobi asks Gy about the nature of heaven and hell, the ghost replies simply that he knows nothing of either, since he has never been to either place (*Yorkshire Writers* 1:301). Similarly, Margaret in *A Revelation* claims that she knows by otherworldly reason but does not have leave from God to tell (65). Apparently, in the fourteenth century, as purgatory became more widely recognized as being a specific place where one could atone for venial sins, direct depictions of hell and heaven became far less important to the faithful. They knew that they could escape hell and make it to heaven, but they wanted more information on how to gain release from purgatory, and these later visions provided that answer.

CRITICAL HISTORY

The history of critical approaches to otherworldly visions divides rather neatly into two periods: before Jacques Le Goff and after Jacques Le Goff. The publication of his *La naissance du purgatoire* in 1981 and its translation into English as *The Birth of Purgatory* in 1984 effectively reinvigorated a field of study that had fallen into a regrettable desuetude, especially among English and American scholars. Analyses of otherworld visions prior to 1980 tend to focus on the generic qualities and origins of the tales and to spend little time on the development of the concepts of the afterlife that these tales preserve. Le Goff's *Birth* changed all that, focusing critical attention on the unique insights these stories provide into the changing popular culture of the Middle Ages. Reactions to this work—both positive and negative—have appeared regularly since 1981, and as a result, a whole new generation of scholars has become attracted to what historian John Benton once called a "real 'growth industry' in medieval studies" (qtd. in McGuire 63).

The most important studies prior to 1980 are those of Ernest J. Becker (1899), St. John D. Seymour (1930), A.B. van Os (1932), D.D.R. Owen (1970), and Howard Rollin Patch (1970). Becker first drew attention to the existence of tales of the afterlife in Middle English literature and compared them with earlier noncanonical Christian works. Seymour followed Becker's lead, but focused on Irish visions and their extensive contribution to the development of the otherworld-visions genre. His signal addition to the study of visions literature was his discussion of the Irish *imram*—the voyage in search of the Earthly Paradise like those of Bran and St. Brendan—and their importance in the development of the geography of the world to come (63). Van Os expanded upon the number of works investigated by either Becker and Seymour, delineated the topoi of the otherworld-visions genre—the use of spirit guides, judgment scenes, and so on—and attempted to pinpoint the first strict delineation between heaven and hell in English in *The Ayenbite of Inwit* (145). Both Owen and Patch expanded upon the type of work these earlier scholars performed and widened the purview to discuss vision literature's origins in ancient Persian or early Buddhist literature (Patch 102). They also sketched its effect on later Middle English literature, particularly on *Pearl*, Chaucer's *The House of Fame* and "Merchant's Tale," Gower's *Confessio Amantis*, and the anonymous *Adulterous Falmouth Squire* (Patch 211–240).

Other encyclopedic works have appeared, most notably texts by Robert Hughes (1968), Alison Morgan (1990), and Alice K. Turner (1993). Hughes's and Turner's texts are popular works, "coffee-table books" redeemed largely by the extent to which both research their topics and the erudition with which they approach their subjects. Hughes develops an extensive study of heaven in both the visual and literary arts, giving an analysis of the topoi employed in describing heaven, particularly the iconography of the nine orders of angels important in *Tundale* and the *Gast of Gy* (22–29). He also gives some attention to visions of hell. Turner, however, focuses on hell and traces the origin of the idea of eternal punishment and damnation from The *Egyptian Book of the Dead* to Freud. Her chapter on the Middle Ages addresses the works of Augustine and Gregory and the visions of Fursey, Drycthelm, and Tundale as well as a host of continental visions. She also provides reproductions of key illuminations from the *Très Riches Heures* of Jean, the duke of Berry, and Simon Marmion's illustrations of *The Vision of Tundale* (c. 1495) made for Margaret of York (figs. 5–10).

Morgan's book, *Dante and the Medieval Other World*, is much more pointed and scholarly than either Hughes's or Turner's works. Her basic purpose is to trace elements of Dante's *Divine Comedy* to earlier, popular sources, rather than from the classical examples of Virgil or Thomas Aquinas. She provides lengthy discussions of topographical motifs, the inhabitants of the otherworld, the spirit guides, and the geography of purgatory and paradise, drawing upon a host of early Christian and medieval visions, including *The Voyage of St. Brendan, The Vision of Drycthelm, The Vision of the Monk of Eynsham*, and *St. Patrick's Purgatory*. Since her focus is on Dante, not on the development of the popular literature itself, she refers to Le Goff's work primarily as a beginning point from which to analyze Dante's choice of the mountain as an image for purgatory (145, 157, 192–195).

Discussions of visions literature as a window into the culture of medieval popular piety date, as stated earlier, from the early 1980s, not only with the publication of Le Goff's *Birth of Purgatory*, but also simultaneously with Peter Dinzelbacher's *Vision und Visionsliteratur im Mittelalter* (1981). The importance of Dinzelbacher's text resides largely in its compendiousness. He provides a listing and overviews of well over two hundred otherworld visions surviving from the sixth through the fifteenth centuries, many of them not listed elsewhere. Not only does Dinzelbacher describe the topoi of these visions, but he also analyzes their effect upon literary dream visions of the fourteenth century and on the visions of women such as St. Bridget of Sweden, Julian of Norwich, Hildegard of Bingen, and Margery Kempe. In *Vision* and later, in a brief article in *Folklore* ("The Way to the Other World" [1986]), he describes what popular visions of the afterlife explain about the world view of the "common person" of the Middle Ages—particularly how the images of mountains, test bridges, and ladders to heaven preserve an idea of the medievals' concept of the integrity of the physical and spiritual realms.

Undoubtedly, though, Jacques Le Goff's study *La naissance du Purgatoire* (1981) has been the single most important event in the recent history of visions-literature criticism. His text describes how medieval concepts of the otherworld developed both spatially and temporally from early Christianity through the fifteenth century and posits that a profound shift occurred between 1150 and 1200 A.D., when writers of otherworld visions switched from a description of a fourfold afterlife—hell, purgatory, paradise, and heaven—to a threefold division consisting of hell, purgatory, and heaven. In this work, and later in a chapter in *Understanding Popular Culture* (1984), he argues that this shift arises from learned authors' refashioning of materials arising from the popular culture of the Middle Ages (*Birth* 289–300; "Learned" 32–33).

Certainly this shift from a fourfold division to a threefold one is visible in the works Le Goff discusses, and it is arguably visible in the few tales described earlier in "Prominent Examples." Early works such as the tales of Drycthelm and Fursey do describe a fourfold afterlife in which heaven and hell are separated by a two-part intermediate state for the "not-so-bad" and the "not-so-good," while later tales like *The Gast of Gy* present a seemingly more tripartite vision of the afterlife. It is not this point upon which subsequent scholarship divides. Opposition has arisen mainly to Le Goff's claim that this shift can be dated to the end of the twelfth century by the initial appearance of one word in Latin texts, the noun *purgatorium* (which before had appeared only in the adjectival forms of *purgatorius)*. The "sudden" appearance of the noun *purgatorium* implies, he claims, that purgatory was not conceived to be a place before the late twelfth century, but rather a state of purgation. In other words, "*the* Purgatory had not yet been born" (*Birth* 3, 362–366).

Those critics who concur generally with Le Goff's findings have employed his discussion of the learned popularization of purgatory in analyses of works he did not cover. This is certainly the case in two important articles by George Keiser, who has looked closely at both *The Gast of Gy* and *A Revelation of Purgatory*. In "The Progress of Purgatory" (1987) he assesses the roles of both these texts, and several others, in the dissemination of purgatorial doctrine (72–86). In "St. Jerome and the Brigittines" he assesses the influence of purgatorial tales like *Gast* and *A Revelation* on Simon Winter's life of St. Jerome (145–146).

Studies that expand upon Le Goff's theories, as Keiser's do, are eclipsed numerically by works that seek to augment Le Goff's major argument—particularly the idea of being able to date a shift in purgatory's spatial conception based upon the appearance of one word. The first of these was R.W. Southern's 1982 review of *La naissance du Purgatoire*, which argues that the medieval conception of purgatory "was deeply rooted in theological tradition, and the process of enlargement was entirely in keeping with other theological developments" around the year A.D. 1050 (652). In another review Alan E. Bernstein also points to the possible oversimplifications involved in using one word to pinpoint the historical development of a concept and argues that the concept of purgatory may have existed long before the word was coined (Review 183). Likewise, Aaron Gurevich, while generally agreeing with Le Goff's analysis of the shift to a threefold partitioning of the otherworld, argues in "Popular and Scholarly Medieval Cultural Traditions" (1983) that the concept of a purgatory as a place "was present in the world of the dead long before theologians pronounced the word *purgatorium*" (83).

Other writers have sought to flesh out Le Goff's dating to give a fuller accounting of the history of otherworld eschatology. Robert Easting has indicated that after 1150 (when Le Goff says that the threefold division took over) belief in an Earthly Paradise reached its apogee, which would indicate that popular belief still held onto a fourfold view of the otherworld. He argues quite convincingly that the development of the concept of purgatory set the fourfold division into stone ("Purgatory" 23–48). This would certainly seem to be the case when one recognizes that even very late works like *A Revelation of Purgatory* and *The Gast of Gy* (with its description of both common and particular purgatories) apparently retain a quartile division of life beyond the grave. Caroline Walker Bynum, in *Holy Feast and Holy Fast*, presents yet another perspective on Le Goff's thesis, indicating that for most medieval visionaries, "Purgatory was, rather, the fact of suffering" (235), and thus this life could be a purgatory, too. This would indicate that "the key question to consider in explaining the evolution of the notion of purgatory is not the opposition of heaven and hell but, rather, the role of suffering in Christianity" (399 n. 54). Similarly, Patrick McGuire's discussion of the Communion of the Saints as a major impetus to the development of purgatorial tales (1989) indicates that recent criticism seeks in general to expand upon the full range of mentalities and social forces that gave rise to the development of otherworld visions (64–66).

Other criticism not focused on Le Goff's findings is largely bibliographic or editorial in nature. Both Eileen Gardiner (1993) and Robert Easting (*Visions*, 1997) have produced annotated bibliographies of sources related to a number of the tales listed by Dinzelbacher, Le Goff, and others. Aside from some minor caveats (Keiser, Review 440), both bibliographies obviously provide excellent insights into the nature of the visions genre and the scholarly work done heretofore on it. Recent editions, such as *Account of a Chaplain's Vision of Purgatory* (Easting, "Peter" 211–229) and *Vision in a Trance* (Youngs 212–234), indicate that there is a great deal of work to be done establishing trustworthy texts of shorter, less widely disseminated visions. Similarly, scholars have only begun to search the corpus of medieval sermons to find other inter-

polated visions. With these two fields of endeavor in mind, it seems likely that
the study of otherworld visions will remain a growth industry for many years
to come.

If the present state of affairs is any guide, future scholarship will most likely
develop along three lines: (1) examinations of the effect of external literary genre
on visions and the effect of visions literature on "high" literature, (2) investigations of how individual visions authors molded the topoi to fit their own
purposes, and (3) analyses of "ghost tales" and the purposes to which they were
put. In regard to the first vein, the literary influence of otherworld visions, some
work has already been done. Aside from Morgan's study mentioned earlier, both
Easting (*Visions* 4–5) and Carol Zaleski (*"St. Patrick's"* 472) draw attention to
particular lines in *Hamlet* that refer directly to Shakespeare's knowledge of the
legends of *St. Patrick's Purgatory*. Zaleski also indicates how *St. Patrick's Purgatory* was influenced by pilgrimage literature (*"St. Patrick's"* 479) and has
elsewhere compared the outlines of visionary tales to modern stories of near-
death experiences (*Life* 30–36). Marta Powell Harley has twice indicated the
influence of otherworld visions on Chaucer's *Canterbury Tales*, once comparing
elements of the legend of Fursey to the Reeve's discussion of the "four gleedes"
of old age ("Reeve's" 85–88) and on a second occasion identifying the literary
background of the Physician's reference to "the Worm of Conscience" ("Last
Things" 1–16). Both these articles follow a much earlier study by Mabel Stanford of the influence of *St. Patrick's Purgatory* on "The Sumner's Tale" (377–
381). To my knowledge, though, no similar analyses of influence exist for other
major works from the fourteenth century in England, such as *Piers Plowman,
Pearl*, or *The Travels of Sir John Mandeville*.

A second possible area for future research involves the molding or augmen-
tation of topoi in vision literature. This direction is best exemplified by Wiesje
Nijenhuis's study of *The Vision of Edmund Leversedge*, in which Nijenhuis
describes Leversedge's truncated versions of the function of the spirit guide, the
focus on the punishments of one sin only (gallantry), and the judgment scene.
He points also to Leversedge's use of the *artes moriendi* (*Book of the Craft of
Dying*) for descriptions of the soul's exit from the body and concludes that
these compressions or truncations create an overly personal vision that "reads
much more like an ego-document than most medieval visions of the afterlife"
(93). Similar analyses might be performed on any of the later visions, but *A
Revelation* in particular might provide ground for an interesting study of how
later Middle English authors reshaped the traditional materials to meet the needs
of their perceived audiences.

A third field, and perhaps the most fertile, into which future studies might
turn involves "ghost tales" and the possible purposes to which these tales were
put. Critical attention has turned to revenant stories only recently, first with R.C.
Finucane's *Appearances of the Dead* (1982), then with Jean-Claude Schmitt's
Ghosts in the Middle Ages (1994) and Nancy Caciola's "Wraiths, Revenants,
and Ritual in Medieval Culture" (1996). Schmitt's work is the most detailed and

complete of these. He traces the history of pious ghost stories from St. Augustine of Hippo's theological pronouncements on the subject through fifteenth-century examples of stories of the returning dead. In the process he describes the development of the social mentalities and the associated functions related to the church's official remembrances of the dead. Perhaps more interesting is the fact that he discusses many tales not heretofore widely studied, *The Gast of Gy*, "The Ghost of Beaucaire," "Spirits of Yorkshire," and "Grandfather of Arndt Buschmann." Caciola likewise addresses ghost tales but focuses more on the reanimated dead as well as the development of churchyard rituals and their relationship to the Dance of Death or graveyard dances like those described in Robert Mannyng of Brunne's *Handlyng Synne* and Walter Map's *De Nugis Curialium* (35–41). Future research should build upon these studies by investigating the possible use of such revenant tales in sermons and the uses to which they were put. *The Gast of Gy*, in particular, would seem to be a major focus of this sort of study, since it was widely disseminated and, as Gerald Owst has pointed out, shows the marks of having been used as a sermon exemplum or sermon dialogue (*Literature* 537; *Preaching* 277 n. 5). Much could be done to show how this tale and a host of others may have been used to strengthen or support dogma attacked by the heresies and schisms that became frequent during the fourteenth and fifteenth centuries, particularly those ideas attacked by the Lollard movement in England.

From this brief survey of the afterlife-vision genre as it developed in the Old and Middle English periods, two things should be readily evident. First, discussion of the nature of the world to come struck a major nerve in the psyche of medieval Europeans. This must be true since we find literally hundreds of such tales produced from the first century all the way through the Middle Ages to the Enlightenment. Many of these works, like *The Gast of Gy, The Vision of Tundale*, and *St. Patrick's Purgatory*, were translated repeatedly into the major European vernaculars, and in some cases the number of surviving manuscript copies of these individual tales outstrips the number of surviving copies of more famous works, like *The Canterbury Tales*. This indicates that afterlife visions provide a unique window into the hopes and dreams of common medieval folk that modern scholarship is just now beginning to peer into.

Second, these tales clearly provide a connection between ourselves and those who have gone before. As every element of modern popular culture indicates, science has not extinguished our hope for a life to come. Our books, our movies, our daily speech all hum with the promise of life after death. Like our ancestors, we cannot imagine a world without us in it, nor the fire of our lives snuffed out and cold. We envision ourselves going on without ceasing, reaping the rewards of a life well lived, while our enemies seethe in the boiling broth of their manifold crimes. It is for this reason that afterlife visions deserve closer study, not only for what they disclose about mentalities past, but also for what they tell us of ourselves.

SELECTED BIBLIOGRAPHY

Primary Sources

*An Alphabet of Tales: An English 15th Century Translation of the Alphabetum Narra-
tionum of Etienne de Besançon.* Ed. Mary Macleod Banks. Early English Text
Society OS 126–127. 1904–1905.
Bede. *Historiam Ecclesiasticam Gentis Anglorum.* Vol. 1. Ed. Carolus Plummer. Oxford:
Clarendon Press, 1896.
———. *A History of the English Church and People.* Trans. Leo Sherley-Price. New
York: Penguin, 1955.
"The XI Pains of Hell." Ed. Richard Morris. *An Old English Miscellany Containing a
Bestiary, Kentish Sermons, Proverbs of Alfred, Religious Poems of the Thirteenth
Century, from Manuscripts in the British Museum, Bodleian Library, Jesus Col-
lege Library,* Etc. Early English Text Society OS 49. London: 1872.
*The Gast of Gy: Eine englische Dichtung des 14. Jahrhunderts nebst ihrer lateinischen
Quelle De Spiritu Guidonis.* Ed. Gustav Schleich. Palœstra I . Berlin: Mayer und
Müller, 1898.
Gobi, Jean. *Dialogue avec un Fantôme.* Trans. Marie-Anne Polo de Beaulieu. Paris: Les
Belles Lettres, 1994.
The Liber Celestis of St. Bridget of Sweden. Ed. Roger Ellis. Early English Text Society
OS 291. 1987.
A Revelation of Purgatory by an Unknown, Fifteenth-Century Woman Visionary. Ed.
Marta Powell Harley. Lewiston, NY: Edwin Mellen Press, 1985.
*St. Patrick's Purgatory: Two Versions of Owayne Miles and the Vision of William of
Stranton.* Ed. Robert Easting. Early English Text Society OS 298. 1991.
The Vision of Edmund Leversedge. Ed. W[iesje] F. Nijenhuis. Middeleeuwse Studies 8.
Nijmegen : Katholicke Universitait Nijmegen/Centrum voor Middeleeuwse Stud-
ies, 1991.
The Vision of Tundale. Ed. Rodney Mearns. Middle English Texts 18. Heidelberg: Carl
Winter, 1985.
Yorkshire Writers: Richard Rolle of Hampole and His Followers. 2 vols. Ed. C. Horst-
man. New York: Macmillan, 1895–1896.

Secondary Sources

Becker, Ernest J. *A Contribution to the Comparative Study of the Medieval Visions of
Heaven and Hell.* Baltimore: John Murphy Company, 1899.
Bernstein, Alan E. "Esoteric Theology: William Auvergne on the Fires of Hell and
Purgatory." *Speculum* 57 (1982): 509–531.
———. *The Formation of Hell.* Ithaca, NY: Cornell University Press, 1993.
———. Review of *La naissance du Purgatoire,* by Jacques Le Goff. *Speculum* 59
(1984): 179–183.
Brashler, James, and Roger A. Bullard, trans. *The Apocalypse of Peter. The Nag Ham-
madi Library in English.* 3rd ed. Ed. James M. Robinson. San Francisco: Harper
and Row, 1988. 372–378.

Bynum, Caroline Walker. *Holy Feast and Holy Fast: The Religious Significance of Food to Medieval Women*. Berkeley: University of California Press, 1987.

Caciola, Nancy. "Wraiths, Revenants, and Ritual in Medieval Culture." *Past and Present* 152 (1996): 3–45.

Chiffoleau, Jacques. *La Comptabilité de l'au-delá: Les hommes, la morte, et la religion dans la région d'Avignon á la fin du Moyen Age (vers 1320-vers 1480)*. Collection de l'École Française de Rome 47. Rome: École Française, 1980.

Collins, John J., and Michael Fishbane, eds. *Death, Ecstasy, and Other Worldly Journeys*. Albany: State University of New York Press, 1995.

Dinzelbacher, Peter. *Vision und Visionsliteratur im Mittelalter*. Monographien zur Geschichte des Mittelalters 23. Stuttgart: Hiersemann, 1981.

———. "The Way to the Other World in Medieval Literature and Art." *Folklore* 97 (1986): 70–87.

Duffy, Eamon. *The Stripping of the Altars: Traditional Religion in England, c. 1400–c. 1580*. New Haven, CT: Yale University Press, 1992.

Easting, Robert. "Peter of Bramham's Account of a Chaplain's Vision of Purgatory (c. 1343?)." *Medium Ævum* 65 (1996): 211–229.

———. "Purgatory and the Earthly Paradise in the *Tractatus de purgatorio sancti Patricii*." *Citeaux: Commentarii Cistercienses* 37 (1986): 23–48.

———. " 'Send Thine Heart into Purgatory': Visionaries of the Other World." *The Long Fifteenth Century: Essays for Douglas Gray*. Ed. Helen Cooper and Sally Mapstone. Oxford: Clarendon Press, 1997. 185–203.

———. *Visions of the Other World in Middle English*. Annotated Bibliographies of Old and Middle English Literature 3. Cambridge: D.S. Brewer, 1997.

Erickson, Carolly. *The Medieval Vision: Essays in History and Perception*. New York: Oxford University Press, 1976.

Finucane, R.C. *Appearances of the Dead: A Cultural History of Ghosts*. London: Junction Books, 1982.

Foster, Frances A. "Legends of the After-Life." *A Manual of the Writings in Middle English, 1050–1500*. Ed. J. Burke Severs. New Haven: Connecticut Academy of Arts and Sciences, 1970. 2:452–457, 645–649.

Gardiner, Eileen. *Medieval Visions of Heaven and Hell: A Sourcebook*. New York: Garland, 1993.

———. *Visions of Heaven and Hell before Dante*. New York: Italica, 1989.

Gurevich, Aaron J. *Historical Anthropology of the Middle Ages*. Ed. Jana Howlett. Chicago: University of Chicago Press, 1992.

———. "Popular and Scholarly Medieval Cultural Traditions: Notes in the Margin of Jacques Le Goff's Book." *Journal of Medieval History* 9 (1983): 71–90.

Harley, Marta Powell. "Last Things First in Chaucer's *Physician's Tale*: Final Judgement and the Worm of Conscience." *Journal of English and Germanic Philology* (1992): 1–16.

———. "The Reeve's 'Foure Gleedes' and St Fursey's Vision of the Four Fires of the Afterlife." *Medium Ævum* 56 (1987): 85–88.

Hughes, Robert. *Heaven and Hell in Western Art*. London: Weidenfeld, 1968.

Japenga, Ann. "Science Looks for Life beyond Death." *USA Weekend* 1–3 October 1999: 18–19.

Keiser, George R. "The Progress of Purgatory: Visions of the Afterlife in Later Middle

English Literature." *Zeit, Tod, und Ewigkeit in der Renaissance Literature*. Vol. 3. Ed. James Hogg. *Analecta Cartusiana* 117.3 (Salzburg, 1987). 72–100.

———. Review of *Visions of the Other World in Middle English*, by Robert Easting. *Journal of English and Germanic Philology* 98 (1999): 439–440.

———. "St. Jerome and the Brigittines: Visions of the Afterlife in Fifteenth-Century England." *England in the Fifteenth Century: Proceedings of the 1986 Harlaxton Symposium*. Ed. Daniel Williams. Woodbridge: Boydell, 1987. 143–152.

Langlois, C[harles] V[ictor]. "Les Deux Jean Gobi." *Histoire littéraire de la France*. Vol. 35. Paris: Imprimerie Nationale, 1921. 532–556.

Le Goff, Jacques. *The Birth of Purgatory*. Trans. Arthur Goldhammer. Chicago: University of Chicago Press, 1984.

———. "The Learned and Popular Dimensions of Journeys in the Otherworld in the Middle Ages." *Understanding Popular Culture: Europe from the Middle Ages to the Nineteenth Century*. Ed. Steven L. Kaplan. New York: Mouton, 1984. 37–48.

MacRae, George W., and William R. Murdock, trans. *The Apocalypse of Paul. The Nag Hammadi Library in English*. Ed. James M. Robinson. 3rd ed. San Francisco: Harper and Row, 1988. 256–259.

Matsuda, Takami. *Death and Purgatory in Middle English Didactic Poetry*. Cambridge: D.S. Brewer, 1997.

McGinn, Bernard. *Visions of the End: Apocalyptic Traditions in the Middle Ages*. New York: Columbia University Press, 1979.

McGuire, Patrick. "Purgatory, the Communion of the Saints, and Medieval Change." *Viator* 20 (1989): 61–84.

Morgan, Alison. *Dante and the Medieval Other World*. Cambridge: Cambridge University Press, 1990.

Nijenhuis, W[iesje] F. "Truncated Topoi in *The Vision of Edmund Leversedge*." *Medium Ævum* 63 (1994): 84–97.

Os, A[rnold] B[arel] van. *Religious Visions: The Development of the Eschatological Elements in Medieval English Religious Literature*. Amsterdam: H.J. Paris, 1932.

Owen, D.D.R. *The Vision of Hell; Infernal Journeys in Medieval French Literature*. New York: Barnes & Noble, 1970.

Owst, G[erald]. R. *Literature and Pulpit in Medieval England*. Cambridge: Cambridge University Press, 1933.

———. *Preaching in Medieval England*. Cambridge: Cambridge University Press, 1926.

Patch, Howard Rollin. *The Other World, According to Descriptions in Medieval Literature*. New York: Octagon, 1970.

"St. Patrick's Purgatory." *New Catholic Encyclopedia*. New York: McGraw Hill, 1967.

Schmitt, Jean-Claude. *Ghosts in the Middle Ages: The Living and the Dead in Medieval Society*. Trans. Teresa Lavender Fagan. Chicago: University of Chicago Press, 1994.

Seymour, St. John D. *Irish Visions of the Other-World*. London: Society for Promoting Christian Knowledge, 1930.

Southern, R.W. "Between Heaven and Hell." Review of *La naissance du Purgatoire*, by Jacques Le Goff. *Times Literary Supplement* 12 June 1982: 651–652.

Stanford, Mabel A. "The Sumner's Tale and Saint Patrick's Purgatory." *Journal of English and Germanic Philology* 19 (1920): 377–381.

Turner, Alice K. *The History of Hell*. New York: Harcourt Brace, 1993.

Utley, F.L. "Dialogues, Debates, and Catechisms." *A Manual of the Writings in Middle*

English, 1050–1500. Ed. Albert E. Hartung. New Haven: Connecticut Academy of Arts and Sciences, 1972. 3:698–700, 864–865.

Wells, John. *A Manual of the Writings in Middle English, 1050–1400.* New Haven, CT: Yale University Press, 1916.

Youngs, Deborah. *"Vision in a Trance*: A Fifteenth-Century Vision of Purgatory." *Medium Ævum* 67 (1998): 212–234.

Zaleski, Carol. *The Life of the World to Come: Near-Death Experience and Christian Hope.* New York: Oxford University Press, 1996.

———. *Otherworld Journeys: Accounts of Near-Death Experience in Medieval and Modern Times.* New York: Oxford University Press, 1987.

———. *"St. Patrick's Purgatory*: Pilgrimage Motifs in a Medieval Otherworld Vision." *Journal of the History of Ideas* 46 (1985): 467–485.

Selected Bibliography

Abbott, H.H., trans. *The Riddles of the Exeter Book*. Cambridge: Golden Head Press, 1968.

Abraham, Lenore. " 'Caedmon's Hymn' and the 'Gethwaernysse' ('Fitness') of Things." *American Benedictine Review* 43.3 (September 1992): 331–344.

Abrahams, Roger D. "The Literary Study of the Riddle." *Texas Studies in Language and Literature* 14.1 (1972): 909–929.

Abrams, M.H. *A Glossary of Literary Terms*. 3rd ed. New York: Holt, Rinehart and Winston, 1971.

Adams, Robert. "*Mede* and *Mercede*: The Evolution of the Economics of Grace in the *Piers Plowman* B and C Versions." *Medieval English Studies Presented to George Kane*. Ed. E.D. Kennedy, Ronald Waldron, and Joseph Wittig. Wolfeboro, NH: D.S. Brewer, 1988. 217–232.

Addison, Joseph, and Richard Steele. *The Spectator*. Ed. George A. Aitken. New York: Longmans, Green, & Co., 1898.

Aguirre, Manuel. "The Riddle of Sovereignty." *Modern Language Review* 88.2 (1993): 273–282.

Alexander, Michael. Introduction. *The Earliest English Poems*. New York: Penguin, 1966.

———. *Old English Literature*. London: Macmillan, 1983.

Alford, John A. "The Idea of Reason in *Piers Plowman*." *Medieval English Studies Presented to George Kane*. Ed. E.D. Kennedy, Ronald Waldron, and Joseph Wittig. Wolfeboro, NH: D.S. Brewer, 1988. 199–216.

Allen, Michael J.B., comp. *Sources and Analogues of Old English Poetry*. 2 vols. Cambridge: D.S. Brewer, 1976–1983.

Allen, Philip Schuyler. *Medieval Latin Lyrics*. Chicago: University of Chicago Press, 1931.

The Alliterative Morte Arthure: A Critical Edition. Ed. Valerie Krishna. New York: B. Franklin, 1976.

The Alliterative Morte Arthure: A New Verse Translation. Trans. Valerie Krishna. Washington, DC: University Press of America, 1983.

Amster, Mark E. "Literary Theory and the Genres of Middle English Literature." *Genre* 13 (1980): 389–396.

Anderson, J.J. "The Narrators in the *Book of the Duchess* and the *Parlement of Foules.*" *Chaucer Review* 26 (1992): 219–235.

Anderson, James. "*Deor, Wulf and Eadwacer,* and *The Soul's Address*: How and Where the Old English *Exeter Book* Riddles Begin." *The Old English Elegies: New Essays in Criticism and Research.* Ed. Martin Green. Rutherford, NJ: Fairleigh Dickinson University Press, 1983. 204–230.

———. "Strange, Sad Voices: The Portraits of Germanic Women in the Old English *Exeter Book.*" Diss. University of Kansas, 1978.

———. *Two Literary Riddles in the Exeter Book.* Norman: University of Oklahoma Press, 1986.

Andreas. Trans. Charles W. Kennedy. *The Poems of Cynewulf.* New York: Peter Smith, 1949. 211–263.

Andrew, Malcolm, and Ronald Waldron. Introduction. *The Poems of the Pearl Manuscript.* Berkeley: University of California Press, 1979.

Aristotle. *The Poetics.* Trans. W. Hamilton Fyfe. Loeb Classical Library. Cambridge, MA: Harvard University Press, 1991.

Arthur, Ross. "Emaré's Cloak and Audience Response." *Sign, Sentence, Discourse: Language in Medieval Thought and Literature.* Ed. Julian Wasserman and Lois Roney. Syracuse, NY: Syracuse University Press, 1989. 80–92.

Ascoli, Albert Russell. "The Unfinished Author." *The Cambridge Companion to Dante.* Ed. Rachel Jacoff. Cambridge: Cambridge University Press, 1993.

Astell, Ann. *Job, Boethius, and Epic Truth.* Ithaca, NY: Cornell University Press, 1994.

———. "Mourning and Marriage in St. Bernard's *Sermones* and in *Pearl.*" *The Song of Songs in the Middle Ages.* Ithaca, NY: Cornell University Press, 1990. 119–135.

Attar, Farid ud-Din. *The Conference of the Birds.* Trans. Afkham Darbandi and Dick Davis. Harmondsworth: Penguin, 1984.

Auerbach, Eric. *Mimesis: The Representation of Reality in Western Literature.* Trans. Willard R. Trask. Princeton, NJ: Princeton University Press, 1953.

Barber, Richard, ed. and trans. *Bestiary.* Woodbridge, Eng.: Boydell Press, 1993.

Barnet, Sylvan, Morton Berman, and William Burto. *A Dictionary of Literary Terms.* Boston: Little, Brown, 1960.

Barnhart, Clarence L., ed. *The New Century Handbook of English Literature.* Rev. ed. New York: Appleton-Century-Crofts, 1967.

Barnum, Priscilla Heath, ed. *Dives and Pauper.* 2 vols. EETS 275, 280. Oxford: Oxford University Press, 1976–1980.

Barratt, Alexandra. "The Five Wits and Their Structural Significance in Part II of *Ancrene Wisse.*" *Medium Ævum* 56.1 (1987): 12–24.

———, ed. *Women's Writing in Middle English.* London and New York: Longman, 1992.

Barron, W.R.J. *English Medieval Romance.* New York: Longman, 1987.

Barron, W.R.J., ed. *The Arthur of the English: The Arthurian Legend in Medieval English Life and Literature.* Arthurian Literature in the Middle Ages 2. Cardiff: University of Wales Press, 1999.

Bately, Janet, comp. *Anonymous Old English Homilies: A Preliminary Bibliography of Source Studies*. Binghamton, NY: COMERS, 1993.

———. "Lexical Evidence for the Authorship of the Prose Psalms in the Paris Psalter." *Anglo-Saxon England* 10 (1992): 69–95.

———. "The Nature of Old English Prose." *The Cambridge Companion to Old English Literature*. Ed. Malcolm Godden and Michael Lapidge. Cambridge: Cambridge University Press, 1991. 71–87.

———. "Old English Prose before and during the Reign of Alfred." *Anglo-Saxon England* 17 (1988); 93–138.

Baum, Paull, trans. *Anglo-Saxon Riddles of the Exeter Book*. Durham, NC: Duke University Press, 1963.

Baxter, Ron. *Bestiaries and Their Users in the Middle Ages*. Stroud: Sutton; London: Courtauld Institute, 1998.

Bayless, Martha. *Parody in the Middle Ages: The Latin Tradition*. Ann Arbor: University of Michigan Press, 1996.

Bédier, Joseph. *Les Fabliaux: Etudes de littérature populaire et d'histoire littéraire du moyen âge*. 6th ed. Paris: Champion, 1964.

Beissinger, Margaret, Jane Tylus, and Susanne Wofford, eds. *Epic Traditions in the Contemporary World: The Poetics of Community*. Berkeley: University of California Press, 1999.

Bennett, J.A.W., and G.V. Smithers, eds. *Early Middle English Verse and Prose*. Oxford: Clarendon Press, 1966.

Benson, C. David. "Their Telling Difference: Chaucer the Pilgrim and His Two Contrasting Tales." *Chaucer Review* 18 (1983): 61–76.

Benson, Larry D. *Malory's Morte d'Arthur*. Cambridge, MA: Harvard University Press, 1976.

Benson, Larry D., and Theodore M. Andersson. *The Literary Context of Chaucer's Fabliaux*. Indianapolis: Bobbs-Merrill, 1971.

Beowulf. Trans. Seamus Heaney. New York: Farrar, 2000.

Bertoni, Giulio. *Il Duecento. Storia letteraria d'Italia*. Milan: Francesco Vallardi, 1910, reprinted 1964.

Beston, John B. "How Much Was Known of the Breton Lai in Fourteenth-Century England?" *The Learned and the Lewed*. Ed. Larry D. Benson. Cambridge, MA: Harvard University Press, 1974. 319–336.

Bettelheim, Bruno. *The Uses of Enchantment: The Meaning and Importance of Fairy Tales*. New York: Knopf, 1975.

Blacker, Jean. *The Faces of Time: Portrayal of the Past in Old French and Latin Historical Narrative of the Anglo Norman "Regnum."* Austin: University of Texas Press, 1994.

Blake, N.F., ed. *The Phoenix*. Rev. ed. Exeter: University of Exeter Press, 1990.

Bloomfield, Morton. "Understanding Old English Poetry." *Annuale Mediaevale* 9 (1968): 5–25.

Bliss, A.J., ed. *Sir Launfal*. London: Thomas Nelson, 1960.

———, ed. *Sir Orfeo*. London: Oxford University Press, 1954.

Boethius. *The Consolation of Philosophy*. Trans. Richard Green. New York: Macmillan, 1985.

Boffey, Julia. "The Reputation and Circulation of Chaucer's Lyrics in the Fifteenth Century." *Chaucer Review* 28.1 (1993): 23–39.

Boitani, Piero. *English Medieval Narrative in the Thirteenth and Fourteenth Centuries.* Trans. Joan K. Hall. New York: Cambridge University Press, 1982.

Boitani, Piero, and Anna Torti, eds. *Religion in the Poetry and Drama of the Late Middle Ages in England.* Cambridge: Brewer, 1990.

Bonjour, Adrien. *The Digressions in Beowulf.* Oxford: Blackwell, 1965.

Borroff, Marie, trans. *Sir Gawain and the Green Knight.* New York: Norton, 1967.

Bozoky, Edina. "From Matter of Devotion to Amulets." *Medieval Folklore* 3 (Fall 1994): 91–107.

Bradbury, Nancy Mason. "Popular Festive Forms and Beliefs in Robert Mannyng's *Handlyng Synne.*" *Bakhtin and Medieval Voices.* Ed. Thomas J. Farrell. Gainesville: University Press of Florida, 1995. 158–179.

———. *Writing Aloud: Storytelling in Late Medieval England.* Urbana: University of Illinois Press, 1998.

Bragg, Lois. "The Modes of the Old English Metrical Charms." *Comparatist* 16 (May 1992): 3–23.

Branca, Vittore. *Boccaccio: The Man and His Works.* Trans. Richard Monges. New York: New York University Press, 1976.

Brehe, S.K. " 'Rhythmical Alliteration': Ælfric's Prose and the Origin of Laȝamon's Metre." Ed. Francoise Le Saux. *The Text and Tradition of La(ȝ)amon's* Brut. Cambridge: D.S. Brewer, 1994. 65–87.

Brewer, D.S. "The Relationship of Chaucer to the English and European Traditions." *Chaucer and Chaucerians: Critical Studies in Middle English Literature.* Ed. D.S. Brewer. University: University of Alabama Press, 1966. 1–38.

Brewer, Derek. "Medieval Literature, Folk Tale, and Traditional Literature." *Dutch Quarterly Review of Anglo-American Letters* 11 (1981): 243–256.

———. *Symbolic Stories: Traditional Narratives of the Family Drama in English Literature.* Cambridge: D.S. Brewer, 1980.

Briggs, Katherine M. "The Fairies and the Realm of the Dead." *Folklore* 81 (1970): 81–96.

Brook, G.L., ed. *The Harley Lyrics: The Middle English Lyrics of Ms. Harley 2253.* Old and Middle English Texts. Gen. ed. G.L. Brook. Manchester: Manchester University Press, 1948; 3rd ed. 1964.

Brown, Carleton, ed. *English Lyrics of the XIIIth Century.* Oxford: Clarendon Press, 1932, reprinted 1962.

Brown, Carole Koepke. " 'It Is True Art to Conceal Art': The Episodic Structure of Chaucer's *Franklin's Tale.*" *Chaucer Review* 27 (1992): 162–185.

Buchan, David. *The Ballad and the Folk.* London: Routledge and Kegan Paul, 1972.

Bullock-Davies, Constance. "The Form of the Breton Lay." *Medium Ævum* 42 (1973): 18–31.

Busby, Keith. *Gauvain in Old French Literature.* Amsterdam: Rodopi, 1980.

Butterfield, Ardis. "Lyric and Elegy in *The Book of the Duchess.*" *Medium Ævum* 60 (1991): 33–60.

Cable, Thomas M. *The English Alliterative Tradition.* Philadelphia: University of Pennsylvania Press, 1991.

Caesarius of Heisterbach. *The Dialogue on Miracles.* Trans. H. von E. Scott and C.C. Swinton Bland. Broadway Medieval Library. London: Routledge and Sons, 1929.

Calder, Daniel. "Ælfric, Wulfstan, and Other Late Prose." *A New Critical History of Old*

English Literature. Stanley B. Greenfield and Daniel G. Calder. New York: New York University Press, 1986. 68–106.

Calin, William. *The French Tradition and the Literature of Medieval England*. Toronto: University of Toronto Press, 1994.

Cameron, M.I. "Aldhelm as Naturalist: A Re-Examination of Some of His Enigmata." *Peritia* 4 (1985): 117–133.

Carley, James P. "England." *Medieval Arthurian Literature: A Guide to Recent Research*. Ed. Norris J. Lacy. New York: Garland, 1996. 1–82.

Carruthers, Mary J. *The Book of Memory: A Study of Memory in Mediaeval Culture*. Cambridge Studies in Medieval Literature 10. Cambridge: Cambridge University Press, 1990.

———. "Imaginatif, Memoria, and 'The Need for Critical Theory' in *Piers Plowman* Studies." *Yearbook of Langland Studies* 9 (1995): 103–114.

Cawley, A.C., ed. *The Wakefield Pageants in the Towneley Cycle*. Manchester: Manchester University Press, 1958.

Chalmers, Rebecca. "Elegy." *Encyclopedia of Medieval Literature*. Ed. Robert Thomas Lambdin and Laura Cooner Lambdin. Westport, CT: Greenwood Press, 2000. 175–176.

Chaucer, Geoffrey. *The Riverside Chaucer*. Ed. Larry D. Benson. 3rd ed. Boston: Houghton Mifflin, 1987.

———. *The Complete Works of Geoffrey Chaucer*. Ed. F.N. Robinson. 2nd ed. Boston: Houghton Mifflin, 1957.

Cherniss, Michael D. "The Oral-Traditional Opening Theme in the Poems of Cynewulf." *De Gustibus: Essays for Alain Renoir*. Ed. John Miles Foley, J. Chris Womack, and Whitney A. Womack. New York: Garland, 1992. 40–65.

Chickering, Howell D., Jr., trans. *Beowulf: A Dual-Language Edition*. Garden City, NY: Anchor, 1989.

Child, Francis, ed. *The English and Scottish Popular Ballads*. 5 vols. Boston: 1882–1898.

Clark, George. *Beowulf*. Boston: Twayne, 1990.

Clark, Willene B., and Meradith T. McMunn, eds. *Beasts and Birds of the Middle Ages*. Philadelphia: University of Pennsylvania Press, 1989.

Clemoes, Peter. "Ælfric." *Continuations and Beginnings: Studies in Old English Literature*. Ed. E.G. Stanley. London: Thomas Nelson and Sons, 1966. 176–209.

———. *Interactions of Thought and Language in Old English Poetry*. Cambridge: Cambridge University Press, 1995.

Coffman, George R. "The *Miller's Tale*: 3187–3215: Chaucer and the Seven Liberal Arts in Burlesque Vein." *MLN* 67 (1952): 329–331.

Coggeshall, John M. "Chaucer in the Ozarks: A New Look at the Sources." *Southern Folklore Quarterly* 45 (1981): 41–60.

Cohen, Shlomith. "Connecting through Riddles; or, The Riddle of Connecting." *Untying the Knot: On Riddles and Other Enigmatic Modes*. Ed. Galit Hasan-Rokem and David Shulman. Oxford: Oxford University Press, 1996. 294–315.

Colopy, Cheryl. "*Sir Degaré*: A Fairy Tale Oedipus." *Pacific Coast Philology* 17 (1982): 31–39.

Conlee, John W., ed. *Middle English Debate Poetry: A Critical Anthology*. East Lansing, MI: Colleagues Press, 1991.

————. *"The Owl and the Nightingale* and Latin Debate Tradition." *Comparatist* 4 (1980): 57–67.

Cook, Albert Stanburrough, ed. and prose trans. *The Old English Physiologus*. Verse trans. James Hall Pitman. Yale Studies in English 63. New Haven, CT: Yale University Press, 1921. Rpt. in *Translations from the Old English*. Hamden, CT: Archon Books, 1970.

Cook, Robert. "Chaucer's Franklin's Tale and *Sir Orfeo.*" *Neuphilologische Mitteilungen* 95 (1994): 333–336.

Cooke, W.G. *"The Tournament of Tottenham*: An Alliterative Poem and an Exeter Performance." *Records of Early English Drama Newsletter* 11.2 (1986): 1–3.

————. *"The Tournament of Tottenham*: Provenance, Text, and Lexicography." *English Studies* 69.2 (1988): 113–116.

Cornell, Christine. " 'Purtreture' and 'Holsom Stories': John Lydgate's Accommodation of Image and Text in Three Religious Lyrics." *Florilegium* 10 (1988–1991): 167–178.

Crawford, Donna. " 'Gronyng wyth Grysly Wounde': Injury in Five Middle English Breton Lays." *Readings in Medieval English Romance*. Ed. Carol M. Meale. Cambridge: D.S. Brewer, 1994. 35–52.

Cross, Tom Peete. "The Celtic Elements in the Lays of *Lanval* and *Graelent.*" *MP* 12 (1915): 585–644.

Crossley-Holland, Kevin, trans. *The Exeter Riddle Book*. London: Folio Society, 1978.

————, trans. *"Storm" and Other Old English Riddles*. London: Macmillan, 1970.

Cullen, Dolores. "Chaucer's *The Tale of Sir Thopas.*" *Explicator* 32 (1974): item 35.

Curtis, R. Churchill. "Kennings." *Encyclopedia of Medieval Literature*. Ed. Robert Thomas Lambdin and Laura Cooner Lambdin. Westport, CT: Greenwood Press, 2000. 331.

————. "William I (the Conquerer)." *Encyclopedia of Medieval Literature*. Ed. Robert Thomas Lambdin and Laura Cooner Lambdin. Westport, CT: Greenwood Press, 2000. 517–518.

Curtius, Ernst Robert. *European Literature and the Latin Middle Ages*. Trans. W.R. Trask. New York: Pantheon, 1953.

Dahood, Roger. "The Current State of *Ancrene Wisse* Group Studies." *Medieval English Studies Newsletter* 36 (June 1997): 6–14.

————. "Design in Part I of *Ancrene Riwle.*" *Medium Ævum* 56.1 (1987): 1–11.

Dane, Joseph A. "Genre and Authority: The Eighteenth-Century Creation of Chaucerian Burlesque." *Huntington Library Quarterly* 48 (1985): 345–362.

————. *Parody: Critical Concepts versus Literary Practices, Aristophanes to Sterne*. Norman: University of Oklahoma Press, 1988.

Dannenbaum, Susan. *"The Wedding of Sir Gawain and Dame Ragnell*, Line 48." *Explicator* 40 (1982): 3–4.

Dante. *A Translation of the Latin Works of Dante Alighieri*. Temple Classics. London: Dent, 1904.

Davidson, Clifford. *From Creation to Doom: The York Cycle of Mystery Plays*. New York: AMS, 1984.

Davies, Constance. "Classical Threads in 'Orfeo.' " *MLR* 56 (1961): 161–166.

Davis, Adam. *"Agon* and *Gnomon*: Forms and Functions of the Anglo-Saxon Riddles." *De Gustibus: Essays for Alain Renoir*. Ed. John Miles Foley, J. Chris Womack, and Whitney Womack. New York: Garland, 1992. 110–150.

Davis, Norman, Douglas Gray, Patricia Ingham, and Anne Wallace-Hadill. *A Chaucer Glossary*. Oxford: Clarendon Press, 1979.

Defoe, Daniel. "The Ballad Maker's Plea" (1722). *Daniel Defoe: His Life and Recently Discovered Writings*. Ed. William Lee. New York: Franklin, 1969. 3:59.

Dillon, Bert. "A Clerk Ther Was of Oxenford Also." *Chaucer's Pilgrims: An Historical Guide to the Pilgrims in* The Canterbury Tales. Ed. Laura C. Lambdin and Robert T. Lambdin. Westport, CT: Greenwood Press, 1996. 108–115.

Donaldson, E. Talbot, trans. *Will's Vision of Piers Plowman*. Ed. Elizabeth D. Kirk and Judith H. Anderson. New York: Norton, 1990.

Donovan, Mortimer J. *The Breton Lay: A Guide to Varieties*. Notre Dame, IN: University of Notre Dame Press, 1969.

Doob, Penelope Reed. *The Idea of the Labyrinth from Classical Antiquity through the Middle Ages*. Ithaca, NY: Cornell University Press, 1990.

———. *Nebuchadnezzar's Children: Conventions of Madness in Middle English Literature*. New Haven, CT: Yale University Press, 1974.

Dronke, Peter. *Dante and Medieval Latin Traditions*. Cambridge: Cambridge University Press, 1986.

———. *Medieval Latin and the Rise of European Love-Lyric*. 2 vols. Oxford: Clarendon Press, 1965–1966.

———. *The Medieval Lyric*. New York: Harper and Row, 1969.

Dudley, D.R., and D.M. Lang, eds. *The Penguin Companion to Literature 4: Classical and Byzantine, Oriental and African*. Harmondsworth: Penguin, 1969.

Duggan, Hoyt N. "Meter, Stanza, Vocabulary, Dialect." *A Companion to the Gawain-Poet*. Ed. Derek Brewer and Jonathan Gibson. Cambridge: D.S. Brewer, 1997.

Duncan, Edwin. "The Middle English *Bestiary*: Missing Link in the Evolution of the Alliterative Long Line?" *Studia Neophilologica* 64 (1992): 25–33.

Dunn, Charles W., and Edward T. Byrnes, eds., *Middle English Literature*. New York: Harcourt, 1973.

Eichmann, Raymond. Introduction. *Fabliaux Fair and Foul*. Translations by John DuVal with introductions and notes by Raymond Eichmann. Medieval and Renaissance Texts and Studies. Binghamton, NY: Center for Early Medieval and Renaissance Studies, 1992.

Elbow, Peter. *Oppositions in Chaucer*. Middletown, CT: Wesleyan University Press, 1975.

Elliott, Charles, ed. *Robert Henryson: Poems*. Oxford: Clarendon Press, 1963.

Entwistle, William J. *European Balladry*. Oxford: Clarendon Press, 1939.

———. " 'Sir Aldinger' and the Date of the English Ballads." 1953. Rpt. in *Saga Book of the Viking Society for Northern Research* 13 (1980): 97–112.

"Epic." *The Compact Edition of the Oxford English Dictionary*. Vol. 1. 1987.

Evans, Murray J. *Rereading Middle English Romance: Manuscript Layout, Decoration, and the Rhetoric of Composite Structure*. Montreal: McGill–Queen's University Press, 1995.

The Exeter Book. Ed. George Philip Krapp and Elliott Van Kirk Dobbie. The Anglo-Saxon Poetic Records. New York: Columbia University Press, 1936.

The Exeter Book. Ed. W.S. Mackie and Israel Gollancz. Early English Text Society O.S. nos. 104, 194. London: K. Paul, Trench, Trübner and Co., 1895–1934; Millwood, NY: Kraus Reprint, 1987–1988.

Ferris, Sumner. "The Date of Chaucer's Final Annuity and of the 'Complaint to His Empty Purse.' " *Modern Philology* 65 (1967): 45–52.

Field, P.J.C. "Malory and *The Wedding of Sir Gawain and Dame Ragnell.*" *Archiv* 219.2 (1982): 374–381.

Field, Rosalind. "Romance as History, History as Romance." *Romance in Medieval England.* Ed. Maldwyn Mills, Jennifer Fellows, and Carol M. Meale. Cambridge: D.S. Brewer, 1991. 163–173.

Figg, Kristen Mossler. *The Short Lyric Poems of Jean Froissart.* New York: Garland, 1994.

Finlayson, John. "Definitions of Middle English Romance." Parts 1 and 2. *Chaucer Review* 15 (1980): 44–62, 168–181.

———. "The Form of the Middle English Lay." *Chaucer Review* 19 (1985): 352–367.

Fisher, John H., ed. *The Complete Poetry and Prose of Geoffrey Chaucer.* New York: Holt, Rinehart and Winston, 1977.

———. "The Three Styles of Fragment I of *The Canterbury Tales.*" *Chaucer Review* 8 (1973): 119–127.

Fisher, John H., Wayne Hamm, Peter G. Beidler, and Robert F. Yeager. "John Gower." *A Manual of the Writings in Middle English, 1050–1500.* Gen. ed. Albert E. Hartung. New Haven: Connecticut Academy of Arts and Sciences, 1986. 7:2195–2210, 2399–2418.

Fletcher, Alan J. "The Dancing Virgins of *Hali Meidhad.*" *Notes and Queries* 40 (238).4 (December 1993): 437–439.

Flint, Valerie I.J. *The Rise of Magic in Early Medieval Europe.* Princeton, NJ: Princeton University Press, 1991.

Foley, John Miles. *The Theory of Oral Composition: History and Methodology.* Bloomington: Indiana University Press, 1988.

Foster, Edward E. "Simplicity, Complexity, and Morality in Four Medieval Romances." *Chaucer Review* 31 (1997): 401–419.

Fowler, David C. *A Literary History of the Popular Ballad.* Durham, NC: Duke University Press, 1968.

Frantzen, Allen. "The Diverse Nature of Old English Poetry." *Companion to Old English Poetry.* Ed. Henk Aertsen and Rolf H. Bremmer, Jr. Amsterdam: VU University Press, 1994. 1–17.

———. *King Alfred.* Boston: Twayne, 1986.

French, W.H., and C.B. Hale, eds. *Middle English Metrical Romances.* New York: Prentice-Hall, 1930. New York: Russell & Russell, 1964.

Friedman, Albert B. *The Ballad Revival.* Chicago: University of Chicago Press, 1961.

Friedman, John Block. *Orpheus in the Middle Ages.* Cambridge, MA: Harvard University Press, 1970.

Fries, Maureen. "(Almost) without a Song: Criseyde and Lyric in Chaucer's *Troilus.*" *Chaucer Yearbook* 1 (1992): 47–63.

Fry, Donald. "*Exeter Book* Riddle Solutions." *Old English Newsletter* 15.1 (1981): 22–33.

Frye, Northrop. *Anatomy of Criticism.* Princeton, NJ: Princeton University Press, 1957.

———. "Charms and Riddles." *Spiritus Mundi: Essays on Literature, Myth, and Society.* Bloomington: Indiana University Press, 1976. 123–147.

———. *The Secular Scripture: A Study of the Structure of Romance.* Cambridge, MA: Harvard University Press, 1976.

Fulk, R.D. *A History of Old English Meter*. Philadelphia: University of Pennsylvania Press, 1992.

Furnish, Shearle. "Civilization and Savagery in Thomas Chestre's *Sir Launfal*." *Medieval Perspectives* 3 (1988): 137–149.

———. "The Modernity of *The Erle of Tolous* and the Decay of the *Breton Lai*." *Medieval Perspectives* 8 (1993): 69–77.

Furrow, Melissa M., ed. *Ten Fifteenth-Century Comic Poems*. New York: Garland, 1985.

Gameson, Richard. "The Origin of the *Exeter Book* of Old English Poetry." *Anglo-Saxon England* 25 (1996): 135–185.

Garbáty, Thomas J. "Rhyme, Romance, Ballad, Burlesque, and the Confluence of Form." *Fifteenth-Century Studies: Recent Essays*. Ed. Robert F. Yeager. Hamden, CT: Archon, 1984. 283–301.

Gardner, John. *The Construction of the Wakefield Cycle*. Carbondale: Southern Illinois University Press, 1974.

Garmonsway, G.N., ed. and trans. *The Anglo-Saxon Chronicle*. London: Dent, 1990.

Gaylord, Alan T. *The Poetics of Alliteration: Readings of Medieval English Alliterative Verse*. Supplement to *Medieval Perspectives*, vol. 14. Chaucer Studio Occasional Readings, no. 26. [Provo, UT]: Chaucer Studio; [Richmond, KY]: Southeastern Medieval Association, 1999.

Gellrich, Jesse M. "The Parody of Medieval Music in the *Miller's Tale*." *Journal of English and Germanic Philology* 73 (1974): 176–188.

Gerould, Gordon Hall. *The Ballad of Tradition*. Oxford: Clarendon Press, 1932.

Glasser, Marc. " 'He Nedes Moste Hire Wedde': The Forced Marriage in the *Wife of Bath's Tale* and Its Middle English Analogues." *Neuphilologische Mitteilungen* 85.2 (1984): 239–241.

Godden, Malcolm. "Apocalypse and Invasion in Late Anglo-Saxon England." *From Anglo-Saxon to Early Middle English*. Ed. Malcolm Godden, Douglas Gray, and Terry Hoad. Oxford: Clarendon Press, 1994. 130–162.

Goldin, Frederick, ed. and trans. *German and Italian Lyrics of the Middle Ages*. Garden City, NY: Anchor/Doubleday, 1973.

———, ed. and trans. *Lyrics of the Troubadours and Trouvères*. Garden City, NY: Anchor/Doubleday, 1973.

Goldstein, David, ed. and trans. *Hebrew Poems from Spain*. New York: Schocken, 1965.

Gollancz, Israel. Introduction. *Pearl, Cleanness, Patience, and Sir Gawain, Reproduced in Facsimile from the Unique Manuscript Cotton Nero A.x. in the British Museum*. Early English Text Society, original Ser. 162. London: EETS, 1923.

Gopen, George D., ed. and trans. *The Moral Fables of Aesop by Robert Henryson*. Notre Dame, IN: University of Notre Dame Press, 1987.

Gordon, R.K. *Anglo-Saxon Poetry*. London: Dent, 1926.

Gower, John. *Confessio Amantis*. Ed. Reinhold Pauli. 3 vols. London: Bell and Daldy, 1857.

Gragg, Florence Alden. *Latin Writings of the Italian Humanists*. College Classical Series. New Rochelle, NY: Caratzas Brothers, 1981.

Gransden, Antonia. "The Chronicles of Medieval England and Scotland: Part I." *Journal of Medieval History* 16 (1990): 129–150.

———. *Historical Writing in England: C. 550 to c. 1307*. Ithaca, NY: Cornell University Press, 1974.

Grattan, J.H.G., and G.F.H. Sykes, eds. *The Owl and the Nightingale*. EETS 119. London: Oxford University Press, 1935, reprinted 1959.

Gravdal, Kathryn. Vilain *and* Courtois: *Transgressive Parody in French Literature of the Twelfth and Thirteenth Centuries*. Lincoln: University of Nebraska Press, 1989.

Green, D.H. *Irony in the Medieval Romance*. New York: Cambridge University Press, 1979.

Greenfield, Stanley B. *A Critical History of Old English Literature*. New York: New York University Press, 1965.

Grendon, Felix. "The Anglo-Saxon Charms." *Journal of American Folklore* 22 (1909): 105–137.

Gros Louis, Kenneth R.R. "The Significance of Sir Orfeo's Self-Exile." *RES* 18 (1967): 245–252.

Guerin, M. Victoria. *The Fall of Kings and Princes: Structure and Destruction in Arthurian Tragedy*. Stanford, CA: Stanford University Press, 1995.

Hacikyan, Agop. A Linguistic and Literary Analysis of Old English Riddles. Montreal: Maria Casalini, 1966.

Hagen, Karl. "*Battle of Brunnanburgh, The*." *Encyclopedia of Medieval Literature*. Ed. Robert Thomas Lambdin and Laura Cooner Lambdin. Westport, CT: Greenwood Press, 2000. 49–50.

———. " 'Battle of Finnsburgh.' " *Encyclopedia of Medieval Literature*. Ed. Robert Thomas Lambdin and Laura Cooner Lambdin. Westport, CT: Greenwood Press, 2000. 50–51.

———. "*Battle of Maldon, The*." *Encyclopedia of Medieval Literature*. Ed. Robert Thomas Lambdin and Laura Cooner Lambdin. Westport, CT: Greenwood Press, 2000. 51–52.

———. "*Beowulf*." *Encyclopedia of Medieval Literature*. Ed. Robert Thomas Lambdin and Laura Cooner Lambdin. Westport, CT: Greenwood Press, 2000. 55–56.

———. " 'Caedmon's Hymn.' " *Encyclopedia of Medieval Literature*. Ed. Robert Thomas Lambdin and Laura Cooner Lambdin. Westport, CT: Greenwood Press, 2000. 73.

———. " 'Seafarer, The.' " *Encyclopedia of Medieval Literature*. Ed. Robert Thomas Lambdin and Laura Cooner Lambdin. Westport, CT: Greenwood Press, 2000. 455.

———. " 'Wanderer, The.' " *Encyclopedia of Medieval Literature*. Ed. Robert Thomas Lambdin and Laura Cooner Lambdin. Westport, CT: Greenwood Press, 2000. 506–507.

Hamilton, Marie Padgett. "The Meaning of the Middle English *Pearl*." *PMLA* 70 (1955): 805–824.

Hanna, Ralph. "Alliterative Poetry." *The Cambridge History of Medieval English Literature*. Ed. David Wallace. Cambridge: Cambridge University Press, 1999. 488–512.

Hanning, Robert W. "The Audience as Co-Creator of the First Chivalric Romances." *Yearbook of English Studies* 11 (1981): 1–28.

———. "Poetic Emblems in Medieval Narrative Texts." *Vernacular Poetics in the Middle Ages*. Ed. Lois Ebin. Kalamazoo, MI: Medieval Institute, 1984. 1–32.

Hanning, Robert W., and Joan Ferrante, eds. and trans. *The Lais of Marie de France*. Durham, NC: Labyrinth Press, 1982.

Harder, Kelsie B. "Chaucer's Use of the Mystery Plays in the *Miller's Tale*." *Modern Language Quarterly* 17 (1956): 193–198.

Hardman, Phillipa. *"The Book of the Duchess* as a Memorial Monument." *Chaucer Review* 28 (1994): 205–15. Rpt. in *Chaucer's Dream Visions and Shorter Poems.* Ed. William A. Quinn. New York: Garland, 1999. 183–196.

Harrington, David V. "Redefining the Middle English Breton Lay." *Medievalia et Humanistica* n.s. 16 (1988): 73–95.

Harrington, K.P. *Mediaeval Latin.* Chicago: University of Chicago Press, 1962.

Harris, A. Leslie. "Tournaments and *The Tournament of Tottenham.*" *FCS* 23 (1997): 81–92.

Hart, Walter Morris. *Ballad and Epic.* 1907. Rpt. New York: Russell & Russell, 1967.

Hartwell, David G. The Wedding of Sir Gawain and Dame Ragnell: An Edition. Diss. Columbia University, 1973. Ann Arbor: UMI, 1973. 7328216.

Hasan-Rokem, Galit, and David Shulman, eds. *Untying the Knot: On Riddles and Other Enigmatic Modes.* Oxford: Oxford University Press, 1996.

Haskins, Charles Homer. *The Renaissance of the Twelfth Century.* Cambridge, MA: Harvard University Press, 1927.

Heffernan, Thomas J. "Sermon Literature." *Middle English Prose: A Critical Guide to Major Authors and Genres.* Ed. A.S.G. Edwards. New Brunswick, NJ: Rutgers University Press, 1984. 177–207.

Heillman, Robert, and Richard O'Gorman, trans. *Fabliaux: Ribald Tales from the Old French.* New York: Thomas Y. Crowell, 1966.

The Heliand: The Saxon Gospel. Trans. G. Ronald Murphy. New York: Oxford University Press, 1992.

Helterman, Jeffrey. *Symbolic Action in the Plays of the Wakefield Master.* Athens: University of Georgia Press, 1981.

Helterman, Jolyon. "The Anglo-Saxon Chronicle." *Old and Middle English Literature.* Vol. 146 of *Dictionary of Literary Biography.* Ed. Jeffrey Helterman and Jerome Mitchell. Detroit: Gale Research, 1994. 61–66.

Henderson, Arnold Clayton. "Medieval Beasts and Modern Cages: The Making of Meaning in Fables and Bestiaries." *PMLA* 97 (1982): 40–49.

Henderson, T.F. *The Ballad in Literature.* New York: Haskell House, 1966.

Hill, D.M. "The Structure of 'Sir Orfeo.' " *Mediaeval Studies* 23 (1961): 136–153.

Hill, Joyce. "Ælfric's Sources Reconsidered: Some Case Studies from the Catholic Homilies." *Studies in English Language and Literature: "Doubt Wisely."* Ed. M.J. Toswell and E.M. Tyler. London: Routledge, 1996. 362–386.

Hines, John. *The Fabliau in English.* London and New York: Longman, 1993.

Ho, Cynthia. "Dichotomize and Conquer: 'Womman Handlyng' in *Handlyng Synne.*" *Philological Quarterly* 72.4 (1993): 383–401.

Hodgart, M.J.C. *The Ballads.* 2nd ed. London: Hutchinson, 1962.

Honegger, Thomas. *From Phoenix to Chauntecleer: Medieval English Animal Poetry.* Swiss Studies in English 120. Tübingen and Basel: Francke Verlag, 1996.

Hornsby, Joseph. *Chaucer and the Law.* Norman, OK: Pilgrim Books, 1988.

———. "A Sergeant of the Lawe, War and Wyse." *Chaucer's Pilgrims: An Historical Guide to the Pilgrims in* The Canterbury Tales. Ed. Laura C. Lambdin and Robert T. Lambdin. Westport, CT: Greenwood Press, 1996. 116–134.

Hornstein, Lillian Herlands. "Eustace-Constance-Florence-Griselda Legends" and "Miscellaneous Romances." *A Manual of the Writings in Middle English, 1050–1500.* Gen. ed. J. Burke Severs. New Haven: Connecticut Academy of Arts and Sciences, 1967. 1:120–132, 278–291; 1:144–172, 298–332.

Horrall, Sarah M. "The Manuscripts of *Cursor Mundi.*" *TEXT: Transactions of the Society for Textual Scholarship* 2 (1985): 69–82.

Howard, Donald R., and James Dean, eds. *The Canterbury Tales: A Selection.* New York: New American Library, 1969.

Hrotsvit of Gandersheim. *Hrotsvit of Gandersheim: A Florilegium of Her Works.* Ed. Katharina Wilson. Cambridge: D.S. Brewer, 1998.

Hudson, Anne. "Robert of Gloucester and the Antiquaries, 1550–1800." *Notes and Queries* 16.9 (1969): 322–333.

———. "Wycliffite Prose." *Middle English Prose: A Critical Guide to Major Authors and Genres.* Ed. A.S.G. Edwards. New Brunswick, NJ: Rutgers University Press, 1984. 249–270.

Hutson, Arthur E. Introduction. *Epics of the Western World.* Philadelphia: Lippincott, 1954.

Hume, Kathryn. "The Pagan Setting of the *Franklin's Tale* and the Sources of Dorigen's Cosmology." *Studia Neophilologica* 44 (1972): 289–294.

———. "Structure and Perspective: Romance and Hagiographic Features in the Amicus and Amelius Story." *JEGP* 69 (1970): 89–109.

———. "Why Chaucer Calls the *Franklin's Tale* a Breton Lai." *PQ* 51 (1972): 365–379.

Hutcheson, B. R. *Old English Poetic Metre.* Suffolk: D.S. Brewer, 1995.

Innes-Parker, Catherine. "The Lady and the King: *Ancrene Wisse*'s Parable of the Royal Wooing Re-Examined." *English Studies* 75.6 (1994): 509–522.

International Reynard Society (Beast Epic, Fable & Fabliau). Online. 2 May 2000. <http://www.hull.ac.uk/french/fox.html>.

Jackson, Guida M. *Encyclopedia of Traditional Epics.* Santa Barbara, CA: ABC-CLIO, 1994.

Jackson, W.T.H. "Allegory and Allegorization." *The Challenge of the Medieval Text.* Ed. Joan M. Ferrante and Robert W. Hanning. New York: Columbia University Press, 1985. 157–171.

———. *Medieval Literature: A History and a Guide.* London and New York: Collier Books, 1966; New York: Collier and Macmillan, 1967.

Jacobs, John C., ed. and trans. *The Fables of Odo of Cheriton.* Syracuse, NY: Syracuse University Press, 1985.

Jacobs, Nicolas. "The Old English 'Book-Moth' Riddle Reconsidered." *Notes and Queries* 35 (1988): 290–292.

Jacoff, Rachel, ed. *The Cambridge Companion to Dante.* Cambridge: Cambridge University Press, 1993.

Jauss, Hans Robert. *Toward an Aesthetic of Reception.* Trans. Timothy Bahti. Minneapolis: University of Minnesota Press, 1982.

Jember, Gregory. Preface. *The Old English Riddles: A New Translation.* Denver: Society for New Language Study, 1976.

———. "Literal and Metaphorical: Clues to Reading the Old English Riddles." *Studies in English Literature* 65 (1988): 47–56.

———. "Prolegomena to a Study of the Old English Riddles." *Journal of the Faculty of Liberal Arts, Saga University* 19 (1987): 155–178.

Johnston, Grahame. "The Breton Lays in Middle English." *Iceland and the Mediaeval World: Studies in Honour of Ian Maxwell.* Ed. Gabriel Turville-Petre and John Stanley Martin. Victoria, Australia: Wilke, 1974. 151–161.

Jolly, Karen Louise. "Anglo-Saxon Charms in the Context of a Christian World View." *Journal of Medieval History* 11 (1985): 279–293.

Jones, George F. "The Tournaments of Tottenham and Lappenhausen." *PMLA* 66 (1951): 1123–1140.

Jones, W. Lewis. *King Arthur in History and Legend*. Cambridge: Cambridge University Press, 1911.

Jordan, Tracey. "Fairy Tale and Fabliau: Chaucer's *The Miller's Tale.*" *SSF* 21 (1984): 87–93.

Kaiser, Rolf. *Medieval English: An Old English and Middle English Anthology* 3rd ed. Berlin: Rolf Kaiser, 1958. Excerpt 173.

Kane, George. *Middle English Literature: A Critical Study of the Romances, the Religious Lyrics*, Piers Plowman. London: Methuen, 1951.

Kaske, R.E. "The *Canticum Canticorum* in the *Miller's Tale.*" *Studies in Philology* 59 (1962): 479–500.

Kaulbach, Ernest N. *Imaginative Prophecy in the B-Text of "Piers Plowman."* Piers Plowman Studies 8. Cambridge: Brewer, 1993.

Keefer, Sarah Larratt. *Psalm-Poem and Psalter-Glosses*. New York: Peter Lang, 1991.

Keeler, Laura. *Geoffrey of Monmouth and the Late Latin Chroniclers, 1300–1500*. Berkeley and Los Angeles: University of California Press, 1946.

Kennedy, E.D. *Chronicles and Other Historical Writing*. Vol. 8 of *A Manual of the Writings in Middle English, 1050–1500*. Ed. Albert E. Hartung. Hamden, CT: Archon Books, 1989.

———. "John Hardyng and the Holy Grail." *Arthurian Literature*. Ed. Richard Barber. Vol. 8. Cambridge: D.S. Brewer, 1989. 185–206.

Kenny, Anthony, ed. *Wyclif in His Times*. Oxford: Clarendon Press, 1986.

Ker, W.P. *Epic and Romance: Essays on Medieval Literature*. 1897. Rpt. New York: Dover, 1957.

Kerby-Fulton, Kathryn. " 'Who Has Written This Book?': Visionary Autobiography in Langland's C-Text." *The Medieval Mystical Tradition in England: Exeter Symposium V*. Ed. Marion Glasscoe. Cambridge: Brewer, 1992. 101–116.

Kiernan, Kevin S. *Beowulf and the Beowulf Manuscript*. New Brunswick, NJ: Rutgers University Press, 1981.

Kitchin, George. "Mediaeval Burlesque." *A Survey of Burlesque and Parody in English*. 1931. New York: Russell & Russell, 1967. 1–37.

Kolve, V.A. *The Play Called Corpus Christi*. Stanford, CA: Stanford University Press, 1966.

Kooper, E.S. "Inverted Images in Chaucer's *Tale of Sir Thopas.*" *Studia Neophilologica* 56 (1984): 147–154.

Krantz, Dennis. *Mocking Epic: Waltharius, Alexandreis, and the Problem of Christian Heroism*. Madrid: J. Porrúa Turanzas, 1980.

Krapp, George Philip, and E.V.K. Dobbie, eds. *The Anglo Saxon Poetic Records*. New York: Columbia University Press, 1931–1954.

Kruger, Steven F. *Dreaming in the Middle Ages*. Cambridge Studies in Medieval Literature 14. Cambridge: Cambridge University Press, 1992.

———. "Imagination and the Complex Movement of Chaucer's *House of Fame.*" *Chaucer Review* 28 (1993): 117–134.

Kubouchi, Tadao. *From Wulfstan to Richard Rolle: Papers Exploring the Continuity of English Prose*. Cambridge: D.S. Brewer, 1999.

Lacy, Norris J., ed. *The Arthurian Encyclopedia*. New York: Garland, 1986.

Lambdin, Laura Cooner. "Arthurian Legend." *Encyclopedia of Medieval Literature*. Ed. Robert Thomas Lambdin and Laura Cooner Lambdin. Westport, CT: Greenwood Press, 2000. 20–28.

———. "Chrétien de Troyes." *Encyclopedia of Medieval Literature*. Ed. Robert Thomas Lambdin and Laura Cooner Lambdin. Westport, CT: Greenwood Press, 2000. 97–98.

———. "Layamon." *Encyclopedia of Medieval Literature*. Ed. Robert Thomas Lambdin and Laura Cooner Lambdin. Westport, CT: Greenwood Press, 2000. 353–354.

Lambdin, Robert Thomas. "Anglo-Norman." *Encyclopedia of Medieval Literature*. Ed. Robert Thomas Lambdin and Laura Cooner Lambdin. Westport, CT: Greenwood Press, 2000. 14–15.

———. "Chivalry." *Encyclopedia of Medieval Literature*. Ed. Robert Thomas Lambdin and Laura Cooner Lambdin. Westport, CT: Greenwood Press, 2000. 97.

———. "*Domesday Book*." *Encyclopedia of Medieval Literature*. Ed. Robert Thomas Lambdin and Laura Cooner Lambdin. Westport, CT: Greenwood Press, 2000. 151.

———. "Wyrd." *Encyclopedia of Medieval Literature*. Ed. Robert Thomas Lambdin and Laura Cooner Lambdin. Westport, CT: Greenwood Press, 2000. 524.

Lane, Daryl. "Conflict in *Sir Launfal*." *Neuphilologische Mitteilungen* 74 (1973): 283–287.

Lapidge, Michael. *Anglo-Latin Literature, 900–1066*. London: Hambledon Press, 1993.

Lasater, Alice E. *Spain to England: A Comparative Study of Arabic, European, and English Literature of the Middle Ages*. Jackson: University Press of Mississippi, 1974.

Laskaya, Anne and Eve Salisbury, eds. *The Middle English Breton Lays*. TEAMS Middle English Texts Series. Kalamazoo: Medieval Institute, 1995.

Lawrence, William W. *Beowulf and Epic Tradition*. New York: Hafner, 1961.

Lawton, David, ed. *Middle English Alliterative Poetry and Its Literary Background: Seven Essays*. Cambridge: D.S. Brewer, 1982.

Leach, MacEdward, and Tristram Coffin, eds. *The Critics and the Ballad*. Carbondale: Southern Illinois University Press, 1961.

Lehmann, Paul. *Die Parodie im Mittelalter: Mit 24 ausgewählten parodistischen Texten*. 2nd ed. Stuttgart: A. Hiersemann, 1963.

Lehnert, Martin. *Poetry and Prose of the Anglo-Saxons*. Vol. 1. *Texts*. 2nd rev. ed. Halle: VEB Max Niemeyer Verlag, 1960.

Lerer, Seth. "Artifice and Artistry in *Sir Orfeo*." *Speculum* 60 (1985): 92–109.

———. *Literacy and Power in Anglo-Saxon Literature*. Lincoln: University of Nebraska Press, 1991.

———. "The Riddle and the Book: *Exeter Book* Riddle 42 in Its Contexts." *Papers on Language and Literature: A Journal for Scholars and Critics of Language and Literature* 25.1 (1989): 3–19.

Lewis, C.S. *A Preface to* Paradise Lost. New York: Oxford University Press, 1961.

Lindstrom, Bengt. "Some Textual Notes on the ME Genesis and Exodus." *English Studies* 77.6 (1996): 513–516.

Lloyd, A.L. *Folk Song in England*. London: Panther, 1969.

Long, Eleanor. " 'Young Man, I Think You're Dyin': The Twining Branches Theme in the Tristan Legend and in English Tradition." *Fabula* 21 (1980): 183–199.

Loomis, Laura Hibbard. "Chaucer and the Auchinleck MS: 'Thopas' and 'Guy of Warwick.' " *Essays and Studies in Honor of Carleton Brown.* London: H. Milford, Oxford University Press, 1940. 111–128.

———. "Chaucer and the Breton Lays of the Auchinleck MS." *SP* 38 (1941): 14–33.

———. *Mediaeval Romance in England.* London: Oxford University Press, 1924.

Loomis, Roger. *Celtic Myth and Arthurian Romance.* New York: Columbia University Press, 1927.

———. *The Development of Arthurian Romance.* New York: Norton, 1970.

Loomis, Roger Sherman, and Rudolph Willard. *Medieval English Verse and Prose.* New York: Appleton-Century-Crofts, 1948.

Lord, Albert. *The Singer of Tales.* Cambridge, MA: Harvard University Press, 1960.

Lucas, Peter J. "An Interpretation of *Sir Orfeo.*" *Leeds Studies in English* 6 (1972): 1–9.

———, ed. *John Capgrave's Abbreuiacion of Cronicles.* EETS 285. Oxford: Oxford University Press, 1983.

Ludlum, Chas. D. "Heavenly Word-Play in Chaucer's 'Complaint to His Purse.' " *Notes and Queries* 23 (1976): 391–392.

Lumiansky, R.M. "Legends of Alexander the Great," "Legends of Godfrey of Bouillon," "Legends of Thebes," and "Legends of Troy." *A Manual of the Writings in Middle English, 1050–1500.* Gen. ed. J. Burke Severs. New Haven: Connecticut Academy of Arts and Sciences, 1967. 1:104–113, 268–273; 1:101–103, 267–268; 1:119, 277; 1:114–118, 274–277.

———, ed. *Malory's Originality: A Critical Study of Le Morte Darthur.* Baltimore: Johns Hopkins Press, 1964.

Lynch, Kathryn C. "The Logic of the Dream Vision in Chaucer's *House of Fame.*" *Literary Nominalism and the Theory of Rereading Late Medieval Texts: A New Research Paradigm.* Mediaeval Studies 5. Ed. Richard J. Utz. Lewiston, NY: Mellen, 1995. 179–203.

Mackenzie, W.R. *The English Moralities from the Point of View of Allegory.* Boston and London: Ginn and Company, 1914.

Mackey, Louis. "Eros into Logic: The Rhetoric of Courtly Love." *The Philosophy of (Erotic) Love.* Ed. Robert C. Solomon and Kathleen Higgins. Lawrence: University Press of Kansas, 1991. 336–351.

Mann, Jill. "Beast Epic and Fable." *Medieval Latin: An Introduction and Bibliographical Guide.* Ed. F.A.C. Mantello and A.G. Rigg. Washington, DC: Catholic University of America Press, 1996. 556–561.

———. *Langland and Allegory.* The Morton W. Bloomfield Lectures on Medieval English Literature 2. Kalamazoo, MI: Medieval Institute, 1992.

Marchalonis, Shirley. "*Sir Gowther*: The Process of a Romance." *Chaucer Review* 6 (1971): 14–29.

Marsden, Richard. "Ælfric as Translator: The Old English Prose Genesis." *Anglia* 109. 3–4 (1991): 319–358.

Marti, Kevin. *Body, Heart, and Text in the "Pearl"-Poet.* Studies in Mediaeval Literature 12. Lewiston, NY: Mellen, 1991.

———. "Traditional Characteristics of the Resurrected Body in *Pearl.*" *Viator* 24 (1993): 311–335.

Martin, B.K. "*Sir Launfal* and the Folktale." *Medium Ævum* 35 (1966): 199–210.

Martin, Richard P. *The Language of Heroes: Speech and Performance in the* Iliad. Ithaca, NY: Cornell University Press, 1989.

Mason, Eugene, trans. *Arthurian Chronicles/Wace and Layamon.* London: Dent, 1976.

Matheson, Lister M. "Historical Prose." *Middle English Prose: A Critical Guide to Major Authors and Genres.* Ed. A.S.G. Edwards. New Brunswick, NJ: Rutgers University Press, 1984. 209–248.

Mathews, John. *Gawain: Knight of the Goddess.* Wellingborough: Aquarian Press, 1990.

Matthews, William. *The Tragedy of Arthur: A Study of the Alliterative "Morte Arthure."* Berkeley: University of California Press, 1960.

McClellan, William. "Radical Theology or Parody in a Marian Lyric of Ms Harley 2253." *Voices in Translation: The Authority of "Olde Bookes" in Medieval Literature.* Ed. Deborah M. Sinnreich-Levi and Gale Sigal. New York: AMS, 1992. 157–168.

McCulloch, Florence. *Mediaeval Latin and French Bestiaries.* University of North Carolina Studies in the Romance Languages and Literatures, 33. Chapel Hill: University of North Carolina Press, 1960.

McCully, C.B., and J.J. Anderson. *English Historical Metrics.* Cambridge: Cambridge University Press, 1996.

McDonald, Richard. "*Anglo-Saxon Chronicles.*" *Encyclopedia of Medieval Literature.* Ed. Robert Thomas Lambdin and Laura Cooner Lambdin. Westport, CT: Greenwood Press, 2000. 15–17.

———. "Geoffrey of Monmouth." *Encyclopedia of Medieval Literature.* Ed. Robert Thomas Lambdin and Laura Cooner Lambdin. Westport, CT: Greenwood Press, 2000. 224–226.

McGalliard, John C. "Characterization in Chaucer's Shipman's Tale." *PQ* 54 (1975): 1–18.

McKnight, George Harley, ed. *Middle English Humorous Tales in Verse.* Boston and London: Heath, 1913.

Menocal, Maria Rosa. *The Arabic Role in Medieval Literary History: A Forgotten Heritage.* Philadelphia: University of Pennsylvania Press, 1987.

Miller, Robert P. "*The Miller's Tale* as Complaint." *Chaucer Review* 5 (1970): 147–160.

Millet, Bella. "*Ancrene Wisse* and the Conditions of Confession." *English Studies* 80.3 (1999): 193–214.

———. "*Hali Meiðhad, Sawles Warde,* and the Continuity of English Prose." *Five Hundred Years of Words and Sounds: A Festschrift for Eric Dobson.* Ed. E.G. Stanley and Douglas Gray. Cambridge: D.S. Brewer, 1983. 100–108.

Minkova, Donka. "Verse Structure in the Middle English Genesis and Exodus." *JEGP* 91.2 (1992): 157–178.

Minnis, A.J., V.J. Scattergood, and J.J. Smith. *The Shorter Poems.* Oxford: Clarendon Press; New York: Oxford University Press, 1995.

Mitchell, Bruce. "The Faery World of *Sir Orfeo.*" *Neophilologus* 48 (1964): 155–159.

Mitchell, Bruce, and Fred C. Robinson. *A Guide to Old English.* 5th ed. Oxford: Blackwell, 1992.

Monroe, James T. *Hispano-Arabic Poetry: A Student Anthology.* Berkeley: University of California Press, 1974.

Moore, Arthur K. "The Literary Status of the English Popular Ballad." *Comparative Literature* 10 (1958): 1–20.

Moore, Samuel, and Thomas A. Knott, revised by James R. Hulbert. *The Elements of Old English.* 10th ed. Ann Arbor, MI: George Wahr Publishing, 1977.

Moorman, Charles. *The Book of Kyng Arthur: The Unity of Malory's Morte Darthur.* Lexington: University of Kentucky Press, 1965.

Morgan, Gwendolyn. "Essential Loss: Christianity and Alienation in the Anglo-Saxon Elegies." *In Geardagum* 11 (1990): 15–33.

———. "Dualism and Mirror Imagery in Anglo-Saxon Riddles." *Journal of the Fantastic in the Arts* 5.1 (1992): 74–85.

———. "Duality in *Piers Plowman* and the Anglo-Saxon Riddles." *Connotations* 1.2 (1991): 168–72.

———. *Medieval Balladry and the Courtly Tradition.* New York: Peter Lang, 1993.

———, ed. and trans. *Medieval Ballads: Chivalry, Romance, and Everyday Life.* New York: Peter Lang, 1996.

Morgan, Gwendolyn, and Brian McAllister. "Reading Riddles 30A and 30B as Two Poems." *In Geardagum* 14 (1993): 67–78.

Morris, Richard, ed. *An Old English Miscellany Containing a Bestiary, Kentish Sermons, Proverbs of Alfred, Religious Poems of the Thirteenth Century, from Manuscripts in the British Museum, Bodleian Library, Jesus College Library, Etc.* Early English Text Society ES 49. London: 1872.

Morton, A.L. "The Matter of Britain: The Arthurian Cycle and the Development of Feudal Society." *Zeitschrift für Anglistik und Amerikanistik* 8 (1960): 5–28.

Motherwell, William. *Minstrelsy Ancient and Modern.* 1827. Rpt. Detroit: Singing Tree, 1968.

Muir, Bernard J., ed. *The Exeter Anthology of Old English Poetry.* 2 vols. Exeter: University of Exeter Press, 1994.

Murphy, James J., ed. *Medieval Eloquence: Studies in the Theory and Practice of Medieval Rhetoric.* Berkeley: University of California Press, 1978.

Muscatine, Charles. *Chaucer and the French Tradition: A Study in Style and Meaning.* Berkeley: University of California Press, 1957.

Nelson, Marie. "Four Social Functions of the *Exeter Book* Riddles." *Neophilologus* 75.3 (1991): 445–450.

———. "The Rhetoric of the *Exeter Book* Riddles." *Speculum* 49.3 (1974): 421–440.

Neuse, Richard. *Chaucer's Dante: Allegory and Epic Theater in* The Canterbury Tales. Berkeley: University of California Press, 1991.

Newman, John Kevin. *The Classical Epic Tradition.* Wisconsin Studies in Classics. Gen. eds. Barbara Hughes Fowler and Warren G. Moon. Madison: University of Wisconsin Press, 1986.

Newstead, Helaine. "Arthurian Legends" and "Romances: General." *A Manual of the Writings in Middle English, 1050–1500.* Gen. ed. J. Burke Severs. New Haven: Connecticut Academy of Arts and Sciences, 1967. 1:38–79, 224–256; I: 9–16, 199–205.

Nichols, Stephen G., Jr. "The Spirit of Truth: Epic Modes in Medieval Literature." *New Literary History* 1 (Spring 1970): 365–386.

Niles, John D. " 'Editing' *Beowulf*: What Can Study of Ballads Tell Us?" *Oral Traditions* 9.2 (October 1994): 440–467.

Nygard, H.O. "Ballad Source Study." *Journal of American Folklore* 65 (1952): 1–12.

Nykrog, Per. "Courtliness and the Townspeople: The Fabliaux as a Courtly Burlesque." *The Humor of the Fabliaux.* Ed. Thomas D. Cooke and Benjamin L. Honeycutt. Columbia: University of Missouri Press, 1974. 59–73.

Oakden, James Parker. *Alliterative Poetry in Middle English*. 2 vols. Manchester: Manchester University Press, 1930–1935.

Oates, Joyce Carol. "The English and Scottish Traditional Ballads." *Southern Review* 15 (1979): 560–566.

Oberhelman, Steven M., Van Kelly, and Richard J. Golsan, eds. *Epic and Epoch: Essays on the Interpretation and History of a Genre*. Lubbock: Texas Tech University Press, 1994.

O'Brien, Timothy D. "The 'Readerly' Sir Launfal." *Parergon* 8 (1990): 33–45.

Ogle, M.B. "The Orchard Scene in *Tydorel* and *Sir Gowther*." *Romanic Review* 13 (1922): 37–43.

O'Keeffe, Katherine O'Brien, ed. *Old English Shorter Poems: Basic Readings*. New York: Garland, 1994.

———. "Orality and the Developing Text of *Caedmon's Hymn*." *Anglo-Saxon Manuscripts: Basic Readings*. Ed. Mary P. Richards. New York: Garland, 1994. 221–250.

Olsan, Lea. "Latin Charms of Medieval England: Verbal Healing in a Christian Oral Tradition." *Oral Tradition* 7.1 (March 1992): 116–142.

O'Neill, Patrick P. "The Old English Introductions to the Prose Psalm and the Paris Psalter: Sources, Structure, and Composition." *Studies in Philology* 78.5 (1981): 20–38.

Orchard, Andy. *The Poetic Art of Aldhelm*. Cambridge: Cambridge University Press, 1994.

Ostman, Jan Ola. " 'The Fight at Finnsburh': Pragmatic Aspects of a Narrative Fragment." *Neuphilologische Mitteilungen* 95.2 (1994): 207–227.

Otten, Kurt. *König Alfreds Boethius*. Tübingen: Niemeyer, 1964.

Owst, G.R. *Literature and Pulpit in Medieval England*. 2nd rev. ed. Oxford: Blackwell, 1961.

Palmer, R. Barton. "*The Book of the Duchess* and *Fonteinne amoureuse*: Chaucer and Machaut Reconsidered." *Canadian Review of Comparative Literature* 7 (1981): 380–393.

———. "Rereading Guillaume de Machaut's Vision of Love: Chaucer's *Book of the Duchess* as Bricolage." *Second Thoughts: A Focus on Rereading*. Ed. David Galef. Detroit: Wayne State University Press, 1998. 133–146.

Payne, F. Anne. *King Alfred and Boethius: An Analysis of the Old English Version of the "Consolation of Philosophy."* Madison: University of Wisconsin Press, 1968.

"Pearl": An Edition with Verse Translation. Ed. and trans. William Vantuono. Notre Dame, IN: University of Notre Dame Press, 1995.

Pearsall, Derek, ed. *The Nun's Priest's Tale*. Vol. 2, pt. 9, of *A Variorum Edition of the Works of Geoffrey Chaucer*. Norman: University of Oklahoma Press, 1983.

———. *Old English and Middle English Poetry*. London: Routledge and Kegan Paul, 1977.

Percy, Thomas. *Reliques of Ancient English Poetry*. 1765. Rpt. London: Russell & Russell, 1921.

Pickering, O.S., ed. *Individuality and Achievement in Middle English Poetry*. Suffolk: D.S. Brewer, 1997.

———. "Newly Discovered Secular Lyrics from Later Thirteenth-Century Cheshire." *Review of English Studies* 43 (1992): 157–180.

Pinto, Vivian de Sola, and Allan Edwin Roday, eds. *The Common Muse*. London: Chatto and Windus, 1957.

Plummer, Charles, ed. *Two of the Saxon Chronicles Parallel*. 2 vols. Oxford: Clarendon, 1892–1899.

Pope, John C. *The Rhythm of Beowulf*. 2nd. ed. New Haven, CT: Yale University Press, 1966.

———. "The Text of a Damaged Passage in the *Exeter Book: Advent, (Christ I)*." *Anglo-Saxon England* 9 (1981): 137–156.

———, ed. *Seven Old English Poems*. Indianapolis: Bobbs-Merrill, 1966.

Porter, James, ed. *The Ballad Image*. Los Angeles: University of California Press, 1983.

Pound, Louise. *Poetic Origins and the Ballad*. New York: Macmillan, 1921.

Prudentius. *Prudentius*. Trans. H.J. Thomson, 2 vols. Loeb Classical Library. London: William Heinemann, 1949–1953; reprinted 1969–1979.

Quinn, William A., ed. *Chaucer's Dream Visions and Shorter Poems*. Garland Reference Library of the Humanities, Basic Readings in Chaucer and His Time, Series 2105. New York: Garland, 1999.

Quint, David. *Epic and Empire: Politics and Generic Form from Virgil to Milton*. Princeton, NJ: Princeton University Press, 1993.

Ramsey, Lee C. *Chivalric Romances: Popular Literature in Medieval England*. Bloomington: Indiana University Press, 1983.

Reilly, Robert. "*The Earl of Toulouse*: A Structure of Honor." *Mediaeval Studies* 37 (1975): 515–523.

Reiss, Edmund. "The Middle English Lyric." *Old and Middle English Literature*. Ed. Jeffrey Helterman and Jerome Mitchell. Vol. 146 of *Dictionary of Literary Biography*. Detroit: Gale, 1994. 392–399.

———. "Romance." *The Popular Literature of Medieval England*. Ed. Thomas J. Heffernan. Tennessee Studies in Literature, 28. Knoxville: University of Tennessee Press, 1985. 108–130.

Renoir, Alain, and C. David Benson. "John Lydgate." *A Manual of the Writings in Middle English, 1050–1500*. Gen. ed. Albert E. Hartung. New Haven: Connecticut Academy of Arts and Sciences, 1980. 6:1809–1920, 2071–2175.

Renwick, W.L., and Harold Orton. *The Beginnings of English Literature to Skelton, 1509*. St. Clair Shores, MI: Scholarly Press, 1977.

Rice, Joanne A. *Middle English Romance: An Annotated Bibliography, 1955–1985*. New York: Garland Publishing, 1987.

Richmond, W. Edson. *Ballad Scholarship: An Annotated Bibliography*. New York: Garland, 1989.

Rickert, Edith, ed. *The Romance of Emaré*. EETS E.S. 99. London: Kegan Paul, Trench, Trübner, 1908.

Ridley, Florence H. "Middle Scots Writers." *A Manual of the Writings in Middle English, 1050–1500*. Gen. ed. Albert E. Hartung. New Haven: Connecticut Academy of Arts and Sciences, 1973. 4:961–1060, 1123–1284.

Ritson, Joseph. *Ancient Songs and Ballads*. 1790. 3rd ed. Ed. W. Carew Hazlitt. London: Reeves and Turner, 1877.

Robertson, Elizabeth. " 'An Anchorhold of Her Own': Female Ancoritic Literature in Thirteenth-Century England." *Equally in God's Image: Women in the Middle Ages*. Ed. Julia Bolton Holloway, Constance S. Wright, and Joan Bechtold. New York: Peter Lang, 1990. 170–183.

Robinson, Fred C. "Artful Ambiguities in the Old English 'Book-Moth' Riddle." *Anglo-Saxon Poetry: Essays in Appreciation for John C. McGalliard*. Ed. Lewis Nicholson and Dolores Warwick Frese. Notre Dame, IN: University of Notre Dame Press, 1975. 355–362.

Rosenberg, Bruce A. "The Three Tales of 'Sir Degaré.' " *Neuphilologische Mitteilungen* 76 (1975): 39–51.

Ross, Thomas W. *Chaucer's Bawdy*. New York: E.P. Dutton, 1972.

Rowland, Beryl. *Blind Beasts: Chaucer's Animal World*. Kent, OH: Kent State University Press, 1971.

Ruud, Jay. *"Many a Song and Many a Leccherous Lay": Tradition and Individuality in Chaucer's Lyric Poetry*. New York: Garland, 1992.

Rumble, Thomas C., ed. *The Breton Lays in Middle English*. Detroit: Wayne State University Press, 1965.

Rumi. *Mystical Poems of Rumi*. Trans. A.J. Arberry, Chicago: University of Chicago Press, 1968.

———. *Mystical Poems of Rumi 2*. Trans. A.J. Arberry, Chicago: University of Chicago Press, 1991.

Russell, J. Stephen, ed. *Allegoresis: The Craft of Allegory in Medieval Literature*. New York: Garland, 1988.

Russom, Geoffrey. *Beowulf and Old Germanic Metre*. Cambridge: Cambridge University Press, 1998.

———. *Old English Meter and Linguistic Theory*. Cambridge: Cambridge University Press, 1987.

Ruud, Jay. "Chaucer's 'Complaint to His Purse.' " *Explicator* 41 (1983): 5–6.

Ryan, Lawrence V. "Doctrine and Dramatic Structure in *Everyman*." *Speculum* 32 (1957): 722–735.

Ryan, Marcella. "Chaucer's Dream-Vision Poems and the Theory of Spatial Form." *Parergon: Bulletin of the Australian and New Zealand Association for Medieval and Renaissance Studies* 11 (1993): 79–90.

Salter, Elizabeth. *Piers Plowman; An Introduction*. Cambridge, MA: Harvard University Press, 1962.

Sands, Donald B., ed. *Middle English Verse Romances*. New York: Holt, Rinehart and Winston, 1966.

Sapegno, Natalino. *Il Trecento. Storia letteraria d'Italia*. Milan: Francesco Vallardi, 1934; 3rd ed. reprinted 1973.

Savage, Anne, trans. *The Anglo-Saxon Chronicles*. New York: St. Martin's, 1983.

———. "The Translation of the Feminine: Untranslatable Dimensions of the Anchoritic Works." *The Medieval Translator, IV*. Ed. Roger Ellis and Ruth Evans. Binghamton, NY: Medieval and Renaissance Text and Studies, 1994. 181–199.

Scaglione, Aldo. "The Mediterranean's Three Spiritual Shores: Images of the Self between Christianity and Islam in the Later Middle Ages." *The Craft of Fiction*. Ed. Leigh A. Arrathoon, Rochester, MI: Solaris Press, 1984. 453–479.

Scanlon, Larry. *Narrative, Authority, and Power: The Medieval Exemplum and the Chaucerian Tradition*. Cambridge Studies in Medieval Literature 20. Cambridge: Cambridge University Press, 1994.

Schipper, Jakob. *A History of English Versification*. Oxford: Clarendon Press, 1910.

Schmidt, A.V.C., trans. *Piers Plowman: A New Translation of the B-Text*. New York: Oxford University Press, 1992.

Scholes, Robert, and Robert Kellogg. *The Nature of Narrative*. London: Oxford University Press, 1966.

Scott, Charles T. "Some Approaches to the Study of the Riddle." *Studies in Language, Literature, and Culture of the Middle Ages and Later*. Ed. E.B. Atwood and A.A. Hill. Austin: University of Texas, 1969.

Scragg, D.G. "The Homilies of the Blickling Manuscript." *Learning and Literature in Anglo-Saxon England*. Ed. Michael Lapidge and Helmut Gneuss. Cambridge: Cambridge University Press, 1985. 299–316.

Scragg, Donald, ed. *The Battle of Maldon, AD 991*. Oxford: Blackwell, 1991.

Seymour, M.C. "John Capgrave." *English Writers of the Late Middle Ages*. Ed. M.C. Seymour. Vol. 3 of *Authors of the Middle Ages*. Aldershot, Hants: Variorum, 1996. 197–256.

Shaw, Harry. *Concise Dictionary of Literary Terms*. New York: McGraw-Hill, 1976.

Shaw, Judith. "The Influence of Canonical and Episcopal Reform on Popular Books of Instruction." *The Popular Literature of Medieval England*. Ed. Thomas J. Heffernan. Knoxville: University of Tennessee Press, 1985. 44–60.

Shenk, Robert. "The Liberation of the 'Loathly Lady' of Medieval Romance." *Journal of the Rocky Mountain Medieval and Renaissance Association* 2 (1981): 69–77.

Shepherd, Stephen H.A., ed. *Middle English Romances*. Norton Critical Edition. New York: W.W. Norton, 1995.

Shippey, Thomas A. "Breton *Lais* and Modern Fantasies." *Studies in Medieval English Romances: Some New Approaches*. Ed. Derek Brewer. Cambridge: D.S. Brewer, 1988. 69–91.

Sievers, Eduard. *Altgermanische Metrik*. Halle: Max Niemeyer, 1893.

Sigal, Gale. *Erotic Dawn-Songs of the Middle Ages: Voicing the Lyric Lady*. Gainesville: University Press of Florida, 1996.

Skeat, W.W., ed. *The Complete Works of Geoffrey Chaucer*. 7 vols. Oxford, 1894–1900.

Smith, A.H., ed. *The Parker Chronicle, 832–900*. 3rd ed. London: Methuen, 1957.

Smith, Elton E. "Charms." *Encyclopedia of Medieval Literature*. Ed. Robert Thomas Lambdin and Laura Cooner Lambdin. Westport, CT: Greenwood Press, 2000. 90–91.

———. "Cynewulf." *Encyclopedia of Medieval Literature*. Ed. Robert Thomas Lambdin and Laura Cooner Lambdin. Westport, CT: Greenwood Press, 2000. 113–115.

———. *"Deor's Lament." Encyclopedia of Medieval Literature*. Ed. Robert Thomas Lambdin and Laura Cooner Lambdin. Westport, CT: Greenwood Press, 2000. 148–149.

———. "Fight at Finnsburgh, The." *Encyclopedia of Medieval Literature*. Ed. Robert Thomas Lambdin and Laura Cooner Lambdin. Westport, CT: Greenwood Press, 2000. 196–197.

———. "Riddles." *Encyclopedia of Medieval Literature*. Ed. Robert Thomas Lambdin and Laura Cooner Lambdin. Westport, CT: Greenwood Press, 2000. 439–440.

———. *"Widsith." Encyclopedia of Medieval Literature*. Ed. Robert Thomas Lambdin and Laura Cooner Lambdin. Westport, CT: Greenwood Press, 2000. 514–516.

Smith, Esther. "Alfred the Great." *Encyclopedia of Medieval Literature*. Ed. Robert Thomas Lambdin and Laura Cooner Lambdin. Westport, CT: Greenwood Press, 2000. 6–7.

———. "Bede, St., The Venerable." *Encyclopedia of Medieval Literature*. Ed. Robert

Thomas Lambdin and Laura Cooner Lambdin. Westport, CT: Greenwood Press, 2000. 54–55.

Smith, Lesley, and Jane H.M. Taylor, eds. *Women, the Book, and the Godly: Selected Proceedings of the St. Hilda's Conference, 1993.* Cambridge: D.S. Brewer, 1995.

Smithers, G.V. "Story-Patterns in Some Breton Lays." *Medium Ævum* 22 (1953): 61–92.

Smithson, George Arnold. *The Old English Christian Epic.* New York: Phaeton, 1971.

Smyser, H.M. "Charlemagne Legends." *A Manual of the Writings in Middle English, 1050–1500.* Gen. ed. J. Burke Severs. New Haven: Connecticut Academy of Arts and Sciences, 1967. 1:80–100, 256–266.

Snodgrass, Mary Ellen. *Encyclopedia of Fable.* Santa Barbara, CA: ABC-CLIO, 1998.

The Song of Roland. Trans. Dorothy L. Sayers. London: Penguin, 1957.

Southern, R.W. *The Making of the Middle Ages.* New Haven, CT: Yale University Press, 1953.

Spaeth, J. Duncan. *Old English Poetry: Translations into Alliterative Verse with Introductions and Notes.* New York: Gordian Press, 1967.

Spearing, A.C. "Marie de France and Her Middle English Adapters." *Studies in the Age of Chaucer* 12 (1990): 117–156.

———. *Medieval Dream-Poetry.* Cambridge: Cambridge University Press, 1976.

———. *The Medieval Poet as Voyeur: Looking and Listening in Medieval Love-Narratives.* Cambridge: Cambridge University Press, 1993.

Spiegel, Harriet, ed. and trans. *Fables of Marie de France.* Toronto: University of Toronto Press, 1987.

Speirs, John. *Medieval English Poetry: The Non-Chaucerian Tradition.* London: Faber and Faber, 1957.

Stanbury, Sarah. "The Body and the City in *Pearl.*" *Representations* 48 (1994): 30–47.

———. "Gazing toward Jerusalem: Space and Perception in *Pearl.*" *Seeing the "Gawain"-Poet: Description and the Act of Perception.* Middle Ages Series. Philadelphia: University of Pennsylvania Press, 1991. 12–41. Rpt. of "Visions of Space: Acts of Perception in *Pearl* and in Some Late Medieval Illustrated Apocalypses." *Mediaevalia* 10 (1988): 133–158.

Stanley, E.G. "Heroic Aspects of the *Exeter Book* Riddles." *Prosody and Poetics in the Early Middle Ages: Essays in Honour of C.B. Hieatt.* Ed. M.J. Toswell. Toronto: University of Toronto Press, 1995. 197–218.

———, ed. *The Owl and the Nightingale.* London: Thomas Nelson and Sons, 1960.

Star, Jonathan, and Shahram Shiva, trans. *A Garden beyond Paradise: The Mystical Poetry of Rumi.* New York: Bantam, 1992.

Stevens, John. *Medieval Romance: Themes and Approaches.* New York: Norton, 1973.

Stevens, Martin. *Four Middle English Mystery Cycles: Textual, Contextual, and Critical Interpretations.* Princeton, NJ: Princeton University Press, 1987.

Stevick, Robert D., ed. *One Hundred Middle English Lyrics.* Rev. ed. Urbana: University of Illinois Press, 1994.

———. "The Oral-Formulaic Analysis of Old English Verse." *Speculum* 37 (1952): 382–389.

Stewart, Ann Harleman. "Double Entendre in the Old English Riddles." *Lore and Language* 3.8 (1983): 39–52.

Stone, Brian, trans. *The Owl and the Nightingale, Cleanness, St. Erkenwald.* Harmondsworth: Penguin, 1971, reprinted 1977.

Stork, Nancy Porter. "Maldon, the Devil, and the Dictionary." *Exemplaria* 5.1 (Spring 1993): 111–134.

———. *Through a Gloss Darkly: Aldhelm's Riddles in the British Library MS Royal 12.C.xxiii.* Toronto: Pontifical Institute of Mediaeval Studies, 1990.

Strohm, Paul. "Middle English Narrative Genres." *Genre* 13 (1980): 379–388.

———. "The Origin and Meaning of Middle English Romance." *Genre* 10 (1977): 1–28.

Sullens, Idelle, ed. *Robert Mannyng of Brunne: The Chronicle.* Binghamton, NY: Medieval and Renaissance Texts and Studies, 1996.

Summerfield, Thea. *The Matter of Kings' Lives: The Design of Past and Present in the Early Fourteenth-Century Verse Chronicles by Pierre de Langtoft and Robert Mannyng.* Amsterdam and Atlanta, GA: Rodopi, 1998.

Sumner, Laura, ed. *The Weddynge of Sir Gawen and Dame Ragnell.* Northampton, MA: Smith College, 1924.

Szarmach, Paul, ed. *Studies in Earlier Old English Prose.* Albany: State University of New York Press, 1985.

Tanke, John. "*Wonfeax wale*: Ideology and Figuration in the Sexual Riddles of the *Exeter Book*." *Class and Gender in Early English Literature.* Ed. Britton J. Harwood and Gillian R. Overing. Bloomington: Indiana University Press, 1994. 21–42.

Taylor, Archer. *English Riddles from Oral Tradition.* Berkeley: University of California Press, 1959.

———. *The Literary Riddle before 1600.* Berkeley: University of California Press, 1948.

Thompson, Stith, ed. *Motif-Index of Folk-Literature: A Classification of Narrative Elements in Folktales, Ballads, Myths, Fables, Mediaeval Romances, Exempla, Fabliaux, Jest-Books, and Local Legends.* Rev. and enl. ed. 6 vols. Bloomington: Indiana University Press, 1966.

Thrall, William Flint, Addison Hibbard, and C. Hugh Holman. *A Handbook to Literature.* New York: Odyssey Press, 1960.

Tigges, Wim. "Romance and Parody." *Companion to Middle English Romance.* Ed. Henk Aertsen and Alasdair A. MacDonald. Amsterdam: VU University Press, 1990. 129–151.

Tillyard, E.M.W. *The English Epic and Its Background.* London: Chatto and Windus, 1954.

Tolkien, J.R.R. "*Beowulf*: The Monsters and the Critics." *Proceedings of the British Academy* 22 (1936): 245–295.

Tolkien, J.R.R., and E.V. Gordon, eds. *Sir Gawain and the Green Knight.* 2nd ed. rev. by Norman Davis. Oxford: Clarendon Press, 1967.

Travis, Peter. *Dramatic Design in the Chester Cycle.* Chicago: University of Chicago Press, 1982.

Tschann, Judith. "The Layout of *Sir Thopas* in the Ellesmere, Hengwrt, Cambridge Dd.4.24, and Cambridge Gg.4.27 Manuscripts." *Chaucer Review* 20 (1985): 1–13.

Tucker, P.E. "The Place of the Quest of the Holy Grail in the *Morte Darthur*." *Modern Language Review* 48 (1953): 391–397.

Tuetey, Charles Greville, trans. *Classical Arabic Poetry.* London: KPI, 1985.

Tupper, Frederick. "The Cynewulfian Runes of the First Riddle." *Modern Language Notes* 25.8 (1910): 235–241.

———. "Originals and Analogues of the *Exeter Book* Riddles." *Modern Language Notes* 18.4 (1903): 97–106.

Turville-Petre, Thorlac. *Alliterative Poetry of the Later Middle Ages: An Anthology.* Washington, DC: Catholic University of America Press, 1989.

———. *The Alliterative Revival.* Cambridge: D.S. Brewer, 1977.

———. "Politics and Poetry in the Early Fourteenth Century: The Case of Robert Manning's *Chronicle*." *Review of English Studies* 39 (1988): 1–28.

Vargyas, Lajos. *Researches into the Medieval History of Folk Ballad.* Trans. Arthur H. Whitney. Budapest: Akademiai Kiado, 1967.

Vaughan, Miceal F. " 'Til I Gan Awake': The Conversion of Dreamer into Narrator in *Piers Plowman* B." *Yearbook of Langland Studies* 5 (1991): 175–192.

Vinaver, Eugène. Introduction. *The Works of Sir Thomas Malory.* 2nd ed. Oxford: Oxford University Press, 1967.

Walker-Pelkey, Faye. " 'Frige hwæt ic hatte': *The Wife's Lament* as Riddle." *PLL* 28.3 (1992): 242–266.

Ward, A.W., and A.R. Waller, eds. *The Cambridge History of English Literature.* 15 vols. Cambridge: Cambridge University Press, 1963–1965.

Warden, John, ed. *Orpheus: The Metamorphoses of a Myth.* Toronto: University of Toronto Press, 1982.

Warhaft, S., and J. Woodbury. *English Poems, 1250–1660.* Toronto: Macmillan, 1961.

Warton, Thomas. *History of English Poetry.* 1774. Ed. René Wellek. New York: Johnson Reprint Corp., 1968.

Webber, Ruth House. "Towards the Morphology of the Romance Epic." *Romance Epic: Essays on a Medieval Literary Genre.* Kalamazoo, MI: Medieval Institute Publications, 1987. 1–9.

Wehlau, Ruth. *The Riddle of Creation.* New York: Peter Lang, 1997.

Weldon, James F.G. "*Ordinatio* and Genre in MS CCC 201: A Mediaeval Reading of the B-Text of *Piers Plowman*." *Florilegium* 12 (1993): 159–175.

Wenzel, Siegfried. "Medieval Sermons." *A Companion to Piers Plowman.* Ed. John A. Alford. Berkeley: University of California Press, 1988. 155–172.

Wetherbee, Winthrop. "Latin Structure and Vernacular Space: Gower, Chaucer, and the Boethian Tradition." *Chaucer and Gower: Difference, Mutuality, Exchange.* Ed. R.F. Yeager. Victoria, British Columbia: University of Victoria, 1991. 7–35.

White, T.H., ed. and trans. *The Bestiary: A Book of Beasts.* New York: Capricorn Books, 1960.

Whitelock, Dorothy, trans. *The Anglo-Saxon Chronicle: A Revised Translation.* Westport, CT: Greenwood Press, 1986.

Whiting, B.J. "The Wife of Bath's Tale." *Sources and Analogues of Chaucer's Canterbury Tales.* Ed. W.F. Bryan and Germaine Dempster. New York: Humanities Press, 1958. 242–264.

Whitman, Frank Herbert. "The Influence of the Latin and the Popular Riddle Traditions on the Old English Riddles of the *Exeter Book*." Diss. Madison: University of Wisconsin, 1968.

Wilgus, D.K., and Barre Toelken. *The Ballad and the Scholars.* Los Angeles: University of California Press, 1986.

Williams, Edith Whitehurst. "Annals of the Poor: Folk Life in Old English Riddles." *Medieval Perspectives* 3.2 (1988): 67–82.

Williamson, Craig, trans. *A Feast of Creatures: Anglo-Saxon Riddle-Songs.* Philadelphia: University of Pennsylvania Press, 1982.

————, ed. *The Old English Riddles of the Exeter Book.* Chapel Hill: University of North Carolina Press, 1977.

Wilson, Peter Lamborn, and Nasrollah Pourjavady, trans. *The Drunken Universe: An Anthology of Persian Sufi Poetry.* Grand Rapids, MI: Phanes Press, 1987.

Wilson, R.M. *The Lost Literature of Medieval England.* London: Methuen, 1952.

Wilson, Robert H. "Malory and Caxton." *A Manual of the Writings in Middle English, 1050–1500.* Gen. ed. Albert E. Hartung. New Haven: Connecticut Academy of Arts and Sciences, 1972. 3:757–807, 909–951.

Wimberly, L.C. *Folklore in the English and Scottish Ballads.* New York: Frederick Ungar, 1959.

Wimsatt, James. *Chaucer and His French Contemporaries: Natural Music in the Fourteenth Century.* Toronto: University of Toronto Press, 1991.

Wirtjes, Hanneke, ed. *The Middle English "Physiologus."* Early English Text Society Original Series 299. Oxford: Oxford University Press, 1991.

Wittig, Joseph S. "King Alfred's Boethius and Its Latin Sources: A Reconsideration." *Anglo-Saxon England* 11 (1983): 157–198.

Woolf, Rosemary. "Later Poetry: The Popular Tradition." *History of Literature in the English Language.* vol. 1, *The Middle Ages.* Ed. W.F. Bolton. London: Barrie and Jenkins, 1970. 267–311.

Wrenn, C.L. "[Prose:] The Beginnings." *A Study of Old English Literature.* London: George G. Harrap, 1967. 195–205.

Wright, Charles D. "The Pledge of the Soul: A Judgement Theme in Old English Homiletic Literature and Cynewulf's 'Elene.' " *Neuphilologische Mitteilungen* 91.1 (1990): 23–30.

Wright, Glenn. "Parody, Satire, and Genre in *The Tournament of Tottenham* (1400–1440)" *FCS* 23 (1997): 152–70.

Wright, W.A., ed. *The Metrical Chronicle of Robert of Gloucester.* 2 vols. London: Rolls Series, 1887. 86.

Wülker, Richard, ed. *Bibliothek der angelsächsischen Poesie.* 3 vols. Kassel: Georg H. Wigand, 1883–1898.

Wyatt, Alfred J., ed. *Old English Riddles.* 1912. Norwood, PA: Norwood Editions, 1973.

Zaerr, Linda Marie, and Joseph A. Baldassarre. "*The Tournament of Tottenham*: Music as an Enhancement to Prosody." *FCS* 16 (1990): 239–252.

Zall, P.M., ed. *A Hundred Merry Tales and Other English Jestbooks of the Fifteenth and Sixteenth Centuries.* Lincoln: University of Nebraska Press, 1963.

Zeeman, Elizabeth. "Piers Plowman and the Pilgrimage to Truth." *Essays and Studies* 11 (1958): 1–16.

Zettl, Ewald, ed. *An Anonymous Short English Metrical Chronicle.* EETS 196. London: Oxford University Press, 1935.

Ziolkowski, Jan M. *Talking Animals: Medieval Latin Beast Poetry, 750–1150.* Philadelphia: University of Pennsylvania Press, 1993.

Index

About the Editors and Contributors

JOHN H. BRINEGAR is an instructor at Virginia Commonwealth University. He is currently working on a book on Alfred's use of Latin sources in his translation of Boethius.

CAROLYN CRAFT is Professor of English at Longwood College, where she has taught courses in Arthurian literature, the alliterative revival, medieval women's literature, and Chaucer, among others. She has served on the Editorial Board of *Cross Currents* for many years and has published there and in many other journals. She is also the English Graduate Program Coordinator as well as the English Program Coordinator.

JOHN MICHAEL CRAFTON is a Professor of English at the State University of West Georgia, where he specializes in medieval literature, especially Chaucer and the history of the English language. He has published numerous articles in these fields. He is currently the editor of *JAISA*, the principal publication of the Association for the Interdisciplinary Study of the Arts.

ED ELEAZAR is Associate Professor of English at Francis Marion University in Florence, South Carolina. His edition of the quatrain version of *Gast of Gy* is forthcoming.

SHEARLE FURNISH is Professor of English and Director of Composition at West Texas A&M University in Canyon. He has an A.B. from Transylvania University (Lexington, Kentucky, 1975) and an M.A. and Ph.D. from the University of Kentucky (1978, 1984). He teaches medieval literature, bibliography and methods of research, English romanticism, and the teaching of college composition. His articles on the Chester and Wakefield plays, the Breton lays in Middle English, and Nicholas Love's *Mirrour of the Blessed Lyf of Jesu Christ* have been published in the *American Benedictine Review, Mediaevalia, Manuscripta, Medieval Perspectives, Essays in Theatre*, and the *Dictionary of Literary Biography* volume on *Old and Middle English Literature* (vol. 146).

BRIAN GASTLE is Assistant Professor of English at Western Carolina University. His research focuses on mercantile institutions in late medieval English literature, especially representations of the *femme sole*.

EMMA B. HAWKINS is Assistant Professor of English at Lamar University. She has presented numerous papers on English and medieval literature. She is also the author of several published articles on Old English and rhetoric.

MICHELLE IGARASHI is an independent scholar who specializes in Old and Middle English literature. Her specialties include the Old English riddles.

SIGRID KING teaches at Carlow College. She has published widely in a variety of fields and journals, including *Black American Literature Forum*. Her chapters and entries have appeared in *Chaucer's Pilgrims* and *Encyclopedia of Medieval Literature*. In addition to medieval literature, her interests include the English Renaissance and literary theory.

DANIEL KLINE is Assistant Professor of English at the University of Alaska at Anchorage, where he specializes in medieval literature, literary theory, and religion and literature, particularly Middle English literature, Chaucer, medieval drama, and medieval women writers. Kline maintains the Electronic Canterbury Tales. He has published in *Comparative Drama, Essays in Medieval Studies*, and MLA's *Profession 95*. His current research examines the representation of children and childhood in Middle English literature.

LAURA COONER LAMBDIN teaches professional communications in the University of South Carolina's Moore School of Business. She and her husband have published four other books together: *Chaucer's Pilgrims, A Companion to Jane Austen Studies, Encyclopedia of Medieval Literature*, and *Camelot in the Nineteenth Century*. She has also published numerous articles, chapters, entries, and reviews, mostly reflecting her interest in Medieval, romantic, and Victorian literary criticism.

ROBERT THOMAS LAMBDIN is Assistant Professor in the Transition Year Program at the University of South Carolina. He has authored or edited many books on Old and Middle English. His interests include Chaucer and hockey.

SCOTT LIGHTSEY teaches at the University of Delaware, Newark, Delaware. His interests include medieval and early modern literature, Chaucer and Ricardian literature, and history of the English language.

KEVIN MARTI is Associate Professor of English at the University of New Orleans. He has published and presented papers on a number of topics, including Old and Middle English.

RICHARD McDONALD is Assistant Professor of English at Utah Valley State College. In addition to medieval literature, his interests include Renaissance literature and literary criticism. He has published and presented a number of papers concerning such diverse topics as Chaucer's Reeve, "The Wanderer," and Jane Austen's *Emma*.

GWENDOLYN MORGAN is a professor of English at Montana State University. She has published extensively on the ballads, authoring several books. She has also cotranslated many Old English poems that have appeared in various journals.

MARIE NELSON received her Ph.D. from the University of Oregon. Her publications include two books, *Structures of Opposition in Old English Poems* and *Judith, Juliana, and Elene: Three Fighting Saints*, along with essays on Old and Modern English literature in *Speculum, Oral Tradition, Language and Style*, and other journals. She has also written a series of "teaching texts": *Words on the Page: Writing about Language, Readings for History of the English Language*, and *Chaucer/Chaucer's Women*, along with three sets of exercises for her undergraduate and graduate courses: "Old English Riddles," "Working Texts," and "Heroes in Transformation." The courses she has taught include writing about aggression, writing about language, fantasy, Old English, Chaucer/Chaucer's women, and history of the English language. She is currently serving as Director of UO's Linguistics Program.

KEITH P. TAYLOR is Assistant Professor of English at Middle Tennessee State University in Murfreesboro, Tennessee. He has published articles on *Beowulf* and the Exeter Book riddles and is a contributor to the forthcoming *Chaucer Encyclopedia*. Currently he is completing a book on *Sir Gawain and the Green Knight* that offers a reevaluation of the poem in light of the context provided for it by its placement in the manuscript.

RICHARD THOMSON is Associate Professor of English at the University of Florida. He teaches courses and has published in the fields of folklore, the ballad, the folktale/myth/legend, Shakespeare, New Zealand literature, indigene writers, and post-colonial studies.